Carrington

D1335135

carrington

A LIFE OF
DORA CARRINGTON

1893-1932

GRETCHEN GERZINA

OXFORD UNIVERSITY PRESS
1990

Oxford University Press, Walton Street, Oxford OX2 6DP

Oxford New York Toronto
Delhi Bombay Calcutta Madras Karachi
Petaling Jaya Singapore Hong Kong Tokyo
Nairobi Dar es Salaam Cape Town
Melbourne Auckland

and associated companies in
Berlin Ibadan

Oxford is a trade mark of Oxford University Press

First published in the UK 1989 by John Murray
First issued as an Oxford University Press paperback 1990

British Library Cataloguing in Publication Data
Gerzina, Gretchen
Carrington : a life of Dora Carrington, 1893–1932. — (Oxford lives).
1. English paintings. Carrington, Dora 1893–1932
I. Title
759.2
ISBN 0–19–282716–2

Printed in Great Britain by
Clays Ltd.
Bungay, Suffolk

For Frances Partridge and Anthony Gerzina, whose patience, assistance, and encouragement made this book possible.

CONTENTS

LIST OF ILLUSTRATIONS ix

ACKNOWLEDGEMENTS xi

INTRODUCTION xiii

PROLOGUE xxi

PART ONE: YOUTH

1 Childhood 3
2 1910–11: The Young Art Student 18
3 The First Triangle: 1912 29
4 Sex and Self-doubt 44
5 Old Trouble and New Friends 60

PART TWO: ARRANGEMENTS

6 The Second Triangle 73
7 London and Lytton 92
8 Separations and Unions 103
9 Tidmarsh Mill House: 1917–18 122
10 Ralph: 1919 137
11 Commitment: 1920–21 154

PART THREE: REARRANGEMENTS

12 Gerald 171
13 Picking up the Pieces 189
14 Ham Spray: 1924 201
15 Retrenchment: 1925 218
16 Compromise 231

PART FOUR: LOVE AND LOSS: 1928–32

17 Fear and Love: 1928   245
18 Disaster Averted: 1929   264
19 The Medal Reversed: 1930   273
20 Foreshadowing: 1931   285
21 The Two-handed Engine   292

EPILOGUE   301

NOTES   307

INDEX   330

LIST OF ILLUSTRATIONS

At Bedford, in her teens
Early posed photograph of Carrington taken in about 1910
Painting a portrait of her father, also in 1910
The 'cropheads' – Carrington, Barbara Hiles and Dorothy Brett
Slade School picnic
Carrington with Lytton and James Strachey
Ralph Partridge in 1914
Carrington with Gerald Brenan
Picnic in Savernake Forest
The last photograph of Carrington, taken at Biddesden House
Carrington's prize winning life studies from the Slade, 1912 and 1913
Lady Strachey, 1920
Lytton Strachey, 1920
Carrington's woodblock self portrait
An early Carrington woodcut

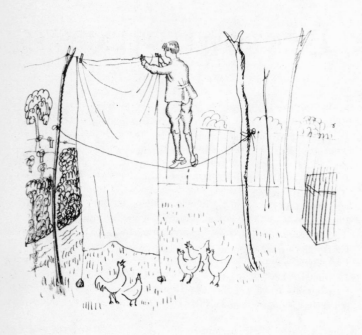

ACKNOWLEDGEMENTS

I wish to thank the following people and organisations for their help in preparing this book:

The Bedford School, particularly Miss Patricia Burnaby, Archivist, for help in research and permission to publish the photograph of Carrington at school.

Sally Bingham, for the information about Henrietta Bingham's life.

The British Library, especially Sally Brown, Curator of the Modern Collection, for use of the letters of Carrington and Lytton Strachey, illustrations from those letters, and the use of Carrington's last diary.

The *Burlington Magazine*, for permission to quote from early articles about the Slade School of Fine Art.

Noel and Catherine Carrington, for permission to reproduce Carrington's paintings, and to quote from Samuel Carrington's letters.

Chatto & Windus Ltd., the Hogarth Press and Harcourt Brace Jovanovich for permission to quote from the letters and diaries of Virginia Woolf.

Constable & Co. for permission to quote from *Today We Will Only Gossip* by Lady Glenavy.

Richard Garnett, for permission to quote from the letters and books of David Garnett.

Luke Gertler, for permission to quote from the letters of Mark Gertler.

Lawrence Gowing, for permission to quote from the writings of Julia Strachey.

Richard and Mary Gray, owners of Ham Spray.

Margaret Hanbury, literary agent for the Estate of Gerald Brenan, 27 Walcot Square, London SE11 4UB, for permission to quote extracts from Gerald Brenan's unpublished papers, © Gerald Brenan and from *Personal Record* by Gerald Brenan, copyright © 1974 Lynda Jane Nicholson Price, published by Jonathan Cape Limited, London.

The Harry Ransom Humanities Research Center of The University of

Texas at Austin, for permission to quote from and reproduce Carrington's letters and drawings.

Lady Pansy Lamb, for the use of letters from Henry Lamb to Carrington.

The Lytton Strachey Trust, most especially Michael Holroyd and Ann Wilson, for research assistance and permission to quote from the letters of Lytton Strachey, and for permission to reproduce the photograph of Carrington, Lytton Strachey and James Strachey at a boarding house. Thank you also to the Society of Authors for permission for the same letters.

Sandra Lummis, for access to and information about the paintings of Vanessa Bell, Carrington, Roger Fry and Duncan Grant.

Frances Partridge, for advice, information and permission to quote from the letters and diary of Carrington and to reproduce her paintings and drawings by Carrington and her photogaphs.

Anne C. Patterson, for permission to quote from the letters of C. R. W. Nevinson.

Max Rutherston, for permission to quote from the letters of Albert Rutherston.

The Scottish National Portrait Gallery, for permission to reproduce 'Lady Strachey' by Carrington.

Richard Shone, for information and permission to quote from our correspondence.

The Slade School of Fine Art, especially Murray Watson, former Secretary, for assistance in research, permission to quote from its unpublished history, and permission to reproduce Carrington's prize winning paintings.

The Tate Gallery Archives, especially Adrian Glew, for generous assistance and permission to reproduce the following: the photograph of Carrington at Bedford in her teens, the 1910 studio photograph of Carrington, the 1910 photograph of Carrington painting her father, the photograph of the 'cropheads', the photograph of the Slade School picnic, the photograph of Ralph Partridge in 1914, and the photograph of Carrington with Gerald Brenan.

The University of Texas at Austin, particularly Dr William Livingstone, for a C.P. Snow Research Grant.

Meg Wolitzer, for her encouragement and assistance in publishing this book, and to Lizzie Grossman and Caroline Dawnay for their indispensable assistance.

Special thanks to my editors Mary Cunnane and Grant McIntyre for their patience and help in preparing the manuscript.

Finally, most heartfelt thanks to Anthony, Simon and Daniel.

INTRODUCTION

Carrington's life was short, and the circle in which she moved was always relatively small. Yet to those who knew her she was recognisable at once as wholly original. Her paintings were not part of any school; her letters could have been written by no one else; she had an ability to entertain, delight and intrigue that singled her out and brought her affection – affection so strong in fact that sometimes its demands upset and disturbed her. She could also, as with Aldous Huxley and D. H. Lawrence, strongly irritate. Those cases draw attention to an essential mystery that underlined her originality, a mystery of course heightened by the – to many – inexplicable nature of the relationship with Lytton Strachey that dominated her life.

Following her death Carrington's reputation and the facts of her life became absorbed into a wider interest in the Bloomsbury group, a coterie of which she was never really a part although she was attached to it through close relationships with some of its members. Only in recent years has she once again become known in her own right. A selection of letters and extracts from her diaries was edited by David Garnett and published in 1970. It was an astonishing success. In the same year the first retrospective exhibition of her paintings was organised in London. Sir John Rothenstein, former Director of the Tate Gallery in London, wrote in 1976 that '. . . she has been the most neglected serious painter of her time.' Two years later her brother Noel published a book of her paintings, drawings and decorations which brought her work to a wider public. That work, once known only to a few private collectors, now hangs in the English and Scottish National Portrait Galleries, in the Tate Gallery, and in several American collections.

While her reputation, both as a painter and as a woman, grows steadily, a full biography seems timely, especially to dispel some of the myths about Carrington which have arisen in the more than fifty years since her death. These myths have in many ways turned her into a cult figure. One finds people inexplicably drawn to her life, even to the point of claiming to be her reincarnation. Occasionally plays and stories are written about her. As well as this infatuation there has been scholarly work, which has brought her into clearer focus. The fascination, whether positive or negative, that so many contemporaries felt still continues. Her life was in many ways her greatest work of art.

Because of her Bohemian lifestyle, connection with the Blooms-bury group, short hair, and rejection of many traditional women's roles, Dora Carrington seemed to symbolise the 'new' and 'modern' woman of the early twentieth century. But though she was born in the Victorian period and died in the Jazz Age she never wholly rejected one century in favour of the other. Her life was a series of unresolved, opposing tensions, and its consistency lay in her ambivalence to many of the problems she faced: she loved truth but constantly lied; she rejected her lovers but continually lured them back; she was happiest when she painted, but her painting frequently depressed her. The stereotype of the carefree, post-war flapper in no way fits Carrington, nor does the stereotype of the frustrated artist *manquée*.

Though most of those who knew her, or thought or wrote about her, found her an enigmatic figure, some have supposed all too easily that they had the measure of her. Described by Lady Ottoline Morrell as 'a wild moorland pony', and remembered by others chiefly for her strikingly blue eyes and Dutch-boy blonde hair, she has been dismissed sometimes as yet another physically attractive but sexually repressed and frustrated artist of the Edwardian and Georgian period. Even some of those who found her most fascinating have described her with too much facility. David Garnett clearly felt he needed to justify an interest in her life and letters when he wrote:

> Tens of thousands of young women have china-blue eyes, talk in little gasps and have sex trouble, but one does not want to wade through their correspondence. Carrington would have always been attractive to her friends; what makes her interesting and fascinating to subsequent gen-erations is her relationship with Lytton Strachey, the critic who sprang into fame with *Eminent Victorians* and his biography of Queen Victoria. Carrington devoted her life to Lytton, and after his death from an undiagnosed cancer of the intestine decided that it was not worth living, and shot herself.[1]

While factually correct, this statement oversimplifies her life. She was, in fact, so complicated that writers of fiction, who several times used her as a model, preferred to reduce her to a single characteristic rather than try to come to terms with her complexity. Wyndham

Lewis portrayed her as a tiny sex therapist in *The Apes of God*, D. H. Lawrence as a frivolous artist's model in *Women in Love* and a gang-raped aesthete in 'None of That', and Aldous Huxley as a jargon-speaking ultra-modern girl out to lose her virginity in *Crome Yellow*. While sexuality, infidelity and modernity were undeniably aspects of her personality, they were equally balanced by a loathing of her own femaleness, a devotion for seventeen years to one man – albeit a homosexual – even while married to another, and respect for many aspects of traditional English country life.

Women in Love, published in 1921 but written in 1916, makes free and ruthless use of Bloomsbury characters. Lady Ottoline Morrell appears as Hermione Roddice, mistress of the country house Breadalby; Lytton Strachey appears as the nerveless Julius Halliday. Carrington herself is thinly disguised as Minette Darrington, an artist's model with short blonde hair and a lisp, and a cruel streak which makes her slice her lover's – Halliday's – hand open. On 24 May 1928, Lawrence published a short story which again appears to use Carrington as a source. This time she appears as Ethel Case, a middle-aged heiress who sought sexual and artistic fulfilment through a Mexican toreador. At the end of this story, entitled 'None of That' and published in *The Woman Who Rode Away and Other Stories*, Case is raped by six men, wills her money to the matador, and commits suicide.

While Carrington as the artist's model Minette Darrington in *Women in Love* is young, pregnant, and manipulative, Ethel is Minette's older version in body as well as in definition of purpose. Minette is small and delicate, arrested in her fifteenth year like Betty Bligh (Carrington was also used as a source for this character), the tiny sex therapist of a Strachey-based character in Wyndham Lewis's *The Apes of God*. Ethel Case, however, is 'between thirty and forty' (Carrington was thirty-five), and approaches middle age: 'she was blonde, with thick, straight blonde hair, and she was one of the very first to wear it short, like a Florentine page-boy. Her skin was white, and her eyes were very blue, and she was not thin.' While 'None of That' is an undeniably vicious story which purports to warn against the dangers of separating the body and the mind, it is curious that Lawrence published it at a time when Carrington was in fact experiencing similar fears.

Most of Lawrence's portrayal of Bloomsbury in *Women in Love* can be explained by his dislike of that privileged group. Despite Carrington's protests he persisted in believing that she had been born with money, had married money, and had inherited money. Her development and difficulties as an artist were unimportant to him since he perceived her (as also did Wyndham Lewis) as someone who adopted the artist's life rather than as someone who was driven to create. As part of the Bloomsbury set, she was lumped with the others in this respect. What had once seemed to set her apart was her relationship with Mark Gertler, and all that Lawrence knew about that was negative; he naturally sided with the young Gertler, who was his friend, whose working-class background more closely resembled his own, and whose sexuality Carrington seemed driven to crush.

Lawrence could not understand how Carrington could fall in love with Lytton Strachey, and he was not the only one. Dorothy Brett, one of Carrington's friends from the Slade School of Fine Art, was another who sided with Mark Gertler when Carrington finally left him to live with Lytton:

> How and why Carrington became so devoted to him I don't know. Why she submerged her talent and whole life in him, a mystery ... Gertler's hopeless love for her, most of her friendships I think were partially discarded when she devoted herself to Lytton ... I know that Lytton at first was not too kind with Carrington's lack of literary knowledge. She pandered to his sex obscenities, I saw her, so I got an idea of it. I ought not to be prejudiced. I think Gertler and I could not help being prejudiced. It was so difficult to understand how she could be attracted.[2]

Because she was used at least four times in literature (Katherine Mansfield also portrayed her in a short story) it is not difficult to see her life as a series of dramatic events, played out by her in different roles. In fact her letters tend to encourage that interpretation, because in them she adopted different voices and tones for different correspondents. To Lytton Strachey she was lightly amusing and very affectionate. To Gerald Brenan she was a story-teller – but became alternately warm and scolding, depending on the state of their relationship. Her letters to Julia Strachey often ended with expressions of physical as well as emotional love: 'Julia, I wish I was a young man and not a hybrid monster, so that I could please you a little in some way, with my affection. You know you move me strangely. I remember for some reason every thing you say and do, you charm me so much.'[3] However, an enormous number of letters to a wide variety of people throughout her life contain similar expressions, and cannot always be interpreted as signs of promiscuity. She was only promiscuous in that she enjoyed having a circle of friends she 'nibbled at', in Julia's words.

After her early relationship with Mark Gertler, when she gained more sexual experience, teasing references to sex occur more frequently. The painter Augustus John, in particular among her friends, also enjoyed this type of conversation; Carrington reported in a letter dated 7 August 1928, that he had 'confided in me all his love affairs.'[4] Fifteen years her senior, he is referred to in her letters as 'the old monster Augustus' who intruded upon her conversations with Dorelia and their daughters Vivien and Poppet. Yet their relations were quite congenial; she travelled to France with them in 1929, and she wrote in early spring of enjoying 'some grand pub crawls with old Augustus.'[5] At the same time, he sent her – apparently unsolicited – a number of 'naughty' drawings and erotic poems.

The sexual remarks that flew between Carrington and Lytton's homosexual friends were more light-hearted. She wrote to Sebastian Sprott in March 1929:

> You really are rather a [drawing of a deer] to give me such a beautiful present [probably for her 36th birthday]. Truly I have never received anything that gave me half-so-much pleasure. What a pity you aren't. . . You might have added so much pleasure to my life, dear boy. But there; 'it's NO good REPINING over lost balls,' said the Countess whilst playing croquet with the Archbishop of Canterbury.[6]

The lack of any possible physical relationship between the two allowed Carrington to indulge in this kind of pun.

However, Carrington's comfort with jokes about sex had its limits. While visiting France with Augustus and Dorelia John in 1929, she and they shared a château with two young American men: 'One is a *bon viveur* bachelor who lives in Paris (great jokes last night about his being a bachelor but *not* our style of joke).'[7] However, references to and jokes about sex found their way into Carrington's other relationships as well. Half in love with both Alix Strachey, James's wife, and Julia Strachey, married to Stephen Tomlin, she frequently wrote to them, expressing in passing her regret at being unable to please them in physical ways. To Alix she wrote at the end of 1928, 'I send you my love. I wish it was 4 some use. Well. Well.'[8]

Several years ago, when I first began working on this book, I had in mind finding the answer to a single question: why was Dora Carrington's work neglected by her friends, and in particular by the Bloomsbury group? That question, however, turned out to be misleading and even inappropriate for it assumed that she wanted her work not only noticed but exhibited. I had fallen into the common trap of assuming that pictures worth painting were created to be exhibited, and that those works not found in galleries and museums were not worth viewing. We tend to think of art more as a finished product than as a process of recognition and creation. Carrington reserved the title 'artist' for the 'gods' of creation: Cézanne was an artist; she and her friends were painters. While perhaps harsh, thinking of art this way gave her a goal. When reading in the pages that follow of her lifelong discouragement with her work, one must remember that this discouragement did not entirely prevent her from painting; it only meant that she never reached the point where she felt that she could lay down her brushes and say, 'I am an artist.'

Among the myths about Carrington is one which I too initially believed: that the men in her life, particularly Lytton Strachey, were to blame for the tapering off of her artistic production. Like many of the other beliefs about her, this oversimplifies the issue. She turned in the last seven years of her life to decorative art (particularly glass pictures and painted tiles) to augment her small income. This did not mean, however, that she gave up her serious art. Some of her finest paintings were done in the years 1925–31, and during some of those years she painted prolifically. But because she frequently painted over canvasses which dissatisfied her many of these works no longer exist.

Reading over the correspondence – much of it unpublished – between Carrington and Strachey forces one to give up the notion that he somehow neglected, disliked, or belittled her talent. On the contrary, he was so concerned that her lack of income forced her to do work which took her from her painting that he offered to give her £100 a year (a fairly substantial income at that time) in order that she should be free to paint.[9] She rarely exhibited after she met him, but when she did it was only because Strachey, believing in her talent, pushed her to submit works to galleries and exhibitions. All but hanging the pictures himself, he helped her to select and price the works she sent off. As his income rose, he paid for her to have studios in each of the houses where they lived. He was as excited by praise of her work as she was herself. Her husband, Ralph Partridge, too 'thought that she was Michael Angelo' and refused to acknowledge any negative criticism of her painting by outsiders.[10]

Most of Bloomsbury saw little of her work; she was secretive, shy and insecure about it. But according to Richard Shone, author of *Bloomsbury Portraits,*

> [Duncan] Grant, in later years when I knew him, was a keen admirer; he denied the idea that Lytton and the household chores held her back from painting more; the paucity of work was due to her own diffidence and sense of failure. Housework was, in a way, an excuse *not* to paint. I went with Grant to the Grosvenor Galleries retrospective in 1970. Lord Eccles made a speech to the effect that Lytton and others in B[loomsbur]y didn't take DC's work seriously. Grant shouted out a protest – 'non-sense' – from among the listening crowd. This was so uncharacteristic of his nature that I felt that he really did think Eccles's view was very mistaken.[11]

Shone goes on to say that he 'didn't write much about Carrington in my *Bloomsbury Portraits* because I never felt there were close aesthetic affinities between her and the Charleston artists. Nor did they emerge from the Slade – which so obviously influenced Carrington for the rest of her life.'

Perhaps the best portrait of Carrington derives from the hundreds of letters she wrote from 1915 to 1932. This biography augments that picture and places her words within the perspective necessary to understand them. I hope it will inspire readers to seek out and enjoy those wonderful letters.

Notes

Carrington was a notoriously poor speller, but she was not the only one in her circle who made mistakes. I have left most of the spelling errors and also those of punctuation, but have not retained one common quirk: Carrington frequently capitalised letters which appeared mid-sentence. It is a vagary of handwriting which is shared by many but which does not translate well into print. Many feel that the errors she made – such as transposing letters in words – were symptomatic of dyslexia or some other learning disorder. This seems to be quite possible.

The drawings by Carrington that appear in the text and at the beginnings of chapters were chosen in many cases without regard for their original contexts or the dates on which they were made. They are intended as decorations only.

PROLOGUE

Early on the morning of 11 March 1932, Frances Marshall and Ralph Partridge were awakened by the telephone in their London flat. The gardener at Ham Spray House in Hungerford, Partridge's former home, was frantic: Dora Carrington, Mr Partridge's wife, had shot herself and was apparently dying on her bedroom floor. The two paused only long enough to telephone the Hungerford doctor, dress, and arouse their friend David Garnett from his rented room upstairs. Then all three, joined by a hired nurse, rapidly made the one-hour drive to Ham Spray, in a state of silent shock.

The doctor arrived before them. Not daring to move her, he had propped her up on rugs and administered morphine; there was little else he could do. Sensing his anxiety, Carrington, although clearly dying, asked him to take a glass of sherry. Her last lucid hours were characteristically spent in seeing to the emotional and physical needs of others.

Lytton Strachey, the linchpin of her short life, had died of cancer only weeks earlier. Although she had promised Ralph that she would not make an attempt on her life, Carrington's nearly successful attempt on the night before Strachey's death and her obvious preparations for her own made it clear that such a promise was only made to calm him. When Ralph and the others arrived at Ham Spray, she said that she 'longed to die'.[1] She later retracted this, and claimed instead that her suicide was really an accident, the result of shooting at rabbits from her bedroom window. This would have been, under other circumstances, a plausible explanation, for rabbits were the scourge of the Ham Spray garden. But this time no one believed her, although she had arranged the room, even to the slipping rug underneath her, to support her story.

Partridge's unceasing attempts to keep her alive had taken their toll; he was made miserable by the recent death of his dear friend Lytton, and exhausted by what he began to sense were futile strategies to keep Carrington from committing suicide. As Frances later wrote, Carrington saw Ralph's 'agony of mind' and promised 'that she would do her best to get well'.[2] Her last promise, however, like so many others, was one she would not keep.

David Garnett stayed outside the room while Carrington was dying, but went in afterwards for 'an intolerable moment': 'There was no sign in her features of the pain she must have suffered,' he wrote. 'It was the face of a proud woman.'[3] When she died that afternoon, she was only eighteen days away from her thirty-ninth birthday. Strachey would have turned fifty-two ten days earlier.

Her final diary entries made it clear that the pain she had suffered during her last hours was nothing compared to that she endured in her last weeks of life. The weather had been incongruously beautiful; Ham Spray had never been so lovely in the spring. This only left her feeling emptier with each day, and she had composed, copied, and pasted poems into the back of the book she had titled – and misspelled – 'D. C. Partride, Her Book'.[4] One, cut from a magazine, read:

> The spring is past, and yet it hath not sprung;
>   The fruit is dead, and yet the leaves be green;
> My youth is gone, and yet I am but young;
>   I saw the world, and yet I was not seen;
> My thread is cut, and yet it is not spun;
> And now I live, and now my life is done.[5]

Her inability to prevent Lytton's death was matched by a sense of failure as an artist. The choice of this poem implicitly brought these two aspects of her life together. She had devoted herself to Lytton, yet he had died; she had continued to paint, yet she 'was not seen'. Like the thread that was 'cut' and 'yet' ... not spun', her artistic work never fully pleased or satisfied her. Several days later Virginia Woolf commented in her diary that 'Lytton is affected by this act. I sometimes dislike him for it. He absorbed her [,] made her kill herself.'[6] Even in death, she felt, he was somehow altered by Carrington's final decision not to live without him.

After the extended and public process of Strachey's death, Carrington's death was isolated, unceremonial, and gruelling. Strachey's body was cremated, and a bronze plaque commemorating him was hung in the Strachey Chapel in the church of St Andrew, in Chew Magna, Somerset.[7]

Frances, Ralph, and their friends, already numbed by Lytton's death, were devastated by Carrington's. Ralph took care of the final arrangements. Apparently there was no funeral. In fact, no one now even remembers what became of Carrington's body.

PART ONE

YOUTH

CHAPTER ONE

CHILDHOOD

'I had an awful childhood,' Dora Carrington wrote in 1920.[8] Like many of those who knew her, in adulthood she found herself hopelessly divided, with frigidity and sexuality, tradition and free-thinking, reclusiveness and sociability uncomfortably mixed in her personality. Unlike many others, however, she was able to trace the origins of her ambivalences directly to her parents and her childhood. In fact, she did so with such facility that her views of those people and that time became rigidly polarised in her memory. She adored Samuel Carrington, her father, and freely and frequently confessed that she hated her mother, Charlotte Houghton Carrington.

Born on 21 June 1832, five years before Victoria began her long reign, Samuel Carrington was the son of a Liverpool merchant, also named Samuel, who had retired to Penrith in Cumberland with his wife Louisa and their children. The younger Samuel was the eldest of eight children and was educated at Cheltenham College. Indian service was something of a family tradition, and various of his uncles and other relations had worked there. Accordingly Samuel was given training in engineering and on 20 June 1857, the day before his twenty-fifth birthday, he boarded a steamer and headed for India to work as a civil engineer with the East India Railway Company. He would spend nearly thirty years there.

Samuel's letters home reveal a young man very much attached to his family. Unlike his daughter, he clearly loved both his parents, and freely admitted it.

My Dear Mother ... It is now 10 days since I last saw you and all, it seems much longer, but one day at sea is so much like another, that I can only count them by the help of my diary. Nothing would give me more pleasure, than to hear if it were possible, a postman's knock with a letter from home. Which knock, however will be a long time before I hear it again. I shall now doubly treasure your good letters, that I have with me – reread them & bring to memory, by-gone time.[9]

His mother copied his letters lovingly into a bound notebook, and tied the originals together with ribbon. Despite their lack of originality, the letters show a family talent for illustration which was passed on to his daughter. Not only are Samuel's occasional drawings of sights he had seen quite competently executed, but also his mother, in copying them into her notebook, managed to improve on them.

Samuel was rather a provincial young man, to whom everything he encountered on his early voyage seemed wonderful. He recorded these things – along with the prices of all the foods and trinkets he saw – in his letters. That naivety vanished quickly as he drew closer to India, however. India was at that time run by the East India Company, to the commercial benefit of Great Britain. Founded in 1600 to compete with Portuguese traders in India, the East India Company had overtaken its European competitors to become the *de facto* ruler of India. When Samuel set out from England in mid-1857, India was not yet officially part of the British Empire, but that situation changed rapidly and violently in the weeks that it took him to get there. The Sepoy Rebellion, a violent revolt of Indian troops known to the British as the 'Indian Mutiny', broke out in 1857, and the British hastened to send their own troops and non-military personnel to quell it. The rebellion was finally put down, and India brought officially under British rule (culminating in Queen Victoria's becoming 'Empress of India' in an elaborate ceremony) in 1858. But for Samuel, as he approached the sub-continent, there was news of massacres at each outpost and of worse to come in the interior.

At first Samuel seemed concerned but confident. 'Every one of the old Indians seem very savaged at the natives, & they certainly will get no mercy, except death,' he wrote home on 9 July. 'And even on board this vessel, so little can the natives be trusted now, that ... the arms are taken out of the stands & put out of reach.' This simple precaution helped, but as they drew closer they saw not only burned-out bridges and 'engineering houses', but dead engineers and inspectors at the stations. 'The natives are very insolent, and demand what they like for hire, and will scarcely serve at all,' he wrote on 7 August 1857.

He reached Calcutta soon after, but by this time had begun to question the motives of both sides. His life was in great danger, as were the lives of all British there, and what was left of his childhood and comfortable innocence soon disappeared in the face of murder, mutilation, theft, and destruction. In August he wrote what he thought might be his last letter home.

And now dear Mother, Father, and all of you, I hope for the best & trust in God above to take care of us, to guide the Rulers of the Land, to do that which will be the best to prevent any more bloodshed on either side. And if the white-faces are to rule these people, let it be for the better in future. And I pray that I may be preserved, under this guidance to do my duty when called upon. I pray for forgiveness through Christ & his mercy, and will try for the future, if I am spared, to lead a better life.

He survived, but lost twenty-one pounds in two months, and learned to sleep with a gun.

He spent the next thirty years, however, in relative peace. Under his supervision, many railway stations and accompanying buildings were constructed. While accepting and working for the British presence in India, over the years he increasingly questioned its repercussions and it was these years that developed the personality which was to form and impress his daughter: a mixture of charitableness, unconventionality, and strong opinion. On 14 May 1867, after ten years in India, he wrote a long disquisition home on the differences between real charity, which was accompanied by moral obligation, and false charity, which only congratulated the giver.

... one digs a well in India for Bono Publico – why – for [the] same reason – altho' from different taste that some people will put a stained glass window in a church at home –

When you see people dieing [*sic*] for want of food and of no fault of their own – can you eat and walk past them like a cow [?] No, instinct makes you feed them. And finding some satisfaction in so doing, you know it's not a bad instinct. And so you go on.

But to be charitable, one should be always helping them and finding out those who want help, not waiting until famine make[s] animals of them ...

He put his feelings into practice, and carried home with him years later a reputation for helping others.

By the late 1870s he had travelled the world, including America, and was beginning to reassess his life. He had moved from youth to middle age in India, with friends but nevertheless alone, and saw the world changing about him. Where his move had seemed permanent, 'nowadays nobody takes any trouble to himself for going home for three to six months if they have anyone to occupy their house – They simply pack-up clothes ... and leave all standing, as you do when you go to Devonshire.' Moreover, the faces around him were changing as well. 'It's queer to look at children I knew [the] other day,' he wrote pensively in 1879, 'now men of business and young men who have turned themselves into Burma sahibs and heads of families – makes one think I've been here too long.' It was nearly time to go home.

He retired and returned to England a few years later, physically active although slightly deaf from overdoses of quinine to cure tropical diseases. He had seen a great deal of the world and collected artifacts from all of the places he had been, and had a large income and savings. Most importantly, he wanted a wife.

In 1888, Samuel Carrington finally married at the age of fifty-five. His choice, much to his family's dismay, fell upon Charlotte Houghton, the sister of the late husband of one of Samuel's nieces. Samuel may have married relatively late in life, but his two sisters had not: each had married at sixteen and each had had a dozen children. By the time he returned from India, those children had in turn married and started families. It was in her capacity as governess that Charlotte lived with her late brother's wife and that she met her future husband. She was in her thirties, some twenty years younger than he, when they married.[10]

His choice seemed an odd one. Charlotte Houghton's family (of whom little is now known) was of a decidedly lower class than Samuel's but their differences in personality were even greater. Where Samuel's outlook on life made room for vagaries of station and character, Charlotte's was limited to what was the done thing. Although both lived in the Victorian age, Charlotte's shorter life had been spent upholding the rigid English codes of behaviour. As a governess, and later as a wife and mother, her devotion to those standards became absolute. Perhaps Samuel felt himself something of an outsider to English family life, and settled on a woman who would be grateful to have him, and who would see to the proper upbringing of the ensuing offspring. For her part, Carrington's mother later confessed that 'she married him out of pity because he wanted looking after'.[11] Even their wedding photograph accentuates their differences: Samuel sits sideways in a chair, one hand casually resting on his cheek, while Charlotte stands rigidly at his side, her hand at her husband's elbow.[12] It is a conventional pose, yet his casualness and her stiffness are their own. It was Charlotte's rigidity, extending through all aspects of life, which would be the bane of Dora's existence.

No one on the Carrington side could forget that Charlotte's background was 'inferior' to theirs. As the keeper of the family propriety, not to mention a former governess, she no doubt felt she must walk a far straighter line than most for whom she could have worked. More was expected of an employee than of a family member. Yet many of her traits were shared with other members of her family. In Noel Carrington's words, 'Samuel Carrington – the rich bachelor from India – surprized and almost certainly disappointed his own relations by marrying the governess. At any rate it was perceptible later that the Carrington connection felt itself a cut above the Houghtons, who came from Erith in Kent and from a less affluent stratum of the middle class ... Our mother's relations were forbidding and finders of fault, perpetually in mourning, perpetually suffering from colds, and apprehensive of draughts.' The Carringtons, in contrast, 'were cheerful, easy-going and spendthrift'. Some of this was reflected in Samuel's 'oriental code of hospitality' which unfortunately encouraged relatives on both sides to visit annually uninvited and to outstay their welcome.[13]

Dora recalled that her maternal grandfather 'was a sanitary inspector (or something like that, he called himself an engineer) [in contrast to her father, who was a 'real' engineer] & they lived at Dulwich, & later at Tooting Bec common'. She remembered being shocked as a child that her maternal grandmother used the word 'ain't'. The Carrington family made an annual trip to Tooting Bec 'and visited these rather vulgar grandparents, & my Mother's brothers, (who frankly weren't gentlemen)'.[14]

In contrast, the Anglo-Indian visitors to the Carrington homes in England were full of praise for Samuel: for one thing he had fed, out of his own pocket, a famine-stricken district. To the Welsh doctor who had once saved his life, he opened his English home for several years, and as a result Dora and her sister and brothers had a new and important view of their ageing father through his eyes. The young Dora, hearing her father discussed in admiring tones, elevated him at times to the level of a myth. He had no concern for the conventions of dress and religion and although he was a devout Christian, his faith was shaped more by the Ten Commandments and the teachings of the New Testament than by public displays of piety. He cared more about being a good man than an ostentatious churchgoer, but this did not save Dora from what she considered to be the ridiculous observations of organised religion. The middle classes of Bedford, where Dora spent most of her childhood, belonged to the Church of England, and since, despite Samuel's unorthodox convictions, he was a God-fearing man, the Carrington children received a highly conventional religious training.

Over the next six years, Samuel and Charlotte produced five children. The eldest, Lottie Louise, later became a nurse and married an orthopaedic surgeon.[15] Their wedding was later to cause Dora great distress. To her, it was a monumental waste of both time and money, and a meaningless convention which served only to legitimise greed and lust. Dora's other three siblings were boys: Sam, later severely shell-shocked during the Great War; Edward, known as Teddy, killed in 1916 at the battle of the Somme, whom she idolised until the end of her life; and Noel, a year and a half younger than she, and with whom she remained close, despite political and personal differences. Dora was the fourth of the five children, born in 1893 when her father was sixty-one. As a girl, and the next to youngest child, she often felt left out of games and exploited by her siblings. The two youngest, Dora and Noel, were also the closest, and frequently banded together against the older three.

Because Dora only knew Samuel in his old age, the exciting parts of his life had already occurred and she knew them only as stories. She saw him as a gentle man who had endured hardship and seen the world, from the East to America; he was, in her eyes, an Odysseus who had reached home at last. This image is particularly appropriate because of the romantic role which sailors would later play in her life: after her favourite brother Teddy was killed, she would refer to him as 'her sailor brother', and the last love of her life would also be a sailor. In sharp contrast to this adventurous and romantic father was Charlotte Houghton, a true example of what Carrington saw as conventional, domestic, and repressive English womanhood.

Noel, Dora's youngest brother, later wrote that 'differences between parents were not voiced openly in front of the children, but they were sensed, and Dora built up a special image of her father's noble qualities'.[16] This loyalty to her father, whether or not based on an accurate understanding of his character, caused her to identify with his refusal to conform and to take his side in the unvoiced dispute between her parents. 'When I used to make jokes my Father always said, "That's balderdash, nonsense, nonsense, gammon-&-spinach,"' she recalled, 'and sometimes in a rage ended up, "not true, not true." He was a fascinating character. It was a pity that he died, & that my Mother lived.'[17]

Noel Carrington, in his book on his sister's art, twice cautions against seeing too much in his sister's relationship with their father: 'That Dora was something of a favourite with her father was undeniable, but for daughters to develop a special relationship with their fathers is not at all unusual.'[18] Later he says that 'it was natural enough for Dora, always an idealist, to feel a deep love for her father, and this surely renders it unnecessary to draw a psycho-analytical moral.'[19]

One cannot, however, discount the profound influence of this early relationship upon her life and career. She seems to have viewed her father as an island of reason and kindness in a sea of strict conventionality. He 'never altered his life to please the conventions or people of this century,' she wrote to Mark Gertler in 1919.[20] 'But I can't forgive [my mother] for taming him as she did, & for regarding all his independence, & wildness as "peculiarities" – and just making out he was a sentimental good husband.'[21] His refusal to keep up the appearances of dress and propriety that were so important to her mother undoubtedly helped give Dora the strength she needed to break away from her mother later, although this was a long and difficult process on both sides. Her father recognised his daughter's need for independence, and in his will left her a small income which she supplemented through her art work.

Undoubtedly Charlotte's obsession with public opinion stemmed from some sense of inferiority. To Noel, his mother's concern with conformity and convention took two forms:

> The first was extreme prudishness. Any mention of sex or the common bodily functions was unthinkable. We were not even expected to know that a woman was pregnant. Even a word like 'confined' was kept to a whisper. The second was church-going and behaviour on Sunday. We all came to hate the whole atmosphere of a Sunday morning. The special clothes, the carrying of prayer books, the kneeling, standing and murmuring of litanies. Yet to lead her family up the aisle, especially on Easter Sunday for communion, was to our mother the true reward of righteousness. I believe Carrington would have refused point-blank to bend the knee had it not been that it would have bitterly grieved our father.[22]

Dora was born at Hereford on 29 March 1893, in a house called Ivy Lodge (she claimed never to be able to recall whether she was born in 1893 or 1894, although she always knew her correct age). On her second birthday the family moved to another house in Hereford, called Belle Vue. She remembered Belle Vue as being 'an enormous house with a huge kitchen'. Like many Victorian houses, this one had the kitchen in the basement and one could look up through the grating outside the window to the garden.[23]

At a time when moving house was a slow and difficult process, the Carringtons 'migrated at regular intervals'. Presumably this was to alleviate Charlotte's rheumatism, but Noel also attributed it to 'a habit acquired in India where "striking camp" was in the nature of Anglo-Indian life'.[24] While she was still quite young the Carringtons moved again, this time to a house called Belmont, in King's Road, Berkhamsted. This house, too, she remembered as being huge, but when she saw photographs of it as an adult she realised that 'it was an ordinary late Victorian detached house with a gravel drive'. They remained at Belmont for two years, and here Dora's memories of particular incidents became quite vivid. As the next to youngest child, she had only the younger Noel to torment when she felt frustrated. Once she managed to lock him outside the gates, which gave her a great sense of satisfaction until they found him and she 'was put in terrible disgrace' and forbidden to attend a party.

Another time, at the age of five, she cut a square out of a blue striped dress 'just there' and tried to cover it with her hands as she walked about. She had made the intriguing discovery that if you folded the fabric in half, the shape doubled when unfolded. Needless to say, her nurse and parents were not as pleased as she at this discovery: 'I was then beaten on my naked bottom by a nurse with pale yellow frizzy hair, rather like Queen Alexandra. I turned my head round as I lay on her knee, & saw my bottom. I was mortified to see it[;] I thought it very large, & pink.'[25]

Around this age, too, she suffered from incontinence. Too shy to ask permission to leave the room, she repeatedly soiled her clothes and repeatedly was punished for it. (This anal stage apparently lasted for some time: she also recalled that once she and Noel, peering through an opening in the outhouse, were given a demonstration of the bodily functions by an obliging brother Teddy, whereupon all three children were caught and punished by the nurse.)

It was during these years that she began to be aware of herself as a separate person.

> At Belmont I first remember drawing, & learning to write my name. My grandfather gave me half-crowns which I remember being forced to put in a money box. I now first remember having a character implanted on me. I was made to feel I was 'good'. I had mixed feelings. I liked being praised. But I also disliked being made to be 'good'. When secretly I wished to do other things.[26]

With this self-awareness came a dissatisfaction with doing things the right way.

The family moved again when Dora was six, to a house called Havenhurst, which was probably in Berkhamsted. There she had a close friend, 'a little girl called Carol who had a red pinafore, & short black hair. My recollections are now so many, & so very visual I can't tell them all.' One of the things she remembered most clearly was having to go to a gymnasium to try to correct her feet. Her toes turned inward, and this remained a problem throughout her life. Many of the cartoons in her adult letters show her with turned-in feet, and one of the things that her later friends recalled about her was her child-like demeanour and stance.[27] Those who disliked her thought that her posture was an affectation, adopted to make her appear more helpless, whereas it was in reality a congenital, orthopaedic problem.

Another early physical problem affected her throughout her life. She was overweight as a child, and as a result clumsy. She fell down a lot, and her brothers and sister gave her the nickname of 'Dumpty'; and even when later photographs proved her to be otherwise she continued to see herself as fat. The baby fat remained until she went off to the Slade in 1910, but was never as much as she imagined. Her school photographs show her to be a plump child who metamorphosed into a smiling, slender, and very attractive young woman with notably slanting, enigmatic eyes.

A picture emerges of a child who was shy, rather rebellious, and insecure, with a low opinion of her body. When she was fourteen and began to menstruate, she was filled with horror and anger at the further shame her body had inflicted upon her. She called this monthly affliction 'the fiend', and it cemented the distaste she felt for her body. It was inevitable that a young woman whose life straddled periods of great social change would have difficulty in coming to terms with her sexuality, but Dora had greater difficulty than most. Her mother's repressive upbringing gave her a disgust with sex and a guilt that never left her. When she left home and entered the far freer world of London artists, she found herself unable to overcome this repulsion for years. She found escape in the occasional wearing of trousers and jodhpurs but adrogynous attire never entirely compensated for the inner conflict.

Samuel, Charlotte and their brood moved to 6 Rothsay Gardens, Bedford, in 1903, and remained there until all the children were educated, some twelve years or so. Bedford was a market town known for its inexpensive schools, and the residents were in large part families headed by men who had retired from the army or, like Samuel, from other overseas careers. The town grew rapidly after the Second World War, and heavy development continues today; the Carrington family would recognise little of it now. Then, the town 'was still something of a religious stronghold where the various churches exercised great influence at all levels of society ... All sects were united in one respect, the strict observance of the Sabbath, to the extent of banning not only sport or entertainment but such private pursuits as painting or playing music that was not hymnal in character.'[28] The schools which the Carrington children attended 'set [more store] on sport than on scholarship as conducive to char-acter-building; and the majority of parents would not have had it otherwise'.[29] The High School acknowledged later that Dora was 'surely more like her father than the average Bedfordian', an opinion with which Dora herself would have wholeheartedly agreed.

She and her sister Lottie Louise were started at Bedford High School in May 1903, when Dora was ten and Lottie fourteen. Neither girl distinguished herself academically: Lottie failed Latin, French, and Botany, but was to 'learn music'. Dora was also to 'learn music' but to have 'no violin or singing'. The records note that she was 'more musical than her sister', that her spelling was bad, and her drawing good. There was no school in the afternoons for younger children, but students whose parents were willing to pay a bit extra sent their daughters back during those hours for classes in subjects such as needlework and drawing. Dora stayed on for drawing lessons in the afternoons, and her ability was quickly 'assessed at Honours

I Design'. Despite her artistic success, however, it took some time for Dora to accustom herself to the new school. The school photograph of 1903, her first year, shows her sitting mournfully on the ground at the end of a row of girls, her long hair over her shoulders and pulled back rather severely at the crown; two years later she graduated to the end of the first seated row, wearing the same unhappy expression and the same hairstyle. Tellingly, she is sitting with a noticeable gap between her and the next girl, the only one in the group to be separated from the others. But by 1908 and 1910 she is smiling and poised, with thick, stylish hair, as befitted her maturity.

Dora was one of about 600 girls at the school, who were divided between boarders and day students. Day girls like the Carringtons arrived on foot and, increasingly, by bicycle. There was no required uniform except for a straw boater worn in the spring, and a felt hat worn in the winter. Under the guidance of Miss Collie, the Headmistress, the girls had a structured day which included both intellectual and physical tuition. The day began with prayers in the School Hall with its moveable podium, to the strains of the grand organ. Bells signalled the end of class, after which the girls had to pass through the corridors in single file, and in silence.

Bedford High School was only the second girls' school in the country to hire a physical education specialist, Miss Stansfield. Before her, army sergeants had instructed the girls in physical exercise. For indoor exercise the school had a gymnasium, a rather small, high room with climbing ropes hanging from the ceiling and gymnastic equipment arranged around the floor. On good days, the girls played outdoors in the playground or went in teams to the playing fields. Dora, however, took little pleasure in physical competition, being by nature uncompetitive, but became as she matured an indefatigable walker and cyclist.

While she was different and perhaps unhappy, Dora was no rebel; in general the Carrington family fitted in well enough, and most of the children grew up happily there. Encouraged to spend time out of doors, they went on long bicycle rides with their father and picnicked, fished on the river, and played games with each other and with their friends. Dora rarely went anywhere without her sketchbook, coercing or bribing her brothers, sister, and their friends to sit for her. When they would not, she drew from memory or drew caricatures. The drawings which so enliven her later letters show her sense of humour, but similar and remarkably sophisticated drawings from her youth reveal how early she developed the quality. Two cartoons of her sister, 'Lottie meeting the Admiral' and a girl shouting with braided hair, seem the work of a much older artist.

Aside from her father, the one person whom Dora adored was her brother Teddy. Like her, he appeared to be an outsider and a misfit in the family. He 'had very dark olive skin, almost black eyes, & pitch black hair – as a little girl I always thought there was a mysterious secret attached to him & that he wasn't really my Father's son because we were all fair.'[30] The best known drawing she did of Teddy gives a different image, of a plump, fair young man, but other drawings show his dark colouring more clearly. As with her father, she romanticised her brother after his early death. It seemed painful and ironic to her that the only two members of her family whom she truly loved should be taken from her.

Samuel believed that children should both work with their hands and develop their innate talents. Dora therefore had materials and encouragement for her art throughout her youth.[31] In recognising her daughter's talent, Charlotte claimed credit for her side of the family since she herself had spent some time at Lambeth Art School in her younger days. This rather unorthodox training for a mid-Victorian girl softens somewhat the harsh portrait of her mother that Carrington drew in later years, suggesting that, whether consciously or not, she later tried to negate or ignore her mother's influence.

Her personality was as much a striving against her mother as it was towards her father. However rigid and repressive Charlotte may have been, it was the tension between the two, and Dora's constant but often internalised struggles against her mother that eventually made her what she became: sexually ambivalent; loving but difficult; unconventional but afraid to rock the boat. Her rarely-exhibited artwork, her long, rambling, misspelled letters, her penchant for lying when confronted, all suggest that these ambivalences were channelled into areas which allowed her to transfer her emotions into less threatening arenas. Her 'awful childhood' thus can be seen as less one of abuse than one whose boundaries were too confining.

The Carrington house differed according to Noel from others in Bedford in that reproductions of works by recognised masters hung on the walls; this was the decision of Charlotte, who claimed that one of the paintings was a Velasquez self-portrait. These were supplemented by a profusion of artifacts, undiscriminatingly chosen by Samuel in his earlier travels in Asia and America. Charlotte visited the Royal Academy's Summer Exhibition in London annually, returning with an illustrated catalogue for her family; in this way, Noel recalled, 'a formal tribute at least was paid to Art, something I cannot recall observing in the homes of my friends. At no stage of her family life did Dora encounter opposition to her desire to become an artist.' On the contrary, her daughter's artistic ability was a source of pride to Charlotte: she could show off Carrington's work at her twice-monthly teas for her friends. This talent also exempted her daughter from musical training after her early lessons.[32]

What seemed to Carrington and Noel to be their mother's annoying allegiance to convention later appeared as an obsession which worsened with time. For Carrington, the carefree life ended in 1908, when she was fifteen and her father, already deaf from overdoses of quinine, was paralysed by a stroke. Charlotte took over the family, assuming the martyr's role she relished. Although partially lame and ill herself, she threw herself into waiting on her disabled husband, guarding him and 'interpreting' him. From then on, his needs and desires became filtered through her very different sensibility.[33]

Preferring secrecy to hypocrisy, Dora began to create a system of 'white lies' which included inventing visits to approved friends in order to visit ones who were disapproved of. Subterfuge increased when she had left home for London, but was still financially dependent upon her parents. It became crucial when she moved in with Strachey.

> I am not frank. It is often a burden to me my deceit ... I had ... an awful childhood, & honestly when I escaped & came to London at the age of 17 I couldn't speak the truth if I wanted to. I had acquired such an art of self protection. And even to Ralph I find I never can give myself completely away. But these people with whom I live Lytton, I mean, Alix [Strachey], & Lytton's brother, & their friends all assume a frankness of conversation, which ... appalled me at first. Then afterwards I saw it was a kind of technique, and behind it all there was a great reserve. I think I've caught rather these habits of conversation, but I never feel I give anyone except perhaps Alix any complete frankness.[34]

Calling this openness a technique made it easier to deal with. She blamed Charlotte and not herself for the development of this trait of reticence and secrecy. Yet to Charlotte, Samuel, and indeed to most Victorians, keeping secrets from one's parents was a cardinal sin. Thus, even in self-protection was guilt.

In her youth, she also began to be both secretive and careless about her correspondence. Letters and letter-writing were to form a major part of her life as she grew older, and she often confided in them secrets which she did not wish discovered by the wrong people. Yet she frequently left her letters lying about, seemingly by accident. In later years she became notorious for reading letters not addressed to her, even when it meant rummaging through others' coat pockets to find them. It is often difficult to discover exactly where she was living between 1910 and 1915, since letters are addressed to places she no longer lived in London, and it may well be that she had friends write to addresses where her parents expected her to be living, when in fact she may have lived elsewhere.

Her letters show that she considered even her name to be almost superstitiously private. She signed her letters with a variety of names over the years. 'Doric' (or its inversion, 'Cirod') was one of her favourites. She used 'Mopsa' (the name of a character in Shakespeare's *The Winter's Tale*) for many of her letters to Strachey. Early in life she dropped 'Dora', and began using her surname only. Her Christian name she felt reflected the eccentricities of both her parents. Her father had apparently misspelled 'Houghton' as 'Hoghton' at the registration of her birth, an error which perhaps reflected a subconscious negligence towards his wife – or that Dora's spelling difficulties were congenital. Dora explained the derivation of her name in 1920 to her friend Gerald Brenan.

> My name. Yes indeed its a closely guarded secret. For like all names it betrays my destiny[.] I can't help feeling I am doomed if once my name is known. So I definitely changed it to DORIC Carrington which is what I have made myself.
>
> DORA de Houghton Carrington ... You here in see the simplicity of my Father. Dora was the name of a lady he once loved in India dimly in the past. He being a virtuous man he doubtless suppressed this reason, & he told my Mother he just liked the name & it was short so I couldn't spell it wrong. My Mother being a woman told me later the reason. Houghton was my Mother's name, so he added 'de' to show that they had French blood in them, & because he was a whimsical character.
>
> There I have told you all. My shame is revealed. You must know I hate my Mother. It is a dull & bare fact. Her name is poison to me I would like to forget I am of Houghton blood [and] I dislike the Victorian sentimentality of 'Dora'.[35]

This preoccupation with names began early. She recalled composing a poem at the age of nine which revealed both her interest in what people were called, and with her own developing sense of guilt:

> He's the poorest of the poor
> See him beg from door to door
> Always asking always pleading
> And his wounds are sometimes bleeding
> 'His name what is his name?'
> There he's asking some good dame
> 'That man's name his name is Sin'
> 'Now my good woman don't let him in!'

She always delivered the line 'with great vigour, as an injunction'.[36]

Dora's perception of her parents' differences shows clearly in a sketch she made around 1910. In it, her mother, stout and stern, plays the piano, accompanied by Teddy on the violin. In the background sits Samuel, hands folded on a lap blanket, with a hauntingly sad expression on his face. Even while she was still in her teens Dora's work was becoming intensely personal. Naturally enough she drew her models from among her family and friends, but these works show a great affection and care. As an adult, her works grew to be notably autobiographical, and many of her best paintings were of people and places she knew and loved.[37]

Whatever the other advantages of Bedford, a cultural atmosphere was not one of them. There was perhaps an occasional concert or Shakespeare play by a travelling group, but nothing to spark or sustain a communal interest in the arts. Dora, despite these disadvantages, blossomed early into a talented and dedicated artist producing sketches which were technically proficient and strikingly composed. She preferred sketching from life, and only later as models became harder to find did she increasingly turn to landscape and still life painting.

At school, Dora's work was indifferent except in natural history and art, but her great talent for drawing and painting was obvious to everyone. She later freely admitted that she was uneducated, and that much of that was her own fault; in her childhood she had had little interest in learning. She cheerfully confessed in 1921 that she had 'not been spoilt by education', even though her later efforts to become a well-rounded reader belie this admission. She got top marks in art and natural history, but, at the age of seventeen, her formal education in everything but art ended.

Even so, her artistic success at Bedford High School was immense. Each year the Royal Drawing Society of Great Britain and Ireland awarded prizes for the best school drawings and exhibited them in a London show. Two years after entering the school, she became a regular winner: in 1905 she won First Class for imaginative drawings in pen and ink, and First Class for imaginative drawings of figures; in 1906 a Bronze Star for figure drawing in colour, Highly Commended for a figure drawing in black and white, and she was awarded a full honours certificate; in 1907, she got Commended Second Class for original figure illustrations; in 1908, Commended First Class for a drawing from life and for original drawings; in 1910, First Class for a figure from life, Second Class for figures from life, Second Class for original illustrations, Fourth Class for original illustrations. She was clearly marked for artistic success.

There was no art school in Bedford, so when her teacher insisted that Dora continue her training and try for the Slade School of Art in London, her family agreed. When she was accepted, her father and her younger brother Noel were particularly proud of her achievement and potential. Although pleased and excited by her success, her mother would soon profoundly regret the decision to send her to London, for 'the Slade ... altered her outlook on life and [gave] her new ideas on middle class conventions.'[38]

CHAPTER TWO

1910-11: THE YOUNG ART STUDENT

London in 1910 was a city of excitement, a hotbed of political and social change, and the location of fascinating or threatening – depending on one's Edwardian view – developments in the arts. Queen Victoria had died in 1901, and her death and the subsequent ascent to the throne of her eldest son, Edward VII, seemed to signal a new age. Already in his sixties when he was crowned, he had whiled away his time as Prince of Wales in the pursuit of the good life, particularly as represented by food, women and country houses. As king, he helped England loosen its Victorian stays until his death in 1910. This relaxing of constraint took a variety of forms. He paved the way for a more comfortable relationship with France, England's traditional opponent, which had both political and artistic ramifications. Germany's power and population were growing, and both England and France recognised the benefits of alliance. In addition, the artiness of the French, once seen as immoral and 'foreign', now gained approval, with profound effects upon English art and literature. The first Post-Impressionist Exhibition was staged by the critic Roger Fry in 1910, and presented the most modern of French art to the English public. In literature, sex began to be discussed far more openly. This was the heyday of the Edwardian novel, of Arnold Bennett, E. M. Forster, John Galsworthy; Conrad and Henry James were still writing, and Shaw's plays began to appear on the London stage.

Other changes were taking place as well. The National Union of Women's Suffrage Societies, joined in 1903 by the Women's Social and Political Union founded by Emmeline Pankhurst and her daughter Christabel, began to take increasingly public and violent action to call attention to their cause. Jailed and force-fed, they held firm in the pursuit of women's suffrage. They appeared in the literature of the period, and many writers supported their cause.

Dora entered the Slade in 1910, at the age of seventeen, and her immediate concerns were both social and educational. She was affected by her more immediate surroundings, yet those surroundings necessarily reflected the changes taking place on a more general level. College life, particularly in an art school, represented freedom in a multitude of ways ranging from increased freedom of artistic thought and performance, to personal freedom from parents and the expected social role for women. These freedoms had little impact upon the communities outside of London, and what conservative outsiders heard led them to fear its possible effects on the young. Since Dora was a product of the protected suburbs, her parents were careful to find a suitable residence for her in London. They placed her at Byng House in Gordon Square, a hostel noted for respectability and discipline.[39] Being lively, mentally quick, and observant, she made friends quickly and for the first time in her life was surrounded by young people whose interests were her own, yet whose social backgrounds often differed greatly from hers. As Noel pointed out, Bedford was only fifty miles northwest of London – barely an hour by train – but it 'might have been almost a thousand for all the cultural influence then exercised on it by the metropolis'.[40] Her new friends came from the poverty of London's East End; from wealthy, titled families; from intellectual and progressive families; from other middle-class, suburban enclaves. The students' sense of freedom derived not only from their talent, which had brought them to the Slade, but from their youth and common interest in art and its creation.

Part of University College London, the Slade School of Fine Art was founded in 1868 when Felix Slade endowed fine arts professorships at Oxford, Cambridge and London Universities. From the first, the Slade set out to be different. Potential students to the Royal Academy and other schools were required to submit elaborate stippled drawings of casts, but the Slade did away with that requirement. Its emphasis was on drawing (at which Dora excelled), an acquaintance with the works of the established masters (which the students reproduced), and life work. Dora had already proven her ability to make such drawings; her pen and ink renderings of the market at Bedford, which both captured the busy atmosphere and paid scrupulous attention to detail, were evidence of the high level she had achieved at the age of sixteen at this kind of work.[41]

Drawing nevertheless remained at the heart of the instruction at the Slade, although they allowed students to move more rapidly from casts to life drawing. The first professor had been Sir Edward

Poynter. He was followed in 1875 by Alphonse Legros who, although he spoke little English, managed to begin the tradition of realistic drawing for which the Slade became famous. Early Slade students included artists of such later eminence as Walter Sickert, William Rothenstein and Augustus John.[42]

Great changes at the Slade, and in the English art world, were taking place in Dora's lifetime. Frederick Brown, at the age of forty-two, was appointed Slade Professor in the same year she was born, and was still at the helm when she arrived as a student. He had been at the Westminster School of Art, and when he came to the Slade he brought with him two new staff members: Philip Wilson Steer, a painter and professor of art, and Henry Tonks, a surgeon whose love for art led him to study under Brown in the evenings. These three men kept tight control over the Slade and profoundly influenced its students for years.

At the time the Royal Academy was still the last – if not the latest – word on English art. The Academy monopolised English taste, which favoured the Renaissance, the Classical, and the sentimental; renditions of mythological and domestic scenes dominated the famous summer exhibitions. The painters who succeeded there attained both fame and fortune and, as Roger Fry's biographer Frances Spalding notes, 'it was here that an artist's reputation was made or broken and though attempts had been made to challenge the Academy's monopoly on artistic taste . . . these had soon degenerated into mere nurseries for the Academy.'[43]

Fred Brown had been among the first to challenge the Royal Academy. In 1886 he and several other artists, including Roger Fry and some formerly from the Slade, founded the New English Art Club. He had written its constitution, which stated that the new venture was to take note of the recent developments in French art, particularly Impressionism. In fact, as the idea for the New English first formed in 1885, someone proposed that it be called the 'Society of Anglo-French Painters'. The English painters of the New English preferred the open-air realism of diffused light to the historical, allegorical and literary works produced and promoted by the Royal Academy.[44] The newer and more progressive English artists like Walter Sickert, William Orpen, and Augustus John, and the artist and critic Roger Fry (who, at about the time that Carrington entered the Slade was himself entering the Bloomsbury 'circle') were, like the Slade professors, exhibiting there.

Yet Brown was no radical. He had a reputation among the students as standing for no nonsense, delivering crushing criticism, and having a great passion for his work. One former student recalled,

His usual method of addressing me was – 'You, Mr What's-your-name,' and I remember well his coming to me and saying in funereal tones – 'I ought to tell you – I think I ought to tell you – that we decided to award you a Scholarship this year. Of course it's much below the standard, but I don't see what we can do.' ... Yet, later, he found me my first commissions, for copies, replicas and decorative designs, and once he bought a drawing of mine from the New English Art Club exhibition.[45]

Wilson Steer was equally laconic but was known to lapse into an occasional, self-congratulatory pun. Stopping before the work of a student named Miss Carmen, he was heard to say, 'Miss Carmen has been very Bizet lately.'[46] Steer was generally reckoned to be the best painter of the three.

About Henry Tonks every student had an anecdote. His love for art was so great that when Brown offered him the position at the Slade, he did not hesitate to give up his job as Demonstrator of Anatomy at the London Hospital, as well as his medical career, to take it. His expertise was in life-drawing, and it was he with whom the students most often came into contact. Many of these encounters were shattering to students, for he was short on praise and long on devastating criticism. He would circulate among the students who were seated on the low drawing seats called 'donkeys' and offer generally negative comments. Sometimes these remarks caused further difficulty, as Randolph Schwabe, a former student, recalled.

Once I witnessed an odd scene. A new student had come into the Antique Room, a very tall, heavy man, in private life an amateur pugilist. He sat as others did on a low 'donkey' near the floor, doing his untutored best to render the cast in front of him. Tonks, from his great height, bent over him and said cuttingly – 'I suppose you think you can draw'. The student collected himself, rose slowly to an even greater height than Tonks and, looking down, replied with suppressed fury (but perfect justice) – 'If I thought I could draw – I shouldn't come here, should I?' He had the better of the encounter. Tonks had nothing to say, and left the room.

  Another reminiscence which concerns Brown, Tonks and Steer, is of a woman student, who, in trepidation, took her work to Tonks for criticism. She went to the Professor's room. It was the ... hour when no teaching was done in the classes. The Professor and his two associates were having tea. Tonks looked through her pictures with more than usually savage comments, which reached a point when the girl could scarcely restrain her tears. Brown could bear it no longer. He seized a picture, carried it to the light and remonstrated, – 'But it isn't as bad as all that, Tonks!' Meanwhile the unfortunate victim felt a warm hand sympathetically squeezing hers. It was Steer's. Somehow she collected the pictures and got away. A few days later she met Tonks in the corridor. He stopped her and began – 'I say – Steer says I've been a perfect beast to you ...' and the *Amende honorable* was made.[47]

Dora entered the Slade in October 1910, listing her London address as 'The College Hall, Byng Place'. Her days, like those of the other students, followed a routine. Each morning she would sign the huge roll book with lined pages divided by alphabet and gender (women on the left page, men on the right – a practice which continues today). Frequently the first under the 'C' section to log in, she often used that printed capital letter as part of her signature. Much of the day was spent in the Antique Room, crowded with students on their 'donkeys', drawing furiously and rubbing out mistakes not with rubber but with pieces of bread. If students were considered competent enough by Tonks and Steer, they would spend the end of the day drawing models in the Life Room.

The Life Rooms were also separated by gender, and the models were generally female. Models and students were forbidden to speak to each other, except for short commands, but naturally this rule broke down after school hours. Still, models were viewed as rather *demi-monde* figures. In earlier days, the women students and the professors could not be in the room with nude models at the same time: '[t]hey had to file out when he came in, and he wrote his criticisms, in their absence, around the margins of their drawings.'[48] Things had progressed past this point before Dora arrived.

The out-of-class hours were nearly as important as the lessons. Dora and her new friends took great advantage of London. They wandered the streets of Bloomsbury around the Slade and went to exhibitions and concerts. They ate out as often as their frequently meagre allowances permitted, usually at the Eiffel Tower restaurant. The more solvent students went to the Café Royal to see and be seen. There one was likely to encounter Augustus John, the former Slade student who was now the Bohemian darling of the London art world. The Slade itself sponsored dances and picnics, and Dora went to everything, dressed in what became termed 'Augustus John' clothing – full skirts and tight bodices, after the women in his paintings – and in general began to re-create herself.

After she had been at the Slade for a while, she was asked to show a new student around. Barbara Hiles, a small, dark-haired, pretty woman, had come to the art school from Paris where her father, a retired Liverpool cotton man, had gone to pursue his first love, art. Dora was somewhat younger than Barbara, but the two soon became close companions and their friendship lasted until the end of Carrington's life. Barbara had studied art in Paris but it was not until 1914, when she won a second prize in the Slade's Summer Competition in painting, that Professor Brown allowed her to pursue painting at the Slade. Tonks was similarly hard on her, but Barbara, unlike other students, stood up for herself. When he declared one

day that 'if she knew anything about dressmaking she had better go
home and do it,' she leaped 'up from her donkey and [told] him, in
a voice quivering with emotion, that she had in fact made every
stitch of clothing she was wearing. Thereafter he treated her with
greater respect.' It was also she who defied the unwritten rule about
keeping off the grass and ate her sandwiches there during the lunch
break. It earned her a visit to the Provost, but it also earned the
other students the right to sit there too. She learned to dance the
tango in the halls of the Slade, unaccompanied by music, but with
a South American partner.[49]

Another friend was Dorothy Brett who was nearly ten years older
than Dora, but who looked the same age. She was nervous and
becoming deaf, but nonetheless was extremely popular, even apparently with Professor Brown. She too remained close to her friends,
but found that friendship became strained over Dora's later affection
for Lytton Strachey. Deaf and lonely later on, Brett would leave
England in 1924 to help D. H. and Frieda Lawrence found a new
community in New Mexico. Dora would remain closer to Barbara
and to Ruth Humphries, another Slade student, both of whom
married and became mothers while fairly young. In these early years,
however, their similarities were greater than their differences, and
they shared not only a sense of excitement but an openness and
devotion to their work.

To many it was clear that Dora was in fact the centre of her circle
of friends, and she caught the eye of many a male student. Paul
Nash, who did not remain long at the Slade, noticed her early on.

> Carrington ... was the dominating personality, and when she cut her
> thick gold hair into a heavy golden bell, this, her fine blue eyes, her
> turned-in toes and other rather quaint but attractive attributes, combined
> to make her a conspicuous and popular figure ... I had noticed her long
> before this was achieved, when as a bored sufferer in the Antique Class
> my attention had been suddenly fixed by the sight of this amusing person
> with such very blue eyes and such incredibly thick pigtails of red-gold
> hair. I got an introduction to her and eventually won her regard by
> lending her my braces for a fancy-dress party. We were on the top of a
> bus and she wanted them then and there.[50]

The distinctiveness of Dora's group of female friends sometimes
put them in humorous opposition to other students, according to
Michael Reynolds, chronicler of the Slade.

> Hiles and her two girl-friends were still at the Slade when another
> notable trio arrived – Lady Violet Charteris and Lady Diana Manners
> (daughters of the Duke of Rutland) and Iris Tree (daughter of Sir
> Herbert Beerbohm Tree), all spectacularly beautiful and dressed in the
> height of fashion. They were at the school for only a short time, but long
> enough to cause a sensation, and their work in the Antique received what

the other trio felt to be excessive attention from the staff, including even Tonks. The crowning touch was the group of handsome young men, in top-hats and frock-coats, who took up position every morning in the entrance hall, waiting to take the beauties out to lunch. In the end Hiles & Co. confessed their feeling of pique to their friend Gerald Shove, who was then sharing a house in Gower Street with Maynard Keynes, and he presented himself at the Slade one day, attired for the occasion in top-hat and frock-coat, and escorted them down the road to No. 3 for a luncheon of scrambled eggs, cooked by Hiles.[51]

This sense of fun and independence was balanced by a deep desire to work. Male and female students met on equal terms; for Dora, as for many of the other women, it was the first time she had gone to school with young men. The young women therefore took their places among their male counterparts with seriousness and enthusiasm, often signalling a break with both their personal and artistic pasts.

The students' Victorian predecessors had turned out technically proficient works for an admiring public, and Charlotte Carrington had undoubtedly been one of these. The public liked what it could recognise; reality for them rested on a traditional representation of subject matter, which in turn consisted of accurate detail, subtle colouring, and faithful rendering of depth and light. The professors at the Slade, however, had other ideas on art. They felt, for example, that shading only served to mask poor drawing. Their moving away from the Royal Academy that Charlotte and so many others had learned to revere, and choosing to exhibit instead at the more innovative New English Art Club indicated an important shift. Yet, even then a new and important kind of art was developing, which would affect Dora and her friends profoundly within her first months at the Slade.

Termed 'Post-Impressionism' by Roger Fry, this new force questioned all the accepted standards in painting, including representation. Impressionism itself had barely begun to gain acceptance on English soil when Fry organised the first Post-Impressionist Exhibition and introduced the British public to the works of van Gogh, Picasso, Matisse, and Gauguin in London's Grafton Galleries from November 1910 to January 1911. When Virginia Woolf wrote that 'on or about December 1910, human character changed,'[52] she was referring in large part to the artistic storm that broke over London at that time.

The public response to the exhibition verged on hysteria. While many who saw the exhibition were reduced to laughter, others found the paintings obscene and were outraged. Few took the works seriously. Many believed it was a huge joke at their expense, and worried that Fry's good name attached to the exhibition might cause people to take the paintings seriously. An article in *The Times* on 7 November 1910 expressed this concern:

> It is to be feared that when [Roger Fry] regards the work of Gauguin and Matisse as the last word in art, the final expression of the genius of to-day, other writers of less sincerity will follow suit and try to persuade people that the Post-Impressionists are fine fellows, and that their art is the thing to be admired. They will even declare all who do not agree with them to be reactionaries of the worst type.[53]

Desmond MacCarthy, who wrote the exhibition catalogue, tried to anticipate and defuse such criticism:

> ... there is no denying that the work of the Post-Impressionists is sufficiently disconcerting. It may even appear ridiculous to those who do not recall the fact that a good rocking-horse often has more of the true horse about it than an instantaneous photograph of a Derby winner.[54]

Such justification only encouraged ridicule, and the Bloomsbury group as a whole, even its non-artistic 'members', found itself at the centre of the controversy.

The Slade's response to the exhibition was swift and negative. Brown broke with his old New English colleague Roger Fry (although he allowed him to continue lecturing at the Slade until 1914) and Tonks, who felt that his commitment to draughtsmanship and realism was now threatened by free style and wild colour, gathered the impressionable young students and announced that although 'he could not prevent students visiting the Grafton Galleries, he would only warn us and say how very much better pleased he would be if we did not risk contamination but stayed away.' Drawing was 'almost a religion' to Tonks, and he saw it as the foundation of all art. In one exhibition Fry seemed to allow the students to sweep away years of meticulous training and 'the entire Slade system'.[55]

Some of the students weathered the controversy without difficulty. Others – and this included Dora – would not be so fortunate, for they were caught in a terrible ambivalence. Belief in what they were being taught and what had brought them to the Slade in the first place was suddenly being compared, and not always favourably, with what was happening with art outside of its walls. This led, predictably, to a new but sometimes lifelong confusion about the value of their work. As one writer on the Slade put it, 'Tonks must take his share of blame for uncertainties experienced by less fortunate artists who wondered of what worth their studies had been' and 'it does not seem unnatural that students who studied during his Professorship should have felt some form of torment.'[56]

Both the Slade and the exhibition opened new worlds to Dora and made it extremely difficult to go back to the old one. Praise at the Slade was for style of art at which Dora excelled. Her drawings were accurate and masterly. One, 'A Cockney Picnic' drawn in 1911, shows not only her eye for detail, but also for arrangement and personally symbolic statement: while the adults lounge on the grass, laughing and eating, a solitary child stands with his back to them, gazing at the distant landscape.[57] At the same time, a new imaginative element was added to her work. 'Dante's Inferno', a pen-and-wash drawing submitted for a Slade competition in 1911, shows the same attention to minute detail, but one is struck most by the grotesqueness of the people condemned to hell.[58]

As the discovery of Post-Impressionism turned the British art world upside down, and the draughtsmanship of the Slade faded in comparison with the startling and innovative French paintings, Dora, still an impressionable teenager, was caught in an artistic bind. A tremendous admirer of the new art, she knew that much of her strength lay in the old. She was happy to experiment, however, and by the time of her first visits home she seemed to have rejected all but modern French and English art. 'None of her letters from that period survive, but I can well remember that even after one term she returned a very changed young person,' Noel recalled.

> Her opinions on art deflated all our previous conceptions; those revered elders, Lord Leighton, Alma Tadema, Herkomer and company were brushed aside as fit only for the dustbin. Who were we to look to, then? Why Sickert, Steer, John, McEvoy: names unknown to Bedford, and even these were not to be mentioned in the same breath as Cézanne.[59]

Cézanne became the patron saint of the younger artists, whether those at the Slade or the more mature painters of Bloomsbury, and his importance to and influence upon them cannot be under-estimated. Her 1915 portrait of her father, for example, bears a striking resemblance to Cézanne's 'Portrait of the Artist's Father Reading L'Evénement'. She uses the same pictorial subject and compositional approach.

The contrast between London and Bedford, school and home, became almost unbearable to her. She had a new life now, and new freedom. Her changed views on painting reflected changed views on any number of subjects, both intellectual and social. The students at the Slade tended to be better educated than she, and she began to develop a hunger for literature and history. While Noel sat for her on her visits home, she picked his brains for information on these subjects; she borrowed his textbooks often without returning them. Younger than she, he remained at Bedford to finish his schooling, but would go off to Oxford within the next year or so. (Teddy, meanwhile, was at Cambridge.) Her reading seemed formidable to him: *Tristram Shandy*, Tolstoy, Mary Wollstonecraft.[60]

The gap between home and school widened further with each visit to Bedford, said Noel, 'and what was opening before her became more frustrating'.

> Gradually she devised a makeshift system of alibis, based on painting commissions or visits to approved friends. All this led to a complicated calendar of deceptions which became a second habit even when no longer necessary. Quite apart from our father's feelings, she was economically dependent on the family, so that evasion was preferable to defiance.... One further consequence of the conflict was that she developed a repugnance for family life as such. As her own friends in turn came to marry she was apt to treat it as a lapse from grace, with maternity an inevitable but none the less deplorable sequel for a person of intelligence.[61]

At the Slade, where women were determined to be the equals of the men, she dropped her first name and used only her last. She would be known simply as Carrington from this time onwards, and even Noel, who shared the last name, never again called her Dora. Evidence that she was in earnest about this decision can be seen in the Slade roll books, where, on 2 June 1911, she signed her name simply as 'Carrington' for the first time. Nine months after her arrival in London, she was in a sense reborn.

In 1911 she made a physical change that symbolised her internal changes: she cut off her long hair, and adopted the style that she would keep for the rest of her life. Her friends did the same – Barbara, whose hair had been cut in Paris, lopped off Brett's – and they became known to Bloomsbury and others as 'cropheads'. Carrington, the originator of the style, in Frances Partridge's words, 'made an impact. She was a leader among the cropheads – she was the first to cut her hair, and was terribly original.'[62] Her sense of humour and unique way of seeing both life and art made her stand out at the Slade, and her golden bell of hair, with a fringe, would both attract and startle people.

In Bedford, short-haired girls were unheard of. She explained to her family that the change was necessitated by a 'fancy-dress party', but this excuse was undoubtedly fabricated solely to appease her parents. Nevertheless, Bedford responded by simply not recognising her, and when she attended a dance there in her new guise it was clear that she no longer fitted in. She wrote to fellow student John Nash that, 'In a rash moment I was taken to a dance in my native town the other night, by my brother.'

> It was sad. For the village lads had quite forgotten me, & taken unto themselves new lasses. They gase [*sic*] askance at my shorn locks – little did they realise who it was who was in their midst! No, sad it is to relate

but I was *not* appreciated[;] hated rivals with blue ribbons & waving locks carried off the erstwhile swains.

This was accompanied by a drawing of her standing unnoticed among the dancers.[63]

There is a sad bravado about this letter, the only one to survive from these years. What she and her friends were developing at the Slade was an androgynous quality which allowed them many – but not all – of the freedoms allowed to the male students: they wore their hair similarly, wore trousers on rare occasions, and were treated as equals in the classrooms. This androgyny allowed them to keep their sexuality in abeyance. Their appearance, which was avant-garde but accepted in London, was unheard of in the suburbs. She found herself one further step removed from Bedford and her family. At the dance it does not seem that the 'erstwhile swains' found her a female at all.

Although she was being rather facetious about her sorrow, it was nonetheless clear that the haircut was more than a convenience; it was a symbol of revolt against a way of life that she no longer could follow. She was joined in this rebellion by others, also artists; a photograph of her with her friends Barbara Hiles and Brett, all three with shorn locks and all staring defiantly at the camera, indicated the seriousness of the confrontation.[64] Cutting her hair meant that Carrington had declared sides, and that London and the world of art had won.

CHAPTER THREE

THE FIRST TRIANGLE: 1912

Carrington soon numbered several young men among her friends. Two, Mark Gertler and C. R. W. ('Chips') Nevinson, became particularly close to her, but only with Gertler did a serious alliance develop. All three were to be involved, stormily, for the next several years, and their relationship would cost Nevinson Gertler's friendship.

Both Gertler and Nevinson entered the Slade in 1908, Nevinson in the second term. To Nevinson Gertler owed an enormous social debt; Gertler's background was very different from the other, often well-heeled, students, and his naivety sometimes made them laugh. When Nevinson arrived he took Gertler under his wing and introduced him to a way of life that others took for granted.[65]

Mark Gertler had been born in London in 1891 to Eastern European Jewish immigrants who were forced by poverty to return to their native Galicia while he was still a baby. They returned to England several years later, and lived in an almost entirely Jewish community in the crowded poverty of the East End. Like the rest of his family – parents and four older brothers and sisters – Mark (or Max, until an English school official 'Christianised' it) spoke only Yiddish for some time.[66]

Although Mark's parents encouraged his artistic talents, they did not at first know what to make of his determination to choose art as a career. They did not believe that he could make a living at painting – or indeed, that painting even existed as a career – but managed to send him to the local polytechnic for further training. Here his progress was good, but not outstanding. His best subject was oil painting, and design his worst. Concerned about the expense and his prospects, his family found him a job as a glass painter in a London business. This helped with expenses, but meant that he had to work a ten-hour day before heading for evening classes at the polytechnic.[67]

Never a healthy child, Mark was in danger of physical collapse from exhaustion when he was granted an interview with the famous painter Sir William Rothenstein. Ironically, it was his young son John who answered the door when Mark arrived with his paintings – the same John who so many years later 'discovered' and was enthralled by Carrington's work. The elder Rothenstein saw Mark's great talent immediately; eager to encourage other Jewish artists, he sponsored Mark for the Slade and wrote a glowing letter to his parents, Golda and Louis.[68]

At the Slade, Mark was at first something of a misfit. He had started school late in life, and had left it at the age of fourteen. His hair was short and his clothes were different. Most of all, however, the other students found him too serious and too intense. He was extremely handsome, with huge dark eyes, pale skin, and a thin body, and he was both solemn and passionate about his art. Only at the polytechnic had he finally been introduced to museums and systematic schooling in the history of art, including the old masters. When he first arrived at the Slade at seventeen, he had the fervour of a convert who has surmounted great obstacles for his religion. In contrast, his fellow students seemed privileged and rather frivolous. Yet his early opinions of them were not untouched by envy.

Nevinson was Mark's opposite in many ways. His physical features, according to their friend Adrian Allinson, earned him the unpleasant nickname of 'Bucknigger'.[69] His family was liberal, intellectual, and philanthropic. To Mark, accustomed to the crowded quarters of the East End, Nevinson's parents' house in Hampstead seemed airy and full of light.

Mark worked hard and was rewarded; he won prizes for his work, earned Professor Tonks's praise, and received scholarships which allowed him more self-sufficiency. Just before Carrington embarked upon her studies, he won prizes in head painting and painting from the cast. By February 1911, his work had been favourably reviewed in *The Morning Post* and *The Sunday Times*; in 1912 he had been praised in the *Observer*, *Star*, *Westminster Gazette*, *Queen*, *Truth*, *Manchester Guardian*, and even the *Glasgow Gazette*.[70] At this point he left the Slade to paint full time.

By the time Carrington arrived at the Slade in 1910, Gertler, Nevinson, and Adrian Allinson were great friends and Mark had blossomed socially as well as artistically. Although still impressed by the social status of students he met, he also became known for his humorous imitations of upper crust and public school accents. And, while Carrington had cut off her hair, Gertler had let his grow into long, artistic curls.[71]

Carrington's progress and success during her first two years at the

Slade were marked, if not quite as spectacular as Gertler's. Where his work was based on his Jewish neighbours and his family and showed a unique flatness, colour, and a square solidity, hers was based on a fluidity which clearly showed her competent drafts-manship. By 1912 she had won the Melville Nettleship Prize for figure composition and a second prize in figure painting. This paint-ing, of a reclining nude with her face turned away, is in many ways a standard student's study. However, it also reflects her aptitude for draughtsmanship and realism, and is carefully executed except for an incomplete or botched foot. The sombre colours are fairly typical of those she often chose; sometimes, particularly in later years, she experimented with brighter colours, but up to this time her work was singularly unaffected by Post-Impressionism. In part this explains why the Slade found it worthy of a prize. Gertler, in contrast, was taking greater chances with his painting. Fame had already begun to come to him, but Carrington was on her way to an equally promising career.

Gertler later recalled first seeing Carrington on the stairs at the Slade, noticing, as Paul Nash had, her turned-in toes and long plait, but being only interested enough to take a second look. It was Nevinson who became her friend first and introduced her to Gertler.[72] That the Nevinson–Gertler friendship was still paramount is made clear in a Slade class photograph of 1912: the three friends, part of the larger group, sit together on the grass. Carrington is slightly separated from Nevinson and Gertler, but the two young men are huddled together, with Nevinson's arm on Gertler's knee.[73] There was nothing sexual about the young men's friendship, but sexuality would be introduced with Carrington's presence.

Unfortunately none of Carrington's letters to the two men have survived, but those from them to her have been preserved. Without her side of the story a rather one-sided view emerges of a young woman caught in the middle of a difficult romantic triangle. Even so, it is possible to reconstruct, through Gertler's and Nevinson's correspondence, the events and emotions of that important time of her life.

Both 'older' men became quickly amorous in their approaches to her, but Gertler's affection soon turned to sexual passion. Nevinson, although hopelessly infatuated, tended to be more instructive about her work. He warned her to keep to her own personal vision and style, although Post-Impressionism had thrown young painters into something of a panic:

... I am convinced there is something in you if only you can find your right track and others do not send you off into wrong ones & now that Art is in this Anarchic & egoistical condition with absolutely no two standards of taste alike in a little time you will probably find yourself hopelessly lost, I know Gertler & I are always getting muddled ... & above all don't get into this post-impressionistic cleverness of pretending to be a great[er] fool than you are & paint your own time & the life about you. I hope you don't object to all these platitudes but they are the only things that are epigrammatic in this paradoxical age.[74]

A few days later, on 2 April 1912, he wrote of his concern that if she did not win the scholarship for which she was competing, she would have to return home to live with her family.[75]

Carrington apparently had already developed into a fascinating correspondent. 'You are a joyful creature Carrington,' Nevinson wrote enthusiastically, 'your manuscript made me really happy, no wonder I cheered up directly I got to know you and am not after your money, my honey, but I simply want you ...'[76] Nevinson became more enthralled with her the more she wrote to him. 'I do not recollect ever having been in such an exotic condition,' he wrote back to her on 8 April. 'I have always said before that a girl's letter consists of four sheets of prosaic balderdash of unemotional fatuity without one original or intimate thought or phrase, or mere cold formality that needs answering but yours were different, you had everything to tell me & I now know you much better than when you left [for her parents' home, on holiday]. I am more and more interested in you & I do like you abominably ...' He called his desire to write to her 'a form of graphomania'.[77]

Already physically attracted to her, Nevinson was intellectually fascinated as well. As their correspondence continued over the next few months, he found himself hooked. 'My honey dear,' he wrote in April, 'I am flattered, I believe you really love me[;] if I should happen to be in a fool's paradise don't tell me I infinitely prefer it to a wise man's puritory [sic]. ... By the way remember this letter is not for publication or rather to be left laying about at the Slade ... I am rather secretive not by nature but by experience ...'[78] Carrington's inability to keep a secret, or to allow others to keep them from her, was apparently already well known. Despite his caution, their relationship was destined to become public. Gertler had also begun to write to her, and by mid-April Carrington found herself with two declared lovers. While each man knew that the other wrote and spoke to her, it is not clear when each realised that the other felt so strongly about her.

So well had the Slade 'last name only' habit succeeded that Mark, unaware of her first name, addressed his first letter to Bedford to 'D. Carrington, Artist'. She was annoyed, not because he had written, but because he had used the word 'artist' so frivolously. Mark was forced to apologise: 'I am sorry that you were offended by the word "Artist" on the envelope. I did not mean it comically. I did not know your Christian name & thinking that you might have dozens of sisters, I was afraid that my "passionate" love letter might fall into their hands –!!' The similarity in Gertler's and Nevinson's concerns about privacy was joined by another similarity: neither could refrain from feeling that his position as a 'senior' painter compelled him to offer artistic advice. 'Remember,' Gertler counselled in the same letter, 'that in art, working hard doesn't mean Quantity but *Concentration*! If you work from ten to four o'clock [and] concentrate, believe me, you shall have done enough.'[79]

Much of their advice concerned her chances to win the scholarships she needed to stay in school. Nevinson, in particular, wrote frequently to urge her on, and to convince her to try every artistic channel in an effort to increase her chances of winning: '... fairly knock off compositions, landscapes, heads & figures in pencil, charcoal, oil, watercolour, tempera & pastel & if you can do any sculpture do a bit of that, I can absolutely guarantee that quantity & versatility are the two qualities that really move Old Brown out of his senile sleep.'[80]

Not only would the scholarship allow Carrington to continue her studies, but it would keep her in London where he could see her. That his anxiety was as great as hers was clear and by May, when he thought she was to hear the results, he wrote that 'I do believe I will be more relieved than you to know the result'. The letter ended with the strongest declaration he had yet made: '... for I do so love you Carrington & am absolutely yours'.[81] When she cautioned him that she was selfish, he excused her because she was an artist, and young:

> ... of course you are selfish so are we all but don't be thoughtless there is a subtle & great distinction between them, don't you see? The difference of an imaginative person & an unimaginative cad [...] however I know you are not the latter but simply a gorgeously egotistical impulsive, unsettled youth and I like you for it, you make me feel younger [he was five years older than she]; ... I went again to the New English yesterday & was much depressed by the tediousness of the work ...[82]

She did get the scholarship, and the Bedford High School magazine noted her honour in a section entitled 'Success of Old Pupils': 'a scholarship of £30 a year for Two Years, tenable at the Slade School of Art, and a Prize for Figure Painting'. Both she and Nevinson were relieved about the award, but a new worry was waiting for them.

Gertler had continued to write, but in a more jocular and friendly tone, still apparently more concerned with her artistic development than with her person. By June all that had changed, for Gertler was no longer willing to share Carrington and considered Nevinson as his rival for her affections. Nevinson had known and loved her first; it was he who had introduced her to Gertler. Mark, however, decided that his feelings for her took precedence and drew battle lines. The passionate nature that he had reserved for art in his first years at the Slade now reappeared, with much greater force, when he fell in love with Carrington. On her side, Carrington seemed to have equal feelings of friendship and affection for both men but a commitment to neither; her work was still foremost in her heart. She was, after all, only nineteen, an age when it is common to have a good time without thinking of the possible repercussions.

To Gertler, such a lack of commitment was inexcusable. He had deified her, and could not bear to find her earthly. One reason for this was certainly physical; she was unlike any young woman he had known in his youth. He was therefore horrified when the woman he so revered admitted to him that she had kissed Nevinson.

> In order to make you understand let me tell you for once always. You are no doubt extremely ignorant that way. Nature, forcibly takes hold of a man, places him on a road where she knows his ideal will pass. She passes: He loves her: madly, horribly, and uncontrollably. Not content with this, Nature implants him with a desire (no doubt for the sake of the preservation of the next generations) to wholly and absolutely honour that woman. This causes him to be jealous of everything she does with other people. He can't stand seeing her own mother kiss her, let alone another man. Of course as I said, it is not for me to tell you who to kiss or who not to kiss, nor will you take any notion of me if I did. The only thing is you mustn't tell me about these things as I can't bear it. I shall try and suffer quietly & alone in future though. Of course it is absurd to ask me to try and be friends with Nevinson, do you think I am made of stone? That I should be friends with the man who kisses my girl . . .[83]

At the same time, he was aware of his attractiveness to women and his growing reputation and prospects as a painter; he knew she cared for him, and regarded that affection as a sacred trust.

> . . . you see our love has now become *The Religion* of my life! . . . How I hate Women who get so sewn into a 'touchy touch' attitude with men & who are ready to kiss at any moment. Surely you are not one of those, because a kiss is a terrible thing. The beauty of you I always in my heart thought was that you stood apart from those woman [*sic*]. Carrington I shall kill myself if I find that you are like the average female. All ready I feel that I can't live I cannot tell you how grieved I am. I don't know what to do I think I shall go mad. What is the good of living such a wretched life . . .[84]

Carrington was caught in a triangle that she could have avoided had she been more experienced. Gertler's volatile temper, and his passion and despair provided a powerful argument on his behalf, but she did not feel that she had to drop Nevinson simply because Gertler demanded it – and she told him so.

After considering the situation and her response to it, Mark decided by 19 June that the answer was to propose marriage. Carrington had written that she wanted to be friends with both; could they not continue that way? But Mark wanted all or nothing. As he saw it, he could offer her a number of benefits, and carefully listed 'the advantages you [would] have by marrying me'.

1. I am a very promising artist – one who is likely to make a lot of money.
2. I am an intelligent companion.
3. You would not have to *rely* upon your people.
4. I could help you in your *art* career.
5. You would have absolute freedom and a nice studio of your *own*.

He offered independence in three ways: artistic, financial, and personal. Yet marriage was in itself a dependency that she would not submit to, at least at a time in her life when her own career looked so promising. She believed strongly that women could not have both marriage and art, and that if presented with a choice, she would select art every time. She had seen few marriages – certainly not her parents' – which seemed worth sacrifice. While she was at the Slade this feeling against marriage began to grow into a positive antipathy; as her female friends began to marry, she saw it as a lapse from sanity and intelligence. Mark knew this and wrote that 'of course you would not agree to this'.[85]

The proposal was a formality, a peace offering; while he would have been ecstatic at an acceptance, he never really expected one. Its greatest advantage would have been freedom from her family, which remained a problem that increased with each visit home. Yet, her links with them were solidified when, after her first year or so at Byng House, Carrington, citing bad food at the hostel, was able to move instead to a small house with her sister Lottie, now a nurse in London. The two sisters had declared a truce and observed, in Noel's words, 'a convenient neutrality'.[86] Gertler's offer, therefore, was refused; he wrote back to ask her to be his friend again, because he found it 'almost impossible to paint without having some person at the back of my mind. I mean that ever since I got to know you I thought of you in every stroke I did. Now I find that I want you badly to see all that I paint and I keep wondering what you will think of my work. I can't bear the idea of developing without you and I am developing so quickly.'[87]

Gertler recognised that despite or because of his success, he needed a peer as both a companion and a critic. While Nevinson had filled both those needs before they met Carrington, Gertler now

wanted not only to drop him, but for Carrington to do so as well.
She made a choice in Gertler's favour, and wrote to tell Nevinson
that when she returned for the next term they would no longer
be friends. She offered no explanation, and Nevinson became as
distraught as Gertler had been before:

> Your note came as a horrible suprise [*sic*] to me. I cannot guess what has
> happened to make you wish to do without me as a friend next term. I
> do hope you will give me some explanation I think I have a right to it
> demand it & I also warn you that I will do everything I can to disuade
> [*sic*] you as I do mean to stick to you during the proverbial thick & thin
> ... I have known hundreds of girls of all classes & kinds & you are
> strangely enough the only girl I have ever wanted as a friend or have
> ever cared to talk in 'intellectual' subjects with & besides your looks &
> appearance appeal enormously to me ... I have thought this out for some
> time & I swear to you I will never speak a word to you as your lover &
> I will do everything in my power to help you in your work & I really
> know a great deal about it & am horribly keen in spite of all my dis-
> couragements ...[88]

Each man used her work as leverage for his suit, but Gertler became
suspicious that this was the only reason she continued with him. In
his view, she preferred Nevinson, but needed Mark's artistic advice.
He believed his work superior to Nevinson's – his success seemed
to prove that – and her enthusiasm for it probably seemed to indicate
that she could learn from it as well. In addition, he was taking greater
risks than she, working on larger canvasses and in newer styles. She
was still very much the student, while he had by now left the Slade
to work on his own.

Nevertheless, he wrote to Nevinson, declaring that their friendship was over; they were now rivals, 'and rivals in love cannot be
friends ... To touch her hand is bliss! to kiss it Heaven itself! I have
stroked her hair and I nearly fainted with joy ...'[89] Nevinson did
not blame Carrington for any of this, but regretted that he had lost
his only friend. He missed 'the companionship of Gertler, our talks
on Art, on my work, his work & our talks in general, God how fond
of him I am, I never realised it so thoroughly till now I have lost
him yet I cannot give you up, you have put a reason into my life &
I am through you slowly winning back my self respect ... it seems
so natural to me for a girl to prefer Gertler to me that I am always
prepared to take a second place purely from a matter of good taste
on the girl's side, if only Gertler was bigger of stature, he would be
absolutely superman with that highly sensitive brain ...'[90] Carrington had only dropped Nevinson at Gertler's demand; now,
moved by his unhappiness, she resumed her friendship with him.

One misses Carrington's letters and her side of the story here. She
appears to have been tossed back and forth between the two as they

battled over possession. She was certainly flattered by the attention and affection, and her liking for both men made her loath to lose either. She found herself in a very powerful position, able to cause joy or misery at will, and at little personal cost. Yet, perhaps greater than the emotional uplift that such a position gave her was the support she received from them as a developing painter. Although Gertler and Nevinson were only a few years older than she, they had more training and Gertler certainly more public success. He was now a *real* painter, out of art school, with a studio and a growing reputation. He, like Nevinson, appreciated her work and was able to advise her when she ran into difficulties. In 1912 she did not yet have Barbara Hiles as a friend and confidante, and it was extremely flattering to have that place filled by a young man so highly esteemed, in some cases nearly idolised, by her fellow students. By the same token, he also recognised her own artistic ability and counted on her to give unbiased and practical counsel on his works in progress.

Despite his apparent success, he often doubted his abilities. His paintings of the Jewish community, including rabbis, his parents and neighbours, had been found fresh and new by the critics for their use of colours and modelling as well as for their subject matter. Yet the Post-Impressionist Exhibition of 1910, and the Second Post-Impressionist Exhibition of 1912, now called into question the validity of his training in facing a changing artistic world. Later in life, when looking back at this crucial period, he said that '[t]he entry of Cézanne, Gauguin, Matisse, etc., upon my horizon was equivalent to the impact of the scientists of this age upon a simple student of Sir Isaac Newton'.[91] Carrington, too, had such doubts, and the support each gave the other was indispensable.

In contrast, Nevinson was meeting with very little professional success, and this caused a double jealousy of his best friend; not only did he get the good reviews, but he got the girl as well. Nevinson's art would not receive any acclaim until several years after the war, when he lived and painted in Paris. Interestingly, the art of all three was extremely different. Willing to experiment with both technique and subject matter, Gertler took great risks. Since the Slade taught that shading masked good drawing, he took this maxim one step further: many of his paintings were now utterly flat, with no shading whatsoever. Nevinson's work reflected more of Cézanne's 'architectonic' qualities, while Carrington's work was highly representational.

Carrington was not willing to give up either of her male friends and, after Gertler had recovered from his anger over the kiss she had given to Nevinson, convinced him to make up with his friend. Nevinson did not believe in this lull: 'I am distinctly amused at you two & congratulate Gertler on his delightful ease & facility with [which] he is able to change from the role of a passionate & over jealous lover to that of a philanthropic platinic [*sic*] friend however only leopards can't change their spots ... Your acquaintance with Gertler I don't think can affect my old friendship with him as I feel there is not much hope of it being regained.'[92] Yet he perhaps got his revenge on 11 July when he responded to an accusation by Carrington: '... though I am quite sure I never did call you an ill-bred shop girl I am humble and mightily fallen ...'[93] He also wrote to Gertler, who decided 'to do my best to be friends with him too'.[94]

Emotionally exhausted, Nevinson planned a trip to France and hoped that although the situation was apparently resolved in Gertler's favour, he had regained his friend and could get on with his life and work. His only fear was that Carrington would drag out the conclusion of this melodrama: 'Oscar Wilde says a woman never knows when the third & last act has arrived but waits for the fourth, tenth & twentieth scenes of anti-climaxes. Well try not to be a woman as much as you are able & realise a thing finished when it is even though it may not have a nice English musical-comedy happy ending.'[95] His letters from then on, particularly those from France, concentrated on art. He was her eyes and ears for modern painters and their works. At the same time, Gertler was converted by a trip to the British Museum to ancient art: 'Egyptian art is *by far*, *by far* the greatest of *all* art ... We moderns are but ants in comparison.'[96] This ancient art was new to him, and he found that its flatness and use of colour resembled his own work. Even in its antiquity he found modernity and he applied it to a portrait he did of Carrington that year. One of the few known paintings of her, it flattens her face and upper body to almost a single plane, stylises and darkens her hair to resemble a short Egyptian wig, and uses almost no shading or background.

Up to this time, Carrington had been enjoying her freedom. The Slade offered her chances for new relationships, new excursions, new art. Certainly the social aspects of this new life were important, and she had been taking full advantage of them: parties, picnics, and trips to museums all played a major part in her free hours. Yet, when she was showered with amorous attention, she reacted like the teenager she was and refused to take it seriously enough to make a break with either person. Nevinson's unhappiness and Gertler's dramatic outbursts pulled her back and forth. The situation was further complicated by the fact that, as secretive as she was about her own life and letters, she apparently sometimes passed Gertler's and Nevinson's letters back and forth between them; they occasionally mentioned details from each other's letters to her in their correspondence. Each day brought a new response and a new episode. It was exciting and dramatic.

It was also the beginning of a pattern. As snide as Nevinson was in quoting Oscar Wilde's remark, he was correct: there was something in Carrington that refused to recognise the end of the play. She had chosen Gertler, but not wholeheartedly. The next step had to be a physical one, and she was by emotion and upbringing absolutely unprepared for a sexual relationship. When Gertler spoke of love he meant physical as well as emotional love, but he did not yet force that issue.

Her sexuality, not surprisingly, had not matured in her time away from home. She was very much the product of a late-Victorian upbringing, and it is doubtful that she knew very much about sex at all. She felt none of the sexual urges that Gertler did, even confessing that she had never been drawn to a man's body in the way he was drawn to a woman's. He was sexually experienced and used every argument he could to try to convince her not only of the 'beauty' of sex, but its appropriateness in a relationship such as theirs. He obviously understood neither her background nor her personality. Full of fun, friendliness, and affection, she was happy to kiss and hold hands. The idea of the sexual act filled her with disgust, and whenever he attempted to touch her, she was filled with shame and guilt. This led to harsh words and frantic letters. Yet whenever Gertler verbally exploded, it was followed by shame and guilt of his own. 'Carrington Dear,' he wrote in July 1912, 'Listen to what I have to say!'

Ever since I wrote you that last letter, I have done nothing but repent for what I wrote. Here then will I state my real feelings and emotions. Emotions that come from my innermost heart.
1. I love you *more* than ever.
2. I never ceased to love you for one second ever since I met you.
3. I only said I did at moments when I was in a rage.
4. You are the best, the most good and beautiful woman I *ever* knew.
5. My only desire is that you should forgive me for my last letter. I shall die of misery if you don't.

I shall do *my best* to remain friends with you, but whether we do or not, I shall always think of you as a person I loved.

You can't imagine how difficult I find it to remain friends. Believe me I do my best, because I know you would prefer it so. However, I shall *really* try [and] am quite willing to sacrifice, in so doing, all my own feelings to yours.

Nevinson also wrote me, in return to my letter to him, how miserable my letter has made him. His letter has made me wretchedly miserable. I shall have to do my best to be friends with him too.[97]

He felt no shame whatsoever at his own sexual drive, but her indignation, 'purity' and threats to end their relationship always caused him to retreat. They would argue, part and find it difficult. After an argument she would either write back to implore his friendship – without sex – or appear, flowers in hand, at his studio.

Later in life, she would again be forced to choose between lovers, and would again, more than once, vacillate between desire and indifference. She would often be swayed by emotional force for, although reluctant to commit herself to certain lovers, she had no desire to hurt anyone. In the meantime, by the end of July 1912 her friendships with Gertler and Nevinson had settled into something more civilised. Nevinson, for example, wrote from Rouen that:

> In landscape I suppose you must have noticed how objects are affected by light, sometimes (when we have not a box of us) we see a gorgeous composition. In triumph one goes the next morning to wonder how on earth one saw anything in it so commonplace it looks ... I am terribly wearied and dissatisfied that I have been able to do nothing or get any suggested ideas from nature. I know it is partly because I am far more hard to please than formerly, but after all nothing to our real artist should appear commonplace except bad art or attempts at decoration or ornamentation which of course is always loathsome whether it is on a canvas, church, house, skirt, arclamp or sewer.[98]

This was not the first time he had written to her about decorative art, nor was it the first time he expressed such disgust. Ironically, when Roger Fry founded the Omega Workshops a year later to produce just that sort of art, Carrington slowly shifted her artistic efforts away from 'pure' art and toward the decorative, precisely because of her own feelings of dissatisfaction with her work. Fry's encouragement of her decorative art at the expense of her serious painting would mirror and influence Bloomsbury's response to her art, and influence her own opinion of her work.

At the end of July Carrington visited her friend Ruth Humphries in Bradford; when she returned Nevinson was also back from the Continent. That his friendship with Gertler was at least temporarily patched up was clear; he wrote to Carrington from an entirely new perspective, saying that her last long letter had 'succeeded in thoroughly chilling me ... You wanted to know why men as a whole did everything to avoid marriage before they eventually succumbed to it. Well, why do you object? Because you think you will lose your freedom, your mind, your soul & your ambitions. Well does not that apply to men, even more so & especially to Artists[?]' This time his compassion was for his prodigal friend, Gertler.

> I simply say how utterly unbalanced you could be sometimes, & a gleam of commonsense strangely enough came & wiped up that madness I once had for you. Thank God ... But poor Gertler was worrying himself silly

& if ever I get again like that & am worried I will run away hard & will *never* see you again ... it has always been so with 'intellectual girls', they have always mistaken anything truthful for lewdness & any decent feeling I may have for sentimentality [.] I know it's not their fault their innocence therefore their upbringing have neither brought them in touch with indecent nature that is 'rending them tooth & claw' their outlook drawing roomy & Arty & know about as much about Life & men & women as an amateur who paints for pleasure knows the revolting horrors & disappointments of a painter.

He ended by lamenting that Gertler, who used to be his close friend, was now 'engrossed in himself & his work & success' and 'naturally has not time for me'.[99] Carrington, once the goddess on the pedestal, was now, in his mind, a tease who had nearly ruined two good men. This did not, however, prevent him from wanting to see her.

Gertler, on the other hand, was now considerably happier. In August he met Augustus John, that illustrious and flamboyant graduate of the Slade, who took him to lunch. While they talked primarily of art, Gertler confided in him that he 'loved a beautiful little girl'. John sympathised.[100] Among Slade students, John represented the apogee of style and success. He was an excellent draughtsman, but with a breeziness and 'rakish glamour about his drawings which drove people wild'.[101] He knew Paris as well as he knew London, and whenever he appeared at the Café Royal dressed in his beret and cape students, former students and independent artists vied for his attention. His noticing Gertler was a mark of great honour but it was Carrington who was destined to become his friend. Once again Gertler had hit an emotional peak; his work went well and his stock was rising in the art world as well as with Carrington, until he discovered that she was still seeing Nevinson.

It did not matter to Gertler that she considered Nevinson simply a friend; he considered her 'behaviour outrageously insulting to me ... I never thought that your nature was such when I saw you on Sat. Your presence was absolutely repulsive to me & I couldn't stand you near me, I was absolutely disillusioned ... There are to me only two kinds of actions: – ugly & beautiful. I can forgive murder or any crime as long as it is done "bigly". But anything mean & low I cannot stand. Yours was such & it was therefore ugly.' Gertler's position as a lover was now clearer. He demanded absolute fidelity, even to the point of not allowing her to see anyone who might make him jealous. He obviously, and perhaps with reason, did not trust her. Her increasingly apparent secretiveness only made matters worse; when she saw Nevinson it was behind Gertler's back, making it appear that the friendship was less than innocent. He was only willing to forgive her because 'you are young yet & perhaps I am expecting too much from you. I think you will improve. You have good things in you. Perhaps next time I shall be able to get over my aversion & then perhaps I may help you.' He reminded her that 'to be a great artist it is necessary to have a beautiful nature'.[102]

An interesting thing was now occurring in her relations with both men: while art had originally brought them together, and love had followed, love and art were now used to define each other. Where Gertler's and Nevinson's roles had originally been those of educators in art, they now took it upon themselves to educate her in life, love, and human nature as well. In doing so, they used the metaphors of painting and painters to try to make her understand their positions. For them, the two passions were so intertwined that each interpreted the other. Perhaps for this reason Carrington began increasingly to paint people and places with which she was emotionally involved, and to gauge her success by the approval of those for whom she cared.

Although Gertler, Nevinson, and Carrington seemed on nearly equal footing as painters, the two men exaggerated their age differences, offered artistic counsel, but sometimes emphasised her female-ness when art, not love, was the issue at hand. They were concerned that others would be prejudiced against her work because she was a woman. Nevinson wrote in September:

> I don't want to discourage you but as you happen to be aiming high you have quite simply a bloody struggle in front of you of course not only with your actual self-expression but that vile dead wall of prejudice & hatred against a woman or still worse that superficial summing out of your work as 'too clever' that so-called people of taste are addicted to ... especially [to] women [as] you lose your youth[.] However remember taste & prejudice are dangerously alike ...[103]

Undoubtedly Nevinson was projecting onto Carrington some of the responses he had received to his own work; certainly he showed frequent symptoms of discouragement in art as well as in love. His summation of her possible reception as a woman artist was based partly on truth, but partly on conjecture. At the Slade the women students were the equals of their male counterparts, and intended to keep it so. His friends, meanwhile, were gaining in importance, Carrington at the Slade and Gertler in the larger British art world.

During his estrangement from Nevinson, Gertler began to frequent the Café Royal where famous and aspiring artists rubbed shoulders, and where he had met Augustus John. He had taken up with a young painter named John Currie, and the two could often be seen at the Café. Like Gertler, Currie exhibited at the Friday Club (like the New English, a young painter's alternative to the Royal Academy) in 1912, and also like Gertler the newspaper critics saw him as facing a promising, perhaps brilliant, career. The two painters shared personal characteristics and histories as well: their backgrounds were of poverty and hard work; both were passionate about art and love; both were possessive. Mark spent much of his time with Currie and Currie's girlfriend Dolly Henry, and often went away on holiday weekends with them.[104]

Nevinson, still optimistic about a full reconciliation, now found himself cut: 'I met him in the Café Royal & he tried to snub and be as cold to me as he could[.] Of course Currie & Olds [another of Gertler's newer friends], I have learnt since have had a large hand in it as they are busy fleecing him & imagining they will get reputations by him & listen with sympathetic eyes to his tales of woe ...'[105] Left in the cold by Gertler, and theoretically rejected by Carrington, Nevinson had lost more than either of his friends. Yet Carrington had made no real commitment, nor did she intend to, to either one. Gertler acted as though she had, but Nevinson, still hopeful of winning one of the two, saw no reason for surprise 'that you cannot be amorously inclined to either of us ... I also see I do not gain you because I lose my best friend on account of you & that ... I was practically compelled to make a choice between losing one of you ...'[106]

In September such a choice seemed unnecessary, for Gertler again resolved to part with Carrington. Meeting Nevinson outside the Café Royal, Gertler informed him of his resolution and Nevinson voiced his approval. He then wrote to Carrington, begging her not to write to Gertler, which would only upset him.[107] So, as the year progressed, the three continued to be entangled.

Gertler's resolution to leave Carrington was short-lived; when she responded to his cold and imperious letter in like terms, he wrote on 12 September to beg her, 'For God's sake don't have that opinion of me Carrington. Carrington Dear I can't live without your friendship. Please Carrington have pity on me & don't leave. Give me one more chance Carrington – I *never I swear, I swear* I loved you all along.'[108]

By this time another pattern was established: one would decide to break with the other, and the rejected one would try to win the other back. Or, the break would be mutual and 'final', then they would continue to correspond and begin the pattern all over again. Neither really knew nor understood the other, either temperamentally or sexually, and as if in proof of this Gertler addressed a letter dated 14 September to 'Miss Dorothy Carrington'.[109] He still did not know her first name.

CHAPTER FOUR

SEX AND SELF-DOUBT

While Carrington's stock was rising at the Slade, Gertler's was rising in the public art world. Nevertheless, in September of 1912 he wrote to her of a new problem: self-doubt. For the first time since he had left the Polytechnic he found that his paintings did not always satisfy him: 'Carrington! I am so dissatisfied about my work ... mediocre art is not only useless, but *criminal* ... No, I am at present more useless than the simplest baker! ... Please God! Give me some more talents so that I may be of some use.'[110] Dissatisfaction with his art made him question its utility, which would never have occurred to him earlier; the 'usefulness' of art was a contradiction in terms. But if one could not make 'good' art, what was the use of trying to produce it at all? Carrington had not yet reached the point in her life where she would begin to question her talent, but she was by now accustomed to acting as a sounding-board for Gertler's work. He trusted her opinions, which she freely offered, particularly because she responded so enthusiastically to all that he did.

Carrington stood out from her fellow students, both in appearance and in originality; as her popularity grew at the Slade, she began to mix more with the other students. She and Gertler had very active social lives, both with and apart from each other. She was forgetful, perhaps deliberately so, and often kept him waiting for appointments or missed them altogether while she worked or met with other friends. As one who had graduated from the student fold, Gertler was now rather outside of her circle, and he felt her absence keenly.

I hope your leg is better – you probably cut it whilst dancing with Pincher. The joy of dancing with him was so great that you jumped for joy! I am nothing! I can be kept waiting a whole hour in a *lonely* studio. The excuse being that Wadsworth's work was *so* interesting, that, that, honestly, Mark Gertler was completely forgotten! Also, the last night, you go to a *rotten* dance in preference to seeing me. That is how you treat me. You take every opportunity to annoy and hurt me. Yet you are the *Lady* and I am the East End boy.[111]

Almost inevitably, their class differences surfaced as his confidence in his art began to decline.

Gertler needed inspiration, so he and Carrington began, at the end of 1912, to plan a trip together to Paris. This was a rather daring thing for a young woman to do, even for a relatively liberated art student; Gertler was so excited that he, the poorer East End boy, sent her ten shillings for her train fare to London to plan the trip. In Paris they would go to all the museums, see first-hand the new continental painters. The trip was planned for 2 January but in December Carrington began to hedge, claiming that difficulties with her parents might force her to postpone it. Gertler, whose last picture was going so badly that he was having headaches which prevented him from working, attempted to spur her on: 'Never mind the affection of your people. Be more independent!'[112]

Despite his encouragement the trip was doomed; probably Carrington had never really intended to go at all. It was delightful to dream about, and even plan, but going alone with Gertler to Paris would have made a sexual relationship with him almost inevitable – or at least she knew he would think so. Carrington was not at all ready for such a relationship, although she had not yet offered him what he considered a real explanation for her reluctance. For him, sex was the natural outgrowth of love, and he loved her passionately; for her, it was intellectually acceptable, but psychologically impossible. Her love for him was more removed, and he complained that when she wrote to him of her love, she always coupled it with the safer term 'friendship'. Her family, which caused her so much difficulty when she wanted to get away during the long holidays from school, also offered her an unimpeachable excuse when she did not want to go away. She therefore could plead inability rather than indifference, laying the blame for not leaving at their doorstep rather than at her own. To make up for his disappointment, she presented Gertler with a Christmas gift: a shirt she had made herself. It was the first time she had attempted such a thing, and he appreciated it even though it was too short in the sleeves.

The gift appeased Gertler for a while, but he was still troubled because Carrington had not given up her friendship with Nevinson. Nevinson, rejected by Gertler and by now no longer a Slade student, found himself almost friendless, though Carrington enjoyed his company and his flattery and did not feel that she must abandon him just because Gertler told her to. Instead, she continued to write to Nevinson and to visit him without Gertler's permission or approval. In mid-January Gertler, still having difficulty with his painting, wrote to her again and ordered her to break it off.

> It is impossible for you to have both Nevinson and myself as friends at the same time. When I first knew you, I hated you for playing with the feelings of two men. A woman is a coquette of the worst type, when she does that. It does not suit you to be a coquette. You will create tremendous harm & no good if you recommence to know Nevinson.

He ended the edict with what he thought was an irrefutable pronouncement: 'Also, my friendship ought to be sufficient for any woman.'[113] It was no doubt true that the young Carrington was reluctant to give up any man who had been involved with her. But it was also true that Gertler's personality, physical attractiveness and artistic success either gave him an inflated sense of his worth, or brought out his insecurities.

Nonetheless, Carrington bowed to Gertler's pressure and wrote to Nevinson that if she did not discontinue their friendship, Gertler would regard their break 'as final'. Nevinson was furious. 'Does Gertler own you?' he asked. 'He is not God Almighty[.] I am going insane with the misery of my life that *he* was the direct cause of . . . why should we separate for a little bounder who despises & abuses you the whole time[?] [O]f course I suppose you are really keener on him than you will admit even to yourself especially as he despises you & bosses you about, that does generally make a woman keen.' More sadly, he added, 'Everybody's dropped me.'[114] Hurt, he fell back on unfair accusations; certainly Gertler did not despise her. In addition, Carrington generally chafed against all authority unless it offered her a way out of an unpleasant situation. As with the proposed trip to Paris, she here was willing to bow to 'authority' in order to resolve a problem that had continued for too long. She had once told Nevinson that she did not love Gertler; now she offered him a 'formal friendship' which he rejected, aptly remarking that she was not engaged to Gertler.

A few days later, however, Nevinson was 'burning all over with shame that I should have behaved in such a way as to make it practically impossible for you to have any respect for me. However the best I can do, I think you will admit, is to say how very sorry I am & try not to give away my meanness to Gertler. I don't think I will ever be able to look him in the face again I feel such a cad.'[115] Carrington may well have written to admonish him for his earlier letter, but Nevinson was admittedly in a terrible bind. He had no friends, and the two who had been closest to him were now siding against him. The previous year he had been forced to choose between them; now it appeared that he had to grovel to have either one at all.

As anguishing as this episode of Nevinson's life was, he put it in perspective in later years. In his 1937 autobiography, published two years before Gertler's death and five after Carrington's, Carrington rates only a nameless mention: '. . . before I left the Slade, affairs of the heart already existed between the gang and the girl students, ultimately breaking up the gang. I coquetted with a girl with whom Gertler was violently in love. Poor girl, she killed herself on the death of Lytton Strachey, years later . . . In some things we were so very young and stupid, and we never hesitated to indulge in every form of dalliance which roused the jealousy of our best friends.'[116] Gertler put a kinder interpretation on this later in life. On 1 March 1932, just after Strachey's death and shortly before her own, Carrington sent Gertler and his new wife Marjorie Hodgkinson a wedding gift. He had recently re-read their old letters and wrote, 'It certainly made most moving reading. It must have been a most extraordinary and painful time for both of us. But we were both very young and probably unsuited. And it is over now and nobody's fault.'[117]

However, her motivation at this earlier time of her life is rather obscure. Certainly flattered by the attentions of the two men, she nevertheless had no desire to use one against the other. When she was angry, she meant it; when she was happy, that was equally honestly felt. After arguing and then making up with Gertler, she would show up at his studio, carrying a gift of flowers or food, and have every expectation that their relationship could continue. Their arguments were based on his jealousy of her friendship with Nevinson and others – he was even jealous of the time she spent with female friends rather than with him – and on her unwillingness to sleep with him.

Clearly her love for Gertler was balanced by pity for Nevinson who was so lonely and isolated. Just as clearly her love for Mark was more platonic than amorous, and she neither understood nor shared his overwhelming physical impulses. Sex was a subject that she did not carefully examine except to reject. Playing the two men off one against another allowed her to avoid a sexual commitment; accepting Gertler on his terms would have been to make one. Furthermore, although most of her friends were also painters, she received absolutely indispensable criticism from Gertler who indeed began to suspect that she was using him for her artistic rather than her emotional needs. As his jealousy of Nevinson waned, probably because Carrington had now twice given him up for Gertler, Mark developed instead a jealousy of her art.

His tactics now changed, and he began to write to her in detail about his flirtations with other women. It was more important to be beautiful than artistic if you were a woman, he counselled. In support of this theory he wrote of an escapade in Brighton, where he had kissed one of the many lovely girls he met there.

> Next to being a great artist I should like to be a beautiful girl. What wonderful creatures you people are, when you are beautiful. To my mind, those that justify their existence most are the beautiful girls and the great artists. A man should be a great artist, and a woman beautiful, I see nothing in between. They are really both the same. The artist creates beauty and the beautiful girl is beauty. Beauty, therefore, is the king of life. My God is beauty, I worship him. A philosopher would immediately stop me here and ask me, 'What do you mean by beauty, what is beauty!?' I would answer, Go to the Devil!!!![118]

While making jibes at the Cambridge philosopher G. E. Moore, whose ideas on the beautiful in *Principia Ethica* had a great effect on the intellectual world and (although Gertler may not have been aware of it) on Bloomsbury in particular,[119] he states that a man is to be an artist, and a woman to be beautiful. Carrington used to be both to him; perhaps his concern about his own work led him consciously or not, to negate hers. Certainly Carrington must have wondered whether by his definition a woman could both be beautiful and create beauty.

Even so, he continued to use her as a sounding-board for his work, and as he pulled himself out of his recent slump their correspondence resumed its old manner. 'I am just writing to tell you, that I am going to make an alteration in my picture of the Old Jew,' he wrote her in May 1913. 'I am going to put another girl's head in the place of the profile one! I think you will approve.'[120] In return, she sent sketches, and sometimes photographs, of her own work. She spent part of the summer of 1913 living in Hertfordshire, with a friend named Constance Lane, where she painted a pastoral fresco in Ashridge House. At home, she worked primarily on landscapes and flowers in watercolour and oil, unless she could coerce someone to sit for her.

By now there was a clear pattern in their relationship. He would scold her; she would become indignant; he would beg her forgiveness. Although he desperately wanted her to change – to love him more and to forsake all others – he knew that he needed her in his life and must inevitably accept her terms and conditions of friendship. His work needed her influence as well.

> You cannot imagine how important you are to my work. You say you like my work, then will you be surprised if I tell you that I think of you in *every* stroke I do?! That you have been a tremendous source of inspiration to me – you are the only personality I've ever met that I've liked *whole-heartedly*.
>
> Having told you this, you will not be surprised in my persistence in knowing you, in spite of your indifference and coldness towards me.

There is only one thing – I feel that I am not worthy of your company. I feel that I am *far* too vulgar and rough for you. But I am hoping through my work to reach to your level.[121]

Gertler had two choices if he wanted to remain with Carrington: either accept her unassailable virginity and accept her merely as an affectionate friend, or elevate her to the level of an inspirational muse or vestal virgin. For a while he tried the latter.

The strain on his relationship with Carrington was eased during this time by the presence of a new patron. Edward Marsh was erudite, well-connected and influential: he was Assistant Private Secretary to Chamberlain, and Secretary, later, to Churchill. He took Gertler under his wing soon after Gertler's friend Currie introduced them.[122] Comfortable but not wealthy, Marsh was a great collector of art and his walls were covered with works he had purchased over the years. Gertler, he became convinced, was 'the greatest genius of the age'. He gave him whatever financial assistance he could[123] and eventually even gave him a key to his flat and the offer of a place to sleep whenever he needed it. Of course Gertler was considerably cheered by this largesse, for he no longer needed to worry about the necessities of bed and board, nor about the 'utility' of art; he could just paint what he wanted. It also no doubt helped his insecurities about his painting.

Marsh also introduced Gertler to a new world: that of intellectuals, writers, and society. He was friendly with D. H. Lawrence, Katherine Mansfield and her husband John Middleton Murry, and Siegfried Sassoon; he had Gertler don evening dress for the first time. Gertler was grateful, but not impressed, after a trip to Cambridge in November and his comments about the coterie he met there parallel his later reactions to Bloomsbury: 'They talk well, argue masterly, and yet, and yet there is something – something – that makes me dislike them. Some moments I hate them! ... But if God will help me to put into my work that passion, that inspiration, that profundity of soul that I know I possess, I will triumph over those learned Cambridge youths. One of them argued *down* at me about painting!'[124] These were exactly the sort of people among whom Carrington would spend her life, and for whom she would eventually forsake Gertler. Then she, like Gertler, would at first feel her lack of education keenly and would sit mute as the 'learned Cambridge' people argued.

In 1913, however, it was Gertler who was testing the intellectual and artistic waters. 'Newness doesn't concern me. I just want to express myself and be personal ... I don't want to be abstract and cater for a few hyper-intellectual maniacs. An over-intellectual man is as dangerous as an over-sexed man. The artists of today have thought so much about newness and revolution that they have for-gotten art . . . Besides I was born from a working man. I haven't had a grand education and I don't understand all this abstract intellectual nonsense!'[125] As he encountered more 'intellectuals', both casually and as critics, he found himself compelled to justify that personal vision.

Another of Gertler's 'new' friends was Augustus John, with whom he had become closer since their meeting in the Café Royal a year or two before. John's artistic integrity in the face of the onslaught of French and Russian art – he appreciated, without becoming a slave to, Post-Impressionism – would be important to both Carrington and Gertler. He knew about the new movements quite well, having spent a great deal of time in France, yet he adhered to his own artistic vision for which the modern English critics rewarded him.

While Gertler's work was becoming more and more progressive, albeit intensely personal, Carrington's was still rather traditional. At the Slade, for the second year in a row, she won a prize for a painting of a nude woman. This oil painting shows a luminescence and a solidity not apparent in her winning work of the year before. Entirely a back view of a standing model in an obvious school studio setting, its dark backdrop allows it to reflect light and put the model into shining relief. Even the pose suggests confidence, for although her face is turned away and her head bent forward, the woman's hands are firmly on her hips and her hair intricately pinned up. Her painting now equalled her drawing in its skill, and suggests the hand of someone older than a twenty-year-old student; it was extremely competent and well-executed, but not overwhelmingly original.

As time went on though, Carrington began to add many imagin-ative and personal touches to her work, but made no wholesale, rapid changes as Gertler did. Her work was obviously progressing, but at a steadier pace which differed from his huge, dynamic leaps. But within the next few years she began to allow herself far freer imagin-ative rein.

She threw herself at this time into an ambitious competition – the Prix de Rome – which if she won would send her to the Eternal City for three years. Her Slade friends wholeheartedly supported her in this endeavour, and on 22 December 1913 she received the following telegram from three of them:

Dear Madam (Sir or Miss) We have much pleasure in stating that we are prepared to advance – and on the slightest provaction [sic] & charging only a nominal interest of 5% tubes of paint, marque 'Prix de Rome' & we trust that this information may interest you. Hoping dear madam (sir or miss) that we may hear from you, we beg to remain yours faithfully

... Brett, Selby [Ruth Humphries's fiancé, John Selby-Bigge] and Roth [Albert Rothenstein].[126]

Undoubtedly this telegram cheered her, for she was at Bedford at the time, spending a typically uncomfortable Christmas holiday with her family.

In mid-1913 Carrington had gained a new correspondent, as the telegram above indicates. Albert Rothenstein, the younger brother of Gertler's early patron Sir William Rothenstein (and therefore uncle to John) had also been a Slade student. In 1913 their letters primarily arranged meetings and outings with groups of friends, including Barbara Bagenal, Dorothy Brett and Ruth Humphries. Unlike Nevinson and Gertler, he was consistently cheerful, friendly, and open to her work without seeming to expect anything further from her friendship.

While on vacation she wrote of her continuing unhappiness at Bedford to Gertler, who advised her to 'try and bear up and remember that it is merely your *superiority* which causes the difficulty and unhappiness ... I think it is hopeless to expect any spiritual understanding between our parents and ourselves. Although in your case I should have thought that they would appreciate you more and would feel happy to have you with them. I am sure that you must make their home less dull and prosaic by your presence.'[127] Certainly the family home was less dull when Carrington was there, but it was not always more peaceful. Both she and her mother were unable to keep their views to themselves, and clashed regularly. To the family, Carrington must have seemed someone they no longer recognised, with her liberal views, 'Augustus John' bodices and skirts and rejection of traditional values. To Carrington, her mother, sister, and, to some extent, brothers were exasperating in the narrowness of their worlds.

She tried to leave Bedford at every opportunity, frequently after she had only been there for a few days. She planned to visit Rothenstein a day or two after Christmas, but her parents were annoyed that she was running off so quickly after arriving, especially during the holidays when families ought to be together. In this instance her parents overruled her, and she wrote to Rothenstein to break the bad news. 'I suppose in a way your parents are insisting only on an affection all feel for you,' Rothenstein responded, attempting to make the best of an unhappy situation, 'they've got the right though & that's one of the advantages of being a parent, one can insist on one's affection. It is hard though & I picture your battles Carrington. I've set my mind so much on your coming that even now I can't give up hope quite. Is it useless to try & battle again? Do, one last fight.'[128] As such occurrences continued, Carrington became stronger in her antipathy to the traditional family structure.

She threw herself during these weeks into writing complaining letters to her friends, who were duly compassionate and consoling. Gertler responded on New Year's Day that 'you must not bother yourself about belonging to the upper middle class; you ought only to congratulate yourself on being such a wonderful exception – it must be very trying for you to be up there with your people[;] I wish I could help you ... You are quite capable enough a person to become independent.' Yet, he went on in the same letter to discourage her from attempting one avenue of independence, the Prix de Rome: '*Don't* think of the Prix de Rome; that is *useless* to you and would spoil you for life. That would mean three years in that decadent city Rome! A city that exists merely on its *past* glories ... What an imprisonment it would be – three whole years !!! No! one must always live in cities that have a future, not merely a past – one mustn't be out of things.'[129] London, he undoubtedly meant, was a city with a future, and that he lived there was not incidental.

During their absence from one another at this time the issue of their sexual relations – or more precisely, the lack of them – again was raised. Gertler felt that he had been more than patient and understanding during the last three years; it was time for her to put aside her girlish fears and have an adult relationship with him. She was, after all, nearly twenty-one-years old. In her turn, Carrington felt that he ought to accept her friendship on her terms. She raised no moral objections to sex, but felt herself absolutely incapable of such acts, and without any desire for them. They made her feel unclean and ashamed. Gertler tried to argue her down; since passion would not sway her, perhaps reason would.

> There can be no real friendship between us, as long as you allow that Barrier – Sex – to stand between us. If you care so much for my friendship, why not sacrifice, for a few moments, your distaste for Physical contact & satisfy me? *Then* we could be friends. *Then* I could love no one more than my friend – *then* I could share all with you.
>
> I am doing work now, which is real work. Far better than anything I have done before & I would like you to share it with, but as long as that obsession for you sexually is there, I cannot. Remember I tried to fight it for three years, without success. Now it cannot go on any longer ...
>
> P.S.S. I am not ashamed of my sexual passion for you. Passion of that sort, in the case of love, is *not* lustful, but *Beautiful*!!![130]

Carrington held firm. As frustrated as Gertler was, she was now undoubtedly a great challenge to him. He loved her but could not fully have her. He could not bear someone else to win the prize. His panic at her kissing Nevinson proved that, although she clearly was not willing to sleep with Nevinson, either.

Carrington herself was not above applying 'reason' to moments of passion. In an undated letter (probably 1915) to John Nash, she recounted a scene with a would-be suitor:

> I had a grand scene with Geoffrey in the kitchen eating chunks of meat pie. He made passionate declarations of his most serious and everlasting love for me. Whereupon I played the Strachey God, & said 'aren't you being a *little* hysterical. You see I know really what you are like & what is going on inside you ...' ... and delivered a long lecture of being insincere, & inventing crises – so he frowned desperately assured me I completely misunderstood him – & then was more humble in the dust, than it is fit for man to be. Whereupon I pounced on him heartily & kissed him violently. Which made him very awkward & embarassed [*sic*]!!![131]

This kind of teasing, applied to three years of her friendship with Gertler, would easily explain his frustration, and perhaps place Carrington, even making allowances for her youth and inexperience, in a less than flattering light. She wanted to discourage sexual advances, but not entirely.

Her stay with her family had been clouded by the possibility that she would not be able, possibly for financial reasons, to return to the Slade the following term. To her relief this was resolved early in January, and she was excited about returning to London and her work: 'I have done no work these hols. of any worth as the family do not encourage my efforts & won't let me use the study to paint in.'[132] She was back in London by 11 January 1914.

The lack of money was a problem that she and Gertler shared. The years she spent in London both in and out of school – for she was soon to leave the Slade – were often painfully poor. She later recalled 'walking from Waterloo to Hampstead because I hadn't a penny. Eating two penny soup packets meal after meal, in a smelly studio in Brompton Rd.'[133] She did not find poverty in the least romantic, but London offered her freedoms that made up for money.

Gertler, in the meantime, was developing new friendships which would strongly influence both him and Carrington. The writer Gilbert Cannan, one of Marsh's young writer friends, was fascinated by Gertler's East End background. He lived with his wife Mary (the former wife of J. M. Barrie) in a mill house in Cholesbury, and in January Gertler spent the first of many weekends there. It was the first time he had spent much time in the country, and he found that the pace and the company suited him well. He and Cannan went for long walks, and in the evenings Cannan played the piano for him and they drank together. All the time they talked, and Gertler found in his new friend an amazingly eager audience. Cannan was fascinated by Gertler's 'exotic' background, his art, his friendships, and his love for Carrington. They agreed on 'the milk and water outlook of Roger Fry and his followers and most of the so-called "advanced" people'.[134] To them, Fry and the Cambridge intellectual painters had a watered-down view of art which was less vital than their own.

This new friendship, which he needed badly, removed a great deal of pressure from his relationship with Carrington. He wrote to her that he 'liked Gilbert Cannan so much that I could scarcely tear myself away. We are already great friends. I will tell you all about it when I see you ... I hope you will be successful in the Prix de Rome. I am sure you deserve it.'[135] Still hard at work on her competition entries, she needed relief from Gertler's demands which had been compounded by living and working in a lonely studio.

She herself needed time and space for her work, and in April Albert Rothenstein offered a solution; his studio would be available for a while, and she was free to use it while he was away. His only caution: '... don't look through all my drawings & probe all the secrets of my life. I couldn't bear it.'[136] He had been working as a set and costume designer at a London theatre where the Russian ballet was performing, and in time he was able to offer her financial assistance as well, in the form of small jobs like tracing designs for the theatre.

While Carrington was hard at work, Gertler was becoming even closer to Cannan. 'He is a *true man*,' he wrote in April. 'There are not many like him. I like him truly. In the evenings we sit in the dimly lit mill, where he plays Beethoven to me and then we talk and talk.'[137] It was inevitable that Cannan, hearing so much about Gertler's life, would want to meet Carrington, and during 1914 she began to join Gertler on his weekend visits to Cholesbury.

Gertler also told Cannan about his artist friend John Currie, who was the cause of a major tragedy in October of that year. His lover, Dolly Henry (whose real name was O'Henry), had moved away from him and found rooms of her own in Paulton Square, Chelsea. Currie went there one evening and they had a terrible argument, in which he shot her and then turned the gun on himself. She died immediately, and he died later in the Chelsea Infirmary, under police guard.[138] Gertler visited him in the Infirmary shortly before he died, and the whole sordid affair deeply affected him. Currie, seven years older than Gertler, had been a mentor to him. He had had little respect for private property, and used to help himself to whatever he desired, even though it might be in a friend's home. He had read Nietzsche earnestly, and had had great self-confidence. He had lived openly with Dolly, and the two of them had taken Gertler to Paris with them, initiating him into great art, petty lovers' quarrels, and foreign culture, all at first hand. As he had done with everything Gertler had told him, Cannan had made careful note of these events and had romanticised them in his fiction.

Through Gilbert Cannan and Eddie Marsh, Gertler was broadening his social horizons. Both moved in very different circles from his and while he did not always appreciate their friends, his growing reputation as an artist and entertaining guest made Gertler something of a social find. His and Carrington's introduction to the Bloomsbury group involved Marsh. In May 1914, Lady Ottoline Morrell, who with her husband Philip Morrell was becoming an important pacifist and patron of the arts at this time, wrote to invite Gertler and Carrington to a production of *The Magic Flute*. Gertler found that he had to break an appointment with Marsh in order to accept, 'But I feel it is so difficult to refuse Lady Ottoline – then there is Carrington too.' Having made the invitation, Lady Ottoline changed her plans, putting it off for a few days and 'was not yet certain whether she can have us to dinner or not on that date'. Behind the scenes Carrington and Gertler were reshuffling all of their plans in order to accommodate hers.[139]

Lady Ottoline, a friend of Gilbert Cannan and half-sister to the Duke of Portland, had introduced herself to Gertler by visiting his studio home in Whitechapel. There she had been saddened by the low ceilings and his obvious poverty, but highly impressed by his work. She soon became his patron and champion, welcoming him (and later Carrington) to her houses in Bedford Square and at Garsington near Oxford. She remained his friend and ally, taking his side whenever Carrington frustrated him, but caring about both of them. They in turn defended her; she was easily caricatured because of her long nose, prominent chin and reddish hair, her sometimes heavy make-up, and flamboyant clothes, and many writers (including D. H. Lawrence in *Women in Love*) portrayed her cruelly in their works. Even her other friends and recipients of her generosity in Bloomsbury frequently made fun of her, which upset Carrington greatly.

Meanwhile, unknown to either Carrington or Gertler, another triangle was developing. Rothenstein wrote to Carrington from Nîmes on 17 May to confess his affection, which apparently an outsider had already brought to Carrington's attention.

Carrington please never believe for an instant that anybody in the world could say or for a moment think seriously, that you gave me the slightest encouragement to think of you save as a friend. I knew always & realised that you regarded me entirely in this light – if it hadn't been for this knowledge, then I would have told you myself before other folks made you realise that it wasn't quite so & that I cared for you differently ... Carrington it wasn't that I didn't wish & long to speak to you but that it was impossible, knowing you to be entirely innocent that I cared for you rather more than I ought to. I'm wretchedly sorry ... I've loved you & all of you, yes, your talent, your delightful insight & wit, & your presence & friendship have brought me golden hours & perhaps great hope & all this given thought I knew that in your eyes I was simply a friend ... I feel you will understand me a little & forgive my clumsiness & it's all so odd & nothing would have made me tell you, knowing how *you* felt if this muddle hadn't come about.[140]

Carrington blamed herself for this 'muddle' of his discovered affections, and wrote to apologise. Just as she had with Nevinson and Gertler, she suggested that they 'cease to be friends "for a time"'.[141] He protested, and their correspondence continued without any further declarations of love. It was, however, increasingly clear that men were strongly attracted to her, and that that would inevitably interfere with her friendships with them. While no doubt flattered, she nonetheless preferred to have a group of friends who were just that. Gertler, who never seems to have discovered this latest rival, was enough to worry about.

As the summer wore on and the fateful August 1914 drew closer, the threat of war affected them all. Gertler was unsuccessfully searching for a cottage to rent near the Cannans, and in the meantime was boarding next door to them. Cannan, far from being inspired to fight, had decided to ignore the whole business of war in favour of his work and was busy typing his latest book. For the Gertler family, things were more serious. As immigrants, they were in danger of being repatriated, and his brothers perhaps forced to fight for Austria. After all these years they considered themselves more English than Austrian (which was not really their nationality to begin with) and were furthermore 'of a peaceful disposition'. Many immigrants were ignorant of the reasons for the war at all; later one heard of old Jewish men returned to 'homes' they barely recalled for reasons they barely understood. Both of Carrington's brothers – Teddy, who was just finishing at Cambridge, and Noel who was going up to Oxford – enlisted when war was declared. Meanwhile at home Samuel Carrington was again ill.

These problems did not prevent the young artists from working. Gertler was living in a cottage near Hastings in July, and Carrington was back home during the summer holiday. He was full of appreciation for her work: 'I hope your work is going well. I *loved* that nude painting of yours [presumably the prize-winning work]. What a good painter you are!'[142] He and Carrington, although not unaffected by the impending catastrophe of war, carefully remained immersed in their work. Gertler of course had to be concerned that he might one day be dragged into it, but Carrington, as a woman, remained for a little while longer on the fringes of the disaster.

Albert Rothenstein was not so sanguine. His letters during and after August 1914, when war had been formally declared, no longer mentioned love; those thoughts had been dispelled during his trip to France where the threat was very real. After his return he was forced to consider the war very seriously.

> It is still hard to grasp what has befallen us all here & it is hard too for one's mind to settle down to anything of a peaceful nature. I have a great desire & longing to help but as yet they don't recognise the untrained ones like myself. I've set my name down in various places for various things but I am told that my chance will probably come only later, when people like myself may be really wanted or really useful.[143]

For the time being he remained in the theatre, waiting for his opportunity to serve. Carrington became more closely affected by the war rather quickly, when Noel returned home, wounded, that autumn. His injuries were not too serious, but his stories of military action brought to life a war that hitherto she had been unable or unwilling to imagine.

Still, life apart from war went on. Rothenstein wrote of a party that he attended, without enjoyment, at 'Lady Utterly Moral's' house, and accompanied it with an amusing drawing of himself in top hat and tails; many of her artistic correspondents, like Carrington herself, frequently illustrated their letters. This one he addressed to 'Doric', one of her several nicknames.[144] In 1914 she had an entirely satisfactory success: one of her drawings, shown at the New English, had been sold. It was a New English rule that buyers remained anonymous, so she wrote to Rothenstein, who had connections with the officials, to beg him to find out who had bought it.[145] 'Do you know I just heard today I sold my picture, the drawning [sic] in the New English for £5, 8.0,' she wrote to Gertler. 'I was so excited! As I have never really sold a drawing before.'

She was enjoying the countryside at her parents' new home at Hurstbourne Tarrant in Hampshire, and she separated herself from them by working hard and taking long walks. As it had done for Gertler, the country was taking on increasing importance for Carrington as a solace, an inspiration, and an escape. 'I am so happy just painting all day, & gardening & in the evenings before supper going long walks,' she wrote to him.

> Only it is a bit lonely as one has nobody to talk to, about the things one feels most. As the people here are for the most part unbearable. The artists are the worst sort. Terrible women who go to Cornwall to sketch

& think everything 'charming & so soft'. Unfortunately people keep on asking me to meet these artists as they think one will like to talk art to them. They are more narrow minded & stuffy i.e. than one could horribly conceive human beings to be.

One woman artist she particularly disliked was 'Mrs Anna Lea Merrit who painted "Love Locked Out" in the National Gallery. She reigns supreme as *the* artist here. Her opinion of [Augustus] John, "disgusting John" she calls him, & his *four* wives most entertaining. I listened in silence. But I will give it her back later.'[146]

Carrington's complaints about her mother centred on what she considered one of her chief sins, lack of artistic taste: 'Mother has no ideas except rotten ones on decorating a home, so spoils it all by putting "artistic" modern friezes round the rooms. I groan. But only a few are born with such keen critical & hypersensitive faculties – applause – thank you.'[147] Despite her complaints, though, she found comfort in a way of life that she liked very much. While at home, she lived in a lovely rural environment where she could take vigorous walks early in the morning and in the evening, paint for much of the day, and write to her friends. The only thing missing was intellectual stimulation.

Rothenstein wrote back to congratulate her on her new life, to express a hope that she was working hard, and to ask why she had not sent anything to the Friday Club exhibition. He was willing to break the 'stringent & sacred rule that we are not told by whom our things are bought', but had no success. His next letter was less cheerful: he had arrived home on 10 December to discover that his father had suddenly died.[148] This, coupled with the military training he had taken up in anticipation of enlistment, left him little time for the short-lived courtship that had taken place only seven months before. His life took an even more marked turn in April 1916: because of the stipulations of an inheritance and because of anti-German sentiment, he changed his name legally to Albert Rutherston.[149]

As old friends began to move out of Carrington's life, new ones began to enter it. In November 1914 she moved even closer to an association with Bloomsbury. She met D. H. Lawrence and David Garnett (who belonged to the younger generation of Bloomsbury) at Gilbert Cannan's, when she and Gertler walked in on an argument between Lawrence and his wife Frieda. Garnett recalled the meeting:

Lawrence was dangerously silent and I foresaw an explosion in which he would turn his wrath on Frieda. Fortunately before it came, the door opened and two other visitors entered – a dark handsome young Jewish painter, called Mark Gertler, and a girl to whom I was at once powerfully attracted. Her thick hair, the colour of a new wheat straw thatch, was cut pudding-basin fashion round her neck and below her ears. Her complexion was delicate, like a white-heart cherry; a curious crooked nose gave character to her face and pure blue eyes made her appear simple and childish when she was in fact the very opposite. Her clothes labelled her an art-student and she was in fact, like Gertler, at the Slade. She concealed her Christian name, which was Dora, and was always called by her surname, Carrington ... My interest in her was returned, though I did not know it, and later we became warm friends until her death.

On this occasion, she scarcely spoke but sat down on the floor to listen, at intervals stealing critical looks at each of the company in turn out of her forget-me-not blue eyes.[150]

Of the five other people in that room, three would portray Carrington in print. Lawrence was to base his characters of Minette Darrington and Ethel Case on her. Gilbert Cannan, who so carefully listened to Gertler in those visits to Cholesbury, published the story of Gertler's love for Carrington in his 1916 novel, *Mendel*, and dedicated the work, with a poem, to 'D. C.'. (Despite his marriage, he had something of a crush on Carrington; he wrote down Gertler's story nearly verbatim, changing Gertler's name to 'Mendel' and Carrington's to 'Greta Morrison'. He also included John Currie's story in that novel.) And David Garnett, so fascinated by her in 1914, edited and published her letters fifty-six years later in 1970.

CHAPTER FIVE

OLD TROUBLE AND NEW FRIENDS

Carrington was quite happy in Hampshire, apart from difficulties with her mother. She had left the Slade in 1914, and spent much time with her parents at Hurstbourne Tarrant while trying to decide on her next step. She did not much miss Gertler's life of wild parties and famous company, although she generally enjoyed a good party as much as he. Despite the cold she was painting landscapes out of doors, learning to ride a motorcycle with her brother ('It is so exciting rushing through the air, with the cold wind hissing in one's eyes and ears'), and reading. She liked *Sons and Lovers* very much, but 'Mr Lawrence I admit tries me sorely.' A few weeks later she read his short story 'Trespassers' and responded: '... How weary one grows of the nape of the neck, & moustache!'[151]

In the country she felt rejuvenated, both emotionally and artistically. 'Since last I wrote,' she told Gertler in early 1915,

> I have been starting some work. I am just going to do a still life, in green, yellow & orange. Of apples, & some little orange pumpkins. Last night I did a drawing of my father. It is rather a good head to draw. But he was suffering so much pain at the time, that in the end I had to stop. In the cold weather his leg gets so stiff & hurts him terribly ... The country round here is wonderful. Two days ago the snow came & fell. It was a fine sight, all the hills & valleys became white, & the little rushes stood out in little spotted patterns all over the hills. And the river rushing on, looking quite green in contrast to the white snow.[152]

Carrington's artistic eye missed nothing, and the stillness of the winter countryside provided her with a visual excitement that rivalled and even surpassed more urban stimulations.

Being in the country also brought out a more domestic aspect of her personality. She decided to learn to cook, she wrote to Gertler, 'to make some puddings & good dishes to cook for you when I come back, as I am sure in time we will get tired of eggs on plates.'[153]

Gertler thought this was a fine idea, responding rather superciliously 'You certainly ought to learn something about cooking. I should always prefer my girl friends to be better cooks than artists. Don't let this annoy you.'[154] She was annoyed, though, that 'you don't care a bit whether I paint a good picture or not! But I *will* learn to cook, so that you will have no fault to find in me.'[155]

Carrington had more than cooking and painting on her mind. Her father's health was both alarming and sad. His deafness seemed worse, as did his paralysis. Early one morning in January she heard a loud crash and, rushing to his bedroom, found that he had fallen out of bed and was unable to get back up.

> It was so terrible to see his big helpless form lying there, & I had to help my brother lift him on the bed again. His brain is so clear & active, it is painful to see his limbs like lumps of carved stone, which his brain cannot make move. He bears it all so patiently & never complains.[156]

His patience in the face of disability (and eventually death) chastened her, and it was largely for his sake that she attempted to live on civil terms with her mother and sister. Carrington returned to her cold studio in the country: 'I wish it was not so cold,' she wrote Gertler on 29 January 1915, 'as one could do such fine things with this landscape. I suffer also from the cold in my studio even though I have a stove to warm it ... Today I had to go out & dig in the garden to get warm ... I am so interested in [the] still life of five apples, & two pumpkins. The colours range from greens to yellow, & then the pumpkins are orange. All on a dark red cloth.'[157]

Although her work kept her busy, she found time to meet up with some of her new friends. The New Zealand writer Katherine Mansfield had joined the widening circle of Gertler's and Carrington's acquaintance. Mansfield and Brett helped Gertler search for a new studio in London, and he had several drunken, 'passionate' scenes with Mansfield at parties. On 1 February David (known as Bunny) Garnett, along with Lytton Strachey's brother Oliver, recently returned from India, Vanessa Bell (Virginia Woolf's artist sister), and Duncan Grant, joined Carrington and her friends John Nash and Barbara Hiles on a visit to the World's Fair at Islington. This is the first recorded instance of her meeting the 'Bloomsberries', and she made it a memorable one for Garnett.

> ... Carrington and I left the others and wandered off round the sideshows, until we came to where the Tattooed Venus exhibited herself. She was a fine woman in her forties with proud expression on her tough face. Her entire back, from the very cleft of her bottom to the nape of her neck and her shoulders and arms were marvellously emblazoned with mermaids, sea-serpents, ships in full sail, sailors, tigers, elephants

with howdahs, British soldiers in scarlet coats and spiked helmets assailed by natives armed with assegais, all intertwined with whorls of red and blue and black so as to give the effect of a Paisley shawl ...

Carrington was spell-bound and gazed at her in silence for a long while. Then, to my horror, I saw her wet her finger with her saliva and rapidly rub a spot on the living tapestry before us. The Venus turned on her indignantly and Carrington at once said 'I beg your pardon ... I forgot that you were ...' She was obviously going to say 'were alive' – but I broke in with some feeble flattery. Venus, however, felt that she had been insulted: her anger rose & her dark beauty was an extraordinary contrast to Carrington's white-heart cherry colouration and her very blue, deceptively innocent eyes. For a moment as the two women faced each other, they made a picture as unforgettable as that of the Westmoreland cottage girl and the wandering Malay, described by De Quincey in the Opium Eater. Babbling apologies, I hastily dragged Carrington out of the tent. I have seldom witnessed such a social gaffe, but Carrington was unperturbed and unrepentant. 'It would be so easy for her to put the patterns on with a transfer,' she said. 'Then she could wash it all off whenever she liked, or if the circus was closed in summer.' But the colours had not run and the pattern had not blurred under the test applied.[158]

While Carrington was shocking Garnett, Gertler's behaviour was shocking to others. He reported that at a party given by Lady Ottoline he had smashed someone's glasses, 'kicked Miss Strachey so that her foot bled, and made a Belgian girl's arm black and blue'.[159] Although both young people were creating unusual reputations for themselves, that did not prevent Lady Ottoline from sending Carrington her love. Yet, since Gertler had been the first of the two to meet Lady Ottoline, it was to him that she was primarily faithful. She took his side in his quarrels with Carrington, and later, for a time, refused to invite Carrington to her home. For the time being they were all friends. The Morrells had bought their famous country home, Garsington Manor near Oxford, which served as a war-time retreat for her circle of writers, artists, and intellectuals. Most of the Bloomsbury figures visited them there. Lytton Strachey, Virginia and Leonard Woolf, Clive Bell and Vanessa, his now separated wife, Duncan Grant, Maynard Keynes, and Bertrand Russell, the brilliant mathematician and philosopher. Many of them, despite their positions, were chronically short of money, and at Garsington they could roam, converse and work for extended periods of time – days, or even weeks. At one point Lady Ottoline invited several of the artists to create a wall of paintings in an upstairs room. Carrington, John Nash, Barbara Hiles, David Garnett (though he was not a painter), and Duncan Grant all contributed. On a later visit, Garnett was shocked to discover that all the works except Grant's had been white-washed over: 'Carrington, who had painted an extremely charming sketch, always regarded this discrimination ... as an out-rage.' Ironically Grant's painting, unknown to Lady Ottoline, was largely Garnett's work.[160]

In London, Gertler also became friendlier with one of the Bloomsbury set. Lytton Strachey had rented a cottage at Lockeridge, near Marlborough, in order to finish writing *Eminent Victorians*. He and Gertler got on well, and Strachey invited him to visit. Their friendship became quite similar to Gertler's with Cannan, for they went for long walks in the country, and talked late into the night. The difference was that Cannan was a married man who regarded Mark as a friend; Lytton, although Gertler did not seem fully to realise it, found him attractive.

Strachey had been searching for some time for his place in life. At Cambridge he had shown great promise. Like many of the other Bloomsbury men – Maynard Keynes, Desmond MacCarthy, and Leonard Woolf, for example – he had been a member of The Apostles, a supposedly secret society which met regularly to present and discuss papers on intellectual matters. It was considered a great honour to be asked to join this group, and the friendships made there frequently lasted for years beyond the university. Strachey came from a large family which lived at 6 Belsize Park Gardens, and he found life there increasingly uncomfortable. Now in his mid-thirties, he had yet to make his mark on any particular career. Writing, particularly on historical subjects, was his bent, but one needed privacy and peace to accomplish that goal.

Strachey's family, like Roger Fry's and Virginia and Vanessa Stephen's, was part of the 'intellectual elite'. These families were sometimes financially comfortable, although rarely wealthy, and shared a history of intellectual vigour and education. The sons of these families generally went to Cambridge, where many of the members of the Bloomsbury group had met.

Strachey by this time had virtually abandoned the unusual clothes which distinguished him at Cambridge – wide brimmed hats and capes – but other characteristics set him apart. He was enormously intelligent and witty, and was known both for his kindness and his humour, which by contrast could be biting. His conversations were accentuated by what many called the 'Strachey voice': normally a baritone, it would shoot up unexpectedly into the falsetto. He was tall and lanky, sometimes – particularly when sitting – appearing to be all arms and legs. His hair was dark and he wore a reddish beard and eyeglasses. He had a reputation as a hypochondriac; he had often been quite ill as a child and as an adult despite his energy for walking would sometimes lapse into weakness and illness. As a result, he sometimes took his minor diseases more seriously than he needed to, but he did have a delicate digestive system and an unfortunate ability to pick up passing diseases.

One of the greatest difficulties in his life stemmed less from his physical conditions than from his inability to find lasting love. He often fell for very attractive younger men who dropped him after a short time. Then he would fall into despair, then begin the search again. His marriage proposal to Virginia Woolf (then Virginia Stephen) had been the result of a meeting of minds, genuine affection and loneliness. When he called it off the next day they were both relieved. He still however needed more than anything an environment in which he could work comfortably, be cared for, and have loving companionship.

Strachey and Gertler seemed unsuited to be friends, for Gertler continued to disparage the Cambridge intellectuals to his own artistic circle. Yet he found Strachey friendly and animated, and enjoyed listening to him talk, despite his voice. Strachey was clearly of the intellectual camp: an *afficionado* of eighteenth-century French literature, he was to make his name as a biographer of nineteenth-century English figures. When Gertler met him, Strachey was still a rather unsettled man of nearly thirty-five, and they were destined to be part of a strange romantic triangle with Carrington at the centre.

In February 1915, however, the two men got along quite happily. 'I have become great friends with Lytton Strachey,' he wrote to Carrington. 'He spends a large part of his time in his cottage, which is in a place near Marlborough – all alone. We carry on a correspondence. He is a very intellectual man – I mean in the right sense. I should think he ought to do good work.' He mentioned in the same letter that he had encountered his old friend and rival, Nevinson, in military uniform. 'He had come back from the Front! Told me in five minutes *all* about it, and you can imagine how ghastly it sounded in "Nevinsonian" language ...'[161]

Gertler's letters to Strachey touched more on the incidents of his everyday life than on his work. Once, while walking on the heath, they were harrassed by young people who, inspired by the sight of Strachey's beard, imitated the sound of goats. Perhaps because Gertler was beginning to understand the nature of Strachey's interest in him, he wrote him in May a very explicit letter about a recent sexual encounter with a woman.[162] This encounter clearly indicated not only his sexual preferences, but the fullness of his social life. He was young, handsome and in demand; there were parties with Brett, Katherine Mansfield and John Middleton Murry, and Gilbert Cannan. But one of the most appealing invitations came from Barbara Hiles, who asked him and Carrington to spend two weeks with her in her family cottage in Wales. Gertler's fear was that two weeks was too long to spend away from his work, but 'what with all these invitations I can't see my way to doing any for a long time!'[163] In the end they did not go, mainly because the train fare was too expensive.

In the past, Gertler's and Carrington's absences from each other had allowed them a respite from their continuing sexual disagreements. In April the issue was again raised when Mark first wrote, 'Whatever you do *don't* mention our sex trouble ... I am heartily sick of it – just write and tell me about yourself [and] the country as usual. And if ever I write about it to you, *please* take no notice,' then himself raised the issue. Carrington, furious, cut out his sentences and attached them to her response.

> You wrote these last lines only a week ago, and now you tell me you were 'hysterical and insincere ...'
>
> Only I cannot love you as you want me to. You must know one could not do, what you ask, sexual intercourse, unless one does love a man's body. I have never felt any desire for that in my life: I wrote only four months ago and told you all this, you said you never wanted me to take any notice of you when you wrote again; if it was not that you just asked me to speak frankly and plainly I should not be writing. I do love you, but not in the way you want. Once, you made love to me in your studio, you remember, many years ago now.[164] One thing I can never forget, it made me inside feel ashamed, unclean. Can I help it? I wish to God I could. Do not think I rejoice in being sexless, and am happy over this. It gives me pain also.
>
> REMEMBER THAT I WOULD SACRIFICE ALL FOR YOU, MY VERY LIFE IF YOU ASKED IT OF ME.
>
> You write this – yet you cannot sacrifice something *less than your life* for me.[165]

It was clear to her, if not to Gertler, that she had a terrible fear of sex. She despised her female body, and found menstruation a hideous burden. She could not share Gertler's enthusiasm over the pregnancy of Ruth Humphries (who was now married to John Selby). The only way Mark could hope to win her would be for her literally to sacrifice herself to him, and this seemed highly unlikely.

She was convinced of the correctness of her position after witnessing her sister Lottie's wedding late that spring to the surgeon R. C. Elmslie. The planning had occupied her family for months, and Carrington was disgusted by it all: the expense, the pomp, the legitimising of sex by church and state which ought to have no part in it. She wrote to Gertler:

> ... you have no idea how terrible a real English wedding is. Two people, with very ordinary minds want each other physically, at least the man does, the woman only wants to be married and have his possessions and

position. To obtain all this they go through a service, which is comprised of worthy sentiments uttered by the old apostles and Christ! Many relatives come and friends all out of curiosity to see this presumably religious rite; afterwards they all adjourn to the house, and eat like animals and talk, and view each other's clothes and secretly criticise everyone and then return home. All this costs a great deal of money . . .

Its just like being in a bird cage here, one can see everything which one would love to enjoy and yet one cannot. My father is in another cage also, which my mother put him in, and he is too old to even chirp or sing.[166]

Although Lottie's wedding was upsetting for Carrington, she grew closer to Gertler after it, writing to him that 'your friendship means so much to me. When you said that the artist's name didn't matter in a picture – and you did not want to be a big artist yourself, only a creator, I felt I loved you more than I ever have before.'[167] Their positions were clearer now, and one unspoken barrier between them had been Gertler's desire for fame, even though he often denied it. Carrington was quite willing to be recognised, but shyness prevented her from seeking publicity for her work. She had been working hard and steadily; though she did not win the Prix de Rome, she continued to work just as regularly. She overlooked chances to exhibit, although she did occasionally show at the New English, preferring instead to perfect her art privately.

Lottie's wedding and the chance to live with Carrington for two weeks in Wales served to prompt his old feelings. Other women enjoyed such relationships; why didn't Carrington? 'The old feelings have returned again,' he wrote on 1 July. 'I mean again I want *all* of you or nothing. I want you to love me properly, or not at all. Like Ruth loves John . . . Painting expresses art and physical contact love. Therefore my physical desire for you is not merely sexual, but a tremendous desire to *express my love* for you.' His own feelings were so strong that he could not understand her lack of sexual inspiration. 'You have never really told me why you don't want physical contact,' his letter continued. 'Why is it? Write to me plainly. Am I repulsive to you? But surely in that case you can't love me and yet sometimes you say you do. Is it simply perhaps because you don't want children? Then we should not have them, like many other couples.'[168] Perhaps feeling that she had run out of legitimate excuses Carrington, to Gertler's joy, at last consented to a sexual relationship. Yet, when the time came to follow through on her promise, she found herself quite unable to do so and remained a virgin.[169] Her fears and shame were simply too great.

Their correspondence reverted to the safer ground of their work. She sent him photographs of a landscape she was working on, and complimented him on his new studio: 'It sounds so perfect in every way. The true life of the artist is I am sure all connected very closely with birds singing, & branches against the sky. And Café Royals & intellectual people talking one against the other.'[170] She was excited about a new picture she was working on, 'a huge clipped yew tree, & figures underneath gardening. The bigness of the tree & the shape is very fine against the sky,' but this happiness had been marred by their recent difficulties and her physical condition. 'Today,' she continued, 'I have been suffering agonies because I am a woman. All this makes me so angry, & I despise myself so much.'[171] As always, menstruation brought her misery.

Nonetheless, the countryside and village offered a wealth of things to draw and paint: ploughboys whose faces seemed to be 'chizelled out of bronze'; gypsies in the post office, one of whom 'had a fine head a big boney structure covered with a net work of wrinkled brownish yellowish skin'; 'big carts of hay ... covered with vivid blue green tarpaulins'; and, of course, her father, that continually captive model.[172] Now that she was no longer a student, she stayed on at Hurstbourne Tarrant, travelling into London to visit friends, go to museums and parties. At one fancy-dress party she sported black eyebrows which prompted Gertler to write that 'I don't think I could love you if you had black eyebrows ... Were your eyebrows black for instance I am sure that a large part of your personality would be different.'[173]

By mid-November 1915 the enforced isolation and dependence on her parents had her chafing at the bit: 'Really I shall come & be a damned teacher I think in London, if only to enjoy the liberty of rushing to see people when I want to.'[174] Her only excitements were a long bicycle ride with an elderly neighbour and having to testify against a Hampstead postman. When arrested for stealing mail, the postman had been carrying a letter from Carrington to Gertler; she was called to be a witness against him. 'How terrible! I feel nothing is safe now. Will my letter be read word for word in court!' she worried.[175] Gertler assured her that it would not. Her instinctive desire for secrecy made this an appalling and terrifying idea to her.

As her circle of friends widened to include Bloomsbury, Carrington found herself increasingly judged by others as well as judging herself. Younger than the rest, she had been influenced by the changes they had introduced into English art. After the first Post-Impressionist Exhibition, Bloomsbury artists increasingly turned their efforts toward decorative art. The Omega Workshops were the scene for some interesting – and sometimes volatile – conjunctions of personality and ideas. Their aim was to make art, through decoration, part of everyday life, and to provide both a workplace and an income for talented but hungry artists. Roger Fry had started the Omega in 1913 with these aims in mind and when it closed in 1919, he had substantially achieved them, despite commercial failure. The two Post-Impressionist Exhibitions which preceded its opening had given the artists a sense of imaginative freedom which canvas painting could not always express. Whole rooms, and all the objects within them, became their canvasses as they turned their brushes to textiles, dishes, screens, furniture and walls.

One crucial result of this new direction was that Carrington, now that she was away from the Slade and becoming painfully protective of her work and unsure of its value, was able to channel her talents into decoration, a much less personal statement of her feelings for her subjects, particularly since one of the main rules of the Omega was that all work was done anonymously. At the same time, she found that she could earn a reasonable income from it, and found herself commissioned to do woodcuts for Virginia and Leonard Woolf's Hogarth Press, and later signboards for local businesses, and tiles for private patrons as well as for the Omega. Fry also enlisted her help in 1916 in restoring a Mantegna painting at Hampton Court.

However, in other ways, the Omega may have done Carrington a disservice: her decorative work was praised at the expense of her serious painting, and neither Fry nor Clive Bell, enormously influential in British art circles, used his position as critic to forward her career. She met them at a time when their artistic allegiances were shifting to France, and with the revelations of the Post-Impressionist Exhibitions, Bloomsbury became predominantly francophile. They looked to that country for a lead in art, literature and way of life. They became friendly with painters in France such as Derain and Picasso (and one of Lytton Strachey's sisters shocked the family by marrying one – Simon Bussy) and with writers such as André Gide. Fry was the first to translate the symbolist poet Mallarmé into English. Strachey himself studied and wrote about eighteenth-century French literature and philosophy. E. M. Forster praised Proust's *Remembrance of Things Past* as the world's 'second greatest novel', second only to *War and Peace*. Vanessa Bell and Duncan Grant took a second home in the south of France. The first generation of Bloomsbury was more willing to sing the praises of their French neighbours than to encourage their British ones.[176] With this emphasis on French art and rejection of English, Carrington lost a valuable avenue of recognition among her peers.

There was, however, a more serious result of Bloomsbury's aesthetic alignments. Both Noel Carrington and Frances Partridge agree that Carrington approached Roger Fry for encouragement and advice about her work around this time, and that something important and permanent took place at that interview. Apparently Fry discouraged her from a career as a serious artist, despite her obvious talent and success at the Slade. (Frances Partridge later called this 'just obtuseness on his part'.[177]) Although she would continue to paint throughout her life, she never again did so with confidence, and from then on satisfaction with her work eluded her. Only recently has she begun to be taken seriously as a major figure of her period, whose work deserves careful attention.

Carrington's fears about her art seem to coincide, too, with the attempted beginning of her physical relationship with Gertler. She could not let him go partly because his views on art were so important to her; although she had other friends who were artists, she respected his work and opinions immensely. Yet her feelings about her own work and her own sexuality uncannily paralleled each other. In both cases her reactions were of disgust and disappointment. 'My work disappoints me terribly,' she wrote to Gertler in 1915. 'I feel so good, so powerful before I start and then when its finished, I realise each time, it is nothing but a failure.'[178]

This, coupled with the increasingly personal nature of her paintings, suggests that the tensions between her work and her life went far beyond simply wanting to paint and to live. Each facet was inextricably tied to the other, and her reaction to the absolute intimacy of sex was necessarily reflected in her reaction to her art. Her fear of exposure, which both exhibitions and sexual intimacy would bring to the fore, was, like her refusal to use her first name, the root cause of her difficulty.[179]

Carrington made her 'formal' entry into the Bloomsbury circle later in 1915 when she spent three days at Asheham house near Lewes along with Barbara Hiles, Vanessa Bell, Duncan Grant, Lytton Strachey and Mary Hutchinson; they had borrowed the house for several days from Virginia and Leonard Woolf. Carrington found their ways much different from hers: they slept late in the morning, were innocent in domestic matters, and gossiped incessantly. In turn they found her sturdy and eager; she rose hours before them each day and went for long walks over the hills, returning redcheeked and invigorated to find them still in bed.

It was much happier than I expected. The house was right in the middle of huge wild downs, four miles from Lewes, & surrounded by a high hill on both sides with trees. We lived in the kitchen for meals, as there weren't any servants. So I helped Vanessa cook. Lytton is rather curious ... They had rum punch in the evenings which was good. Yesterday we went a fine walk over tremendous high downs. I walked with Lytton ... What traitors all these people are! They ridicule Ottoline! even Mary

> H[utchinson] laughs at the Cannans with them. It surprised me. I think
> it is beastly of them to enjoy Ottoline's kindness & then laugh at her.[180]

She wrote this to Gertler, who was also their friend, but to a girl
friend she told a somewhat different version.

> Duncan Grant was there who is much the nicest of them. and Strachey
> with his yellow face and beard. Ugh! ... We lived in the kitchen and
> cooked and ate there ... Everyone devoid of table manners. The vaguest
> cooking insued. Duncan earnestly putting remnants of milk pudding
> into the stockpot ... What poseurs they are really![181]

In neither of these two letters had she told the entire story of the
weekend that had changed her life. While on that long walk with
Lytton Strachey, she told Barbara, he had suddenly and inexplicably
stopped to hold and kiss her. She was horrified; she found him very
unattractive. Indeed they were physical opposites: Lytton, thirteen
years her senior, tall and thin with dark, lank hair, eyeglasses, and a
peculiar voice; Carrington, twenty-two, was shorter and solidly
built, with heavy, fair hair and a voice that often came out in little
gasps. When she returned to the house she recounted the upsetting
incident to Barbara, who tried to reassure her. Lytton was a known
homosexual, and Barbara knew well (if Gertler did not) the nature
of his attraction to Mark. Carrington apparently did not even understand the meaning of the word 'homosexual'. When she was enlight-
ened, she was even angrier and swore to take revenge.

As the story goes, she crept into Lytton's room late that night
with a pair of scissors, prepared to cut off the offensive beard. Just
as she leaned over to make the first clip, Lytton's eyes opened. From
that moment, until the end of her life, she was absolutely in love
with him.[182]

PART TWO

ARRANGEMENTS

CHAPTER SIX

THE SECOND TRIANGLE

Undoubtedly there were similarities between Lytton Strachey and Samuel Carrington which made Carrington's attraction to Strachey understandable. Both men were rather dominated by somewhat overbearing women (in Lytton's case his mother). Both seemed to her to be of earlier centuries and countries – her father reminded her of an Elizabethan and had lived abroad for thirty years, while Strachey wrote about and studied eighteenth-century France. Both men lived, by choice, largely outside of traditional English society. Both were now frequently ill and gave the impression of needing looking after. Finally, as Freud would undoubtedly have noticed, Samuel's paralysis and Strachey's homosexuality prevented either of them from being sexually threatening to her. Her attachment to Strachey, and his to her, was unexpected but not unreasonable. As Frances Partridge later wrote, Carrington's 'craving for independence and privacy made it no accident that she concentrated her intensest love on someone who made no emotional demands on her, and was thus in a sense unattainable'.[1] As a product of the late Victorian period, she shared with a great many young women a personal dilemma. Her adolescent rebellions had been against the restrictions of religion and social convention, as interpreted by her mother, yet to a large extent these prejudices lasted throughout her life. Although she had fought against sexual repression, she herself remained sexually 'repressed' for years. And although she had struggled to quit the regimented Victorian household, she later found that she could be happy and work only in that well-oiled machine, the smoothly-run house.

Carrington had long regretted her lack of education, and since first attending the Slade had embarked on a long course of self-education. She expressed her determination to do so in a letter to Noel: 'I am going to insist ... that seriously you teach me English History, and French – see? Because I am determined to no longer be so stupid & lacking in knowledge.' She was quick to understand, criticise, accept or reject, but had lacked a structured plan or approach to her reading. In the long days at Garsington which followed her falling in love, she discovered in Strachey a teacher who was eager to share his own insights and knowledge with an equally eager student.

Garsington quickly became the weekend (and frequently longer) retreat for Bloomsbury and other Londoners. There, in a virtual fairyland of landscaping, peacocks and vividly coloured walls, one could meet the Prime Minister as well as the intelligentsia, the titled as well as struggling artists. According to David Garnett,

> The oak panelling had been painted a dark peacock blue-green; the bare and sombre dignity of Elizabethan wood and stone had been over-whelmed with an almost oriental magnificence: the luxuries of silk curtains and Persian carpets, cushions and pouffes. Ottoline's pack of pug dogs trotted everywhere and added to the Beardsley quality, which was one half of her natural taste. The characteristic of every house in which Ottoline lived was its smell and the smell of Garsington was stronger than that of Bedford Square. It reeked of the bowls of potpourri and orris-root which stood on every mantelpiece, side table and window-sill and of the desiccated oranges, studded with cloves, which Ottoline loved making. The walls were covered with a variety of pictures. Italian pictures and bric-à-brac, drawings by John, watercolours for fans by Conder, who was rumoured to have been one of Ottoline's first conquests, paintings by Duncan and Gertler and a dozen other of the younger artists.[2]

There Carrington saw Lytton frequently, and began to know the other members of Bloomsbury better; there was even a rumour that Asquith flirted with her in the garden.

While Carrington was now associating with some of the political luminaries of her time – Philip Morrell's position as an M.P. meant that she would have frequently met not only Asquith, the Prime Minister, but other influential people as well – there is little indication in her letters of this. She presumably took part in the political discussions that must have taken place at Garsington and elsewhere but little mention of them is made in her correspondence. Like the others in Bloomsbury she was a pacifist, and perhaps partly for that reason the war still raging on the continent and in which her brothers fought rarely figured in her daily life and letters. Similarly, the nature of her training at the Slade reinforced for her and the other women a sense of equality with the male students, yet the battle for women's suffrage which occasioned so much publicity through Mrs Pankhurst and others during those years seems to have affected her little. It was, to borrow E. M. Forster's term, a 'failure to connect'. In any case, the young men she surrounded herself with had nothing to do with the war except to escape it. They were medically unfit or conscientious objectors finding alternative service. In this atmosphere it was easy to ignore the terrifying outside world.

She undertook a concentrated course of study, reading everything that Lytton recommended, and began to study languages as well. French was the obvious choice, and she began to address him in that language as 'Uncle' or 'Grandfather', signing herself less flatteringly as 'Votre grosse bébé'. Keeping their relationship on such safe, familial grounds could have been merely humorous, but it also could have been a subterfuge for both of them, for they were in many ways unprepared for the relationship that was developing, and for the stories that would soon be spread by the notorious gossipers of Bloomsbury.

In the meantime, a three-way correspondence had developed between Carrington, Strachey and Gertler. Mark wrote to Lytton in May that 'I knew you have been in London from a certain friend of mine ... Really I was hurt that you had not called on me.'[3] Strachey wrote to Lady Ottoline, asking whether Carrington might be there during his next visit. And Carrington herself was trying to pave the way slowly for the chance to see Strachey more openly; Gertler's jealousy, as she well knew, could be a terrible thing, and neither she nor Lytton wanted to provoke it. She began by reassuring Mark that she loved him. Did that make him happy? He replied:

> You ask me if I am happy now that you love. Well, firstly, nothing can make me absolutely happy and secondly I have such a mistrust of human nature that I sometimes mistrust your love for me! Forgive me, I can't help it! Besides your love is so unusual and difficult to understand; some moments however I believe in it and then I must say I am happy. But I never know whether or not those moments are concoctions merely of my own feelings and imagination.[4]

Only ten days later, however, she had somehow angered him again.

> If only I could believe in you more, all would be different, but I can't. You do and say things which disprove the whole. One small detail can upset the whole for me. Besides, physically I am no use to you – you would hate me. I have a small wretched skinny body, worn out by continual nervous strain. All my limbs speak of my wretched life. On my body, more than on my face, my unhappy life has told. You alone have tormented me for five years and now after all I find you unsatisfactory. Please leave me, I cannot bear any more. *I have a reason for writing this letter*. It is not just out of my head. I feel now so tired and ill that I can't think how I will go on living.[5]

Carrington wrote back the next day to sympathise, but also to argue for and justify her right to see other people.[6] Yet, her 'love' was indeed 'unusual and difficult to understand'. Its basis was an affection not founded upon conventional ideas of fidelity. She had no theories of love, but clearly and simply her love for Mark was neither as singular nor as strong as his for her. Still, she cared for him deeply and could not bear to hurt or lose him. She craved independence but refused to let go.

In need of a confidant, Gertler had long ago turned to Gilbert Cannan. In a situation reminiscent of that with Nevinson, Mark became enraged by an innocent kiss between the two friends, although he spent many, perhaps most, of his happiest hours at Cannan's mill house in Cholesbury, frequently with Carrington. On his visits there alone, he unburdened himself to his friend. In May 1916 he wrote proudly and rather ingenuously to Strachey that 'Gilbert is *not* writing, but *has* written a book (it took two months) about a young man who, I believe, is supposed to resemble me, but I don't know.'[7] This book, *Mendel*, would appear within a few months.

Although Carrington was now emotionally involved with Strachey, she was not yet willing or able to sever her emotional ties to Mark. They had been seeing each other for five years, and had, to a large degree, 'grown up' together artistically and personally. While increasingly independent of one another in their movements, their attachment anchored them in a very real sense. They tried, perhaps too hard, to fulfil the potential that each of them sensed in their relationship, and despaired that fundamental differences would inevitably prevent them from reaching, in Mark's words, 'that state of spiritual friendship both you and I desire so much'.

> The reason is that we both have different ways of reaching it. And the two ways are so different that they clash and fight and they always will clash and fight so that we shall therefore never be able to succeed together. Your way of reaching that state of spirituality is by *leaving out sex*. My way is *through sex*. Apparently we neither of us can change our ways, because they are ingrained in our natures. Therefore there will always be strife between us and I shall always suffer.[8]

Mark never could accept nor understand Carrington's deep aversion to sex. Extremely passionate himself, he had probably been initially attracted by Carrington's cool sexual reticence. Although correct in sometimes ascribing her reluctance to a lack of love, he could not control his fiery, aggressive advances either in his letters or when alone with her. Not solely sexual, this desire was also a longing for ownership. As time wore on and he realised that she felt absolutely no physical desire for him, he employed other tactics: logical argument, artistic inspiration, jealousy, and his allies at Garsington.

As with her relationship with Nevinson and Gertler, Carrington again found herself in a bind. This time, however, there were differences: Lytton and Mark were opposites in personality and temperament, and therefore their expectations of her were different. In fact, there was little choice, for Carrington and Lytton were becoming fonder of each other almost daily, yet she found herself as unable to admit this to Gertler as Lytton did to admit it to his friends. In the meantime, Gertler had reason to worry. Carrington was attempting to discourage their relationship – but not entirely – by resorting to metaphor:

> ... I know how miserable you have been. It makes such a big gap and makes me realise how little you believe in me. Do you not see an island in the middle of a big lake? Many islands of adventures which one must swim across to? But one will always return to the mainland. You are that mainland to me. I will leave you sometimes perhaps, but always I shall come back, and when the best state of our friendship is arrived at you will love my adventures as you do your own. Mental and physical adventures perhaps, perhaps none. This world is so big and full of surprises but the great thing is an implicit faith in you, and a greater love for you than mankind. Do you never feel the excitement of this big world, and ships, and many people?
>
> I will not fail you. Do not fear. But I am human also. You have had phases and moods. I also am mortal and am like unto you. I may have had phases also. You must never be surprised or distressed because you know I shall come through and we are in the whole part together.[9]

This nautical terminology, which she also used to describe her brother Teddy, was a red flag to Mark. Even months later, in September, he recalled it: 'How I hate the coldness of life!... Life has made you cold ... Your ego has never been surpassed ... You are always writing to me of the many ships on the sea – etc; etc; ... But my poor virgin. You have known *no* man yet!'[10] Mark's fears were perfectly reasonable, for Carrington was keeping him dangling, while trying to warn him that a temporary split was inevitable.

Gertler's anger and frustration found vent in poetry, and in 1916 he composed the following poem:

I

If my love were not impassioned,
　　　Or could will be moderate,
I could bask in pleasant friendships
　　　Lukewarm sun, contentedly;
But Love's beauty once perceived,
　　　Mere friendship can no longer satiate;
So when I saw your love's immensity,
　　　Now coffined by virginity,
Pain turned my love into hate.

II

Hatred sprung from too great love,
From perception, then desire,
　　　Of your great love's intensity;

From possessors greed, from your alcove,
That shouted you from all
        Embracing love's eternity;
From your bolted door, Virginity,
        Ever mocking, mocking from above.

III
From too great love I hated you,
        I hated your Virginity;
And hated soon, my devilish
        Lips began to screw,
Artfully, to kill all incongruity,
Into a butterfly of Blood Red Hue.

IV
Then hovered it revengefully,
        Oh! Disguised devil,
Above your flower, and then around,
Then lower, lower, its smell circles made,
        Until on level, until,
Alighting then, as it innocently a
        Pretty rose had found,
Not honey then, but your blood
        It sucked, that virgin roote Devil.

V
So did your cherished virginity,
Turn God into Devil,
Love to Hate, Desire, to pain,
        But futility,
So would Love forged into Hate,
        On coy virginity's anvil.
So murdered cruel Virginity,
        All embracing love's immensity![11]

Strachey knew of her predicament and sympathised with both Carrington and Gertler. Unlike Nevinson, he was not trying to steal
her away, but he was becoming increasingly fond of her. Their
correspondence begins in earnest at this time, with letters passing
between them several times a week for the next year or two. The
most noticeable thing about these letters is their contrast to hers and
Mark's. Absent is the tension; instead there is warmth and humour;
they are funny, friendly, comfortable, and as they progress, increasingly loving. They were changing each other's lives. Lytton, the
older intellectual, thrived under Carrington's youthful sense of fun.
Carrington, the young gadabout, was gaining a stronger sense of
purpose. Her creativity shines in her letters, and Strachey begins to
copy her style of writing and of illustrating. When she wrote on 2
July that she had bought 'some lovely red boots' and drew a picture

of one,[12] Lytton wrote back the next day to say that 'I bought no red shoes – only a sponge and hair brush,' and included a drawing of each, signing it with a drawing of himself.[13]

There is no doubt that she – and perhaps Lytton as well – enjoyed the privacy of their relationship. Carrington had a big secret, which she wanted to keep from everyone: Gertler, her family, the Garsington and Bloomsbury sets. She wrote to Strachey at Garsington on 4 June 1916, a week after writing Gertler the 'many ships' letter: 'I will start by using violent language so that you do not show my letter, as is your wont to the whole of the company at the breakfast table,' signing it with a drawing of Lady Ottoline's pug dogs.[14] Lytton wrote back on 7 June that '[i]t was a pleasure to get your letter, which you may be glad to hear I perused in the privacy of my four-poster – and no further attack has been allowed upon its chastity.'[15]

Carrington's chastity was becoming a topic of conversation at Garsington mostly because of Mark's complaints about it. Lytton, though by no means chaste himself, defended her and sent her a gift: a long pencilled translation of Rimbaud's 'Le Bateau Ivre', writing her to 'Forgive this scratch, which I realise is no fit reply for a single one of your PUGS – mais que veux-tu? I hope Rimbaud may make up for my exiguity.'[16] He also praised a painting of hers of flowers in a pot, which he had seen at the New English Art Club. From her letters it is clear that she was back in London, at least occasionally, painting. In February 1916 Duncan Grant, leaving to do farm work in Suffolk with David Garnett as their alternative war service, left her his studio for several days until his lease expired and she could find one of her own.

The art that she and Gertler frequently discussed in their letters was transmuted in her letters to Lytton into verbal representations of her visual surroundings. Back in London, discouraged both by her work and by the ugliness around her, she now occupied a studio at 16 Yeoman's Row, Brompton Road, and spent frequent weekends at Garsington with Brett, Strachey, and whoever else happened to be visiting the Morrells.

My greatest pleasure is a motor bike which I am going to learn, and then all England is within my grasp . . . I am so miserable over my work just now. All grey stones compared to what I want to paint.

. . . My studio is incredibly dirty and I sit knee-deep in crockery, and old letters, and everywhere drooping flowers, with pools of deep-red petals and on the mantel shelf long spines with vertebras hanging brown and musty by little threads. These were once lupins.

The buses and tubes disappoint me, only aged hags, and men with yellow teeth sit and chuckle, and the soldiers have pink raw faces with boils.[17]

She signed the letter 'Votre grosse bébé'.

The Rimbaud poem thrilled her, however: 'You will believe me I know when I tell you,' she wrote on 13 June, 'that the poem made me ill with excitement. I cannot understand how all these people go on so calmly ... We have just been down to Wittering for Whitsun [visiting the Hutchinsons] ... I had a wonderful walk from Chichester late at night there, with only a half sucked acid-drop of a moon for company ... Do you know I can ride the motor bicycle now all round Regent's Park before breakfast tearing quicker and quicker leaving gaping faces of city clerks behind on either side.'[18]

Barbara Hiles was also learning to ride a motor-bike, but not for pleasure. She helped the London war effort by delivering messages in the city. Carrington seemed strangely detached from the war, rarely mentioning it in her letters, even though there was little else on the world's mind. At home, all three brothers volunteered for service before conscription began in 1916: Sam, the eldest, was already commissioned as a regular soldier after leaving school. Teddy, like his father, had been studying engineering at Christ's College when the war began. He and some of his friends joined a mine-sweeping unit on the east coast (which is why Carrington referred to him as a sailor). He later took a commission in Sam's Wiltshire Regiment. Noel, the youngest, joined the same regiment in 1914 and was sent across the Channel. None of the brothers was lucky in this regiment. When the war finally ended in 1918, Sam was badly shell-shocked, Teddy was dead, and Noel was wounded in the elbow by a German sniper and nearly lost his arm.[19] Even with the war so close to home, Carrington frequently left her family in favour of her friends. One can imagine their unhappiness at having all their children gone – three of them in constant danger – during these difficult years.

While Carrington divided her time between London, Garsington and Hurstbourne Tarrant, the members of Bloomsbury were moving to the country. At Wissett Lodge in Suffolk, David Garnett and Duncan Grant toiled under the tutelage of farmers – Garnett was keeping bees for honey in addition to his other duties – doing alternative work which kept them out of active military service. They later moved to Sussex with Vanessa Bell where on weekends they were joined by Clive Bell and Maynard Keynes. The city people made a strange contrast to the local country folk, as Garnett wrote to Carrington in 1916:

Country folk are queer creatures – we gave a tea to our black currant pickers & they ate cream puffs to the gramophone accompaniment of

'Keep the Homefires Burning', & then played games. Maynard offered old women cigarettes which they smoked with relish. Clive winked and laughed and was in high feather, but Nessa who had on an African native witchdoctor's hat, was professionally mournful in character like a mute at a first funeral.[20]

Undoubtedly the fruitpickers found them even stranger. Carrington aided Garnett in this enterprise by drawing over and over again designs for woodcuts which would be used on the labels for his honey.

With his friends beginning to scatter, Strachey was at this time living a rather rootless life. His family still lived in Belsize Park Gardens, but he lived in a series of long visits to friends, returning to the family's old, dark, large Victorian home only when necessary. He was trying to write his masterpiece, *Eminent Victorians*, while making these rounds to the country homes of Lady Ottoline and Philip Morrell, Virginia and Leonard Woolf, and Vanessa Bell and Duncan Grant. He loved his friends but was becoming increasingly annoyed by Garsington and its inhabitants, and was not entirely thrilled by the family life of Vanessa and her small children. And he missed Carrington, as he wrote from Suffolk.

> In spite of a certain sordidness in the surroundings (about as much below par as Garsington is above) I find that I'm enjoying myself, as I like the company, which is at present simply Vanessa, Duncan, & Bunny [David Garnett]. By the bye, why shouldn't you come down here for the week-end after next? There'ld be plenty of room, and it would give me a good excuse for staying on here, instead of going back to a rather funeste party at Garsington.
> ... Please tell me – is it true that you & Brett are going to take up your residence at the Garsington pub for the month of July? I gathered it was projected, and I should like to know whether it's really likely, because my future is extremely vague, and if there was a reason to think that was about to happen, it would be a considerable weight in the scale in favour of my returning to that Haunt about then. Let me know, do. I would translate the whole of French literature for you, and give you lectures on the whole of English – Latin, Greek, Portuguese, and Low Dutch to follow. Without your support I doubt whether I should be able to face the place any more: the last few days there, with Philip back from Parliament, were pretty acute.
> ... The 2 little boys are here, and tend to come over and cover one with hay every five minutes, which is trying. But no doubt you would join them. Only just wait till *you're* 65 with a red beard.[21]

He signed it, 'ever your Grand-père'.

She was tempted, she responded, and 'the prospect of learning French down to Low Dutch with you certainly is enticing. But what of Philip the King & the Pugs? also now I know from Brett *what was said* when I sat enthralled beside you on the lawn, & when we came back glowing with inspired eyes from the Clumps! Wissett sounds a long way off. It will need much persuasion to make me walk so far I fear. Besides you are not very kind, are you? You laugh much & often. Next week I shall love you no more, for I shall have a Rimbaud of my own all the way from France!'[22] That they enjoyed each other's company so much had been fully noted by their friends, who assumed that their platonic friendship had become a sexual one; she as usual asked him to '[p]romise you will *not* show my letter to a Wissett breakfast or I will *never never* write to you again quickly. Promise,' and related that she had dined with Lady Ottoline. After dinner they 'went to the Palladium where we heard the incomparable song: "I'm Burlington Bertie of Bow" '.[23]

As the friendship between Carrington and Strachey developed, things became more complicated with Gertler and her other friends, many of whom remained at least as close to Gertler as to her. Brett was in many ways a ministering angel to him, dropping in at his studio, bringing him food, discussing his painting, and even helping him to wash his hair: the kinds of thing Carrington used to do before she met Lytton. While Carrington and Lytton planned their trip to Garsington, Mark was already there, miserable, as he wrote to his new friend S. S. Koteliansky (or Kot, as he was called): 'But I am tired, tired of speaking of my eternal worry ... It gets more and more complicated with C. I get so tired and worn out some moments I can scarcely stand. And I have to pretend I am happy here. If only the torment would end. It is like some terrible disease and incurable. We both put our heads together to try and end it, but we can't. It goes despite our both being tired and worn out ... it has neither beginning nor end.' This was perhaps Gertler's greatest insight into their frustrating relationship; for once he admitted that he, as well as Carrington, was unable to end it. Many have said that Carrington preferred to be pursued, and when that ceased became the pursuer. While there is truth in this, clearly Mark also switched roles and the relationship crawled on.

When Lytton returned to London from Suffolk, Carrington began to put him off as she had Mark. 'It seems slightly absurd not to see you till Thursday,' Strachey wrote on 1 July 1916. 'Pourquoi pas, mysterious woman? There is Monday. Couldn't we have tea together then – either here or there? – Or dinner?'[24] She answered immediately to propose Tuesday; 'Monday never, the Jew would slay you, if you lured me from him.' 'Are you in the Jew's arms at the present moment?' Lytton responded. 'So near, and yet so far. Oh! Ah!'[25] There was of course a curious ambiguity to this last remark; was he jealous of Mark or of Carrington? His initial attraction had been to Mark after all, but Mark had made it clear that he was not interested in a physical relationship with Lytton – or any other man.

Mark's painting reflected his state of mind, and his latest painting upset most who saw it. Lytton, who went to his studio to select a drawing he had paid for in advance, reported that 'he showed me his latest whirligig picture. Oh lord, oh lord, have mussy upon us! – it is a devastating affair, isn't it? I felt that if I were to look at it for any length of time I should be carried away, suffering from shell-shock. I admired it, of course; but as for *liking* it – one might as well think of liking a machine gun ... Well, well! These jewboys!'[26] In October, D. H. Lawrence wrote a much longer but similar letter to Gertler himself: 'your terrible and dreadful picture has just come. This is the first picture you have ever painted: it is the [most] *modern* picture I have seen: I think it is great, and true. But it is so horrible and terrifying. I am not sure I wouldn't be too frightened to come and look at the original.'

> I think this picture is your arrival – it marks a great arrival. Also I could sit down and howl beneath it like Kot's dog, in soul-lacerating despair. I realise *how* superficial your human relationships must be, what a violent maelstrom of destruction and horror your inner soul must be ... You are all absorbed in the violent and lurid thing that makes leaves go scarlet and copper-green at this time of year. It is a terrifying coloured flame of decomposition ... – But dear God, it is a real flame enough, undeniable in heaven and earth – It would take a jew to paint this picture. It would need your national history to get you here, without disintegrating you first. You are of an older race than I, and in these ultimate processes, you are beyond me, older than I am. But I think I am sufficiently the same, to be able to understand.[27]

Gertler's emotional well-being had been tested by his physical illness, the war, and not least by the endless struggle with Carrington. To understand that she simply did not love him as much as he loved her would have devastated him, and inevitably his frustrations found release in his work. But since he did not yet know the nature of Strachey's and Carrington's feelings for each other, the worst was yet to come.

Meanwhile, Lytton's and Carrington's friendship was about to move to a different level. While they had been staying at Wissett Lodge with Vanessa and Duncan, David Garnett went for a long country walk with Lytton. Lytton had been invited to Wales as a chaperon for Barbara Hiles and her fiancé, Nicholas Bagenal. Carrington had been invited too, and Lytton desperately wanted her to go. The secrecy he and Carrington had imposed on themselves was proving a strain for him, and he needed to 'confess'. Said Garnett later,

Lytton then said that he thought he was in love with Carrington. This was told me in a hesitating mixture of eagerness and deprecation. He had burst out because he needed to make a confidence. And then came the fear that he had been indiscreet. I was asked to swear not to repeat what he had told me to either Duncan or Vanessa. Duncan would tell Vanessa, and she would relate it in a letter to Virginia, and the fat would be in the fire. Ottoline would hear of it, which would be fatal. I did not breathe a word of Lytton's secret.[28]

The view, then, held by many that theirs was an entirely one-sided love is obviously false.

There were two major difficulties regarding the Wales trip: Carrington's parents, and Carrington's finances. Although she was twenty-three and had been living primarily in London for nearly six years, she could not disappear for two weeks without explanation. In addition, she still depended on their allowance for her support. Despite these obstacles, Lytton begged her to come: 'I went this afternoon to your studio in the dim hope that you might have been there – ... What is happening to *you*? Please tell me. Have you abandoned Shandygaff Hall [their secret name for Garsington Manor] yet? and the Jew? ... Write, write, write for Jesus' sake! You *must* come to Wales.'[29]

Carrington's response made it clear that another, more upsetting, problem had now arisen. In her absence, Mark's affection had increased. Since she had first come to Garsington under Mark's wing, and since Mark remained a great favourite of Lady Ottoline, anything that Carrington did to offend him by extension also offended those at 'Shandygaff Hall'. She wrote cheerfully to Lytton that 'I want so much to go to this land of mountains – and – (since this disgusting cult of truth has begun,) so much to be with you again,' but that evening at Garsington Manor something occurred which upset her.

I spent a wretched time here since I wrote this letter to you. I was dismal enough about Mark and then suddenly without any warning Philip after dinner asked me to walk round the pond with him and started without any preface, to say, how disappointed he had been to hear I was a virgin! How wrong I was in my attitude to Mark and then proceeded to give me a lecture for a quarter of an hour! Winding up by a gloomy story of his brother who committed suicide. Ottoline then seized me on my return to the house and talked for one hour and a half in the asparagrass bed, on the subject, far into the dark night. Only she was human and did see something of what I meant. And also suddenly forgot herself, and told me truthfully about herself and Bertie [the mathematician and philosopher Bertrand Russell]. But this attack on the virgins is like the worst Verdun on-slaughter and really I do not see why it matters so much to them all. Mark suddenly announced that he is leaving today (yesterday), and complicated feelings immediately come up inside me.[30]

In this letter, Carrington evidently equated the sex act with violence. Clearly she felt violated by Gertler's unrelenting attempts on her virginity. Furthermore, the 'complicated feelings' that arose in her eventually led to Ottoline's closing the doors of Garsington, at least temporarily, to her. Lytton immediately wrote back to support her, counselling a literary solution: 'What Devils they all are, with their proddings & preachings, & virginity-gibberings. Won't you write a poem on them in the style of the Librarians? – Have you looked at Donne's Satires? *They're* rather in that style. ... (aspara*grass*? ...)'[31]

This episode helped Carrington to decide that going to Wales with Lytton was probably a very good idea. 'At last I have left!' she wrote to him a few days later, after departing from Garsington. 'It seems strange to be out of that mass of intrigue. You have no idea how *incredibly* complicated it became just before I left ... Ottoline in one of the many farewell interviews that I had with her yesterday morning, asked me if I was really a fraud. All very embarrassing.' Trying to find a way through her financial difficulties, she proposed taking a train as far as Gloucestershire, and then bicycling through Wales, '[b]ut all this will depend on how soon I can escape from my parental home'.[32]

Long trips away from London or Hurstbourne needed her parents' approval, and had to be chaperoned. Strachey was to be Barbara and Nick's chaperon in Wales, but who would be Carrington's? She needed either to lie or to break with her parents to go, and she was reluctant to do the latter. Garsington, as the country home of a Member of Parliament, was naturally approved.

Carrington and the other guests at Garsington during this visit would appear, thinly disguised, in Aldous Huxley's novel *Crome Yellow* and in D. H. Lawrence's *Women in Love*, both written in 1921. Carrington herself attempted to inspire a literary journal of sorts: 'The Garsington Chronicle'.

> In this dark and monotonous land these days at Garsington seem to the humble inhabitants precious and varied and perhaps they may have a thread of eternity in them.
> To test this we the dwellers in this small island of freedom wish to weave a chronicle of the days as they pass. We ask you to stretch forth your skill & coloured fantasy to aid us weave this tapestry which will hang we hope before us in the future. Coloured with the gaiety, and the gravity of the varied lives of these that crossed and intertwined here. We wish for no faded & sentimental arras of the past, but a frank & ruthless record of these brightly coloured days.

On the back it read:

> The 'Garsington Chronicle' will appear twice a year
> A chronicle of essays, poems, pictures

Serious, fantastic, truthful & otherwise.
No censor.
Contributions which may be annoynous [*sic*]
    if too libellous
to be sent to Lady Ottoline Morrell
By September 30 written on foolscap clearly.[33]

Lytton was at breakfast with his brother Oliver in August when '[t]he "Garsington Chronicle" [came], in green ink. Oliver was nearly sick when I showed it him . . . Can't you contrive to stamp it out? Oh dear – after all these years! – To be so very far from the correct *ton*! – A "thread of Eternity" – mon dieu! – The gaiety and gravity of varied lives that cross and intertwine . . . most distressing! No. I will *not* stretch forth my skill and coloured fantasy, no, *no*. Mais que dire, que faire? I beg you to waft it all into oblivion.'[34] Carrington, refusing to 'agree with you about the Garsington chronicle as I invented the idea', recognised that it probably would not work out as planned. 'But as it will be plentifully filled with a long discourse with her Ladyship . . . your valuable services will be easily dispensed with!'[35] The 'Garsington Chronicle' died a quiet death.

On 5 August 1916, Carrington wrote to Strachey that she 'liked Alldus [*sic*] Huxley at Garsington. We used to sleep on the roof together, as it became so unbearably hot in those attics. Strange adventures with birds, and peacocks, and hordes of bees. Shooting stars, other things.'[36] Like Gilbert Cannan, Huxley was taking careful note of all that went on around him, and their friendly (but not sexual) rooftop discussions as well as the almost universal 'assault' on Carrington's virginity were incorporated into his novel *Crome Yellow*. Two days after Carrington's letter, Huxley wrote to a friend that he had been spending the nights at Garsington with Carrington. Most of the time, he reported, they talked or sang 'to the stars.' In the mornings they were awakened by Ottoline's noisy peacocks.[37]

Carrington appears in *Crome Yellow* as Mary Bracegirdle, a young virgin of 'advanced' ideas who decides to lose her virginity while she is a guest at a country house based on Garsington Manor, called Crome, owned by the Wimbush family. One of the candidates for this honour is a sculptor, Gombauld (Mark Gertler, who was experimenting with sculpture at this time). Other occupants are Anne Wimbush (Dorothy Brett), Denis Stone, the young protagonist and poet; and a red-haired, Tarot-card-reading version of Lady Ottoline as the lady of the house, Priscilla Wimbush.

Like Carrington, partially trapped by Bloomsbury's francophile enthusiasm, Mary finds herself in thrall to the opinions of a cosmopolitan intelligentsia: 'She was accustomed in London to associate with first-rate people who liked first-rate things, and she knew that there were very, very few first-rate things in the world, and those were mostly French.'

Huxley did not portray Mary Bracegirdle as an artist; rather, she is a young and singularly impressionable young woman with no ideas of her own. Her decision to lose her virginity is based on an intellectual system of thought which parodies Bloomsbury's early infatuation with the work of the philosopher G. E. Moore. The choice of Carrington to voice and satirise Bloomsbury's beliefs demeans both the people and the ideas; Mary Bracegirdle clearly is a creature of little original thought, but with a laughably serious demeanour. 'If you had read Mr Aldous Huxley's latest book,' Carrington wrote to Gerald Brenan when the book appeared five and a half years later, 'you would realise that a certain young lady called Mary Bracegirdle always talks about complexes. But its a book which makes one feel very very ill. I don't advise you read it.'[38] At the end of the novel, when Mary completes her sexual mission on the roof with the late-arriver Ivor, he plucks a peacock's feather and offers it to her. This symbolic act may also have represented Huxley's own mixed feelings for Carrington. As he later indicated to Brett, he was always 'losing [his] heart to her completely so long as she is on the spot, but recovering it as soon as she is no longer there'.[39]

Back at Garsington, Lady Ottoline, now alone with Brett, wrote consolingly to Gertler: 'Carrington is like some strange wild beast – greedy of life and of tasting all the different "worms" that she can find without giving herself to any mate. Sometimes I wonder if she ever will find a mate that fulfils all her desires. I wish she would concentrate more on her work. But I hope she will soon – for nothing is so important as that. It would get her proportions straight ... I love Carrington too and you. I hope you will always tell me anything you feel like and when you feel like it ...'[40] Gertler passed this information on to Carrington at once: 'There's a nice thing to write to *me*!' he complained. '*Never* to be mated! She meant well, however.'[41]

It seemed to Ottoline that Carrington's new life was far too exciting to permit her to paint. Her work did slack off during this period, but whenever she was in London or Hurstbourne Tarrant – away from Garsington – she painted. She worked mainly in oil, but she experimented with the more difficult medium of watercolour from time to time. Part of the problem was that she differed from her newer friends in her artistic bent. They had been hit harder by Post-Impressionism, and their work reflected that influence in inventiveness and freer use of colour. She was far more closely aligned to her Slade contemporaries than to Bloomsbury and older painters.

Where Vanessa Bell and Duncan Grant were turning to a Mediterranean influence in terms of colour, imagery and spontaneity, Carrington worked in close handling of smaller spaces. Like Bell, Fry and Grant, she loved the work of the Post-Impressionists, but by and large they did not profoundly influence her own work. Indeed, her landscapes in particular more closely resemble those of John Nash and Gilbert Spencer.[42] Carrington worked more slowly, and her tightness and control ran counter to the new artistic religion. While they admired each other's work, she may well have been reluctant to share hers with people moving in such a different direction. Like her friends from the Slade, there was a split between what they produced and preferred to produce, and what they admired in others. This was undoubtedly yet inadvertently compounded by the company she now kept. She started to lose the self-confidence her Slade success had given her now that she no longer had the regularity and structure of that institution.

Carrington by now had decided to accompany Lytton and Barbara to Wales. Her letters delighted Strachey, who wrote, 'It was a relief to get your très-aimable letter in these somewhat cloistral (though to be sure also pregnant) surroundings [of Durbins, Roger Fry's home where he was staying]. I laughed at several passages at breakfast, and the middle-aged visitors ... raised their eyebrows.' With this letter he enclosed a pound note 'to induce you to go by train, rather than bicycle, which I'm sure would be most uncomfortable, and I fear you may only propose to do because of the expense of railway tickets. Don't be angry, please. I apparently have a large balance at the bank,' he added tactfully, 'and it's only reasonable that you should not be ruined by having a holiday in my company.'[43] With that obstacle overcome, only her parents remained as a deterrent. Apparently that difficulty was resolved in typical Carrington fashion: when Carrington's mother discovered the plan and refused to let her go, Carrington made up her mind to leave and went anyway. The three met at the Welsh railway station on 12 August 1916.

Gertler, who still did not consider Strachey a threat, knew of and supported the idea of the trip. Carrington wrote to him on her arrival that she was very happy in Wales.

We go out most of the day for long walks, and bathe in a wonderful pool with waterfalls. The mountains are quite high, and one gets Cézanne landscapes of mountains with dull green trees, and ugly white cottages with slate roofs. Lytton has brought John Donne so I read to him in the garden.
... I miss you. The intimacy we got at lately makes other relationships with people strangely vacant, and dull.[44]

Mark was overjoyed by her letter, not suspecting that she was not being honest about her feelings for him. 'Imagine my delight when on the tray with tea ... I found a letter from you!!' he exclaimed.

> Oh what joy. How I loved you for it! And I didn't expect one from you for ever so long. Wales seems so far off. Thank you, dear friend, for it. It was such a good letter too ... What you say is so true, about how all other relationships beside our own intimacy seem lifeless. How well I feel that. But you must be happy and enjoy yourself where you are, as I am always with you in spirit – I never leave you for a moment. I am always talking to you and I have never loved you more and felt more thankful to you or more happy.[45]

Carrington's lies to Gertler, like most she told throughout her life, were as much to protect him as to protect herself. Affectionate words gave him so much pleasure; he blossomed under her warmth, and she was loath to hurt him. She continued to encourage him without realising that their inevitable break would be that much more painful for him. At the same time, she had never spent so much time with Lytton in such relative solitude, and found that her love for him only increased with time and isolation. She wrote to Gertler from Wales that 'I ... feel that you do not appreciate Lytton very much. Probably as you say because that other objection [his homosexuality] comes so much always before you. I have altered my views about that, and think one always has to put up with something, pain or discomfort, to get anything from any human being. Some trait in their character will always jar, but when one realises it is there – a part of them and a small part – it is worth while overlooking anything bigger and more valuable ...'[46]

Perhaps now sensing that he was about to lose Carrington, Gertler wrote to her immediately 'not [to] think that by keeping away from me you will find yourself. *Never*! You can *only* find yourself through *me*! Just as I am finding myself through *you*!! You are afraid of telling me all or coming near to me in case you lose yourself. You are *absolutely* wrong. Your mind, if you are not careful, will lead you hopelessly astray.'[47] But it was already too late.

The weather in Wales was often bad – cold and rainy – and Lytton, frequently in poor health, fell ill. While Barbara and Nick were off by themselves, Carrington sat by Lytton's sick bed listening to him recite from Shakespeare and Donne. She also began one of her most famous works: a painting of Strachey lying in bed, reading. She sketched him over and over again, finally putting brush to canvas when she returned home.

At the end of August, when the Welsh trip was nearly over, she and Lytton struck off on their own for a journey through western England. Gertler, becoming certain that a permanent change was taking place wrote desperately on 29 August: 'My dear Carrington, Please write at once, as your silence has made me miserable with apprehension.'[48] But on the night before, Carrington had broken her long-standing vow of virginity when she and Lytton shared a bed at The George Hotel, Glastonbury, Somerset.

While their sexual preferences and difficulties boded ill for a physical relationship between them, the remarkable thing was that they cared enough about each other to attempt it. On the same day that Mark sent his frantic note, Lytton and Carrington sent off a note to Maynard Keynes which shows that they had indeed attempted a sexual experiment.

> When I'm winding up the toy
> Of a pretty little boy
> – Thank you, I can manage pretty well;
> But how to set about
> To make a pussy pout
> – *That* is more than I can tell.

Carrington appended to Lytton's poem a drawing of a cat sleeping on a pillow.[49] It seems likely that they did indeed have a physical relationship, but how far it went and exactly how long it lasted (it did not last very long) will never be known. The most important aspects are their willingness to try, and the fact that Carrington offered herself to Strachey first.

The entire trip was a delight. Lytton wrote to David Garnett that he 'was in Bath for a day or two with Carrington. Do you know it? Really it's a most charming town ... And then, the infectious enthusiasm of my youthful companion ... you smile but you are mistaken.' With this remark, Garnett believed, Strachey began 'the facade of being entirely homosexual'.

> He was alarmed lest his liaison with an apparently unsophisticated young woman should excite the malicious hilarity of Lady Ottoline Morrell – hilarity spiced perhaps with jealousy? He had to keep up his reputation of being indifferent to, and rather horrified by, attractive young women. There were solid reasons also. Carrington's parents had to be kept in ignorance, and Gertler's jealousy not excited ... It was also convenient for Lytton to know that he was always a welcome guest at Lady Ottoline's country house ... it would be impossible to stay at Garsington if he were to be constantly teased about having fallen victim to the charms of a countrified girl.[50]

During the rest of their walking trip, they visited secondhand book-shops (where Carrington 'discovered accidently an early Voltaire which gave Lytton great joy, as he had been looking for it for a long time'), toured old houses, and studied local architecture.[51] By their return at the beginning of September, they had made a mutual commitment to look for a country cottage, where Strachey could finish writing his book, and where Carrington could paint and be free of her parents' restrictions.

When they returned, they missed each other terribly and wrote to each other at once. 'Oh! I am feeling so desolate!' Lytton wrote to her. 'Lunch is over, tea is over, dinner is over, and here I am lying in my solitary state on the sofa among the white cushions – silent, nieceless, sad! ... I hope I shall hear from you ere long – and that I may hear that you have discovered a large cottage with an orchard in the depths of Berkshire, close to a station on the main line, to let for £15 a year.'[52] For her part, Carrington wrote, 'Home! No discoveries! As I expected, the most utter boredom and peevishness. They suspected I was in London, and sent wires up there on Wednesday! ... I did enjoy myself so much with you, you do not know how happy I have been, everywhere, each day so crowded with wonders. Thank you indeed.'[53]

CHAPTER SEVEN

LONDON AND LYTTON

In early September of 1916 Clive Bell, then visiting Garsington where Carrington was spending the day, subjected her to 'numerous questions' about Lytton and their trip to Wales, but she 'restrained from all enthusiasm – which you will hardly believe, and created no mysteries'. In the same letter to Lytton she repeated that 'Ottoline dislikes me! Rather plainly.' Nor was Clive the only curious one: 'There is great excitement at Garsington because I refrained from any excitement about our journey and merely gave a short decription of the landscape! To hell with them! If one is ecstatic they accuse one of being superior and uplifted. If one is silent, and tempered, of being cryptic and exclusive!'[54] Carrington had, no matter what the reasons, no intention of revealing the secrets of their journey. Keeping secrets from the Bloomsberries, who loved gossip and shared letters, was a serious offence, and this, added to Carrington's treatment of Gertler, seemed to compound her guilt.

From her parents' home at Hurstbourne Tarrant Carrington, who was active and energetic, could bicycle over to Garsington, even for a day, if her friends were there. In September 1916 she rode there one evening to visit Brett, and discovered their friend Katherine Mansfield was there as well. The three women were hoping to rent floors in Clive Bell's London house in Gower Street, near the Slade, along with Maynard Keynes and Katherine's husband John Middleton Murry. Carrington wrote to Gertler that Katherine's presence helped make up for Lady Ottoline's obvious coolness.

> Late Tuesday evening I bicyled over to Garsington to see Brett about this house business, & Katherine was there. I shared a room with her. So talked to her more than anyone else late at night in bed & early in the morning. I like her *very* much. It is a good thought to think upon that I shall live with them & Brett ... What parties we shall have in Gower Street in the evenings. Katherine was full of plans. She was splendid at a concert there was at Garsington and sang coon songs, &

acted a play. It was a curious night all very strange. I am out of favour now! *Completely*! I do not know why – But her ladyship loves and fondels [*sic*] me no more! and Brett was rather severe. I got rather lonely & depressed there. Except for Katherine I should not have enjoyed it much. But she surprised me I did not believe she would love the sort of things I do so much. Pretending to be other people & playing games & all those strange people with their intrigues ... Katherine and I wore trousers. It was wonderful being alone in the garden. Hearing the music inside, & lighted windows and feeling like two young boys – very eager. The moon shining on the pond, fermenting & covered with warm slime.

How I hate being a girl. I must tell you for I have felt it so much lately. More than usual. And that night I forgot for almost half an hour in the garden, and felt other pleasures strange, & so exciting, a feeling of all the world being below me to choose from. Not tied – with female encumbrances, & hanging flesh.

Almost as an attack on Gertler himself, to whom she was writing, the last sentence attacks the woman's body that Gertler desired so much. Clearly she intended to continue to discourage him from a sexual relationship, but she ended the letter enticingly: 'If I find many more poems by Donne urging me to forsake my virginity I may fall by next spring when the sun is hot once more. I think he is a man of such rare wisdom that I take his words very seriously. Far more so, than Philip & Ottoline & all these worthies with good intentions. But I ought not write this to you. As my moods varey [*sic*] like a sky of clouds!'[55]

Carrington knew of Gertler's homophobia (very likely encouraged both by her growing friendship with Strachey and by Gertler's friendship with D. H. Lawrence, a notorious homophobic), and this letter indicates both her dawning recognition of her own bisexuality as well as a plea for a neutral and all-encompassing androgyny. Mansfield was herself bisexual, but there is no indication that their relationship became a physical one. Mansfield allowed Carrington to express her concerns about her sexuality without necessarily encouraging her to act them out. Others in Bloomsbury apparently recognised this aspect of Carrington for, twelve years after Carrington posed nude, simulating a statue, for a photograph in Garsington, Vanessa Bell painted a panel entitled 'Bacchanale', featuring a figure astonishingly similar to it with one important exception: the figure is clearly an hermaphrodite. Bloomsbury's sexual relationships crossed lines Carrington in her youth assumed to be firm. Maynard Keynes had relationships with men before marrying in middle age; Duncan Grant, despite fathering a child with Vanessa Bell, was primarily homosexual and had an affair with David Garnett who later married Duncan and Vanessa's daughter Angelica; Virginia and Leonard Woolf had a celibate marriage; Lytton was, of course, homosexual and continued to have affairs with men despite his relationship with Carrington. At the time naturally not all of these facts were known to her, but clearly the sexual assumptions she had been raised with no longer appeared valid.

She hoped that the house at 3 Gower Street, which she, Brett and Mansfield moved into at the end of September, would make up for the unpleasantness, 'the mice, and the general dirt of that studio of mine in Yeoman's Row' which 'rather suffocated one'.[56] The plan was for Mansfield and Murry to take the bottom floor, Brett the second, and Carrington the attics, for which she would only pay £9 for the nine months. Keynes and John Tressider Sheppard, a former fellow Cambridge 'Apostle' of Keynes' and Strachey's and with whom Strachey had once been besotted, would take the middle floor. Aside from the price and the freedom, Carrington looked forward to living with Katherine, for '[s]he will play all the games I love best. Pretending to be other people and dressing up and parties!'[57]

This plan to share a house in London paralleled the idea for a country house which she and Lytton had discussed on their holiday. Since Lytton needed a place to write away from his family home, yet had very little money, a proposal was made among his friends to subscribe jointly to a country house where he could live and work in peace, and which they in turn would be allowed to visit on weekends. Lytton and Carrington planned to share the house, despite her own lack of funds, both in order to give her a place to paint and live in independently, and to enable them to spend more time together.[58]

Lytton, always wary of his friends' response to this new, and for him unusual alliance, played down her position in this scheme. Writing to Maynard Keynes in mid-September, Strachey asked, 'Have you heard of the scheme for a country cottage? Would you be willing to join? ... Oliver [Strachey, his brother] and Faith [Henderson] are going to take shares – also perhaps Saxon [Sidney-Turner] ... Oh, Carrington, too.'[59]

By mutual consent Carrington, with the frequent assistance of her friend Barbara, was to search for a cottage while Lytton toiled away at *Eminent Victorians*. She rode her bicycle for miles along country roads, looking for houses and following leads from friends and estate agents, sending Lytton reports, drawing maps and sketching cottages.

> I was just flying into a tangent at not hearing from you. Considering I had sent you a map of the best land in Europe, and plans and diagrams worthy of Inigo Jones! But I might have known that (without that treasure of a niece), you would leave no [forwarding] address behind. Fool. Oh aged Fool!

... And I feel too enraged at the present moment to write it all again!
And the energy lost! 40 miles in one morning did I bicycle for your sake
revered uncle! Searching the highways and hedges, for your blasted
house! 40 miles!!
   ... In anger I remain your niece DORIC ... And I told Ottoline I
was vague as to *your* future plans. And you tell her I am busy with
Barbara finding you a house???[60]

As usual, she assigned herself a familial relationship to him, most
likely to satisize the 'unsuitability' of their age difference but also
perhaps to downplay the nature of their connection to each other.

Carrington was not the only one looking for a house. Conscientious
objectors Duncan Grant and David Garnett had been working on
the Wissett Lodge fruit farm, but in 1916 a government committee
on alternative service refused to let them continue there. Vanessa
Bell, who had been living with Grant since her estrangement from
her husband Clive, found work for them and a house to let: Charleston Farmhouse near Lewes in Sussex, which was close to her
sister Virginia's house, Asheham.[61]

The move to Charleston brought about Carrington's first, and
inadvertant, close contact with Virginia and Leonard Woolf. David
Garnett, who was to begin working before Charleston was ready,
convinced Carrington and Barbara to go down to Sussex with him
for a few days. They took bicycles, but leaving them at an inn,
walked over the downs to Asheham to visit the Woolfs. Surprised
by not finding them at home, they were in an awkward position; it
was too cold and dark to walk back, so they climbed through an open
upstairs window and, as the linens were locked up, spent the night
huddled in one bed. The next morning they put the place to rights.
Although they helped themselves to a few apples, a more serious
offence was Garnett's 'borrowing' one of the Woolfs' books. They
hoped the incident would never be revealed, but it occasioned some
rather frantic letters from Carrington to Garnett. On 11 October
she wrote that '[i]t was very difficult not to tell [Lytton] about
Asheham and Charleston in detail. And other things!!! Bunny you
must not tell anyone about Asheham, promise truly. Because you see
Vanessa will get all the blame and dishonour thrown on her and as
we did succeed in doing it all so well, why should they ever know
and cause confusion and desolation in the camp? Lytton saw Virginia
on Saturday at Richmond, actually. I nearly said "Had she found
out?" quickly.'[62]

By 14 October 1916 their secret was at least partly revealed.

   All is discovered Bunny, I saw Roger on Thursday (yesterday) and he
asked me if we stayed there as Virginia was in rather a panic as strange

people had broken in, eaten all the food and *moved the beds*!!!! some old hag had written a wild letter telling of our outrageous frightfulness. 'Of course I knew at once it was a fabrication about the beds being moved and the furniture. But told Virginia you had possibly just got in to look at it' said the worthy Roger. So I told him to confess to Virginia about the apples being eaten and us looking at the house and agreed with him that the other rumours must be an invention of the heated brain of the old hag!! [Apparently the Woolfs' charwoman.] But I saw Vanessa and Duncan, so lovely in a new suit, last night and confessed the truth ... You *must* put that book back can you in the dead of night quietly without any commotion? It is all very exciting!! I was very tempted out of wickedness to make a mystery of it and deny everything just to aggravate the wolf.[63]

For some reason Virginia placed the blame solely on Carrington, and duly summoned her to Asheham to explain. Carrington was terrified, which pleased Virginia: 'It flatters us a good deal to see what a reputation for temper we've got. I telephoned to Miss Carrington, and heard her quake at the sound of my voice miles off!'[64] Carrington was certain that the versions of the story told by herself and Garnett were not the same: 'Dear Bunny, *What* have you written to Virginia? Everything is in such a blasted muddle now and I have to go to dinner with Virginia and her wolf on Thursday to "explain about Asheham" – so for god's sake write *by return* and tell me exactly what you have told Virginia.' Barbara added a commiserating postscript to this letter: 'Poor Carrington has to face the he-wolf all alone to dinner she is dreading it and I don't envy her.'[65]

Garnett wrote back from Charleston that 'I've just written to Virginia and told her that we broke in, had a meal and went over the house and that I had a bath. Please stick to this tale.'[66] The whole situation was too complicated, and the multiple lies began to double back on them. In the end, she was rescued by Lytton's presence. Carrington dashed off a note to Garnett as she departed for the confrontation, warning him that 'I am just going in a few minutes with grandfather Lytton to the Wolves den. And make a hash of it for you, as I do not feel in an untruthful diplomatic mood tonight! But I will try my best.'[67]

The matter was smoothed over, but it had been a trying month. Garnett, who was what Frances Partridge called a 'pouncer', had attempted to make love to Carrington, despite Barbara's presence in the same bed, that night at Asheham. She rebuked him and they remained good friends. (He wrote many years later, however, that later in her life he 'was sometimes able to console her as a lover when she was unhappy'.)[68] In November she sent him off on his bicycle to inspect a farmhouse near Wilmington as a possible answer to the country cottage problem. At the beginning of that month, however, two much more unpleasant things happened: Gilbert Cannan's novel, *Mendel*, based on Gertler's life, was published, and her favourite brother, Teddy, was reported missing in action.

It was apparent that Cannan had changed little in his presentation of Mark's life: he portrayed him as the impetuous but talented immigrant painter Mendel Kuhler, struggling to find his position in art and among the 'Christians'. Mendel was in love with a Christian girl from the country, whose name showed little imagination in its transference from Dora Carrington: Greta Morrison. Most upsetting was his unabashed portrayal of the friendship between Gertler and John Currie, one of Gertler's more recent and close artist friends in London, and the subsequent murder–suicide of Currie and Dolly Henry. D. H. Lawrence called it 'a bad book – statement without creation – really journalism. Gertler ... has told every detail of his life to Gilbert – Gilbert has a lawyer's memory and he has put it all down, and so ridiculously when it comes to the love affair. We never recognised ourselves.'[69]

In *Mendel*, the stereotype of Carrington as countrified schoolgirl is presented in its most extreme form. The novel was dedicated to 'D. C.' and it became clear that Cannan, despite his marriage, had been in love with her for the past five years; but the character of Morrison is so ethereal and poorly developed that one finds little reason for that love. No matter how complimentary Cannan may have intended to be, Carrington was not pleased: 'How angry I am over Gilbert's book. Everywhere this confounded gossip, and servant-like curiosity[.] It's ugly and so damned vulgar. People cannot be vulgar over a work of art, so it *is* Gilbert's fault for writing as he did ...'[70] Virginia, on the other hand found it 'rather interesting, and makes me think of Barbara, not that she occurs in it, I suppose, but all the young do, and I wonder if they're so very different from us. I think life for us was more complicated at that sort of age.'[71]

Whether or not life as a young adult had been more complicated, many of the young men of Virginia Woolf's generation – most of whom were in their thirties at the war's outbreak – had not faced the threat of extinction as those of Carrington's now did. The disappearance at the front of her brother Teddy finally brought the war home to Carrington. It had now been going on for over two years, and had caused changes even within Bloomsbury. Most of the circle were pacifists, and the men attempted to achieve conscientious objector status, particularly when military service became compulsory in 1916. Gertler, primarily concerned with the terrible interruption which being drafted would cause his work, wrote that he believed he was a 'passivist', an ironic misspelling which captures his understanding – or misunderstanding – of the outside world. As it happened, when he was finally called up he was found physically unfit for military service.

Yet, with three brothers involved in the fighting, Carrington was forced to make a connection in a frightening way. She often found Noel and Teddy pompous and overly conservative, but they were dear to her nonetheless. Like many young women of her generation, she opposed the war in principle but it otherwise had relatively little effect on her. Only after she was personally touched, through her brothers, did she finally understand the magnitude of the destruction. She made no attempt to upset or dishearten them while they were away and in danger. Some of her frequent letters to Noel at the front have survived, and show that she tried hard to keep him connected to the domestic world outside of the war. She sent books, asked him for the drawings he had been making, and described, humorously, her various adventures.

Earlier in 1916 she combined her love of theatre with a desire to aid the British troops. A Slade acquaintance Beatrice Elvery (by that time Lady Glenavy) recalled that Carrington went round among her friends in London, gathering performers for 'a monster matinée in the Chelsea Palace Theatre in aid of Miss Lena Ashwell's Concerts for the Front. It seemed that everyone in the social, theatrical and intellectual world of London was to appear in it. Carrington was on one of the numerous committees among the duchesses and theatrical celebrities.'

It was to be a sort of history of Chelsea, with little plays about Rossetti, Whistler and others, with songs and dances ending up with a grand finale in praise of Augustus John. Carrington's job was to collect a chorus of about forty people for the final scene. She was designing the dresses, which were to be made by Roger Fry's Omega Workshop. She had got a lot of distinguished names for her chorus (but doubted whether any of them could sing) . . .

The rehearsals started. They were held in any theatre where we could get a stage . . . Our song had six long verses with choruses, each chorus having different words. The words of the song written by Harry Graham and the music by H. Fraser-Simson.

It began:

> Some people will squander their earnings away
> On paintings by Rankin or Steer
> For Brangwyn or Conder huge sums they will pay,
> And they buy all the Prydes that appear.
> But if you'd be smart as patrons of art
> It's almost a *sine qua non*
> To prove your discretion by gaining possession
> Of works by the wonderful John.

At this point we came on, singing:

> John, John, how he's got on,
> He owes it, he knows it, to me.
> Brass ear-rings I wear and I don't do my hair
> And my feet are as bare as can be.
> When I walk down the street, the people I meet
> All stare at the things I've got on.
> When Battersea-Parking, you'll hear folks remarking,
> There goes an Augustus John.

Our producer, Harry Gratton, had at first tried to make us enter with little steps and kicks like a trained music-hall chorus, but the result was chaos. We kept kicking the people in front and in turn got kicked by those behind. Then we had the brilliant idea that we should slouch on and take poses about the stage like John's drawings.
... The show was such a financial success that they decided to repeat the performance in June of the same year.[72]

Augustus John's influence on Carrington's generation was more than artistic; she was not the only one who had taken to wearing the kind of clothing depicted in John's work, proof that life follows art.

Later that year, possibly about the time of Teddy's disappearance, Lady Glenavy recorded another, much more upsetting reminder of the war. Gertler, Carrington, and some other friends had spent the evening with Lady Glenavy and her husband Gordon, when 'suddenly the whole outside world seemed to burst into a roar of fierce, terrible, savage cheering'.

> Pulling the curtains apart, I saw the whole sky was crimson and all the houses and trees lit up. I went down the stairs like an avalanche, gasping, 'Zeppelin coming down – burning'. Carrington shot out of her room, and we both clawed at the hall-door and dashed out into Norfolk Road. There it was, creeping and dripping down the sky, head first, mighty and majestic, a great flaming torch, and away above it the little light of the plane, signalling to the guns. There was an Artillery barracks at the end of our road. The great roars of cheering, rising and falling in crescendo and diminuendo, came from there, but it sounded as if all London was cheering.
> Carrington burst into terrible sobbing and rushed back to her room: I felt almost unconscious with excitement, and was on a plane of living where human suffering no longer existed. It looked as if the remains of the Zeppelin had come down on Hampstead Heath, though in reality it was much farther off, in rural Essex. I wanted to get a taxi and go to where it had fallen, and went to Carrington to get her to come with me, but she was crying so bitterly she could not speak, so I left her.[73]

While the war dragged on in Europe, Carrington's relationship with Gertler dragged on also, even while moving toward its inevitable end. Gilbert Cannan, away from Cholesbury, had offered Gertler the use of his mill house in his absence at the end of 1916. Gertler had invited Carrington, who in turn invited Strachey ('I promise you vast quantities of food and drink, and raiment for the night season. A fire in your bedroom and our love shall out-heat the very fires and be hotter than the very soups and curries,' she wrote seductively).[74] Lytton diplomatically declined. What the exact nature of her physical relationship with Lytton was at this point no one really knows, but it seems most likely that it had been relegated to sexual jokes and innuendos in their letters.

Even while it was clear that it must at last end, Carrington and Gertler's relationship reached another turning-point at Cholesbury: at long last they embarked upon a sexual relationship, with a predictable result. Carrington failed 'to get really interested' and it proved a tremendous disappointment after the years of difficulty that preceded it.[75] Perhaps she felt that her loyalty lay with Lytton now, but that at the same time she owed something to Mark who had been waiting for so long. Now that she had taken a big step with Lytton, sleeping with Mark lost some of its importance. Further, an inability to enjoy herself physically with Mark meant that she could sleep with him without being 'unfaithful' to Lytton. It was inevitable that her sexual relations with Mark would be doomed to failure; according to Garnett, Lytton felt this was 'due to Gertler's violence and Carrington's worry and disgust over contraceptives'. Garnett himself believed that 'the real reason was that she was not in love with him, but with Lytton. Blaming herself did not improve matters.'[76] Nevertheless, she and Mark continued to sleep together, unsatisfactorily, for some time.

Although she found that sex improved her understanding of literature, Carrington felt compelled by her shame and lack of real interest to ration such experiences.

> I read Marlowe ['To His Coy Mistress' by Andrew Marvell] again last night and knew what one thing meant more than I did last week! It certainly is a necessity if one wants to understand the best poets. No she's not going on to say that is *why* she takes sugar in her coffee now. But taking sugar incidentally does make one appreciate those poets more fully. But I only like sugar some times, not every week and every day in my coffee. I think you would like it so much and take it so often in your coffee that you wouldn't taste anything in time, and miss the taste of the coffee. But darling I shall look after that alright and only allow you three lumps a month. You've had more than three for this month. So no more till next year, you sugar-eater you![77]

She signed this injunction playfully – 'Yr PERIWINKLE CRINKLE CRINKLE' – but Mark was exasperated. Her falsely playful tone masked the fact that her objections were strong and fundamental. Sex with Mark was more than unpleasant – it was vulgar, possibly because of his unrelenting pressure over the years, beginning when she was young and unprepared for such a relationship. Yet it is probable she had not found it so with Strachey, indicating a deep and difficult ambivalence which it would take years to resolve, but which would gradually fade with time.

Desperate to retain her love, his letters clearly showed his torment.

> ... For God's sake don't torture me by not letting me see much of you – I must see you *very* often. I shan't worry you for much 'sugar' if only I can see you and talk – I must, I must. And if any other man touches any part of your beautiful body I shall kill myself – don't forget that! I could not bear such a thing. Give me time – give me at any rate a year or so of happiness. I deserve it – you have tortured me enough in the past. Perhaps later I shall be able to be 'advanced' and reasonable about your other friends. Then you can have other ships ... Don't believe those 'advanced' fools who tell you that love is free. *It is not* – it is a *bondage*, a beautiful bondage. We are bound to one another – you must love the bondage. How I hate your 'advanced' philosopher self! Yes I hate that part of you – you have lately added hateful parts to yourself. If you really loved me you could not be so advanced. A person really in love is *not* advanced. I loathe your many ships idea ... Also you would not call love-making 'vulgar' if you were in love. You would not arrange for it only to happen three times a month ...
>
> I hate you for three things:
> 1. Because you can't love passionately.
> 2. Because of your advanced ideas.
> 3. I hate you because I love you and am therefore in the power of your cruel, advanced and unpassionate self![78]

He knew that she found love-making 'vulgar', but was undoubtedly pleased that she had seemingly surrendered her virginity to him. He did not know that she had first offered it to Strachey.

Carrington, once again surrounded by the peacefulness and beauty of the countryside at Hurstbourne Tarrant, was conciliatory. She was even willing to try the contraceptive device he had apparently given her:

> I am sorry if I have annoyed you lately about that business and making such a fuss. It is only my inability to really get interested I am afraid and really I did try that thing. Only it was much too big, and wouldn't go inside no matter what way I used it! But I won't be so childish any longer ... I am so excited about my painting now. I want to do nothing else all day long. Today I shall go for a long walk over the Downs. But it is cold. Almost too cold out to be really happy.[79]

She was working on a watercolour – one of the few she completed – of the 'Hills in Snow at Hurstbourne Tarrant', which demonstrates a shift in her style. The scene has a rather fantastic quality to it, with its almost Japanese trees and the strong contrast between the trees and their shadows and the stark snow on the hills. So much did it show the Slade influence rather than the Post-Impressionist that it has been taken for a work by John Nash. Yet there is an expansiveness and a freedom that did not show in the more restrictive studio environment. While there is great attention to detail, it captures the sweep of the downs and the coldness of the winter without being locked into stifling precision. Carrington loved to paint outdoors, no matter what the weather, in order to get the correct effect of the scene and to be true to the work itself; when she felt it was successful, such painting exhilarated her.

At the close of 1916, despite a Christmas party at Garsington which included Katherine Mansfield, John Middleton Murry, Bertrand Russell and his friend Maria Nys, Brett, Strachey and herself, Carrington apologised to Gertler for being 'tiresome and in bad humours, but the difficulties that go on inside me, in spite of my fat exterior. I envy often amiable people who can love more simply, and get on.'[80]

CHAPTER EIGHT

SEPARATIONS AND UNIONS

The Gertler–Carrington alliance limped on into 1917, but sleeping together presented them with new difficulties rather than solutions. They did not see each other often for Carrington was very busy painting, giving private art lessons to bring in money, seeing other friends, and trying to find a cottage to share with Strachey. When they were together they tended to quarrel, partly because Mark now began to pressure her to live with him. Although she was clearly in love with Strachey, she claimed not to understand why she and Mark could not get on: '... it makes me a thousand times more frantically wretched to know you are also sad, and I am the cause of it all. But you must know it is not that I dislike you. Its something in between us – that is hateful. Really inside me. I am going to think seriously and simply find out what it is – and then I will come back to you.'[81] She was simply buying time.

The cause for Carrington's and Gertler's difficulties was obvious to everyone but Gertler. Carrington's deep and growing love for Strachey made it impossible for her to love anyone else fully. His homosexuality inevitably would dictate the course of their affections; each, in the coming years, would have to look elsewhere for lovers. Their attachment to each other however was undeniable and powerful. Thus after finishing Lytton's portrait, Carrington looked at it every evening in his absence, and described this ritual in her diary – as though it were a letter addressed to Strachey – at the beginning of 1917.

I wonder what you will think of it when you see it ... now tonight it looks wonderfully good, and I am happy. But then I dread showing it. I should like to go on always painting you every week, wasting the afternoon loitering, and never never showing you what I paint. Its marvellous having it all to oneself. No agony of the soul. Is it vanity? No because I don't care for what they say. I hate only the indecency of showing them what I have loved ... If I was a man I should heap you with presents, bags of soft something, until you *had* to cry out thanks because they overflowed on top of you, and weighed you down. I would love to explore your mind behind your finely skinned forehead. You seem so wise and very coldly old. Yet in spite of this what a peace to be with you, and how happy I was today.[82]

Lytton's love was non-threatening, and, unlike Gertler, he was gentle and warmly witty. He did not want to restrict her freedom, nor did he make any 'crude' sexual demands. Lytton's way of life, shaped by his class and education as well as temperament, was more cerebral, reasonable and orderly than the life she had experienced with Gertler. They could go beyond the purely physical and enjoy together literature, travel, and their own humour.

In any case, her times with Mark were short and infrequent, and left both free to develop new friendships and to work without deciding what to do about their own relationship. Now that the dust from the Asheham fiasco had settled, Carrington was drawn even closer to those in Bloomsbury. Virginia and Leonard Woolf offered her the use of the house in January 1917; she went there with Barbara and one of Lytton's friends from Cambridge, Saxon Sydney-Turner, at the end of that month. A member of the Bloomsbury coterie, Sydney-Turner had been ordered by his doctor to get some rest, but a greater enticement for him was Barbara herself: around this time he fell in unrequited love with her and this continued for most of his life; even through Barbara's happy marriage he quietly nourished that futile affection.

Life at Charleston and at Asheham presented interesting contrasts to well-appointed, well-to-do country houses such as Garsington. Bloomsbury may have been known for certain intellectual and sexual freedoms, yet discussions on these subjects frequently took place in appalling physical discomfort. Indoor plumbing and central heating were luxuries and, when they existed, were not always efficient. Even the healthy Carrington later would find herself frequently felled by frigid temperatures and resulting illnesses in her country homes and in those of others. When she arrived at Asheham with Barbara and Saxon on the evening of 29 January, she found the house freezing and the old woman who took care of the house and cooking ill. 'Should you contemplate coming,' she wrote facetiously to Lytton, 'do I beg you bring only the lightest of summer clothing and some antidote for mosquitoes & gnats which infest the garden in the evenings.'[83] Lytton, well-accustomed to such conditions, responded cheerfully, 'Eh bien, ma chère – niece? tante? petite-fille? – I was glad to hear you were having such a grilling time among the tropics of Asheham. It must just suit your delicate constitution and fragile

frame. I hope you & your co-mates continue to enjoy yourselves. Do you wear muslin or alpaca?'[84]

Despite the cold, there were visual and social compensations. Carrington and Barbara made a huge fire in their bedroom and awoke the next morning 'finding amazing downs clear and sharply defined sun shining at them through the window'. That afternoon Adrian Stephen (brother to Virginia and Vanessa), his wife Karin, David Garnett and Duncan Grant walked the four or five miles from Charleston for tea, eating 'like starving stags'. In the evening Saxon read Swinburne to them. They all spent the days happily, sliding down the snowy hills near Charleston ('I slid all the way down the Firle Beacon on Maynard's despatch case, a terrific rate'), painting landscapes while warmed by hot water bottles, and cooking dinner for Vanessa, Duncan, Maynard and David.[85] In a letter to Lady Ottoline, Lytton said, 'It sounds a singular party, and I fear we shall never hear a true history of its goings-on. I gather they spend much of their time tobogganing down the Downs on tea-trays.'[86] The evenings were spent in typical Bloomsbury fashion, as Carrington reported to Gertler:

> ... they sat and talked very seriously about what was certain in life and what one did like to live for, and believe in – whether good or evil were positive, and beauty, and pleasure. Everyone agreed that pleasure was certain, but argued over the good and evil and beauty.[87]

This cheerful spell was followed by more difficult times. In early February Louis Gertler, Mark's father, suddenly fell ill. Mark arrived home to find him dying and his family in a terrible emotional state. Carrington expressed from Asheham the 'hope [tha]t your father will recover', but he died, leaving Mark miserable and his mother inconsolable.[88] Guilt troubled both Carrington and Mark, she for not being able to comfort him better, and he for having left his family and returned to his work shortly before the death unexpectedly occurred.

Her brother Teddy was still missing in action and Carrington became terribly depressed as his February birthday passed with no news of him. He had to be presumed dead, and his loss drew her even closer to Lytton, who tried to comfort her. 'You will not mind if I want to see you often', she wrote. 'For its wretched being alone & knowing how he went – without ever being seen or loved. He had the independence of a child ... his joys all contained inside himself – made by himself. Forgive me for writing – only I think you would have loved him too ...'[89] The tragedy of unfulfilled potential in life as well as in work depressed her terribly.

Lytton, too, had family problems. The Strachey house at Belsize Park Gardens had run out of coal, and therefore could have no fires. Never one to enjoy 'roughing it', he lamented to Carrington in a letter addressed from 'Lunacy Lodge' that '[i]t seems improbable that we shall meet until my coffin passes down Gower Street on its way to the Paupers' Cemetery.'[90] Carrington responded, 'I am grieved to hear of your sad state and the near approach of

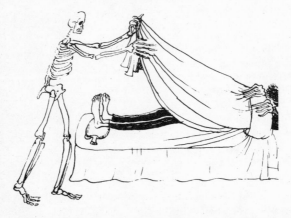

Try no more to elude his boney figures. They will be warmer far than those you sit round in the padded room lighted by that perfidious gas fire.'[91]

Lady Strachey became ill and Lytton had to give up seeing Carrington when his mother 'had a rather bad attack'. He continued the letter a few days later, on his birthday on 1 March, composing a poem which began a tradition of birthday poems for them. Yet none of these difficulties changed his or Carrington's desire for a country home for, as Lytton wrote, 'It strikes me as maniacal to live anywhere but among trees & grasses, open skies, fresh butter, wood fires, & days that are empty and endless.'[92]

Carrington's deepening affection for Lytton was by no means unwelcome, although at times it made him nervous – particularly when he was surrounded by his Bloomsbury friends. His friendship and correspondence with her had become an established part of his life, and he missed her when they were apart even though such absences were necessary to make their friendship work. 'I wish you could have shared the chicken & the claret tonight, and then drawn up your chair by mine in front of the fire,' he wrote her from Alderney, where he was staying with Augustus and Dorelia John.

> The arrangements in this world are sometimes rather tiresome. I had dimly hoped that I might have heard from you today, but not a word has reached me from the world – not a letter, and – thank the Lord! – no newspapers. So I haven't any idea of what may or may not have happened. I hope, at any rate, your silence has not been caused by annoyance. I don't know in the least what at; but I fear I *am* at times a trifle ... unsatisfactory. Is it age, sex, or cynicism? But perhaps it's really only appearance – of one sort or another. The fellow, as they say (only they don't), is good at heart. I wish I could be of more avail. I often think that if the layer of flesh over my bones were a few inches thicker I might be. But that is one of the tiresome arrangements of this world. Ma Chère, I'm sure I do sympathise with your feelings of loneliness. I know what it is so horribly well myself.

He indicated his age, physique and fidelity in the closing: 'From your très-vieux, très-maigre, et très-fidèle Lytton.'[93]

When he was delayed at Alderney Manor by a blizzard, he tried to convince Carrington to join him there: 'Why *not* come & share it with me? ... And then, if I had a telegram from you tomorrow, you should have a taxi at the station ... Is it all a vision? We could return on Monday perhaps. And, if you once got here, you would hardly find it colder than London, and much less confusing – also one bed is warmer than two –.'[94] Carrington telegraphed that she could not join him, but it is not clear whether her reasons lay in work commitments, in her parents' refusal, or her financial condition. She was on her way to stay with her parents and wrote to Lytton of her affection: 'I missed you horribly today ... & felt slightly angry for having confessed to you that I did care so much ... often I would tear you to pieces, & eat you up ... You must write me very long letters in the country.'[95]

'Will you do any painting down there, I wonder?' Strachey responded. ' – I miss you too, you know. – That was such a divine hour – why regret any of it? A great deal of many kinds of love, from Lytton.'[96] She, as usual, ran into difficulties with her parents; her mother 'is more erratic & insane than I expected even ... My Father just delivered in his best O. T. manner, with the solemness [*sic*] of

Isaac a grand lecture on my sins.'[97] Lytton found that Carrington's 'relatives are a queer lot'.[98]

Whether she was in London, at Garsington Manor, or with her parents, the problem of Mark stayed with her. She knew that her feelings for Lytton surpassed what she had ever felt for anyone, and that it was a terrible injustice to Mark not to be honest with him. Self-revelation, whether of emotion or work, caused her terrible pain even as she fully realised the pain that not revealing herself caused others. At last, in mid-April, she arranged to meet Mark and tell all. She had decided it would be best to see him in his studio, and then to see Lytton after supper that same evening. She then wrote the main facts – of her love for Strachey – in a letter; when Mark received it, he telephoned to confirm the meeting. He surprised her by being calm. He had fully expected some kind of disclosure and anticipation prevented him from working: 'Lately I have been unable to work much as I have been far too preoccupied with life itself and the problems of life. These troublesome thoughts have put my work for the time being in the shade. As long as they go on I don't suppose I shall be able to do any continuous work. I am passing through terrible changes. I don't know what awaits me the other side, but I am not frightened. But in the meantime I am suffering much – more than you can imagine. Veil after veil I keep tearing off my eyes and the disclosures are more and more terrible. What I see is ghastly, almost too much to bear.'[99]

On the day of their appointment, 13 April 1917, Carrington 'awoke after a horrible dream' in which she first saw photographs of the lost Teddy, then had him returned to her, alive: 'I remember rushing at him, telling him how I had thought he was dead and how I closed my fingers into his hard fat cheeks. Very brown and kissed him and hugged till I nearly crushed him to atoms. After all this I awoke and felt rather miserable, as I remembered soon I should have to see Mark.'[100]

The break was as painful as she had expected. Mark was dispassionate rather than angry. In fact, 'His calmness amazed me and his complete unselfishness and generosity', she wrote in her diary.

> I became more and more wretched and wept. It seemed like leaving the warm sun in the fields and going into a dark and cold wood surrounded by trees which were strangers. I suddenly looked back at the long life we had had between us of mixed emotions. But always warm because of his intense love and now I had to leave it all and go away. Then suddenly he saw it also: the end of all this closeness, the final goodbye, the separation of two brothers, with a life between them, and he broke down and sobbed, and then it was agony. For he wanted to die and I thought how much this love mattered to him, and yet in spite [of] its greatness

I could not keep it, and must leave. His loneliness was awful. We left the studio and had tea in a Suisse cafe in a dark back room. He didn't talk much, hardly at all about Lytton; only – 'Will you live with him?' 'No.' 'But he may love you.' 'No he will not.' That I thought made it easier a little. He begged to still be friends and see me. But we both knew it could not be so and it was separation.[101]

Even at the point of revealing all, Carrington tried to protect Mark's feelings. In fact, she continued to deny that she planned to live with Lytton, even after they had moved into a house together. Never forward-looking in this respect, she did not anticipate what would occur when Mark eventually discovered the truth. Whether she truly believed that Lytton would not love her is unclear.

What is clearer is that Lytton was not told until afterwards the complete nature of her confession to Mark. When she arrived at Lytton's later that evening they had the following conversation, which she also recorded in her diary.

(C) I thought I had better tell Mark, as it was so difficult going on.
(L) Tell him what?
(C) That it couldn't go on. So I just wrote and said it.
(L) What did you say in your letter?
(C) I thought you knew.
(L) What do you mean?
(C) I said that I was in love with you. I hope you don't mind very much.
(L) But aren't you being rather Romantic and are you certain?
(C) There's nothing Romantic about it.
(L) What did Mark say?
(C) He was terribly upset.
(L) Did he seem angry with me?
(C) No. He didn't mention you.
(L) But it's too incongruous. I'm so old and diseased. I wish I was more able.
(C) That doesn't matter.
(L) What do you mean. What do you think we had better do about the physical.
(C) Oh I don't mind about that.
(L) That's rather bad. You should. I thought you did care. What about those boys, when you were young.
(C) Oh that was just being young. Nothing.
(L) But do you mind me being rather physically attracted.
(C) I don't think you are really.
(L) Why? Because of your sex.
(C) Yes partly. I don't blame you. I knew it long ago and went into it deliberately.
(L) They will think I am to blame.
(C) They needn't know.
(L) Mark will tell them.
(C) No he won't.

(L) But my dear aren't you being rather romantic. You see I'm so very ancient, and well –

(C) It's all right. It was my fault. I knew what I was doing.

(L) I wish I was rich and then I could keep you as my mistress.

(C) (I was angry then inside) It would not make any difference.

(L) No it wouldn't, true . . .

She continued,

> . . . The misery at parting and my hatred of myself for caring so much. And at his callousness. He was so wise and just. Then he left and I went down later and talked long into the night with Alix [Alix Sargant-Florence, her good friend]. But there was no consolation. Still it was good to be able to talk of it.[102]

The next day she recorded Gertler's misgivings in her diary. He was most annoyed that 'after all these years in 3 months you should love a man like Strachey twice your age (36) and emaciated and old. As I always said life is a crooked business.' She felt 'as if [her] nose had been cut away'.[103] This was perhaps the most difficult thing she had ever had to do. Not only did she finally reveal at least part of the truth to Mark and send him away – at a time of loss in both their lives – but she also had to reveal the depth of her feelings to Strachey and take the consequences. He had made no such demand of her, although he undoubtedly felt the unfairness of Mark's position. She made her position clear to both men, and thereby made a commitment to Strachey, which, although they had planned to find a cottage together, nevertheless began to make him nervous. Up to this time, their love was mutually recognised but undeclared. With her confession to Mark, their private relationship became public. Carrington was careful not to make him feel responsible for her emotional condition, but recognised that 'it all ends like this about as crooked as it could be'.[104]

For several weeks Mark and Carrington were on a 'dear friend' basis. They continued to write to each other and were very self-congratulatory about the maturity with which they handled the break. 'I in no way blame you for anything that's happened,' Mark wrote on 18 April. 'We have done well to part at last, and this time it does seem the end of that long and terrible struggle. I shall commence right away to build up my future life, brick by brick, and I have hopes. My work will be the basis. From now onwards my life will be a more decent and spiritual thing than it's ever had a chance to be before. I hope you too will find yourself soon on your feet and with a better knowledge of your mind and feelings.'[105] By May, however, Carrington was again covering up the truth ('I *don't* want to live with him. Honestly [I don't] want to. But I only said if [he wanted me to I would not] oppose him.'),[106] and even trying to woo

Mark back ('Mark, you never write to me. I wonder why. I am agitated already in case you are not happy. Do write to me soon please again ... I am working on a little "Giotto" for you').[107] Yet later that month she and Mark had again begun to sleep together, and she wrote that the news of their split and resumed friendship had made its way to 'all those fly catchers at Garsington'.[108]

Their reconciliation seemed complete; in fact, a letter Carrington wrote to Gertler in May suggests that their resumed sexual relationship brought with it fears of pregnancy.

> I am sorry to have made such a commotion about it. But what really upset me was:
>
> (1) That you had not been *quite* honest in not telling me. Everything.
>
> (2) That seeing that you did not know whether it might not by chance have gone right up, that you took any risk. Through (I still maintain) selfish and lazy motives. That was really what upset me so much. I care so much for living. That the prospect of that [pregnancy?] fills me with, for a moment even[,] with absolute horror. If you ever lie to me again, even a fraction of a lie, no matter what your motives are, I shall not forgive you.[109]

Their new 'friendship' did not keep Gertler from criticising her, but she refused to allow it. 'I am sorry you take up that stupid attitude about wearing breeches as its rather absurd,' she retorted to his censure of her 'unfeminine' attire. 'I don't want to look like a boy as I know I'm female and it would be useless to be anything else. But I like definitely wearing them much better. So pish! for thee my Iceland dog!'[110] Never glamorous in her appearance, she had discovered the comfort of trousers which in her active life were a welcome, if still occasional, addition to her wardrobe.

All of these developments kept her away from her work, and on 29 May Roger Fry wrote asking 'when and where are you discoverable'.[111] He wanted her to help him with art restorations at Hampton Court but, unknown to most of their friends, Lytton had taken Carrington to Cambridge for several days. This was an important occasion for her, for it helped her to fit together the pieces of Strachey's past and to help her better understand Bloomsbury. Additionally, it was important that Lytton, previously so anxious to keep her hidden in the wings, now took her where he was so well known, in effect publicising their relationship.

Her reaction to Cambridge was very different from Mark's when Eddie Marsh had taken him there several years earlier; she was comfortable with the people and the place, perhaps because she was now more comfortable with people who came from there. Mark had found the students pretentious and had felt like a fish out of water; Carrington was able to see Cambridge as an important backdrop to the life she had chosen with Strachey. That Lytton wanted her to see it was, she felt, an honour; 'Thank you so much for taking me there,' she wrote, 'Very Very Much.'[112]

She returned to her work with relief, hoping to finish Lytton's portrait as well as her obligations to Fry at Hampton Court. Lytton returned much less peacefully to face the tribunal, or draft board, about his ability to serve in the military. With war still raging, the army was relaxing its standards in an effort to draft more men. Lytton tried to obtain conscientious objector status, and on 17 March 1916 he had appeared before the Hampstead Tribunal, accompanied by numerous friends and supporters, to plead his case. He carried with him a travelling rug, and Philip Morrell handed him an air cushion – he was suffering from piles. He blew up the cushion and seated himself carefully before the procedures could begin. When asked if he had a conscientious objection to all wars, he replied, 'Oh no, not at all. Only this one.'

'Then tell me, Mr Strachey, what would you do if you saw a German soldier attempting to rape your sister?'

He replied gravely and ambiguously, after looking at his sisters, 'I should try and come between them.'[113]

He was turned down for conscientious objector status but received a medical exemption soon after that hearing. In June of 1917, however, he had to be re-examined by doctors and his status reviewed. He telegraphed the results immediately to Carrington, and followed that with a more explanatory letter. The tribunal had not given him a total clearance, but he did have a reprieve: 'So far as I can make out, the result is ... of course not so good as absolute rejection. It means that I shall be called up again in six months – unless I put in a conscience claim. There's more than a week to think it over. At present I incline towards letting sleeping dogs lie.'[114]

Meanwhile, Carrington was having problems of a different sort. The allowance her parents gave her did not stretch far in London, skimp as she might. She resorted to borrowing from the equally insolvent Gertler (to pay her art supply debts), and from her brother Noel for her living expenses.

> Dearest Noel, I am up a gum tree as the debts close in about me. And next week on the 14 we have to move from here [3 Gower Street] and I have no wherewithal. Dear Brother hearken unto my prayer. Lest I be utterly consumed. I swear faithfully I am making earnest attempts now to earn the bright sovereigns and give up my profligate life. Oh Saint Lewis hearken upon my supplications. The nett amount of bills is £8.10 But I swear the golden day will come when all will be returned to you.

She signed this letter 'Miserably your sister Dora', using her rejected name as an indication that she was on her best suburban behaviour

in writing to him, despite the humour, and included a drawing of
herself weeping on top of a tree.

Noel responded to her plea and she was appropriately grateful:
'Dear Noel, Bless you. And thank you. Alas! The gum tree was not
"fruitful" *but* by a miracle has now grown fruit even 5 large pears!'[115]
Another drawing showed her this time happily eating pears in the
tree.

Despite money problems, the summer of 1917 was going well for
her. She and Mark were friendly; she was seeing Lytton; and in
June she was delighted by a new occurrence: Lady Strachey was
recovering at Roger Fry's home, Durbins, after surgery, and in her
absence the house at Belsize Park Gardens was shut. Lytton therefore came to stay with Carrington for several days in her new studio
at 60 Frith Street. When he left to join his mother at Durbins,
Carrington wrote to Barbara of her joy: 'I've never been so happy
in my *life* before. Hurray ... It was fun persuading Mrs Reekes, my
housekeeper that Lytton was my uncle. But I think the general
uproar that went on in the early morning in his room rather upset
her belief in me!'[116] On his arrival at Durbins, Lytton found it
'curious this morning waking up with no virginal bodyguard at hand
... Je t'embrasse.'[117]

Carrington's happiness was not undiluted; Lytton would be away
for two months that summer; such absences, though not generally
so prolonged, would be commonplace. As disappointed as she was
about this, she nonetheless wrote to Mark not to think 'I am unhappy
for it is not true'.

> I am very happy nearly always. If anyone runs Lytton down you ought
> rather to say, he must be better than we think since Carrington loves
> him. Do you not see that if you love me, you *must* believe in what I love,
> and not agree with the public who are stupid, and prejudiced in saying
> it is ill sorted, and I am misled. But rather you, and you alone since you
> know I am honest, ought to believe in me. Will you?[118]

Mark did not agree with her logic; this was a great request for
someone who had endured what he had, and who was still in love
with her. Yet, as Lytton was later to say about the war, 'even the
worst peace is peace'.[119]

July was an extremely busy period for Carrington. While in
London she went to the opera, museums, parties, and gave art
lessons 'to [a] brat in St Johns Wood'.[120] Both in London and
at Hurstbourne Tarrant she worked on woodcuts for the Woolfs'
Hogarth Press, and painted. The woodcuts took much time and
effort, for which she was paid the miserly sum of fifteen shillings,
but she was rewarded by praise when Virginia and Leonard liked
'the wood cuts immensely'.[121] They were to illustrate Virginia's *Two*

Stories, which eventually sold 135 copies, but there were difficulties in printing. When the woodcuts' margins did not seem quite right, Virginia and Leonard 'bought a chisel, and chopped away, I am afraid rather spoiling one edge', Virginia confessed. Lytton complained, 'Damn them. They haven't put enough ink on your cuts,' but added, 'I adore the Snail. Virginia I consider a genius.'[122]

In Hurstbourne, Carrington began a painting of her old friend Alix Sargant-Florence, who she had known since her early London days, but was unable to finish when the wilful Alix departed, leaving her 'all alone, except for these imbecile parents, and the bloody Scotch nurse'.[123]

Back in London by 25 July, Carrington was overcome by the city heat and wrote Lytton a wonderfully evocative and descriptive letter in the style that was uniquely hers, and which delighted him.

> The cats drink the water in the gutters of the Square. The hair falls out from the backs of dogs, & lies on the footway. The very pavements are greasy with sweat which oozes from the holes in the boots of the passers. Steam rises up from the rotten fruit in the barrows, & mingles with the dark grey air which hangs heavily over the city ... yes, & many worse things could I relate to you sir.
>
> Life here is dominated by the insect world, flies cover the jam laden faces of the children, & nest in the thick warm powder of the prostitutes. Till one might well be living in a populace of negroes, so seldom does one see any white skinned creatures.
>
> ... Went to Percy Young [her art supplier] & got thoroughly miserable & savage over the war. His son & two nephews had been killed, & his fury against the government was great. Do you know they actually sent his nephew out with a *wooden* foot again, & he is in the Flying Corps & has to drive a machine!!
>
> Je pouverais t'embrasse un mille mille des temps.[124]

With Lytton still at Durbins, helping to watch over his mother and agonising over the 'General Gordon' section of *Eminent Victorians*, Carrington could indulge herself in both work and play. Finishing a wood block for Roger Fry, she got her 'canvasses all ready & paints laid out in a row'. But at the same time she was planning a walking tour with her brother Noel, who soon would be coming home on leave from the war. Lytton took all this to mean that she was neglecting her cottage-finding duties and avoiding making arrangements for a proposed September trip to Cornwall. 'Madam!' he chastised her, 'You fiddle while Rome is burning ... You'll wake up one fine morning and discover that it's the first of September, and that you're in no. 60 Frith Street, with no prospect of getting out of it for the rest of your natural life ... It's annoying that you can't nip down here in some form or other – preferably your own.'[125] To which she responded, 'O Frêle creature. Why do you doubt the powers of the female napolean? Will verse restore your lost confidence[?]'

> Whilst playing her fiddle this valiant maid,
> Gave orders loudly to the fire brigade
> Who quelled with water the fierce fires of Rome
> Thus saving many lives, & St Paul's vast dome.
> * * * *   Moral.   * * * *
> Fear not, therefore that this same Maid will fail
> To obtain, O ancient, Cornwall's Holy Grail.[126]

She worked in her studio on a still life which pleased her, but related an embarrassing incident at the opera 'Figaro', where she and a friend were 'crushed in with all the Lords & paper-mache Ladies, swam up the crowded stairs, presented my tickets, in that neglige which stamps all members of the upper classes, when the harsh, & vulgar voice of the flunkey said, "What are you about *missy*? These are yesterday night's tickets."' When the box office refused to acknowledge an error, she ended up watching from the pit. She faced such instances with good humour, but also revealed a penchant for practical joking. Lytton was completely taken in by her false report – a mischievous joke on her part – that his newly-wed friend, George Reeves, was unhappy in his marriage. Several days later he discovered 'that the George story was a flam. Petite diablesse!'[127]

He and she were now regarded as a couple by many of their friends; Lytton was invited to Charleston in August and reported that 'Vanessa expects you to accompany me'.[128] Virginia, well aware of Carrington's virginal reputation, found it all rather curious and teased her about it in a letter. 'A swarm of bees conglobulated suddenly over our heads on the terrace – in an ecstacy of lust – drove us in – then made for the chimney, and all settled in the attic. Please tell us what to do. We want the honey; the males were all dead – But I forgot: you dont like the fact of copulation, only the theory – What an odd generation yours is!'[129] While this underscored Woolf's knowledge of Carrington's character and reputation, it was a decidedly acidic remark – particularly from a woman with even greater sexual difficulties.

Separately and together Carrington and Lytton visited Asheham and Charleston; Lytton continued to frequent Garsington but Carrington was, for some time, *persona non grata* there. Wherever Lytton went, the letters flowed between him and Carrington. 'Your letters are a great pleasure', he wrote on 7 August. 'I lap them down with my breakfast, and they do me more good than tonics, blood capsules, or iron jelloids ... It's also excellent that your paintings are progressing. As for Gordon, he is going on, and I am feeling less crushed.'[130]

They had now entered on a new stage of their relationship: feeling free to express their feelings for each other. On 12 August Carrington wrote to Strachey,

> Norton [one of Lytton's friends, Harry Norton] told Alix it was of course just the infatuation of a school girl for a mistress – But since last summer I have never thought of anyone else. Every moment, when something definite is not being done – I am thinking of you. And if it was not that in another ten days I shall be with you at Charleston – these days here would be miserable. But my ambition for you is great, & lately I have felt that perhaps time, which you might have spent working, was wasted with me this year. You must always refuse to see me if this is so – Dear Lytton if you knew how much I thank you for what you have taught me. Even if the results are not very apparent![131]

Despite his pleasure in her letters, he felt compelled to correct the more egregious of her spelling errors. She deferred, both to his greater knowledge and to his character. He protested, saying 'I consider your letters perfect – so pray don't improve them. You know I can hardly be expected to share your flattering views, you dearest creature! But how can I hope to explain how much *I* have got from *you*?'[132]

On 10 August Lytton made a woodcut of his own, claiming it was a 'beautiful object I've just found, lying about. It'll show you how things should be done.'[133] Carrington was delighted: 'You cunning old wretch to work away like the ferret in the rabbit-hole all this time and then surprise me by this beautiful creation! But no more woodcuts for your frontispieces! Now you have surpassed me in your skill you can do your own centaur!' She went on to tell Lytton of her ability to withstand the advances of a rival, a young man named Geoffrey: '... he told me of his passionate love for that girl Carrington. Which I received with all sympathy, & sarcasm, and delivered him a long lecture on his humility ... and told him not to go about with those degraded Café Royal pole-cats. – His methods of making love were practically Pre-Raphaelite – or rather more

Burne-Jones. – so there was *not* much chance for lust to urge up &
overcome the female!'[134]

Besides the walking tour with her brother, Carrington was planning another excursion. Despairing of finding a cottage on her own,
she and Lytton decided that she should disguise herself as a boy and,
accompanied by her 'Uncle Lytton', roam the villages of southern
England to find one.

> Hours were spent in front of the glass last night strapping the locks back,
> and trying to persuade myself that two cheeks like turnips on the top of
> a hoe bore some resemblance to a very well nourished youth of sixteen . . .
> But dear, promise you'll come even with a female page for a companion. I
> think those cursed military authorities make the other rather more
> difficult, as the life of a village policeman is so drear, that the sight of a
> fat cheeked boy and a German bearded spy would throw him into
> a spasm of alertness and bring up all this stupidity surging into his
> gullet . . .
>
> But the probability of us both being arrested the first night, *you* for
> the *offense* that I am not a disguised female, and me for the offense that
> I *am*! But one might find out first whether it is a criminal offense![135]

Perhaps deterred by these war-time difficulties, they never actually
made this journey.

The trip with Noel she undertook with greater success. Still
involved in the war, he looked forward to a carefree tramp through
the English countryside and wrote Carrington asking her to plan
one. This depended on his promised military leave coming through,
and when he did not appear on the expected evening, she was
'uneasy' – as much because she thought it might mean she would
have to give up the impending Charleston visit as out of concern for
him. She was excited at the prospect of seeing him again, but certain
'that we won't really get on, and I shall be disappointed'.[136] He
arrived in London the next day, and they began their trip from

their parents' home at Hurstbourne Tarrant, under the auspicious appearance of a double rainbow.

After taking a taxi to Oxford, they stayed at the Bear Inn in Wantage, which they found 'so very pleasant and Noel became entangled with some people' that they lingered another day or two. From Wantage they proceeded to Aldbourne, walking on through Great Bedwyn, discovering the little 'village called Ham at the foot of the big Combe downs', where Carrington would eventually settle in 1924, and 'toiled up this vast mountain, barefoot, groaning under weight of haversacks . . .' Indefatigable and determined walkers, they covered 107 miles in their short trip.[137]

As happy as she was with Noel, she looked forward even more to meeting Lytton at Charleston where soon 'I shall be wrapt in the folds of your octopi arms'[138] and from which they proceeded to Cornwall for the month of September. They were joined on this trip by Lytton's brother James, and by their female friend Noel Olivier. Their destination, Beeny Farm, was a terrible disappointment. Run by an 'old hag' and her offspring, the farm included less than romantic appointments: a pig sty, fleas, no hot water, 'all rather ramshackle, and decayed'.[139] There Lytton worked on revisions to General Gordon, read to her in the evenings and went with her on long walks.

Having made the best of an unpleasant situation for ten days, they sent wires to other farms, finally discovering a gem of a place to which Carrington would return, warmly welcomed, several times in the future. Run by a Mrs Box, Home Farm, Welcombe, near Bude, proved a dream come true: comfortable, clean rooms with double beds, plentiful food and easy access to the sea. Carrington went for icy swims with Noel Olivier and she painted, at first indoors, because 'I have had a great bother to get a pass to paint. A policeman came the other evening, and spent a long time taking all particulars of my origin. I was furious. It's been so absurd, and idiotic. Not to be allowed to paint a tree within four miles of the sea, because one might be giving information to the enemy!!! But next week he said I might have it.'[140]

Carrington found Cornwall perfect, and remained for some time inspired by both its landscape and its inhabitants. There she began one of her finest pictures: a portrait of Mrs Box. This work shows how much her ability had matured since she had first begun to win prizes at the Slade. Looking like a quintessential Cornish farmer's wife, Mrs Box is dressed in the oldest of fashions: a large, beribboned bonnet, and full, patterned clothes, sitting grimly with her hands folded on her ample lap. This portrait is extremely subtle in colouring; the red-orange of the patterned sleeves is counterpointed by the

dark background of the armchair and the blue-greens of the wall
and her other clothing. But the greatest artistry appears in the
figure, for both the hands and the face, while partially shadowed, are
illuminated to reveal a finely detailed realism.

As she painted more, she resumed contact with Mark. He wrote
back a decidedly unfriendly letter from Garsington.

> I am afraid that your passion for L. S. estranges me more & more from
> you – I can't stomach it at all. It's poisoning my feelings and belief in
> you. I don't feel the same about you as I used to. Also I think now that
> you have been so unnecessarily cruel to me in the past. It's difficult for
> me to forgive you.[141]

This letter made Carrington suddenly realise that in choosing
Lytton, she had truly lost Mark. She could not bear such a final
ending and she wrote to him immediately: 'Oh Mark, dearest friend,
I was so glad to get [your letter] that I almost cried for joy, although
it hurt me also ... Only be merciful, do not hate me.'[142] Mark,
however, was adamant.

> It has been difficult for me to write because honestly, I do not feel the
> prospect of returning to you at all enticing. I get on so much better
> without you. I don't see why the future should be any better than the
> past, and the past visualised in perspective is pretty ghastly. You have
> treated me abominably, Carrington – always until the last moment – and
> it is hard not to hate you for it.[143]

These were harsh words and terrible truths; Carrington could only
deal with them by trying to win back his good feelings through their
common interest in art. 'May I come and see your paintings when
I come back?' she ventured. 'Please, Mark do not think of me vilely
and try and forgive me. So that I shall not be timid to come because
of your anger. Brett wrote to me the other day, and told me what
good paintings you had done. I am trying hard to do a good portrait
of the old lady Box. But its so difficult to get the forms simplified.'[144]
His reply to this particular supplication is unknown.

Despite the continued – and probably unjustly prolonged – struggle with Mark, the Cornwall expedition was a success. Lytton completed his revisions, and Carrington did a number of paintings. She
also grew closer to James and to Noel Olivier who, in her medical
career, would assist Carrington later on.

When Carrington returned on 18 October 1917 to Hurstbourne
Tarrant, it was to news which drew her even closer to Lytton.

> I did not realise how happy I had been until this evening ... You have
> spoilt me for too long, and now I feel as if suddenly I had walked into a
> greenhouse in the winter. For in the paper I saw the first thing on the
> red clothed table when I came in, Teddy's death. It was a year ago, and
> now they announce it officially. Its rather worse being here with all his

books & things about – and where I saw him last – and the remoteness of my parents. Forgive me for writing but I wanted you so badly. One is not even left alone to cry. Dearest Lytton I love you so much.[145]

Clearly she now felt that Lytton was her true 'family' and, with the possible exceptions of her brother Noel and her friend Alix, her only sympathetic intimate. It was equally clear that with the loss of Teddy and Mark, the only person she could live with was Lytton who, despite his nervousness about their relationship, shared and encouraged her visions.

By an odd and interesting twist of fate, it was Carrington's mother who found a solution.

> 1 mile from Pangbourne The Mill House
> *Tidmarsh* Old fashioned House.
> ground cover 1 acre small orchard
> Hall 3 recpt rooms Kitchen etc.
> *Electric Light*, 6 bedrooms box
> room. *Bath H & C*
> Rent £52   3 years lease
> Nr. Church & P.O.   London 65 mins

Mother just gave it to me with an order to view what she had received. I've just telephoned the agents & its still to let. So will go over tomorrow & see it. Sounds too good to be alright!
             Mopsa[146]

That evening she wrote to him again, 'I have made two large pots of blackerberry jam with the sugar of this house. For our future residence! . . . My Mother is knitting you a pair of red & grey mittens. Little did she know . . .' Certainly Charlotte Carrington could not have realised the truth about the living arrangements. Carrington led her to believe that the house was to be shared by former Slade students – all women – who needed a retreat away from London in order to paint. She had no idea that the longed-for cottage was to be shared – albeit in separate bedrooms – by an unmarried man and woman.

Carrington rushed down to Pangbourne on 20 October 1917 and was so excited by the Mill House that she stopped at a tea shop in Newbury to write and send Lytton the news. '. . . Tidmarsh Mill it is to be. Its very romantic and lovely.'

> Vast big rooms, 3 in number,
> 2 very big bedrooms and 4 others,
> Bathroom; water closet;
> very good garden and a shady grass lawn
> with river running through it.

The house is very old with gables and some lattice windows. It is joining on to the Mill. A charming miller showed me over it. Very well

built in good condition ... More apple trees fruit trees vegetables. 2 miles from Theale St. 1 mile Pangbourne ...
Oliver etc must go and see Tidmarsh on Tuesday. Electric light in every room. I'm wildly excited. Hooray![147]

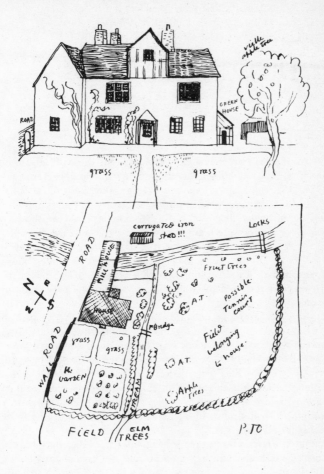

CHAPTER NINE

TIDMARSH MILL HOUSE: 1917-18

As soon as Oliver Strachey signed the lease for the Mill House in Tidmarsh in early November, Carrington flew into action. She spent the rest of 1917 in busy but excited preparations, including 'raids' for furniture, cookware, gardening tools, plants, and anything else she could find. The heaviest looting took place at Hurstbourne Tarrant; her parents were planning another move and she managed to find 'in the stable some water-cans & jugs which will be useful. And I've got free permission to devastate the garden and green house of trees & plants.' She also came up with a table and camp bed, with permission, but the bulk of what she packed up she took without their sanction.

> At last it is all packed, without the heavy looting having been discovered. But the escapes have been as narrow as the way to Heaven. Everything is packed with apples artichokes & potatoes instead of straw & paper! This method will probably insure all the china being smashed. But anyway the food supply is guaranteed for some months!!![148]

She began to move into the house on 22 November, in order to start renovations before Lytton's arrival, and wrote to him happily on 7 December, 'Do you know old Yahoo of a Lytoff this is going to be a good life here.'[149]

Carrington's friend Barbara Hiles – now Barbara Bagenal – moved in for a while to help with the preparations. The two stained floors, measured and laid carpets, and painted walls. They were justifiably pleased with their work; 'I don't know what you think,' Carrington wrote to Lytton triumphantly a few days later, 'but *we* think it's almost as good as Charleston and mind you without any wall decorations. Of course the female favouritism will be rampant.'[150]

Virginia Woolf noted in her diary that '[T]he work of furnishing has fallen of course upon Carrington',[151] who willingly took on that task, but there was no expectation that she should take on the more mundane aspects of running the house as well. An older village woman, Mrs Legg, was soon hired to do the cooking, cleaning, and laundry; her grown son Donald helped out with the heavier tasks of cutting wood, hauling, and gardening under Carrington's close supervision. Carrington was charmed by Mrs Legg from the first, and learned from her the most useful bits of local information: where to buy the best wine and vegetables, post office hours, etc. At first the two women spent many hours together, working out a careful system for running the house, enjoying each other's company and preparing the house for Lytton's occupation in December.

In the meantime, both Carrington and Lytton had some explaining to do. Carrington was still corresponding with Gertler, who continued to be upset about her love for Strachey. What particularly angered him was that while he himself had adored her physically as well as emotionally, Lytton he felt could not perform even the most rudimentary heterosexual functions. In November Mark drew and sent to Carrington a vulgar and vindictive picture of the three of them, naked. In this drawing Mark, walking sadly away, has a large erection. Carrington's body is boyish and chunky. Lytton, holding her arm, has a scrawny, stooped body with exaggerated ribs and a limp penis. An arrow pointing to Mark labels him 'New lover doing his "bit"'. Another labels Carrington 'The maiden in question'. The whole drawing is captioned, 'I move aside – graciously – and make room for your newer – more beautiful lover', and a final note states, 'It would make rather an immoral drama, would it not?'[152]

Such bitterness clearly indicated that Mark, far from coming to terms with the new situation, found it increasingly disturbing. Carrington recognised the danger in his condition, and tried to put him off the track. 'No, I'm not going away with Lytton!' she protested in November. 'But my people are leaving Hampshire, and are going to live in a little town, Cheltenham, so I've got to go home for a little while when they move to help them, and take away my goods and furniture. Then I'll be back in London all the winter I expect.'[153]

His letters to her alternated between friendliness and fury. He followed every angry outburst with a letter asking for her forgiveness. His biggest explosion thus far came in a long, angry – but honest – letter late in 1917.

> ... I feel I must once and forever tell you fully what I think of your love for LS. I have not told you before, because I felt it was useless. If you had come and told me that you thought LS was a wonderful man & that you had an admiration for him, I should have tried to dissuade you because I do not think that he is. I think very much the contrary in fact. But you came and told me that you *loved* him. When I know I was

powerless and that it would only be a waste of breath to be critical. However, now that we are on the subject, I must tell you that I regard your relationship with LS with abhorrence and I shall never change my mind. You have by your love for that man poisoned my belief in love, life, & everything...

... for years I wanted you – you only tortured me, then suddenly you give your love to such a creature, and you yourself said if he wanted your body you would without hesitation have given it to [that] emaciated withered being. I young & full of life you refused it, tell me Carrington what am I to think of life now ... I long to fly very often to another country where I shan't smell the stench that fills my nostrils constantly from the combination of your fresh young self with that half-dead creature who is not even man enough to take your body – your beautiful body – thank God he can not, because if that happens, I shall be sick all day! ...

... he will deaden you in time & that is what hurts me so. You are absolutely at his feet. You follow him about like a puppy, you have lost all self respect. I shudder to think of it ... I only hope soon this nausea of this wretched relationship of yours will poison the spirit of my love for you & so diminish the stink of it. But never as long as I live will I ever get over it.[154]

His sentiments were shared by Brett, who later wrote that she could never understand how Carrington could be attracted to Lytton, and that Carrington had submitted herself completely to him.[155] Yet Brett apparently kept such views to herself at the time, for she contributed 'a big chest of drawers' to Tidmarsh.

Regardless of Mark's emotional outbursts, Carrington found pleasure in caring for Lytton, even through the post. Altering the words of a newspaper advertisement for a tonic, she wrote to the ailing Strachey, 'Have you taken your sana-to-GIN, if not will you please do so at ONCE without further delay. If I find on investigation you have dared to DISOBEY my commands. Henceforth be gone. I have done with you ... I shall never part with your [drawing of stomach]. It is now mine. I feel like [a] strong man with electric sparks flying out. But really I shall see you tonight at old Pozzo [Pozzo de Borgo, Lytton's nickname for Maynard Keynes] – you wretch! Of course you'll be there, curvetting on the High Toe. Did you get the socks this morning at old Madame White-Fuz-Bush? Dearest Yahoo, Good morning.'[156] And the next day, 'Never again are you going to behave like this! After November you will start a regular life at Tidmarsh, supported by glasses of milk, & vigorous walks.'[157]

Lytton had never been cared for like this, and he loved the attention she showered on him. While ill at the Woolfs' house, Asheham, in April 1918, he lamented, 'Imagine the venerable Count, spewing into a basin and gasping in agony, with no Mopsa to comfort him!'[158]

Strachey's health had always been difficult, and most of his problems centred on his delicate digestive system. His physical ailments were well known to his Bloomsbury friends, who humoured him and sympathised – up to a point. Carrington, in contrast, made his health and well-being her first priority.

Virginia recorded in her diary a conversation she had with Lytton about Carrington, in which he 'spoke of her ... with a candour not flattering, though not at all malicious'.

> 'That woman will dog me' – he remarked. 'She won't let me write, I daresay.'
>
> 'Ottoline was saying you would end by marrying her.'
>
> 'God! the mere notion is enough – One thing I know – I'll never marry anyone –'
>
> 'But if she's in love with you?'
>
> 'Well, then she must take her chance.'
>
> 'I believe I'm sometimes jealous –'
>
> 'Of her? thats inconceivable –'
>
> 'You like me better, don't you?'
>
> He said he did; we laughed, remarked on our wish for an intimate correspondent; but how to overcome the difficulties? Should we attempt it? Perhaps.[159]

Carrington never learned of this conversation, but Lytton wrote her an abbreviated and contradictory version of its tone: 'I had a long tête-à-tête with Virginia on Sunday, in which she became distinctly flirtatious, but (needless to remark) I remained calm.'[160]

During the initial months of the Carrington–Strachey alliance, Woolf frequently commented on the two in ways that seemed tinged with more than a little jealousy. Gertler, often at Garsington, warned Carrington away from Virginia and her set: 'Your "Bloomsburies" as they are called, are the most capricious and vicious – I know more than I care to tell you. But they all back-bite the supposed love and best friend! It is all so small – so hateful – and *you* will *not* see it – you are blind or hypnotised – I don't know which – you my dear girl, deserved a better fate.'[161]

Carrington's 'fate' was viewed at first as an impediment to Strachey. After they visited Virginia in March, she noted that 'Lytton & Carrington came to tea – she apple red & firm in the cheeks, bright green & yellow in the body, & immensely firm & large all over ... Carrington going out of the room for a second, Lytton explained that he would like to stay with us without her, could it be managed.'[162] Lytton felt the nervousness normally attributed to bridegrooms, and to a certain extent these nervous feelings were stronger when he was with his old friends who would sympathise. Sometimes his friends surprised him, though. When Virginia 'complimented him on the change in Carrington – he has improved her', Lytton responded, 'Ah, but the future is very dark – I *must* be free. I shall want to go off. [Virginia] suggested that [Carrington] might follow suit, which did not perhaps quite please him.'[163]

By June, Virginia was looking at Carrington more carefully, writing in her diary that,

> She is odd from her mixture of impulse & self consciousness. I wonder sometimes what she's at: so eager to please, conciliatory, restless, & active. I suppose the tug of Lytton's influence deranges her spiritual balance a good deal. She has still an immense admiration for him & us. How far it is discriminating I don't know. She looks at a picture as an artist looks at it; she has taken over the Strachey valuation of people & art; but she is such a bustling eager creature, so red & solid, & at the same time inquisitive, that one can't help liking her.[164]

In July she considered Carrington's position in the relationship, rather than Lytton's: 'If one were concerned for her, one might be anxious about her position – so dependent on L., & having so openly burnt the conventional boats. She is to run her risk & take her chances evidently ... She kisses him & waits on him & gets good advice & some sort of protection.'[165] Not the least consideration was class difference: Carrington's background was decidedly middle class, unlike the predominantly upper-class Bloomsberries. They must have viewed her as in some sense bettering herself, in spite of the notional classlessness conferred on her by becoming an artist. An August entry in Virginia Woolf's diary confirms that Carrington, now a fairly frequent visitor, had been scrutinised and accepted.

Carrington came for the weekend. She is the easiest of visitors as she never stops doing things – pumping, scything, or walking. I suspect part of this is intentional activity, lest she should bore; but it has its advantages. After trudging out here, she trudged to Charleston ... She trudged off again this morning to pack Lytton's box or buy him a hair brush in London – a sturdy figure, dressed in a print dress, made after the pattern of one in a John picture, a thick mop of golden red hair, & a fat decided clever face, with staring bright blue eyes. The whole just misses, but decidedly misses what might be vulgarity. She seems to be an artist – *seems*, I say, for in our circle the current that way is enough to sweep people with no more art in them than Barbara in that direction. Still, I think Carrington cares for it genuinely, partly because of her way of looking at pictures.[166]

It was the contrast between Carrington and Strachey that made everyone so dubious at first: their ages, physiques, interests, not to mention sexual preferences seemed unbridgeable gaps to outsiders. As time passed, these differences appeared for what they were: complementary, rather than opposing, attributes. Everyone assumed that theirs was a sexual relationship, and Woolf recounted an amusing afternoon at Tidmarsh in July:

... after tea Lytton and Carrington left the room ostensibly to copulate; but suspicion was aroused by a measured sound proceeding from the room, and on listening at the keyhole it was discovered that they were reading aloud Macaulay's Essays![167]

Lytton's new life with Carrington, symbolised by the move into Tidmarsh, began under less than auspicious circumstances, but quickly changed to pleasure. 'We had rather a still time of it a few days ago, arriving in the extreme cold – pipes frozen and various supplementary horrors', he wrote to Ottoline on 23 December. 'But things are settling down now very comfortably, and I really think the house will turn out quite a pretty one, though it won't be in proper trim till the warm weather. Carrington is most energetic – painting walls, staining floors, creating carpets, etc. etc. etc. I (as you may imagine) am less so. Today the sun has come out for the first time, and I feel what a blessing it is to be in country.'[168] The year thus ended happily for Lytton, in a new home, and with an acceptance by Chatto & Windus of his second book, *Queen Victoria*.

Yet the trouble with Mark was still unresolved. Lytton and Carrington were settled in Tidmarsh, but Carrington continued to deny this both to her parents and to Gertler. As always, she lied in order to avoid unpleasant repercussions and to avoid making people unhappy. Mark knew that his 'real life will not commence before my passion for Carrington ends', and she hoped that this emotional change would occur before he ever discovered the truth.[169] But by 24 February 1918, he had found out. 'I know that you live with Lytton', he wrote, and the only surprise was that it had taken him two or three months to find out.[170] An event which occurred nearly ten days earlier had alarmingly pointed to such a discovery.

On the night of 14 February 1918, Carrington, Lytton, Maynard Keynes, and their friends Harry Norton, John Sheppard, and Monty Shearman were leaving a party near Ravenscourt Park in London. Mark, drunk, came upon them in the street and suddenly attacked Lytton, who later wrote that '[a]nything more cinematographic could hardly be imagined, and looking back it wears all the appearance of a bad dream. All the same it was at the time extremely painful, especially as a little more presence of mind on my part might have prevented the situation: but it all came about with a speed. Poor Mark! The provocation was certainly great and I am sorry for him.' Carrington was immediately hustled away by Sheppard, 'and Harry supported my trembling form from the field. It was really an intervention of providence that they should all come up at the psychological moment, as otherwise Heaven knows what might have happened.'[171] The 'incident' came to a calmer conclusion the next day, when a sober and contrite Gertler saw Strachey lunching at the Eiffel Tower restaurant, and walked over to his table to apologise.

Although letters continued between Carrington and Gertler, and she felt responsible for the attack, she nonetheless adopted a new, annoyed attitude toward him. 'What's to be done?' she asked a few days later. 'Frankly I wish you had some better friends to keep you from getting dissipated, and wasting your time in the evenings ... Remember I care always very much for you. Just as much as I used to. It is in no way changed and if you knew how much I felt your pains and grief it would lessen them for you.'[172]

He threw himself, in despair, into his work, but this episode had really signalled the end of their relationship. After a few letters their long correspondence almost ceased, to the benefit of both. Carrington's happiness at Tidmarsh was undoubtedly marred by guilt over Mark, but her new life also allowed her to gain some perspective on a relationship that could never have worked. She and Mark had begun with many differences, and over the years those differences had multiplied. By now what they had most in common was a difficult mutual history. Carrington must have known that they could not last much longer when, out of a sense of guilt, she had finally agreed to sleep with him. After the final break some of Mark's peace of mind returned, but not for long enough. His health

continued to be precarious, and he faced a future of severe respiratory disease and depression.

Life at Tidmarsh quickly settled into a routine that would typify Lytton's and Carrington's subsequent time together. Lytton read, wrote, or corrected proofs; Carrington painted and gardened and wrote her famous letters. When either was away, as often happened, they wrote to each other almost daily. And on 1 March, Lytton's first birthday since they had lived together, Carrington wrote him the first of her series of birthday poems.

To GLS on his thirty-eighth birthday[173]

Eight and thirty years are gone,
Since the day that you were born.
You shall read my song of praise
Long before the sun's mild rays,
Slant across your window panes.
Or sounds of fierce March rains
Steal into thy sleepy ears
Filling thee with horrid fears.

Of your thirty years and eight
It alas has been my fate
To love you for only two
Which is thirty-eight too few.

Rise and greet me with a kiss
For the labour writing this
Alone deserves that dear salute ...
Why dear poet are you mute?
True, I bring no present Fair,
In my hand no snuff-box rare,
Do my ill rhymes cause you pain?
Is my Song of Love but vain?
Forgive me, from your Bed of State
Since you today are Thirty-Eight![174]

Their life, although not unmingled with troubles, was filled with high spirits. A letter from Carrington to Strachey written in August to arrange a trip was typical of their playfulness.

> I hope you'll be economical & cancel the room for Tues. night and meet me (unless I wire or anything frantic happens) at Wooler Station at 7.40 on Wednesday. Then a High Old Dinner, ale & chop. Then High old jinks and chops of a very different nature. 'Well,' said the Philosopher 'we shall see we shall see' Oh Dear one. Wednesday Wednesday & then x x x x[175]

In addition, they shared their life with many friends. Nearly all of these visited Tidmarsh, and rarely did a weekend pass without overnight guests. Many – particularly Lytton's brother Oliver and his not always welcome lady friend Inez – were financial contributors to the Mill House and therefore had almost unrestricted visiting rights. Others were simply friends, but all caused extra work:

> ... when we returned from Gordon Square here, Mrs Legg announced brightly that she was going away the next day for a week's holiday ... So nearly all my time has been taken up preparing food for human consumption and cleaning rooms which I with much greater speed make dirty again. Then last Wed. Clive [Bell] and Mary [Hutchinson] were to have come so there was great commotion. Pies were baked, partridges roasted (which to give Clive his due, he sent). Then they played us false two days and then went to Roger's instead. They said the trains weren't running because of the strike. But it was truly incompetence on Clive's part, as we found out the trains did run. Anyway, it wasted the devil of a time.[176]

Carrington's own special friend at this time, and indeed for the rest of her life, was her old friend Alix Sargant-Florence. She had taken up with Lytton's brother James, the psychoanalyst, and therefore had a double bond with the Tidmarsh inmates. Sometimes coming down alone, she would be set to work in the garden or made to sit as a model for Carrington. She had a strong personality, mirrored in her angular face and tall, thin body, and could be delightfully capricious. She easily developed and dropped infatuations or manias; later in life, for instance, she threw herself into jazz dancing. During one visit with Harry Norton in April 1918, Carrington worried that 'Alix is a woman of moods and fancies & who can tell whether she will not leave Harry N. with me on Saturday because "she cannot stand it a moment longer." '

> Fortunately I just averted her committing suicide by hanging herself from the W.C. chain – For her boredom had excelled its limits playing 'patience' the entire day ... So this morning after dislodging her from the plug [I] introduced her to the art of acrostics – She was delighted & promptly wrote to the London Literary demanding all their volumes on

the subject. And tried in vain to solve the very obscure riddle I set her –[177]

This fascination for word games was a Tidmarsh staple; Oliver and Inez played them so often that Carrington described them as having 'an acrostic affection'.[178]

Life at Tidmarsh still alternated with life at London and at friends' country homes, and they frequently spent time with friends in Gordon Square, both separately and together. While Strachey was away on his literary and social pursuits, Carrington painted, worked in the garden, and wrote him daily of her pleasures and trials, frequently illustrating her letters. She was now in what was probably her most fertile painting period, one which showed change and experimentation as well as productivity. 'The Mill House at Tidmarsh, Berkshire', painted in 1918, shows a use of colour, form and imagination not seen in her earlier works. Like most of her other paintings, it was done in oil. Full of the painstaking details which mark her style, this picture uses swathes of orange for the entire roof of the house and its reflection in the water. The River Pang flows under the house through a black tunnel which is the focal point of the painting, and the sky is painted in swatches of blue against a pale background. Noel called the figures of two exotic black swans in the foreground 'an imaginative introduction', but it seems no frivolity; instead it appears deliberate and symbolic. Tidmarsh was not only the first house she could control, but it was the first house she shared with someone she loved. The two swans on the river in front of the house are a peaceful, elegant and solitary pair, inescapably suggestive of Carrington (a swan with its neck bent, facing the other and the house) and Lytton (a swan with a straight, erect neck, looking outward) in a setting which perfectly suits them, despite their difference from the rest of the world.

In early June country life took its toll on Carrington's health, for she was badly bitten on the face by an insect. Her eye swelled so much that she could neither paint nor read, yet she managed to turn this mishap into an amusing fable for Lytton's enjoyment.

And the Lord, who was Lytton Strachey, overheard from his turreted bower at Garsington, the conversation of young females, as they lay in the hayfield. For the dark haired one said ... 'Come, everyone will be there, & it will be fun'[.] the other said – 'I should like to bu...' – 'Then why not' – 'Just for the night'? – 'Yes' – 'Yes'? – 'Yes, and I'll give you a dinner party first' – – – '*This shall not BE*', said the Bearded Trinity. So he called his favourite spirit, GNAT by name, and said 'Away over hill & dale, fly unto Tidmarsh. There you will find a fairhaired wench bite her with your poisoned fangs. Attack her in the rear, in her favourite parts, render it impossible that she shall with pleasure enjoy the day or night season ... But do not completely destroy.' So the spirit departed

on his errand. In the evening, he found as he had been told the young ladies & their companion talking on the lawn. Dazzled by the beauty of his victim, and realizing her glory lay in her azure eyes he flew down, settled on her eyelid & rapidly thrust in his envenomed dart, then flew away – –. The Lord said 'Thou has done well. Behold I give thee now thy liberty.' Last night I felt my eye rather sore, & noticed an almost imperceptible swelling – The night passed as usual in horrid nightmares, & tossings – this morning on attempting to ope my eyes & greet the morning gloom, behold the left eye was stuck, & would not open . . .
How completely satisfying you are. What a good thing it was I fell in love with you before you were famous: – or . . . I might have been refused.[179]

This was a real fear. *Eminent Victorians* – his reworking of biography to present short lives of four Victorian figures – which had occupied Lytton for so long, was published in 1918 and had an immediate and astonishing success. He had taken a great risk in his irreverent handling of the lives of General Gordon, Florence Nightingale, Cardinal Manning and Dr Arnold, but the English, after more than three years of war, were quite willing to see these previously revered people treated with wit and irony. Not only did the book completely revise the art of biography from something long and dull to a quick-paced and creative form, but Lytton suddenly found himself a well-known and socially desirable character. Further he began to enjoy, for nearly the first time in his life, a comfortable and independent income.

A new friend, Rex Partridge, who had also studied (and rowed) with him was easing into the circle at this time as well. He was a friend and fellow officer of Noel Carrington's at Christ Church, Oxford, before the war. He had met Carrington briefly through her brother, but got to know her much better in July when she, Noel, Partridge, and the daughter of one of Partridge's Scottish friends took a trip to Scotland together. Carrington found him very friendly and sympathetic, and wrote to Lytton that

Partridge shared all the best views of democracy & social reform – wine

& good cheer and operas ... He ... wants after the war to sail in a schooner to the Mediteranean [*sic*] Islands & Italy, and trade in wine without taking much money, and to dress like a brigand. I am so elated & happy. It is so good to find someone who one can rush & on & on with, quickly ... Fortunately he is to be in England 3 months. So I hope I shall see him again – not very attractive to look at. Immensely big. But full of wit, and recklessness.[180]

Strachey was pleased by her find and enthusiasm, but also issued a warning.

The existence of Partridge is exciting. Will he come down here when you return, and sing Italian songs to us, and gesticulate, and let us dress him as a brigand? I hope so; but you give no suggestion of his appearance – except that he's 'immensely big' – which may mean anything. And then, I have a slight fear that he may be simply a flirt.[181]

His fears proved to be unfounded. Partridge was the opposite of the kind of man who normally attracted her. He was tall and broad-shouldered and, in spite of her critical assessment of his looks, very handsome. He was in many ways a 'man's man', who wore his uniform as if he were meant to and was an athlete. Her friends in Bloomsbury took to calling him 'the major', and wondered how to assimilate such a seemingly stereotypical and masculine member of the English upper middle classes into their circle. They were to find that he fitted in rather well.

Carrington wrote long, detailed letters to Strachey whenever she travelled, which were not only one way of sharing the trip with him, of having him near her, but were also, most importantly, a gift. For, particularly with the success of *Eminent Victorians*, he appeared to her far greater than she. Her words and views were what she had to offer him when they were apart, and she was keen to keep him amused in her absence. She was charmed by the lochs and landscape of Scotland, and particularly by one lake she had seen, with a single boat. When she teased that she might have run off with the boatman, Lytton responded, '[you] now, I daresay, are enjoying quite a new kind of honeymoon, in a wild-cat's cave, among red deer and eagles, and I shall never see my Mopsa more!'[182]

Strachey was enjoying a world of double pleasures. Since *Eminent Victorians* had catapulted him into an unexpected sphere of fame and society, he was invited everywhere, and by everyone. While Carrington was in Scotland he received '[p]ositively today, a letter from a Duchess! Her Grace of Marlborough', who invited him, along with Mrs Asquith and Lady Astor for a weekend at 'her "little place"' in Surrey. He worried about the state of his clothes and manners, '[a]nd what I really want is the Gentleman's Complete Guide to Society.'[183]

Yet while society beckoned, Carrington had been indoctrinating him into the ways of country life. He learned to weed the garden while sitting on a little chair, and to pick vegetables for Mrs Legg to prepare for his meals. Left without Carrington's guidance, some of these tasks seemed beyond him. He managed to pick peas, but '[t]he beans frighten me. I was told to pick some of them, but they frighten me. As for the raspberries, I feel as if I should never worm my way under the nets. La Legg confesses herself baffled by the hens – after pretending last night that she could catch them without the slightest difficulty. I am in favour of making them tipsy – it seems to me, short of shooting them, the only plan. She, of course, thought I was mad to suggest it . . .'[184]

Lytton's physical ailments impeded, from time to time, his productivity in the garden and in his writing. An episode of shingles, which caused his hand to swell up in October of 1918, was Carrington's first real experience with being 'a ministering angel, hewer of wood and drawer of water'.[185] This was the role in which popular opinion cast her, and still does today. This misconception, according to David Garnett, is as false as 'the picture of Lytton as an exhausted lily left over from the nineties . . . So is the view of Carrington as a country hoyden occupied in setting ducks' eggs under broody hens. She was a reader with a taste of her own before she ever met Lytton.'[186] Yet her place in Lytton's life was a confusing one to outsiders, even when they knew of her existence. Bloomsbury frequently invited him for long visits without her (although they did this with many others as well) and 'when famous hostesses such as Lady Cunard, Margot Asquith (afterwards Lady Oxford) and Lady Colefax invited the literary lion Lytton Strachey to their houses they would no more have thought of including Carrington than of asking him to bring his housekeeper or his cook'.[187] In many ways she was forced to forge a social life of her own apart from his which, although they often overlapped, found her more comfortable with those she had known from her Slade and London days than with the Bloomsbury artists – and in Bloomsbury she was more comfortable with the painters than with the others.

Carrington celebrated Armistice Day with parties in London, where Alix played a practical joke on her.

Alix said, . . . 'I was going to write & tell you – but I will tell you now instead, that I met yr mother today, who asked me, whether you had come back with me – I said I had never seen you – She said you had written to say you were spending the weekend with me (Alix) at Marlow' – Alix then denied having ever seen me – whereupon my mother broke out her pent up suspicions etc you can imagain [sic] my state! And this circle of people gaping – Honestly my heart stood still at least 5 mins – still – Then Oliver came to the rescue & said Alix was only pulling my leg – 'Too hard – she has pulled too hard' – murmured poor Dora, & collapsed dead as a door nail on the floor.[188]

In this letter to Strachey, it becomes abundantly clear how strong her ties to her family still were. Although she was now twenty-five years old, she still had to lie to them in order to gain time away from them.

In the meantime, the parties and the links to Bloomsbury continued. Two nights later, at a party at Gordon Square, conversation flourished and 'the conclusion however arrived upon by everyone was that French letters must be more advertised to reduce the population, and that all the black races must be castrated. But it was astonishing apart from the arguments to see the characters of all those people, their faces, & attitudes.'[189] She implies that she did not share those attitudes which were, in the drawing room, flippantly snobbish.

Her relationships with old friends continued as well, and the next morning she visited her friend Barbara Bagenal, who had just given birth to her first child. Carrington's horror of pregnancy and childbirth was reinforced by this experience. 'What is the female body made of?' she wrote to Lytton. 'For she told me it took nearly 24 hours coming out, with acute pain *all* the time, in the end they had to pull with pincers . . . The next morning she woke up & had coffee, & eggs for breakfast, & now feels quite well!' The baby itself was 'a Japanese grub in the cot beside her'.[190] She returned with relief to Lytton and the Mill House.

Their pleasure in their new life, even when they were apart, seemed endless. Their house on the Pang river – Virginia referred to it as the 'Mill on the Pang'[191] – was a delight and an adventure; the river sported leaping fishes in spring and summer, cows were in neighbouring fields, and they supplied many of their meals from their own garden. They acquired a kitten, Nero, which later had to be destroyed because it killed chickens. Both were able to pursue their interests, and Carrington painted constantly.

Carrington had always suffered from time to time from nightmares. These now became more pronounced during Lytton's absences, but in spite of that they both felt a peacefulness in the knowledge of their country home. Their letters, even when rushed and brief, reflected their happiness, as when Lytton wrote from London, 'This is only to give you a kiss. No time for anything more. How are you?'[192] And when Lytton was away, Carrington imagined herself with him.

Dearest Lytton I send you my love, & a great many kisses. How I long to steal away from here, & climb the heights of Firth [actually Firle]

Beacon, & one day perchance you would come walking by – & I hidden in a hillock would see you pass. And after whisper to the April Hare in his hole – *That* man I love. For he is Lytton Strachey.[193]

CHAPTER TEN

Ralph: 1919

Life at Tidmarsh, through Carrington's unflagging devotion to it, was maintained in a careful and delicate balance. Carrington saw to it that all of Lytton's physical and emotional needs were met; his very presence seemed to ensure that hers were. But it could not be considered a marriage, even a celibate one, by normal standards. Each of them required a certain independence which translated into trips to London and the countryside, or visits to friends, but that freedom was held in subtle check by their devotion to their life together and to Tidmarsh itself. Carrington was terrified of losing him and so regaled him in his absence with letters and gifts of food and clothing which ensured that he would return to her. Although his social world was large and constantly expanding, he had no desire to do otherwise.

The first year of living with him and of living away from the confusion and difficulties of her family and of London allowed changes in her to take place. Her desperate need for independence had been fulfilled, and while she still regularly withheld information on her life from her parents, life lost much of the frantic aspect it had had with Gertler. Lytton and country life had a soothing effect upon her, and this allowed other attitudes to develop. She was terribly romantic, and while her relationship with Gertler had certainly been romantic, it was one-sidedly and melodramatically so. He was too ardent, too desperate. Lytton's acceptance of his own sexuality led to jokes between them, and a sympathy for sexuality itself. She knew that he had, and would continue to have, affairs with men, and this did not bother her; they presented little threat to the life they were developing and could be easily incorporated into it. And while she did not particularly pine for similar affairs, it left the door ajar for other relationships of her own. It was at this point that Rex Partridge appeared on the scene.

While Carrington's old friends were always as welcome at the Mill

House as Strachey's friends, she was reluctant to introduce new people there – particularly if she was unsure of how they would get on with Lytton. Partridge's first visits were timed to intrude as little as possible on the Tidmarsh routine, and the fact that he spent some of his first hours there outdoors on the river indicates just how uncertain she was about his ability to fit in.

By 17 August 1918, Partridge wrote to Noel that he had 'been initiated into the Mill House, but as a great part of the [festivities] took place on the river, I viewed the proceedings very favourably. Old man Strachey with his billowing beard and alternating basso-falsetto voice did not play a great part.'[194] While he thought things had gone well, the visit had in fact been a failure. He had argued on about the war in an arrogant and callous manner, claiming among other things that all pacifists ought to be shot.[195] Like a bull in a china shop, he made his way through the conversation by virtue of brute strength. His feelings about the war later proved to be quite different, but Carrington was embarrassed and Lytton appalled by this initial encounter between the two men.

Noel and Partridge were now colleagues at Oxford, like many other veterans, completing the studies which the war had inter-rupted. Their friendship and Oxford's proximity to Pangbourne ensured that they would visit Tidmarsh fairly often. But Carrington wanted to be sure that Lytton would not complain about their presence.

Carrington herself expressed ambivalence about Partridge. She found him attractive in a large, athletic way but she had hitherto been attracted by less strapping men, more immersed in the aesthetic. Partridge was a physical force to be reckoned with. Yet she claimed to find 'his face . . . that of a Norwegian dentist', and his conversation unstimulating.[196] Apparently the charm of shipboard talk that had so intrigued her on the Scottish trip wore off as he became concerned with the more mundane issues of demobilisation, academic studies, and making a living. These concerns, which mirrored Noel's, she found 'boring'.

At the beginning of 1919, though, a much more distressing issue concerned her. Her family had moved again, this time to Chelten-ham, where, after years of deafness, paralysis and pain, Samuel Carrington had died in December 1918 at the age of eighty-two. Carrington, who had spent the last few years complaining bitterly about her parents and the restrictions they placed on her, was overcome with guilt and anger. His helplessness had sometimes upset her terribly. Her mother, she believed, had put him into a 'bird cage' and made herself a martyr to the cause of controlling him in his state of powerlessness. Most upsetting was the way her mother and sister responded to his death. They were preoccupied by the funeral trappings, and forced Carrington, to her dismay, to shop for mourning clothes, and to make public demonstrations of her acute and private grief.

Her relations with her mother had not improved over the years and even after achieving the peacefulness of Tidmarsh she found her obligatory visits home increasingly uncongenial. 'Its pretty dreary here', she had written to Garnett earlier. 'My mother is as vulgar & tiresome as Mrs Bennet in Pride and Prejudice which I've just been reading. Oh yes, its pretty horrible! But I've discovered an amusing method of enjoying it. By behaving like a Strachey & reducing the poor woman! I see Strachism is a fascinating occuptation [*sic*]. How are you? . . . I see this letter is doomed to failure as the woman keeps on interrupting me with trivial conversation such as: "If only you let me do *up* your brown velvet with buff facings, & black velvet which my dear is so much worn this winter it would make you a very smart costume." Can you imagain [*sic*] it. I doubt whether you can. But I've got a superb pair of riding breeches from my brothers wardrobe which delight me beyond anything this morning & Mary's [Hutchinson?] written to say Lytton slept well. So I am quite happy.'[197]

She sent Garnett some discarded clothes – this was a habit of hers throughout her life, and these had probably belonged to Teddy – but included a note for him to copy out: ' "Dear Mrs C. Thank you for the clothes which your daughter sent me. They fit me very well and I was glad of the overcoat in this cold weather. Yours sincerely David G." *Not a word more or less* or I'll strangel [*sic*] you dead as a doornail.'[198] She wanted her mother to have no clues about her new life, and feared disclosure either because it would create a row, or because she simply needed privacy from her mother.

Samuel's body was laid in its coffin in his bedroom at Cheltenham. The house was arranged so that one had to pass through this room in order to enter the downstairs lavatory. The temptation to take a final look was great and when Carrington went in and lifted the white cloth from his face, she was startled into a greater understanding of her loss.

When I lifted a napkin, oh Lytton, there was not his face, but a face very small, and pale yellow. So dim, and icy cold. Then I knew how much I loved him, and now how lost it all was. That crazed hoary old man, with his bright eyes, and huge helpless body but so big always, now lay in this narrow box in white linen,– and it was a ghost compared to that man, that lay there. And then a vision of all those people whose faces I have loved came. Teddy too, must have gone all pale like that –
. . . Oh Lytton why didn't I love him more when he could feel. I might

have fought for him – he was so helpless himself. I knew what he cared for, how my mother tormented him, & yet I did so little ... He was so like me, that I felt always he understood & was on my side – now I am all alone with these two.[199]

With her father gone, her circle of familial sympathisers had shrunk; only Noel remained, and he was at Oxford. Lottie was married but Carrington saw her as perhaps even worse than their mother. Now the only unmarried sister, Carrington was expected by the other two women to fill the dutiful daughter's role and to remain at home as a companion to her mother, 'I gather indefinitely'.[200] This was utterly unthinkable, even if they had got on well together; Carrington's life and way of thinking had altered too radically in the nine years since she had left for the Slade, and the life at Tidmarsh was a stronger pull than any call to duty. Her mother accused her of being selfish. In the throes of her mourning Charlotte could not see that Carrington could not possibly cheer her. The next day, Carrington's understanding showed signs of maturity: 'I think my mother does care very much, and thinking it over I suppose she must occupy herself with something to keep herself together, perhaps that is why she turns so desperately to the little details of funerals, and mourning.'[201]

Part of what upset her, Carrington realised after she returned in relief to Tidmarsh, was that very similarity between herself and her father. 'He was so like me in many ways', she wrote to Gertler. 'Sometimes I feel almost glad he has gone off this planet, & that I am now not joined by that curious link.'

[My mother and I] both loved a totally different person. I loved my father for his rough big character. His rustic simplicity & the great way he lived inside himself & never altered his life to please the conventions, or people of this century. He would have been exactly the same if he had lived under Elizabeth. My mother hated all this, & even admitted to me she married him out of pity because he wanted looking after. She's a character like Mary Cannan; she adores making a martyr of herself, toiling unnecessarily & working off her sensual side in religious outbursts. But it all has a dreadfully upsetting affect on one.[202]

Perhaps what Carrington found so upsetting in her similarity to her father was a sense of powerlessness; after having been independent for so many years as a bachelor in India, Samuel had married and become an invalid. Carrington was still trying to break away from the family life which he had created, and which indeed had created her, yet was still unable to sever completely the ties or even deal with them honestly. When her father died, she felt as many children do when faced with the death of a parent: that she had not told him how much he meant to her, and that she had too often stood by while her mother misunderstood him. She wrote to Lytton from Cheltenham that,

> I didn't want them [her mother and sister] to weep, but at least they might not have taken such a cold hellish interest over his relics. I couldn't help remembering all that time that a dead body lay in the next room, across the passage. Instead of that human being in the bath chair in front of the fire. You are right, there's nothing so crushing and wretched as hard human beings without feelings. They were simply like two pieces of furniture conversing. The piano, & the marble mantelpiece could not have felt less. They say the funeral will not be until Thursday. So I suppose I shall have to stay till then. If I was a little braver I would run out of the house.
>
> I don't believe they can [have] felt physical affection for a person. It used to be so different when I came home, & went into the dinning [*sic*] room, he used to hug me, & almost cry because he was so glad to see me. They sat eating cold turkey, and made some polite address, & then discussed my clothes, & what I must buy. The little cook with her wizened face feels more grief.
>
> ... As a little boy running in these lanes of Prestbury, my father little guessed he would die among these women folk, in such captivity in the same village.[203]

While her parental home had been the scene of many arguments, Carrington had often managed to get her own way by making up stories about her whereabouts; although she had disobeyed, rarely had she defied them under their own roof. It is not surprising, then, that she had a disturbing dream about a furtive encounter with the creator of the virginal 'Mary Bracegirdle' which took place in her mother's house, only weeks after her father's death, as she wrote to Strachey.

> Such a nightmare last night, with Aldous in bed. Everything went wrong, I couldn't lock the door; all the bolts were crooked. At last, I chained it with a watch chain to two nails. Then I had a new pair of thick pyjamas on and he got so cross because I wouldn't take them off and they were all scratchy. Everything got in a mess, and he got so angry, and kept on trying to find me in the bed by peering with his eyeglass, and I thought all the time how I could account to my mother for the mess on my pyjamas![204]

Huxley had seen her recently, and made it clear to Brett that a sexual relationship with her was out of the question.

> I saw Carrington not long ago, just after the armistice, and thought her enchanting; which indeed I always do whenever I see her, losing my heart completely as soon as she is no longer there. We went to see the show at the Omega, where there was what I thought an admirable Gertler and a good Duncan Grant and a rather jolly Vanessa Bell. Carrington and I had a long argument on the subject of virginity: I may say it was she who provoked it by saying that she intended to remain a vestal for the rest of her life. All expostulations on my part were vain.[205]

This was a strange conversation, for Carrington was no longer a virgin at this time. Either she felt that her sexual experiences were so unsatisfactory that they did not qualify as loss of virginity or, more likely, she preferred that the world still view her as a virgin. She had, in a sense, a reputation to uphold. Huxley put this conversation to use in *Crome Yellow*.

One unsurprising result of Samuel's death was that Carrington became, as she put it, 'stuck somehow' in her painting.[206] She wrote to Mark to inform him of her father's death, and of her difficulties with her work, but never saw the loss of her father and the difficulty with her painting as cause and effect. He counselled her that although 'that "blankness" you speak of is indeed terrible', at the same time it was 'quite a healthy state. It usually means that one is growing, that one is too dissatisfied to go on working in the old way, that something new and more interesting must be found.'[207] Mark's own work was going well, and Carrington was pleased that 'Roger [Fry] liked your work so much. He is one of the *best* people I think, as he really cares so much for good work and is aloof from criticising people for their personal weaknesses and characters.'[208] Because she had such a high opinion of Fry's critical abilities, she trusted his evaluation of her work. Both Roger Fry and Clive Bell wrote extensively about the work of their friends, but never mentioned Carrington's work at all. Therefore, although Gertler and she had virtually ceased to write to each other, he was nonetheless an important confidant at this particular time especially, since, having lost his own father so recently, he understood both her feelings of loss and her distance from her family.

She longed to have some prearranged work which would require no thought but now she could think of nothing to paint. She began a picture of two local boys sitting side by side, but as it progressed it grew too large for the canvas and she had to glue on additional strips. All this added to her growing sense of failure, a feeling which was to plague her throughout her life, although never before had it stopped her from trying. Generally she found inspiration in looking at pictures by her favourites: Goya, El Greco, Cézanne. Sometimes, though, this had the opposite result and she ended by feeling artistically impotent. After she had fallen in love with Strachey, her aims for her work changed: rather than working for competitions or exhibitions or even entirely for herself (although this last aspect remained important), she wanted to offer him the gift of her creativity. 'Lytton, you give me such a happy life,' she wrote to him at the end of 1919 from her mother's house. 'One day I really hope I shall be an artist, & then you'll see my affection.'[209]

Her artistic efforts in the first part of 1919 were chiefly decorative, but in a manner which infuriated her. She was hired by a wealthy woman on Marlborough Street in London (whom Carrington dubbed the 'Duchess of Marlborough') to decorate a trunk, for which she was paid only a nominal wage. Carrington spent most of her weekdays from 25 January until the first week in March working in an icy attic, with little food, and being treated worse than a servant. This uncomfortable experience only served to bring out a socialistic indignation against the rich.

By March she was ready for a change, and Noel unwittingly offered her the opportunity. He and his friend Rex Partridge had decided to go off to Spain on a steam trampship, and 'I incline rather to forcing myself on them. What do [you] think?' she asked Lytton. 'Madrid, & BilBayo (or however it *is* spelt). Of course one might have better company. But on the other hand, will one ever get the chance to go again?'[210] Noel and Rex managed to book four berths – the fourth was for Partridge's sister – and the only obstacle was getting passports. That achieved, they met on the dock on 19 March, Carrington's illness of a swollen throat notwithstanding. 'The young men met me at the shipping office,' she wrote cheerfully to Lytton. 'Horrified by my appearance. Good for them however. I will not renounce a single scarf for any god much less man ... What a vile Devil this Mumpsa was to come between us & ruin these last few days. They might have been so much better & more cheerful. I am afraid I became an awful bore with my old neck, & mopping [*sic*] cat-like attitudes in every chair.'[211]

She wrote Lytton extended accounts of the trip, acting as his eyes and ears on the journey. The four played poker and talked; she learned more about Partridge – and his opinion of her – from his sister Dorothy who did not quite approve of Carrington and her effect on Rex. As bunkmates the two women had to get along, but privately Carrington found in her every female characteristic she despised.

> Watched D. P. dress. How revolting women are. It came over me suddenly all their apparatus stays, & hideous underclothes – & worst of all that bunchy shape – like a stuffed pin cushion. She has a pretty fat face with pink cheeks, very dark brown eyes & pale yellow straight hair. As I always imagine young German girls must look. She is always smiling, & happy. And is one of those perfectly nice characters, without any surprises ... Her generalisations on life made me boil with rage inside. She said people ought not to be unhappy or morbid but ought to control their feelings – But it was very stupid. And not worth repeating to you.[212]

The male Partridge Carrington found equally exasperating. He made potentially humorous remarks about sexual relations between men, 'rather amusing but spoken – all wrong'.[213] He spoke good Spanish, but persisted in having only the most banal conversations with the natives.

Under Carrington's influence, Partridge's behaviour began to change, but not always pleasantly. He took to ridiculing his sister constantly, which made everyone uncomfortable. He could argue in the Bloomsbury fashion, but with what Carrington saw as an Oxford rather than a Cambridge slant: 'A kind of wit for discountenancing one ... putting a different interpretation on one's words, & arguing with one – taking one's point for granted before one has announced it'.[214] Frustrated, Carrington asked Lytton for lessons on arguing rather than history. The boat journey, which Carrington compared to Virginia Woolf's first novel, *The Voyage Out*, ended on a happier note. There was music, to which Dorothy Partridge sang, capturing the heart of the boat's captain, and there were flirtations all around. Carrington changed her mind, and decided that 'Miss Partridge's nice character overpowers me'.[215]

Spain proved to be an enchanting experience, despite several setbacks. Old women stroked Carrington's fair hair and called her a beauty, so that 'besides having a permanent Spanish bore you'll also have an insufferably vain creature to put up with this summer'.[216] Starting at Malaga, they walked to Ronda, Burgo, and Sedella. This was a very long, mountainous, and often remote journey, unusual for travellers. They had to stay in humble 'posadas' or cottages rather than hotels, sometimes knocking on doors to ask to buy food and drink from cottagers. This was the beginning of a lifetime of trips to Spain for both Carrington and Partridge; his friend Gerald Brenan would spend most of his adult life there. Back at Malaga, Carrington took out her sketch book while waiting for dinner and attracted a crowd while she drew a Spanish soldier. Later '[t]he charming fat soldier ... came and found us, & carried on a great deal of Spanish eye movement with me, RP on the other side carried on knee & hand pressure.' This double flirtation, like all of her other experiences, found its way into her letters to Lytton. In several places her sketchbook caused local chaos: villagers demanded she do their portraits when they saw her drawing their neighbours.

Perhaps most important of all, as a painter she was won over completely by the Spanish landscape and architecture, having years before begun preferring the Spanish painters to most others. 'You know I always thought Innes & John must be rather extravengacas [*sic*] in their Spanish landscapes,' she recorded in Granada. 'But truly they are just rather dull realists. One does see green, pink & grey mountains all ... against the most remarkable skies ... On Sunday morning we went very early to look at the Alhambra. It really is very remarkable. So complete, & romantic, that I found my prejudices vanishing, & my "significant form" eyes closing.'[217] In Córdoba and in Madrid at the Prado, she saw at last the works by her heroes, Goya and El Greco, and found them different but even better than she had expected, 'the pictures are so large, & the colour incredibly beautiful'.[218]

Meanwhile two difficulties cropped up. Dorothy Partridge thought that Carrington was ruining her brother – and told her so. He was, she felt, being permanently changed for the worse by Carrington's unconventional attitudes. And later, an argument with Noel nearly ruined the end of the trip. Always rather extravagant financially (this would later become a major source of argument between herself and Partridge), she wanted to buy Strachey a large reproduction of a Goya painting, 'but Noel wouldn't give me any money. Because with his damnable prudence he said unless it was absolutely necessary etc. etc. I lost my temper inside then, & said it didn't matter. Then they never came to fetch me as they promised that afternoon, and I didn't know enough Spanish to buy one myself. Even if I had had enough money. I am disappointed because I shall have nothing to give you dearest.'[219]

Partridge, she found, 'improved' with time, even though he still sometimes lapsed into long and boring conversation, but he unexpectedly redeemed himself just before they returned to England by a charade acted out in a suburb of Madrid. Because of their dress, they were refused entrance to an unexpectedly fancy nightclub. The porter led them to a café and made it clear that he thought they were American acrobats, '[a]ll of which RP answered in the affirmative ... He was evidently very anxious to persuade us to stay – & to try & get us to show him our turns. I must say RP was rather good at lying.'[220] This revelation turned the tide for the unpromising relationship.

After their arrival back in London on 22 April, he became a Tidmarsh acquisition, where he found himself at first on probation, then accepted in body but not in title. Lytton changed his regal name to 'Ralph' (pronounced 'Rafe'), which meant that all three now went by names other than their Christian names: Lytton's first name was Giles, Carrington's Dora, and Ralph's Rex, none of which was ever used again.

At first Ralph appeared at Tidmarsh as a messenger or by his own invitation. When Noel could not make a planned visit, 'the Bird Partridge however flew over to tell me' on 11 May. He obviously wanted to see her again, and was a willing victim when she set him to work.

I joined him to my minor battalion of slaves in the garden and made him plant beans & peas without a break till lunch!! Whilst the small boys watered the garden & cut grass, I rode an imaginary steed around the footpaths cracking my whip & giving orders. [She had a headache.] I think its the fug of the valley & general heat. – Not that I am in heat. How could one be with a chest of drawers?[221]

Her first motive seemed to be to assure Strachey that she was not attracted to Ralph, and indeed her feelings toward Partridge were uncertain. At the same time she did feel a strong physical attraction to him (despite her denial of his and her own attractiveness), and when she drew him nude in the garden on the 1st of June, 'I confess I got rather a flux over his thighs, & legs. So much that I didn't do very good drawings.'[222] Under Lytton's relaxed attitude toward sex, Carrington was relaxing her own. Mark had simply been the wrong person for her, and she had been too young.

By the 18th, when they were planning another trip with Noel (to Cornwall), she had given in to her instincts. 'Drawing the bird Partridge in my studio was not without its bass accompaniament this afternoon. He is so naive and young. [He was one year younger than Carrington.] I felt like some mature hag boosted up with a complete knowledge of mankind!! ... UGH – I see it means a large bed in that cottage [in Cornwall] if one is to put up with him for a fort-night, and painting *all* day long so that one doesn't have to talk.'[223] Later that summer she found she did not like his written words either, and loaned him a published volume of selected letters as a hint, 'but it doesn't seem to have had much effect'.[224] In contrast, Strachey who was being lionised in London, found hers excellent: 'How charming your letters are! I never say thank you for them; but I hope you realise how much I like them.'

Lytton's appreciation of Carrington was beginning to be shared by his friends. Virginia Woolf, who had at first been so sceptical of the Tidmarsh arrangement, found that Carrington had 'increased his benignity'.[225] In fact, she began to find fault with her old friend, and with all Stracheys, for being 'unadventurous'; '[e]ven in the matter of taking Tidmarsh Lytton had to be propelled from behind, & his way of life insofar as it is unconventional, is so by the desire and determination of Carrington'.[226] When she and Leonard planned their move to Monk's House near Lewes, she wrote to Carrington that '[o]ne of the chief decorations [was] going to be a large showpiece by Carrington, found in an attic at Asheham; doesn't that make you blush all over – upset the tea – and scald the cat?'[227] She knew well Carrington's shyness about her work, and imagined her 'a little absorbed with household duties; secreting canvas in the attic'.[228]

While romance and gardening progressed at Tidmarsh, the other aspects of running the house were not doing as well. Mrs Legg, their adored servant, had decided that she was too old and too ill to continue working for them. The search for a suitable replacement occupied both Lytton and Carrington. While visiting Garsington, (where 'The [T. S.] Eliots went off yesterday. Aldous like a piece of sea weed, remained'[229]), Lytton interviewed Miss Crozier, one of Lady Ottoline's servants. She went to Tidmarsh in the middle of May to meet Carrington. Clearly disappointed in the ramshackle Mill House, and probably daunted by the weekly series of guests trooping through what she considered insufficient facilities and quarters, she made a series of demands if she were to remain: she wanted a different bedroom from the one intended for her; a sitting room made for her out of the library; new wallpaper. In return she would bring a lot of furniture which could be put to general use in the house.

Carrington was so anxious to settle the problem and get some help that she was willing to make any compromise. She proposed to Lytton that she move her painting equipment out of the library into the attic, but he was concerned about her work and raised objections: 'I think so far as the Library goes, it all depends on what *you* think – viz. will you really be able to manage your painting satisfactorily in the attic? If you thought so it doesn't seem to me that there's any real objection, as the room is hardly ever entered by anyone else. But it is important that your painting shouldn't be hampered.'[230] Even though Carrington made this concession, 'La Crozier' had too many demands to be met. The situation was resolved when the blacksmith's young niece, Annie Stiles, agreed to work as housekeeper without living in.

Life at Tidmarsh had changed a great deal in the year and a half since their arrival. Lytton was now a famous man, with a reasonable income, which meant that his trips were more frequent and more luxurious. Carrington's pride in him was great, and she felt honoured that he continued to use her as a sounding-board for his works in progress. As her attachment to Partridge grew, her letters to Strachey became even more affectionate. On 30 June 1919 she wrote to him,

Dearest, now you've gone I am dreadfully sorry that I didn't see more of you. I am furious that the poor Partridge came, & ruined two evenings, and a walk. The only thing will be if you'd accept, & like the picture I did on Sunday when its finished I have hopes for it ... It *is* a privilege to have your great pies hot from the furnace. I always feel tremendously honoured every time you come down, & stay here, and when you read me your work more delighted than at any moment in my life. Forgive me if I express what I want to say so vilely. Only I had to write immediately to tell you that I was in love with you. There now its said, I'll go on with my letter in an orderly fashion.[231]

And on 25 August,

> It was good of you to let me glimpse under the coverlet at the infant
> Victoria [his biography of Queen Victoria, in progress]. From the struc-
> ture of the bones, & the quality of her clothes, I see she will be a
> prodigious child. But most of all because I have such confidence in that
> red bearded old nurse in the bonnet who suckles her.[232]

She saw him as father and mother to his own works and in many
ways to herself. His success also made her feel honoured by his good
opinion of her own work, which she did not feel rivalled his. Lytton
however consistently believed in the importance of her painting for
its own sake.

There was, however, a paradox about the newly developing
triangle. She did not want Lytton to regard Partridge as a rival for
her affections; if anything, Lytton was *more* important to her than
before. Yet she also wanted to be free to develop relationships which
could give her what his did not. The closer she became to Partridge,
the more self-abnegating she became to Strachey. 'Do you remember
those plaintive pen wipers made of red & blue felt with jagged edges,
with "use me" embroidered in green on the cover?' she asked him
in September, after her visit to Cornwall with Ralph. 'That's what
I would like you to remember, that I am always your pen wiper
Mopsa.'[233] 'I don't approve of the pen-wiper theory', Lytton
responded to this remarkable and revealing statement.

While submitting herself emotionally to Strachey, she emphasised
that in her opinion Ralph was not his intellectual equal; in fact, she
implied, she only liked him for his physical uses. Her attitude toward
sex had changed radically in word if not yet in deed since she had
given up Gertler for Strachey: 'There's no denying that the Major
with all his dullness is in the Shakespearian use of the word "A most
excellent bed fellow"'! If only as in the story of Psyche he appeared
every night, & was invisible by day!'[234] Perhaps sensing that Carrington represented him unfairly to Strachey, and certainly realising
that Strachey's approval of him was absolutely essential to any
further relationship with Carrington, Ralph expressed his suspicion
to her that Strachey did not like him. On the contrary, Lytton
replied. 'I really like him more than anyone else – he seemed so
modest; but I wish he had rather more forehead.'[235]

But by July, when Carrington and Partridge set off for Cornwall,
Lytton found himself distinctly attracted to Ralph, who left him a
basket of raspberries as he departed.

> They were indeed heavenly. I suppose he would be shocked if I suggested
> that you should give him a kiss from me. The world is rather tiresome,
> I must say – everything at sixes and at sevens – ladies in love with

buggers, and buggers in love with womanisers, and the price of coal going up too. Where will it all end?

Not that I am in love with anybody – oh, no! no! a thousand times no.[236]

By the end of the year, however, it was clear that he was.

The trip to Cornwall was a combination of bicycling (for which Carrington had purchased a new bicycle) and travelling by train to Bath, Glastonbury, Cheddar, ending at Welcombe, in Bude. On her departure, she left Lytton a wifely note, pointing out arrangements made for him. It ended, 'Orange in noble plates on side board. Wood (cut) in greenhouse. Love for you inside yr Mopsa.'[237] He was to work on 'Victoria' and some plays in her absence. Ralph and Carrington went ahead and were joined later by Noel. This gave them a chance to live alone as a couple; it was, although neither said so, a test of their compatibility.

They got on wonderfully. Ralph was kindness personified; he fetched wood, did all the cooking. Carrington's old friend Mrs Box and her servants 'of course thought the major the most lovely young man they'd ever seen ... & inwardly thought what a nice pair we made!'[238] Yet when Lytton expressed the wish to be twenty-four and have blue eyes like Ralph, Carrington protested, 'But *I* like brown eyes best! Besides who except you isn't, or wasn't, or wouldn't be a bore at twenty-four! Stupid stoopid old man!'[239] For the first time since they had lived together, Carrington was developing a strong attachment to another man, and she took pains to make that attachment secondary to hers to Lytton. At the same time that he did not want to lose her, Strachey compared himself to the younger, more robust man – and found him attractive. But Carrington made it clear that she intended to spend her life with Strachey: 'There's no doubt that eventually in our old age we shall both have to come and live here in Cornwall just because the people are so kind and sympathetic', she wrote.[240]

In Cornwall, despite the mist and cold, Carrington did a lot of painting. One picture, 'of the valley with the cottage', she thought 'would be rather good if I can finish it.'[241] Strachey, pleased that she was working so hard, tried to convince her to get over her fear of exhibiting her work. He realised that revelation was painful to her, but was nevertheless necessary to her development and recognition as an artist. 'Don't you think the time has come to think seriously of beginning to show your pictures?' he wrote from Tidmarsh on 22 July 1919. 'Unless you do, I don't see how you can hope to sell them, and that will really be essential, if you ever want to stand on your own legs.'[242] There is no record of Carrington's reply. There was no question that he thought her work good enough to exhibit and sell; Carrington herself was the only obstacle. When she finally did begin to show her work, it was only at Strachey's insistence. Like Strachey who had needed her 'push from behind' to take the Mill House, Carrington needed his propulsion to exhibit her work to the public.

As usual, concentrated daily work at her painting put her into a good mood and she began to view Partridge more favourably. 'The major is so sympathetic that if he was only silent I might unbend considerably more to him', she said on 20 July.[243] When they returned to Tidmarsh a few days later, she decided that '[t]he weekend hasn't been bad, by dint of continual painting I get into such an angelic frame of mind that I can't be upset even by a major'.[244] That the relationship continued was due to Ralph, who had decided that he wanted her. Despite her reluctance, he tried to wear her down by kindness and usefulness. Yet they were so dissimilar in temperament that Carrington had strong doubts about continuing on with him; in the autumn, after receiving a 'gloomy letter from La Major', she thought perhaps she 'had better abandon that business. I confess my incompetence to deal with him.'[245] She did not abandon him, but still felt she had to keep him out of Lytton's way in October: 'I say do you mind if La Majora comes over on Sunday to till our soil. He seemed so lonely, & bleated so winningly that I gave in. I will keep him on the potato patch, so you won't hardly notice him.'

Part of the difficulty stemmed from the steady stream of weekend guests to Tidmarsh. Saxon Sydney-Turner, still in love with Barbara despite her marriage and children, came often that autumn. In fact, he and Carrington travelled to 'Boxland' in Cornwall (from which she addressed her letters 'Chez Boxina') together that autumn. Other guests were Oliver Strachey with his companion Inez; Clive Bell, who annoyed both Lytton and Carrington with his inflated conversation; Lytton's sisters Marjorie and Pippa; and his brother James and Carrington's friend Alix, who were now a bona fide couple. Alix expressed her egalitarian friendship by sending Carrington and James each £100; she had made £300 on the sale of her car, and shared the profit equally. In spite of the affection they felt for their friends and relations, Lytton and Carrington sometimes felt the strain of such continual and regular guests. When Saxon wrote of plans to visit in October, Carrington wrote to Lytton that she would 'frustrate it if possible – but remembering your principals [*sic*] about "shareholders" I will also not dissemble'.[246] The shareholders, those who financially enabled Strachey and Carrington to live at Tidmarsh, could not be refused without good reason. Yet Annie, sometimes with Carrington's help, had to work exceptionally hard to cook for and look after the visitors. In January 1920, Carrington had noted that

> ... Clive Bell, & Mrs Hutchinson [Bell's 'lady friend'] came here last week end. They aren't my style. Too elegant & 18 cent. French ... for that's what they try & be – I felt my solidity made them dislike me.
>
> Then I had to make their beds, & empty chamber pots because our poor cook Mrs Legg can't do everything & that made me hate them because in order they should talk so elegantly, I couldn't for a whole weekend do any painting, & yet they scorned my useful grimy hands.[247]

Introducing a new suitor to this ménage was a serious proposition.

In November, yet another figure entered their lives. Gerald Brenan, another former soldier and friend of Noel and Ralph, had been introduced to her some months before in London. He had been a fellow officer of Ralph's for a time during the war, but since then had a more remarkable history. When he returned from the war he found that he wanted no part of the future mapped out for him by family expectations. Instead, he set out to educate himself, first in England and later in Spain. His family was strongly opposed to what they viewed as a lazy, pointless existence and he was given little financial support. Spain was inexpensive, and he therefore packed up his books and set out for a monastic life of study and writing in the remote regions of Andalusia on 13 January 1920. Yegen was poor but visually stupendous. At 4,000 feet above sea level, one could see the Sierra Nevada chain of mountains rising behind it. Streams ran down the hillsides, and houses seemed suspended along the incline. It was full of light and air, with wonderful colours, and at night the stars were brilliant and multitudinous. Up these hillsides Gerald Brenan transported 2,000 books and in due course found a house and a servant, and quickly learned the language. His friendship with Partridge was based on common backgrounds: born in the same year – 1894 – both had spent their early childhoods in India before being sent back to England for a more or less traditional education, Ralph to Westminster and Gerald to Radley. Always a rebel, Brenan left home at the age of seventeen intending to walk to the East, but with the outbreak of war returned to join the army. Partridge spent a brilliant year at Christ Church, Oxford before joining the army. Both had outstanding military careers. Brenan was awarded the Croix de Guerre and served as an officer at the front; Partridge won the Military Cross and the Croce de Guerra and became a major at twenty-three. Now, both were experiencing similar changes in their rejection of traditional careers and lives.[248]

Before departing he met Carrington. 'It was in the spring of 1919 that I saw Carrington for the first time,' Brenan recalled.

We met casually in London, after which Ralph brought her over for a two day walking tour of the Cotswolds and I joined them. Then in July I went down to Tidmarsh for the night. It was, as I remember, one of those dark, overcast summer days. The trees and the grass had turned to a uniform tint of green and the air was heavy and stagnant. I came down a straight road shaded by elms and then saw a low brick and plaster building, in size a small farmhouse, standing by an open meadow which must once have been the marsh. This was the Mill House. Carrington came to the door and with one of her sweet, honeyed smiles welcomed me in. She was wearing a long cotton dress with a gathered skirt and her straight yellow hair, now beginning to turn brown, hung in a mop round her head. But the most striking thing about her was her eyes, which were of an intense shade of blue and very long-sighted, so that they took in everything they looked at in an instant. Passing a door through which I saw bicycles, we came into a sitting room, very simply furnished, in which a tall, thin, bearded man was stretched out in a wicker armchair with his long legs twisted together. Carrington introduced me to Lytton who, mumbling something I did not catch, held out a limp hand, and then led me through a glass door into an apple orchard where I saw Ralph, dressed in nothing but a pair of dirty white shorts, carrying a bucket. He came forward to meet me with his big blue eyes rolling with fun and gaiety and carried me off to see the ducks and grey-streaked Chinese geese that he had recently bought ... After this I was introduced to the tortoiseshell cat, which to his delight was rolling on its back in the grass in the frenzies of heat, and taken on to the kitchen where a buxom, fair-haired village girl of twenty, whom he addressed in a very flirtatious manner, was busy among the pots and pans.[249]

Carrington soon began a correspondence with Brenan, adding him to the number of people to whom she penned (and pencilled) her beguiling letters. She struggled at first to find the correct approach to take in writing to him, for each person required a different tone. 'I wonder what sort of letters you like?' she asked on 21 November, in her first communication with him. Immediately, though, she began to confide in him as she had to no one else but Strachey. Even that early in their friendship she found him a kindred spirit. 'First let me say how much I would like to come & make jam for you', she began. '... I was horribly untruthful to you in London. But it causes one curious pain raking up truths nakedly.'[250] Brenan later recorded that he had found this a distinctly 'oncoming' letter.[251]

As a friend of Ralph's, he was, Carrington felt, someone to whom she could speak about Partridge. She and Ralph had been bickering, yet they continued to meet and soon it was clear that he, like Gertler before him, wanted Carrington to commit herself to him. But her commitment to Lytton and their life at Tidmarsh precluded any tie to another person; she would have been happy to see him and even to be fond of him, provided he understood that he was one – and not the only one – of her loves. Ralph seemed finally to accept this, she told Brenan on 15 December.

I've become much fonder of R. P. He has become so much more charming, & has given up his slightly moral character which used to tire me. So we never quarrel now, & have become a perfect pair of pigeons in our affections. I certainly will never love him but I am extremely fond of him – I believe if one wasn't reserved, & hadn't a sense of 'what is possible' one could be *very* fond of certainly two or three people at a time, to know human beings intimately, to feel their affection, to have their confidences is so absorbing that its clearly absurd to think one only has the inclination for one variety. The very contrast of a double relation is fascinating – But the days are too short, and then one has work to do. So one has to abandon some people, & the difficulty of choosing is great, don't you find it so?[252]

CHAPTER ELEVEN

COMMITMENT: 1920-21

By January of 1920, Carrington was able to report to Brenan that Ralph and Lytton had become great friends '[w]hich is an immense improvement all round. As Lytton delights in teaching anyone literature. Its made R much happier, & less diffident, and I can have him here as often as I like. I am doing a large oil painting of him every day which gives me greater pleasure than it does the unfortunate victim.'[253] Partridge spent his winter vacation at Tidmarsh, and while Carrington painted him, Lytton read to them: 'Edward II' and poetry by Marlowe, 'lovely songs' by Campion.[254] The three of them began to settle into a comfortable life which centred around Carrington. The more deeply in love with her Partridge became, the more Strachey became attracted to him. Soon Lytton was in love with him as well.

Carrington held everything together. She made Tidmarsh possible, in every sense, and neither man would have been there without her. If she remained in love with Lytton, that only made the Mill House a home based on love as much as on convenience. Ralph's presence did not change that, despite their recognition that her fondness for him could not equal hers for Lytton. Realising this, it behoved Ralph to become fond of Lytton as well. Yet, no matter how direct a route that was to Carrington's heart, it also occurred honestly and naturally. The three fell into a comfortable routine and, during his visits to Tidmarsh, Ralph shared Carrington's bed.

Despite speculations to the contrary, Ralph's only physical relationship was with Carrington. As Frances Partridge later put it, Lytton quickly realised that Ralph was 'completely heterosexual' and that any other kind of relationship with him was 'no go'. Imagining that the three lived in a sort of free-love ménage à trois simplifies what was a much more complicated triangle. Ralph certainly grew to love Lytton, and their friendship was very deep and warm. They called each other 'dear' and 'darling' in letters and met on intellectual grounds. Theirs was an extremely strong and mutual affection which sometimes excluded Carrington because she was a woman. Lytton could tell Ralph things of a sexual nature which he felt he could not confide in Carrington, but this did not mean that their own relationship spilled over into the sexual realm.[255]

If Ralph brought an extra dimension to Tidmarsh, the Mill House provided him with something as well. He had returned from the war without a strong sense of direction or of belonging. His parents lived separately; his mother lived in Italy for a time, and his father suffered from depression and suicidal tendencies. And, like Carrington, he had little personal income. At Oxford he was reading literature, but despite his aptitude his heart was not in it. Unlike many of his classmates, he knew he would have to make his own living and wavered in his selection of a career. Then, just as he was taking up with Carrington, her brother Noel left for India for three years to work for the Oxford University Press, leaving Ralph without a close friend in England. Ralph found in Tidmarsh and Carrington a refuge. There he could tend the garden in season, provide and care for ducks and chickens, talk to Strachey about his thoughts on books, and be painted – and admired – by the woman he loved. He did not want to lose any of it, as he wrote to Noel.

> I have turned gardener at Tidmarsh, and we view my lusty youth with a spade every week-end; in a barrow I import dung & spread it a-field – I uproot metals from their inveterate pasture, I sift cinders, clip hedges, burn, overturn & level to the ground all that comes in my way – & have sent an order for many pounds worth of seeds to Suttons. Land, my boy, is the best material thing in life to aim at. A landholder has a proprietory joy that is unparalleled in any other walk of life.[256]

More than a simple refuge, however, Tidmarsh and its occupants served as an education to him. Not only was he searching for a career, he was also searching for a new way to *be*. The old world had died in the war along with his old self. Through Lytton and Carrington he learned a new way to live and face the world. In that sense, his sister was right: Carrington had permanently altered him. Yet this led to some seeming contradictions. He was more accepting, more gentle, more open to people's sexual and personal idiosyncrasies. Never again, for example, would he make crude jokes about homosexuals. Yet his Army training had been as a leader, so that Carrington often found him stubborn, bullying and regimented. But those characteristics rarely appeared when he was contented, as he was now at Tidmarsh.

That his presence pleased both Lytton and Carrington (who undoubtedly felt the need for physical affection as much as Ralph did) shows in Strachey's annual birthday poem ritual. In March

1920 he turned forty, and as usual Carrington's literary offering was pastoral and joyful. It ended,

> None must stand aloof today
> All must sing, and none may pray,
> Lytton, dear, *I* have no song.
> *I* cannot join the birdies throng,
> *I* have no scent, no petals bright,
> To lay before you to delight.
> Only this little wish I give
> That you for eighty years may live,
> ... But that's too short! Pray let it be
> Forty thousand years WITH ME.[257]

This time, however, Lytton responded with a poem of his own, dedicated to both Carrington and Ralph.

To D.C. & R.P.   *March 1st 1920*

> Suppose the kind Gods said 'Today
>   You're forty. True: but still rejoice!
> Gifts we have got will smooth away
>   The ills of age. Come, take your choice!'
>
> What should I answer? Well, you know
>   I'm modest – very. So, no shower
> Of endless gold I'ld beg, no show
>   Of proud-faced pomp, or regal power.
>
> No; ordinary things and good
>   I'ld choose: friends, wise and few;
> A country house; a pretty wood
>   To walk in; books both old and new
>
> To read; a life retired, apart,
>   Where leisure and repose might dwell,
> With industry; a little art;
>   Perhaps a little fame as well.
>
> At that, I'ld stop. But then, suppose
>   The Gods, still smiling, said 'Our store
> Of pleasant things still overflows.
>   Look round; be bold; and choose some more.'
>
> Hum! I should pause; reflect; then 'Yes!'
>   Methinks I'ld cry, 'I see, I see,
> What would fill up my happiness.
>   Give me a girl to dwell with me!
>
> A girl with genial beauty dowered,
>   A healthy and vigorous liberty,

By supreme Nature's self empowered
    To live in loveliness and glee,

And clothe her fancies with fair form,
    And paint her thoughts with vivid hue;
A girl within whose heart, so warm,
    Love ever lingers – oh, so true!'

Enough! – But hush! – if once again,
    Once more, the Gods the gates of joy
Threw wide, and bade me take! – Ah, then
    I'ld whisper 'Let me have a boy!

Yes, yes, a charming boy, whose soul
    With tenderest affection flows;
Young, yet not too young – the rich whole
    Of manhood blooming in youth's rose;

Gentle as only strength could be;
    With something of a Grecian grace,
And – sweeter, fairer still to me! –
    The loved light of an English face.'

x x x x x x x x x x x x x x x x x x x x

Dreams! Dreams! For never, sure, high heaven
    – And yet . . . to one . . . they *have* been given:
    For, dearest creatures, they are mine![258]

Since the trip to Spain the year before, Carrington had longed to show that country to Strachey. Ralph could act as organiser in a way that Carrington could not, and could speak the language. When Carrington found Lytton studying a Spanish grammar book in bed, she wrote to Gerald Brenan excitedly that perhaps the three of them could visit him in Yegen after all. Lytton, who loved the physical comforts of civilisation, would find Gerald's mountain retreat rustic but beautiful, she thought. When Brenan, responding to one of her letters, wrote jokingly that she should announce her 'secret feelings & complexes' in *The Times*, she thought it a good idea marred only by the fact that 'my Mother takes in that journal [so] surely it would be folly. For then there would be no Spain – and a convent.'[259] Now nearly twenty-seven years old, she only managed to get away by telling her mother that she would be travelling with the female cousin of a friend.

Ralph booked three berths for 18 March 1920, to sail from Liverpool to Lisbon. They were to stop for a day at Corunna before landing at Lisbon, then travel by train to Madrid, Córdoba, and Granada. From Granada the plan was to take a bus to Almería on the coast, finally reaching the heights of Yegen by mule. Lytton put all his faith in Ralph to see that the trip would be fulfilling without being fatiguing or troublesome.

Yet troublesome it was. Train travel was slow and bumpy; the oily cuisine played havoc with Lytton's delicate digestive system; both Lytton and Carrington found Ralph's masterful energy and organisational abilities as relentless as they were capable. He had them scheduled so tightly that their only break was three lovely days spent in Córdoba. By the time they reached Granada, where Brenan was to meet them, their disenchantment with each other was great. Carrington and Partridge bickered constantly, while Lytton remained stonily silent. When Brenan did not appear – he was ill in bed with influenza, but they did not know this – they sent him a wire and headed for the bus to return. He managed to scramble weakly down the mountain to meet them just in time.

The mules which took them to Yegen were nearly their undoing. The road was flooded and the journey took twelve hours, spent in fording streams and paths, mounting and dismounting. Brenan was genuinely ill, and Lytton threatened to be so. Holding a sunshade over his head and suffering from piles, Lytton repeatedly had to climb on and off of his mule on a trip he later described to Virginia Woolf as 'death'. They reached Brenan's retreat at midnight, Carrington and Brenan having rushed ahead to see that his servant, Maria, had prepared a meal and beds.

Once there things became more pleasant. From Brenan's house one could see both the mountains and the blue Mediterranean. While Lytton recovered and braced himself for the return trip, Carrington revelled in the beauty of the surroundings, and found that, despite his 'vagueness', Brenan was a pleasant companion who shared many of her feelings about life and literature. She and Ralph went for long walks with him once he regained his health.

Even so, the trip was not entirely successful. Worried about Lytton's physical and emotional well-being, as well as being annoyed with Ralph's regimentation, Carrington was irritable as she balanced her life among the three men. Far more relaxed by the end of their visit, they left Yegen in the middle of April, stopping at Toledo for two days before moving on to Madrid and, to Lytton's pleasure and relief, Paris. Carrington wrote a letter of thanks and apology to Brenan from Madrid.

At last I have time to write you a letter, so warm of thanks that your fingers would get burnt, if you knew how much I loved the Yegen life, those four days ... I feel like apologising because I feel I didnt 'show up' very well. I was rather tired, & anxious, & selfish. I am afraid you didnt enjoy our visit as much as we did. I shall I promise you if it is possible come out with our dear RP next September, in a different frame of mind armed with pots & paints, & no griefs.[260]

And no Strachey, she must have silently added. As much as she loved him, as a travelling companion he was at his best 'flanning' on cosmopolitan streets, sitting in cafés, and looking for first edition books in shops. When they met Barbara and Nick Bagenal in Paris, all five of them headed immediately for the refined and ordered elegance of Versailles.

Carrington and Lytton were not the only ones frustrated by the visit to Spain. Ralph wrote to Noel in exasperation on 5 May that 'Lytton, when well & lively, was an incalculable asset, when ill, depressed or tired, an almost . . . immeasurable drawback. Mark this, my Noel – be wary before you go on expeditions with men over 40 and women over 25 – the one are devils for comfort and the others comfort the devil . . .'[261] He found their minds an odd mixture of intelligence and disorder:

L. S. & D. C. are far worse than an embattled batallion, but neither has any discipline to speak of, and both have fertile imaginations without the requisite decision to attain their imaginings without a system. I did a course of pictures in Madrid under the guidance of the muchacha. She is equipped with a curious fund of knowledge on her art, that one hardly gives her credit for, as she is so inexpert at setting it out. I've become much more definite in my likes & dislikes and actually can give a reason or two why I think a picture good.[262]

Carrington had even greater physical discomforts awaiting her than long rides on mules' backs. Before setting off for Spain, she had consulted a doctor about her seemingly endless colds and swollen throats. Deciding that she was 'low in health', he prescribed 'vile medicines' which she had to drink with every meal.[263] When this brought no relief by May, she saw a London specialist who found that she had 'a defective nose'. He 'discovered I had bent the cartilage in the centre, & that until it was straight I would never get better. So next week I have to go into a hospital in LONDON, & have it cut out. I confess I am not looking forward to it. As it will make one rather weak & also increase, & ruin, my already too large nose.'[264]

She went into the Royal Free Hospital on 18 May (regretting that she could not afford a private nursing home) and was operated on the next day. Her only pleasures were in finding that she weighed just 120 pounds, and in having her friend Noel Olivier, a medical student in that women's training hospital, in attendance. Otherwise she found the whole experience, from the anaesthetic to the recovery on a ward, a horror. 'Well here I am with two great wooden tusks in my nostrils lying in bed', she wrote Lytton on 20 May 1920.

It was all over yesterday about 10 ock, Noel was there so can give you all the details. I hated going off more than anything one couldn't believe it wasn't death & nothingness & I yelled to be allowed to stay. I expect drowning must feel like that. Noel said I fought three of them very valiantly and I find bits chipped off my fingers & bruises this morning. Noel said it was a very bad nose. She saw inside two twists instead of one like Alix and most people have.[265]

She spared Strachey greater details of the operation and he visited her promptly.

To Brenan, however, she wrote a long 'journal' letter which set a precedent for other such letters in the future. On over fifteen long pages, she scrawled her feelings about life, her childhood, and the people around her. Although complaining about her surroundings – she referred to the hospital as a 'dungeon' and a 'death hole' – she found ample opportunities to express her humour. Nearly at the end of her tether after a week of moaning patients, nurses who spoke in the first person plural, bed pans (she managed to sneak off to the lavatory on her own, and then lie to the nurses when they came around) and visiting parsons, she composed a long poem titled 'Thoughts on lying in a hospital on WhitSunday'. It began,

> Encased in dark green walls I lie.
> Somewhere swing boats float high!
> Eighteen beds in two long rows,
> I in one, with battered nose.

She longed for her release and the sight of 'intelligent loving faces'.[266]

Tidmarsh, when she returned, was not entirely a paradise. Ralph bicycled the twenty miles from Oxford regularly, but they could not manage to get on well for any sustained period of time. He wanted more from her; she wanted her life to continue just as it was. This made him unhappy, which she could not bear, but neither could she see a solution. She would not marry him, as he wanted, because she felt he wanted to possess her. She wrote sadly to Brenan, one of their few mutual friends, that she could see 'no solution. It seems apalling that in this world when one gets on with so few people, when one does care for some one as much as I do for him, & he does me, one must part because of these difficulties. It is impossible to go one being perpetually unhappy & worried which is what he is doing now. Yet I know even if I did not think of myself, to marry him, would not make it any better. Because one cannot change a spirit inside one. And it is that he cannot possess.'[267] Yet she was forced to think rather more seriously about marriage. She had long ago made a 'spinster' pact with her closest friend, Alix Sargant-Florence. Alix was about to break that pact and marry James Strachey.

Perhaps even more upsetting, she discovered that her beloved Mrs Legg, who still did much of the cooking at Tidmarsh while

Annie was learning the ropes, 'has systematically robbed us these three last years, & in spite of all my affection for her said the most vile things, & admitted with relish that she had cheated me & tried to egg on the new housekeeper to do the same. What I disliked most was she had read all my most private letters & documents which she made vulgar gossip of. It is despairing!' Under this double betrayal, Carrington began to feel the sanctity of her idyllic life at Tidmarsh violated. While Ralph grew more and more comfortable there, making himself indispensable in innumerable ways, she felt threatened both by and without him. 'How divided one is really', she lamented to Brennan.[268]

During the summer, things took a better turn. She and Ralph, who now had access to a car, took a motoring trip to Stratford-on-Avon and the Lake District. They visited Shakespeare's cottage and Dove Cottage, where Wordsworth had lived. Inevitably both she and Lytton compared their life at Tidmarsh to Wordsworth's with his sister Dorothy: the rural atmosphere; the brother and sister relationship; the 'great man' reading to the woman in the evenings. In the North Country they climbed mountains and Carrington painted constantly. They spent a great deal of time with Ralph's friend Alan MacIver, at Windermere, and Carrington worked on a portrait of him.

While they were there, Lytton wrote with great delight and excitement about Carrington's work. His brother-in-law Simon Bussy, a prominent French painter, had visited Tidmarsh with his wife (Lytton's sister Dorothy). There Bussy had noticed Carrington's paintings and was overwhelmed by her talent. He was particularly impressed by her 'Mill House' painting.

> He was ... enthusiastic is not the word. – Looked & gazed, talked, praised, extolled – on & on he went. 'Better than anything at the London Group' – but that was by no means all. 'Better than most French things – better than Marchand 'et tous ces gens' – *much*'! ... There was no doubt about the genuineness of it all. 'I am not a French complimenter', he said in his curious English, and it's quite true. At last, after he had been going about it for almost half an hour, I really began to feel rather bored! ... So there's no doubt that you'll very shortly have to have a one woman show![269]

Lytton felt great pride in Bussy's reaction to Carrington's work; she never believed his compliments, but here was one she could not doubt.

She reacted with pleasure. 'Thank you for making me so happy. You know in a curious way one feels what one means to do, & then when nobody sees it in one's work, & when Duncan & Vanessa like not what I tried for, but for something else, I was confused. I tried so hard when I painted that Mill picture for a certain vision, & I felt depressed afterwards because I thought I must have failed completely, as no one saw. Only a small part of it did come off, but that Simon should have seen that delighted me.'[270]

Lytton wrote back immediately to reassure her. Simon had not found her work merely that of a talented student; 'Pas du tout!' As for Duncan and Vanessa, 'I rather felt that [they] were not quite perfect critics – they tend to want you to be like them, and not like yourself – which is really the only thing it's worth anyone's while to be. Simon has the power of appreciating a great many kinds of work.'[271] Carrington's work had long ago diverged from a derivative path. As she struck off on her own, her paintings were very much products of her personal vision. This of course made her even more reluctant to reveal herself through exhibition. Lytton once more, however, made a plea for her to show her work: 'So you see you will really have to appear before the public! The advantage of that will be that all sorts of other people will appear who will understand what you're up to. – Very likely people one's never heard of – but they certainly exist.'[272]

All this brought her back to Tidmarsh in a better frame of mind, and all would have been well had Ralph not been more determined than ever to have her as his wife. She steadfastly refused, and he took his problems to Lytton. Lytton could not bear to see either of them unhappy, and found himself in the position of the wise counsellor; indeed, Carrington referred to herself and Ralph as Lytton's 'children', and thanked him for his wisdom on both sides. He managed to cheer Ralph a great deal, for he at first advised patience with the assurance that Carrington would slowly come around if not pressured.

Carrington had several reasons for not wanting marriage. First of all, she was extremely jealous of her independence and privacy. Trained throughout her childhood and adulthood to keep her plans private, and to guard them by lying if necessary, the thought of having to share herself legally with someone else was terrifying. Second, her life with Strachey had been well nigh perfect up to now, in the nearly three years she had been living with him. She had learned so much from him, and he had softened so much with her, that she saw little to be gained by the permanent intrusion of a third party. While she was enormously fond of Ralph, she could not give herself up to him as she had already done with Lytton. As she had written to Brenan earlier that year,

> Sometimes with Lytton I have amazing conversations. I mean not to do with this world – but about attitudes, & states of mind, & the purpose of living. That is what I care for most in him. In the evenings suddenly

Early posed photograph taken in about 1910, the same year that Carrington started at the Slade School of Art

At Bedford School in her teens

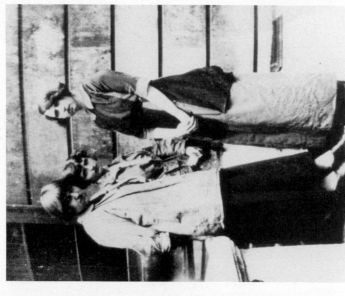

Painting a portrait of her father, also in 1910

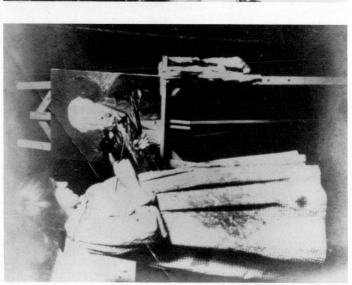

The 'cropheads'—Carrington with Barbara Hiles (later Bagenal) (centre) and Dorothy Brett (right) outside the Slade in 1911—shortly after all three had cropped their hair

Slade School picnic with Carrington in the front row at left. To her left, without jackets, are 'Chips' Nevinson and Mark Gertler. Also in the photograph are David Bomberg (back row, third from left) with Professor Frederick Brown on his left. Isaac Rosenberg in kneeling at the left of the middle row, and Stanley Spencer is second from right in the front row

With Lytton and James Strachey, most likely at a boarding house

Ralph Partridge in 1914, as a pre-war undergraduate

Carrington with Gerald Brenan

Picnic in Savernake Forest: Frances, Ralph, 'Beakus' Penrose, and Rachel MacCarthy

Carrington at Biddesden House with Pamela Mitford, Ralph, David Garnett and Frances. This was the last photograph taken of Carrington

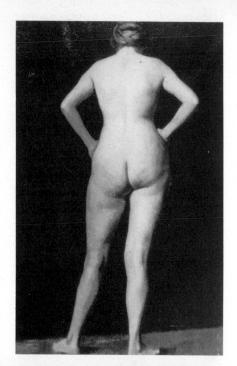

Carrington's prize winning life studies from the Slade, 1912 and 1913

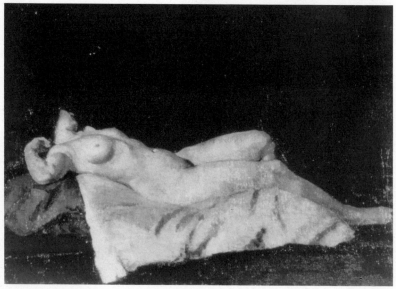

Lady Strachey (Oil, 30 in. × 24 in., 1920)

Lytton Strachey (Pen and ink, 1920)

Carrington's woodblock self portrait, with the C inadvertently reversed, meant to be used as a bookplate

An early Carrington woodcut, probably commissioned by the Hogarth Press

one soars without corporeal bodies on these planes of thought. And I forget how dull & stupid I am – & travel on also.

Its rather a responsibility having someone in love with one. One's behaviour becomes so much more important & it ties one to the earth in a curious way. But the interest is enormous. Do you know even at the most intimate moments, I never get the feeling of being submerged in it. I find myself outside, watching also myself & my workings as well as [Ralph's] from the detached point of view. But I confess it has made me much happier his affection. For owing to the fact that I deserted almost everyone, except Alix, for Lytton. There were moments when Lytton did not want me – when I recognised the isolation of it all – when one turned in despair for some relation with a mortal to assure one, that one wasn't entirely cut off – Now it is good to tell one's feelings, & feel his fondness at such times.[273]

The final, and perhaps most important, reason for resisting marriage was her art. Marriage almost inevitably involved children, and she knew of no woman artist who successfully managed motherhood and her career (apparently she forgot or ignored the example of Vanessa Bell). Carrington could not abide the thought of having children – her friend Barbara's example reinforced her resolve every time they met – and Ralph wanted them. 'One cannot be a female creator of works of art & have children', she wrote to Brenan.

That is the real reason why so few women have reached any high plane of creators. And the few that did become artists, I think you will admit, were never married, or had children. Emily Bronte & her sisters, Jane Austen, Sappho. Lady Hester Stanhope. Queen Elizabeth, and even lesser people like the French female artists Berthe Morrissot, Le Brun, Julie de Lespinasse & Dudeffand ... My real reason however is that I dislike merging into a person, which marriage involves, & I do *not* care for children. They seem too tedious & interrupting. I prefer the friendships of grown-up human beings. If when I am 38, I am not an artist, & think it is no good my persevering with my painting, I might have a child. But I doubt if I shall ever have maternal feelings enough to go through the bother & tedium of child bearing. Amen ... I *hate* those little self centred worlds which married people live in.[274]

On 24 August 1920, Virginia Woolf wrote to her sister Vanessa Bell words which were to start an inexorable chain of events: 'We've got Carrington and Partridge for the weekend. Dont [sic] you think it would be a good thing to bring about a legitimate union?'[275] One of Ralph's chief concerns had been to find suitable work. The Hogarth Press which, while running on a shoe-string budget and publishing at first chiefly the works of Virginia and their friends, was now becoming successful enough to need additional help. Ralph was most interested in the position; he met them; Lytton helped to arrange suitable conditions in terms of salary and duties. This accomplished, Ralph renewed his proposals to Carrington.

Carrington's inability to make up her mind about Ralph reflected her history of such decisions. As with Gertler, she was unable to commit herself to him, yet equally unable to let him go. If they moved to London so that Ralph could work for the Press, she would be giving up the life she loved more than any other. If she refused, she would keep Tidmarsh, but at the price of Ralph's attention and affection. Furthermore, she worried that their continued bickering and indecision would in some way drive Lytton away from her. Finally a compromise was proposed: Carrington and Ralph would spend the autumn and winter in London at 41 Gordon Square, a building which housed over the years so many Bloomsberries, while Ralph worked for the Woolfs. They would spend their weekends at Tidmarsh.

As a result, Ralph became more loving and less bullying, and Carrington's love for Strachey was strengthened. When she wrote to him at Charleston to thank him for all his help and patience in the affair, he replied, 'My dearest, I am sure that all is really well between us, which is the great thing. Some sort of embarrassment chokes me sometimes, & prevents my expressing what I feel. You have made me so happy during the last 3 years, and you created Tidmarsh as no one else could have, and I seem hardly to have said thank you. But you must believe that I value you and your love more than I can ever say. It seems to me that your trying the Gordon Square experiment is probably right. But whatever happens you must rely on my affection.'[276]

What Strachey wanted, in the midst of trying to produce 'Victoria', was peace, without losing either of the people he loved. Nevertheless, Carrington's subconscious brought to the fore the idea that if she were a man, this situation and its attendant difficulties would never have arisen. 'Last night I dreamed I was a man,' she wrote to Lytton on her way from Vanessa's home at Charleston to Virginia's at Rodmell, '& had an implement which I could take off & examine in my hand & then put back again into a satchel. It came I think from struggling with a new camera which I bought yesterday at Winchester, & in the evening I took its inside out & then couldn't put it back again. I hope it will turn out a good machine. But I was sorry to wake up this morning a woman again.'[277] As a man, she could have been everything to Lytton.

Forty-one Gordon Square belonged to James and Alix Strachey, who had recently married. James was a psychoanalyst, and Alix was training to be one, and they were spending some months in Vienna studying under and being psychoanalysed by Freud. They were to be the first translators into English of Freud's writings (and their translations are still well known today). At their house Carrington could have a studio, and her distaste for city life would be tempered by weekends at Tidmarsh. After moving in in October, she was at first preoccupied with getting settled and with, at last, submitting some works to an exhibition. At Lytton's instigation she sent three paintings, including that of the Mill House, to the London Group show. Vanessa advised her to price it at £15 but, following Lytton's advice, she put a price of £30 on it: 'Which I thought would be alright either way. It's a great mercy to have them shipped off, and to have been so brave. Bless you dear, for spurring me on.'[278]

She began to paint continuously during the day, frequently going to parties and to visit 'Bloomberries' with Ralph in the evenings. As promised, they spent most weekends at Tidmarsh. Yet, despite all this activity, she found herself unhappy and unable to adjust to the new life. To Gerald she stated emphatically that '[t]he married state is *not* a good one and I *won't ever* get married so there. And that's a TRUTH of great importance.'[279] To Lytton she was less gallant: '*you* said the middle of the week would go so quickly, but the weekends, they go quicker far. And I saw so little of you ... yet I must try honestly to forget now that I have given my promise to stay here with him. Perhaps in a few weeks I will either numb some senses or realise I cannot bear it. He is so good to me. He tries to make me happy. But I have to hide my pain, which makes it harder. For I do miss you so frightfully.'[280]

By mid-November she had accustomed herself to the new life, but was disheartened by 'having to fetch my pictures unsold from the London Group. As you know only 2 pictures sold in the whole exhibition. It was an awful spectacle ... work men already putting up carved brackets & revolting furniture where once those pictures hung ... the pictures? Faces against the wall waiting like umbrellas at the club to be fetched.'[281] Carrington rarely exhibited again.

She did, however, score one major coup. Lady Strachey, Lytton's mother, agreed to let Carrington paint her. Her spirits soared while she planned the painting, until the other Bloomsbury painters, Roger Fry, Vanessa Bell and Duncan Grant, heard of her success and insisted on joining her 'in a confusion of easels and conversation'.[282] Lytton's sister Pippa fortunately interfered, an action which Lytton applauded: 'How supreme of Pippa to keep that hound barking pack away!'[283] Carrington was excited about this painting.

> [I] was completely overcome by her grandeur, & wit. I am painting her against the book case sitting full length in a chair, in a wonderful robe which goes into great El Greco folds. It is lined with orange. So the effect is a very sombre picture with a black dress, & mottled cloak, & then brilliant orange edges down the front of her dress. She looks like the Queen of China, or one of El Greco's Inquisitors.[284]

She sold the portrait to Lady Strachey for £25, and each time Lytton was in London he could see it. 'The more I look at her Ladyship', Lytton wrote with pleasure, 'the more I admire it.'[285] Perhaps spurred on by this success, when at Tidmarsh she worked on a portrait of the new servant, Annie. Her disappointment with the London Group exhibition did not prevent her from painting all the time.

The winter passed, with Carrington growing more accustomed to life with Ralph. By February she was able to report to Brenan that 'Ralph is very happy working with the Woolves at Richmond every day. We get on very amicably now.' To her delight, Lytton was spending a lot of time down the road, at 51 Gordon Square. By the time of Lytton's forty-first birthday on 1 March 1921, she wrote his poem as from both herself and Ralph.

> Forty-one today! Forty-one today!
> Oh Lytton pause, fly not so fast.
> Remain with us, speed not away
> To join the veillards of the past,
> You are to us so young & gay.
> Oh if a wish a God would grant me
> Now I should chuse you would stay
> Even with us Forty-One! . . . until we
> Growing older . . . one day may
> Lytton, forty-one also be, but find you,
> Still as young, as dear, as True.[286]

That spring, however, she tried to spend more and more time alone, seizing on a commission to paint a Pangbourne shopkeeper's signboard as an excuse to remain at Tidmarsh without Ralph. She missed her solitude, 'the pleasure of being able to breakfast at 7.30, wander about aimlessly, do numbers of stupid things, eat fried eggs, & currant cake at every meal & never talk to anyone all day . . . man was not made to be united or merged into another person. As the handles of the scissors.'[287] Part of their difficulties stemmed from their small income, which forced Ralph to work with little time off. Carrington thought that 'he is ill suited for any continuous labour'.[288] Lytton's plans to go to Florence early in May only made the daily grind more frustrating, as it precluded their joining him there.

Although her paintings had not sold at the London Group, she decided to allow Roger Fry to hang another – a picture of four tulips – at the Grosvenor Gallery in May. Rather than being pleased at her bravery this time, she was depressed. 'It never seems anything like as good as what I conceive inside. Everything is a failure when its finished. They start off so full of hope.'[289] By now there was a definite link between her life and her art. When she was happy, she liked the work she produced; when she was not, she was completely disheartened. Like her paintings, her relationship with Ralph had begun full of hope but seemed to be heading for a very different ending. They quarrelled frequently, this time because Ralph 'had a mania for getting married lately'. She had hoped that the issue would be held in abeyance as long as they were living essentially as man and wife.

In despair, Ralph wrote to Lytton who was then in Italy. Before he could respond to this, Carrington dashed off a letter to assure Lytton that all was well, taking the blame upon herself and resolving to make it all right the next day. Finally, though, Ralph could bear it no longer and broke down at work, in front of Virginia and Leonard. His feelings for Carrington had affected his work as well as his private life, and they advised him to deliver an ultimatum: either marry him, or leave him. On 13 May Ralph and Carrington met at a coffee shop in Reading, halfway between London and Pangbourne, to resolve the issue. After that meeting Carrington wrote Lytton a heartbreaking letter.

He looked completely ill, & his mouth twitched – I'd really made up my mind some time ago that if it came to the ultimate point, I would give in. Only typically I preferred to defer it indefinitely, & avoid it if possible. You see I knew there was nothing really to hope for from you – well ever since the beginning. Then Alix told me last spring what you told James. That you were slightly terrified of my becoming dependent on you, and a permanent limpet, & other things. I didn't tell you, because after all, it is no use having scenes. Ralph repeated every word you once told him ... of course because he was jealous & wanted to hurt me. But it altered things, because ever after that I had a terror of being physically on your nerves, & revolting you. I never came again to your bedroom. Why am I raking all this up now, only to tell you that all these years I have known all along that my life with you was limited. I could never hope for it to become permanent. After all Lytton, you are the only person who I have ever had an all absorbing passion for. I shall never have another. I couldn't now – I had one of the most self abasing loves that a person can have. You could throw me into transports of happiness and dash me into deluges of tears & despair, all by a few words ... So in the café in that vile city of Reading, I said I'd marry him.

... So now I shall never tell *you* I do care again. It goes after today somewhere deep down inside me and I'll not resurrect it to hurt either you, or Ralph. Never again. He knows I am not in love with him. But he feels my affections are great enough to make him happy if I live with him. I cried last night Lytton, whilst he slept by my side sleeping happily. I cried to think of a savage cynical fate which had made it impossible for my love ever to be used by you. You never knew, or never will know the very big and devastating love I had for you. How I adored every hair, every curl on your beard. How I devoured you whilst you read to me at night. How I loved the smell of your face in your sponge.

Then the ivory skin on your hands, your voice, and your hat when I saw it coming along the top of the garden wall from my window... Ralph is such a dear, I don't feel I'll ever regret marrying him. 'Though I never will change my maiden name that I have kept so long – so you mayn't ever call me anything but Carrington.[290]

Lytton was devastated at this letter: 'Oh my dear, do you really want me to tell you that I "love you as a friend"! – but of course that is absurd, and you *do* know very well that I love you as something more than a friend, you angelic creature, whose goodness to me has made me happy for years, and whose presence in my life has been, and always will be, one of the most important things in it. Your letter made me cry, I feel a poor old miserable creature, and I may have brought more unhappiness to you than anything else. I only pray it is not so, and that my love for you, even though it is not what you deserve, may make our relationship a blessing to you – as it has been to me. ... Oh! My dearest dear, I send you so very much love.[291]

On short notice, at great expense, and with great happiness, Ralph ordered a marriage ceremony at the registry office in St Pancras, selected an 'infinitely thin' wedding ring at a pawn shop, and arranged passports and financial affairs.[292] Lytton paid for them to join him in Italy, after a brief honeymoon in Paris, as a wedding gift.

On Saturday, 21 May 1921, Carrington married Ralph.

PART THREE

REARRANGEMENTS

CHAPTER TWELVE

GERALD

'R[alph] will tell you I am a poor mistress, & make promise of being an ill-favoured wife,' Carrington wrote to Gerald eighteen days after her marriage.[1] She had come to terms with her decision to marry, but that decision had been made under duress and with the encouragement of all the people she admired and cared for most. Professing great fondness for her new husband, she nonetheless recognised that she did not love him in the way that a wife 'normally' loves her husband. Despite this inauspicious beginning, she and Ralph left England happily for France and Italy, relieved that the issue had at last been resolved; Ralph had captured his girl, and Carrington had preserved intact the two pillars of her life.

The only uncomfortable part of the process had been letting her mother know of the decision the afternoon before the civil service ceremony. Virginia, who had no small part in arranging the marriage, and who was proud to have been 'in the thick of it and [to have given] motherly advice', described the awkward meeting to Vanessa: 'She had to break the news to her mother, who endeavoured to explain that there is a certain thing the man does on the first night, by pointing to a bee copulating on a flower – but she broke down – and Carrington couldn't get her to proceed. "I think that lump on the back is a gentleman bee" was as far as she got.'[2]

In Paris, Carrington and Ralph went to an Ingres exhibition with a friend Carrington had made the previous December. Valentine Dobree[3] was to have a lasting effect on the newly-weds and on their marriage. Carrington had been immediately taken with Valentine when she met her at the Slade years before, and their friendship was renewed at this time. 'She sings divinely very old XIII & XIV century French and Italian songs,' she wrote excitedly to Gerald. 'She can draw & has painted two most remarkable pictures I think. She is wild, & full of southern passion. Her ancesters were Basques, & her name was Pechelle [actually Brooke-Pechell] before she married Bonamy Dobree. They have unfortunately left England for ever, & are going to find a house in the south of France, or northern Spain to live for the rest of their lives. [. . .] We only had three weeks friendship. But I enjoyed her company to the fullest when I was with her.'[4]

Virginia Woolf referred to Bonamy, who was a writer and literary scholar, as 'a nimble second-rate man'.[5] Valentine was the more vivacious and popular of the two, but they were, in any case, an odd couple. Lytton found that Bonamy 'has mildly literary and pedantic tastes. He is dull but harmless – I fear he is writing a series of sixteenth century lives in the style of Eminent Victorians. She is rather more interesting – perhaps a Saph – much attached to Carrington – but oh, not what might be called clever.'[6] Michael Holroyd goes further, and describes her as 'voluptuous, highly sexed and unstable... Dark and beautiful, though, with some malformation which made hearing difficult. . .'[7]

Her beauty, sexuality and instability caused tremendous trouble later on, but they were also what attracted Carrington to her. She was exactly the kind of woman Carrington admired: attractive, artistic, independent, and unconventional. Hoping that Gerald would be taken with her as well, Carrington wrote to him that the Dobrees were unable to find a place to rent or buy in France. Would he put them up for a few weeks while they continued their search in Spain? 'She is much more talented beautiful, & charming than your Doric', she added, knowing he would not necessarily agree, but nonetheless believing it herself.[8]

The Strachey-funded trip took Carrington and Ralph to Siena, Perugia, and Assisi, all of which delighted them. From Assisi they took a 'three day walk over the Appennines to Rimini, on to Ravenna, & join Lytton in Venice'.[9] Their honeymoon was as free from strife and tension as the preceding weeks had been full of them. They arrived back at Tidmarsh, relaxed, around 21 June, at almost the same time that Brenan arrived in England, making his annual visit to his parents in the Cotswolds.

Tidmarsh, as if in expectation of their return, had outdone itself in beauty and fecundity, as she informed Lytton, who was away, on her return.

My dear, its too agitating the size of everything. The goosies! the ducks! the hens! When we left them they were enveloped in a cage five feet high. Now they look over the top & dwarf the privet hedges. The garden is a mass of confused vegatation [sic], the orchard a wilderness of hay, and the dinning [sic] room possessed by the devil of a giant bookcase! We simply sit crushed; the labour necessary to control the establishment seems endless. Even Ralph is in despair. But really its superb. [. . .]

There are masses of pears to eat, gooseberries, cherries, broad beans & new potatoes. But we groan & groan at the labours before us. Annie is blooming more beautifully than ever, & calls me 'Miss Carrington & Mrs P' alternately in great confusion. [...] How happy we have been, how happy we are going to be! You don't know how much we both love you ... Your books looked a little sad when you didn't appear to greet them. They stand in such perfect order brimming with pride at having remained so erect, so well behaved all this time...[10]

The summer promised peace and productivity. Carrington had begun receiving commissions from local businesses for her sign-boards, 'a greater honour to my mind than becoming a member of the London Group'.[11] Ralph returned to his work with the Hogarth Press, taking the train to London each day, and returning home at 7.30 in the evening. Carrington loved having her days thus free to paint, and her evenings with Ralph and Lytton, when Lytton was not in London himself.

This tranquillity was nearly destroyed by Gerald's return to England. Carrington had begged him to visit them at Tidmarsh, promising to 'feed you as I feed my geese, for nothing, & you shall eat strawberry ices, & cream, & cheese straws & home made marmelade, & drink Lytton's port'.[12] She wanted to paint his portrait, and Ralph of course joined her in desiring Gerald's company. With some misgivings and confusion, Gerald agreed to come down for one night.

While Ralph was at work, Carrington and Gerald met on their bicycles at an inn near Uffington, on 7 July 1921. They planned to picnic on White Horse Hill, and accordingly Carrington had packed sandwiches. After a long and comfortable conversation, they had progressed to the point of holding hands and kissing. Gerald professed later that the kisses meant little to him at the time; to Carrington they seem to have been the natural outgrowth of a warm friendship strengthened by steady correspondence. In any case, little was said about it, and it seemed an isolated incident which posed no threat to her marriage. They bicycled back to the station and took separate trains to separate homes.

Two weeks later, however, things changed drastically for Brenan, if not for Carrington. He returned to Tidmarsh for a visit of two or three days, and had an experience which rivalled in intensity Carrington's first recognition of her love for Strachey.

I was sitting in an armchair in the sitting room when Carrington passed across in front of the window, outlined against the setting sun. She just passed across and all at once something overturned inside me and I felt that I was deeply, irretrievably in love.

An avalanche of feelings followed, unlike anything I had ever experienced before. In that quarter of a minute the whole orientation of my life, all the thoughts in my head had been changed. Like a Pacific Islander who succumbs to an attack of flue [*sic*] brought in by a foreign sailor, I was struck down and overwhelmed. Nothing had happened to prepare me for such a situation and I sat there helpless, dazed by the welter of new emotions that flooded over me.[13]

Carrington's feelings developed through their letters and meetings more slowly and less intensely. They were in many ways soul-mates. Gerald was imaginative in a way that Ralph was not, and this showed in his letters to her and his extreme sensitivity. Carrington was an incurable romantic, a trait which had got her into trouble before. Over the next days they met privately again, exchanged more kisses, and discussed what, if anything, should be done. Gerald wanted to tell Ralph, but Carrington did not. She was happy to write and receive letters, kiss a great deal when they met, and keep things pretty much as they were. It was lovely to have such a relationship; she did not at all see that it interfered with her marriage, despite what it might have looked like to outsiders.

In this respect she was a true innocent who had a child-like faith in the present and in the power of many kinds of love. To her, sex really did not enter the picture at this juncture. They had not committed adultery, nor did they intend to. For his part, Gerald would not have been able to sleep with his best friend's wife, nor did he equate sex with 'good' women. There was a purity of feeling involved, a warmth and closeness which Carrington believed disclosure would only vulgarise. Furthermore, this was Carrington's secret, a part of her private self and feelings which she felt had nothing to do with Ralph. She felt that what he did not know could not possibly hurt him, yet her secrecy and privacy, so precious to her, were exactly what Ralph hated most.

They continued to correspond, with Ralph always a presence in their letters and thoughts: he read all of Carrington's mail, despite her objections. They wrote in their letters of their 'fondness' for each other, but rarely went beyond that. If Gerald, overwhelmed by his feelings, stepped beyond those bounds, Carrington wrote back in fury. No matter what happened, she did not want to hurt Ralph. Even when they met in London on 4 August, they kissed by the hour but would go no further, like two adolescents involved in a first puppy love.

The relationship was thus at first a very innocent one, marked by awkwardness and naivety, but not deviousness or prurience. Gerald later wrote that '[w]hat must seem strange and indeed almost incredible is that I felt no sexual attraction for Carrington, using that word in its narrower sense. I seemed to have been carried to heights where I was above all physical desires ... Finally, Carrington's body was flat and boyish and offered nothing to the sensual imagination. No one would wish to sleep with her unless he loved her.'[14] It seemed instead that a strong, but not wholly recognised, androgyny attracted them to each other.

Unlike Ralph, Gerald resembled Carrington in uncanny ways. He was moodier and more impetuous than she, but Ralph remarked to Gerald that they 'even peeled an apple in the same clumsy way. He could see that, unlike himself, we were neither of us dominating nor aggressive. We stuck out for what we wanted, but we were unworldly and ingenuous in the sense in which young artists and writers frequently are. He admired us for living for something which he could not share, but he also found us irresponsible, vague, muddle-headed and generally unreliable.'[15] Ralph had so little sense of being threatened by the true nature of their friendship (which he knew nothing about, of course) that he invited Gerald to join them, along with Lytton, Alix and James on their holiday at Watendlath in August. Ralph and Gerald were very close, and had a friendship that would last for more than forty years. Gerald admired Ralph's manliness, and Ralph admired Gerald's courage and his writing.

Before starting off on his second trip of the summer, Ralph had to clear the air at the Hogarth Press, for he had become increasingly dissatisfied with his job there. Hired as a secretary, through Lytton's intervention and negotiation, he was now primarily a printer and salesman. According to Leonard Woolf, Ralph worked only two or three days a week, by agreement, for which he was paid an annual salary of £100. Although the hours were relatively easy, he began to resent not having even more free time at his disposal. Living with Lytton and Carrington, who worked to their own timetables, made it a greater annoyance.

However, personality conflicts provided the greatest frustration. He found Leonard and Virginia – particularly the former – too paternal and authoritative. Unlike Carrington, he made no allowances for genius in personal relations. For their part, the Woolfs saw little of the carefree side of Ralph which endeared him to Lytton and Carrington. Carrington found him a completely different person when in the company of the Woolfs: business-like, tight-lipped, and stiff. As the business relationship continued, the chafing increased. Finally, the two couples met at Monk's House, Rodmell, to discuss what Carrington called 'The Situation'.

Placing friendship first, they had tea and a long walk over the downs, from which Carrington 'came back filled with enthusiasm for Virginia. Its impossible not to fall in love with her I find. She was so friendly to me I couldn't help colapasing [sic] completely.' After dinner they sat down to business. First Leonard gave his point

of view, then Virginia gave hers; '[t]hen Ralph rather tentatively returned the fire – And I summed up the proceeding at the tail end of everything', Carrington reported to Gerald.[16] Then they adjourned to their separate homes to think the matter over. It was under this cloud that they left for the Lake District at the beginning of August for a month.

Carrington and Lytton, joined that evening by Alix and James, arrived at Watendlath on 6 August. Ralph was visiting his Liverpool friend, Alan MacIver, whom Carrington had painted on a previous visit. They shared the farm not only with the family that ran it, but with 'two very plain young North country ladies' whom they secretly referred to as the 'white roses', and 'a North country man in tweeds'. Over dinner the first night this gentleman engaged Lytton in conversation, but 'opened his mouth & nearly droped [*sic*] out the lamb when Lytton first spoke. He had never heard such a voice before!'[17]

Despite cold rains, Carrington delighted in the countryside. She sent for her easel and paints and, until they arrived, sketched in and out of doors. The only problems were her continuing arguments with Ralph, whom she refused to accompany to Liverpool, and who did not want to make the long walk over to Watendlath. As his wife, she was expected to make social calls to his friends, but she found the beauty and tranquillity of the country too engaging, and his friends too 'bourgeois', to leave. 'As for D. C.,' Ralph wrote to Noel, 'I have deserted her or she has deserted me – as yet I cannot decide which – for a week or two. Whether it is that she prefers Alix's society to that of the MacIver family, or that I prefer that of the MacIvers to that of Alix's and James, or that we are both naturally cantankerous, or both uncommonly obliging to each other, it's a psychic phenomenon that I cannot elucidate. A great deal of our time at any rate is always spent in these mental tugs of war . . .'[18] She finally gave in, and wrote to Gerald from a dismal Liverpool boarding house on 9 August.

> The evenings are the worst part of this house. The men play bridge, & the females sew, & talk to each other. I can do neither. G.r.r.r.r.r. Preserve me from such society in my old age, children, babies, & golfing men & females.
>
> PS. I will not have any children, ever.
>
> PS. There are 12 children, & 3 babies in this house.[19]

Just before they left for Watendlath, Barbara gave birth to a blue baby. 'Nick is regarded as responsible for the baby', Ralph continued to Noel, 'and Twilight Sleep for its colour.' Carrington became even more firmly committed to her childless state. At the house, Ralph attempted 'to convert me to a country house lady, & tried to teach me ping-pong! But I confessed after a few minutes it was hopeless because I don't care for winning, or playing seriously. I really was sorry, as he enjoys games so much.'[20]

Her lack of competitiveness constituted an important difference between them. As a rowing man, Army major, and student, Ralph had been compelled to be competitive. He enjoyed this, but in many ways was attempting to leave this behind him. Still, Carrington's continual self-effacement and lack of competitive spirit, although it in no way inhibited her sense of self, frustrated him because it led to the problems that always plagued her: financial strain (he contended that she let local merchants cheat her on her signboards); an unwillingness to exhibit her work; and difficulties with servants. Increasingly, she escaped into secrecy, and when Gerald's first letter to Watendlath arrived, she did not share it with Ralph: 'For some reason I liked to pretend it was only for me. So I hid it in my pocket & read it in my bedroom secretly.'[21]

They returned to the serenity of the farm, and in the company of friends fared rather better. The group went for long walks together; Ralph swam and fished with Carrington by his side. One day Lytton made them little boats out of paper, 'which we christened & launched upon the dashing stream. It was fun, all tearing down the bank watching the brave little vessels dash the rapids.'[22]

Even with such company and innocent pleasures, Carrington began to miss Gerald, and finally offered to send him £5 for his fare to join them before he returned to Spain. Although Ralph was always pleased to see his friend, and indeed had already asked him to come, Carrington made the offer surreptitiously. Gerald arrived, and during the two weeks of his visit, the situation became increasingly tense. He was in love with her, but needed to conceal his feelings. She wanted to spend time alone with him, but did not want the holiday to be one of illicit meetings. When alone, they talked and kissed as constantly as before, but had a very close call when Ralph nearly caught them.

To Carrington, this seemed 'a warning from the Heights',[23] and she told Gerald it would probably be better if he left. Although he agreed, it caused sorrow for all three: Gerald was about to return to Spain, and did not know when he would see her again; Carrington knew she would miss him, but also knew that she was playing with fire; Ralph would also miss him, but accused Carrington of quarrelling with Gerald and causing his departure. Carrington found the irony of that accusation 'dreadful'. When Gerald left Watendlath on 30 August, their relationship was still technically chaste.

Gerald boarded a ship at Newhaven on 8 September, stopping in the Basses-Pyrenées on his way to Yegen to stay for several days with Carrington's friends Valentine and Bonamy Dobree. They had found a house in France, and therefore had never come to stay with him in Spain as planned. He found, as many did, Bonamy to be rather pedestrian in both taste and intellect, while Valentine he found open and interesting – although she did not sing for him. He learned of her training under the French painter Derain (in fact she was rumoured to have been his mistress at some point), and discovered that she and her husband had what was, in modern terms, an open marriage – that is, Valentine had extramarital affairs (primarily when her husband was away in the war), and Bonamy tolerated them. Gerald found this 'a true and touching marriage, each of them satisfying the other's need', and when he moved on, they all made plans to meet again.

Carrington may not have known about the affairs, but she did find 'Valentine's life interesting'.

> She has given so much out of herself to the world, lived so fiercely. It is splendid. Then I admire the way she has no preconceived conception of how a woman, & an artist should live. She is as worldly as she feels worldly. She is business like, & generous, gay, & very melacholly [sic],

unprincipalled [*sic*], & yet virtuous, & does not think it wrong to bake good cakes, & trim a hat with ribbons, & yet paints 5 hrs a day, & will not be interrupted for all the men in the world. I feel when I think of her, & Alix, that I have been priveledged [*sic*] to know two such remarkable women.[24]

Many of the things which Carrington found so exciting about Valentine were traits she shared with her, and found validated by her. At the same time she was undoubtedly besotted with her. Lytton's observation that Valentine was 'perhaps a Saph' provides another clue to her attraction for Carrington. Carrington's own sexuality had been an issue ever since she had known Mark, and while she was clearly attracted to men it was evident that she was also attracted to women.

Lytton left Watendlath only a week after Gerald. When seeing him off in the pouring rain, Carrington and Ralph reached another breaking point, arguing all the way back from the station at Keswick after tea. Ralph 'admitted it was partly because he found life too inactive, & wanted to go off abroad somewhere, perhaps to N. Africa as a war correspondent'.[25] This confession seemed to clear the air, for Ralph cheered up and Carrington began painting a landscape from the window of Alix's room, and another one outside of the farm.

Like her earlier work, 'Farm at Watendlath' uses subtle colouring, this time in shades of blue, green, brown and grey. The foreground features squares of white on the stone farmhouse and fence, and mother and daughter figures, while in the background the hills recede and ascend dramatically. 'I sat and drew a white cottage and a barn ... sitting on a little hill until it grew too cold ...', she wrote. 'The trees are so marvellously solid, like trees in some old Titian pictures, and the houses such wonderful greys and whites, and the formation of the hills so varied.'[26] Less detailed than many of her paintings, this one relies on the careful blending of colour to contour and define.

Most striking about the picture are the hills and mountains, which are highly suggestive in the female voluptuousness of their rolling curves. The two female figures stare back at these curves, hand in hand. She rarely painted children – partly because she knew few who would sit for her – so it is notable that one of the two figures is a child. In a more directly Freudian sense, she selected women at different stages of their lives directly contemplating their own femininity. At a time when her sexuality and sense of romance were divided between two men, she seems to have channelled much of those feelings into her art and, given the turmoil of her sexuality, this painting probably conveys something of Carrington's own sexual feelings. The female figures are tiny and utterly dwarfed by the sensual background, suggesting a sense of intimidation by her own womanhood. The theme of sensual rolling hills occurs again in her works, most notably in 'Mountain Ranges at Yegen, Andalusia', painted in 1924. With the Watendlath painting Carrington achieved a posthumous success: it was used on the cover of the British edition of Gerald Brenan's *Personal Record* (for obvious reasons) and now is owned by the Tate Gallery in London.

Ralph and Carrington left the farm only a few days after Strachey, Carrington paying a visit to Vanessa and Duncan at Charleston before returning to Tidmarsh. Anxious to return home, she found the people at Charleston friendly but lacking in fastidiousness. Even by the fairly relaxed standards of Tidmarsh, Charleston was poorly maintained. 'The sordidness of this establishment is a trifle trying', she wrote to Lytton. 'Everything is allowed to rot from year to year ... including the rats killed by poison, whose smell is now wafted through the house. "It will be gone in a day or two", says Vanessa dreamily. Well, *I* shall be gone tomorrow.'[27]

Before returning to Tidmarsh she paid a visit with Ralph to one of his old girlfriends, now married, then went on to Hereford to visit Barbara and her family. Carrington was not at all impressed with Ralph's 'former love': 'She was so sweet & pure I nearly laughed. So refined, with a gentle voice. R tried to pretend she was full of qualities & virtues, but he wasn't very convincing in his enthusiasm. "What an escape", I kept on murmuring for the rest of the evening. How kind chance is to us to be sure. I shiver sometimes when I think what escapes I had, and when I see the ghostly, or substantial forms of my past husbands in the streets of London, I almost thank them for their mercy.'[28] One of her 'past husbands', Mark Gertler, had not fared as well as she in recent years. Suffering from both nervous and respiratory disorders, he had been released from a sanatorium in the same month that she married Ralph.

Back at Tidmarsh, she grew lonely again. Freed from the grinding work of writing and revising 'Queen Victoria' at long last, Lytton was spending some of his weekends there, but much of the week in London and Cambridge. At Cambridge he gave a paper and met the new undergraduates and Apostles, some of whom he brought back to Tidmarsh with him: Sebastian Sprott, F. L. Lucas, James Doggett were among these new visitors, and old ones continued to come as well.[29] 'I miss him so much when he leaves', she wrote to Brenan. 'I love his appearance so much, & there is an emptiness in the rooms & garden when he has left.' In addition, she suffered physical and mental torments, in the form of a stomach flu and nightmares. 'What divine spirit prompted you to write a discourse on the ills of the stomach?' she asked Gerald.

> For when your letter came I lay under my canopy of blue, limp & worn after a night of the most horrible visitations. Empty as a new coffin, hollow as a tea-caddy. I now write crouching over a fire thinking only of my stomach, and wondering what fiendish germ it was yesterday that set all Heaven in a tumult, & cast out all the contents of my inside in such anguish. At three this morning it started. Four journeys in the ice cold morning. Another journey downstairs to drink a tumbler of brandy. And then when Ralph awoke at 7.30 he was ignorant of my illness! Lytton's more finely tuned stomache [sic] woke up at hearing the cry of a neighbouring vessell [sic] in distress & was all sympathy this morning when I called him. I am sure all my talents lie in that crater, for I feel divested, & shorn this morning, even my affections for you are dimmed ...[30]

In the meantime, she busied herself with work, beginning a 'new composition of men gathering apples on long ladders in a tree. Its rather a good design, but I see it will [be] almost impossible to carry out.' She worked sporadically, spending whole days in her attic studio, alternating with days of laziness and days of 'concentrated industry and virtue' around the house.

Only two weeks after returning home, she and Ralph left again, this time for a bicycle trip to Surrey, which proved disappointing, and to visit her mother who had moved again. She was now staying in Lottie's cottage in Hindhead, and regaled them with complaints about Carrington herself, her brother Sam '& his misdemeanours, the failures of the dividends, the repetition of incidents about many people whose names & faces I have forgotten ...'[31] Charlotte was pleased, nonetheless, about her prodigal daughter's married state, and Ralph and Carrington wanted her good feelings about them to last, partly because each time she moved they raided her belongings for things they could use at Tidmarsh. An unpleasant visit to Carrington's brother Sam, now living on a farm in Spain with an Irish wife, convinced Charlotte Carrington that her wayward daughter was not so bad after all. According to Mrs Carrington, Sam and his wife forced her to pay for her keep, help around the house, and berated her for not lending them money which she apparently did not have. She returned to England with relief, bearing gifts for her daughter and new son-in-law.

Carrington felt no more sympathy for her sister Lottie than she did for her brother. She was concerned only about social matters: marriages, incomes, and status. Far from having financial troubles, Lottie and her physician husband had, in Carrington's estimate, £3,000 a year, a car, and a house in Portland Place. Even so, '[h]er saggy discontented face still haunts me. And to think for at least 10 years we lived side by side, & slept in the same room together. Now I feel she is more removed from me than Mrs Lloyd George or Princess Mary.'[32]

They fared rather worse with Ralph's parents. His suicidal father had once threatened to kill himself because the government refused to acknowledge that he owed back taxes. Only when Ralph wrote on his behalf did the government respond to his letters and enable him to pay what he owed. Clearly there was little support to be expected from that quarter. His estranged wife, Ralph's mother, never approved of Carrington as a daughter-in-law, treating their marriage as something barely to be acknowledged and endured rather than celebrated. Carrington found that Ralph's parents 'treat me [...] as if I was a harlot, or a charity child'.[33] Their lack of children made this worse, yet a November trip to Barbara in Herefordshire, where Carrington had to share a room with a crying baby, convinced Carrington – if she needed further convincing – of 'the tediousness, & purposeless[ness] of [children's] conversations and actions. My cat is a noble animal in comparison . . . I felt destroyed & unsettled.'[34]

Although both her father and Ralph's had been civil servants in India, like most of Bloomsbury his family was of a higher class than hers. This, and the fact that she was an unconventional artist, made them feel that he had married beneath him. In November she took a kind of revenge when she refused a invitation, or summons, from Mrs Partridge to meet Mr Partridge 'who has never recognised or noticed the fact I've married Ralph'.[35] Then, in December, she gloated over Mrs Partridge's being confined to a nursing home. Now ill, she made friendlier overtures to Carrington. 'I will take her wretched gifts', Carrington wrote bitterly to Brenan, 'but she does not take me in. And I will *never* become a presentable daughter in law.'[36] Her self-confidence did not extend to other areas of her life; that night she 'cried in [her] sleep, and woke up in a cold sweat . . . because Annie told me some trivial lies'.[37] When Carrington chastised her, she felt worse than the guilty servant. Annie was, after all, more important to her than her relations by birth or by marriage.

Nevertheless, staying in the good graces of their respective families was important. As much as she and Ralph differed with their parents and siblings, their financial futures to a large extent depended on possible inheritances. The situation with the Hogarth Press was still unresolved, and Ralph knew that soon he would have to face the 'the Woolves' and reach a decision about the direction his career – such as it was – should take. This impasse, coupled with their depressing financial situation (Ralph had earned only £130 that year, and was £30 overdrawn at the bank), made Carrington resolve to 'support him in taking up something more active' if things had not improved with the Woolfs by Christmas.[38] In the meantime, they acted the proper married couple only to the extent required by the outside world. Not surprisingly, her painting suffered during these difficulties. '[S]omehow I have no heart for it', she wrote Gerald. 'It starts so well, & then I lose grasp, & heart & the pictures remain unfinished. I think for a little I will do wood blocks, & give my brushes & that side of my brain a rest.'[39]

The annual round of Christmas visits to Tidmarsh began early. Clive Bell and Mary Hutchinson, never Carrington's favourite guests, arrived early in December and upset her as much as ever. They directed all their intellectual conversations to Lytton, although Carrington had read all the works they referred to; they had 'a subtle way of forcing one to become a certain character. "Well how many hens houses have you made since tea"? "Poor Carrington seems to do all the work." ... I do not work as you think at chicken houses because I am not in the room with you ...' she imagined herself replying.[40] Bell was willing to accept her as a labourer but not as an artist.

Other difficulties developed as well, but these were internal. Her greatest fear, that Lytton might leave her, manifested itself in fears that he would find her stupid. 'He is such an amazingly sympathic [sic] man, and so amusing, we often laugh all dinner over the most absurd jokes', she wrote to Gerald.[41] As long as he was amused, or working hard, she had no worries. But now that he was spending so much time with his more 'intellectual' friends she felt threatened.

> I've felt so stupid lately, and then I get dreadful misgivings that I am boring Lytton – sometimes I literally dread lunch as I used to in old days. I dread being alone with him, I dread my vapidity, & the almost imperceptible wince he gives, when I offend his good taste, or irritate him with my stupidity. Its rather too Russian at times. My terror, & the way I plunge deeper & deeper into the bog – yet of course we have a great deal in common, & he is generally very lenient & forgiving. It is only when he is depressed, or exhausted that I feel the strain.[42]

Their Christmas guest was their friend Maynard Keynes, who read to them from his new book on war reparations, and was intelligent and charming. Like Keynes, Boris Anrep, the Russian mosaicist[43] was Bell's refreshing opposite. He arrived on New Year's Eve bearing gifts and affection, and 'praised everything. He noticed all my favourite pictures ... Even my sign board.'[44] He returned in January, this time offering lemons and fifty oysters which the three – Lytton did not eat oysters – devoured for dinner. The season was marred only by the publication of Aldous Huxley's *Crome Yellow* and its portrait of the repressed Mary Bracegirdle.

In contrast to the end of 1921, Carrington began the new year of

1922 with pleasure. An aristocratic friend from Slade days, Phyllis Boyd, was about to marry a Frenchman named Henri di Janzé and move to Normandy. Carrington bought an infinitely respectable outfit and prepared to 'go to the function, & elbow the Duchesses out of the front pews'.[45] She found Phyllis 'very upper class and immoral, but full of character', and also terribly attractive. During the days before the wedding the two women spent several hours talking, with Phyllis holding court from her bed, and Carrington admiring her. 'I actually suffered torments because I longed to possess her in some vague way,' she confessed to Gerald. 'To make her realise somehow that I was important to her. But she only prattled away in her bed, about her château in Normandy, her parents, her past lovers, & the scandals of London.'[46] This confession of a lesbian impulse passed unremarked by either of the correspondents, and Carrington moved cheerfully on to other subjects.

A second object of her affections was not to be so easily forgotten. Carrington had been eager for Brenan to meet the Dobrees, and was thrilled when Valentine wrote at the end of January that she and Bonamy were planning to see him at Yegen. Carrington felt both envy and delight that two objects of her intense affection were to be together. She expressed herself openly to Gerald, saying that her feelings for Valentine were 'far from ordinary – Everything she does moves me strangely & to think of her singing to me, dressed in a yellowish shawl in her room at Hampstead playing at the piano, throws me into a state of . . . sentiment.'[47]

This visit to Yegen was to start a terrible chain of events. While there, Valentine told Gerald that she wished Lytton, Ralph and Carrington to visit her and Bonamy in their new French home at Larrau, in the Pyrenées, in a remote mountain cottage. Guessing something of the feeling between Gerald and Carrington, she asked Gerald to join them there and, according to Gerald, 'promised to take Ralph off my hands so that I could sometimes be alone with Carrington'.[48] Gerald, who had suffered in silence, opened up to her. She encouraged him to talk and was all the more sympathetic to him because of the stories she had been told about Ralph's London behaviour from her close friend and correspondent, Mark Gertler. Apparently many had noticed what Carrington and Lytton had not: that already Ralph had been unfaithful to Carrington, and probably more than once.

Gertler had never recovered from Carrington's marriage, and knew or had heard rumours about Ralph's London infidelities while employed by the Hogarth Press. He was furious with Ralph's behaviour and did not hesitate to report it to Valentine. Perhaps he knew that it would get back to Carrington through this route. Carrington herself had tea with Mark at the beginning of February, the first time the two had written or met for almost a year. He did not repeat his accusations then, but Ralph's affairs would soon enough become public knowledge.

Blissfully ignorant of these behind-the-scenes developments, Carrington turned her wit to a practical joke against a not unexpected target. Clive Bell had criticised George Bernard Shaw in an article for the *New Republic*. Carrington thought the criticism unjustified and, with Ralph's help as typist, forged Shaw's signature and sent Bell the following letter:

> Dear Clive Bell, Thank you for the numerous compliments you have paid me in this week's New Republic. I am sorry I cannot return the compliment that I think you, or your prose, 'Perfectly respectable'. . . . You do not, it would appear, lead a very enviable aesthetic life; to me it seems dull. Yours Bernard Shaw.[49]

The letter had unexpected results, as Lytton wrote to Carrington gleefully from 51 Gordon Square: '– What do you think? – Clive was completely taken in by the Bernard Shaw letter! "He wrote me a perfectly preposterous and furious letter – too absurd! – Poor old man – quite gaga – I replied that he was the last person in the world whom I wanted to hurt the feelings of. He wrote again, pretending he hadn't written before – quite gaga, poor old fellow!" etc. etc. So you see the signature must have been forged very brilliantly.'[50]

Carrington could not have been more pleased. 'I see a new aspect: a new avenue in life now!' she wrote back on 15 February. 'Forgery between lovers, enemies, dukes and duchesses.'[51] By 24 February, however, the situation had got out of hand. All of Bloomsbury was privy to the secret, and found Clive's response most embarrassing. Virginia wrote Lytton that he must tell the truth; Clive carried the letter around with him, showing it to all who would listen, and was 'evidently ... the laughing stock of London'.[52] He was accordingly informed and, writing of the incident in his memoirs, said that although he had 'never cared for practical jokes and hoaxes', he and Carrington had 'remained fast friends to the day of her death'.[53] It was true, however, that Clive and Carrington did not get on well. But it is also true that her letters paint a rather one-sided picture of him.

When she was not quarrelling with Ralph, they got on quite well; it was either feast or famine. He proved his affection for her in February when Alix Strachey, studying with James under Freud in Vienna, became frighteningly ill with pleurisy. James wired to Tidmarsh for special foods, as he was unable to find any to her liking in Austria. Soon Carrington realised that Alix's condition was far worse than they had first understood: the doctors had to open her chest without an anaesthetic due to the weakness of her heart, 'cut a big piece of rib away to clean out the lungs, and she can use only one lung to breathe with now'.[54] As she hovered close to death, James's emotional condition was equally precarious. Ralph, who could speak some German, hastened Carrington to Vienna, leaving her there almost immediately after their arrival; she arrived only two days after receiving the frightening report, leaving without time to pack sufficient clothing or any art supplies for her to pass the long hours of waiting for news.

She found James in a nursing home, and her arrival comforted him enormously. Taking charge after Ralph returned home, she cooked special meals on a small burner in her room to compensate for the Viennese cuisine which both he and Carrington loathed: 'Life here is just as expensive as England, & the food is horrible. Everything has an overcoat of batter, the meat often wears two waistcoats, & two mackintoshes to conceal its identity. The very cakes wear masks. The butter is ashey pale and tasteless. I had chicken last night that tasted of fried mongoose ...'[55] She was not allowed to see Alix, whose temperature rose whenever Carrington's name was mentioned, so she passed her time by taking German lessons, visiting with Freud's daughter Anna (who brought Alix a hard-to-get pint of milk each day), and visiting galleries. She also fiendishly sent Clive Bell a letter purporting to be from Freud, knowing this time that its real author would be obvious. Despite James's and the doctors' desire to keep her there, Alix's doctors finally realised that there was little chance of Carrington's seeing her for quite a while. The patient was progressing, albeit very slowly, and so Carrington returned home 'terribly miserable at never seeing her' about 10 March 1922. Ralph met her at Victoria Station.[56]

In London, before returning to Tidmarsh, Carrington saw Valentine again, but the meeting proved disappointing. 'I wanted our meeting to be different', she wrote wearily to Gerald. 'I suppose that means I am a romantic. I wanted her to come here, to be alone with her. Instead I was too tired, & feeling dreadfully ill with the Fiend.' Despite Alix's recovery, Carrington was depressed and unable to 'throw it off'.[57]

In spite of this disappointment, Carrington decided that their next holiday should not be spent at Yegen, as originally planned, but with the Dobrees at Larrau. She asked Gerald to join them there, arguing,

> ... we are worse off than ever. Lytton has had to pay for the Vienna trip & many other expenses so we couldn't hope for help from him. It will be cheaper to send you £20 than to spend money on going to Yegen. [...] I *do* mind, Gerald & you will also, I know. But if you don't accept our gift and come to Larrau, it will mean we shall n't meet at all.[58]

When Gerald objected, Carrington lamented her inability finally to find happiness with anyone.

> As you say everything proves this to be a senseless & idiotic world. I have loved Lytton for 6 years. He might have had my love for the rest of my life if he wanted it. He might have made me his boot-black, or taken me to Siberia, and I would have given up every friend I had to be with him ... and now its all been melted down, smothered with pillow after pillow of despair, and finally put away in an envelope the day I married R. – and R. can make me care for him in every way except the way he wants me. And we who perhaps only want a month together on the mountains of Yegen & get thoroughly tired of each other have hardly been alone 6 hours ...
>
> ... I only want to be very happy with you, & have as few regrets as possible. I have a feeling we might achieve this at Larrau. Valentine's diplomacy will count for much.[59]

Carrington and Gerald, in their naivety, made a serious error in placing their trust in Valentine. She and Ralph planned to visit the towns of Poitiers, Périgueux, and others along the way, and she would carry along her painting equipment. They left on 30 March, Gerald on 5 April. He joined them in France five days later.

The excitement was short-lived. Ralph, who had not known Valentine well beforehand, now discovered that he 'had taken a violent dislike to [her] which he made no attempt to conceal'.[60] In fact, the feeling appeared to be quite mutual and Ralph and Valentine, both hot-tempered people, quarrelled constantly. Ralph had to make the best of a bad situation while Carrington painted Brenan's portrait in Valentine's attic, and went for short walks among the lilacs and daffodils. In the evenings Bonamy droned on from his Elizabethan book, and Valentine's father, Sir Roger, a retired general who insisted they dress for dinner, told long stories about his days in Kashmir. Ralph was thoroughly exasperated with all of his hosts and his trip, so when Valentine planned a day trip by car with Carrington and Brenan to Pau on 15 April, he announced his preference to remain at Larrau and await their return. As luck, good or ill, would have it, the car broke down for lack of oil and the travellers were forced to spend the night in a hotel. This was the would-be lovers' chance. They ordered dinner sent to their separate rooms and that evening Carrington, whose room was below Gerald's, called out 'Cuckoo!' to signal him to join her.

Up in his room, Gerald agonised. Wanting more than anything to make love to her, he feared that impotence would overcome him, causing not only sexual failure but embarrassment. He spent the night awake and miserable, and early the next morning crept down to her room to explain himself. Sitting unhappily on the edge of Carrington's bed, he found her completely understanding and sympathetic. His relief was short-lived, however, for a few moments later Valentine walked in on them unexpectedly. Certain that she had caught them at the end of a night of love, she turned around and left immediately.

When they returned to Larrau, the situation took an even more bizarre twist. Valentine was sure she had information about Carrington and Gerald – just as she had had information about Ralph and his lovers. Ralph was exasperated after his night with Bonamy and Sir Roger. And to cap it all, it began to snow. There was tension and emotional electricity in the air and it finally ignited: Valentine and Ralph, fell suddenly, passionately, and inexplicably in love.

Everyone left soon after. Unknown to Carrington, Valentine was following them back to England. By the time everyone had returned to their respective homes two weeks later, it was obvious that Ralph and Valentine were having an affair.

CHAPTER THIRTEEN

PICKING UP THE PIECES

For nearly two months, things nevertheless went smoothly. Ralph's involvement with Valentine was not his first dalliance, but Carrington's acceptance of it seemed to mark the end of their marriage of less than two years as a sexual and social convention. She now felt free to write to Gerald, seeing herself as a Fanny Brawne to his Keats, and their own affair began at this time. While feeling some guilt over their sexual union – she was, after all, still married – she felt little acrimony (but a certain small amount of jealousy) when Ralph would bring Valentine to Tidmarsh or go off with her to London. Her greatest concern was that the structure of their life at the Mill House be preserved, even though the relations and sleeping arrangements of its occupants might change. The only news that saddened her that spring concerned Alix, who required a second operation and the removal of a rib. Carrington worried more about the lasting effects of this surgery than its immediate difficulties, for '[s]he will always be crooked. That is awful. For she was so superb, & straight, & moved so erectly.'[61]

Although she enjoyed her time with Gerald (who spent the last two weeks of May with her at Tidmarsh while Ralph was off with Valentine), and endless numbers of lengthy letters passed between them, she did not want their fondness for each other to threaten the stability of the Tidmarsh ménage. Accordingly, she warned Gerald not to 'expect anything from me. I can't give you anything worth much, except my friendship. Don't let us spoil the pleasure we get from being friends by having complications & too many secrets from Ralph.'[62] Although marrying Ralph might have been a mistake, in a way it had cemented the union of three lives. Lytton remained supremely important to her, and Ralph had managed to fit into their lives in a comfortable and important way. Should Ralph depart, Carrington feared the whole emotional structure would collapse.

There was reason for her fear, and this threat soon became horribly real. On 8 June 1922 Gerald, who was then in London, received the following telegram: 'Wire or telephone me 1917 Club 4 Gerrard Street must see you urgent. DC.'[63] He received another telegram from Ralph, also demanding an interview. An explosion, the first of many, had occurred. Apparently Valentine, unsure of her position with Ralph, but convinced of her sexual superiority to Carrington, had told him that his wife was having an affair with his best friend; that everyone knew of it but him; that it had begun at Pau; that the trip to France had been the result of a plot. Ralph, furious, grabbed a bottle of whisky and drove off to confront Carrington immediately. She denied the existence of a plot, confessed to her affection for Gerald, but denied that they were having an affair. She reasoned to herself that her affair had begun after Ralph's own infidelity with Valentine, and (as she had by now learned) that this was not his first. Nevertheless, she knew that he would consider that no excuse for her own conduct and decided that it was safer to keep her subsequent behaviour with Gerald a secret.

Carrington begged Gerald not to give her away and when, the next day, he met Ralph at Hogarth House in London for a similar grilling, he endeavoured to be as honest as possible without compromising her. In *Personal Record* he recalled that,

> ... I told him the whole story of my love for Carrington down to my last visit to Tidmarsh. He began to press me on certain physical details – had I put my hand down the front of her dress and so forth? I could see that they were of immense importance to him. If I had told him that I had, I felt that he would have been overcome with loathing for her and would almost certainly have refused to go back to her. But, keeping my mind firmly on what had happened to us at Watendlath and [Larrau], I could assure him truthfully that I had done nothing of the sort, and he appeared to believe me. Luckily for me he asked no questions about our recent relations at Tidmarsh, since in that case I should have had to lie to him. Then the story of the supposed plot with [Valentine] came up. Every ten minutes he left the room and went upstairs to consult with her about what I had said. That, at least, was what he told me, though I have since gathered that it was a hoax and that she was not there. At the end he said that he would have to consider what he would do and whether he would return to live with Carrington or not.[64]

Gerald's love for Carrington led him to do whatever he could to help her preserve the life that was so important to her. He knew, despite her protests, that his love for her was greater than hers for him, and that it was based on absence and correspondence rather than presence and physical affection. 'What else could I do?' he asked rhetorically in his memoirs. 'I had nothing to offer her that could possibly make up for the loss of her present civilised mode of life. We might be "in love" with one another, but in her deeply rooted situation at Tidmarsh such love was not enough. Lytton came for her before everyone.'[65]

That 'black day', as Carrington later called it, was the beginning of months of heartbreak and nightmare. Forbidden by Ralph to write to Gerald, her fate lay in the hands of an unfaithful husband and the undeniable and unquestioned existence of a double standard. Ralph continued to see Valentine quite openly, and Carrington's greatest fear was that Valentine would poison him against Tidmarsh and its 'civilised mode of life'. Her once admired friend now became a source of pain and in one of her last letters to Brenan before Ralph forbade her to write again, she said that 'Gertler once said that V. did everything she touched with a touch of genius. I agree. This is altogether so masterly.'[66] As far as Gerald was concerned, 'the famous plot' consisted of nothing more than his 'thought that if Valentine and R went about together, we should sometimes be alone'.[67] Since they had not yet slept together at that time, he apparently had expected nothing more than the kissing episodes of their earlier meetings.

Both Carrington and Gerald felt that they had lost not one, but two friends in the loss of Ralph and the other. The issue was far more complicated than a straightforward case of adultery, for it involved three complex personalities. Ralph made no effort to deny or excuse his own affairs, but he did not consider that the main point. At the heart of the problem, for him, was Carrington's character: he abhorred lies and secrecy, while she constructed much of her life around them. That deception itself was not her ultimate aim did not matter to him, and the simple fact of deceit was enough for him to condemn her. He was unremitting in his search for the truth in the matter, yet he would not believe her since he knew she had kept the liaison secret thus far. At the same time that he probably finally realised that an affair had not taken place when Valentine claimed, he treated them as though it had. Once he established the basic facts, he subjected Carrington to two kinds of silence. He only spoke to her when necessary and would not allow her to write to or receive letters from Gerald. Valentine, already his lover, now also became his ally and reinforced his anger against his wife and friend, and he felt free to see her in London, go on trips with her, or even bring her to stay at Tidmarsh, whenever he liked.

Gerald was frustrated by his enforced absence and his inability to communicate with Carrington or Ralph. Lytton, caught in the middle of his dearest friends' difficulty, was equally miserable. And Carrington never *really* felt she had done anything wrong, since her original attachment had been romantic – a meeting of kindred spirits – rather than sexual. And it was not until Ralph's infidelities became obvious through his latest liaison with Valentine that she began to sleep with Gerald, probably feeling that he was the only one apart from Lytton who understood her.

But it was Lytton himself who was Carrington's greatest concern. She spent her days crying and praying that somehow the pieces could be picked up before their life together was irremediably broken, and in this she too had many allies. Lytton himself was a great source of comfort, even after he discovered that she had lied about her later sexual relationship with Brenan. In the first days of the breach, he offered to go in her place when Gerald asked her to see him in London. Although Carrington admitted that Lytton had 'lost confidence' in her, he was full of compassion for both parties, and tried to do everything in his power to reconcile them.[68]

Like Carrington, Lytton feared that the Tidmarsh ménage might be ruined by these events, and he shared her feelings about Valentine. 'I have talked it over often with Lytton', Carrington wrote in an unposted letter to Brenan. 'He agrees that with her temperment [*sic*] its impossible for her to make R happy, or be in our lives. If they had really loved each other, & gone off after that June episode then I would accept the situation, but they didn't, so its different. And now R admits that he is no longer in love with her, merely fond of her.'[69] Lytton had arranged to go off to Paris and Italy with his friend Sebastian Sprott just before the chaos hit Tidmarsh. Reluctant to leave them alone in their highly-charged state, he wisely arranged for Barbara Bagenal to stay there in his absence. Finally, exhausted both physically and emotionally by the turmoil, he left in the third week of June.

There was some reason for Lytton's and Carrington's concern. Even if the fact that Ralph preferred to remain at Tidmarsh seemed comforting, he returned from each visit to Valentine 'cynical about Tidmarsh, suspicious & cynical about me, & even about Lytton. When he is left alone he is as we used [to] know him before all this happened,' she told Gerald.

> Its only when he gets with her, & she writes to him everyday, that Tidmarsh seems rather dull, & Lytton & me 'cold fishes' to use her favourite expression. ... As I am not an adventuress & don't want a succession of lovers, & I *do* want this particular life here with Lytton & Ralph, no one can force me to accept Valentine's grant of 'Freedom'. I don't want Ralph to be my 'tame cow'. And I don't want intrigues with you. You know we cared for each other in a fashion not common to everyone, and one great point of our relation was it was not 'possessive'.[70]

Carrington's other allies were Alix, who was still in Europe, and Virginia. To Alix she wrote a far more biased explanation of the problem.

At Watendlath perhaps you observed Gerald Brenan conceived a passion for me. It had started before Watendlath really. However we both knew it was hopeless because (a) I wasn't in love with him and (b) because R would be in a state if we went to bed together. So nothing happened except embrasades. Then he went off to Spain and it all faded away ... Lytton says R's complex about my virtue is almost insane. It has made him dreadfully wretched and reduced him to a man of nerves. You, of course, will be cynical and say 'why do I put up with it?'. Well, I suppose its because I care a great deal more for living with Lytton and R and Tidmarsh, than I do for occasional affaires and Gerald's friendship, and I really am very fond of R ... R now says he can't face living with me at moments because I am such a fraud etc. Lytton thinks it will be alright in time ... but that I mustn't if I am going to live with R have any more affaires. As they were not even affaires, romances I suppose is the only word for this one and as I have had no others, it isn't much of a sacrifice to give up this imaginary life of rouee. I am now feeling as you'll see rather grim – I mean now to paint and become very serious. So perhaps the end of this rather wretched business will be I'll paint and be some good as an artist.[71]

One of the most complicating factors in the whole situation was Ralph's problem with the Hogarth Press. His already strained relations with the Woolfs had no doubt contributed to his marital difficulties, and now the situation was deteriorating. While Carrington literally adored the Woolfs and found them 'charming, good people' who were 'slightly worn with poor R's outpourings and Leonard insists it should not be mentioned again till July 23rd',[72] she understood the strain Ralph faced in working under demanding people and not being in control of his life. She also knew that Virginia and Leonard could be very trying to work under; they were 'perfect people to know as friends, but rather difficult as overseers, & business people'. After examining possibilities for improvement, he and Carrington thought that working on his own either by starting his own press or a bookbinding business might do. In the meantime, however, everyone was miserable: Carrington, to whom Ralph rarely spoke, and then usually in anger; Ralph, who felt betrayed at home and badgered at work; Lytton, who remained nearly helpless while those he loved battled; and the Woolfs, who felt their press threatened by a belligerent employee. For Carrington herself Virginia and Leonard felt great sympathy. 'Please excuse illiteracy,' Virginia wrote to her on 8 November, 'I have had to scribble all day to finish an article and this leaves one very much out of language. Not, however, out of affection, which is always very strong for Carringtonia; so you must come and see me, and Leonard joins in this.'[73]

The Woolfs' worry over the Press was mingled with their concern for Carrington. Virginia felt partly responsible for their marriage, since she and Leonard had encouraged Ralph to issue his ultimatum, and was miserable for Carrington's sake. She found Ralph's position untenable, and his double standard ludicrous. She tried not to let her personal feelings interfere with her professional interests, but it was clear that the situation only got worse as the months passed and that it was only a matter of time before a final break would take place. When the battle-weary Partridges took a motor trip in September and stopped to see Virginia and Leonard in Sussex for one night, Virginia noted that Carrington was 'rather bitter against the institution of marriage still; but she is going to paint it down'.[74] Ralph stopped seeing Valentine temporarily, partly because he had grown tired of her and partly because the previously patient Bonamy demanded her return to France. Carrington had not seen or written to Gerald since early June, and their 'affair' had been limited to his May visit to Tidmarsh. There is some indication that she and Ralph were trying to pull their marriage back together, but despite Ralph's surprising suggestion that Carrington have a baby to improve their marriage – an idea which seemed the more unreasonable since he knew of her almost pathological antipathy to childbirth and child-rearing, and their own lack of a sexual relationship – it was clear that his marriage and his job were both doomed.

Although their life moved along somewhat more smoothly by early autumn, Carrington complained to Lytton that Ralph's feelings 'change very rapidly – and partly because of my position, & partly because I dislike these scenes, I know & ask very little of his present feelings now, & of what has happened since [Valentine – who had left for a few weeks] came back. But I do know a great deal of his *past* feelings, & her conduct. So my moments of alarm aren't quite groundless.'[75] She sat humbly at Tidmarsh, working on pictures she had sketched while in Austria, and thankful for Lytton's continued support and intercession on her behalf.

By October, Gerald and Ralph began to write to each other again. Gerald tried to explain himself and his feelings for Carrington, but Ralph was exasperated by the whole matter.

My mind is perfectly restored to its balance. What are your feelings for me, what for D.C., what value are you prepared to give your own judgement of your own feelings, what are your aims with me, with D.C., how certain are you of your aims? These are a few of the pertinent questions that are a great deal more to the point than the mere lapse of time! The only reason for time to elapse before something is done between us is because you or D.C. require the lapse of time to settle your own minds. I am not going to alter from my present attitude unless for something a good deal more sensible than the fact that I'm 28 instead of 27. It is too insulting that my suspicions must be lulled. I have renounced my suspicions, but I retain my judgement. I should like to know why you and D.C. are determined to be unhappy indefinitely; it strikes me as absurd – unless your feelings on both sides are dimmer than you care to admit. I confess I lose patience.[76]

Carrington, still forbidden to write to Gerald, took solace in painting and in the writing of a long, but unposted, journal letter to him which chronicled the events and feelings of those bleak months.

In December, Carrington received a respite from her misery when she went to Normandy to visit Phillis de Janzé, whose wedding she had attended earlier that year. There she was pampered by servants who brought hot chocolate to her in a lovely country bedroom, was instructed about farming by Phillis's young husband who was running their large estate very successfully, and learned to ride. Unwinding at last, she admired her friend's 'charming character of Moll Flanders ... We have such fun together we laugh all day over absurd bawdy jokes, I feel so young again. We have known each other since we were 17 at the Slade. Ten years ago? Who will tell? I would not have missed this adventure for anything.'[77] She returned rested, and excited about the possibilities for Christmas. One of her most prized possessions was a toy theatre, for which Lytton had promised to write a play, and Maynard Keynes was to bring his new love, the tiny Russian ballerina Lydia Lopokova who excited so much Bloomsbury gossip, to stay at Tidmarsh with him.

Ralph met Carrington at Victoria Station, and the two talked for hours 'until we became tired with talking'.[78] Before returning to Pangbourne, they engaged in a round of social activities: visits to Ralph's mother in Francis Street; a lecture by Roger Fry 'tracing the development of design, "significant form" in painting'; a party at Duncan Grant's studio, where 'earnest Cambridge men twisted & turned on their toes, & shrieked in high nasal voices, Vanessa drooped like a flower with a too heavy head over some coffee boiling on a stove. Duncan moved about with sprightly steps with trays of biscuits, & beer in glasses.'[79]

The return to Tidmarsh was peaceful. Ralph had some holiday time, and Carrington, inspired by Fry's lecture, wanted to paint him. 'Suddenly reviewing my last year's work it seems disgracefully amateurish & "little". So I shall now start this Christmas after they have all gone a composition of a[n] interior scene in this kitchen. Only I shall paint it *very* big. I do not want to tackle anything too difficult or I know I shall then despair & give up the composition before it is finished.'[80] Her characteristic worry about her painting did not prevent her from embarking on a new period of sustained work. The prohibition on writing to Gerald was at long last lifted and although their cat had died ('Dead as a Ducat'), a new peace seemed to descend on troubled Tidmarsh.

Just before Christmas, the split with the Hogarth Press, so long anticipated, at last took place. When it came, 'by whom I can't say, but not consciously or deliberately by me', Ralph informed Gerald, it was almost an anticlimax.[81] Virginia promised Carrington that 'all friendships remain intact'; (thanking her for her Christmas gift, she also said, 'I don't know which was nicer – your letter, or your sweets – both completely unlike anything else in the habitable globe')[82] and for the time being all was well. However she never fully forgave Ralph for his treatment of Carrington.

The Christmas season brought only a temporary relief from their low spirits, however. Even though things were moving along more peacefully – aided in great part by Valentine's split with Ralph and subsequent return to Bonamy and Larrau – there were new difficulties to face. In January 1923, Katherine Mansfield died of tuberculosis in France. Carrington, who had not seen her since they had shared the house on Gower Street, described her to Gerald as 'a great life-enhancer. Her writing was the least interesting part of her ... Even Lytton was impressed by her. She was so witty, & had so much courage. She lived every sort of life. She knew every sort of person. It was queer that she wrote so dully. For she was the reverse of that when one talked to her. I always think she was doomed through her connection with Murry [her husband, J. Middleton Murry]. I think he ate her soul out of her.'[83] She later added that she was 'very much a female of the underworld, with the language of a fishwife in Wapping. Murry's circle in Hampstead is now making her into a mystical Keats.'[84]

Another death, that of Ralph's father in August, was to have a greater effect upon them. Their financial difficulties seemed endless, and Carrington hoped, rather morbidly, that he would die and leave them some money. She did not apologise for these feelings, for she felt that the Partridges' treatment of her merited nothing better; in her long journal letter earlier that year she told Gerald that 'the Partridge family are making overtures to Ralph now, & actually invited us both to Devonshire. But we could not face it. I would lick their boots once a month if they would give R. £100 a year, but he says he is certain they won't. Really it makes one's blood boil that R's parents, & yours, should be such shits and such rich shits.'[85] Both Ralph's and Gerald's parents strongly disapproved of their sons' choices in life: they were too Bohemian, too unprofessional, and too insecure, they felt. Nevertheless, at the beginning of 1923 an inheritance seemed the only solution to their money problems. In August, however, this hope was disappointed.

> ... at the most we shall gain £60 by old Perdrix's death. Mrs Partridge will have about £4,000 a year. Dorothy £400 of her own, another married sister about £300 plus her husband's money. & Ralph will have his own past earnings etc. about £80 a year, & 4 insurances which come to fruit when he is a pot bellied bald headed old gentleman of 54!! (and possibly the £60 solid cash.) Have you any comment to make on that!
>
> 'Of course dear if you had children, then naturally we would give you an allowance, Rex's father was of course terribly disappointed at having no grandchildren etc. etc. ... and of course even if you do have children these insurances in 1954 will be of the greatest assistance ...' Secretly I think his mother hopes to force him into a respectable business[man] through sheer poverty ... Ralph has the character of Saint Francis, & simply refuses to squabble with his mother. I wish some malignant disease only to be contracted by middle aged – middle class parents would sweep through England ... and swallow them all up. I would only allow one exception to be made and that couple to be preserved in the B[ritish] M[useum]. [I]n a special gallery.[86]

Their support, both financially and emotionally, continued to be Lytton. It was to him that Carrington bared her heart, and looked for guidance; that had not changed in the six years of their life together. When he was at Tidmarsh they went for walks every afternoon before tea, and talked and read before the fire every evening. To Gerald she wrote, '[y]ou can't think how fascinating my country life is with Lytton. Every afternoon he gives me a discourse on what he has been reading.' That life showed no signs of diminishing in its fascination.[87]

What did happen, and they hardly seemed aware of it, was that Tidmarsh itself began to lose its appeal. Carrington confessed in October that 'I've grown bored with these damp meadows, & the Ibsen-esque drip of the rain, & the night mist from the fjord.'[88] Their beloved home had become tainted by their difficulties. Consciously or not, they began to spend more and more time away, either on holidays or working in London.

On one such trip in early February Annie, who had never been to that metropolis, was treated to a day on the town by Carrington. It rained all day long, but they managed to take in Madame Tussaud's (where Annie 'examined every wax work with great care'), lunch,

Covent Garden where they saw the market and a show ('An American Revue' in which Lydia Lopokova was dancing), St Paul's, the Houses of Parliament, and a walk on the Thames. By six o'clock Annie was overwhelmed and, rushing out of a restaurant, was sick in the street. The next day, however, she was well and regretted that they had not seen more.[89]

As much as Carrington admired London, she loved her country life even more; '[d]irectly I am alone in the house, I send Annie away before lunch, & sit on the floor eating my meals off a chair. It is only Lytton & Ralph's standards that keep me from sinking into a cottage slut.'[90] Ralph still spent much of his time in London, at first working off the three months' notice the Woolfs had given him and training the young woman who was to replace him. With this woman, Marjorie Joad, he became amorously involved for a short time. He had decided some time before not to start a rival press, and when his work with the Woolfs ended, he began to train himself in bookbinding by visiting places where this was done, sometimes in the company of Noel Carrington who had been transferred back to England from India by the Oxford University Press.

Soon afterwards he began to bind books on his own at Tidmarsh, but his social life revolved to a large extent around the people he knew in London: David Garnett and Frankie Birrell, who owned a bookshop which was a favourite with Bloomsbury, were at the centre of this other life. 'I keep seeing new people, a younger generation than Bloomsbury,' he told Gerald.

> There is a Marjorie Joad, who has taken up my duties at Hogarth; Frances Marshall, who sits in Birrell and Garnett's shop; various Cambridge young men with good looks and posts at the *Nation*; rising talent, dancers and party-goers; the 1917 Club, new faces, with a hope of new minds.[91]

It was within this new life that he would eventually find his happiness. Carrington was pleased, although sorry that he spent so much time away now that they were getting along better, but did not mind that he 'has at least four intrigues on foot with various lovely creatures in London'.[92] She was amused to discover that Valentine's real name was Gladys.

That winter Lytton, Carrington, and Ralph planned a trip to northern Africa to coincide with Ralph's 'liberty from Woolfdom',[93] hoping to leave in the middle of March 1923 and stop in France, meet Alix and James in Tunis, and return home via southern Italy. They did not manage to leave until a week later than they expected, and the trip was punctuated by illnesses: Carrington as usual was seasick on the crossing, then developed another illness a few weeks later, suffering from fever, chest pains and vomiting. Alix caught bronchitis halfway between Tunis and Constantine. On 10 May, Lytton nearly fainted on a train in Sicily when a tram conductor smashed a beggar boy's face against the tram, and was sick in bed for a week after they left Palermo. Ralph, who had also been seasick on the crossing, had a nosebleed on an African train. In Sicily, Carrington suffered the indignity of having an Italian man shove 'his hand up my private parts' as she was mounting a mule.[94] Despite the company of friends and relatives – they were joined at various points by Marjorie Strachey and Noel Carrington, as well as Alix and James – the trip was often a rather dismal one. Never yet had they been exposed to the poverty and smells that they encountered this time, even though they were rewarded by a final, lovely week in Italy before Lytton's poor health forced their early return.

Although Tidmarsh seemed an oasis of sanity and peace upon their return, by May they were evidently considering a more permanent move. 'I am contemplating buying a studio, & putting it up in the garden', Carrington wrote Gerald on 31 May 1923. 'I find the room space is too cramped. But perhaps we shall leave Tidmarsh next year then it won't be worth while. I want to find a house on the Lambourne Downs. I think its a mistake to become sentimental over any place & I can't quite get over my hatred for this garden & the dull green fields since our return from Rome.'[95] She settled for moving her studio into the attic, where she hoped the 'elevated change will have a great effect on my work'.[96] This suited her for the time being.

That summer they planned yet another trip, this time to France. This time they wanted to take their car; that way Carrington could be dropped off at an inn with Barbara to paint, and Lytton would spend two weeks 'with some French people in an old monastery',[97] where he had been invited to join a group of writers and intellectuals, including the novelist André Gide. Leaving England on 2 August, they picked up their car in Dieppe and motored to Rouen, accompanied by Lytton's friend Sebastian Sprott, who charmed Carrington despite his taste in clothing and art. 'I somehow feel he hasn't a very inventive brain,' she wrote to Gerald from France. 'But he [is] very interesting because he has read so much ... But perhaps too much of a bugger for your taste. I should think he is 28. His aesthetic taste is what really grieves me. I don't mind the absence of it completely. But two rather vulgar topaz, & emerald rings, a large black sombrero, an orange tie, & violet socks are really almost too much to sit beside, without protest ... and he thinks it all out very carefully.'[98]

This trip, too, was to have its disasters. Barbara, barely recovered from a serious bout of scarlet fever which caused much of her hair to fall out, became bedridden with rheumatism, and Carrington was extremely careful to shield her from rain and draughts. While in France, Ralph's father died and he had to leave, after depositing the two women at a country inn. Carrington painted indoors every morning, lunched at the 'commercial table' downstairs, then went off to paint outdoors every afternoon. Barbara was only able to leave her bed for dinner, but Carrington managed to do three paintings, and forced herself to wander into shops and converse in French with the shopgirls.

The final trip for 1923 was to be the most important, for it would mark the end of a difficult period of their lives. While in France, they began to discuss the possibility of another visit to Gerald in Yegen. Lytton was strongly opposed to this visit, proposing instead that Ralph go alone, and Carrington go out the following year when more time had passed. His great concern was for Gerald, whom he felt might find his feelings for Carrington stronger than ever. Ralph, according to Carrington, was untroubled about the reunion.

> You must not think Ralph is alarmed at us meeting. He thinks *nothing* of it. He is only concerned about the money etc & his work. *Lytton* is concerned chiefly from affection for R and me, & a certain wisdom which makes him treat the feelings of *all* people very considerately. This earnestness affected me by the end of our conversation. And I suddenly saw I might be acting very selfishly towards you by going to Spain. If the result was unhappiness for us both afterwards. Could you tell me?[99]

Ralph's seeming lack of concern was caused by the fact that he was 'carrying on some intrigue in London at the moment'.[100]

Gerald's situation in Spain was quite different. Although sometimes joined for months by friends – his friend John Hope-Johnstone was there for some time, as was Augustus John's son Robin – his was basically a lonely life spent reading and writing. His love for Carrington had not diminished with absence, but he was subdued by the events of the previous fifteen months.

Nonetheless, Lytton was won over and 'a decent lengthened month' was planned in Spain for Carrington and Ralph.[101] Having come full circle in their relationship, they were about to face enormous and permanent changes which included new loves and a new home.

CHAPTER FOURTEEN

HAM SPRAY: 1924

'Amigo', Carrington wrote to Gerald on 20 November 1923, 'a despair has fallen over me. Not a reason that will draw forth sympathy from you.

I am in love with a house.'[102]

The Tidmarsh trio had begun house-hunting in October, and on the 23rd of that month had seen the place that caused Carrington to be 'in a fever of excitement'.

> It is called Ham Spray House. That's a good title to begin with. It is within a mile of the village of Ham & the village of Inkpen and a stone's throw (if one threw well) from the most marvellous downs in the WHOLE WORLD – Tibet excluded – Inkpen Beacon. It is four miles from Hungerford. We saw a ram shackle lodge, a long avenue of limes but all wuthering in appearance, bleak, & the road a grass track. Barns in decay, then the back of a rather forbidding farm house. We walked to the front of it & saw to our amazement in the blazing sun a perfect English country house. But with a view onto downs before it that took our breaths away ... Inside the house was properly built, simple & good proportions. It faced south so one would never shiver with the damp & cold as one does here. And there were eight bed rooms, & numerous queer lofts, & outhouses, also a small cottage separate from the house. The price is prohibitive I fear, but Ralph is negociating with the agents ... to think Mrs Partridge has £40,000 ... as Lytton says, it's a direct incentive to poison, or murder.[103]

This house represented more than a more comfortable home; it represented the possibility of a new beginning for the Tidmarsh ménage, and an end to the terrible and divisive difficulties of 1923.

It seemed particularly prophetic that they discovered their dream house shortly before leaving for Spain. Now that Lytton's objections had been overcome, Carrington was both excited and cautious about the impending visit. She did not want to lose, either through actions or words, the good will that she had so carefully nourished in the last miserable months. When Carrington and Ralph left for Spain on 17 December, Lytton continued the negotiations from Tidmarsh. Despite the offers and obvious interest, the owners were difficult to bargain with and Carrington was horrified to see another advertisement for Ham Spray in *The Times* as they left from Paddington station.

The common goal of the house drew the three closer together, and Carrington and Ralph set off in good spirits for Paris, from which they would travel south. That 'Ralph is such a dear, & we are both very happy' was due in some part to a redefinition of their relationship.[104] Now that Valentine was out of the picture and Gerald back in it as their mutual friend, they had entered a friendly state of not being married while being married. Their futures remained linked while their marital commitments did not. Ham Spray would reaffirm their fondness for each other and their agreement to continue their triangular friendship with Lytton.

The reason for Ralph's 'highest spirits' was Frances Marshall, and Carrington welcomed the relief that his new emotional attachment brought. 'Ralph is in love with a black haired beauty, & thinks life perfect', she wrote Gerald before they left. '... he is in love with a beautiful Princess that lives in Birrell & Garnett's bookshop. So you need not fear there will be any glooms!'[105] Ralph had met her in London while he was still employed by the Hogarth Press, and had been impressed by her intelligence as well as looks. She worked, rather than 'lived' at the bookshop, and therefore had encountered him on his numerous professional and personal visits there.

Later, as he studied bookbinding at the Polytechnic in preparation for his own bookbinding venture at Tidmarsh, they met 'several times a week. We lunched, dined and danced together, and whenever it was impossible to meet I got a letter', Frances recalled. 'That was the beginning of a long, high-powered and concentrated courtship such as I had never been subjected to before.' David Garnett, married to Frances' sister Ray, was aware of Ralph's recent philandering and issued 'a brotherly warning ... which amused but did not offend me. It amounted to the fact that Ralph had a roving eye, and wasn't a man to be trusted.'[106] She trusted her instincts instead and continued to see him, but not to sleep with him.

This new relationship pleased rather than upset Carrington and Lytton. While they found Frances young and inexperienced – she was twenty-three to Carrington's thirty – she clearly had none of Valentine's hostility toward the other inhabitants of Tidmarsh. In fact, she was yet to be convinced that Ralph was the man for her; she had been quite popular in her university years at Newnham

College, Cambridge (where women could attend, but at that time still were not given a formal degree), and another young man was still very much in the picture. And not to be taken lightly was the fact that Ralph, however attractive and seemingly free, was still married and still lived with his wife. These were lines which were difficult for a properly brought up young woman to cross, and their relationship remained a chaste and almost traditional courtship.

Nevertheless, before Carrington and Ralph left for Spain, she accompanied him to Tidmarsh for a weekend. There she 'was alarmed by Lytton, charmed by Carrington, amazed that we ate stewed plums and milk pudding at every meal (the latter was apparently a necessity to all Stracheys)'.[17] She began to melt, and the others seemed prepared to accept her, at least provisionally. They were to meet again in Paris, on the Partridges' return trip from Yegen.

Although Ralph was now involved with someone else, Carrington approached Yegen and Gerald with caution. He met them at Posada de los Pescadores, Orgíva, on 22 December, and the next day they began the arduous trek to his mountain retreat. 'Left for Harza de Lino by motor bus', Gerald recorded in his diary. 'Walked along Contraviesa to Venta Cuatro Camiones. Tea. Met muleteer. By moonlight to Yegen. Ralph told me of his affair[s...] D. C. rode on mule, we walked ahead. Got in at 8, & had a boiled chicken.'[108] The matter-of-factness of this account reflects what he later recalled: that '[o]n seeing Carrington I felt nothing'. On the contrary, '[a]ll my old affection for [Ralph] came surging back and he told me of the brief affairs he had had' and of his newer, more serious interest in Frances.[109]

The weather at Yegen, unlike the trip they had made there with Lytton, was perfect. It was hot enough for Carrington to sleep on the roof and to paint outdoors during the day, while Ralph and Gerald went for long walks and swam. Together the three went on wild shopping sprees, buying so much china and pottery, and so many jugs and plates, that they were not sure how to pack and return with them all at the end of their stay. (This was a project not destined to succeed. Every single dish was broken when they went through French customs on their way home.) The only bad news was in a letter from Lytton, who informed them that their offer for Ham Spray had been rejected, but that 'the owner [according to the Harrod's estate agent] has promised to let us have his definite decision before the end of the month'.[110] Lytton hoped that the bad English winter and poor state of the stock market would prevent any other offers from coming in.

Gerald spent much of his time with Ralph, with Carrington carefully keeping her distance, so it was 26 December before they saw each other alone. Complimenting her on her appearance, he was instantly rebuffed: 'You must no longer say things like that', she immediately responded. He begged her for half an hour's conversation, and having obtained Ralph's permission they set off on a short walk. They agreed that Gerald ought to approach Ralph and request 'the same friendship he has with F[rances] M[arshall], liberty to go about together and kiss'. Later that afternoon Gerald spoke to Ralph making 'it clear that I was no longer in love with her, but only very fond of her. He replied with great cordiality that he had no objection whatever to our going about together or kissing.'[111] A few nights later, however, Ralph felt unwell and went to bed early. Carrington and Gerald stayed up late in front of the fire, talking freely for the first time in nearly six months. The next morning Ralph was upset with them both and they realised that little had really changed except for Carrington's broken spirit.

> So the days flew by [Gerald wrote]. I went for walks with Ralph while Carrington painted. Then I went out alone with her to carry her easel and for the first time since her arrival we kissed. But her kisses were timid ones. Strongly subject as she was to guilt feelings, Ralph's conduct during the past eighteen months had got her down. Her old feeling of independence seemed to have gone forever.
> ... It was easy to see that she was as much attached to me as ever, though in a different way, as a person who had been through a great deal with her.[112]

With this realisation came unhappiness, which the weather reinforced. Rain set in, and a trip into town where they visited the cinema – with Ralph sitting between them – and dined intensified their low spirits. Carrington cried in her hotel room because of Gerald, and 'sent in R. to comfort [Gerald] because she thought me unhappy. So charming a character he has!'[113] Neither of them blamed Ralph, but their depression continued, culminating, Gerald recorded in his diary, on 8 January.

> Perpetual, heavy rain. All extremely depressed ... R. said he would leave us to return to hotel. We went to cathedral – shut – I suggested one café after another – all seemed wrong – in a rage I said, lets go back to Ralph. But I saw D. was on the verge of tears, and suddenly repenting of my bad humour, I took her to tea shop. For $1\frac{1}{2}$ hours we talked in extreme happiness. Returned at 5 to R.[114]

The next day they received a triumphant telegram from Lytton: Ham Spray was to be theirs. In a much different mood Carrington and Ralph started home via Madrid, and Gerald concluded, 'Not very unhappy. No zone of despair to cross this time.'[115] Nonetheless, when Carrington spoke of Gerald to Ralph in Madrid, he replied, 'Whatever *I* may do you know I shall always mind just as much as I did before about you, & I couldn't bear you to live with anyone, does G. know that?'[116]

They met Frances in Paris, and stayed in an hotel room which adjoined hers. Carrington wanted to return to Lytton and Tidmarsh but Frances was 'obviously rather agitated lest her people should discover'[117] that she was in Paris with a man, so Carrington had to stay on as a chaperone for her husband and his girlfriend. To make matters worse, she could hear them talking in Frances' room at night, while she waited for Ralph to return to their room.

> ... I behaved rather badly last night ... After dinner we went to a cafe, it was terribly hot, & the French all looked revolting. Their faces are made of soap, & their hair looks false. My depression grew worse & worse. R & FM grew gaier and gaier. At last I saw I was on the point of fainting, so I left the cafe, with excuses & came back to the hotel about 9 ock. I went to bed, but I couldn't sleep. Suddenly the pointlessness of these next days seemed unbearable & the lack of privacy impossible ... FM has a room adjoining our bedroom. So it is impossible to talk to R alone or even sit in our room by myself, since one can hear almost every word spoken in the next room.[118]

When Carrington announced to Ralph the next day that she wanted to return home, he told her she was selfish; after all, 'he had given two weeks' for her to see Gerald in Spain. She realised that if she left and Frances got into trouble no forgiveness would be possible, and that she certainly would be unable to spend time with Gerald in May when he was to return to England.

Once again, however, things worked out well. On 13 January a telegram arrived from Lytton announcing that he would be in Paris the next day. The clouds cleared, and Carrington reported to Gerald that Frances 'is a very delightful companion. Perhaps almost too perfect, beautiful, & unselfish. I think I would like her better if I could detect one fault!'[119] Leaving them alone in the daytime, she tested her independence by visiting the Louvre alone, although admitting that she both enjoyed and resented their happiness. 'Do you know,' she wrote ruefully, 'sometimes I dislike myself intensely. Last night I thought I could hardly bear to be inside my cow's skin.'[120] Lytton's arrival made everything all right, even though he characteristically refused to speak a word of French, leaving it to Ralph to do all his speaking and food ordering for him.

Back at Tidmarsh, they could talk of nothing but Ham Spray and lay plans for landscaping, gardening, painting and furniture. Lytton had paid £2,300 for it, the greatest purchase he had ever made, but he considered it a home for the three of them. Carrington was to learn to drive, which would enable her to reach the nearby villages quite easily. They had an optimistic projected possession date of 25 March, but were still involved in negotiations over payments and rights to certain buildings and grounds. Initially she had hoped Gerald could stay with them in the house while he was in England, but in the light of Ralph's opinion of their relationship, decided that a nearby cottage would be more suitable.

As the time for moving drew closer, she also began to worry that Ralph's happiness with Frances might pose a threat to their Tidmarsh and Ham Spray arrangements. What if Frances were really in love with Ralph? Would that mean that he would divorce Carrington? And if he did, what would Lytton do? On the positive side, she 'suspect[ed] Frances is having a good influence on Ralph. She took my side in Paris several times in disputes, which rather weakened R.' Having an ally in her arguments with Ralph made things easier, and she decided that, in the long run, she preferred that Ralph 'continued his friendship with her'.[121]

Her fears about Lytton were less easily dispelled. Always present even in the happiest of times, they began to force themselves into her dreams. Her difficulty with nightmares was with her throughout her life, and often affected her waking as well as sleeping hours. On 14 February 1924 she was awakened by a dream which proved that her link to Strachey was by now clairvoyant as well as apprehensive.

... a cart horse very young and violent approached just down a road it reared & plunged. Ralph thought we could walk past safely on the grassy side of the road. I saw by a certain look it gave us, it meant to try & kill Lytton. So I stood in front of Lytton, I was terribly frightened, the horse leapt up, & jumped over us, just touching me. Lytton crouched on the grass behind me. Then I woke up, & then slept again with more nightmares – This morning Lytton instead of being better (for yesterday he was almost well from his influenza except for a cold) was worse. He had a temperature of 101° again, & would eat nothing. He has been in bed since Sunday now.[122]

Even in her dreams Carrington was willing to sacrifice herself in order to protect him. This time, rather than her life, she sacrificed her work: she had 'a head bursting with ideas' but was unable to paint because she gave Lytton the only lamp from her cold attic studio while he was ill. While he slept, she worked hard at a landscape of Yegen which, years later, would grace the cover of the American edition of Brenan's *Personal Record*.

Up to now her landscapes had been of familiar English locations. The Andalusian countryside, however, presented new possibilities. The most noticeable contrast was in colour; where England was cool and therefore presented in blues, greens, greys, and whites, these mountains were orange, yellow, brighter blues and greens. According to Richard Shone, 'the Andalusian landscapes mark a change in mood (and rather "hotter" colour)'.[123] Like the Watendlath painting, 'Mountain Ranges from Yegen, Andalusia' shows steep and rolling 'feminine' hills. The jagged and pointed mountains receding into the background, however, like the black swans in the Tidmarsh picture are 'an imaginative introduction'. No such hills exist there, or perhaps anywhere; they resemble the backs of prehistoric animals guarding the distant blue sea from the softer hills of the foreground. The upper left corner still bears the scar of her displeasure. Another Andalusian picture, painted earlier after her visit to Yegen, is full of light. 'Hill Town in Andalusia' contrasts the curves of hills with the architectonic qualities of the white buildings carved into the hillside. Carrington's visits to Yegen, then, marked a complete change from her normal life; there, and in the pictures she painted of it, the world changed visually as well as emotionally. The weather was warmer, the colours 'hotter', and there was an appealing unreality about it which allowed her freer rein in her work, both in terms of imagination and execution.

Lytton's illness went on for several weeks, eventually developing so seriously into flu and lumbago that his sister Pippa was called in to assist. She had nursed her brother often and provided the calm efficiency which the situation required. Carrington, on the other hand, was nervous enough to make mistakes; one night, mixing his medicines 'in the dim light of a lamp', she inadvertently poured out iodine instead of his sleeping potion. As she wiped her fingers she noticed a brown stain on the towel and realised her mistake immediately: 'With great control, I did not shriek, but poured out the right mixture. But as Lytton was drinking it, I suddenly felt hysterical, & nearly burst out laughing for no reason. But it shook my faith in myself, & unnerved me considerably.'[124]

Taking a break from her constant nursing chores, Carrington went up to London in early March to attend a farewell party for D. H. and Frieda Lawrence. They were off, with Carrington's old Slade friend Brett, to begin an idealistic community in the American southwest.

Of course on examination it comes out it is New Mexico that they go to, which is a state of U.S.A. But they speak about it as 'Mexico' – 'We lead a very primitive life, we cut our own wood, & cook our own food' 'and

Lawrence makes the most beau-ti-ful bread' Frieda always comes in like a Greek chorus, the moment D. H. L. has stopt speaking. I nearly said he could come to Tidmarsh if that was all he wanted by 'Primitive' –

'And here is Carrington, not very much changed, lost a little of her "ingenue" perhaps, still going to parties, still exactly the same, except I hear you are very rich now, & live in a grand country house.'

I took the shine off his Northampton nose, & his whining 'ingenue' accent. I told him I had £130 a year which I had always had 'ah but yet married a rich husband!' He has £80 a year. 'And yer don't mind ther change, that's very fortunate.'[125]

Before returning home on Saturday, she passed through Knightsbridge and noticed a little shop called 'the Knightsbridge Kennels' which sold dogs. 'Ushering a doggie lady of 60 out of the shop was a red faced young man, with a yellow waistcoat, & neat navy blue suit, & spats', she wrote Gerald. Looking again, she realised that it was her brother Sam, and 'felt the gulf was a sea between us, so I did not stop'.[126] She was turning her back upon days long gone by and upon people she had ceased to care about. Ham Spray loomed as a prophetic and beneficent beacon.

That Carrington so easily accepted Ralph's attachment to Frances was due in part to a new relationship of her own. In March of 1923 she met someone who was to change the course of her future attachments, for better or for worse. At that time, she and Ralph and Lytton had been looking for someone to rent Tidmarsh during their excursion to North Africa. David Garnett, hearing of this, sent two American women out to Tidmarsh.

One of them was lovely. Very tall with an olive skin, dark shiny eyes like jet beads, & perfect slim figure, & short black curling hair. Her friend was my style, pink, with a round face dressed in mannish clothes, with a good natured smile. Her name was Henrietta.

Henrietta Bingham, the second woman, was the daughter of Judge Bingham, the American ambassador to the Court of St James. She was living for a time in England with her friend Mina Kirstein. She was taking courses at the London School of Economics and, unknown to Carrington, she was breaking any number of English hearts, both male and female.

Lytton took an instant dislike to Henrietta. When a letter came announcing her desire to take the house, he refused to let it to her. Instead, Carrington's mother was to move in temporarily and act as caretaker. Nevertheless, Carrington had been fascinated by her initial glimpse of Henrietta, even though the 'lovely creatures wander[ed] round the house taking about as much interest in me as if I'd been the housekeeper!'[127] Captivated, she hovered about them at

Tidmarsh, and saw Henrietta once more at a party given by Garnett just before they left for Tunisia. The rich, rather quiet foreigner with 'the face of a Giotto madonna' sang negro spirituals – the Binghams were from Kentucky – and accompanied herself on the mandolin. Carrington was hooked: 'She made such wonderful cocktails that I became completely drunk, & almost made love to her in public. To my great joy Garnett told me the other day she continually asks after me & wants me to go & see her ... Ralph cut my hair too short last week. When it has grown longer & my beauty restored I shall visit the lovely Henrietta & revive my drunken passion.'[128]

For the first time in her life, Carrington was in active pursuit of a particular lover. Men had always been attracted to her, but she had never taken on the chase herself. With an eagerness and openness that could only yield disappointment, Carrington threw herself into the courtship. Lytton's instincts were entirely against this involvement, and she was forced into subterfuge, pretending that when Henrietta accompanied the sculptor Stephen Tomlin and Alix to Tidmarsh, she had not invited her. She was 'self-conscious about [her] feelings' for the woman, and wanted no criticism, particularly if it were justified.

For her part, Henrietta apparently saw Carrington as one of many suitors. Flattered and interested, she nonetheless had a full social and romantic life and felt little compunction at breaking appointments at the last moment, even when Carrington had cooked and cleaned all day in anticipation of her visit. Henrietta failed to materialise twice in one week and while Carrington grew cynical enough to stop cooking when she was due to arrive, she recalled her own similar actions in earlier years and forgave her. Others who knew Henrietta were less forgiving. Frances later called her actions 'semi-deliberate cruelty', for Henrietta obviously enjoyed the power she held over her lovers.[129]

The matter was complicated, as all of Carrington's romantic relationships had been, by yet another triangle. Henrietta was at that time the lover of Lytton and Carrington's friend, the sculptor Stephen Tomlin, or Tommy as he was called. He and Carrington shared the same emotions and frustrations over Henrietta, but Carrington was forced to suppress hers in his company, as well as in the company of Lytton and Ralph. Even so, by mid-June Henrietta and Carrington had become lovers, meeting at least once in Knightsbridge at 'Henrietta's secret house'. Alix, herself bisexual (though she and Carrington were never sexually involved with each other), was Carrington's only confidante at first, and Carrington wrote to her freely of this new discovery about herself.

Really I confess Alix I am very much more taken with H. than I have been with anyone for a long time. I feel now regrets at being such a blasted fool in the past, to stifle so many lusts I had in my youth, for various females xx[.] But perhaps one would have only have been embittered, or battered by blows on the head from enraged virgins. Unfortunately she is living in London now with a red haired creature from America, so as she tactfully put it, 'You must wait, if you can. My passions don't last long, but at the moment...'[130]

Carrington ought to have heeded such an obvious warning, but the discovery of her own bisexuality and first real sexual passion clouded her judgement.

In this she had only to look to her beloved Lytton as an example: he was now involved with a young man named Philip Ritchie who, she suspected, 'isn't nearly so fond of Lytton as he pretends to be. Perhaps he doesn't pretend, & Lytton imagines it himself.'[131] The eldest son of Lord Ritchie of Dundee, Philip was still an Oxford undergraduate destined for a legal career when he was introduced to Lytton by a mutual friend, C.P. Sanger, at a Tidmarsh tea. Carrington, always friendly with Lytton's friends, was not impressed this time.

[Philip] is rather tedious because he talks of nothing else but of b*****y, not in the gay fantastic way Sebastian does, but very seriously. As if it was a public duty to talk about rapes, young men, tarts, & catamites every ten minuets [sic]! I suspect he must have been very pruddish [sic] in his youth, so feels it is rather exciting to have bawdy conversations, & to be 'outspoken'.[132]

But Lytton, who never formed a lasting attachment to another man – not for lack of trying, but more often because his eye often fell upon the young and the flighty – was anxious that she and Ralph like his companion.

Please, however, both of you, try to like – or at any rate not dislike – my Philip. I assure you he's a great rarity. It's true that he's not immediately attractive to look at, and that he probably has no taste in pictures; but he's intellectual (a good point); and he's sensual (also good); and he gives not the slightest value to anything but what is really valuable (very good indeed). Also when he gets tipsy...[133]

In the meantime, Ham Spray needed attention. They had hoped to move in March, but it took months to iron out the details of ownership and occupation, and even longer to make it habitable. Repairs and cosmetic improvements became a community effort, with Frances, Carrington, Ralph, and sometimes Henrietta and Tommy pitching in. 'Frances M. was very angelic, & helped me paint & do very dull things', while Henrietta turned out to be 'a wonderful painter of walls. Far better than I was, to my surprise!'[134] She was magnificent when she appeared, but disappeared almost immediately for days without writing. She turned up again on 5 July in her car with 'two large American boys' – Mina Kirstein's brothers – and threw herself into the painting once again. When she appeared she was sympathetic and a good listener to Carrington's feelings, and seemed 'to be composed of perfections & sensibilities. I feel rather a dull cow in her company by comparison.'[135] When she was gone, she seemed to vanish.

Gerald also knew of Carrington's new involvement. He was back in England for a prolonged stay, and they wrote to each other daily and met often in London. He had become good friends with both Alix and Frances, and it was unlikely that he could remain in the dark for long. Interestingly enough, he was not overwhelmingly jealous, and perhaps did not know at first of the physical nature of the relationship. Carrington, when in London, ran back and forth between the two and confessed that 'I get carried away by Kentucky princesses who after all compared to my amigo are not worth one half minuet's [sic] thought.'[136] Like an unstoppable train, a metaphor which Brenan would use a year later to describe her headlong rush towards heartache, Carrington saw the dangers but could not prevent them.

By mid-July 1924, they were ready to move into the new house. Carrington's new bedroom had been painted a clean, Mediterranean white,[137] while the other rooms blossomed in carefully chosen colours. Tidmarsh was a mass of boxes, and Carrington wrote her last letters from that house in 'our last hold on civilisation': Lytton's bedroom. In a burst of nostalgia, she proposed to write a sonnet entitled, 'Thoughts on seeing Tidmarsh Mill for the last time'.

> Dear mill whose friendly whitened face,
> Has been for long my resting place
> Today we part as lovers must
> Leaving sad memories to dirt, &
> dust . . .

Frances arrived on the 15th to help, and once things got underway the next morning, Carrington's spirits soared. 'All is beautiful! And we are growing happier', she wrote to Lytton, who had gone to

France with Pippa to preserve his health and avoid the commotion.[139] Once settled, she threw herself into staining floors, hanging pictures, and making jam, while Ralph set up his bookbinding equipment and commenced work.

Gerald, woefully neglected through Carrington's domestic and romantic affairs, began to chafe. He had allowed Carrington and Ralph, separately or together, to use his London rooms while in town if he were absent. He withdrew that privilege from Carrington (but not from Ralph, who paid back his hospitality by breaking the lock in a fit of anger and frustration one night) during the summer; she had broken an appointment once too often, and with too little remorse. His life differed so greatly from hers that he had difficulty understanding her. Alone with his books (he was trying to write a life of Saint Theresa) in a cheap and smelly London room, he lived for the days they could spend together. Despite his profession to Ralph in December that he was no longer in love with Carrington, his feelings had re-ignited in her presence.

His solitary life, broken by occasional Bloomsbury parties, gave him much more time than she had to reflect on his feelings, her feelings, and their inequality. 'You seem to have hardly any of the feelings or sensibilities of human beings', he accused her that summer. 'Do you really think that to behave like this is nothing? It is hard not to believe there is some profound malice in your behaviour towards me: you know exactly how to produce the greatest quantity of unhappiness: and then you seem altogether unconscious of it ... you have got to choose between being sufficiently fond of me & losing me.'[140]

Carrington was contrite. 'I agree with you entirely', she wrote back. 'I *am* impossible. I say this in no particular mood of depre- cation ... but the result of a week's thinking alone. The solution to all my difficulties lies up stairs in my studio. Henrietta repays my affection almost as negatively as you find I do yours.'[141]

The fundamental problem was that she meant more to him than he did to her. She cared for him very deeply, but cared even more for the life that she was rebuilding at Ham Spray. Leonard called her a 'classic female' who ran when pursued and chased when ignored, but that oversimplifies her character and ignores the fact that she never, despite Gerald's accusation, acted with malice. Even Gerald recognised what he called her 'essential goodness', and that her 'life [was] too full & too interesting. Since I have been in England the acquisition of Ham Spray has made it more so. Then I play my part badly...'[142] They made it up soon, but were on a seesaw of quarrels and reconciliations, almost exactly like those between her and Mark Gertler years before, while he remained in England. A time of peace arrived for both, as well for the enamoured Tommy, when Henrietta went off to Scotland for a month in August with her father and brothers, and when Brenan went off to the Kent seaside to act as tutor to Igor and Anastasia (Baba) Anrep, and their mother Helen.

Helen Anrep and Boris, her husband, were having difficulties, not the least of which was his insistence on having his young lover live with them. Helen had gone off to Warren's End for the summer, and there Boris joined his family at weekends. Both Gerald and Carrington found Helen admirable, and became increasingly involved in their marital difficulties the following year when Helen finally deserted her husband for Roger Fry. Boris, according to Frances, 'became furiously angry, and threatened to tar and feather Roger.'[143] This new relationship, however, was destined to last until Fry's death. The summer on the coast served several purposes: it provided a respite in the Anreps' problems, provided Brenan with an income and conversation in the evenings, broke the tension between Gerald and Carrington, and occupied the Anrep children.

At first the separation from Carrington was extremely difficult for Gerald. When she did not write, he would throw himself down upon his bed and weep. When she did he was either ecstatic or sceptical. He became more peaceful under Helen's influence and by 22 August was able to write, 'Now it gives me only pleasure to think of your love for Henrietta, whereas lately I have thought of it with a little bitterness. For if you tell me such secrets, then I see you are fond of me also.'[144] Hers was not a confiding nature, and he felt honoured by her confidences. However, Henrietta decided to stay in England another six months. Even without that additional time, Carrington's feelings had altered towards him.

They agreed, after much debate, that Carrington would join him at Warren's End for several days. She arrived on 8 September, and that first night together they made love over and over again. Brenan was thrilled, and dreamed that night 'that we were two drowned bodies drifting through green fathomless seas, clutched tightly together, and that this was the end I desire, the supreme and ultimate happiness'. The four days she spent with him, while affording him at times great happiness, also showed a side of her that he had never seen, and that apparently she rarely demonstrated. 'I had to watch on her face her growing anxiety to return to Ham Spray, I had to hear her say in her scolding censorious manner that such meetings as this would be very rare and that I must consider myself lucky to get anything.'[145]

He later attributed this unpleasant shift in personality to her attraction to Helen, now that Carrington had discovered her own lesbian tendencies. While it seems a facile excuse, he could hardly think otherwise without accepting part of the blame, or without acknowledging the tremendous emotional upheavals she had undergone during the previous year. The final blow came when he discovered a letter she had written to Helen in which she referred to him as 'that ridiculous Brenan'. He wrote her a scathing letter, which, typically, he later retracted.

Arguments arose whenever they met, and abated when they separated. She planned to meet him in London every two weeks, but had entered on a new period of intense painting which sometimes meant they could meet only every three weeks. Her fondness for him never diminished, but the intensity of their arguments increased throughout the autumn. Gerald could not see her without wanting to make love and '[f]rom the moment that she entered the room, dressing in her rather absurd and ugly London clothes – for no formal clothes became her – and carrying a bunch of garden flowers and a home-made cake or pot of jam, her whole face irradiated by her honeyed smile, I was thinking only of that and could listen to nothing she said until the matter had been decided. This was not because my physical urge was so great, but because making love had become the proof that she still loved me ... In her sexual feelings she was unpredictable.'[146]

Henrietta still loomed in the background as erratically as ever. Carrington could count on her for nothing, but found extraordinary pleasure in any mark of attention from the 'femme fatale', which erased her frustration whenever she managed to meet her. There is a poignancy in her desperate romance, which shows up in her accounts of their meetings.

H. said on the telephone she would come & see me off [from Paddington station]. So I dashed up & down the platform looking for her. No sign of her, & one minute for my train to start. All the windows blocked with beastly little school girls saying goodbye to parents. The platform crowded. I felt it was some terrible dream & that I would go mad. Suddenly in the distance I saw H. walking down the platform very slowly with that enigmatic smile on her face – I pushed the school girls from the carriage door brushed through the parents & dashed towards her. The smoothness of her cheeks again returned, & I remembered nothing but that she is more lovely to me than any other woman. We talked for one minute I leap into the train. She kissed me fondly, & the train moved away.[147]

In contrast, Brenan could offer little. Their relationship had persisted for nearly three years, with little hope of improvement. They would never marry, clearly, nor could Brenan really settle for sharing her with others. Their letters were their most important link, and they needed each other for certain kinds of emotional outlets. In fact, Carrington was happiest when they were apart.

Yet their love occupied a very special place for them, which the secrecy it had necessitated for so long had preserved. Giving nicknames to those she cared for had always been of crucial importance to Carrington. For Brenan she had invented Kunak, Amigo, and later, Sweegie, referring to herself as Doric or backwards, Cirod. The maintaining of these very private and affectionate pseudonyms proved to her their mutual tenderness and trust, despite their obvious difficulties.

But Gerald wanted more, and pressed her to give it. He denied that he wanted her to give up her painting for him, and recognised that she could never give up the security of her Ham Spray life. His worries, like hers, began to affect his dreams, and on 25 October he recorded a frighteningly prophetic nightmare in his diary: 'I dreamed of [Cirod] last night: she was very ill: Ralph had given her a child and Alix Strachey said to me "she will probably commit suicide". . . . I awoke trembling, with a feeling of pity not only for [her] but for the fragility of all human existence.'[148] Carrington had written him a similarly prophetic letter the year before: 'I often hope I shall die at forty, I could not bear the ignominy of becoming a stout boring elderly lady with a hobby of sketching in water colours.'[149]

He decided on 30 October that they should no longer write, but less than a week later received a dressing-down from an unexpected source: Ralph. Partridge 'convinced me once & for all that my behaviour had not been so considerate or so reasonable as I had imagined', and he wrote to apologise.[150] Their letters crossed; Carrington wrote back to break off everything. 'The real truth is I know I can't make you happy in the way you want, & I can't bear to be the person who makes you unhappy', she said.[151] Life was far too complicated at that time for her, and she knew that she brought him more pain than pleasure. But by December 1924 she had a heartache of her own when Henrietta dropped her unexpectedly and without explanation.*

Although she regretted that she had cared for her so unreservedly and lay awake at night because of it, she now threw herself into her work and 'family'. Now that Ralph and Frances were undeniably a couple – Frances spent most weekends at Ham Spray – her quarrels with Ralph were rare. She tried to paint her way out of her unhappiness, and slowly began to return to the peacefulness that Ham Spray had promised but that she had not had time to enjoy. 'So the months passed', Frances later said, 'with Lytton arranging his books in his library, Carrington beautifying the house with charming tiles and painted papers, Ralph cutting down trees and binding books.'[153] Carrington painted portraits of both Frances and Catharine Alexander, Noel's young girl friend from the Slade. Tranquillity had returned.

The first Christmas season at Ham Spray fulfilled all their expectations. They threw a Christmas party which was a great success, at which they performed a comic play Lytton had written. Afterwards

---

* There is, however, an interesting explanation offered by James to Alix Strachey. Their friend Ernest Jones had psychoanalysed Henrietta, and according to him 'the real reason why she threw over Carrington was because she (Carrington) wasn't a virgin'.[152] Henrietta had a difficult life. At ten she was in the car when an accident causing her mother's death occurred. Her father had a series of unsuccessful marriages, which left her without positive male or female rôle models. In her fifties she married briefly, but died a lonely alcoholic in the 1960s. Her niece, Sallie Binsham, later remarked that with the exception of Carrington, Henrietta never hurt anyone.

everyone danced until dawn. Henrietta had been invited, but 'of course telegraphed the day before the party, & said she couldn't come. But as I had already given up expecting her, I hardly felt her last blow.'[154]

CHAPTER FIFTEEN

RETRENCHMENT: 1925

As with all of Gerald's and Carrington's previous separations, this one did not last. He sent her a crystal snowflake for Christmas of 1924, and she allowed it to grace her mantelpiece. Their correspondence resumed, but cautiously. Although they agreed that she would again visit him in his London rooms every couple of weeks, Carrington did not want a renewal of the possessive and highly-charged emotions Gerald had exhibited in the past.

She went out of her way to indicate that she would not be jealous if he were seeing – or even sleeping with – other women, and to argue against more frequent meetings: 'I think our relation is more romantic than any other relation can ever have been!' she wrote on 16 January 1925. 'I like the complete change that makes our meetings so different from any other. Then by not seeing each other continuously I believe we will never be bored, or dulled as other people do.'[155] She clearly preferred a relationship that existed primarily on paper, but Gerald could not be content with such an arrangement.

Because Ralph felt entitled and even obliged to read Gerald's and Carrington's letters, they had developed over the years a two-letter system which placed important discussions in postscripts on separate sheets of paper for private perusal. Often a furious correspondence, quite different from what Ralph read, raged subterraneously. The focus of this correspondence at the beginning of 1925 was Gerald's dissatisfaction with the portion of Carrington's life allotted to him, and this naturally had sexual overtones to which she took exception.

> You are again I see going to press in a direction which will cause difficulties. Every sentence of your post script confirms what I felt only too acutely last winter. That by becoming your lover I would make the situation more difficult. Because the responsibilities would be greater. Since our relations are circumscribed because my life is so arranged that I can only give you a small portion of it it is a very difficult matter the arranging of that portion ... But I tell you there are few things that hurt

me more than to think I am cared for just because of ∼.[156] The whole difficulty in my relation with M[ark] G[ertler] was always that he could take little interest in seeing me unless he made love.

... If you find no point in seeing me because you cannot make ∼ to me, you have only not to see me. But I refuse to be intimidated by your saying before hand you are going to make a scene. You know making you unhappy doesn't give *me* pleasure. But life is so arranged. When I formed an attachment for Lytton I could not foresee it would then make another attachment more difficult. One is not made of iron, one cannot say 'because I shall also give pain as well as pleasure to this person I must not form an alliance with him'. One forms attachments which complicate life, & also make life durable.

... It is unfair of course that I should have this very complete life here – & only give you a small portion of it – but that is outside me – I cannot alter that now. No one, not even you, can make me care less for Ralph, & Lytton – & Ham Spray – my own life – no one but you could ever make me care so much as I do for a third person. But it is no use your continually blaming me for something I cannot help –[157]

Gerald replied, as Gertler had in the past, that the sexual act was a natural outgrowth of mutual fondness, that one 'cannot separate in this way the intellectual & the physical'.[158] Carrington, though, could and did.

In order to understand the situation and the person from whom he could not extricate himself, he took to analysing her in long, closely-written passages of his diary. Sex with any man caused her to resent her partner afterward; she had no idea that it could be simple and uncomplicated (she claimed it disrupted her painting emotionally as well as in terms of lost time); she felt she had lowered herself, and compromised her pride and dignity. Some of these silent accusations were no doubt true, but as the year progressed his analyses became more complicated and more desperate. He needed to understand why she could not love him.

They reached an agreement, and things went along fairly smoothly for about six weeks until Ralph, glimpsing a withheld page protruding from her pocket, demanded to see it. What Ralph read confirmed his suspicions of Gerald's and Carrington's greater attachment to each other and caused him to regain interest in her. Gerald found himself pushed to the side; composing unposted letters to Carrington and to Helen Anrep (who, since the previous summer, had been his confidante), he confessed that what upset him most was 'the ease with which you yield to force when you would never yield to reason'.[159] Again plunged in misery, alternately hating and loving her, he realised they were heading for yet another breach, and that again Ralph might be the cause.

He had reason for concern. Recognising but not truly understanding the desperation she felt over the threat to her life at Ham Spray, he nonetheless knew that in any struggle between that life and one with him, he would emerge the loser. Such a battle was inevitable as life at Ham Spray became more exciting and involving. Carrington had entered a period of creativity, in which both her serious and 'commercial' art took on new life. Visitors to Ham Spray abounded, and scarcely a week went by when there were not several guests, many of them new. Ralph, Lytton and Carrington, with years of a mutual life behind them, were again affectionate and harmonious. Lytton had never lost his feelings for either Carrington or Ralph – by now, they were equally split between them – but Ralph and Carrington probably got along better precisely because there was no longer any sexual tension between them. Finally, Ham Spray itself, with its comforting beauty, proved as serious a rival to romance as any lover would be.

Late in 1924, Carrington began to experiment with a new art form: glass pictures. Painting directly on the backs of small panes of glass, and incorporating bits of silver paper into her designs, she created unique pictures which were novel enough to sell rather easily. They had the further advantage of being relatively quick to produce, and when Frances found she could sell them with little difficulty in Birrell and Garnett's bookshop, Carrington found a new and badly needed source of income. Keeping them separate from her more serious painting, she tried to make enough of them to earn £2 a week in profits.

Gerald took exception to the low artistic status she accorded these pictures: 'You underestimate, I think, the value of this art and do not treat your work seriously. It is criminal to leave so many of your lines just cuts with scissors. No artist is so careless.'[160] Carrington did not consider them on a level with her other work, however, and continued to turn them out rapidly. Her friends and guests saved their foil candy wrappers for her, and she was delighted with her success, as she told Alix in early February.

> The pictures only take about 2 hours to make & some sell for 35/ = or £2. So really the profit is enormous. My plan is to keep this minor talent in the winter as a means of making money, & in spring and summer do my serious painting. I will do you a very lovely picture as a present on your return. In any style, on any subject. Flower piece, boxers, balloons, volcanoes, tight rope dancers, Victorian beauties, soldiers, tropical botanical flowers, birds & fruits, are a few of my subjects. I cater for every taste. Ravishing soldiers in Busbies for the gentlemen, & elegant ladies for the Clive Bells.[161]

Boris Anrep, seeing some of the glass pictures, was willing to act as her broker for them but had advice for their improvement: she needed to use freer, bolder designs; to trust herself; to use thinner glass. The last point was most troublesome, for she found several times that, finishing a picture, it would break. Although frustrated, she valued Anrep's opinion and tried to develop new ways of creating them for beauty and durability. Sales went into a temporary slump by late February, and although Carrington still tried to produce some for Frances to take back to London after her weekend visits to Ham Spray, her thoughts returned to more serious works.

For her more serious painting she found great support from both Ralph and Lytton. When Boris criticised her glass paintings to Ralph in Gerald's presence, Ralph became 'very angry with Boris, he really thinks you are Michael Angelo & that one must praise everything', Brenan reported.[162] Carrington, while pleased, demured: 'Ralph thinks rather too much about my paintings – But then he is not an artist, & truly I would never discourage any one from liking my work! I haven't so many admirers that I can dispense with even R! I particularly value Boris['s] opinion because he is so broad minded. If I succeeded in pleasing him I should be very glad.'[163]

Her paintings in this year took two forms: portraits and flowers. During the preceding few years she had concentrated on landscapes, but now she narrowed her focus to particular, rather than panoramic, beauties. She found willing sitters in the Ham Spray weekenders, and in addition to painting Frances, Ralph, Alix, Lytton's nieces Janie Bussy and Julia Strachey, and Noel's fiancée, Catharine Alexander (they married that March), she did a large sofa picture and a study of 'Suzanna in her bath', all within a year. Of all these portraits, only three – those of Janie, Julia and Catharine – are known to survive. The paintings of Julia and Catharine, like her earlier pictures of E. M. Forster, David Garnett and Gerald Brenan, are close-up studies of head and shoulders. Julia and Gerald, in theirs, look with almost unnerving directness at the viewer. All make relatively little use of background, placing only the face of the sitter in full focus. Janie Bussy's portrait, however, represents a departure for Carrington. She rests on a chaise longue, with views of two Ham Spray rooms in the background. The detail so representative of her earlier works is there, but it all appears more relaxed through what the art critic Richard Shone calls 'a free handling of paint'. Whereas most of her works show 'a tighter, more miniature handling of a given space',[164] this one is looser and more expansive – and, at twenty-four by thirty-three inches – bigger.

Flowers, representations of Ham Spray's bounty and of more exotic locations, became a favourite subject. She bought botanical prints, which Ralph bound into books for her. She frequently gave and received flowers as gifts, and friends scoured florist shops and country gardens for pleasing specimens for her. If she received a gift of a flower, all other work ceased while she painted it during its brief life. The painter Henry Lamb brought her 'a most superb Mexican lily, a great red lily on the top of a thick purple stalk'[165] at the end of March, and when Lytton went on holiday he sent her gentians from the continent.

In these new artistic interests, and in her execution of them, she further distanced herself from Bloomsbury and French painters. She admired Duncan's work immensely and found him and Vanessa to be 'good' artists in the way they structured their lives around their work, but they were still fundamentally influenced by the French. In contrast, Carrington had little, if any, respect for her contemporaries in France. 'I could write you a long letter on the modern French painters', she wrote to Lytton on 27 April 1925, referring to unnamed artists.

> Really they filled me with an unspeakable rage. They are fifty times worse, I think than any other painters, English or German. Because they are morally wicked, being charlatans, cheats and imitators and outwardly they produce hideous, vulgar pictures. Really they have an exact parallel to those French women of 50, all made up to look beauties and under-neath they are hags of iron. I shall be interested to hear what Roger and Clive have to say on these most modern monsters when they come back.[166]

But confidence in her critical opinions did not translate into a new confidence in her own work. In June she lamented that she was 'really only capable of "beginning" pictures. I always ruin them after a week's work.'[167] This meant that, despite Ralph's and Lytton's enthusiasm and encouragement, she no longer submitted serious works to galleries or exhibitions.

It did not mean, as so many have assumed, that she ceased to paint seriously as her life became more involved with Lytton and Ralph. Because many of these paintings have disappeared, not infrequently painted over by herself, many people have come to the mistaken conclusion that they were not painted at all. Her continuing lack of lack of confidence in her own works shows on examination of the Yegen landscape: it bears a linear scratch on one side, evidence of the time it spent on its side, allowing the paint to drip, in her studio.

When not painting, she was enjoying herself immensely with those who were fortunate enough to be invited to Ham Spray. Gerald rarely went there, preferring to meet Carrington in London where he would not have to be always under the inspecting eye of its inhabitants. An invitation there was considered quite special by many of their acquaintances; when Henry Lamb was first invited, he responded that 'There is something too much like a Holy of

Holies about Ham Spray (in my mind) for me not to feel rather nervous about such an intrusion & then I hardly know you two speckled partridges.'[168] He passed inspection, and returned several times in the company of Dorelia John, Augustus' lovely wife.

This year brought other friends and visitors: Lytton's friends Dadie Rylands, Sebastian Sprott, and Philip Ritchie; Simon Bussy's wife Dorothy and their daughter Janie; Catharine Alexander; Stephen (Tommy) Tomlin, now recovered from his passion for Henrietta Bingham, in the much more suitable company of Julia Strachey.

Carrington was particularly pleased with Dorelia John and Julia Strachey. Julia, the daughter of Lytton's brother Oliver, was also a lifelong friend and contemporary of Frances Marshall. They had known each other as children, and had been away at school together for several years. Carrington first spoke to her in late June at a party given by Roger Senhouse; while she seemed rather cool, lovely and aloof, Carrington 'made a brave dash at' her, finding her 'underneath all that stucco rather simple [this was not true], & intelligent'.[169] Julia spent increasing amounts of time at Ham Spray, and she and Carrington became great friends. Dorelia she also considered lovely and 'completely fascinating'.[170] Always perfectly dressed, and sometimes in the company of her children, she charmed Carrington by her poise and interest. Like Julia, she would become one of Carrington's closest friends in the last years of her life.

Ham Spray life, in short, had become irresistible. Visitors spent their time talking, playing music on the gramophone, eating and drinking, playing poker and ping-pong, and going for walks. Evenings were high-spirited occasions, and Frances recalled that time as being full of fun, unending jokes, and conversation. When not with company, Carrington spent her time gardening or working in her studio, which she loved. 'Really it is marvellous to have a great big light room like this all of one's own. In London one would pay 15/- a week for such a room. I am tremendously happy whenever I think of my extreme good fortune, I mean living in such a lovely place & with such amiable companions & then to have London as an extravagance whenever I feel in the mood for a change...'[171] Only two things marred the happiness of those early months of 1925: servant difficulties, and Carrington's inability to forget about Henrietta.

The first problem was painful, but easier to resolve. Annie Stiles, who had been with them since the traitorous Mrs Legg had betrayed them at Tidmarsh, was now determined to leave. She had grown from a girl to a young woman, and Carrington found her often insolent and difficult to manage. Annie's boyfriend, who wanted her to move away to be near him, issued an ultimatum in January of 1925, and Ham Spray lost. It was a mixed blessing, for although Annie was in Gerald's words 'an impudent little creature and would in any case soon be leaving',[172] Carrington imagined that anyone else would be even worse. With some trepidation she set out to find a new servant, and she and Ralph combed the nearby towns in their car looking for a replacement.

She found a sixteen-year-old who would have to be completely trained, and an eighteen-year-old who 'knew some cooking' but had a 'certain animal look that always terrifies me in the lower classes. So I don't think I will go & see her again. I know she would dominate me if she came here. And I must have a weaker character than my own, whom I can control.'[173] She opted for the younger girl and, after interviews with her mother at the end of February, it was agreed that she would come over to inspect Ham Spray. Olive Martin was the daughter of the local carpenter, and Carrington later discovered that she was only fifteen.

She turned out to be a perfect choice; at the end of March Carrington stated tentatively that 'I think Olive our new maid is going to be charming. She is very energetic & hard working & I think a nice character.'[174] She quickly learned how to cook, under Carrington's tutelage, and her enthusiasm was unimpeachable. They were astounded to return one hot afternoon to find her galloping across the lawn, breathlessly pushing a mower.

The problem of Henrietta was more difficult to handle. Carrington had refrained from writing to her for several weeks, but felt her loss acutely, as she told Alix:

> Now I've recovered slightly from my misfortunes, & misadventures. I dream only once a week – instead of every night – of that wretch H & I think of her only 2 hours out of the 24 ... Someday – if you ever return you shall have the whole story. At least my side – she is still a mystery & I only know her version of my fall & disgrace through eavesdroppers but its left me a warped, gnarled old tree, with a pain in my head whenever I hear the name of 'H' or the word American. I did not loose [*sic*] her through pride as you suggested in your letter, but through excess of L... I suspect she found my affections so cheap that she doubted they could be worth very much. And as she has an income of £8000 a year I expect she thinks even L... ought cost a few hundreds ... I still can't help being a little embittered ... 'God's neck! – as Katherine Mansfield used to say – it is very mortifying. Lytton curiously enough was the one person who sympathised. Although he was no admirer of that Lady.[175]

Henrietta was due to return to America shortly, and Carrington hoped that that distance would make things easier. With Henrietta still in London, the temptation to go see her was great; 'I keep on forgetting she is cruel, & indifferent,' she wrote to Brenan, '& I can only remember her Beauty, & her charm.'[176]

Five weeks later she wanted to return a cocktail shaker that Henrietta had left at Ham Spray and found, with classic Freudian behaviour, that she could not remember the address.

No, I refrained from writing to H. I merely sent back her cocktail shaker in a cardboard coffin with a black cross on the outside and snowdrops round the cocktail shaker corpse inside and on a piece of paper [a drawing of a box containing the words 'R.I.P. DC. Dec 15 1924'] leaves of balm at the corpse's head and box at her feet. Wasn't it queer, I simply couldn't remember H's address. I nearly went mad on Sunday night looking for it. Then I looked it up on a map of London & couldn't find it. On Monday suddenly by a sort of instinct I looked in a certain box of papers & found it. But the complete forgetfulness of the address, although 3 months ago I wrote a letter twice a week to her, was very curious.[177]

This occurred shortly after she had unexpectedly and upsettingly seen Henrietta at a party. Gerald also saw Carrington at that time, and the meeting prompted him to dream of seeing her 'face very haggard and marked with tears and blood looking down on me from the branches of a tree'.[178] The repercussions of that unusual triangle were to last a long time, and for the time being sometimes prevented Carrington from seeing Gerald, who was also in London.

The pleasures of Ham Spray and its occupants to a great extent made up for other miseries, or at least Carrington tried to make them do so. Lytton, always the true focus of her life, now afforded her even more happiness. She found his wisdom and his sense of humour great sources of comfort and pleasure. Returning with her from London at the beginning of 1925, 'Lytton was delighted with his riding gloves [although he did not ride], & nearly gave an elderly dowager a shock by pretending to be riding on a horse, & clicking his tongue, when I gave them to him in the railway carriage.'[179].

Taking advantage of the readily available friends, Lytton wrote two plays that year. The first, a Greek play, was acted under the

Ham Spray ilex tree; its cast included Dadie Rylands 'as a Greek God*dess* appearing from Olympus (ie the Downs) ...'[180] Lytton's relationship with Philip Ritchie still continued, and under the influence of that happy stability he found himself returning to his writing. The second play, 'The Son of Heaven', was produced more formally, with a professional actress, in London that summer, although it had been written in 1913.

Gerald's worries about Carrington and Ralph began to appear less unreasonable as winter slowly moved into spring. Lytton went to Lyme Regis with Sebastian for his health at the end of March, and Carrington and Ralph were often alone at the house. Frances still came down most weekends. There was no question of Ralph's love for her, but there was also no question that he and his wife were getting along better than before. He thought that Carrington, who had been working very hard, needed a holiday before the spring gardening engulfed her, and accordingly wrote to Lytton that he and Frances were going to Paris for Easter, and hoped that Carrington could be persuaded to join them a few days later.

After some hesitation Carrington went, arriving in Paris the evening of 15 April. While Frances was off with a friend, Carrington and Ralph visited art galleries, seeing works by Derain, Rousseau, and Picasso ('he certainly is a very formidable artist', she reported, apparently reserving her strong negative opinions for lesser French artists); they attempted to see an exhibition of African sculpture but the gallery was closed. After several days in Paris she and Ralph took a walking tour, hiking in the countryside near Arles, visiting Provençal cottages, Ralph picking flowers for her. She reported all of this to Brenan, who assumed – perhaps with reason – that she did so in order to make him jealous. They returned to Ham Spray on 25 April. Lytton, still rather ill and weak, returned on 28 April.

Gerald, at Carrington's suggestion, had taken rooms in the house of a farmer in nearby Shalbourne early in May. It was cheaper than London and, since he was still trying to write his biography of St Theresa (which he never completed), provided the solitude he needed. From there he could bicycle over to Ham Spray, but he found that his presence was not always welcome. Their letters had settled into a pattern of anger and apology; he would be made miserable, would write to complain bitterly, then, when she replied, would repent.

His moods in all the years he was involved with her ranged from romantic ecstasy to caustic abuse. That winter he had written that 'You take me into a world which is quite different from the one in which I ordinarily live. I cannot explain this at the time, because it is impressed on the deeper & more articulate layers of myself and I am scarcely aware of it. I have to wait till a few more hours have passed ... Then I see how happy I have been and what a pure and aesthetic current it was that flowed through my mind while I was with you.'[181] Such sentiments were strangely reminiscent of Gertler's letters, and so were those which expressed his fury and frustration. The result was that Carrington, withdrawing more and more into increasingly satisfying Ham Spray life, drew further and further away from him. Ralph, Gerald felt, was responsible for this, and the situation reached an unpleasant climax in June.

> R. could not conceal his jubilance at my 'downfall', but mixed it with some pity – not much, because he said I *deserved* it, my treatment. They were now allies banded together against me – I could feel the hard pressure.
>
> After dinner I walked with [Cirod] on the lawn. 'I have lost all physical feelings for the time being. I cannot say how long it will last.' Yet she had to confess she had lost them for me only. She & R had begun again to be lovers & certainly wd be so that night, as soon as I left them. She would not look at me, would not touch me, spoke in a voice of feigned kindness, yet still, because she did not wish to lose me, promised everything for the future. Next day I returned to London.[182]

Gerald had no proof – only his untrustworthy instincts – that Carrington and Ralph were once again acting as man and wife, but that suspicion alone was enough to unnerve him. In fact, he was wrong about this. Carrington and Ralph were able to get along better now precisely because they were not sexually involved. They accepted that their marriage was over, and lived as brother and sister far more comfortably than they ever had as husband and wife. He was so distraught over Carrington's treatment of him during these months that his judgement, as he later admitted, was unreliable. In any case, his fondness for both made him feel doubly betrayed, as did the recognition that he would never really fit in there, did not 'belong to her menage', as he said in an unposted letter to Helen Anrep. 'I cannot be moved about & dusted with the furniture. And did you ever see a woman more absorbed in physical objects? If one looks for her interests, her affections, her desires, one will find them not lying coiled up in her head but stuck on to the garden, the meals, the furniture, the hot-water bottle.'[183]

In early June, Carrington and Ralph made another trip, this time by automobile. Lytton was giving a lecture at Cambridge, and she and Ralph motored down and stayed with David and Ray Garnett in their beautiful home at Hilton Hall. On the way they stopped for a picnic lunch on Boxmoor Common, and she took him to see the frescoes at Ashridge House, which she had painted in the summer of 1913. They were – and still are – remarkably well preserved.

The summer of 1925 passed pleasantly. The high point was Lytton's play 'The Son of Heaven', about the Dowager of China, which was performed for several days at the Scala Theatre in London. Gerald and Ralph had small parts in it – Carrington professed to Gerald that Lytton was particularly impressed with his acting ability, although he only had a line or two – and Duncan Grant designed the sets. Carrington was hard at work painting dresses. Ralph and Carrington acted as Lytton's eyes and ears at the July 19 performance, for he had fled to Austria. The reviews, they found, were lukewarm, mainly because they 'expected, (God knows why,) that it would be exactly the same as "Victoria" '.[184] Desmond MacCarthy alone of the reviewers discussed the play itself, but no one even mentioned the painstakingly created scenery and costumes.

The second night of the performance, however, proved disastrous to Brenan. At a party given for the actors, Carrington stayed in a corner and kept her distance from him. Upset, he became drunk and flirted heavily with Marjorie Joad. Finally, he approached Carrington and expressed his anger. Distressed, she searched for Ralph, who had left the party, and finally fled alone. What followed was a strange drama.

It was two o'clock in the morning and Carrington, carrying a heavy rucksack and nearly dropping with exhaustion, had to walk a mile to the railway station at King's Cross. Gerald followed her down Tottenham Court Road, begging to be allowed to carry her sack and, when she refused, became upset. 'I ran after her. "No, you are tired", she said. "You must go home." She kept on repeating this all the way to King's Cross, her face very pale, her eyes enlarged and fixed in a kind of icy misery.' When they reached the station there was an hour to wait and they sat, not touching, miserable, on the kerb. They both knew that these emotionally wrenching scenes would have to stop, but Gerald extracted 'fresh promises for the future' from her. Finally, 'Ralph appeared and she drew towards him, while I walked home.'[185]

The next day she wrote him perhaps the most painstakingly honest letter she ever had, trying to express herself carefully.

Oh my amigo what an awful thing it is to be so divided. So unhinged. How much easier it would be if one felt definite & positive feelings, like other people. If only our feelings for each coincided more often. You want perpetually something from me which it is not in my power to give you, & I feel always a sense of guilt & depression because I cannot give it to you.

... I want so hard to try & be very exact ... You know I have always hated being a woman. The Fiend [her term for menstruation] which most women hardly notice fills me with such disgust & agitation every time, I cannot get reconciled to it. I am continually depressed by my effeminacy. It is true *au fond* I have a female inside which is proved by ~ but afterwards a sort of rage fills me because of that very pleasure ~. And I cannot literally bear to let my mind think of ~ again, or of my femaleness. It is partly because R treats me not like a woman now that the strain has vanished between us. All this became clear really last summer with H. Really I had more ecstacy with her, & no feelings of shame afterwards.

... Its really nothing to do with *you*, but some struggel [*sic*] in myself between two characters. I think H. although she gave me nothing else, gave a clue to my character. Probably if one was completely S[apphic] it would be much easier. I wouldn't then be interested in men at all, & wouldn't have these conflicts. Its not true to say I don't care for ~ with you. Because you know I did ... Somehow it is always easier if I am treated negatively, a little as if I was *not* a female ... I have never completely told R this, or anyone. It is a confidence I make only to you. Merely thinking of this makes me so agitated I feel I can hardly bear any relations with anyone again. In the past everything I believe went wrong for this reason. Always this struggel [*sic*] with two insides, which makes one disjointed, unreliable, & secretive.[186]

Gerald replied that 'for your own happiness you should give up men and become a complete sapphist. Yet that is not the only thing that has separated us. An alteration in your feelings for R. has altered your behaviour towards me. You have given up so many of your human qualities to become a little tame bird that flutters about the house & garden assisting, looking in, serving, inspiring.'[187] They did not write to each other again until mid-September.

Carrington's portrait of Brenan, painted when he was twenty-eight, provides one of the most fascinating psychological keys to their relationship. The picture divides into two distinct sides: the left side is dark, the right side light. While the hair on the left is long and smooth and Brenan's features are regular, the hair on the right is short and chopped about, his right eye turns inward, and his right ear is oddly shaped and full of angles. Most importantly, the scarf is covered with red stains, again on the right side. Even the fabric of the coat is predominantly smooth on the left, mottled on the right. All these seem to indicate Carrington's ambivalence toward Gerald, and her love–hate frustration with him.

Bitter as it was, Gerald's assessment of her recent actions had some justification. That summer she had humiliated him in bed at Ham Spray; he had waited impatiently for her to come to his bedroom and when she arrived after midnight she offered herself as a sacrifice to him. Afterwards, according to his account, she asked coldly, 'Are you finished?' and went back to her own room.[188] He saw her reattachment to Ralph and retrenchment as a last desperate act to preserve the Ham Spray arrangement.

Ralph was by now clearly in love with Frances and no doubt this contributed to the more peaceful atmosphere between him and Carrington. Frances was more suited to him in any number of ways: where he could fluster and defeat Carrington in philosophical argument, Frances, trained at Cambridge in Moral Philosophy, would lock horns with and often defeat him. She was not inclined to moods or inconsistencies, and they spent hour upon hour talking and laughing together. And, as Gerald remarked, she was one of the prettiest girls in London, with glossy dark hair and a ready smile.

The main obstacle to their happiness was Frances' own indecision. She was at the time still seeing a man in the Foreign Office who, as he was single, had none of Ralph's marital liabilities. And although they got along well, she was not sure that she was in love with Ralph. For these reasons they had not become lovers, despite her frequent weekends at Ham Spray. As long as this state continued, Carrington could be sure that her life would remain intact. However, that was about to change.

In October, Ralph persuaded Frances to go off to Spain with him. She no longer cared what her parents might think of such an arrangement; she had a mind and life of her own (she was now twenty-five) and later said that they had by now given up expecting to control her movements and actions, even though she still lived with them in London. She and Ralph lived roughly, travelling on inexpensive tickets and staying in cheap hotels. Nonetheless it was extremely romantic and decisive. By the time they returned, Frances recalled, 'Ralph and I were both very much in love, and our one desire was to spend our lives together.'[189] The day Carrington had so dreaded had arrived.

CHAPTER SIXTEEN

COMPROMISE

For several months after Ralph and Frances returned from Spain, Ham Spray was plunged into confusion and turmoil which the outside world knew nothing about. Frances returned to 27 Brunswick Square and her mother, where Ralph wrote her impassioned letters from Ham Spray and London.

Back at Ham Spray, Carrington was becoming desperate. It seemed almost certain that Lytton would decide to take up residence in London should Ralph desert them at Ham Spray, and she desperately sought a solution that would allow Ralph – along with Frances – to remain in their lives, for he had grown to be an integral and crucial part of Lytton's and Carrington's life. This was clear when Lytton bought Ham Spray: he wrote a will leaving the house to Ralph, assuming that since Ralph and Carrington were still legally married, it would of course belong to both of them. Lytton found Ralph's masculine presence comforting and steadying. Although there had been situations in which Ralph did not always act rationally, by and large Lytton found him extremely efficient and capable. Carrington, too, was capable of running the house efficiently, but after several years of Ralph's presence Lytton began to find the idea of living with only Carrington less satisfying. He loved her no less, and had long ago forgotten any sexual designs he might have had on Ralph, but he felt that Ham Spray life would be altered by Ralph's absence, in which case he himself might prefer to move back to London. Ralph was caught in the middle, and did not want to be responsible for anyone's unhappiness.

Finally resorting to what she herself termed 'intrigue', Carrington wrote to Julia Strachey in London, asking her if Frances might not share her flat.[190] If the point were for Frances to gain her independence, and thereby allow Ralph to spend as much time with her as he wished, this seemed to Carrington a plausible possibility. Among the benefits she cited to Julia were having someone to share the burden of housekeeping, and living with her old friend. She knew that such a request was only buying time and giving herself 'a straw to cling to', and begged Julia not to write back 'as Ralph returns next Monday and please burn this letter ... I've very little spirit left. For which reason I've rather taken to the other "spirits".' She added movingly in her postscript that '[m]y only hope rests with your diplomacy'.[191] Julia's answer has been lost, but presumably she knew that this would not be a good solution.

Weeks passed but no resolution appeared. Lytton finally took charge and invited Frances to lunch at the Oriental Club in London, in the only room 'allowed to be sullied by the presence of females'. Feeling that she was defending herself in a court of law, Frances carefully presented her case: she loved Ralph and wanted to live with him; she did not want to deprive Carrington and Lytton of his presence. Lytton listened patiently before presenting his side.

> 'You see', he said, 'I rely very much on Ralph's practical support, sound sense and strength of character. Fond as I am of Carrington I fear she loses her head sometimes. So that I think I ought to warn you that if you and Ralph set up house together I can't promise to stay at Ham Spray with Carrington, and I think you know what this would mean to her. What would become of her?'[192]

In the guise of worrying about Carrington, Lytton in fact revealed his own, more selfish, fears. Of course Carrington's life was inextricably bound to his; nevertheless his main objective was to keep Ralph from moving out, rather than actually to move out himself.

Frances was horrified at suddenly having the fates of four people in her hands. She knew well that everything in Carrington's life revolved around Lytton and his approval; all her art work, decoration, meals, and even moods depended upon him for sustenance. Gerald and her other friends were nothing compared to this. How could Frances make herself responsible for taking all that away from her?

She went down to her sister's house in Kent to think things over, but of course could confide in no one that she was in love and having an affair with a married man. Yet, her desire to live with Ralph under those conditions was proof of her love; to a well-brought-up and well-educated young woman of her class and her time, living 'in sin' with any man – let alone one who already had a wife – was a tremendous undertaking. She would never have considered it had Carrington's and Ralph's marriage not, for all intents and purposes, ended years before.

The door to compromise opened when the two women involved began to communicate, at last, with each other. While in Kent, Frances received a long letter from Carrington herself. Up until then,

Ralph had served as message-bearer and interpreter. Carrington, realising defeat, called upon Frances to deal with her fairly and compassionately.

> We each know what we have all three been feeling these last months. Now its more or less over. The Treaty has to be drawn up. I have to face that owing to a situation, which cannot be got over, I must give up living with Ralph. I simply now write quite frankly, to beg you to try, while these adjustments are being made, to see the position from my point of view and to try and see if its not compatible with your happiness and my relation with Ralph. I can't get away from everything, because of Lytton. Even although the happiness of my relation with Lytton, ironically, is so bound up with Ralph, that will be wrecked. I am obliged to accept this situation; you must see that. All I can do is beg you to be, at any rate at first, a little generous.
>
> You see I've no pride, I write a letter which I suppose I oughtn't to write...[193]

She ended the letter with a confession that Ralph's position was the most difficult of the three, and with assurances of her fondness for Frances.

Frances responded with equal warmth.

> You have always been such an angel to me and I am so fond of you that it makes it all the more intolerable – this horrible knot in which our happinesses have got involved...
>
> I don't know what the position is or what is going to happen. It is practically impossible to talk to R. about it – but whatever happens this is the main thing. I never never never feel that if R. should live with me I should want him not to see you very often and go on being fond of you.[194]

Just as things seemed to have reached an intolerable state, a solution presented itself: James and Alix needed tenants for the first floor of their house at 41 Gordon Square (where, ironically, Carrington and Ralph had lived during their 'trial marriage') to share expenses and housekeeping responsibilities. It was agreed that Frances and Ralph could move in in the spring, and that they would spend as much time as possible at Ham Spray. Ralph would go down for two or three days every week, and Frances would join him for two or three weekends every month.

Relieved and delighted that such a civilised solution had been reached, Lytton and Carrington went to Falmouth for a week's holiday in early March of 1926. The situation had been draining for both of them, but now it was a pleasure to have each other's company without fear of losing what they had so long shared. Lytton's health had been poor for some time, and he needed to get away for reasons of physical as well as emotional well-being. In Falmouth they regained their stability. Carrington returned to Ham Spray on 18 March –

Lytton remained behind to try to recover his health – and wrote to him on the train, 'You gave me such a lovely holiday. I have been thinking of you nearly all the time since I left you this morning. Thank you very, very much.'[195] Lytton, too, enjoyed the trip and immediately wrote back, 'Yes, it was a perfect holiday. And for me the enjoyment all depended upon you. I am a mere ghost now; but I am glad to say a more healthy and cheerful one.'[196]

With the new arrangements, life moved into a new phase at Ham Spray. All of them were spending more time in London, Ralph and Frances painting and preparing their new home, Carrington painting walls for Alix. Ralph met Carrington at Paddington on her return from Falmouth and took her to the cinema to see a Valentino film.

Gerald, too, was in London, but was about to set off to spend several months in Toulon, France. He had been kept in the dark about the recent Ham Spray turbulence, and spent part of his time going over and over Carrington's letters, trying to understand her moods and behaviour. Her letters, he felt, expressed only a portion of her personality: 'Going by letters, how good, how charming, how reasonable she appears in comparison to myself! And so she was in my absence, and sometimes in my presence, yet was there ever a creature more expressly created to torment those who loved her?' He found her 'character impossible to live with except for someone endowed like Lytton with yogi-like indifference'.[197]

These were important conclusions, for it was true that she could live with no one but Lytton. The more a lover made demands upon her life and love, the more she pulled back. The more desperate a lover felt, the more threatened she felt. Lytton, on the other hand, made no demands; he remained reasonable; and she gave freely. When Ralph disclosed the events of the autumn and spring to Gerald on 23 April over dinner, Brenan resolved that it was 'better far to keep out of this, to avoid her, since clearly she has nothing to offer me!'[198]

She, too, was examining relationships during the spring. She wrote to Brenan asking to borrow the 'diary' she had kept on Henrietta; she wanted to write a '*temps perdu*, beginning with the American invasion'.[199] He claimed that she had instructed him to burn it. They planned to meet briefly before he left for Toulon, but she fell ill and was confined to her bed. While she was sick the conventional Ham Spray roles temporarily reversed. Lytton sat in her bedroom 'on the low Spanish chair framed against the black ilex in the window, reading Tambulaine [aloud]. – At these moments I wish life would stay still.'[200] Rather than tear them apart, the recent developments had drawn Carrington and Lytton closer together. When he was at

Ham Spray, they spent their mornings in 'artistic pursuits', their afternoons going for walks, and their evenings reading by the fire.

There were other signs that Ham Spray would continue, with alterations, to offer a reasonable life. Dorelia and Augustus John planned to settle nearby, and Tommy was to spend the summer at or near Ham Spray. Carrington began painting again, and on 6 May began a still life of tulips. Later that year she worked on other serious paintings: a landscape and a painting of a 'rustic'. Only her mother's illness in May disrupted this tranquillity.

When Charlotte Carrington fell ill with pneumonia, Carrington's 'Goneril of a sister' Lottie sent wires demanding that she go down to care for her.[201] A longer visit to Cheltenham was put off till 23 September 1926, but when Carrington arrived she was filled with 'horror ... coming back to this life of dead ghosts again. The gargoyle-sideboard & the small details, the inkstands, & the sugar spoon, with arum lily handle, & the chipcarved photograph frames ... The awful thought is that one is tainted with the same blood, & perhaps my manias for treacle prints, & old tea pots is just as bad as Japanese cases, & Indian brasses!'[202] Her reaction to her mother is more informative than their actual relationship. They had established a pattern in which Charlotte complained and badgered, and Carrington, irritated, sought escape in letters, walks and painting. Yet it was more what her mother represented than what she did that bothered Carrington. To her, Charlotte was everything Carrington hated and refused to be: conventional, petty, repressed, lacking taste. She was nomadic, moving every year or two after Samuel's death in search of some undefined comfortable home, while Carrington became very attached to her two homes. Her attitude to her mother was shared, to a certain extent, by her siblings. Recalling that his children called their grandmother 'granny with a stick' (because of her arthritis), Noel acknowledged that she was rather difficult to get on with. Carrington was thankful to return to Ham Spray after her short but compulsory visits.

The previous year Carrington had achieved one of her dreams and acquired a horse, Belle, which she rode over the downs, and housed in a small stable next to the main house. From the top of the downs that she and Lytton walked over, she was filled with delight at the sight of the white figure grazing in the distance. Belle provided a much needed physical release for her and, when things became difficult, she would go for long and wild gallops over the hills. The downs behind Ham Spray are steep; from their wind-blown tops one can see for miles in every direction. The house and neighbouring farms lie far below, while at the very top there remains to this day a gibbet as a reminder of earlier rough country justice. Carrington would often walk or ride there, surveying with pleasure the endless countryside, the sheep on the hillsides, the farms spreading down the downs. (That summer she found a small animal there, which appeared to be half rabbit, half cat, and brought it home to the Ham Spray menagerie. Lytton found it too peculiar for his taste.) It was also, as she and her friends learned, a wonderful place for tobogganing and kite-flying.

On 14 May 1926, Ralph and Frances took possession of their new home. Not much later Lytton decided to take the ground floor of the same house as a *pied à terre* for his frequent trips to London. This home did not mean that he would spend more time away than he already did, but rather that he would spend it in one place rather than staying as a guest of various friends. It also gave Carrington a base for when she came up to London.

In early June Lytton left for Paris with his sister Pippa, and for the first time Carrington got a taste of what the new life, with Ralph in London during the week along with Lytton's frequent absences, would really mean.

> You can't think Lytton darling how much I've loved being with you alone lately. And how I love you for being so kind to me always. It seems ridiculous after 10 years to still tell you that I care so much, but everytime you go away it comes back to me, and I realise in spite of the beauties of the ilex tree & the Downs, Ham Spray loses more than half its beauty robbed of its Fakir.[203]

In order to combat her loneliness, she avoided solitude by inviting friends to stay with her in the country or attending rounds of drinking and dancing parties in London.

Soon, however, she found she preferred the beauties of Ham Spray and her horse to the dissipations of urban life. And she was, as her earlier letter to Frances indicated, drinking more than she had before. Most often this was in the company of others, but occasionally it occurred when she was alone. Her bad dreams had returned – they did not seem particularly dependent upon unpleasant occurrences during her waking hours – but by and large the summer and early autumn passed peacefully.

In early November Gerald tentatively resumed his correspondence with her from France. She replied, though he said that she 'scarcely concealed from me that at the time she was having an affair with Stephen Tomlin. He had been spending the summer at Ham Spray and, as I gathered later, the possibility of his taking Ralph's place in that three-cornered relationship had been broached.'[204] Whether this was conjecture or based on fact is unclear. In any case, Gerald planned to return to England shortly, and hoped she might be able to meet him in Paris for a few days and make the return trip in his company. Again finances posed a problem, for she was chronically short of cash, but when Ralph heard of the plan he offered to loan her £8 for the trip. She confessed to Alix that she felt 'rather weak, (in spite of my apparent dash, & courage,) being alone in a train bound for France. I hope the new coat and shirt will put courage into me tomorrow.'[205] It was the first time she had crossed over to the continent alone, but she was indeed bolstered by the new clothes she had bought and by the thought of seeing both her old friend Phyllis de Janzé (who now had a posh dress shop in Paris) as well as Gerald.

Like so many of their other meetings, this one between Gerald and Carrington was doomed to failure. She wanted to see Phyllis alone, and Gerald felt that this was because he 'was not well-dressed or fashionable enough to be taken to call on her, so I spent the day walking about the streets by myself. That evening she did her best to atone for this, but underneath there was a feeling of strain.'[206] When it was time to return to England, she decided she wanted to sleep separately on the boat from Calais to Dover. Gerald attributed this to a 'sudden access of respectability' and to her guilt feelings for having spent the nights with him in Paris.

However, it appears more likely that, having come to terms to a certain degree with her new life, and not having communicated with Brenan for several months, she was most reluctant to jump back onto the treadmill of their relationship. If there had been any reasonable future for them they surely would have discovered it by now. Nevertheless, as she was going up to London more frequently that autumn (whenever, Brenan said, Lytton went up) they continued to meet. Gerald found her changed by recent events; she was more independent, out of necessity, and although he quickly decided that he wanted to resume a serious relationship with her, this was a fresh obstacle to it.

They continued to write and to meet occasionally, but his place as her most regular correspondent was now taken by Julia Strachey. Despite their eight-year difference in age, Carrington and Julia got along extremely well. She could stay for longer periods than the other guests, and kept Carrington company at Ham Spray when everyone else had gone. 'For some reason she always makes one very high-spirited, & gay', Carrington wrote to Gerald in early December. 'She is such a fantastic character.'[207] Later that month she reiterated her appreciation of her: 'I am very happy here with Julia[.] I find her most lively & sympathetic. We laugh nearly the whole time we are together.'[208]

The pleasure of her company was enhanced by Carrington's open attraction to Julia; she flirted with her outrageously in her letters although with no hope of – and most likely no desire for – a sexual relationship. After her experience with Henrietta, she was reluctant to begin another such liaison, and this allowed her to be completely frank in her admiration. She wrote to Gerald on 31 December 1926 that '[t]he maddening thing is that I actually have (or rather don't "HAVE") a lily white lady with Chinese eyes & arms of purest milk sleeping night after night in my house, & there's nothing to be done, but to admire her from a distance, & steal distracted kisses under cover of saying good night'.[209] This was enough for her, but such sapphic remarks began to appear more frequently in her letters to both men and women – even to Frances. She apparently felt free to indulge her humour and comments when there was no hope or expectation of reciprocation. In any case, Julia was involved in an on-again, off-again relationship with Tommy and planned to move to Paris with him.

Carrington now led a rather split existence, with days passing fairly pleasantly, weekends spent with Lytton, Ralph, Frances, and others, but with nights that were 'heavy & unbearable' with night-mares.[210] Most of her letters from this period, however, show little of this disjunction. In fact, because they are full of comic drawings, jokes, and high spirits, they bear a remarkable resemblance to those of her early years with Lytton. She began 1927 by painting for days at a time, and spending other days with Helen Anrep and her children, who were wintering nearby. She went tobogganing with Olive on the downs, but at the same time wrote an almost ominous letter to Gerald on how she spent her nights.

> What does Miss Moffat do all day & all night? Gase [*sic*] out the window at the snow covered fields, & watch the moon like a huge orange steal up behind Inkpen, & rise like a balloon higher & higher, & paler, & paler, till at last the whole garden is lit up, & huge shadows like stains of purple ink, lie across the lawn. Then Miss Moffat loads her gun . . . and creeps out into the still night, with the snow & frost crackling under her feet, & hides in the jasmine bush looking for the rabbits that eat up the winter salads. But the rabbits are peeping out the laurel hedges, & never come out till Miss M is in her bedroom, & all the lights in the windows of Ham Spray have been turned out.[211]

It was an eerie foreshadowing of her death.

Her humour served her well in mid-February, however. She and Henry Lamb had gone horseback riding in Richmond Park, London, and she was thrown. At first it was thought that she was seriously injured and, as she described the scene to Julia, she 'was picked up for dead and carried by 10 stalwart men to a car and driven to the hospital amidst a gaping crowd of admirers longing for death'.[212]

There she was X-rayed and examined and was found to have sprained her back.

The recuperation required that she spend nearly two weeks in London, having daily back massages by a 'terribly sadistic' masseuse recommended by Carrington's doctor – who was also Lytton's cousin – Ellie Rendel. She passed the rest of her time beautifying Lytton's rooms at Gordon Square, wondering, in passing, if she were 'cutting [her] own throat' by making them 'so elegant and lovely'.[213] Gerald, too, had taken new rooms (in St James's Street), and she painted them as well. Alix commissioned her to decorate a gramophone, so the period of her recovery was spent, perhaps unwisely, in physical labour. She suffered for this all spring, finding that the gardening she so loved caused her back to ache.

By the time she returned to Ham Spray, near the end of March 1927, she and Gerald were quarrelling again. He found her too secretive about her life; she found his curiosity intrusive. 'If my Mother hadn't *ruined* my life by her interference, & espionage', she retorted, 'I should n't now be so adolescent about the pleasures of having a secret, or a locked room of my own. You have never known these feelings so you have no right to call them absurd.'[214] Although this appears at first to be an allusion to Virginia Woolf's *A Room of One's Own*, that book was not published for another two years.

She turned her attention with renewed energy to Ham Spray and Lytton. James had given them a wireless set, which added a new diversion to their lives. Lytton 'looked very comical moving the "condensers" with his "ear phones" on his head'.[215] Far from losing affection for her after Ralph left with Frances, he seemed careful to express his feelings in a number of ways. The previous October, having left for London in a bad mood, he immediately sent off an apology which made clear his feelings for her: 'My dearest, I am afraid I was rather dim as I went off – what with the rain ... – but I didn't mean to be – far from it. You are an angel – and perhaps I am a trifle absurd and tiresome. I love you very much.'[216]

Travelling back from London together in April, he bought her a first-class ticket and regaled her with jokes and funny stories all the way home. In May he delighted her by appearing on the lawn, where she was sewing a quilt for Gerald, and crying, 'Is this Mohemet's [*sic*] carpet?'[217] For her, such flights of fancy reinforced their compatibility, and they drew closer that spring than they had been since the strain of her marriage. They resumed their life of walks and reading and work (he was writing 'Elizabeth and Essex' and they invented a play together), and when he was in London she spent time with James and Alix, Dorelia John and her children. On weekends there were Ralph and Frances. Gerald suspected, rightly, that there was now little room for him in her life.

Finally, Brenan was invited down for a Ham Spray weekend at the end of May. He 'had not been there for two years, partly owing to the peculiar taboos that regulate their week-end visitors, partly to the hostility or coldness of Lytton. I knew that in C. R. D.'s eyes my visit was a critical one and that I should be judged upon the finest shades of conduct. Even for casual visitors Ham Spray was a sort of Tom Tiddler's ground from which, whether they realised it or not, they emerged exalted or disgraced. I made up my mind to do my best to be agreeable and to fall in with the special, where she was concerned, almost religious tone of the place.'[218]

But once again he was to be disappointed. Taking opposite sides in a philosophical discussion with Ralph and Frances on the value of art, he and Carrington found hostility – at least on her part – rising, and she slept that night in her own room, without him. He remained awake all night and left the next morning without seeing or speaking to her.

By now it was evident that a final break was necessary and imminent, yet they saw each other several more times that summer, even sleeping chastely in the same bed. They also planned a picnic to White Horse Hill, which was, they knew, to bring them full circle in their association; it was the scene of their first picnic and kisses, years before. However, before this was to take place she went to visit Alix in Munich. When she returned, she sent a letter to Gerald calling for an end to their relationship.

The truth seems to be that I am almost diseased in the head over some matters, & probably its lunacy for me to try to have an intimate relation with anyone. Lately, I mean the last two months, I've had rather an obsession on the subject of c[opulation?]. The result is I sleep badly, & get nerves about it. It seems out of my control. I mean when these

feelings come, & go. – However – I see its maddening for you to have anything to do with me, & the knowledge that my behaviour affects you so considerably, & makes you bear me grudges only makes me feel disinclined to see you, & depressed. I feel at the moment its no good you seeing me. For I only irritate you, and I'm incapable of promising before hand what my moods will be, as I do not know them myself.[219]

Even though Gerald knew and agreed that their relationship must come to an end, he bitterly referred to this letter as having been written 'in the usually apologetic, self-blaming manner'. In any case, their affair was over.

It had been a year of changes: Julia and Tommy, to Carrington's delight, married that summer, but in September Philip Ritchie, Lytton's recent lover, died suddenly of pneumonia, through a complication of surgery. Lytton and Roger Senhouse, who had already begun an affair and did not know how to break the news to Philip, comforted each other and were brought even closer together by this event. Such a juxtaposition of happy and tragic occurrences seemed unfortunately to represent the events of the years of change that had just passed.

PART FOUR

LOVE AND LOSS
1928-32

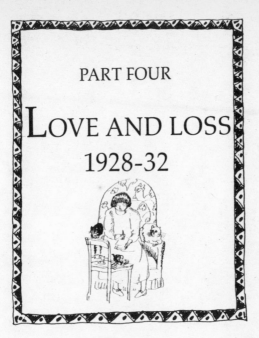

CHAPTER SEVENTEEN

FEAR AND LOVE: 1928

Beginning in late 1927 and early 1928, Carrington's life began to combine familiar themes with portents of trouble. Her love of nature, Ham Spray, and Lytton continued unabated, as did her dissatisfaction with her painting, but they were joined by efforts to deal with her increasing loneliness, fears about ageing, and horrifying nightmares. Her life began to take on a more frantic tone as she attempted to cope with changes.

Early in the winter of 1928, she visited Augustus and Dorelia John's home at Fryern, writing to James Strachey that they were 'very much to my taste. Boozing, galloping on wild horses, painting, endless gossiping over huge fires, & lovely cooking. Dorelia is fascinating I could – almost – live there for the rest of my life in her company. But of course its not often that one gets her alone without the great monster Augustus.'[1] The Johns, Henry and Pansy Lamb, and Julia and Stephen Tomlin were among her most important and most faithful friends during the last four years of her life.

Although the men in all three couples were artists, there is not much evidence that Carrington discussed aesthetic issues with them. Rather, an appreciation of their way of living, which appeared to her much more carefree and uncomplicated than her own, drew her to them, as did an appreciation of the beauty of the women. As Frances Partridge has said, Carrington 'loved "presenting" women, appreciated creating them as works of art'.[2] Julia had been a fashion model in Paris and wore clothes well. Carrington envied Rosamond Lehmann her lovely wardrobe. Dorelia John, or Dodo, combined beauty with maternal ease and a sense of adventure. Because of the Johns' more affluent position, they were able to provide relaxation and comfort for their guests. They sincerely welcomed Carrington's visits, (and would do so even in the distressing weeks after Lytton's death).

While at Fryern Carrington painted a portrait of Augustus John's daughter Vivien, but even her pleasure at the success of the picture could not entirely dispel her general dissatisfaction with her work.

> I did a portrait of Vivien John which turned out better than most so I feel in rather better spirits about my painting at the moment. Its rather maddening to feel one ought to paint so much better than one does & to be filled with ideas. & to, in reality, produce messes that ought to be consigned down the [drawing of a lavatory].[3]

Other things caused 1928 to open badly as well. She wrote in her diary on 1 January that she had caught a bad cold, with resulting chills and fever. Lytton had been spending a great deal of time away from Ham Spray, returning on weekends, often along with Ralph and Frances. Carrington's weekdays were therefore frequently solitary. Although ill, she continued to work, drawing in her studio all day, and going out across the field that afternoon to put her horse Belle into the stable. In the meantime, 'R[alph] and F[rances] went tobogganing [sic] all afternoon'.[*4] Being in the company of Ralph and Frances so frequently at Ham Spray, particularly during Lytton's absence, was becoming irritating to her. When she was ill, it was an even greater source of annoyance and increased her sense of being intruded upon. Undoubtedly, part of her discomfort stemmed from being odd man out. Lytton was now involved with Roger Senhouse up in London and frequently had him down to Ham Spray, Ralph and Frances were obviously happy, both in London and at Ham Spray, and Carrington's closest friends were married. She naturally now began to feel her unattached situation more acutely. 'The year ended rather melancholly [sic]', she wrote in her diary at the beginning of 1928.

> The great distinction suddenly seemed to appear between couples supporting each other – & isolated figures unattached. Then as one grows older there is no doubt one becomes more particular – fastidious ... If one becomes detached there seems a danger of becoming eccentric, & old maidish. A dislike against the melange of living too closely against other people.[5]

Since she was unable to alter the circumstances of her life, her dreams bore the weight of her frustrations. She dreamed that night of 'sitting on a bus that I couldn't stop – felt unable to move from my seat'. Mark Gertler was riding the same bus with her and she 'pressed one by one, six pennies into his hand. And felt sad, for some reason, that I should soon be leaving him. Woke up early feeling ill with headache & cough found it rather an effort to be good tempered,

---

* This letter continued 'Read G's letter in R's pocket. He suddenly seemed to me rather cold, & egotistical. & I minded less in consequence the idea of not seeing him again.' Rather than feeling guilt over her improper action, she used what she discovered to justify her feelings about those she was involved with.

& bear being even touched. . ."[6] She still saw Mark very occasionally when she was up in London, and perhaps this dream is what inspired her to write to him in March, inviting him down to Ham Spray. He was still painting and exhibiting, and his pictures were selling, but he did not have the spectacular success he seemed destined for earlier. He responded with a brief but fairly friendly letter: 'I should like to stay a week-end with you. Please when the time comes try and give me a week or ten days' notice, as I generally become rather involved with engagements. Meanwhile if you are in town do come and see me. I enjoyed your last visit.'[7] But when he and Marjorie Hodgkinson, his future wife, were invited in June, his poor health prevented them from coming.

Never good at ending relationships – preferring, in fact, to prolong them long past their ability to give pleasure – Carrington in her dream seems to have realised both the necessity of certain endings and her inability to alter her behaviour. Indeed, she was still legally married to, and in some ways still dependent upon, Ralph. But, as Clive Bell later remarked, there were no divorces in Bloomsbury: only reshufflings. As much as she enjoyed her married friends, Carrington had found her own love affairs 'complicating' and disruptive to her art. 'I would like this year (since for the first time I seem to be without any relations to complicate me,) to do more painting', she wrote. 'But this is a resolution I have made for the last 10 years.'[8]

The next night, however, she suffered from one of her most terrifying dreams yet, one which undoubtedly resulted from her resentment of the Ralph–Frances relationship.

I was lying in the verandah in a chair. Looking out across the Park late in the evening . . . Suddenly I noticed the grey mists creeping over the lawn, & obscuring the Park so that the ilex tree became a shadow . . . very gradually, as I watched the mists, & felt the cold I began to get frightened. Then I saw a shadow of a farmer I thought on the lawn, so I tried to call out to send him away . . . But then another shape came, a sort of cow, & this time *on* the lawn, so I called to R who I knew was talking upstairs I could hear his voice but I couldn't make any words carry, so then I crawled because I was so terrified on my hands and knees in doors to the foot of the stairs, & cried, Ralph . . . & tried to cry louder, but only made noises in my throat. I thought how stupid I shall look how annoyed he will be, to see me crawling here on the stairs, but I got more & more terrified. Then I suddenly heard quite clearly his voice arguing with F saying 'The point about Ibsen is' and I realised with terror, it was no good I couldn't interrupt, & I woke up trying to cry loud.[9]

Clearly she felt excluded both from the relationship between Ralph and Frances and from their intellectual discussions. As in her waking hours, her feelings of guilt and inadequacy, of somehow being a child who would annoy by looking 'stupid' and who 'couldn't interrupt', caused her suffering and made her unable to act.

The following morning, possibly out of guilt, 'making me either a martyr, or behaving badly', she rose from her sick bed to cook breakfast for Ralph and Frances before their trip back to London.[10] To atone for the strain which Frances noticed during this visit, she sent Carrington the next day a 'lovely book ... which means that is what they call "wiped out". But the conclusion is it doesn't work for more than 3 or 4 days. And not when I am below or above ... a certain temp. inside & if its very cold outside.'[11] Although on the surface the two women had reached a truce over Ralph and Ham Spray, there was a noticeable strain between them. Frances considered Ham Spray her weekend home, as did Ralph. The original agreement had called for Ralph to spend one or two weekends a month there without her, but she was appearing nearly as often as he did. Even Lytton began to feel that he never saw Ralph without her, and felt that the arrangement was not in fact what it had been in principle, and finally wrote gently to Ralph to ask for a change.

> My dearest, I am writing this without telling Carrington, and perhaps you may think it best not to show it to Frances, but of course you must do just as you like. I have felt for some time rather uneasy about F. – but have been unable to bring myself to say anything. What worries me is her coming down here with you so much, and staying for so much of the time you are here, so that we see so little of you alone. It is not quite what I had expected would happen – and I think not exactly what you intended either. I am afraid you may suppose that this indicates some hostility on my part toward F, but this is far from being the case ... I know that this must be painful to you, but it seems better that I should tell you what is in my mind than that I should continue indefinitely with a slight consciousness of a difficulty not cleared up between us. Perhaps it can't be cleared up – but at any rate I think it's better open than secret.[12]

No compromise is wholly satisfactory, as both Lytton and Carrington were coming to understand, but there was a brittleness to this situation that made everyone nervous about offending any of the others. No one wanted the difficulties of 1927 to recur.

With Carrington's illness and increasing loneliness came thoughts of death. She took to her bed at last, and reflected, 'Suddenly I see what my grandmother must have felt when she refused to have a doctor at Ivy Lodge, & locked the door & died ... I think the retort is Ha Ha I am a private individual – I can sleep alone. I'm not afraid of the dark, & if one brings it off a great feeling of pride, & to utterly condemn one-self if one doesn't.'[13]

The twin concerns of solitude and death remained with her

throughout this period. She thought about making a will, but 'I am ashamed to ask anyone to sign it, as it looks so melodramatic'.[14] At the same time, she tried to convince herself of the pleasures of solitude which, if one succeeded in making it 'nice enough it obviously [could] be quite as good as the other thing. What is difficult is to put energy into things for oneself to enjoy.'[15] So accustomed to trying to please others, Carrington had fallen out of the habit of thinking only of herself. She recognised, however, that painting, when it succeeded, brought her a degree of satisfaction: 'if I paint the windows I shall be even a little happier than I am now', she wrote in her diary on 4 January.[16] But painting involved risk as well as satisfaction; decorative work could be therapeutic, but if a canvas did not meet her exacting standards she would become discouraged and paint over it. Many of the paintings from this period of her life have disappeared, some of them undoubtedly lying undetected under existing works.

Thoughts of the past, and of death, led her to assert that 'one always chooses one's antecedents. I kept on thinking I am so like my grandmother C[arrington] and S[amuel] C[arrington, her father] but when I was drinking the whiskey [one night during her illness] I suddenly remembered Grandfather Houghton in that shiny pin-cushion arm chair, & the reek of whiskey. & his mania for barometres, & the weather reports, & his cutting snippits out the Times, & reading the Times from cover to cover! I wish I could have seen Grandmother C.' And later, 'It's awful to think of the stable OWL being DEAD'.[17]

She seems to have been attempting, in E. M. Forster's words, to 'only connect'. With all of the important connections in her life either gone or becoming less certain – her father (and *his* parents) and her brother dead, Lytton more frequently away, Ralph living with Frances – she looked back into her family's past to explain herself and find reasons for her habits, her likes and dislikes, and perhaps even to predict her future. Like Proust's tea and madeleine, her glass of whisky triggered long-forgotten memories at a time when it was important that she reformulate her expectations of life.

This process, conscious or not, was a painful one. Along with events and people of the past, fears about her future began to surface: 'I think so much about the tulips. One of my terrors is we may n't, by some chance, be here when they come out.'[18] She feared more and more her own as well as Lytton's absences from the Ham Spray haven and, as some of her closest ties began to move further away from her, being alone seemed only a step removed from death itself.

Carrington grappled with this dilemma by trying to convince herself that solitude and loneliness were not the same; she should appreciate, in turns, the weekends with Lytton, Ralph, and their guests, and the quieter weekdays. Her diary reflects this conscious effort to strengthen and congratulate herself.

> Feel pleased at having got through these rather gloomy days (being ill I mean) so happily. Pleasing other people one may *think* is what one likes doing, but probably it is against one's flesh underneath – and then a sense of freedom, not affecting any one except myself by what I DO. Not being in the wrong, a great mercy. I feel more even all day, less torn up & down, which is rather a relief.[19]

Confidence about being alone was essential to her sense of self preservation. This first week of January 1928 was in some respects a milestone for her. She had weathered bad colds in the past, and almost certainly had done so alone before. What she needed this time, however, was to come to terms with what she sensed might be a permanent situation.

Her newly-discovered strength was short-lived. In London after her recovery, she did without lunch rather than face Ralph and Frances. As with her search for the past through her grandparents while at Ham Spray, she found herself looking at old photographs, and feeling depressed. Not even dinner with Lytton kept her from having another 'bad night'.

Returning to Ham Spray she worked seriously on a portrait in water colour and decorative painting, but was unable to stave off more dreadful nightmares 'about having my neck cut off, & blood running down my chest'.[20] Looking at her Audubon books, particularly at the pictures of owls, brought consolation but, as she tentatively wrote to Lytton that same day, 'it does make a very great difference having a Ham Spray without a Fakir'.[21] Her valiant attempts to enjoy life without him were clearly not working. The next day she returned to London, where 'Lytton [was] very gay and amusing, [it was] charming to see him again'. Even so, she 'felt rather in despair slept badly'.[22]

The problem erupted publicly a few days later at the cinema with Ralph, when Carrington was inexplicably seized by an 'awful attack of shivering, and depressions during a wild west horse film'. It was strong enough to make her 'almost cry with misery'.[23] She worked hard all the next day at finishing the gramophone which Alix had commissioned her to decorate, and with despair and relief caught the five o'clock train back to Ham Spray.

What was to be done? Unhappy at her beloved Ham Spray, and unable to relieve her misery by trips to London or hard work, she was unprepared for the situation in which she found herself. She had only recently returned from Fryern; another trip away would have provided, in any case, only a temporary solution. The answer seemed to lie in either rekindling old attachments or forming new ones. Yet, when Gerald Brenan unexpectedly wrote and asked to see her, she replied:

> I have (as you probably have) TWO minds about seeing you again. I had *not* 'no doubt guessed' you had long ceased to have 'unfriendly feelings'. I imagained [*sic*] to tell you the truth, that I had ceased to exist. But perhaps you've said and felt rather more than is compatible with being friends again? And then I have found curious pleasures in my isolation, and being exempt from any responsibilities, or blame ... But what can [one] do when one is a divided character?[24]

As far as Carrington was concerned, Gerald was a closed door, even though she rarely, as she well knew, closed any door forever. 'One of the pleasures resulting from having explored the bottom of the sea is that afterwards one has full liberty to break all rules and be as capricious as one likes. So there are no irrevocable endings, final letters, unforgivable insults, or closed doors.'[25] In her view, having seen the depths that their relationship could reach gave her certain privileges. It is not clear that she thought this gave Gerald any.

The nightmares continued. One night she was so frightened by the wind, and by worries about Lytton, that she asked Olive, the Ham Spray servant, to sleep with her. Another night she dreamed of a wizard standing in a grove and surrounded by green scum through which Carrington had to wade, only to have him laugh and tell her that the 'water [was] reeking with syphilis, & I felt doomed'. Several nights later she had a violently lesbian dream. She apparently discussed her sense of 'absolute despair' with Lytton, who told her not to worry; it was probably due to her recent illness. There is no evidence that she turned to James and Alix in their professional capacity as psychoanalysts. They had only two patients in England since psychoanalysis was a new field, and in any case they were out of the country.

She was beginning to be self-conscious about her age. She refers to herself in the letters of these years as 'aged' and 'middle aged', although she was only in her mid-thirties. Julia noticed that,

> She used to smoke her cigarettes with elbows poised high, like the half-unfurled wings, and usually balancing on the edge of the chair, in readiness for all eventualities – an angular elf, turning her face from the daylight in the window, restlessly shaking flies – or whatever they were? – out of her bobbed golden hair ...
>
> She was such a changeling, at once too old and too young, Such people are often artists, or have some queer streak or gift. She wore the progression of youth into age (which is the usual lot of humanity and can be a quite respectable overcoat) like something hired, 'off the peg', thrown on 'all anyhow' and of a most farcically clownish fit.

Carrington had large blue eyes, a thought unnaturally wide open, a thought unnaturally transparent, yet reflecting only the outside light and revealing nothing within, just as a glass door betrays nothing to the enquiring visitor but the light reflected off the sea – something he feels of a 'take-in', considering that it stands ostentatiously wide open, as if inviting him in. From a distance she looked a young creature, innocent and a little awkward, dressed in very odd frocks such as one would see in some quaint old picture-book; but if one came closer and talked to her, one soon saw age scored round her eyes ... She had darkly bruised, hollowed, almost battered sockets; and the strange eyes themselves, wide, clear and light as a Northern sky, were not particularly comforting, because of her look of blindness – a statue's blindness, screening her own feelings.

Emotional herself, though she was afraid of others depending on her emotionally, she had an immense richness and range of feeling: was a productive creator, showering jokes, elegancies, and perceptiveness wherever she went, possessing a great gift for 'seeing the point' of another person's wit or style. A lot of her qualities were essentially feminine – her sly teasingness, her lightness of touch, the fact that her whole life was a creation in fire, feeling and style: her lack of general knowledge and education also and the remarkable impression of sunlight she made.[26]

Her sister-in-law, Catharine Carrington, remarked much later that one certainly could not imagine her as an old woman. In any case, Carrington began to feel that time was running out for love affairs. While she wrote cheerfully that Ralph advised her to begin to act her age, it is more likely that she feared she would soon be forced to live the more sedentary and virginal life of a middle-aged spinster. Carrington felt that her days for romance were numbered.

She was not looking for marriage; she already had a husband. She felt no particular need to divorce him, just as Frances felt no particular need to marry him. Nor did she necessarily seek a less orthodox permanent alliance; Lytton provided that. His needs always came first, and he now needed her again. His book on Queen Elizabeth I, 'Elizabeth and Essex', was proving extremely difficult to write, and as he neared its painful completion – under pressure from his publishers – he fell ill. Carrington, herself tired from decorating Lytton's friend George (Dadie) Rylands's rooms at Cambridge (she called the walls 'a complete failure'),* 'rather worn down by nightmares and the difficulty of reconciling myself to the fact that my painting isn't any better (if as good) as Douglas's [Davidson]', threw herself into her familiar and comfortable domestic role:

> Now I must run to the telephone and ring up the doctor in London and ask for a tonic for Master and order some chops and feed the horse and – you know the hundred and one little things that there are for a busy housewife to do after breakfast on a Wednesday morning.

---

* George Rylands is still at King's College, Cambridge, and Carrington's decorations look, according to him, as good as new. He writes that 'he loved her dearly'.

The facetious tone barely masks her cheerfulness at once again nursing Lytton, running Ham Spray as she had in the past, and painting. Even so, her painting was not going as well as it could, as she wrote to Lytton, who was in Cambridge, on 7 March: 'I wish I wasn't so "tied up in knots" over my painting. I feel as if I was painting behind iron bars, in a cage, unable to do really what I want to do.'[27]

Spring brought another chance to visit Dorelia and Augustus John at Fryern Court near Fordingbridge. As usual during her visits to them, her worries faded and inspiration returned. The lovely Dorelia and her daughters cheered Carrington enormously, the days beginning with them all lying on Dorelia's bed and having long talks after breakfast. 'Everything here is so lovely,' she wrote to Lytton in April, 'the house, the garden, these females and the galloping horses. I am happy all day long. In fact if it wasn't for a bearded El Greco saint living in an Ilex bower, I think I could spend the rest of my days here, painting pictures and riding.'[28]

The pleasures of Fryern were followed closely by an even greater one: Lytton at last completed 'Elizabeth and Essex', and he and Carrington set off in May for a month abroad, touring Provence. Despite bad rain and wind for the first several days, she enjoyed herself tremendously, and the trip was therapeutic for both of them. Lytton preferred sitting in cafés, while Carrington was more adventurous, swimming in the mineral baths at Aix-en-Provence. The hotel and the coast were exotic in a way she had begun to miss in England. As with her other trips to France and Spain, landscape and people excited her visually:

> One's head instantly becomes filled with a hundred ideas for painting. And even if one doesn't paint it is pure pleasure to watch these curious black widows, old men with white moustaches, and portfolios, nuns herding petites peuples in white dresses to confirmations and the students of the University of Aix arguing with each other outside the cafés.[29]

Travel always stimulated her, particularly if it were with someone she loved. Furthermore, her confidence seemed to increase when she left home and she trusted her own artistic instincts and critical opinions much more while abroad.

As much as she loved her life at Ham Spray, her self-doubts and preoccupation with her day-to-day life had forced her into a creative corner: in order to paint without risk, she took as subjects things which were less aesthetically and psychologically complex. At the same time, she was reinforcing the importance of her daily life. The subjects included flowers given to her by Lytton and others, vases, and things which began as gifts and which she transformed into paintings. Unlike many of her earlier works at the Slade and Tid-

marsh – the pen-and-ink 'Dante's Inferno' or the Andalusian paintings – she was now afraid to take risks in her art. While sticking
closer to her subjects, whether they were people or flowers, she
managed to make them fuller than she would have earlier. Backgrounds become as important as the subject itself, and are frequently
spotted and detailed. Richard Shone writes that 'she does show a
certain progression and was obviously, towards the end, in a period
of change'.[30] Shone cites her oil painting 'Dahlias, with its spotted
background', an unfinished work from 1927, as an example of this
change. Rather than wild, sweeping landscapes, she moved in closer
and closer to the subject, filling it with detail without taking great
liberties with its intrinsic uniqueness. Or, when decorating for
instance George Rylands's rooms at Cambridge, she channelled her
art into functional design.

It is not clear that she did much painting during this trip, but it
is almost certain that she continued to sketch. Her greatest pleasure
was the uninterrupted four weeks with Lytton, although on their
last day they made a disheartening find in Nîmes: 'a library with
160,000 books all 18 cent., & bound in the purest style. Poor Lytton
felt very ill at ease at seeing three enormous rooms with books
mounting up to the ceiling. He now feels it hardly worth while going
on with the Ham Spray Library.'[31]

Carrington returned to Ham Spray renewed in body and spirit,
and set to work on a major redecoration of the house. But Lytton,
finding the noise, dust, and confusion of workmen overwhelming,
often took himself to London or to visit friends. This project invigorated Carrington, but could not substitute for what she knew she
truly wanted: someone to share herself with. She wrote to Julia that
her 'life is nothing but a whirl of carpenters, engineers and schemes
for improvements. I'm getting quite a mechanic over the car now.
But perhaps it would be better if I did a little less mechanizing and
a little more: who can say? I wish I had a lover.'[32] And to Sebastian
Sprott, her confidant in many affairs of the heart, she confessed,
'Suddenly in the middle of tea this afternoon I felt cross I had no
one to go to bed with when I wanted to. But then, if I had, I should
probably be cross because it wasn't to my taste! I rather envy you
your animal variety. My life is rather too untouched by human hand
at moments. Reading *Phèdre* with Lytton of course is a very good
substitute, curious as it may seem. I mean I get tremendous pleasure
you know by living here. It's so lovely, and Lytton is such an angel
to me.'[33] This was a marked change from her more independent self.
Where before she desired above all autonomy, now her failure to
attach herself to anyone (except Lytton) in any meaningful way left
her longing to share her life with someone; to be in love.

Reading with Lytton, or having Lytton read to her had always been one of her happiest pastimes, but could not entirely compensate for the lack of a physical relationship. Carrington and Lytton were like a happily married couple after Ralph and Frances left to live together and when Lytton was at Ham Spray without Roger. Once the initial tension had been resolved, they were full of good humour and pleasure in each other's company. Yet Frances could not later recall ever seeing them touch, and this was a great difference between them and other non-sexual couples. There was no doubting their mutual love and affection, but they demonstrated it only in ways that were not physical. Lytton did so by bringing Carrington gifts and reading to her, Carrington by creating a home. They went elsewhere for the touch of the human hand.

Lytton's financial resources allowed him to be 'such an angel'. In June he, Ralph and Carrington went shopping for a new car, a Sunbeam. In July, he provided the monetary means for a new studio for her.

> I don't know – in a whisper – if you realise how grateful I am for your goodness in promising to make me such a lovely studio. I shall show my gratitude by making you a book plate this week, and a design for your library.[34]

Despite his generosity Carrington still had to augment her own small income, and was now painting tiles for bathrooms and fireplaces. She bought the tiles wholesale, then decorated them and sold them through London shops. 'The wood for the studio has arrived', she wrote to Lytton in July. 'My brain thinks of nothing but tiles. I wish there wasn't such a gulf between one's images in the brain, & putting it down with a brush.'[35]

Although Lytton's income rose steadily with his literary success, Carrington could not and would not become financially dependent upon him. His money went into the house, which he and Ralph owned, and therefore benefited Carrington as well. The inheritance from her father allowed her to live rather modestly, but did not provide enough money for all her needs. She was, financially and personally, an independent member of the household. Her increasing involvement with decoration, including painting tiles and glass pictures to be sold in stores, as well as room design, was generated as much from a desire to produce an income as from a fear of attempting 'serious art'. However, she no doubt at times exaggerated her need for money in order to justify spending time away from art.

Lytton's *Elizabeth and Essex* was published that fall, and had 'a huge but dubious success'.[36] At least one Bloomsbury person, Virginia Woolf, found fault with it. She recognised her own jealousy of others' literary successes, and found herself 'secretly pleased to find Lytton's book a bad one', but was also depressed because of her response to it. It was in her opinion 'so feeble and so shallow; & yet Lytton in himself is neither'. Lytton had had great difficulty in writing it, and it had only been the continual prodding of his editor that forced him, at last, to do so. He later agreed with Woolf that the book was a disappointment, yet one doubts that she informed him of where she had placed the blame: 'one ... accuses the public; & then the Carringtons & the young men'.[37] The implication was that Carrington's lack of literary discernment offered faulty encouragement to Lytton, and that his 'young men' distracted him from his real work and talents. His relationship with Roger, like that with Philip, was a May–December romance. Roger was in his twenties, while Lytton was nearly fifty. In either case, not until the day before Carrington's suicide, in 1932, did Virginia fully understand the depth of Carrington's devotion to Lytton and forgive her for removing him from the Bloomsbury fold.

Lytton went to Sweden with Roger in June. Carrington, as usual when faced with loneliness, resolved to work harder at her painting. She vowed that when her new studio was finished she would 'completely change my character and become a very hardened recluse and paint pictures all day. Then all these spinster ravings will no longer blast my letters ...'[38]

Ralph and Frances, freshly returned from a trip to Brittany, came to Ham Spray to spend Whitsun with her, but their presence only aggravated her feeling of being 'rather "out" of the present'.[39] It brought back memories of Tidmarsh when she preferred not to dwell on the past. Ralph and Frances were obviously happy, and Carrington was sincerely fond of them both, but their presence at Ham Spray during Lytton's absences continued to make her feel resentful. Little of it, though, found its way into her letters to Lytton. To him, she wrote of a pleasant day the three spent at Fryern, where they swam in the river and 'Ralph looked so lovely naked, very brown with the sun, swimming like an enormous Neptune amongst these sirens'.[40] Indeed, her unhappiness seemed based more on a dissatisfaction with her own life than with a resentment of theirs. Yet she was genuinely excited by the prospect of the refurbished studio and looked ahead to her work.

'My life is conducted on a sort of fugue basis', she wrote to Gerald in August. 'I go forward a few bars and then retreat and pick up the old theme ... I did not even tell Ralph I had seen you twice! My life is so poor in secrets I was forced to turn you into one!'[41] Problems she thought buried in the past resurfaced with this letter. Her secrecy and Gerald's relative lack of importance in her life could not help but make him feel he was being taken lightly, and she compounded the injury by sending some of Lytton's old clothes to Gerald.

The greatest difficulty in the Gerald–Carrington affair had been her refusal to commit herself to him in any way, the reason being that she felt committed elsewhere. Leaving aside her earlier tendency to try to attract a man and then run from him when she had done so, it is clear that Lytton stood squarely, abeit unintentionally, between Carrington and any other man.

The tensions between Carrington and Gerald had never been resolved. She believed that their past history had destroyed whatever chances their relations had of settling into friendship. Gerald, on his side, remained quick to take offence at any slight, whether intentional or not. Yet it was he who had resumed their correspondence in 1928. Carrington took this as a sign of a renewed, and perhaps peaceful, friendship. But when she characteristically but unthinkingly wrote to Gerald and offered him Lytton's cast-off things, 'she was presenting a red rag to a bull'.[42]

She had always believed in sharing what could be used. Notoriously unstylish, she even offered the fashion-conscious Julia her unworn jerseys. Lytton's old clothing was frequently dispatched to his friends in Bloomsbury, to artists, and even to local farmers. Because Gerald was living under difficult financial circumstances, he appeared an ideal candidate for such an intimate offering. And offering it was meant to be, for in Frances' words, 'everything of Lytton's is so hallowed to her that she feels anyone ought to be delighted to be given it'.[43] Carrington in her 'generosity' ignored both Gerald's old hurts and his peculiar personal taste. Whether or not she meant to offend, her act rekindled an animosity that was to last for many years.

This bad situation was made worse when Gerald saw Frances wearing a scarf that he had given Carrington. This happened innocently enough – Carrington had left it behind at Gordon Square and Frances, without realising whose it was, put it on – but Carrington became frantic when Gerald accused her of giving away his gifts. Her overwhelming sense of secrecy often made her complicate simple issues and in this instance, rather than confess that she did not understand what had happened she instead said, 'Yes, she had given away some of his presents, because (unlike him) she was so upset by these relics of the past that she couldn't bear to keep them.'[44] Perhaps she intended to hurt him. Accusations flew, and both parties took refuge in self-righteousness.

Gerald returned all her gifts to him 'and existed for some days in a fine frenzy, reading his old diaries and brooding over his wrongs'. At the end of several days he came to two conclusions: he would return to Spain in the spring, and once there would take what he called an 'honourable revenge' through writing about Carrington.[45] This latest episode seemed to him the last of a very long series of serious offences, and in such a mood no dispassionate picture could possibly emerge in his writing.

As though to garner support for his plan, Gerald asked Frances to read all the diaries he had kept during his affair with Carrington. She found them extremely moving, particularly when he wrote of sobbing on his bed after Carrington had neglected to telephone or had cancelled appointments. Nevertheless, she 'told him it was no use trying to disguise the fact that he felt wickedly inclined and would probably behave wickedly. He said that he would probably act blindly, but when he is in a wicked mood Gerald is never blind.'[46] He finally attempted to influence her by listing the people who took his side against Carrington. This was precisely what Frances, Ralph, Carrington and Lytton had tried to avoid through their warm yet cautious dealings with each other. Gerald did go on to write about those difficult years in *Personal Record*, his memoirs of the years 1920–72, and what becomes clearest in that account is the lack of understanding on both sides.

All this increased Carrington's general unhappiness. As the year drew to a close she faced the further unhappiness of Christmas without Lytton, whose mother had died on 15 December. Ham Spray, lovely in all seasons but almost unbearably cold in winter, seemed even more so when she was alone with only her cats for company. 'A good setting by Synge,' she wrote to James, 'but a poor setting for a lonely middle aged old haggis.'[47] The thought of having Julia with her for the holidays cheered her, for Julia was more than a friend: she was one of the masterpieces that Carrington had created, for she also got an artist's pleasure from the younger woman's beauty and in finding ways to augment it by producing 'powders and perfumes, hats, beads, and ribbons; she helped dress me up to go out to parties, and entered into all my most fantastic projects for plays or performances'. The younger woman's calm yet dramatic looks contrasted with Carrington's less sophisticated appearance. Julia found all this attention a two-edged sword: on the one hand, she felt tremendously pampered and humoured by it. On the other hand, Carrington actually seemed to be taking on something of the other person, in a kind of secret voodoo rite. Julia went so far as to call Carrington 'a modern witch'.

Perhaps the envelope of deafening guilt, which, as someone remarked, surrounded her like a cloud of loudly buzzing mosquitoes wherever she went, had something to do with the preternatural acuteness of her vision of others. Maybe she felt that her need to reach out towards their essential natures had an acquisitive, greedy and aggressive side to it – I think she even thought of it as 'stealing'. I believe she saw herself as some kind of witch, who would creep out under cover of darkness, call someone's name, run away under the bushes with him, hoard him and nibble him, all the time patting him this way and that with a paw. There was a sort of black magic in her proceedings: first getting hold of the waxen images, then sticking them with pins, then by starlight or rushlight melting them down and refashioning them, perhaps only slightly, but into someone different.[48]

Julia meant 'witch' both in the benign sense of being bewitching, and in the more negative sense. Her interpretation is startling and probably acute: from Gertler to Partridge, people were indeed bewitched by Carrington. She was irresistible to many, although few were able to explain why, and this had a dark side, which bears on her painting. Paintings could work a very important and personal kind of magic, for through them she was able to gather to herself the transformed images of the people and places she loved.

Further, her constant dissatisfaction with her art could have resulted from the 'envelope of deafening guilt'. If Julia's interpretation were correct, Carrington when painting might actually have felt she was 'stealing' the soul of her subject. The painted-over canvasses could be unconscious penance paid for the theft, and the move toward decoration and away from serious, 'pure', art an emotional disengagement from a risky business.

A portrait of Julia painted at the end of 1928 demonstrates this. The picture is unquestionably a good likeness, from the unemotional expression to the aristocratic features. Yet it displays the same ambivalence demonstrated in her portrait of Gerald Brenan, done seven years earlier: the left and right sides of the picture show completely different attitudes about the subject. Julia's portrait has, as Fry said successful pictures must, a diagonal line running through it – from the upper left hand corner to the lower right. But when the division is viewed, Julia is seen to be represented in such a markedly different way on each side that a psychological interpretation is unavoidable.

On the left side, the eye is sharp and angled upward at its outer edge; the pupil is elongated, and the eyebrow joins the nose. The whole side of the face is obscured by shadows on the temple, under the eye, along the nose, down the jaw and throat. The upper lip is blurred. The impression is that of an older woman, a faded blossom. It is also the 'busier' side of the portrait, with a profusion of details creating a sense of clutter: there is a large rose on the headscarf, and the scarf drapes forward to cover one shoulder. The collar is wrinkled. The background, including the back of the chair, shows a profusion of brushstrokes which form the patterns of wallpaper and fabric.

The right side strongly contrasts with the left. Julia is painted in full light, with no shadows. The scarf is plainer and rests behind the shoulder; the collar is neat. The only sign of disorder is the necklace, which twists on the right. Julia looks younger on this side by years, despite the serious expression on her face.

There are several ways to interpret this painting. As she had about Gerald, Carrington had mixed feelings about Julia. She found her 'fascinating' but also suspected that she lived 'in a world of rarefied dreams, & found us all rather coarse and materialistic'. This comment in a letter to James was followed by her usual caution: 'Don't leave this on the mantelpiece now.'[49] At the same time, she felt a physical attraction to Julia, which became even more pronounced while she painted her portrait:

> I had a pleasant day yesterday with Julia, painting, & talking. I can't help being strangely moved by that Young Lady, but I suppress my feelings manfully ... I fear I've mushed up Julia's head [in the portrait] I worked at it yesterday, & reduced it to chaos. Probably its better to be less grandiose, & achieve – well – something pleasant to look at –.[50]

There is, of course, a direct correlation between the choices of attempting the 'grandiose' versus 'something pleasant to look at', and having a love affair versus being content to dress Julia up. Carrington did not attempt the affair, opting instead for a close friendship full of sexual innuendoes and some regret. She did attempt the grandiose painting, and tried to transform Julia, once and for all, into art. That she would feel she had 'not pulled it off' was inevitable. It was also inevitable that in practising her magic, she would incorporate her own feelings into the picture, fusing, in a sense, herself and Julia in a way that could not occur physically.

The left side of the picture could be said to represent Carrington herself – older, living a complicated life in the shadows of secrecy and perpetual guilt; spending so much time on interior decoration; neglecting her appearance; seeming 'coarse and materialistic'. Julia, on the right, was eight years younger, and appeared to Carrington to live in the metaphoric light – open, beautiful, composed, and clear.

Julia was a dear friend, but Carrington wanted someone to be more than a friend. That she discovered someone who might possibly fill that gap in her life is clear from a humorous valentine she sent to Lytton that February:

A Dove brought back to me
My love on a Wave of the sea,
A Dove brings my Love for you
Obscured in the Wool of a Ewe.[51]

Above was a drawing of a dove pulling a ship; below, a dove pulling a wheeled sheep to Lytton. There was someone she was interested in, and perhaps sleeping with, but who was not yet a major part of her life. By sending a valentine about a new 'love' to Lytton, she showed that she associated her new love with her older one. As always, she felt that anything belonging to her also belonged to Lytton. A gift of love to her was, in turn, also an offering to him, as was clear in her relationship with Ralph. Yet Lytton would never be enthusiastic about Bernard (or Beakus, as he was called) Penrose.

Beakus was an attractive, young, self-styled sailor who at twenty-five was Carrington's junior by ten years. 'Beakus', Frances Partridge writes, 'wasn't in the Royal Navy but was a well-off young man, romantic about the sea, who sailed several times in windjammers and later bought his own Brixham trawler.'[52] David Garnett called Beakus 'the last great passion of [Carrington's] life', and says that '[t]hough reserved, often silent and slow of speech, Beakus Penrose already had his own strong aesthetic tastes and a clear sense of values'.[53] The brother of Alec, Lionel and Roland Penrose (Alec was one of Lytton's new, young Cambridge friends whom he described as 'a complete womaniser' and 'a man of character'[54]), Beakus literally sailed into her life when he was most needed to stave off her loneliness and many fears, especially of ageing. Yet this affair was different from her previous relationships, for Carrington appears to have initiated it, perhaps as an antidote to those increasing fears. Quiet and unintellectual, Beakus posed no threat to her continuing life with Lytton.

As a rugged and ruddy-faced sailor, he offered her the novelty of a physical life aboard ship, and a diversion from the often empty, and certainly more scholarly, life at Ham Spray. Still, she felt compelled to refer to these attributes negatively in an undated letter to Alix:

> Beakus (sailor Penrose) came in after supper. He lives on a sailing ship
> ... in the harbour ... its a pity – that – so beautiful – he should be so
> young – & don't leave this letter on the mantelpiece, for Lionel to read –
> a little dense ... I shall try to seduce Beakus to take me a pub crawl one
> night, & to the Cinema ... My dreams are really getting too much of a
> good thing – I wish you would give me a remedy – there's no doubt it's
> almost time my head was purged out, as well as the lower system. Perhaps
> they are interinvolved ...[55]

Where before she sought release through hard work, she now sought to 'purge' her 'head ... as well as the lower system' by sexual means – another change from her younger self, inspired in part by a sense of adventure, romance and desperation.

Although Lytton never became fond of Beakus, Carrington never hid what was going on from him. Nevertheless, in late December she 'deserted' her beloved Dorelia and Fryern and pretended to return to Ham Spray. Instead, she went to Southampton with Beakus where, despite 'drizzling rain' and 'slushing mud' they spent a romantic night aboard his ship, the *Sans Pareil*, with 'a black cat keeping watch on deck'. She apparently knew him well enough by this time to assign him a pet name: 'the Seagull'.

> Its an infinitely romantic ship, with brown varnished cupboards and cut
> glass handles and a little fire place with a brass mantelpiece. I don't think
> I ever enjoyed an evening more in my life, the rain beating down on the

deck above, sitting in the cabin lit by lamplight, cooking eggs and sausages over the fire and drinking rum. The Seagull is fascinating on board. He is so in love with his ship that he moons about in a trance opening cupboards and eulogizing over its beauties, in his slow voice. The only disadvantage is, if I may say so, that the bunks aren't built for two sailors alongside. The black puss is a great charmer and sat on the rails of the little balustrade that goes round the bunks peering with green eyes at the midnight feast. The next morning I washed up and cooked an omelette for breakfast and chatted to some sailors who were mending the cabin door.

The Seagull suffered a good deal from my un-nautical language. But was impressed by my lamp-trimming. I dashed back to Ham Spray yesterday after lunch, in time to set the house in order, and meet Lytton at the station. I shall tell nobody but you of my romantic evening because nobody but you discerns the beauty of varnished wood and silver suns behind lamps...[56]

Quite likely this secrecy heightened her sense of romantic adventure, as did using Julia as a confidante.

Nevertheless, by the end of the year she appeared to be happier. She mentioned only casually in the same letter that Lytton seemed well and was going away again for a week. By September the studio was finished and Lytton was now spending most of his time in London, working at the British Museum. 'You can't think how often I think of you & how much I love you', she wrote to Lytton. 'Everytime I sit in my beautiful studio ... You are really very, very kind, and I feel utterly unworthy, yet sign myself your devoted (female) servant, Mopsa.' Much of the time spent in the new room was in painting tiles, which were, not surprisingly, nautical designs 'mostly of shells, fishes and ships'.[57] The year ended completely differently from the way it had begun: she was healthy, painting again, and in love – but determinedly and desperately so.

CHAPTER EIGHTEEN

DISASTER AVERTED: 1929

The renovations to Ham Spray, financed by Lytton's literary successes of 1928, began shortly after that Christmas. Meanwhile Carrington had been hired to decorate rooms for various friends, including Dadie Rylands's rooms up at Cambridge, and a small room for Dorelia John. Now she was able to turn her efforts to Lytton's rooms in London, and Ham Spray itself. This of course involved the inconveniences of carpenters, plaster dust and paint pots, and consequent minor disasters. After Carrington returned from France she discovered that her instructions to paint the back sitting room at Ham Spray cream had been misinterpreted: 'on my return I found my favourite blue front sitting room painted out! For they call the "back" of the house the "front" and vice versa. So I am rather bored with internal beautifying at the moment!' The 'beautifying' took its toll on her dreams, as she wrote to Lytton.

> Terrible dreams last night. I saw a crack in the walls of the house by my bedroom window, & as I was pointing it out to you, standing on the lawn by the aspen tree the whole window with a chunk of wall, clean out of the house, fell with a sickening thud into the lawn. And I thought 'how typical, that just as I have had the house painted, & cleaned it should fall to pieces'. – Then terrible enemies pursued me in the kitchen & tried to put my eyes out with a very small bent fork. – As he was doing it, I thought of our new Harrods forks, & wished it wasn't such an old one. – If it wasn't for my grim nightmares I should lead a very happy life.[58]

Her special pride in the little library she created in an upstairs room at Ham Spray for Lytton, who 'seems tolerably pleased with it which means – very much so'. She designed a wonderfully realistic imitation bookcase, filled with false bookbacks, over an unused door. (It still exists, and continues to take in people who see it.) She invented and wrote in titles, many of which reflect her recent difficulties with workmen.

Deeds Not Words	by A. Carpenter
Vols. I, II	
A Catastrophe	by Tiberius [Tiber was her cat]
The Empty Room	by Virginia Woolf
Bangs	by Georges Carpentier
The Lad	by Leonard Woolf
Deception	by Jane Austen
Œvres	by Le Conte Lytoff

She hoped that two improvements to the house would increase both her comfort and her creativity. Central heating was installed, and her studio was renovated. Ham Spray was so devastatingly cold in the winter months that Carrington and Lytton sometimes took to their beds to keep warm. 'The central heating certainly makes life far less grim in the winter here,' she wrote to Sebastian, 'sort of pads over the deficiencies of wayward lovers and cold hearted young men.'[59] This was a reference to Beakus, for the relationship with him was not a steady one. If his boat were close enough by for them to meet, they did. If not, she rarely heard from him. He did not share her penchant for letter-writing, and she had to settle for seeing him when she could. Lytton still held the centre stage in her life.

This same letter to Sebastian reveals the beginning of a problem which was to plague her for most of the year: 'Olive is away in bed [at her parents' home] with lumbago', she wrote to him in March, 'so Lytton and I have to cook for ourselves. (Lytton is a first-class bedmaker.)'[60] Because she thought the problem was temporary, she could treat it lightly. In fact, she was able to turn it into art.

What a horrid scene to see before one when one starts a letter to an orderly young gentleman *of taste* in Nottingham. Breakfast, lunch and tea mingled with fragments of Vita Wheat. Jam on the plates, whisky jostling with ink pots. You see to what a pass I am reduced and my chamber pot is still unemptied and the beds NOT made, or is it merely an excuse for drawing a still-life apres le grand maitre Monsieur Fry? Who can tell indeed?[61]

When Olive's illness lasted through a second week, Carrington and Lytton finally fled domestic responsibility, she to London and he to Cambridge. Ham Spray was too large to care for alone, and Lytton's perpetual digestive problems meant that separate meals had to be prepared for him. In any case, he was hardly an ideal domestic helper.

Carrington returned to Ham Spray several days later to find Olive still ill: 'The doctor says she is "run down" but I have a sickening feeling it may be something worse so really most of my time lately has been spent cooking and emptying chamber pots.' Ralph kindly offered to bring his London servant Mabel and her sister down for

Easter, but even so 'I suppose I shall have to try and get a temporary, or a new girl. Its a frightful bore.'[62]

Throughout the winter and spring she had continual problems with servants, redecorating, and loneliness. She spent her quiet weekday evenings drinking alone, writing her famous illustrated letters. 'Since I started this letter', she wrote to Sebastian in the spring, 'the stove has gone out and as usual I've drunk too much.'[63] And to Julia, at about the same time, she wrote, 'I've just tidied up my studio and directly this servant crisis is over I shall draw up my "plan" for your inspection and start on a new era of work and discipline. The spelling seems rather drunk today. I am sorry.'[64] Ham Spray had a well-stocked cellar; she, Lytton, and Ralph would buy barrels of wine in France and bottle it themselves at the house. This of course was another major – although voluntary – job which she faced periodically, and which when she wanted it gave her another excuse not to paint. On 21 May, the eighth anniversary of her marriage to Ralph, she wrote to Lytton,

> Ralph is coming back on Friday evening. And what shall we drink for supper tonight??? What indeed. When the cat is away the mice will make hay. [This was followed by a drawing of mice drinking bottles of wine.]
> You can't think how much I miss you. I would like you to only go away on wet gloomy days. It seems monstrous to waste a beautiful evening like this without you.[65]

And to him again the next afternoon,

> I am rather boozed and befuddled with drink [after lunch with the Johns] so forgive a poorish letter ... Dorelia loved your library and our botanical Dutch books. I wish she could have stayed, but she had Augustus and a tribe of visitors shrieking at Fryern today. In a moment I shall go to sleep but I must first order the wine bottles. I shan't drink another drop now, till you return, and tomorrow I shall start a painting of tulips.[66]

She signed this letter, 'Your devoted loving intoxicated Mopsa XXX'.

The resolution did not last long. A week and a half later she and Beakus attended a party at Fryern; he drove her there in his racing Bentley, and she found him 'a very careful driver, curiously efficient and on the spot'. They arrived home late, and the next morning she felt 'a little dim in the head with too much sherry ... We bottled one cask of white wine on Saturday. I'll get Olive to help with the red perhaps this week. It's really very simple with the new system.'

Carrington visited Holland with Sebastian Sprott in July 1929, while Lytton went on holiday with Ralph. She found the people dull, the coffee good, and 'some of the architecture very beautiful'.[68] The pictures in the galleries pleased her most, and she saw many modern paintings, including some by van Gogh, Seurat, and Renoir whose work, unlike the 'modern French painters', she admired. Viewing the paintings brought on her usual depression about her own work, causing her to caution Julia that 'my life has been frittered away without producing anything worth looking at. You must at least learn by my sad example and finish your novel.'[69] She expanded on this subject toward the end of the year when she read Virginia Woolf's *A Room of One's Own*: 'I still don't agree that poverty and a room of one's own, is the explanation why women didn't write poetry. If the Brontës could write in their Rectory, why not other clergymen's daughters?'[70] August found her happily painting again, this time a thorn-apple tree at Fryern. Her disappointment was never enough to prevent her from trying again.

As usual when she felt lonely or depressed, she went to stay with the Johns at Fryern. A 'picture of a thorn apple tree in flower in the garden on a huge canvas' occupied her for at least two days, and Beakus accompanied her on an errand to choose wallpaper samples for Lytton's Gordon Square bedroom.[71] The following evening she and Dorelia were to visit Beakus's ship at Southampton, and she was able to write that she was enjoying herself very much. While at Fryern she met T. E. Shaw (Lawrence of Arabia), whose portrait Augustus was painting, but found him 'a measly little man'.[72]

The summer of 1929 was a time of experimenting in another artistic direction. Beakus Penrose bought a motion picture camera, which inspired the production of several amateur films. The first was made at Hilton, David Garnett's home: the cast consisted of both Beakus and Alec Penrose, Frank Ramsey (a young philosopher) and his wife Lettice, Angus Davidson, and Frances Marshall. Frances, made to wear a pink dress and play the heroine, later remarked that she 'never had the smallest gift for acting'.[73] The film took two days to complete. David Garnett found it 'marred by insufficient lighting for the indoor scenes', and 'though [he] was intensely proud of this film, ... [he] had to admit that one produced shortly afterwards at Hamspray by Carrington and Tommy and shot by Beakus, was infinitely more imaginative.'[74]

When Beakus 'dropped in for a weekend, very vaguely of course', in mid-August and brough his movie camera, everyone was inspired. Lytton was away, but Ralph, Frances, Saxon Sydney-Turner, Rachel MacCarthy (daughter of Desmond, an original 'member' of the Bloomsbury group), and Stephen Tomlin were there. They spent Saturday evening planning, with some minor setbacks: 'Of course Ralph was very tiresome and destroyed every idea that was suggested until he had to be ignored', Carrington wrote to Lytton.[75]

She rose early on Sunday morning to make 'dummies' and masks, and prepare props; by noon the production officially began. Carrington set the film in a mental institution, with Saxon Sydney-Turner as head doctor – forgetting until later that this was his father's real profession.

> I must say it was great fun. Saxon in the leading role as Dr. Turner acted superbly. Rachael was a simple girl called Daisy, the rest of us were lunatics in Dr. Turner's mental home. (Of course I forgot that Saxon's father kept a 'Home'!! But I am sure Saxon didn't mind the coincidence.) We didn't have lunch till 2.30 and the whole afternoon was given over to drowning Rachael in the bath by the greenhouse ... puss played a large part in the film with great success. It is to be performed next Thursday at 41 Gordon Square. I suppose you won't be able to come?[76]

David Garnett described the Ham Spray film in even greater detail.

> The setting was Dr. Turner's private lunatic asylum, where the inmates were experimented upon and reduced to the condition of animals, the subject being Saxon Sydney-Turner's sinister attempts to experiment upon the innocent heroine who was played by Rachel MacCarthy, wearing a daisy chain. The scene of Saxon, as Dr. Turner, peering around the bathroom door at her, had a macabre quality which I have never seen achieved in any other film. My sister-in-law Frances also achieved a success as a human quadruped lunatic wearing riding boots on her arms.[77]

The entire production lasted several days, finishing on Monday morning, and Carrington then faced 'the mess and confusion left after all the acting'.[78]

The film enjoyed great success among her friends. Film-making, had it been possible, might have been a natural next artistic step for her. It combined her love of costume design, designing rooms (or sets), humour, directing people, and theatre. She liked going to the cinema and when she finally saw a Mickey Mouse cartoon 'laughed until [she] nearly cried'. Music-hall productions, especially those which involved rustic humour and 'naughty' jokes, delighted her. Not only would film-making have provided a new medium for her personal and artistic strengths, but films like the one made that summer might have provided an outlet from some of her nightmares and fears.

Inevitably, the excitement over the film was short-lived. A few days later she was alone and feeling low, '[p]artly because it seems a bit hollow and empty after the wild shrieks and gaiety of the weekend, and then one of those tiresome moods of craving for a little ~ ~ ~ ~ came upon me. But I expect it will soon pass, only it's boring to feel so gloomy.'[79] Lytton's reply to this letter undoubtedly cheered her: 'I cannot try to say all you are to me', he wrote.

Perhaps because of a reluctance to be alone at Ham Spray for long, Carrington travelled a great deal in 1929. She left for France

on 18 September with Augustus and Dorelia, but their celebration of the night before left her unpleasantly hung over for the crossing.

> I had rather a collapse last night. We went to dinner at the Tour, where I got very drunk on hock, in spite of all my intentions to keep a clean palate for Burgundy.
> ... After dinner, we went ... to a Russian restaurant in Picadilly, a dreadful place with sham cossacks, where I regret to say, to my shame, I passed away insensible after drinking some glasses of vodka, and had to be removed home by Dodo, a sad ending to a charming evening. So this morning 3 very wobbly wobblers sailed for France, accompanied by 2 Siamese cats.[80]

The letters from this period reveal above all her determination to have fun at all costs. Her trip to France with the Johns was an extended party: champagne and oysters for breakfast, 'half a bottle for lunch every day with cheese, and a salad at some small inn. Then another half bottle and a brioche for tea and a whole bottle of very grand wine for dinner.'[81] Yet worry and guilt about leaving Lytton followed her; she offered to return home immediately if he needed her, and sent wires if he went too long without writing. Above all she needed to be needed and her dissipations were diversions and ways of filling her time.

When Carrington returned from France Olive had finally recovered, but in early October 1929 delivered bad news:

> I've had an awful blow ... Olive leaves me, for ever, the end of this month. She has to go into a family business, a baker. Its mostly I am fond of her. But then I dread starting all over again teaching someone to cook and our habits. My mind wavers between getting a Swede or Finn, two sisters, a Chinese boy, an elderly housekeeper, a country girl. But whatever nationality they are, or sex, or age, they are bound to be terrible. It's a bad moment for I must do some glass pictures for a commission, and earn a little money this week. Then there are Lytton's rooms in London which *must* be painted and at once – he is in despair about them – and between all this I have three weeks to find a servant.[82]

She was still quite uncomfortable in the role of employer and 'gave orders with a curious sort of diffidence', recalled Frances.[83] When Olive left in October she was replaced temporarily by Kitty, 'an ice cold maid' who 'reigns in the kitchen'. A new servant meant spending hours each day in training, and leaving her studio to 'see if Kitty has made a sauce for the fish'.[84] When all these difficulties began to interfere with Carrington's social life, she regretted that friends – Henry Lamb is mentioned in one letter – 'would think all my reasons, i.e. servants and perpetually working for Lytton's new rooms, mere cockey-eye excuses'.[85] In a way they were just that, of course. All these things needed doing, but there was no question that she was afraid to face her easel and the inevitable, though not always warranted, disappointment of artistic creation. Flo, the new servant, replaced Kitty near the end of 1929, and there had to be lessons in cooking omelettes, making soup, and using the vacuum cleaner. Flo learned quickly but needed guidance, and it was more than a year before the house was running smoothly again.

Carrington paid for this latest holiday with hard work on her return. In London, she worked at commissioned decorating jobs, and at finishing Lytton's rooms. Then, back at Ham Spray, there were visitors: along with Ralph, Frances and Lytton there appeared that autumn many of Lytton's friends – Morgan Forster, Stephen Tennant, Arthur Waley, Willy Walton – all immediately following Olive's departure. The difficulties raised by decorating, guests, and servants were nothing, however, compared to a real nightmare which occurred late that autumn when Carrington discovered she was pregnant.

Her response was entirely predictable. She became so profoundly depressed that both Ralph and Lytton, recently returned from their holiday, feared that her mood verged on the suicidal. Over the years she and Lytton had expressed strong opinions on children, or 'les petits peuples', as they called them. Her brother Noel writes that at neither 'Tidmarsh nor Hamspray ... were children welcome, and this was not entirely because "le petit peuple" would be a bore for Lytton's circle of intellectuals'.[86] Despite this antipathy, Carrington had shown at least an artistic appreciation for children, painting them in France, Spain, and England. When younger, she had given art lessons – although not always with whole-hearted enthusiasm – to children, and mentions in early letters enjoying teaching a child to swim. But having a child of her own was an entirely different matter.

Pregnancy was not only the ultimate reminder of her femaleness, but it would also completely upset the very delicate balance of life at Ham Spray. Lytton would undoubtedly wish to spend even less time at Ham Spray if a child were living there. The negotiations over the resettling of Ralph and Frances had been very delicate, and even though three years had passed since then, life at Ham Spray was still subtly shifting and settling. Ralph and Frances liked children, and Carrington, before her death, urged them to have a baby (which Ralph thought indicated her intention to die, and to be 'replaced' by their child).

There was no doubt that if Carrington were to remain pregnant it would surely have led to an attempt on her own life. Lytton was extremely kind and understanding to her during this crisis. She wanted both him and Ralph to know how much she appreciated their help but did not 'really see why such foolishness should be rewarded!'[87] Yet, she also wanted to reassure Lytton and herself that she was all right, when she was not: 'I've been working in my studio all this morning ... Truly I am quite happy here. If I feel gloomy I will motor over to Julia, and Tommy for a visit. I hope you will enjoy London this week ... I love you so much, and I shall never forget your kindness lately to me.'[88] She wrote to him daily, bravely, but the letters show a steady shift towards a serious depression. The next day she tried to use her usual humour when writing to him, saying 'I go for a "jog" on Belle and then I shall sit down and listen to the wireless and twiddle my thumbs, and repeat old proverbs about stable doors and steeds ... I pin all my faith on the jog-trot!'[89] This apparent attempt to cause a miscarriage did not succeed, and the third letter of that week to Lytton shows her struggle to be brave:

The rain pours down and the Downs are obliterated by clouds. Je pense je suis perdu. I took a very violent ride on Belle all yesterday along the top of the Downs, mais, sans effet. It is a little difficult to keep one's spirits up, and preserve a sense of humour. Especially with thick grey clouds hanging over one's head and obliterating all the light![90]

Frances remained an outsider while Ralph and Lytton tried to reach a solution. Apparently concerned that Frances would feel some unease about the situation, Lytton again met her for a private conversation, this time in a taxi, where he expressed his appreciation of her understanding. Frances had no real involvement in the problem, except as the lover of the man who would legally become the child's father. She found that Carrington's 'attitude to the situation was brave as well as tragic', but everyone knew that only one solution was possible: Ralph arranged, and largely financed, an abortion at a London nursing home. When she visited Carrington there, Frances found 'the change in her state of mind ... miraculous. Ralph's reward was her boundless gratitude, as well as "undying love" on the part of the author of the episode, who wrote to him saying, "I think you have been *damned nice*".'[91]

The 'author of the episode' was of course Beakus, but he was strangely absent from most of the discussions and arrangements. He was something of a shadow figure, visited by Carrington or appearing at Ham Spray mainly in Lytton's absence. He was not really admired by her but was attractive and important to her stability and feeling of self-worth. Because of the sense of romance his way of life afforded her, she clung to the relationship and he actually became more, rather than less, important to her as time passed.

While the immediate change in Carrington's state of mind may have been 'miraculous', it did not last. Olive was thinking of leaving, Beakus was away, Lytton was gone most of the time, and now there was an abortion to end the year. She pinned her faith on Lytton, the person who 'give[s] me a standard of sensible behaviour which makes it much easier to be reasonable'. Difficult though the last year had been, she had survived – and Lytton and Ralph, not Beakus, had helped her.

CHAPTER NINETEEN

THE MEDAL REVERSED:
1930

Carrington had originally been attracted to Beakus by both his physical appearance and his life as a sailor, and was well aware that in both he reminded her of her dead brother, Teddy. As the months passed, her infatuation became more of an obsession, and she began to see herself and Beakus as characters in a continuing story. Any unkind word from him seemed to signal the end of the relationship, and any night spent aboard his shop seemed the height of bliss. Her pregnancy, which brought on such an alarming depression, added to the melodrama. In one diary entry she hinted that, at least at first, she kept the pregnancy a secret from him: '... as he hugged me in the kitchen I thought "you little guess what you hug between us!" '[92] While there is no question that her intense response to the pregnancy was genuine, this comment raises the likelihood of another, simultaneous response: this was possibly the greatest secret she had ever had, and it suited the dramatic nature of their relationship (or indeed, of every relationship she had ever had). Just as in fiction, it was the climax of the affair.

The diary entries of late 1929 and early 1930 prove that she thought of the affair dramatically. Several entries are presented as short stories, complete with titles, when in fact they are long descriptions of actual occurrences and her responses to them. One entry entitled 'A Short Love Affaire or The Danish Grave' begins and ends with the assumption that her affair with Beakus is ending, an event which she takes philosophically, preferring 'a short love affaire' to none at all. Sandwiched in between this resignation is a celebration of romance.

Not very much curiousity [sic]. Yet that is probably the main attraction. Perhaps the most beautiful moment with a shirt in dark close fitting trowsers and a brass belt. Do men know the beauty of their appearance as exactly as females do? Their best advantages? ... The pleasure of kissing in taxis. The cinema holding hands ... and the resolution that another twenty kisses are worth giving up a party for.

... Standing looking out of my studio window at the landscape and the oak and kissing. Thinking its like being at a light house window with a sailor. Making toast in the kitchen over the fire, and cooking eggs. And then the going away and listening to Handel and Beethoven and the steady hum of hive life again.

This was precisely why she chose a male and not a female lover: she may have found a sexual awakening with Henrietta – and there is no evidence that she ever had another woman as a lover – but ultimately it was romance with a man which she craved. Those who knew her felt that this sense of the romantic superseded for her more 'animal' instincts. She grew to accept and even enjoy sex with men, as her comments after she met Ralph prove, but what she really craved was the aura of an imaginative setting. This was something Beakus could offer in abundance, as well as allowing her, through his resemblance to Teddy, to regain a crucial loss and finally express her affection for her 'sailor brother'. As the affair increasingly took on the form of an obsession, it began to fill her days at Ham Spray. By the beginning of 1930 some of her loneliness began to lift. With it went some of her worries about her age and she replied to a letter from Julia: 'Too old for kisses am I? Well, well every cat her day I suppose.'[93]

In January 1930 she wrote to Lytton that 'life is so rushed and whirling – as you rightly guessed we dash about the country to Fryern, and Combe Bissett and drink and talk like magpies without a pause. I painted a picture for the Lambs, in a panel in their passage, which seemed to please them.' In addition to this cheerful visiting, she began to take more of an interest in her wardrobe, ordering a 'very grand' dress to be made. Her spirits were lifted even further by a new person to add to those she admired: Iris Tree's mother (Carrington had attended the Slade with Iris), whom she found 'fascinating. I got tired with laughing she was so amusing.'

> ... I was completely bowled over by her punning humour and high spirits. No wonder Iris is such an amusing good humoured character with such a steel to sharpen her wits upon. And again I am not surprised she prefers Lady Tree's company to any husband.[94]

Carrington's life in the first half of 1930 took a definite turn for the better. She had weathered a crisis that could have proved disastrous. She had loving and happy friends to visit and to support her, was in love with a handsome young man, and was getting over the difficulties she and Lytton faced after Ralph moved to London. In her time and thoughts were now so occupied by Beakus that it was Lytton who needed to look elsewhere for the sympathetic conversation he usually found with Carrington – particularly about his current affair with Roger Senhouse.

When she was alone, however – less often now that she attempted to spend as much time as possible with others – she found that she still missed Lytton as much as ever. 'Poor Tiber [the Ham Spray cat] isn't very well today', she wrote him on 22 February. 'An attack of depression. He mops [sic] sadly in front of the fire. I hope it is nothing serious. Its curious how much you take away with you when you go. Do you know that? More than half my purpose in living seems to vanish, and your empty library looks a different room. I love you always so much.'[95] She turned again to her painting, and in March selected two pictures, at Augustus John's request, to show at the Salisbury Picture Gallery. As usual her lack of confidence posed a problem made worse when she went to see the exhibition: 'Went to look at the Picture Gallery. Alas, mine looked just as dingey [sic] as the others. Filled me with despair & neither sold. So I whirled back to Ham Spray with a SAD Heart.'[96] A few weeks later she wrote Lytton that she was 'trying to brace up my self to start a campaign of painting. Its rather awful that I've done none this year! [This was not true.] When you come back I shall have a fine exhibition I hope to show you.'[97]

By early summer, although she and Lytton seemed to be spending more time apart, they were actually growing closer. In June he visited Rome with George Rylands for three weeks, and Lytton and Carrington spent the evening of 3 April together before his departure. Much sadder than usual at separating, they wrote to each other nearly every day to express their love.

> Just to send you my fondest love for your journey. I did so love spending last night with you. – I shall be very happy when you are away starting my reformed life of painting. – You mustn't think I mind in the least you being in Rome. – I mean I do. – But at the same time I shall be very happy so you mustn't think of me. On the whole I think you ought not to ask me to join you. a) Because of the expense, & b) then it will be so nice at Ham Spray, that I am sure Italy can't compare with it. c) and then I have so much painting to do I ought not to go caravansing [sic] across Europe. – Give Dadie my love.[98]

Lytton, however, quickly became homesick for both Ham Spray and Carrington, writing to her that he wished she could be there with him. In these last months they obstinately put their lives into high gear, visiting friends, travelling, working (she at her painting, he – with the help of Ralph and Frances – editing the memoirs of Charles Greville in the British Museum), yet feeling closest to happiness when they were alone together.

While Carrington painted a rosy picture of Ham Spray life, all was not entirely well there. In Lytton's absence the servants began to squabble among themselves, carrying tales to Carrington for her to resolve. In annoyance she refused to have anything to do with them, preferring to spend her time, when possible, with Beakus. 'I still rather adore my strange Gull, & pub life among the sailors,' she confessed to Lytton before his return on 23 April.[99] But even there all was not well. When Beakus arrived at Ham Spray on 10 June for the weekend, she decided 'with my gypsy's warning' but no other evidence than his distant manner that he had been to bed with someone else.[100]

He seemed distracted throughout the weekend, and Carrington, already nervous about her age, took this to mean that she had lost his affection. Apparently there was reason for this worry. Gerald later said that since Carrington was obviously older than Beakus, his other women friends made fun of her behind her back. She wrote about these two days in his diary, adopting a short story format which allowed her to both dramatise and examine the situation. She entitled it 'The Reverse of the Medal' to signify that their love had suffered what she thought was a permanent setback. At thirty-six she felt that every reversal in love was forever, and her obsession with Beakus expressed itself in two ways: resignation to every difficulty and to the obsession itself, and a quiet but increasing panic that this love, like all the others, would not last. The only love she could count on was Lytton's, and nearly losing him after Ralph's departure with Frances made her even more frantic over the possibility of losing Beakus.

In fact, in 'The Reverse of the Medal', she clearly likened her situation with Beakus to Lytton's situation with Roger Senhouse, who was also staying for the weekend, along with Ralph and Frances. Indeed, there were a number of similarities. Both Carrington and Lytton were involved with much younger lovers, which made them not only appreciate their good luck, but also to worry that it could not last. Both found their lovers extremely attractive physically, and worried about their fidelity. They both had reason to believe that they loved more than they were loved. These handsome young men were in fact to be the last great loves of Carrington's and Lytton's lives.

At Ham Spray that weekend, one member of each of the three couples wanted something which she or he expected her or his partner to know instinctively. As a result, there is no dialogue at all in her account of it, and the characters appear as silhouetted dancers against the backdrop of the house. Carrington, as in several of the 'stories' she wrote in her diary is the interpreting observer of all the action. She begins *in medias res*, and ends with a dramatic explanation of the symbolism of the title.

The Reverse of the Medal[101]

Directly he arrived I saw he was changed. I thought I would leave him to see how long it would be before he joined me. He was only occupied by the lateness of the time he went to bed the night before, that he did not get any sleep till 3 o'ck. I knew with my gypsy's warning that he had really been to B., with B., and was exhausted and was starting to explain his indifference by sleepiness.

We played badminton, after that ping-pong after dinner. There was a wireless. I hoped he would sit alone with me or go for a walk, but he insisted on listening. I couldn't listen. I watched him half asleep in his chair, and thought he was probably after all a figure head. I remembered how all day I'd been looking forward to his coming and now how bored and flat it seemed. And I felt not the slightest interest in me.

After the wireless, I suggested going to bed and left the room. F[rances] with what I call the 'frustration of the lover's movement', at once put on the wireless. I told R[alph] that Lytton was longing to go to bed and begged him to put off the wireless. He was cross, in the engine house. I saw Lytton wandering disconsolately in the sitting-room; it was half past ten. I saw F[rances] was determined to play the wireless dance music. Then Roger and B[eakus] started ping pong.

I suddenly saw the similarity between Lytton and my position. Both unable to do anything because we longed for our bed companions who were equally indifferent, to put it bluntly, about coming to bed. I couldn't bear to see Lytton unhappy, so I went out and sat in the moonlight on a stump under the ilex with Tiber who was prowling about on our lawn. I watched Lytton flapping the pages of the Nation restlessly on his chair in the sitting room. I could hear the dim strains of the wireless and hear the ping of the ping pong balls.

After half an hour Ralph passed through the dining room and went, I knew by instinct, into the kitchen for ice to make drinks. He seemed to take a long time. I got colder and colder. Suddenly Lytton got up, and went to see if Ralph was R[oger] perhaps I thought, then went back to his paper in the chair. At last Ralph went back with drinks. Then Lytton got up and went upstairs to his library.

I was afraid he'd see me under the tree, so I went round to the beech tree and lay on the motor mower cover. Puss running after me and lay on my lap; I could see Frances playing ping pong and B[eakus] sitting in a chair staring in front of him. I looked at the moon through the beech leaves which had a fine grey edge against the sky. And listening to the sad pee-wee cats got very cold. I thought B[eakus] has never once wondered where I have got to.

At last the light was put out. I went and lay under the ilex and watched Ralph look for me in the bedroom, undress and put out the light, Lytton go to bed. Two lights down the passage windows. Roger undressing. B[eakus] very slowly standing by his bed, finally pulling off his shirt and putting on blue striped pyjamas. Lytton evidently came to Roger's room for suddenly Roger pulled his curtains. B[eakus] put out his light. I heard the door in the lavatory shut. No light turned up in my empty eyed windows. He had gone however for after ten minutes there was a light turned up in his bedroom. But I was not, after that, going to go to his room. It was after half past twelve.

Lying in the cold grass I suddenly realised that he was completely indifferent to my sensations, incapable of any love. Only quite ready to go to bed if there was anyone ready to go to bed. Probably thought it was expected of him by me ... I can't stand being treated so casually. But I was undetermined whether I could bear to part all together, and I knew if I accused him of being in the wrong he would seize the excuse probably of quarrelling with me. As he can't bear criticism.

We played badminton all the morning and I saw such hostility to me in his play. Very slight but different from other times. After lunch we went bathing and met Noel and Missie [Noel Carrington and his wife Catharine]. I saw all day he took no opportunity to kiss me when we were alone so the rather chagring [sic] truth wore into me ... Monday we played badminton ... The rest indifferent[.] I saw he was restless and critical and not enjoying himself. Went bathing I felt a positive hostility as we had tea, and an avoidance to be alone with me. The beauty of the scene restored me and darling Lytton's sympathetic company ...

Afterwards in the bathroom he came in he never kissed me. I felt I was ugly. He had a bath I washed his back and thought I can forgive your little monkey body covered with spots. But you have no love in you for me ...

I lay in bed for about ten minutes wondering if he realised how hurt I'd been by his hard voice and indifference. I thought tomorrow it would be different to [word missing] over such a parting. Because I should think of it alright. I was miserable. I went to his room and said goodnight. He was nice but far away and clearly unaware of my unhappiness. I thought if he asked to come back to my room [I] will, not otherwise. So I said goodnight and went away realising suddenly everything, that this was the reverse of the medal ...

AT any rate I didn't as I always have in the past love too little. It could not have been more perfect. The difficulty now is to get accustomed to wearing on my necklace the medal reversed.

Any number of explanations are possible for Beakus's behaviour, including his having another lover, but the most likely is the simple one that by now they had been lovers for about two years. Carrington still acted as though they were in the first stages of their love affair, when the relationship had obviously nearly run its course. Her greatest sympathy was for Lytton, who was undergoing similar treatment by his lover, yet even this simply reflected and heightened her own unhappiness.

'The Reverse of the Medal' demonstrates another, and perhaps more interesting, aspect of Carrington's character. In the piece she acts the part of a *voyeuse*, a role at least partly rooted in her artist's sensibility and acute powers of observation. She watches for hours outside the house people who do not know that they are being observed; one wonders if she would have continued to watch had Roger Senhouse *not* pulled the curtain. This voyeurism can be seen also in another of her less than admirable practices, such as reading others' mail, and vindicates Julia's characterization of her as a kind of 'witch' who wanted to make off with everyone's innermost secrets. Because she was so aware of everyone else's habits and movements, she guarded hers more closely, yet resented it when no one attempted to discover them.

Carrington knew that she was responding irrationally to Beakus's moods:

> Its difficult to describe my feelings because they are so illogical. Its partly the effect of having laid two years in the coffin untouched, so as to speak, that these months of animal affection rather ruined my moral [*sic*]. Its difficult to go back to coffin life again and with my numerous complexes not very easy even if one wanted to, to get a transfer ticket onto some one else. Fortunately its mostly a matter of bodily lusts I have to deal with in other respects.[102]

This was, in several respects, a new situation for her. With other men – Mark, Ralph and Gerald – she had been the one pursued. Now she was not the centre of Beakus's life as she had been in the past with other men. Much of her frustration in 'The Reverse of the Medal' resulted from her belief that he should not only anticipate her needs and desires, but be constantly aware of her whereabouts and follow her.

When he was not and did not she was crushed and began to long for her solitary days before she had been involved with him. At the same time she was no longer satisfied with her former life of sexual and emotional dormancy. Even while she resented this feeling, she needed to feel connected. She began to find fault with everyone around her, beginning with Beakus himself: '. . . Beakus, who I found so beautiful two days ago . . . that I could hardly take my eyes off him, seemed now dull & monotonous.' When he complained about her white stockings – he preferred black silk which 'show off the leg so much better' – she 'realised our PATHS lay differently. I shall mourn in secret this week, painting my tiles and then go back to my coffin and enjoy the company of my friends again.' She resented the time spent washing dishes for 'this unworthy Gull', time which might have been more happily spent with Julia and Tommy, or Dorelia and Augustus. *They* did not complain about her clothes.[103]

At Ham Spray, she had more problems with the new servant Flo, and found that with so many guests, her life had become a succession of 'coal skuttles [*sic*] & endless meals'. The evenings were marred by 'shrieking conversation & bunchy groups over the fire'. Her list of complaints included one about Ralph, whose 'jocular intimacy, mixed with conversations in the bathroom with F, is n't to my taste'.[104] Most annoying was that Lytton, her most sympathetic confidant, was away. She felt alone in the crowd, rejected by her lover; forgetting the miserable loneliness and nightmares which marred her 'coffin life' of the late 1920s, she longed to return to solitude.

These anxieties manifested themselves in sleeplessness. She found herself more tired when she rose in the morning then when she went to bed at night. During the day she felt separate from the jovial conversations of Ralph, Beakus, and the others, and her work in the studio was frequently interrupted by household responsibilities which the others either did ineffectually or not at all.

> ... a sort of overboiling seizes me sometimes when I am interrupted in my studio to turn off the water, & have to put logs on the fires, & order all the meals, to hear these perpetual shrieks in the sitting room & nobody stirring – what they call – a finger – to do any work in the house. The inclination to cut this nautical knot, & retreat back to my former solitude is so great, that I find it difficult not to DO it ... But in spite of reasoning that one's feelings are unnaturally egotistical, I long for the wings of an owl that I might FLY.[105]

Even when this problem was eased by the departure of the visitors, her work depressed her. By this time nearly all of her art was channelled into the painting of tiles, which she both sold and gave as gifts.[106] Although quite successful, this business was a mixed blessing. It absorbed much of her time, and her letters are sometimes little more than a tally of the number painted and ready to be fired. By 13 June she had completed another lot of 120 tiles, and felt 'as if the brain was about to give way'. At such times she fled in the Sunbeam to visit friends at Fryern or Combe Bissett, or delivered newly-painted tiles to London to be fired before sending them on to the stores that sold them anonymously. These trips to London also gave her a chance to visit Lytton in his rooms at Gordon Square, or go to parties and restaurants with other London friends.

Lytton began to be concerned about the time she spent on unfulfilling projects, and on 11 June 1930, made her an offer which she apparently refused. 'Have you been slaving away at the tiles?' he wrote from Cambridge. 'I wonder if you feel an absence of money. If so, would you like a sort of salary or pension of £100 a year? – I could very easily manage it, if it would in any way be a comfort to you. Why not?'[107] He had known of her financial difficulties for years, but oddly it was not until now that he realised just how hard she had to work to earn money. No letter exists to indicate her response.

Her resolution to care less about Beakus was short-lived. Only a week or two after his departure from Ham Spray she began to compose sentimental poems full of nautical symbols and themes. In one, she likened herself to a 'faded passion flower' who has lost 'the love of my Paramoor [sic]'. A few days later, apparently convinced that he had left her for another, she forgot her anger during his recent visit and wrote 'On a Picture of a Ship':

> A cross stitch ship in a frame of wood
> Could life be once again as good,
> As the day he gave me that picture rare
> And I rumpled my hand in his wind-swept hair.
> But good Days are past, and before me lies
> An eternity of Dull Blank Skies.[108]

This mood, as with most of her reactions to Beakus, did not last long. She spent half of her time depressed by their relationship, and the rest resolving to reconcile herself to its difficulties. Beakus was not really aware of her fluctuating moods; in any event, she was happiest with him when they were away from Ham Spray: in London, on his boat, or visiting friends.

She recognised that 'aiming at being a stoic' was unlikely to succeed. Try as she might to convince herself that she preferred to live alone, she *did* mind – and found that fact 'ignominious'. Her nightmares seemed to have abated but she woke up one morning in June 'in an ecstacy of love . . . to find my mouth full of sheets which I was biting passionately'. She hoped that the arrival of weekend guests would cheer her, 'but the difficulty is not to let one's mind wander off into abysses of gloom that lead but to munching sheets by moonlight in bed'.[109]

A letter to Sebastian Sprott in July sheds light on her uncomfortable feelings towards Beakus.

> I am sorry the food was such cold comfort at the weekend. I'm afraid Flo isn't very bright in the head . . . The Seagull was particularly charming and I may say that I am so badly gone on the boy that one 'night' sets me up for days afterwards. We had a lovely time in London last Friday evening: a cinema and sipping sherry in the little bed room at Gordon Square out of a tooth glass.
> . . . I wish I wasn't so mashed on this sea captain. I can hardly think of anything else and I can't bear to make any plans in case I might see him . . . Next week I go to London to draw designs for Phyllis de Janzé's library. She says 'I hope it will lead to great things for you.' So do I.[110]

Her infatuation interfered with and controlled her life to a great extent, but her success at interior design and decoration offered hope for a new direction.

In August Carrington learned a secret from Ralph, and true to form immediately wrote to tell Lytton of it. Gerald Brenan was engaged to Gamel Woolsey, a poet from the American south. She had been living with the literary Powys family in England and Gerald, their neighbour, had been attracted by her languorous beauty, her unusually 'artistic' style of dress, and her intelligence. They later moved to Spain, but were not formally married for many years. If Gerald himself told Ralph of his engagement, it is likely that he did so to be certain that Carrington found out. Gerald had never truly forgiven her treatment of him during their long affair, and he would surely have wanted her to be one of the first to discover his serious involvement with another woman. As trustworthy as Ralph was, it was unlikely that he could keep such an important secret from her. It was even less likely that she could keep it to herself, although she cautioned Lytton that it was 'a deadly secret so you're not to tell anyone!'[111] In any case, her involvement with Beakus was by now so deep that Gerald's news was merely a matter for surprise, curiosity and poetry.

> When a camal
> Weds a Gamal
> What sort of mamal
> Will appear?

'Camel' was one of her pet names for Gerald.[112]

Lytton went off to Ireland in August, and Carrington spent much of the rest of the summer making a conscious effort to enjoy herself. Although she was commissioned to paint a series of tiles for Alec Penrose, the work went slowly while she frequented friends' houses, the cinema, music-halls, and pubs. On 8 August she and James Strachey 'saw a lovely film together and at last I've seen a Mickey Mouse. I thought it was almost a work of genius! We laughed tremendously (aloud!) over it.'[113] In September she, along with Julia and Tommy, John Strachey (one of Lytton's nephews), and others, found amusement in tracking down unusual pubs and music-halls. One theatre provided a show that she found delightful as a perfect example of the genre.

> It was a *marvellous* performance. Indescribably English. Two very good comedians ... The audience was mostly soldiers and Salisbury yokels and they rocked backwards and forwards with shouts of laughter at the jokes about illegitimate babies and coming home with the milk. It was so perfect we could hardly bear it to end.[114]

She also found 'fine pubs' in Southampton.[115]

In contrast to this bucolic amusement, the rage in London was for 'Hermaphrodite Parties' for which guests dressed up in dual-sex clothes and make-up. Frances Marshall, reporting on one given by Eddie Sackville-West, found it hot, noisy, and degenerate: 'all the creative energy of the participants goes on their dress, and there are none of the elaborate performances of earlier parties. Personally I think this is a sad come down, a sign of decadence.'[116] Carrington's outings seem very innocent in comparison.

It was a busy summer for her, and the rest of September offered even greater diversions. Dorelia and Augustus John invited her to a castle off the coast of Scotland, she had a chance to be a ship's cook on the way to France (perhaps through Beakus or one of his friends), and the Tomlins invited her to stay with them. In the meantime, Beakus still sometimes visited her at Ham Spray. All this activity and prospective activity prompted her to write to Julia that 'high jinks may be alright for girls in their teens but old Harridans ought to be pushed by old sea salts in Bath-chairs on the sea front instead of being pushed – fill up at your pleasure'.[117] She expressed this concern with age most frequently with Julia, always linking it to sex. Sex was a measure of youth, and to enjoy it now – in contrast to her younger days – was to ward off age.

After writing to Julia, Carrington confided in her diary:

> Happiness in life is largely a matter of time relationships – some experiences come too early others too late with relation to ones [sic] other situations and affairs or to one's age. At 37 one should be settling down over tea cups, bottling gooseberries, instead of which I have Shelley cravings to sail and leave these quiet rural scenes for Greek Islands. Ridiculous.[118]

Even so, thoughts and jokes about sex remained more satisfying than the act itself. As her affair was playing itself out, she began to revert to her earlier feeling of dissatisfaction.

> 'Was this really the character that I have thought about these three weeks night and day? Can this be the nose, the mouth, that I craved for? Can this be the evening that I was frustrated of, this the body that I longed for?' And as we talked of Durer etchings, motor engines, Alec's character, I thought how dim all this is from what has obsessed me all these weeks. How completely uninterested he is. I am dressed in black tonight, a sudden reversion from colour. Mercifully what was revealed wasn't endearing. I didn't love *more* tonight like some nights. I am sinking back into that previous state of *not* being a female. Hating undressing, hating getting into bed, after hours of thinking about an evening, it is curious how completely uneventful it can be.[119]

She found Beakus 'quite incapable of understanding my odd cravings and feelings about him', and began to long for quiet days with Lytton at Ham Spray. Yet, she wrote to Lytton in an attempt to untangle feelings that were 'getting as involved as a mooncalf's labyrinth', it was always better to have loved than not to have loved,

> Although I know its absurd, I mind so much, (partly because I see him

so little) if I do see him, he isn't happy. And yet really of course the whole thing is a chimera, a mirage of my own making ... Yet in spite of my miseries I would not have had anything different. Would you? For, one perfect evening seems to me, even in memory, to make days of gloom worth putting up with.[120]

CHAPTER TWENTY

FORESHADOWING: 1931

On 20 March 1931, Lytton suddenly said to Carrington while they were having tea, 'Remember, all the bird books and flower books are yours.' When she asked why, he replied, 'Well after I am dead it would be important.' She in turn verbally bequeathed him all her 'pictures and objects', adding 'but if I died first...' Lytton, noting her unhappiness 'like a wind sweeping across the lawn through the laurels', changed the subject.[121]

Later that evening she recalled similar thoughts she had had while glueing in bookplates in Lytton's library.

> I suddenly thought of Sotheby's and the book plates in some [books] I had looked at when Lytton was bidding for a book and I thought these books will one day be looked at by those gloomy faced booksellers and buyers. And suddenly a premonition of a day when these labels would no longer [be] in this library came over me, and I longed to ask Lytton not to stick in any more. And I felt unutterably gloomy at my thoughts.[122]

To Carrington, such thoughts were terrifying. Lytton's musings may have been prompted by the proximity of their birthdays: he had turned fifty-one on 1 March, and Carrington would celebrate her thirty-eighth birthday on 29 March. It was the month when they traditionally gave each other gifts.

Carrington and Lytton had less than a year to live. A premonition of their closing lives seems, in retrospect, to have made them begin disposing of material objects. This last year would see several such uncannily prophetic events.

Several weeks later, on 16 April, Dorelia and Caspar John appeared at Ham Spray in an aeroplane. Carrington, always much more adventurous than Lytton, immediately agreed to a flight. Thrilled by the experience, she tried to convince Lytton 'to have a go'. Predictably he refused, even though Caspar promised him a mild experience, and Dorelia teased that he would never 'be able to discipline Carrington if he wilted where she braved'. This kind of physical adventure was against Lytton's nature and he remained earthbound, asserting that 'he was the wrong *shape* for flying and that his beard presented a hazard that was likely to foul the controls'.[123] Another friend was not so wise: Stephen Tomlin's brother Garrow would die that autumn while practising spins in his plane.

That spring there was a closeness and comfortableness with Lytton, despite his absences, that pleased Carrington. She was still seeing Beakus whenever possible and although their relationship had seemed completely doomed the previous year, it continued to ebb and flow. Some of her favourite times were spent aboard the *Sans Pareil*, watching the harbour lights and cooking and sleeping aboard ship.

In mid-May she decided to extend a visit in Falmouth and wrote to Lytton about household matters: he was to get the cook to order meat, fish and vegetables for his meals; to arrange to pick up the car from the garage in Newbury. Her letter is comfortably domestic except that she also asks him to send on more clothing to her: 'a red silk dress ... black and green check silk blouse', and a pair of pyjamas. These were a far cry from her customary white stockings and cotton print dresses, and showed that she was still sufficiently close to Beakus to accommodate his tastes in clothes. In a reversal of their usual roles, Carrington imagined Lytton at Ham Spray, 'happy with puss and your fire'.[124]

The weekend before she went to Falmouth, Carrington and Lytton had made an excursion to the forest at Savernake, one of her favourite places. They spent the weekend alone together, which she loved. Complaining to him in French of a broken heart which she was trying to 'rivet' back together, she assured him that 'your friendliness means more than I can ever express. Coming in the train ... I thought of you and how happy you made me by living at Ham Spray.'[125] Since Ralph's move to London, Carrington felt that Lytton was doing her a favour by continuing to live with her. Weekends alone with him were rare and precious, and even the thought of him inhabiting Ham Spray in her absence was comforting.

In early June, however, she realised that her relationship with Beakus had in fact now virtually reached its end. This occurred to her at Ham Spray, where he became ill with what first seemed a fairly minor complaint, chiefly of headaches. But when the doctor advised against sending him back to the Penrose family home, Oxhey, she knew it was something more serious. The complaint was later diagnosed as jaundice, and Carrington had to nurse him through illness and depression for several weeks. She had a great deal of experience in this area, since she had been nursing Lytton through illnesses for years. This time, however, she found the role rather exasperating. Had Beakus been ill aboard ship the experience would have been romantic. At Ham Spray he was in the way and disrupted her routine. 'Rather ironical', she wrote to Sebastian, 'to realise one's mission in life is Florence Nightingale!'[126] During those weeks she 'learnt everything there was to know about him and in some ways cured my illgotten passion'.[127]

Lytton was far too kind to complain about his weekend visits, but having him in the house constantly as a patient was a different matter. Carrington herself had to curtail her social life, giving up a trip to London. At last she admitted to Rosamond Lehmann what she had told no one else:

> I suppose you wonder sometimes why I am so fond of him. Its really very little to do with him actually, but because he is so like my brother who was killed. I couldn't say this to anyone. Please don't show my letter to Wogan [Phillips, Rosamond's husband], as I am awfully self conscious of being a romantic, and rather stupid. My brother was very silent and removed. I hardly ever was allowed to be intimate with him and I always put it off, thinking one day I'd be able to show him how much I cared and then it was too late. And partly because he wasn't reported killed, it took me ages to ever believe consciously he was dead.[128]

Her connection to Rosamond Lehmann was important in other respects. Although her senior by several years, Carrington admired Rosamond greatly as a woman and a writer. Always ready to warn other women to avoid procrastinating about their work, Carrington advised Rosamond not to let her domestic responsibilities get in the way of her writing.

> I think it's NO good being anything but what you are and the great thing is never to do anything one doesn't feel genuinely inside oneself. (This is Lytton's creed, not *my* invention!) And actually one can be very tame inside in spite of all one's dashing about ... I think your writing is what is really important and if you found the house and domestic things hampered *that*, I would agree with you about it being bad for you ... I am sure really everyone had to find their adventure in different ways ...

Ralph is always blowing *me* up for not settling down to a purple sprouting old age and hates me going off to parties and boozing![129]

That summer Carrington and Ralph performed a final duty as a married couple, paying a visit to his mother, who was suffering from cancer, in Devon. The next day they visited Gerald Brenan and Gamel Woolsey in Dorset, and returned to Ham Spray to find weekend guests already arriving. Lytton brought Sebastian Sprott, and informed them that Clive Bell would also be coming. In Ralph's words, 'Carrington sends up a shriek'.[130]

July also saw what would later seem a startling coincidence when the following announcement appeared in the *Week-End Observer*: 'Mr Lytton Strachey has just published a set of six thumbnail sketches of six English Historians. Let us suppose that to these a seventh is added – that of Mr Strachey himself. We offer a First Prize of TWO GUINEAS and a Second Prize of HALF-A-GUINEA for the last 250 words of this essay.'[131]

Writing under the name of 'Mopsa', Carrington won easily with the following submission.

Crouching under the ilex tree in his chaise longue, remote, aloof, self-occupied, and mysteriously contented, lay the venerable biographer. Muffled in a sealskin coat (for although it was July he felt the cold) he knitted with elongated fingers a coatee for his favourite cat, Tiberius. He was in his 99th year. He did not know it was his last day on earth.

A constable called for a subscription for the local sports. 'Trop tard, trop tard; mes jeux sont finis.' He gazed at the distant downs; he did not mind – not mind in the very least the thought that this was probably his last summer; after all, summers were now infinitely cold and dismal. One might as well be a mole. He did not particularly care that he was no longer thought the greatest biographer, or that the Countess no longer – or did she? Had he been a woman he would not have shone as a writer, but as a dissipated mistress of infinite intrigues.

But – lying on the grass lay a loose button, a peculiarly revolting specimen: it was an intolerable, an unspeakable catastrophe. He stooped from his chaise longue to pick it up, murmuring to his cat 'Mais quelle horreur!' for once stooped too far – and passed away for ever.[132]

Dyneley Hussey, competition judge at the *Observer*, called the entry 'almost too good to be true ... If Mopsa be thought cruel ... the victim is, after all, only getting as good as he gives.' Not only did Hussey find her style a perfect imitation of Lytton's, but found the context perfect as well. 'Considering how often Mr Strachey ends his essays with the death of his hero, I was surprised that only one other competitor followed his example.'[133]

The contest was *not*, as David Garnett later asserted, to write Strachey's obituary. That Carrington chose to set her piece in his 'last summer', and that it proved to be just that, later amazed and haunted all who recalled it. At the time, however, there was nothing but good humour surrounding the episode. Lytton, unaware of the entire proceeding, read the results in the newspaper and sent her a telegram. She responded happily, 'My most venerable Biographer, knitter of coattees, most dissipated of masters, do you know your wire gave me more pleasure than anything in the world? . . . Terrible to think I nearly lost my two guineas through cruelty! Ralph is really more delighted than I am, I believe!'[134] Her pleasure was replaced by guilt at the end of the year, when she thought that her essay actually in some way caused, or at least contributed to, Lytton's death.

Shortly after this she left for another visit to Fryern, where Dorelia John gave her some rare cacti for her greenhouse.[135] As usual with such gifts, the cacti found their way into a painting and two glass pictures. Her last serious works tended to be either of plants or natural settings: 'The Winter' (oil, 1928); 'The Downs from Ham Spray in Winter' (oil, 1929); 'Cattle by a Pond' (oil, 1930). Her final known portrait was of Janie Bussy, Lytton's niece, in 1928.

When she refers to her painting it is not always clear that they are works on canvas. In this last year they were just as likely to be on glass. Her glass paintings, china, and tiles had been enormously successful, but something of an artistic compromise. This last autumn, at Biddesden, the home of Bryan Guinness, she painted what she later announced to have been her only successful work – because Lytton had liked it. It was a *trompe l'œil* painting of a woman and a cat sitting by a window. The Ham Spray cat, Tiber, earlier immortalised in print, was now immortalised in this picture. She was so serious about this work that she worked outdoors in all types of weather to complete it: 'Darling Lytton! Oh dear! Inanimate objects are very animated down here! I can pay no attention to elections and tariffs when motorcars refuse to start, scissors disappear and gloves walk off and hide themselves. I got up at half past 7 this morning in order to start my picture at Biddesden early. Then, typically as you would say, the moment I started to paint it came on to rain. So all my paints got mixed with water. My hair dripped into my eyes, and my feet became icy cold.'[136]

In many ways she felt that her artistic future hung on others' opinion of 'the cook and the pussy cat'. Yet, because she trusted no one to be completely honest with her, and perhaps dreaded that they might be, emotionally she stacked the cards against herself. Asking Julia whether she found this painting 'an improvement', Carrington went on to say, 'If you'd tell me that, I should then know whether to go on with my painting, or take to poker-work. But nobody speaks the truth. So its all no use.'[137] So, in her thirty-ninth year, she still continued to paint and to crave the approval of those she loved, but who were the least qualified to give it her. To those who were qualified she rarely showed her work.

Decorative art work and a love of the theatrical combined in an exciting way, and she wrote under the utmost secrecy to Tommy about a new and different project, a proposed ballet. Asking his opinion on the design and idea, she also asked for his help on costume and set design; if he thought there was nothing in them 'will you say so and say no more?' She was very excited by the project, as her hurried letter shows:

> I am too impatient to draw it out nicely, also I've a terrible cold and a temperature so can't concentrate. The dairymaids would be dressed in my favourite rustic china-figure-1840 style. You would have to make my masks and help with the inventions, please. I then thought, supposing you thought it possible, we might draw it out neatly, with colours, and ask Lydia [Lopokova, former ballerina now married to Maynard Keynes] and Constance Lambert to give us £1,000 and put it on the stage. Or shall we ask Mr Cochran and get £1,000 and sink art and ambition?
> PS. The moral I confess of this ballet seems a little obscure. The triumph of Lesbianism?[138]

She wrote nothing more about the plan, which came to nothing, but it demonstrated an interest in the theatre that had been developing since she had solicited singers for the War Relief stage show in 1916. As late as the beginning of November of 1931 she wrote happily to Lytton that her friend Angus Wilson [not the writer] 'knows Rene Clair, "Le Million" film producer, and is going to ask him to Tidcombe. So perhaps after all I shall end up by being a film-produceress.'[139] This outlet for her talents and her energies would undoubtedly have taken her into new and exciting directions, but it is equally certain that her self-doubts would never have deserted her.

One of Carrington's last pleasurable outings was to a fair at the nearby town of Marlborough. Taking a break in September from the cook and 'the ghostly cat', she spent an exhilarating day with Alix Strachey and a friend named Paul Cross hitting the hammer ('but couldn't sound the bell'), riding the merry-go-round, and shooting at bottles. Alix perhaps had the best time of all, for she 'went quite mad in those little electric motor cars and charged everyone to pieces'.[140] Carrington hoped to finish the picture the next day. Not long after she managed to do so, Lytton fell ill again.

Lytton was so frequently ill with minor complaints that few took his complaints as seriously as Carrington used to do. Yet when he wrote from Brighton that he had not been feeling well, she answered simply that 'I do hope you are better', and continued on with other news.[141] His affair with Roger, like hers with Beakus, had been deteriorating. This not only made her feel closer to him, but allowed her a companion in her bouts of unhappiness; quite possibly she attributed his low spirits and poor health to unrequited love. By early November, however, they both knew the problem was much more serious.

Ralph and Frances looked for ways to lift the spirits of the Ham Spray occupants. The four of them had planned to spend the winter months in Spain, closing Ham Spray during their stay. Not only would a change of scenery be beneficial, but the warm climate would help Carrington get over her perpetual winter colds and Lytton to recover from his 'seediness'. Lytton particularly counted on Ralph's support for all sorts of problems ranging from Ham Spray's plumbing to physical ailments. Although they all knew that Carrington was quite capable of handling most problems, that she could drive and make arrangements for any situation, Lytton was still comforted by Ralph's strong, masculine presence. Nevertheless, Lytton hesitated at the prospect of the trip, even though they had all apparently looked forward to it enough to contact travel agents and look into passages and hotels.

Carrington's continuing nightmares and illnesses, and Lytton's reluctance to make a commitment to the Spanish trip, seemed to augur the worst. When Lytton returned to Ham Spray on 5 November and was put to bed with a high fever, the real nightmare was about to begin. As Frances was to write later, 'the two-handed engine was at the door'.[142]

CHAPTER TWENTY-ONE

THE TWO-HANDED ENGINE

It was not long before the full accoutrements of serious illness took over Ham Spray. Lytton had a fever that would not go away; he was weak and tired, sometimes speechless; there were haemorrhages. Nurses attended him round the clock, and doctor after doctor was called in. No one could accurately diagnose his illness. It seemed at first to be typhoid fever because of the high temperatures, but there was no evidence of that in the blood cultures. 'The grandest pathologist in the world' agreed with another specialist that it was probably ulcerative colitis, and recommended a new treatment which included 'more drastic washing outs and pills'.[143] No one suspected the real disease: terminal cancer of the stomach, determined later only by an autopsy. Lytton, through it all, remained the perfect patient.

Meanwhile, it seemed that the whole world had rallied round him. Stracheys, including Pippa and James, took up residence nearby at the Bear, an inn in nearby Hungerford. Gerald Brenan and Stephen Tomlin also stayed there, coming up to the house to offer support to Carrington. Frances Marshall stayed closer, in the village of Ham, and walked up daily to do household chores and take Ralph for walks whenever he could be spared. Newspaper reporters telephoned each day for bulletins on the great man's health.

By December there was little change in his condition. Ralph, as usual, seemed to bear the brunt of it all, for not only did he have to see that Lytton was well cared for, but that those who cared for him were also supported. Carrington, who had stopped seeing Beakus in this crisis, particularly worried him, and he made sure to soften for her every pronouncement of the doctors. 'Carrington cries every time she goes in to see him, as soon as she gets out', he wrote to Frances on 10 December. 'She can only view it emotionally and is an equal patient. It is with her I am trying to deal. I talk to her hour after hour to prevent her rushing into panics, and she flings herself into running the house.'[144] His greatest fear was that if Lytton died, Carrington would kill herself.

It was well that there were nurses to attend to Lytton's medical needs, for Carrington became far too flustered if she had to answer his bell. She and Pippa would wipe his forehead with sponges and sit by his bedside. They cared for those few people who were allowed to stay in the house, sometimes preparing meals for them and the others. Carrington, when not being domestic, shut herself in her studio for hours, from which, Ralph said, 'enormous glass pictures find themselves hastily brought into the world'.[145]

Christmas passed with little improvement. Carrington wrote letters to everyone who had kept in constant communication with her throughout this trial: Diana and Bryan Guinness, at whose house she had painted the *trompe l'œil* picture of the cook and the cat; Dorelia John, whom Ralph hoped would come and stay with Carrington; Sebastian Sprott; Lady Ottoline Morrell. From her home Virginia Woolf imagined the scene at Ham Spray and described her own with Leonard: 'This is a scene I can see; & see Lytton too, always reasonable, clear, giving his orders; & dying as he thought; & then, as reasonably, finding some strength returning, deciding to live. And L. & I sobbing here. And I expect Nessa & Clive sitting over the fire late, with some tears, at Seend.'[146]

On Tuesday, two days before Lytton's death, he suddenly said, 'Carrington, why isn't she here? I want her. Darling Carrington I love her. I always wanted to marry Carrington and never did.'[147] This was the most consoling thing he could have said to her. Throughout her final weeks she carried that deathbed confession with her as her only happiness.

The next day, on Wednesday afternoon Carrington, who was sitting by his bedside, noticed that although Lytton still slept his breathing had changed. 'I thought of the Goya painting of a dead man with high light on the cheek bones', she wrote in her diary. She noticed also that he had the hiccups, and ran for the nurse, who instructed her to ring the doctor for the correct dosage of strychnine. Passing Pippa and James on the stairs without speaking to them, she ran for the telephone, and then back to Lytton's room. As she held his arm while the nurse gave the injection, 'it became clear to me he could not live'.[148]

Round-the-clock watches were ordered; Carrington's turn was to be at six o'clock the next morning. She was unable to sleep, and at three o'clock went into Lytton's room to ask the nurse if there were any chance that he might live. 'Oh no – I don't think so now', the nurse replied. Carrington kissed his forehead, finding it cold and damp, and left the room. Then she looked for Ralph and kissed him also, requesting that he not wake her. When Ralph went into Lytton's room and James went downstairs, Carrington quietly descended the back stairway and headed for the garage. What happened next she recorded in painful detail in her diary.

The garage door was stuck open I could hardly move it. Every movement seemed to scriech [*sic*] through the still night air. At last I got the door closed. Then sitting in the car I touched the horn, & my heart stood still, for I felt R. must have heard as the landing window was open. I stood in the yard watching for a light to go on in the passages. After some time I crept back again, & made every preparation all ready that I could start up the car directly the milking engine started in the farm yard. But not a sound outside. It was very cold in my dressing gown. I thought the milkers started at 4.30. It was 4.30 by the car clock, & still no body stired [*sic*]. I longed to go round the garden but I feared to be too far from the garage to run back, so I stood under the beech tree by the back door. On the edge of the gutter on the roof, perched 6 pigeons asleep silhoutted [*sic*] against the pale dawn sky. The moon sunk lower. The faint noise of a wind blowing up, came across from the trees in the garden.

I thought how different one feels everything to what one usually does. As if one was almost transparent, so without any emotion. I was only terrified the cow men had overslept & that it would be 6 ock before they would start. The moon disappeared behind a cloud. I went indoors, & drank whiskey in a tea cup in the dinning room [*sic*]. The house was very warm after outside. I went back to my watch under the tree – Suddenly I heard sounds across the yard and movements in the milking shed. I ran into the garage & shut the doors & got in the car. I started it up one minuet [*sic*] after the milking machine which was half past 5 by the car clock but that is 10 mins fast. I was terrified by the noise[;] once [I] nearly stopt to turn on the petrol more. There seemed no smell. I got over in the back of the car & lay down, & listened to the thud of the engine below me & the noise of the milking machine puffing away outside. At last I smelt it was beginning to get rather thick. I turned on the light inside the car & looked at the clock only 10 mins had gone. However Ralph would probably not come exactly at 6 ock. the windows of the car looked foggy & a bit misty. I turned out the light again, & lay down. Gradually I felt rather sleepy. & then the noise grew fainter, & further off. Rather like fainting I remember thinking. And not what Ellie [Rendel] had told me about a pain in one's throat. I thought of Lytton, & was glad to think I shouldn't know anymore. Then I remember a sort of dream which faded away.

Suddenly long after, waking up in my bed with a buzzing in my ears, & Dr. Starkey Smith holding my arm & injecting a styringe [*sic*]. I cried 'No NO go away' & pushed him, & his hand away, & saw him vanish away like the chesire cat [*sic*]. Then I looked & saw my bedroom window, and it was daylight. And Ralph was there. Ralph held me in his arms & kissed me and said 'How could you do it?' I felt angry to at being back after being in a very happy dream, sorry to be awake again. A buzzing in my ears & something wrong with my eyes. I couldn't see my hands or focus on anything.[149]

No one had believed that Carrington would make her move while Lytton was still alive. But Lytton had had a bad attack early that morning. This had roused the household and, once up, they noticed Carrington's absence. Ralph, already distraught about Lytton's inevitable death, 'found her in the garage with the car engine running, rushed in and dragged her out'.[150] She stayed in her four-poster bed until noon, feeling 'no remorse' but 'so defrauded & angry that fate had cheated me in such a way & brought me back again'. At twelve o'clock she went into Lytton's room and looked upon his still living but pale form, and upon Pippa's tear-streaked face. With Lytton's breathing the only sound, she saw their life together pass before her: other mornings spent together in that room; *Pride and Prejudice*, the book they had been reading together last, still on his table. Suddenly she felt ill and, fleeing the room, was 'violently sick' in the chamberpot of her bedroom.

An hour or so later Lytton took a turn for the worse. Pippa and Carrington stood by his bedside, Carrington's arm tightly around Pippa's waist, with James and Ralph standing behind them. The nurse tried to force the two women to leave, and Carrington hated her for it. Lytton's breathing slowed and seemed to stop, then began again. Carrington recalled hearing a blackbird singing outside his window. Then his breathing stopped. Carrington kissed his forehead and eyes, and left the room. In Frances' words, 'the poor creature had the cruel fate of witnessing what she had so desperately longed to escape – Lytton's death'.[151]

There was no funeral. During the next two days, before his body was taken away for cremation, Carrington saw him twice more. The second time, Ralph had given her some bay leaves which she made into a wreath which she tried on her own head before placing it on his. Each time she kissed his face and eyes, feeling them growing colder and colder. She moved through the day in a daze.

On Friday she went with Ralph, Frances and Tommy to Savernake Forest, where the last photograph of her was taken. She knew that the purpose was to get her out of the house while Lytton's body was being removed. Frances recalled that Carrington 'got out of the car and took a few steps, walking like a weak invalid'. The forest was incongruously beautiful and full of life, even for winter; they saw a deer and a stag but Carrington thought of nothing but her loss and of the irony 'that Lytton by that early attack at 6 o'ck saved my life. When I gave my life for his he should give it back.' Having given back her life by rescuing her a few days before, Ralph was now faced with the tremendous task of keeping her alive. 'This outing', said

Frances, 'marked the beginning of Ralph's elaborate plans to pin her to life ... Yet no-one who was with her at this time could fail to be moved by the pathos of someone dragged forcibly back to face a life she had deliberately decided was unbearable.'[152] Her suicide attempt, according to Ralph and Frances, had had two motivations: to offer herself as a substitute sacrifice in order to save Lytton, and to avoid having to witness Lytton's death, should he die. After Lytton's death Carrington's thoughts, when she allowed them to, revolved around her loss and the futility of her life. Although rarely alone at first, she would fill the pages of her diary with heart-rending poems.

> My sweet companion and my gentle peer
> Why has thou left me thus unkindly here?
>   Thy end forever and thy life to moan,
>   O, thou has left me all alone.
>   Thy soul and body when death's agony
>   Besieged around thy noble heart,
>   Did not with more reluctance part
> Than I, my dearest friend, part from thee.

> My dearest friend, would I have died for thee?
> Life in this world henceforth will tedious be.
>   Nor shall I know hereafter what to do
>   If once my griefs prove tedious too.
>   Silent and sad I walk about all day.
>   As sullen ghosts stalk speechless by.
>   Where their hid treasures lie;
>   Alas! My treasure's gone. Why do I stay?

She thus began an internal argument on the admissibility of suicide. Ralph, sensing this, arranged that she be kept busy. It was a good sign when she returned to her domestic tasks but, to be safe, he arranged that Tommy stay on with her while he and Frances went to London and Wales for a short while. Some of those tasks, sorting through her belongings, for example, seemed ominously like preparations for her own death.

Tommy was the best possible choice of a person to anchor her to life. She loved her friends, but that love alone would not keep her alive. Tommy, on the other hand, was suffering almost as much as she, for he was still inconsolable over the recent death of his brother Garrow, and now Lytton was gone. Ralph was certain that Carrington's compassion for him would not allow her to add to his miseries and his unstable emotional state by killing herself in his presence. Further, he got her to agree to put off such a decision until a month or two had passed. She agreed, but no one relaxed the vigil.

At least one of her friends thought suicide was a reasonable option. 'They cant [sic] leave Carrington alone', Virginia wrote in her diary on 30 January. 'She says she will kill herself – quite reasonable – but better to wait until the first shock is over & see. Suicide seems to me quite sensible.'[153] As 'reasonable' and as inevitable as another attempt on her life appeared, no one, especially not Ralph, could allow such an opportunity to present itself.

Over the next weeks, as she dug in the garden under the ilex tree, planting flowers in the spot where she had hoped Lytton's ashes would be buried, Ralph became convinced that she had 'some desperate plan up her sleeve'. She was doing entirely too much straightening up and arranging, and her talk of the future included Ralph and Frances (she wanted them to have a child 'as a suicidal compensation' for her) but not herself. He did not trust her not to read his letters, even when they were buried in his coat pockets, and when he stayed at Ham Spray he instructed Frances not to write to him there. Finally, he found a paper she had written which arranged for the disposal of her possessions; he was to have the £10,000 which Lytton had left her in his will.[154]

Behind her hollow eyes a battle raged. She had already decided to die, but tried to hang on a little longer to please Ralph. He was so miserable about Lytton's death that another following so closely on would devastate him. She made him promises that he did not expect her to keep, and filled her diary with page upon page of grief.

> What point is there now in what I see everyday – in conversation, jokes, beautiful visions, pains, even nightmares. Who can I tell them to who will understand? One cannot find such another character as Lytton. & curious as it may seem to G[erald] B[renan] these friends that he talks of as consolers & substitutes for Lytton cannot be the same ... I just feel I must get through the days and pray they won't be very many more.[155]

She recalled discussions she and Lytton had had on the permissibility of suicide, and essays they had read on it. What had been a purely intellectual exercise now took on particular meaning.

Ralph, asking Frances to understand his absence, spent a great deal of time at Ham Spray. Eventually though he needed a respite and he arranged for Carrington to go to Dorelia John at Fryern for a week. She dutifully went off, but the change of scene and proximity of her formerly adored friend did little to help her.

> By not allowing oneself to think of the reality of the situation I can bear life. But then it is not life. It is a contradiction. I pretend to myself this week at Fryern that I am on a holiday. I avoid allowing my thoughts to even approach Lytton. If for a moment they break through my fences I at once feel so utterly miserable that its only by thinking there will be only a few more weeks I can bear the pain. That there is nobody any longer to serve & love completely & entirely makes everyday pointless.
>
> Really I have deceded [sic]. And if I may bring myself to think of

reality for a few hours how could I bear the emptiness and loneliness of life without Lytton?[156]

Ralph still tried to wrestle her back to life, and arranged on her return to keep people around her. On 12 February 1932 he wrote to Frances that James and Rosamond Lehmann were to come down, and that he would stay on for a couple more days himself. This 'depressed [Carrington] markedly. I think she intended to leave no loose ends outstanding after this weekend . . . Now she is faced with a future engagement she is at a loss how to proceed . . . all I can do is keep putting a hook in her as fast as she unhooks herself.'[157]

In the meantime, her discussions of the deserted Beakus showed no emotion and her diary took on the form of a constant conversation with Lytton. 'What can I do', she wrote to him. 'I do not care about anything now. R's love is a reproach to me. For I feel so cold and melancholy. I can do nothing for him. Oh why did I not know – not believe the warnings, premonitions that I sometimes had . . . Oh Lytton darling you are dead. The impossible terrible thing has happened. & all is utterly cold and grey on this earth now.'

> They say one should keep your standards & your values of life alive. But how can I when I only kept them for you. Everything was for you. I loved life just because you made it so perfect & now there is no one left to make jokes with or talk to . . ,. I see my paints, & think it is no use for Lytton will never see my pictures now, & I cry. And our happiness was getting so much more. This year there would have been no troubles, no disturbing loves . . . Everything was designed for this year – Last year we recovered from our emotions, & this autumn we were closer than we had ever been before. Oh darling Lytton you are dead & I can tell you nothing.[158]

She spent much of her time reading over his letters and, until they were taken away, going through the clothes she had helped him choose. On 16 February she made a bonfire of some of his things, and threw his eyeglasses into the flames.

Each day she found harder rather than easier to bear. She seemed outwardly to be improving, and Ralph found her grumpiness in the bathroom one morning a sign that she was returning to normal. During the nights, though, she dreamed of Lytton, feeling in the mornings as though he 'had died afresh'. A near escape from death – being thrown from one of the Guinness's horses at Biddesden on 18 February – she found only ironic: 'That I who long for death find it so hard to meet him.'[159]

With her seeming recovery, Ralph thought it worth trying to leave her alone. Lytton had been dead for a month without her attempting to kill herself, and the experiment had to be tried sooner or later. Dorelia John and Helen Anrep came for lunch, and she was looked in on from time to time by others. No one put pressure on her to make any decisions, although it was suggested that she might like to help with an edition of Lytton's letters. Ham Spray house had been purchased in Ralph's name and was therefore legally his, but he made it absolutely clear that it was her home, to be shared with whomever she wished.

While at Biddesden at the end of February, she had casually asked to borrow a shotgun; rabbits were once again overrunning the Ham Spray garden. 'We all heard the request', Frances wrote, 'but it was rather vaguely given, and I think everyone hoped it would be as vaguely forgotten.'[160] When the subject was dropped Carrington went back for the gun in secret, keeping it hidden until 11 March.

Virginia and Leonard Woolf were the last people to see her alive. They arrived for lunch at 1.30 on Thursday, 10 March. 'She was pale, small, suffering silently. Very calm.' Clearly they had come to check on her, and conversation was difficult as they sat down in the cold dining room. After lunch they wandered round the garden, and Carrington excused herself to write some notes. Later she returned, and asked them to stay to tea with her. She and Virginia went up to Lytton's study and, looking out of the window arm in arm, Carrington mentioned that she had seen Dorothy Wordsworth's house, where her brother's things had been preserved exactly as they had been left. Turning, Carrington broke down and sobbed in Virginia's arms.

'There is nothing left for me to do. I did everything for Lytton. But I've failed in everything else. People say he was very selfish to me. But he gave me everything. I was devoted to my father. I hated my mother. Lytton was like a father to me. He taught me everything I know. He read poetry & French to me.' I did not want to lie to her – I could not pretend that there was not truth in what she said. I said life seemed to me sometimes hopeless, useless, when I woke in the night & thought of Lytton's death. I held her hands. Her wrists seemed very small. She seemed helpless, deserted, like some small animal left. She was very gentle; sometimes laughing; kissing me; saying Lytton had loved his old friends best . . .

Then, as we were leaving the room to go she suddenly picked up a little French box with a picture of the Arc de Triomphe upon it & and said 'I gave this to Lytton. Take it. James says I mustn't give away Lytton's things. But this is all right. I gave it him.' So I took it. There is a coin in it. How frightened she seemed of doing wrong – like a child who has been scolded.[161]

Carrington walked them back to their car at the front of the house. There she kissed Virginia, who said 'Then you will come & see us next week – or not – just as you like.'

'Yes', Carrington answered. 'I will come.' She paused. 'Or not.'

They kissed for the last time and, as Virginia and Leonard got into their car, Carrington walked back to the house, where she turned to pause and wave good-bye. Then she walked into the house and closed the door.

EPILOGUE

Lytton and Carrington's friends, still not recovered from his death, now had to cope with Carrington's suicide. Their misery left them numb. Ralph had to pull himself together long enough to arrange for Carrington's cremation. The fact that neither Carrington's brother Noel nor Frances later remembered whether she had, in fact, been cremated, or what had become of her body, shows how devastated they were. She had planned to have her ashes and Lytton's buried side by side under her favourite ilex tree at Ham Spray, but she probably did not know that James had taken charge of Lytton's ashes. The manner of Carrington's death meant that there was also an inquest to be suffered. The verdict was of accidental death. After that, Ralph and Frances went to France where Ralph, perhaps in an act of purgation, visited the battlegrounds of the war in which he had witnessed and survived great horrors.

Shortly after Carrington's death, Gerald Brenan wrote the following letter to Alix Strachey:

> One or two things transpired after you left. It was proved [at the inquest] that her last letter to Ralph, found in the drawer, was written within three days of that Friday. Then instead of wearing her own yellow dressing gown, she put on Lytton's purple one and died in that. It was a kind of ritual act. Then a paper was found, written in fresh ink, a fair copy of the dirge from the White Devil, covered with birds and crosses and weeping willows. On it the word *Wolf* was especially underlined –
>
> > But keep *the wolf* far hence – he's foe to men
> > For with his claws he'll dig them up again.
>
> But perhaps there is not much point in these conjectures.
> She killed herself mainly, I think, to emphasise the importance of Lytton's death but time races away from that Friday and soon very few people will ever remember it. I do not know whether great tragic acts occur out of literature, but this, I feel, was not one but something childish and thoughtless and pitiful. Or perhaps it is merely that I am

obliged to go on reproaching her – for the last act as for so many other acts of her life.[162]

Thus the bitterness he had felt during Carrington's life continued after death. Years later he regained his perspective, taking part of the blame for the failure of their relationship, although still assigning her a portion.

In 1957, when he was in his sixties, Gerald fell in love with Carrington's twenty-five-year-old niece, the daughter of Noel and Catharine. Like her aunt, whom she had never met, Joanna Carrington was unhappily married, and her feelings for Gerald were mixed. They eventually settled into a peaceful friendship, and his marriage to Gamel was preserved. He had a successful career as a writer, and his book on the Spanish Civil War, *The Spanish Labyrinth*, published in 1943, is a small masterpiece. After a long and full life, Brenan died in Spain at the end of 1986.

Virginia Woolf found it difficult to shake off the deaths of Carrington and Lytton. Previously a defender of suicide, after the event she had second thoughts.

> So Carrington killed herself; & again what L[eonard] calls 'these mausoleum talks' begin again. We were the last to talk to her, & thus might have been summoned to the inquest; but they brought it in an accident. She maintained this, even to Ralph. Her foot slipped as she was shooting a rabbit.
>
> And we discuss suicide; & I feel, as always, ghosts dwindling, changing. Lytton's affected by this act. I sometimes dislike him for it. He absorbed her[,] made her kill herself.[163]

The talks continued the next day: 'Talk of Carrington: how long shall we talk of Carrington? Dispute as to how she got her gun.'[164] And about a week later: 'I am not sure of the precise day, save that it is Thursday & tomorrow is Good Friday & therefore we are at Rodmell on the loveliest spring day: soft: a blue veil in the air torn by birds voices. I am glad to be alive & sorry for the dead: cant [*sic*] think why Carrington killed herself & put an end to all this.'[165] Nine years later, Virginia killed herself on 18 March 1941.

Mark Gertler was deeply shocked by Carrington's death, as he reported to Dorothy Brett. His marriage to Marjorie Hodgkinson was initially a happy one, although marred by ill health. He had tuberculosis, she a miscarriage; when their son Luke was born, he too had medical problems for some time. Mark found that family life was a disruption to his work, which was not going well. He loved his wife and son, but they agreed to separate for a while in January 1939 until he could get back on his feet. On 23 June 1939, short of money, fearing a recurrence of tuberculosis, and worried about his work, he locked the door to his studio and turned on the gas ring and gas stove full force. When he was found he had been dead for several hours.[166]

Frances and Ralph were devastated by the succession of deaths during that dreadful winter of 1931–2. But life gradually returned to normal and they married a year later. They left London and returned to Ham Spray, where they lived for more than thirty years. As Carrington had hoped they would, they had a son, Burgo, who was raised in the house. Theirs was a long and happy marriage.

Those who knew Carrington insist that her life was tragic only in its ending. Her great originality, ability to entertain and intrigue others, and love, offset, in their opinion, the misery she experienced in her final months. I hope this biography has made clear those aspects of her life.

At the same time, she was a very complicated woman whose difficulties cannot be summarily dismissed as idiosyncracies. What makes her life merit a close look are the things that made her different: her unique outlook, her strong artistic ability, the environments she created for those she loved. These things combined with characteristics which often made them hard to achieve. Her outlook estranged her from her family; her insecurity about her painting kept her from popular or commercial success; some, like Gerald Brenan, believed that the living spaces she created were more important than outside relationships, and ultimately damaged those relationships. But all these qualities found harmony and near perfection with Lytton Strachey.

Paradoxically, his homosexuality both kept her from achieving true perfection and allowed her to come as close to it as possible. Had he been heterosexual, she might well have seen him as sexually threatening – particularly in light of the state of her relationship with the more sexually aggressive Mark Gertler – and never become involved at all. His homosexuality allowed them full rein in all other aspects of their relationship, and both were productive in their life together. Strachey had begun *Eminent Victorians* before he knew her well, but managed to complete it while he was involved with her. The love and security and confidence she gave him made possible his extremely successful writing career. Carrington, under the shadow of the more successful Gertler, was losing confidence in her art when she met Strachey. As her love developed she began taking chances in her work, turning out most of her best works in their early years together. She never fully recovered that confidence, of course, but this was no fault of Strachey's. He admired her work unreservedly and did whatever he could to buoy her spirits and her career. There is no way of knowing if he tried to convince his friends Fry and Bell to give her paintings the serious attention they deserved, but like Ralph Partridge he praised them highly, valued them as gifts, and encouraged her to take her career seriously.

The question most often raised is whether her life with Lytton and Ralph caused her to give up her art and channel her talents into housekeeping and decoration, or whether those things gave her a convenient excuse not to tackle more difficult works. This is something of a chicken-and-egg proposition. She had many artistic talents, and the creation of beautiful rooms, tiles and dishes ought to be rated highly. Her life, and the atmosphere in which she lived it, was for her an art of a different kind, to which these objects contributed. But there is no question that she found such things easy to create and more immediately rewarding. Serious painting was draining, and she had to dig into herself – including her loves and insecurities – to produce it. This, coupled with her almost inevitable disappointment with the finished product, was frightening.

Even so, she continued to paint until nearly the end of her life. That she gave up portrait painting four years before her death does not mean that she laid down her brushes. Some of her wonderful paintings of flowers, cactuses and vases painted in those last years are only now coming to light and show her development in a new direction. As Vanessa Bell and Duncan Grant were experimenting with wider brushstrokes and simpler colours and designs, Carrington miniaturised, filling spaces with small strokes and abundant details. Each object painted was presented to her with love, and she tried to incorporate that into these late works. Frances Partridge thought, in fact, that Carrington became so attached to them that she ultimately showed too much respect for the object itself. But she did continue to paint, in one form or another.

Love, with all its accompanying difficulties, insecurities, risks, subterfuges and rewards is what her life – as well as her death – was all about. Her love for her father and brother helped shape her subsequent loves. Her love for Gertler was based partly on their mutual affection and talent, and partly on his love for her, but her inability to end the relationship was also based on her unwillingness to lose someone she had felt so much for. Like her relationship with Gertler, those with Partridge, Brenan and Penrose were ultimately overshadowed – and destroyed – by her love for Strachey. She wanted romance and physical relationships, but these were always complicated by her 'real' life at Tidmarsh and Ham Spray. Certainly by today's standards she had few love affairs (there were perhaps brief affairs with David Garnett and Stephen Tomlin in addition to those with Henrietta Bingham and the other three men) in her nearly forty years of life. This reflects perhaps her complicated sexuality, but more likely emphasises the overwhelming importance of Lytton Strachey in all aspect of her life. Many profess not to understand how she could have such an 'unsuitable' love when so many others desired her. But Lytton was civilised, caring, witty, intelligent – and he needed her. She provided similar qualities and comforts for him. This question, however, cannot be answered any more easily than questions on why any person loves another. Love is love and hard enough to find.[167]

NOTES

INTRODUCTION

1. Garnett, David, ed. *Carrington: Letters and Extracts from her Diaries* (London: Jonathan Cape, 1970), p. 10.

2. Dorothy Brett to Michael Holroyd, quoted in Holroyd, *Lytton Strachey: A Biography* (London: William Heinemann; New York: Holt, Rinehart and Winston, 1971), p. 669.

3. Carrington to Julia Strachey, October 1929, in *Carrington: Letters and Extracts from Her Diaries*, p. 427.

4. Carrington to Lytton Strachey, 7 August 1928, British Library.

5. Carrington to Julia Strachey, end of March or beginning of April, 1926, in *Carrington: Letters and Extracts from Her Diaries*, pp. 408–9.

6. Carrington to Sebastian Sprott, early March 1929, ibid., pp. 404–6.

7. Carrington to Lytton Strachey, 21 September 1929, British Library.

8. Carrington to Alix Strachey, 18 November 1928, The Lytton Strachey Trust.

9. Lytton Strachey to Carrington, 11 June 1930, British Library.

10. Gerald Brenan to Carrington, late February 1925, Harry Ransom Humanities Research Center, University of Texas, Austin.

11. Richard Shone to the author, 5 May 1988.

PART ONE

1. Frances Partridge, *Love in Bloomsbury: Memories* (London: Victor Gollancz; Boston: Little, Brown and Company, 1981), p. 210.

2. Partridge, p. 210.

3. David Garnett, *Great Friends* (London: Macmillan London Ltd., 1979), p. 159.

4. Since Partridge was a name she only used with the grocer, farmers, and others, it was telling that she misspelled it on her diary.

5. Carrington, *D. C. Partride [sic], Her Book*, 1931–2, unpublished. Now housed at the British Library.

6. Anne Olivier Bell, ed., *The Diary of Virginia Woolf, Vol. 4, 1931–5* (London: Chatto & Windus; New York: Harcourt Brace Jovanovich, 1982), Thursday, 17 March 1932, p. 83.

7. Michael Holroyd, *Lytton Strachey: A Biography*, p. 1067.

8. Carrington to Gerald Brenan, 6 October 1920, University of Texas, Austin.

9. Samuel Carrington to Louisa Carrington, 21 June 1957, India Office Library, London. All subsequent letters from him are from this collection.

10. Noel Carrington, *Carrington: Paintings, Drawings and Decorations* (London and New York: Thames & Hudson, 1978), p. 17.

11. Carrington to Mark Gertler, January 1919, in *Carrington: Letters and Extracts from Her Diaries*, p. 123.

12. *Carrington: Paintings, Drawings and Decorations*, p. 15.

13. Noel Carrington, 'Carrington's Early Life' in *Carrington: Letters and Extracts from Her Diaries*, p. 502.

14. Carrington to Gerald Brenan, 26 June 1924, unpublished letter, Harry Ransom Humanities Research Center, University of Texas at Austin. This was a long journal letter written to Brenan about Carrington's childhood; most of the information which follows about her early life is taken from this letter.

15. Unpublished letter, Noel Carrington to Gretchen Holbrook Gerzina, 21 June 1986.

16. *Carrington: Paintings, Drawings and Decorations*, p. 19.

17. Carrington to Gerald Brenan, 24 January 1924, Harry Ransom Humanities Research Library, University of Texas at Austin.

18. *Carrington: Paintings, Drawings and Decorations*, p. 19.

19. ibid., p. 20.

20. Carrington to Mark Gertler, January 1919, in *Carrington: Letters and Extracts from Her Diaries*, p. 123.

21. Carrington to Lytton Strachey, 1 January 1919, British Library.

22. *Carrington: Letters and Extracts from Her Diaries*, p. 504.

23. See Note 14.

24. *Carrington: Paintings, Drawings and Decorations*, p. 16. Charlotte Carrington herself adopted this habit. After Samuel's death at the end of 1918, she herself began to move at regular intervals, buying or renting cottages in various towns. Inevitably disappointed in the house, she would soon move again and call upon Dora to assist her each time.

25. See Note 14.

26. See Note 14.

27. See Note 14.

28. *Carrington: Paintings, Drawings and Decorations*, p. 18.

29. ibid, p. 18.

30. Carrington to Gerald Brenan, 6 March 1923 (in a letter begun 1 March 1923), University of Texas, Austin.

31. His encouragement was crucial, for, according to noted psychiatrist Phyllis Greenacre, the encouragement of parents – and particularly of fathers – can determine whether or not a talented woman follows her artistic instincts:
Inhibition of artistic interest to the extent of its actual suspension seems particularly likely to occur if the parents, especially the father, react with disfavor towards this interest of the daughter ... On the other hand, the father's approval and encouragement ... may permit the girl to develop a predominantly positive oedipal relationship, together with a limited identification with him, in such a way as to salvage or even free her artistic interests. (Phyllis Greenacre M. D., 'Woman as Artist' [New York: *The Psychoanalytic Quarterly*, Volume 29, 1960], p. 96.)

32. *Carrington: Paintings, Drawings and Decorations*, pp. 18–19.

33. *Carrington: Letters and Extracts from Her Diaries*, p. 502.

34. Carrington to Gerald Brenan, 6 October 1920, University of Texas, Austin.

35. Carrington to Gerald Brenan, 26 December 1920, University of Texas, Austin.

36. ibid.

37. In a 1978 review of an exhibition of Carrington's paintings, Christopher Neve made a similar observation: 'There is nothing new in the notion that an artist paints his or her own landscape best. But in Carrington's case, there is a sense that she identified place so strongly with people – the people she shared them with –

that they become portraits of a kind as well.' (Christopher Neve, 'The Passionate Landscape: Dora Carrington 1893–1932,' in *Country Life*, 9 March 1978, p. 610.)

38. Noel Carrington to Gretchen Holbrook Gerzina, unpublished, 21 June 1986.

39. *Carrington: Letters and Extracts from Her Diaries*, p. 503.

40. *Carrington: Paintings, Drawings and Decorations*, p. 18.

41. Reproduced in *Carrington: Paintings, Drawings and Decorations*, p. 16.

42. Mary Chamot, *Modern Painting in England* (London: Country Life Ltd.; New York: Charles Scribner's Sons, 1937), pp. 37–8.

43. Frances Spalding, *Roger Fry – Art and Life* (London: Paul Elek; Berkeley: University of California Press, 1980), p. 32.

44. Chamot, pp. 28–30.

45. Randolph Schwabe, 'Three Teachers: Brown, Tonks and Steer' (London: *The Burlington Magazine*, January 1943, pp. 142–3.

46. ibid., p. 146.

47. ibid., p. 145.

48. ibid., p. 142.

49. Michael Reynolds, *The Slade: The Story of an Art School, 1871–1971*, unpublished, pp. 184–7.

50. Paul Nash, quoted in Reynolds, p. 181.

51. Reynolds, p. 186.

52. Virginia Woolf, 'Mr Bennet and Mrs. Brown', in *The Captain's Deathbed and Other Essays* (London: The Hogarth Press, 1950).

53. *The Times*, 7 November 1910, p. 12.

54. *Manet and the Post-Impressionists* (exhibition catalogue), The Grafton Galleries, 8 November to 15 January 1910–11 (London: Ballantyne & Company Ltd, 1910), p. 9.

55. *Made at the Slade: a survey of mature works by ex-students of the Slade School of Fine Art, 1892–1960* (Brighton: Brighton Polytechnic Faculty of Art & Design, 1979), pp. 5–6.

56. ibid., pp. 5–6.

57. Reproduced in *Carrington: Paintings, Drawings and Decorations*, p. 27.

58. ibid., p. 23.

59. ibid., p. 20.

60. ibid., p. 20.

61. *Carrington: Letters and Extracts from Her Diaries*, pp. 504–5.

62. Author's interview with Frances Partridge, unpublished, 11 June 1986.

63. Carrington to John Nash, undated, Tate Gallery Archives.

64. Photograph at the Tate Gallery Archives. Reproduced in *Carrington: Paintings, Drawings and Decorations*, p. 21.

65. Anon., 'Mark Gertler', *Studio*, September 1932. Quoted in Woodeson, *Mark Gertler: Biography of a Painter*, pp. 58–61.

66. ibid., pp. 2–29.

67. ibid., pp. 37–43.

68. ibid., pp. 48–9.

69. ibid., p. 59. This kind of word was unfortunately used rather frequently. One finds it in Gertler's correspondence, Vanessa Bell's correspondence, and more surprisingly, in Clive Bell's published discussions of African art.

70. ibid., p. 79.

71. ibid., pp. 64–5.

72. Mark Gertler to Carrington, quoted in Woodeson, p. 85.

73. Photograph at the Tate Gallery Archives.

74. C. R. W. Nevinson to Carrington, 28 March, 1912, University of Texas, Austin.

75. ibid., 2 April 1912.

76. ibid., 2 April 1912.

77. ibid., 8 April 1912.
78. ibid., 9 April 1912.
79. Mark Gertler to Carrington, 15 April 1912, University of Texas, Austin.
80. C. R. W. Nevinson to Carrington, Thursday 28 March 1912, University of Texas, Austin.
81. ibid., May 1912.
82. ibid., 10 June 1912.
83. Mark Gertler to Carrington, 7 July 1912, ibid.
84. ibid., no date.
85. Mark Gertler to Carrington, 19 June 1912, quoted in *Mark Gertler: Selected Letters*, Noel Carrington, ed. (London: Rupert Hart-Davis, 1965), p. 36.
86. *Carrington: Letters and Extracts from Her Diaries*, p. 503.
87. Mark Gertler to Carrington, June 1912, quoted in *Mark Gertler: Selected Letters*, pp. 36–7.
88. C. R. W. Nevinson to Carrington, 21 June 1912, University of Texas, Austin.
89. Mark Gertler to C. R. W. Nevinson, July 1912, quoted in *Mark Gertler: Selected Letters*, pp. 38–9.
90. C. R. W. Nevinson to Carrington, 5 July 1912, University of Texas, Austin.
91. Anon., 'Mark Gertler', *Studio*, September 1932. Quoted in Woodeson, *Mark Gertler: Biography of a Painter*, p. 94.
92. C. R. W. Nevinson to Carrington, no date, University of Texas, Austin.
93. ibid., 11 July 1912.
94. Mark Gertler to Carrington, quoted in *Mark Gertler: Selected Letters*, p. 40.
95. C. R. W. Nevinson to Carrington, July 1912, University of Texas, Austin.
96. Mark Gertler to Carrington, July 1912, quoted in *Mark Gertler: Selected Letters*, pp. 42–3.
97. *Mark Gertler: Selected Letters*, p. 40.
98. C. R. W. Nevinson to Carrington, July 1912, University of Texas, Austin.
99. ibid., August 1912.
100. Mark Gertler to Carrington, August 1912, quoted in *Mark Gertler: Selected Letters*, p. 44.
101. Andrew Forge 'The Slade: 1871–1960', unpublished, p. 25.
102. Mark Gertler to Carrington, 15 August 1912, University of Texas, Austin.
103. C. R. W. Nevinson to Carrington, 9 September 1912, University of Texas, Austin.
104. Woodeson, pp. 97–103.
105. C. R. W. Nevinson to Carrington, 28 August, 1912.
106. ibid., 22 August 1912.
107. ibid., 9 September 1912.
108. Mark Gertler to Carrington, 12 September 1912.
109. ibid., 14 September 1912.
110. Mark Gertler to Carrington, 24 September 1912, *Mark Gertler: Selected Letters*, p. 46.
111. ibid., December 1912, p. 47.
112. ibid., December 1912, p. 48.
113. Mark Gertler to Carrington, 13 January 1913, University of Texas, Austin.
114. C. R. W. Nevinson to Carrington, 16 January 1913, University of Texas, Austin.
115. ibid., 20 January 1913.
116. C. R. W. Nevinson, *Paint and Prejudice* (London: Methuen, 1937), p. 29.
117. 1 March 1932, *Mark Gertler: Selected Letters*, p. 235.
118. Mark Gertler to Carrington, 2 April 1913, *Mark Gertler: Selected Letters*, p. 51.
119. The young philosopher had been like a 'thunderclap' to the members of Bloomsbury while some of them attended Cambridge University. They found in

him and his important book *Principia Ethica* someone whose ideas gave credence to the questions they raised and the answers they needed. Lytton Strachey, for example, found in Moore's stressing of 'the pleasures of human intercourse' a justification for homosexuality (Paul Levy, *Moore: G. E. Moore and the Cambridge Apostles* [London: Weidenfeld and Nicolson, 1979], p. 238). Young Bloomsbury found Moore's method of raising and answering questions of ethics scientifically and impeccably organised; they were able to pick and choose among those ideas to find the perfect combination of academic structure and innovative insight which they could apply to their own lives. To the painters, as to most modern readers, it was dry and difficult reading; while they agreed with much of what Moore believed, his methods were not theirs.

120. Mark Gertler to Carrington, 10 May 1913, University of Texas, Austin.

121. Mark Gertler to Carrington, October 1913, *Mark Gertler: Selected Letters*, p. 57.

122. Woodeson, p. 106.

123. ibid., p. 105.

124. ibid., p. 115.

125. Mark Gertler to Carrington, December 1913, *Mark Gertler: Selected Letters*, p. 60.

126. Telegram, 22 December 1913, University of Texas, Austin.

127. Mark Gertler to Carrington, 25 December 1913, *Mark Gertler: Selected Letters*, p. 60.

128. Albert Rutherston to Carrington, 26 December 1913, University of Texas, Austin.

129. Mark Gertler to Carrington, 1 January 1914, *Mark Gertler: Selected Letters*, pp. 60–1.

130. Mark Gertler to Carrington, 2 January 1914, University of Texas, Austin.

131. Carrington to John Nash, no date, Tate Gallery Archives.

132. ibid., 4 January 1914.

133. Carrington to Gerald Brenan, 'About January 12 1920', University of Texas, Austin.

134. Mark Gertler to Dorothy Brett, January 1914, *Mark Gertler: Selected Letters*, pp. 63–4.

135. Mark Gertler to Carrington, January 1914, University of Texas, Austin.

136. Albert Rutherston to Carrington, 8 April 1914, University of Texas, Austin.

137. Mark Gertler to Carrington, April 1914, *Mark Gertler: Selected Letters*, p. 68.

138. Reynolds, p. 184, and Schwabe, p. 9.

139. Mark Gertler to Edward Marsh, *Mark Gertler: Selected Letters*, May 1914, p. 69.

140. Albert Rutherston to Carrington, 17 May 1914, University of Texas, Austin.

141. Albert Rutherston to Carrington, no date, University of Texas, Austin.

142. Mark Gertler to Carrington, July 1914, University of Texas, Austin.

143. Albert Rutherston to Carrington, 17 August 1914, University of Texas, Austin.

144. ibid., no date.

145. ibid., no date.

146. Carrington to Mark Gertler, no date, University of Texas, Austin.

147. ibid., no date.

148. Albert Rutherston to Carrington, 10 December 1914, University of Texas, Austin.

149. ibid., 13 April 1916. Max Rutherston notes that the date is given incorrectly in several published works as 1915.

150. David Garnett, *The Flowers of the Forest* (London: Chatto & Windus; New York: Harcourt Brace and Company, 1955), pp. 9–10.

151. Carrington to Mark Gertler, University of Texas, Austin. Letter says August 1915, but is apparently misdated from January or February. Carrington's family had just moved again, to Hurstbourne Tarrant in Hampshire.

152. ibid.

153. Carrington to Mark Gertler, see Note 151 above.

154. Mark Gertler to Carrington, January 1915, *Mark Gertler: Selected Letters*, p. 81.

155. Carrington to Mark Gertler, 29 January 1915, University of Texas, Austin.

156. Carrington to Mark Gertler, see Note 151 above.

157. Carrington to Mark Gertler, January 1915, University of Texas, Austin.

158. David Garnett, *Flowers of the Forest*, pp. 106–7.

159. Mark Gertler to Carrington, *Mark Gertler: Selected Letters*, p. 83.

160. David Garnett, *Flowers of the Forest*, p. 111.

161. Mark Gertler to Carrington, 4 March 1915, in *Mark Gertler: Selected Letters*, pp. 86–7. Nevinson was to lend his artistic talents to the war effort as a war painter, and later became part of the Futurists' movement which in its manifesto extolled the modern machine and denounced women.

162. Mark Gertler to Lytton Strachey, 23 May 1915, in *Mark Gertler: Selected Letters*, p. 92.

163. Mark Gertler to Carrington, 15 June 1915, University of Texas, Austin.

164. This was something of an exaggeration. Their relationship was not yet consummated.

165. Carrington to Mark Gertler, 16 April 1915, *Carrington: Letters and Extracts from Her Diaries*, p. 17.

166. ibid., May 1915, pp. 18–19.

167. Carrington to Mark Gertler, May 1915, University of Texas, Austin.

168. Mark Gertler to Carrington, 1 July 1915, *Mark Gertler: Selected Letters*, pp. 97–8.

169. Woodeson, p. 210.

170. Carrington to Mark Gertler, no date, University of Texas, Austin.

171. ibid.

172. ibid.

173. Mark Gertler to Carrington, 14 November 1915, in *Mark Gertler: Selected Letters*, pp. 102–3.

174. Carrington to Mark Gertler, 19 November 1915, University of Texas, Austin.

175. ibid., December 1915.

176. In rejecting Victorianism and Edwardianism, they also rejected those who remained firmly entrenched in English soil and culture. Richard Shone, in his book *Bloomsbury Portraits*, supports this view when he says of Vanessa Bell, 'About most of her contemporaries she was dismissive; little English work interested her. French are constantly held up for praise in her letters but English painters rarely figure.' And, 'Clive [Bell] seemed more prepared to encourage a second-rate French painter than any English one.' (Richard Shone, *Bloomsbury Portraits: Vanessa Bell, Duncan Grant and their Circle* [London: Phaidon; New York: E. P. Dutton and Company, 1976], pp. 87 and 196.)

177. Frances Partridge interview with the author, 11 June 1986, unpublished.

178. *Carrington: Letters and Extracts from Her Diaries*, p. 23.

179. Dr Phyllis Greenacre says of this phenomenon that '... many gifted people develop at least two and sometimes more than two self-images with more or less separate identities – that of the ordinary citizen and that of the artist ... Inevitably the invasion of the artistic work is the greatest when the personal life is the dominant one or when the two are fused.' (Greenacre, p. 218.)

180. Carrington to Mark Gertler, December 1915, University of Texas, Austin.
181. Carrington to Mary Ruthentall, 6 December 1915, Tate Gallery Archives.
182. Holroyd, *Lytton Strachey*, pp. 634–5.

PART TWO

1. Frances Partridge, *Love in Bloomsbury: Memories*, p. 96.
2. David Garnett, quoted in Holroyd, *Lytton Strachey*, p. 596.
3. Mark Gertler to Lytton Strachey, May 1916, *Mark Gertler: Selected Letters*, pp. 110–11.
4. Mark Gertler to Carrington, *Mark Gertler: Selected Letters*, 20 May 1916, pp. 112–13.
5. ibid., 30 May 1916, p. 114.
6. Carrington to Gertler, 31 May 1916, ibid., p. 114.
7. Gertler to Lytton Strachey, May 1916, ibid., pp. 110–11.
8. Gertler to Carrington, 27 February 1916, ibid., pp. 108–9.
9. Carrington to Gertler, 31 May 1916, ibid., p. 114.
10. Gertler to Carrington, 4 September 1916, ibid., p. 219.
11. Gertler, no date, University of Texas at Austin.
12. Carrington to Lytton Strachey, 2 July 1916, ibid.
13. Lytton Strachey to Carrington, 3 July 1916, ibid.
14. Carrington to Lytton Strachey, 4 June 1916, ibid.
15. Lytton Strachey to Carrington, 7 June 1916, ibid.
16. ibid., 7 June 1916.
17. Probably a result of mustard gas employed in the war. Carrington to Lytton Strachey, June 1916, British Library.
18. Carrington to Lytton Strachey, 13 June 1916, *Carrington: Letters and Extracts from her Diaries,* pp. 28–9.
19. Noel Carrington to Gretchen Holbrook Gerzina, 22 January 1988, unpublished letter. Some parts quoted verbatim.
20. David Garnett to Carrington, 1916 from Wissett Lodge, unpublished.
21. Lytton Strachey to Carrington, 16 June 1916, British Library.
22. A friend was bringing a copy for her. Carrington to Lytton Strachey, 19 June 1916, *Carrington: Letters and Extracts from her Diaries*, pp. 29–30.
23. ibid.
24. Lytton Strachey to Carrington, 1 July 1916, British Library.
25. ibid., 3 July 1916.
26. Lytton Strachey to Lady Ottoline Morrell, 3 July 1916. Like the nickname given to C. R. W. Nevinson, this word reflects a common side of Bloomsbury: the use of a derogatory word to express what is not necessarily a derogatory feeling.
27. D. H. Lawrence to Mark Gertler, copied out in Gertler's hand, 9 October 1916, University of Texas at Austin. Interestingly, like Strachey Lawrence felt compelled to attribute this painting to Gertler's Jewishness.
28. David Garnett, *Great Friends*, p. 150.
29. Lytton Strachey to Carrington, 28 July 1916, British Library.
30. Carrington to Lytton Strachey, 30 July 1916, *Carrington: Letters and Extracts from her Diaries*, pp. 32–3.
31. Lytton Strachey to Carrington, 1 August 1916, British Library.
32. Carrington to Lytton Strachey, 5 August 1916, *Carrington: Letters and Extracts from her Diaries*, pp. 34–5.
33. Carrington, no date, 1916, University of Texas at Austin.
34. Lytton Strachey to Carrington, 1 August 1916, British Library.
35. Carrington to Lytton Strachey, 5 August 1916.
36. ibid.
37. Aldous Huxley to Frances Peterson, 7 August 1916, quoted in *Letters of Aldous Huxley*, Grover Smith, ed. (London: Chatto & Windus, 1969) p. 109.

38. Carrington to Gerald Brenan, 18 December 1921, University of Texas at Austin.

39. Aldous Huxley to Dorothy Brett, 1 December 1918, *Letters of Aldous Huxley*, p. 172.

40. Ottoline Morrell to Mark Gertler, 8 August 1916, quoted in *Mark Gertler: Selected Letters*, p. 117.

41. Mark Gertler to Carrington, 14 August 1916, ibid., pp. 116–17.

42. I am indebted to art critic Richard Shone for many of these observations.

43. Lytton Strachey to Carrington, 9 August 1916, British Library.

44. Carrington to Mark Gertler, August 1916, *Carrington: Letters and Extracts from Her Diaries*, pp. 36–7.

45. Mark Gertler to Carrington, 15 August 1916, *Mark Gertler: Selected Letters*, p. 118.

46. Carrington to Mark Gertler, August 1916, quoted in *Mark Gertler: Selected Letters*, pp. 120–1.

47. Mark Gertler to Carrington, 24 August 1916, ibid., pp. 120–2.

48. ibid., 29 August 1916, p. 23.

49. Lytton Strachey and Carrington to Maynard Keynes, August 1916, *Carrington: Letters and Extracts from Her Diaries*, p. 37.

50. David Garnett, *Great Friends*, pp. 152–4.

51. Carrington to Mark Gertler, quoted in Holroyd, p. 667.

52. Lytton Strachey to Carrington, September 1916, British Library.

53. Carrington to Lytton Strachey, 1 September 1916, *Carrington: Letters and Extracts from Her Diaries*, p. 58.

54. Carrington to Lytton Strachey, 6 September 1916, ibid., pp. 39–40.

55. Carrington to Mark Gertler, September 1916, University of Texas at Austin.

56. Carrington to Lytton Strachey, 8 September 1916, *Carrington: Letters and Extracts from Her Diaries*, pp. 40–1.

57. ibid., pp. 40–1.

58. Lytton did not, as Gerald Brenan wrote, take a house and then invite her to live there as his housekeeper. Nor did she move in, as Huxley later stated, 'to be his secretary and housekeeper'.

59. Holroyd, *Lytton Strachey*, p. 673.

60. Carrington to Lytton Strachey, 16 September 1916, *Carrington: Letters and Extracts from Her Diaries*, pp. 42–4.

61. Today Charleston is under the protection and management of the Charleston Trust, and visitors there can see in every room examples of Bloomsbury and Omega art in the house where Vanessa and Duncan lived until their deaths, and where Vanessa's sons Quentin and Julian, and her daughter Angelica by Duncan, were raised.

62. Carrington to David Garnett, 11 October 1916, *Carrington: Letters and Extracts from Her Diaries*, pp. 44–5.

63. ibid., 14 October 1916, pp. 45–6.

64. *Letters of Virginia Woolf*, Vol. 2, N. Nicolson ed. (London: Hogarth Press, 1976), [23?] October 1916, p. 124. This was perhaps the first time that they had spoken, which would further explain Carrington's fear and embarrassment.

65. Carrington to David Garnett, 17 October 1916, *Carrington: Letters and Extracts from Her Diaries*, pp. 46–7

66. David Garnett to Carrington, no date, unpublished.

67. Carrington to David Garnett, 25 October 1916, *Carrington: Letters and Extracts from Her Diaries*, p. 47.

68. David Garnett, *Great Friends*, p. 159

69. D. H. Lawrence, 2 December 1916, quoted in Woodeson, p. 238.

70. ibid.

71. *Letters of Virginia Woolf*, Vol. 2, [3?] December 1916, p. 128.

72. Beatrice Elvery, Lady Glenavy, *Today We Will Only Gossip* (London: Constable, 1964), pp. 83–5.

73. ibid., pp. 104–5.

74. Carrington to Lytton Strachey, 10 December 1916, *Carrington: Letters and Extracts from Her Diaries*, pp. 49–50

75. Garnett, *Carrington: Letters and Extracts from Her Diaries*, note page 50.

76. ibid., footnote, p. 50.

77. Carrington to Mark Gertler, December 1916, ibid., p. 50.

78. *Mark Gertler: Selected Letters*, December 1916, p. 134.

79. Carrington to Mark Gertler, December 1916, *Carrington: Letters and Extracts from Her Diaries*, p. 51.

80. ibid., p. 51.

81. ibid., 5 January 1917, p. 53.

82. Carrington's diary, 1 January 1917 (misdated 1916), ibid., p. 52.

83. Carrington to Lytton Strachey, 29 January 1917, British Library.

84. Lytton Strachey to Carrington, 31 January 1917, ibid.

85. Carrington to Lytton Strachey, January 1917, British Library. This letter also appears in Garnett's edition of Carrington's letters, but is misdated as 4 February.

86. Lytton Strachey to Ottoline Morrell, 6 February 1917, British Library.

87. Carrington to Mark Gertler, 5 February 1917, University of Texas at Austin.

88. ibid, 5 February 1917.

89. Carrington to Lytton Strachey, 26 February 1917, British Library.

90. Lytton Strachey to Carrington, 9 February 1917. Quoted in *Carrington: Letters and Extracts from Her Diaries*, p. 58.

91. Carrington to Lytton Strachey, February 1917, British Library.

92. Lytton Strachey to Carrington, 6 March 1917, ibid.

93. ibid., 8 March 1917.

94. ibid., 9 March 1917.

95. Carrington to Lytton Strachey, 22 March 1917, ibid.

96. Lytton Strachey to Carrington, 23 March 1917, ibid.

97. Carrington to Lytton Strachey, 23 March 1917, ibid.

98. Lytton Strachey to Carrington, 26 March 1917, ibid.

99. Mark Gertler to Carrington, April 1917, *Mark Gertler: Selected Letters*, p. 141.

100. Carrington's diary, *Carrington: Letters and Extracts from Her Diaries*, p. 63.

101. Carrington's diary, 13 April 1917, ibid., pp. 63–5.

102. ibid., pp. 63–5.

103. *Carrington: Letters and Extracts from Her Diaries*, 14 April 1917, p. 66.

104. ibid., p. 66.

105. Mark Gertler to Carrington, *Mark Gertler: Selected Letters*, p. 142.

106. Carrington to Mark Gertler, May 1917, *Carrington: Letters and Extracts from Her Diaries*, p. 68.

107. ibid., p. 68.

108. ibid., pp. 68–9.

109. Carrington to Mark Gertler, May 1917, University of Texas at Austin.

110. ibid., no date.

111. Roger Fry to Carrington, 29 May 1917, University of Texas at Austin.

112. Carrington to Lytton Strachey, 17 June 1917, British Library.

113. Quoted in Holroyd, *Lytton Strachey*, pp. 628–9.

114. Lytton Strachey to Carrington, 9 June 1917, British Library.

115. Carrington to Noel Carrington, no date 1917, *Carrington: Letters and Extracts from Her Diaries*, pp. 70–1.

116. Carrington to Barbara Bagenal, quoted in Holroyd, *Lytton Strachey*, p. 694.

117. Lytton Strachey to Carrington, 22 July 1917, British Library.

118. Carrington to Mark Gertler, 13 July 1917, University of Texas at Austin.

119. Lytton Strachey to Carrington, 24 July 1917, British Library.

120. Carrington to Lytton Strachey, 27 July 1917, ibid.

121. Virginia Woolf to Carrington, 13 July 1917, *Letters of Virginia Woolf*, Vol. 2, p. 16.

122. Lytton Strachey to Carrington, 15 July 1917, British Library.

123. Carrington to Mark Gertler, July 1917, University of Texas at Austin.

124. Carrington to Lytton Strachey, 25 July 1917, British Library. Written from her new studio at 60 Frith Street.

125. Lytton Strachey to Carrington, 28 July 1917, British Library.

126. Carrington to Lytton Strachey, 30 July 1917, ibid.

127. Lytton Strachey to Carrington, 7 August 1917, ibid.

128. Lytton Strachey to Carrington, 31 July 1917, ibid.

129. *Letters of Virginia Woolf*, Vol. 2, 5 October 1917, pp. 184–5.

130. Lytton Strachey to Carrington, 7 August 1917, British Library.

131. Carrington to Lytton Strachey, 12 August 1917, ibid.

132. Lytton Strachey to Carrington, 14 August 1917, ibid.

133. Lytton Strachey to Carrington, 10 August 1917, ibid.

134. Carrington to Lytton Strachey, 11 August 1917, ibid.

135. Carrington to Lytton Strachey, 10 August 1917, *Carrington: Letters and Extracts from her Diaries*, pp. 80–1.

136. Carrington to Lytton Strachey, 12 August 1917, British Library.

137. Carrington to Lytton Strachey, August 1917, ibid.

138. ibid.

139. Quoted in Holroyd, *Lytton Strachey*, p. 699.

140. Carrington to Mark Gertler, September 1917, University of Texas at Austin.

141. Mark Gertler to Carrington, 12 September 1917, *Carrington: Letters and Extracts from her Diaries*, p. 152.

142. Carrington to Mark Gertler, September 1917, University of Texas at Austin.

143. Mark Gertler to Carrington, 4 October 1917, *Mark Gertler: Selected Letters*, p. 152.

144. Carrington to Mark Gertler, October 1917, University of Texas at Austin.

145. Carrington to Lytton Strachey, 18 October 1917, British Library.

146. Carrington to Lytton Strachey, 19 October 1917, ibid. This seems to have been the first time she used this name, which she would use to sign nearly all of her subsequent letters to Lytton.

147. Carrington to Lytton Strachey, 20 October 1917, *Carrington: Letters and Extracts from her Diaries*, p. 83.

148. Carrington to Lytton Strachey, 20 November 1917, British Library.

149. Carrington to Lytton Strachey, 7 December 1917, ibid.

150. Carrington to Lytton Strachey, 10 December 1917, ibid. This was a reference to the distinctive Charleston decor. Vanessa Bell and Duncan Grant, not content to paint only on canvas, turned to walls, furniture, fireplaces and textiles. The result was an entirely Omega-like environment: unique, distinctive, and colourful.

151. *Diary of Virginia Woolf*, Vol. 1, 13 December 1917, p. 91.

152. Mark Gertler to Carrington, November 1917, University of Texas at Austin.

153. Carrington to Mark Gertler, November 1917, ibid.

154. Mark Gertler to Carrington, no date, ibid.

155. Dorothy Brett to Michael Holroyd, quoted in Holroyd, *Lytton Strachey*, p. 669.

156. Carrington to Lytton Strachey, 8 November 1917, British Library.

157. Carrington to Lytton Strachey, 9 November 1917, ibid.
158. Lytton Strachey to Carrington, 1 April 1918, ibid.
159. *Diary of Virginia Woolf*, Vol. 1, (8–12) December 1917, pp. 89–90.
160. Lytton Strachey to Carrington, 11 December 1917, British Library.
161. Mark Gertler to Carrington, 13 November [1917?], University of Texas at Austin.
162. *Diary of Virginia Woolf*, Vol. 1, 18 March 1918, pp. 128–9.
163. ibid., 31 July 1918, p. 176.
164. ibid., 6 June 1918, pp. 152–3.
165. ibid., 23 July 1918, p. 171.
166. ibid., 16 August 1918. pp. 183–4
167. *Letters of Virginia Woolf*, Vol. 2, July 1918, p. 212.
168. Lytton Strachey to Lady Ottoline Morrell, 23 December 1917, University of Texas at Austin.
169. Mark Gertler to S. S. Koteliansky, *Mark Gertler: Selected Letters*, p. 158.
170. Mark Gertler to Carrington, 23 February 1918, *Mark Gertler: Selected Letters*, p. 158.
171. Lytton Strachey, quoted in *Mark Gertler: Selected Letters*, 18 February 1918, p. 156.
172. Carrington to Mark Gertler, February 1918, quoted in *Mark Gertler: Selected Letters*.
173. Lytton's full name was Giles Lytton Strachey.
174. Carrington to Lytton Strachey, 1 March 1918, British Library.
175. ibid., 23 August 1918.
176. Carrington to David Garnett, 2 October 1918, *Carrington: Letters and Extracts from her Diaries*, pp. 104–5.
177. Carrington to Lytton Strachey, 4 April 1918, British Library. The 'London Literary' was probably the London Library at 14 St James's Square, at which several Bloomsbury members held subscriptions.
178. ibid., June 1918.
179. ibid., 9 June 1918.
180. ibid., 4 July 1918.
181. Lytton Strachey to Carrington, 6 July 1918, ibid.
182. ibid., 9 July 1918.
183. ibid., 7 July 1918.
184. ibid.
185. Carrington to Virginia Woolf, October 1918, in *Carrington: Letters and Extracts from her Diaries*, pp. 105–6.
186. David Garnett, *Great Friends*, p. 152.
187. David Garnett, Preface to *Carrington: Letters and Extracts from Her Diaries*, pp. 10–11.
188. Carrington to Lytton Strachey, 12 November 1918, British Library.
189. Carrington to Lytton Strachey, 12 November 1918, British Library. It is difficult to get a real understanding of Bloomsbury's attitudes on race and religion. They made frequent racist remarks, yet it seems to have been the fashionable thing to do. Clearly they did not question the implications of such remarks, nor did they often know many people to whom they applied. They were, it is clear, snobbish and unthinking in this respect.
190. Carrington to Lytton Strachey, 15 November 1918, British Library.
191. *Letters of Virginia Woolf*, Vol. 2, p. 205.
192. Lytton Strachey to Carrington, 12 June 1918, British Library.
193. Carrington to Lytton Strachey, 3 April 1918, ibid.
194. Ralph Partridge to Noel Carrington, 17 August 1918, University of Texas at Austin.
195. Holroyd, *Lytton Strachey*, p. 761.

196. Carrington to Lytton Strachey, 9 June 1919, British Library.

197. Carrington to David Garnett, no date, from Tatchley, Prestbury, Cheltenham, Gloucestershire. Courtesy of Richard Garnett.

198. Carrington to David Garnett, no date, from Tidmarsh, unpublished, courtesy of Richard Garnett.

199. Carrington to Lytton Strachey, 1 January 1919, British Library.

200. ibid., postscript 1 January 1919.

201. ibid., 2 January 1919.

202. Carrington to Mark Gertler, January 1919, *Carrington: Letters and Extracts from her Diaries*, pp. 124–5.

203. Carrington to Lytton Strachey, December 1918, from Cheltenham, British Library.

204. Carrington to Lytton Strachey, 22 January 1919, British Library.

205. Aldous Huxley to Dorothy Brett, 1 December 1918, *Letters of Aldous Huxley*, p. 172.

206. Carrington to Mark Gertler, January 1919, *Carrington: Letters and Extracts from her Diaries*, pp. 124–5.

207. Mark Gertler to Carrington, 12 January 1919, *Mark Gertler: Selected Letters*, p. 169.

208. Carrington to Mark Gertler, 8 December 1918, *Carrington: Letters and Extracts from her Diaries*, pp. 118–9

209. Carrington to Lytton Strachey, 11 December 1919, British Library.

210. ibid., 3 March 1919.

211. ibid., 19 March 1919.

212. ibid., 21 March 1919, written in a 20 March letter.

213. ibid.

214. ibid.

215. ibid.

216. Carrington to Lytton Strachey, on the road to Malaga, 30 March 1919, ibid.

217. Carrington to Lytton Strachey, 6 April 1919, ibid. 'Significant form' was a term coined by Roger Fry and used by Clive Bell in his book *Art* to define that most important aspect of any work of art.

218. ibid., 15 April 1919.

219. ibid, 18 April 1919.

220. ibid.

221. ibid., 11 May 1919.

222. ibid., 1 June 1919.

223. ibid., 18 June 1919.

224. ibid., 2 July 1919.

225. *Diary of Virginia Woolf*, Vol. 1, 22 January 1919, pp. 234–5.

226. ibid., 24 January 1919, p. 236.

227. *Letters of Virginia Woolf*, Vol. 2, 15 June 1919, p. 367.

228. *Diary of Virginia Woolf*, Vol. 1, 15 November 1919, pp. 311–12.

229. Carrington to Lytton Strachey, 12 May 1919, British Library.

230. Lytton Strachey to Carrington, 15 May 1919, ibid.

231. Carrington to Lytton Strachey, 30 June 1919, ibid.

232. ibid., 25 August 1919.

233. ibid., 9 September 1919.

234. ibid., 12 July 1919.

235. Lytton Strachey to Carrington, 19 June 1919, ibid.

236. ibid., 11 July 1919.

237. Carrington to Lytton Strachey, [9?] July 1919, ibid.

238. ibid., 14 July 1919.

239. ibid., 12 July 1919.

240. ibid., 14 July 1919.

241. ibid., 18 July 1919.

242. Lytton Strachey to Carrington, 22 July 1919, ibid.

243. Carrington to Lytton Strachey, 20 July 1919, ibid.

244. ibid., 25 August 1919.

245. ibid., 28 October 1919.

246. ibid.

247. Carrington to Gerald Brenan, 'About Jan. 12, 1920', University of Texas at Austin.

248. Xan Fielding, *Best of Friends: The Brenan–Partridge Letters* (London: Chatto & Windus, 1986), p. 3.

249. Gerald Brenan, *Personal Record*, (London: Jonathan Cape, 1974) p. 23.

250. Carrington to Gerald Brenan, 21 November 1919, University of Texas at Austin.

251. Gerald Brenan, *Personal Record*, p. 24.

252. Carrington to Gerald Brenan, 15 December 1919, University of Texas at Austin.

253. ibid., 2 January 1920.

254. ibid., 1 February 1920.

255. Perhaps a tongue-in-cheek play written by Peter Luke and produced by the BBC, in which the three chased each other around a large bed, gave rise to this misinterpretation. There is no evidence whatsoever, either in documents or in the memories of those involved, to support speculation of an affair between Strachey and Partridge. When asked about this Michael Holroyd, Strachey's biographer, said he had never discussed it in that book simply because it never occurred to him or anyone he spoke to that there might have been anything sexual in Strachey's and Partridge's friendship.

256. Ralph Partridge to Noel Carrington, 7 February 1920, University of Texas at Austin.

257. Carrington to Lytton Strachey, 1 March 1920, British Library.

258. Lytton Strachey to Carrington and Ralph Partridge, 1 March 1920, ibid.

259. Carrington to Gerald Brenan, long letter begun 1 February 1920, University of Texas at Austin.

260. ibid., 18 April 1920, Hotel Terminus, Madrid.

261. Ralph Partridge to Noel Carrington, 5 May 1920, University of Texas at Austin.

262. Ralph Partridge to Noel Carrington, May 1920, University of Texas at Austin.

263. Carrington to Gerald Brenan, long letter begun 1 February 1920, University of Texas at Austin.

264. ibid., 5 May 1920.

265. Carrington to Lytton Strachey, 20 May 1920, Royal Free Hospital, London, British Library.

266. Carrington to Gerald Brenan, Royal Free Hospital, London, 23 May 1920, University of Texas at Austin.

267. ibid., 5 May 1920.

268. ibid., 23 May 1920, Royal Free Hospital.

269. Lytton Strachey to Carrington, 19 July 1920, British Library.

270. Carrington to Lytton Strachey, 21 July 1920, ibid.

271. Lytton Strachey to Carrington, 22 July 1920, ibid.

272. ibid.

273. Carrington to Gerald Brenan, 'About Jan. 12, 1920', University of Texas at Austin.

274. ibid., October 1920, 41 Gordon Square, London.

275. *Letters of Virginia Woolf*, Vol. 2, 24 August 1920, p. 442.

276. Lytton Strachey to Carrington, Charleston, 4 September 1920, British Library,

277. Carrington to Lytton Strachey, 8 September 1920, on her way from Charleston to Rodmell, ibid.

278. ibid., 12 October 1920, 41 Gordon Square, London.

279. Carrington to Gerald Brenan, 18 October 1920, University of Texas at Austin.

280. Carrington to Lytton Strachey, 25 October 1920, British Library.

281. ibid., 16 November 1920.

282. ibid., 24 November 1920.

283. Lytton Strachey to Carrington, 25 November 1920, ibid.

284. Carrington to Lytton Strachey, 21 November 1920, ibid.

285. Lytton Strachey to Carrington, 9 February 1921, ibid.

286. Carrington to Lytton Strachey, 1 March 1920, ibid.

287. Carrington to Gerald Brenan, long letter 24 April–2 May, 1921, University of Texas at Austin.

288. ibid.

289. Carrington to Lytton Strachey, 8 May 1921, British Library.

290. ibid., 14 May 1921.

291. Lytton Strachey to Carrington, 20–21 May 1921, ibid.

292. Carrington to Lytton Strachey, 17 May 1921, ibid.

PART THREE

1. Carrington to Gerald Brenan, 8 June 1921, University of Texas at Austin.

2. Virginia Woolf to Vanessa Bell. *Letters of Virginia Woolf*, Vol. 2, 22 May 1921, pp. 470–1.

3. The name 'Clare Bollard' was used for Valentine in David Garnett's edition of Carrington's letters, in Gerald Brenan's *Personal Record*, and in Michael Holroyd's biography of Lytton Strachey, apparently to protect the living. In those works her husband Bonamy Dobree is called 'Septimus Bollard'.

4. Carrington to Gerald Brenan, 28 December 1920, University of Texas at Austin.

5. Quoted in Fielding, pp. 22–3.

6. Lytton to James Strachey, 9 April 1922, quoted in Holroyd, *Lytton Strachey*, p. 837.

7. Holroyd, *Lytton Strachey*, p. 837.

8. Postcard from Carrington to Gerald Brenan, 4 June 1921, University of Texas at Austin.

9. Postcard from Carrington to Gerald Brenan, 24 May 1921, ibid.

10. Carrington to Lytton Strachey, 22 June 1921, British Library.

11. Carrington to Gerald Brenan, 5 July 1921, University of Texas at Austin.

12. ibid., 28 June 1921.

13. Gerald Brenan, *Personal Record*, p. 27.

14. ibid., p. 31.

15. ibid.

16. Carrington to Gerald Brenan, (mid-July) 1921, British Library.

17. Carrington to Gerald Brenan, 6 August 1921, University of Texas at Austin.

18. Ralph Partridge to Noel Carrington, 6 August 1921, ibid.

19. Carrington to Gerald Brenan, 9 August 1921.

20. ibid.

21. ibid., 15 August 1921.

22. ibid.

23. ibid., August 1921.

24. ibid., 21 September 1921.

25. ibid., 1 September 1921.

26. Quoted in *Carrington: Paintings, Drawings and Decorations*, p. 57.

27. Carrington to Lytton Strachey, 5 September 1921, British Library.

28. Carrington to Gerald Brenan, 10 October 1921, University of Texas at Austin.

29. Holroyd, *Lytton Strachey*, pp. 809–10.

30. Carrington to Gerald Brenan, 12 October 1921, University of Texas at Austin.

31. ibid., 21 September 1921.

32. ibid., 18 December 1921.

33. ibid., 27 November 1921.

34. ibid., 23 October 1921.

35. ibid., 27 November 1921.

36. ibid., 9 December 1921.

37. ibid.

38. ibid., 10 September 1921.

39. ibid., 27 November 1921.

40. ibid., 9 December 1921.

41. ibid., 28 October 1921.

42. ibid., 27 November 1921.

43. Quite a number of his mosaics, many featuring Bloosmbury people, are on display in the vestibules and landings of the National Gallery, London.

44. Carrington to Gerald Brenan, 31 December 1921, University of Texas at Austin.

45. ibid., 14 January 1922, from 'Tidmarsh-in-the-snow'.

46. ibid.

47. ibid., 27–9 January 1922.

48. Fielding, p. 23.

49. Carrington to Clive Bell, around February 1922, *Carrington: Letters and Extracts from Her Diaries*, p. 202.

50. Lytton Strachey to Carrington, 13 February 1922, British Library.

51. Carrington to Lytton Strachey, 15 February 1922, *Carrington: Letters and Extracts from Her Diaries*, p. 202.

52. Lytton Strachey to Carrington, 24 February 1922, British Library.

53. Clive Bell, *Civilisation and Old Friends* (Chicago: University of Chicago Press, 1973), p. 106.

54. Carrington to Lytton Strachey, 28 February 1922, British Library.

55. ibid.

56. Carrington to Gerald Brenan, 12 March 1922, University of Texas at Austin.

57. ibid.

58. ibid.

59. Carrington to Gerald Brenan, 14 March 1922, University of Texas at Austin.

60. Gerald Brenan, *Personal Record*, p. 43.

61. Carrington to Gerald Brenan, 3 May 1922, University of Texas at Austin.

62. ibid.

63. ibid., 8 June 1922.

64. Gerald Brenan, *Personal Record*, p. 50.

65. ibid.

66. Carrington to Gerald Brenan, 11 June 1922, University of Texas at Austin.

67. Gerald Brenan to Carrington, 11 June 1922, *Carrington: Letters and Extracts from Her Diaries*, p. 221.

68. Carrington to Gerald Brenan, 19 October 1922, University of Texas at Austin.

69. ibid.

70. Carrington to Gerald Brenan, 20 October 1922, University of Texas at

Austin. This is part of a very long journal letter which Carrington wrote to Brenan but held aside for months until they were 'allowed' to correspond again.

71. Carrington to Alix Strachey, 19 June 1922, in *Carrington: Letters and Extracts from Her Diaries*, pp. 225–7.

72. Carrington to Lytton Strachey, 22 June 1922, British Library.

73. Virginia Woolf to Carrington, 8 November 1922, in *Letters of Virginia Woolf*, Vol. 2, p. 563.

74. Virginia Woolf to Barbara Bagenal, *Letters of Virginia Woolf*, Vol. 2, p. 558.

75. Carrington to Lytton Strachey, 25 September 1922, British Library.

76. Ralph Partridge to Gerald Brenan, 10 October 1922, Fielding, p. 30.

77. Carrington to Gerald Brenan, 12 December 1922, University of Texas at Austin.

78. ibid., 20 December 1922.

79. ibid.

80. ibid.

81. Ralph Partridge to Gerald Brenan, 22 December 1922, Fielding, p. 42.

82. Virginia Woolf to Carrington, 25 December 1922, *Letters of Virginia Woolf*, Vol. 2, p. 596.

83. Carrington to Gerald Brenan, 29 January 1923. University of Texas at Austin. This is another long journal letter, added to almost daily but posted much later.

84. ibid., 18 February 1923. This is a continuation of the journal letter noted above.

85. ibid.

86. Carrington to Gerald Brenan, 8 October 1923, University of Texas at Austin.

87. ibid., 18 February 1923. Long journal letter begun 6 February.

88. ibid., 22 October 1923.

89. ibid., 6 February 1923.

90. ibid., 18 February 1923. Long journal letter begun 6 February 1923.

91. Ralph Partridge to Gerald Brenan, 17 October 1923, in Fielding, pp. 54–5.

92. Carrington to Gerald Brenan, 26 July 1923, University of Texas at Austin.

93. ibid., 18 February, 1923. Long journal letter begun 6 February.

94. ibid., 3 May 1923. Journal letter begun 24 April 1923.

95. ibid., 31 May 1923.

96. ibid., 5 June 1923.

97. ibid., 26 July 1923.

98. ibid., 27 August, 1923.

99. ibid., 27 August 1923.

100. ibid, 15 September 1923.

101. ibid.

102. ibid., 20 November 1923.

103. ibid., 23 October 1923. Carrington was exaggerating Mrs Partridge's wealth.

104. ibid., 17 December 1923.

105. ibid., 20 November 1923.

106. Frances Partridge, *Love in Bloomsbury: Memoirs*, p. 97.

107. ibid.

108. Gerald Brenan's diary, 23 December 1923, University of Texas at Austin.

109. Gerald Brenan, *Personal Record*, pp. 67–8.

110. Lytton Strachey to Carrington, 21 December 1923, British Library.

111. Gerald Brenan's diary, 26 December 1923, University of Texas at Austin

112. Gerald Brenan, *Personal Record*, p. 68.

113. Gerald Brenan's diary, 6 January 1924, University of Texas at Austin.

114. ibid., 8 January 1924.

115. ibid., 9 January 1924.

116. Carrington to Gerald Brenan, 11 January 1924, University of Texas at Austin.

117. ibid.

118. ibid., 13 January 1924.

119. ibid., 15 January 1924.

120. ibid.

121. Carrington to Gerald Brenan, 22 January 1924, University of Texas at Austin.

122. ibid., 14 February 1924.

123. Richard Shone to the author, 5 May 1988.

124. Carrington to Gerald Brenan, 10 March 1924, University of Texas at Austin.

125. ibid., 4 March 1924.

126. ibid.

127. ibid.

128. Carrington to Gerald Brenan, 8 June 1923, University of Texas at Austin. A long journal letter begun 31 May.

129. Frances Partridge in a note to the author, March 1988.

130. Carrington to Alix Strachey, no date, the Lytton Strachey Trust.

131. ibid.

132. Carrington to Gerald Brenan, 15 October 1924, University of Texas at Austin.

133. Lytton Strachey to Carrington, 17 October 1924, British Library.

134. Carrington to Gerald Brenan, 23 June 1924, University of Texas at Austin.

135. ibid., 5 July 1924.

136. ibid., 22 June 1924.

137. This is what Carrington says in a letter, but Frances Partridge remembers it as being a very pale blue.

138. Carrington to Gerald Brenan, 15 July 1924, University of Texas at Austin.

139. Carrington to Lytton Strachey, 16 July 1924, British Library.

140. Gerald Brenan to Carrington, summer 1924, University of Texas at Austin.

141. Carrington to Gerald Brenan, 25 July 1924, ibid.

142. Gerald Brenan to Carrington, 31 July 1924, ibid.

143. Frances Partridge to the author, March 1988.

144. Gerald Brenan to Carrington, 22 August 1924, University of Texas at Austin.

145. Gerald Brenan, *Personal Record*, pp. 82–3.

146. ibid., p. 85.

147. Carrington to Gerald Brenan, 27 September 1924, University of Texas at Austin.

148. Gerald Brenan's diary, 25 October 1924, ibid.

149. Carrington to Gerald Brenan, 8 August 1923, a long journal letter from France begun 26 July 1923, ibid.

150. Gerald Brenan's diary, 30 October 1924, ibid.

151. Carrington to Gerald Brenan, 7 November 1924, ibid.

152. James Strachey to Alix Strachey, 5 July 1925, in *Bloomsbury/Freud The Letters of James and Alix Strachey 1924–5*, edited by Perry Meisel and Walter Kendrick (New York: Basic Books, Inc, 1985), p. 259.

153. Frances Partridge, *Love in Bloomsbury: Memoirs*, p. 101.

154. Carrington to Gerald Brenan, 24 December 1924, University of Texas at Austin.

155. ibid., 16 January 1925.

156. This was her symbol for sex.

157. Carrington to Gerald Brenan, postscript on 19 March 1925, University of Texas at Austin.

158. Gerald Brenan to Carrington, 24 March 1925, ibid.
159. ibid., in an unposted letter, March 1925.
160. ibid., 25 January 1925.
161. Carrington to Alix Strachey, 4 February 1925, Lytton Strachey Trust.
162. Gerald Brenan to Carrington, late February 1925, University of Texas at Austin.
163. Carrington to Gerald Brenan, 27 February 1925, University of Texas at Austin.
164. Richard Shone to the author, 5 May 1988.
165. Carrington to Lytton Strachey, 30 March 1925, British Library.
166. Carrington to Gerald Brenan, 27 April 1925, University of Texas at Austin.
167. ibid., 21 June 1925, University of Texas at Austin.
168. Henry Lamb to Carrington, 3 April 1925, University of Texas at Austin.
169. Carrington to Gerald Brenan, 28 June 1925, University of Texas at Austin.
170. ibid., 30 March 1925.
171. ibid., 23 January 1925.
172. Gerald Brenan to Carrington, 24 February 1925, ibid.
173. Carrington to Gerald Brenan, 25 February 1925, ibid.
174. ibid., 30 March 1925.
175. Carrington to Alix, 4 February 1925, unpublished, Lytton Strachey Trust.
176. Carrington to Gerald Brenan, 5 February 1925, University of Texas at Austin.
177. ibid, 17 March 1925.
178. Gerald Brenan's diary, 15 March 1925, ibid.
179. Carrington to Gerald Brenan, 7 January 1925, ibid.
180. Carrington to Alix Strachey, 22 February 1925, Lytton Strachey Trust.
181. Gerald Brenan to Carrington, 1 February 1925, Uniersity of Texas at Austin.
182. Gerald Brenan's diary, 3 June 1925, University of Texas at Austin.
183. ibid., 8 June 1925.
184. Carrington to Lytton Strachey, 20 July 1925, British Library.
185. Gerald Brenan, *Personal Record*, pp. 109–10.
186. Carrington to Gerald Brenan, 21 July 1925, University of Texas at Austin.
187. Gerald Brenan to Carrington, 23 July 1925, ibid.
188. Gerald Brenan, *Personal Record*, p. 105.
189. Frances Partridge, *Love in Bloomsbury: Memoirs*, p. 105.
190. Carrington to Julia Strachey, spring 1926, in Carrington: *Letters and Extracts from Her Diaries*, pp. 331–2.
191. ibid.
192. Frances Partridge, *Love in Bloomsbury: Memoirs*, pp. 180–1.
193. Carrington to Frances Marshall, in *Carrington: Letters and Extracts from Her Diaries*, pp. 332–3.
194. Frances Marshall to Carrington, ibid., pp. 333–5.
195. Carrington to Lytton Strachey, 18 March 1926, British Library.
196. Lytton Strachey to Carrington, 19 March 1926, ibid.
197. Gerald Brenan's diary, 29 March 1926, University of Texas at Austin.
198. ibid., 24 April 1926.
199. Carrington to Gerald Brenan, 14 April 1926, University of Texas at Austin.
200. ibid.
201. Carrington to Alix Strachey, early May 1926, Lytton Strachey Trust.
202. Carrington to Lytton Strachey, 23 September 1926. British Library.
203. ibid., 19 September 1926.
204. Gerald Brenan's diary, autumn 1926, University of Texas at Austin.
205. Carrington to Alix Strachey, November 1926, Lytton Strachey Trust.
206. Gerald Brenan, *Personal Record*, p. 175.

207. Carrington to Gerald Brenan, 8 December 1926, University of Texas at Austin.

208. ibid., 30 December 1926.

209. ibid., 31 December 1926.

210. ibid., 10 January 1927.

211. ibid., February 1927.

212. Carrington to Julia Strachey, in *Carrington: Letters and Extracts from Her Diaries*, pp. 357–8.

213. ibid., p. 361.

214. Carrington to Gerald Brenan, 31 March 1927, University of Texas at Austin.

215. ibid., 6 April 1927.

216. Lytton Strachey to Carrington, 29 October 1926, British Library.

217. Carrington to Gerald Brenan, 10 May 1927, University of Texas at Austin.

218. Gerald Brenan's diary, 28 May 1926.

219. Carrington to Gerald Brenan, 13 August 1927, ibid.

PART FOUR

1. Carrington to James Strachey, winter 1928, The Lytton Strachey Trust.

2. Frances Partridge to the author, 1986.

3. Carrington to James Strachey, winter 1928, The Lytton Strachey Trust.

4. *D.C. Partride, Her Book*, 1 January 1928, British Library.

5. ibid.

6. ibid.

7. Mark Gertler to Carrington, 28 March 1928, in *Mark Gertler: Selected Letters*, pp. 227–8.

8. *D.C. Partride, Her Book*, 1 January 1928, British Library.

9. ibid., 2 January 1928.

10. ibid., [3] January 1928.

11. ibid., 4 January 1928.

12. Lytton Strachey to Ralph Partridge, 6 November 1928, quoted in Holroyd, *Lytton Strachey*, p. 978.

13. *D.C. Partride, Her Book* [3] January 1928, British Library.

14. ibid., 4 January 1928.

15. ibid.

16. ibid.

17. ibid.

18. ibid., 5 January 1928.

19. ibid.

20. ibid., 16 January 1928.

21. Carrington to Lytton Strachey, 16 January 1928, in *Carrington: Letters and Extracts from Her Diaries*, p. 385.

22. *D.C. Partride, Her Book*, 17 January 1928, British Library.

23. ibid., around 20 January 1928.

24. Carrington to Gerald Brenan, 9 February 1928, in *Carrington: Letters and Extracts from Her Diaries*, p. 386.

25. ibid., 11 February 1928, p. 387.

26. Julia Strachey in *Julia: A Portrait of Julia Strachey by Herself & Frances Partridge* (Boston: Little, Brown and Company, 1983), pp. 119–20.

27. Carrington to Lytton Strachey, 7 March 1928, British Library.

28. ibid., 10 April 1928.

29. Carrington to Gerald Brenan, 10 May 1928, University of Texas at Austin.

30. Richard Shone to the author, 5 May 1988.

31. Carrington to James Strachey, 22 May 1928, The Lytton Strachey Trust.

32. Carrington to Julia Strachey, no date, in *Carrington: Letters and Extracts from Her Diaries*, p. 394.

33. Carrington to Sebastian Sprott, Whitsun 1928, ibid., pp. 395–6.

34. Carrington to Lytton Strachey, 4 July 1928, British Library.

35. ibid., 18 July 1928.

36. Holroyd, *Lytton Strachey*, p. 984.

37. *Diary of Virginia Woolf*, Vol. 3, 28 November 1928.

38. Carrington to Sebastian Sprott, Saturday, Whitsun 1928, in *Carrington: Letters and Extracts from Her Diaries*, pp. 395–6.

39. ibid.

40. Carrington to Lytton Strachey, 7 August 1928, British Library.

41. Carrington to Gerald Brenan, 30 August 1928, University of Texas at Austin.

42. Frances Partridge, *Love in Bloomsbury: Memories*, pp. 152–4.

43. ibid.

44. ibid.

45. ibid.

46. ibid.

47. Carrington to James Strachey, no date, The Lytton Strachey Trust.

48. Julia Strachey in *Julia*, pp. 118–20.

49. Carrington to James Strachey, right after Christmas 1927 or 1928, The Lytton Strachey Trust.

50. Carrington to Alix Strachey, no date, The Lytton Strachey Trust.

51. Carrington to Lytton Strachey, February 1928, in *Carrington: Letters and Extracts from Her Diaries*, p. 387. Presumably Carrington had knitted him a gift.

52. Frances Partridge to the author, 1986.

53. David Garnett, *Carrington: Letters and Extracts from Her Diaries*, p. 386.

54. Quoted in Holroyd, *Lytton Strachey*, p. 829.

55. Carrington to Alix Strachey, no date, The Lytton Strachey Trust.

56. Carrington to Julia Strachey, late December 1928, in *Carrington: Letters and Extracts from Her Diaries*, p. 401.

57. Carrington to Lytton Strachey, 10 September 1928, British Library.

58. ibid., [21?] March 1929.

59. Carrington to Sebastian Sprott, early March 1929, in *Carrington: Letters and Extracts from Her Diaries*, pp. 404–6.

60. Carrington to Sebastian Sprott, early March 1929, ibid., pp. 404–6.

61. Carrington to Julia Strachey, end of March or early April 1929, ibid., pp. 408–9.

62. Carrington to Julia Strachey, end of March or early April 1929, in ibid., pp. 408–9.

63. Carrington to Sebastian Sprott, early March 1929, ibid., p. 404.

64. Carrington to Julia, end of March or early April 1929, ibid., pp. 408–9.

65. Carrington to Lytton Strachey, 21 May 1929, ibid., p. 410.

66. ibid., pp. 410–11.

67. Carrington to Lytton Strachey, 3 June 1929, British Library.

68. Carrington to Julia Strachey, 1 July 1929, in *Carrington: Letters and Extracts from Her Diaries*, pp. 412–13.

69. ibid.

70. Carrington to Lytton Strachey, 6 November 1929, British Library.

71. ibid., 27 August 1929.

72. ibid.

73. Frances Partridge, *Love in Bloomsbury: Memories*, p. 159.

74. David Garnett, *The Familiar Faces* (New York: Harcourt, Brace & World, Inc., 1062), p. 46.

75. Carrington to Lytton Strachey, 17 August 1929, in *Carrington: Letters and Extracts from Her Diaries*, pp. 413–14.

76. ibid.

77. David Garnett, *Flowers of the Forest*, p. 46.

78. Carrington to Lytton Strachey, 17 August 1929, in *Carrington: Letters and Extracts from Her Diaries*, pp. 413–14.

79. Carrington to Lytton Strachey, 19 August 1929, British Library.

80. ibid., 18 September 1929.

81. ibid., 27 September 1929.

82. Carrington to Julia Strachey, 7 October 1929, in *Carrington: Letters and Extracts from Her Diaries*, p. 426.

83. Frances Partridge in conversation with the author, 1986.

84. Carrington to Julia Strachey, 29 October 1929, in *Carrington: Letters and Extracts from Her Diaries*, pp. 428–30.

85. ibid., end of October or early November 1929, pp. 430–2.

86. Noel Carrington in *Carrington: Paintings, Drawings and Decorations*.

87. Carrington to Lytton Strachey, 4 November 1929, British Library.

88. ibid.

89. ibid., 5 November 1929.

90. Carrington to Lytton Strachey, 6 November 1928, in *Carrington: Letters and Extracts from Her Diaries*, p. 434.

91. Frances Partridge, *Love in Bloomsbury: Memories*, pp. 167–8.

92. *D.C. Partride, Her Book*, 'A Short Love Affaire or a Danish Grave'.

93. Carrington to Julia Strachey, (January 1930), in *Carrington: Letters and Extracts from Her Diaries*, pp. 437–8.

94. Carrington to Lytton Strachey, 7 March 1930, British Library.

95. ibid., 22 February 1930.

96. ibid., 19 March 1930.

97. ibid., 1 April 1930

98. ibid., 4 April 1930.

99. ibid., 17 April 1930.

100. *D.C. Partride, Her Book*, 10 June 1930.

101. ibid. Although Carrington used no paragraphs in her diary, I have done so here to make it easier to read.

102. Carrington to Julia Strachey, 10 June 1930, in *Carrington: Letters and Extracts from Her Diaries*, p. 442.

103. ibid.

104. *D.C. Partride, Her Book*, June 1930.

105. ibid.

106. They were prized by those to whom she gave them. When Noel and Catharine Carrington moved to Long Acre Farm after Carrington's death, the tiles she had painted for them as a wedding gift – incorporating their initials as well as designs of fish – were removed from the first house and reinstalled in the new bathroom.

107. Lytton Strachey to Carrington, 11 June 1930, from Cambridge, British Library.

108. *D.C. Partride, Her Book*, 20 June 1930.

109. Carrington to Julia Strachey, June 1930, in *Carrington: Letters and Extracts from Her Diaries*, p. 447.

110. Carrington to Sebastian Sprott, July 1930, ibid., pp. 447–8.

111. Carrington to Lytton Strachey, 9 August 1930, British Library.

112. ibid., 10 August 1930.

113. ibid., 9 August 1930.

114. ibid., 14 September 1930.

115. ibid., 24 September 1930.

116. Frances Partridge, *Love in Bloomsbury: Memories*, p. 178.

117. Carrington to Julia Strachey, 1930, in *Carrington: Letters and Extracts from Her Diaries*, pp. 451–2.

118. *D. C. Partride, Her Book*, 25 August, no year, British Library.

119. ibid., 30 October 1930.

120. Carrington to Lytton Strachey, 31 December 1920, British Library.

121. *D. C. Partride, Her Book*, 20 March 1931.

122. ibid.

123. Holroyd, *Lytton Strachey*, pp. 1032–3.

124. Carrington to Lytton Strachey, 12 May 1931, British Library.

125. ibid.

126. Carrington to Sebastian Sprott, July 1931, in *Carrington: Letters and Extracts from Her Diaries*, p. 470. Florence Nightingale was one of the people Lytton wrote about in *Eminent Victorians*.

127. ibid.

128. Carrington to Rosamond Lehmann, early June 1931, in *Carrington: Letters and Extracts from Her Diaries*, p. 464.

129. ibid.

130. Frances Partridge, *Love in Bloomsbury: Memories*, pp. 188–9.

131. *Week-End Observer*, pasted into Carrington's diary on 18 July 1931.

132. Cut from newspaper and pasted into Carrington's diary on 18 July 1931.

133. ibid.

134. Carrington to Lytton Strachey, 18 July 1931, British Library.

135. ibid.

136. ibid., 29 October 1931.

137. Carrington to Julia Strachey, no date, in *Carrington: Letters and Extracts from Her Diaries*, p. 477.

138. Carrington to Stephen Tomlin, July 1931, ibid., pp. 471–2.

139. Carrington to Lytton Strachey, (5) November 1931, British Library.

140. Carrington to Frances Marshall, September 1931, in *Carrington: Letters and Extracts from Her Diaries*, p. 474.

141. Carrington to Lytton Strachey, (5) November 1931, British Library.

142. Frances Partridge, *Love in Bloomsbury: Memories*, p. 191. The allusion is Milton's 'Lycidas': 'But that two-handed engine at the door/Stands ready to smite once, and smite no more.'

143. *D. C. Partride, Her Book*.

144. Frances Partridge, *Love in Bloomsbury: Memories*, pp. 192–3.

145. ibid., pp. 193–4.

146. *Diary of Virginia Woolf*, Vol. 4, 1 January 1932, pp. 61–2.

147. *D. C. Partride, Her Book*, no date.

148. ibid., 21 January 1932.

149. ibid.

150. Frances Partridge, *Love in Bloomsbury: Memories*, p. 199.

151. ibid.

152. ibid., pp. 199–201.

153. Virginia Woolf, *Diary of Virginia Woolf*, Vol. 4, 30 January 1932, pp. 65–6.

154. Frances Partridge *Love in Bloomsbury: Memories*, pp. 203–4.

155. *D. C. Partride, Her Book*, February 1932.

156. ibid.

157. Frances Partridge, *Love in Bloomsbury: Memories*, pp. 203–4.

158. *D. C. Partride, Her Book*, 12 February 1932.

159. ibid.

160. Frances Partridge, *Love in Bloomsbury: Memories*, p. 209.

161. *Diary of Virginia Woolf*, Vol. 4, 12 March 1932, pp. 81–2.

162. Gerald Brenan to Alix Strachey, no date, The Lytton Strachey Trust.

163. *Diary of Virginia Woolf*, Vol. 4, 17 March 1932, p. 83.
164. ibid., 18 March 1932, p. 83.
165. ibid., 24 March 1932, p. 85.
166. Woodeson, p. 330.
167. Paraphrased from Carolyn Heilbrun, *Towards a Recognition of Androgyny.*

INDEX

NOTE
Entries for Brenan, Carrington, Partridge and Strachey have been arranged in two sequences: chronological for life events; alphabetical for general references. Carrington's relationships are indexed chronologically.

Aldbourne 118
Alderney Manor, Strachey at 107
Alexander, Catharine (later Carrington) 253
  on C 252
  C's portrait of 216, 221
Allinson, Adrian 30
Andalusian paintings 180, 206–7, 222, 254
Anrep, Boris 183
  and C's glass paintings 220–21
  marital difficulties 213
Anrep, Helen 238, 298
  as Brenan's confidante 219
  C's relationship with 213, 214
  marital difficulties 213
Apes of God, The (Lewis) xiv
Apostles, The 63
artist, the, C's view of xvii, 32
Asheham House, nr Lewes:
  C at 69–70, 104–5
  C breaks into 95–6
  life at 104
  Strachey at 124
Ashridge House, Herts, fresco 48, 228
Ashwell, Lena 98
Asquith, H. H. 74
Assisi 172

Bagenal, Barbara, see Hiles
Bagenal, Nicholas 159, 177
  in Wales 83, 84, 85, 88–91
Barrie, J. M. 53
Bedford: Carringtons at 11–12, 13, 16, 27–8, 51

Bedford High School 11–12, 16, 33
Beeny Farm, Cornwall 118
Bell, Clive 80, 92, 130, 150
  on Bloomsbury reshufflings 247
  and C's art 68, 183
  C plays joke on 185–6
  criticises Shaw 185
  at Garsington 62
  at Ham Spray 288
  relationship with C 183, 186
Bell, Vanessa 61, 80, 95, 165, 195
  art 87–8, 304
  at Asheham 69–70
  on C's bisexuality 93
  in France 68
  at Garsington 62
  motherhood 163
Belle, C's horse 235
Belle Vue, Hereford, Carringtons at 9
Belmont, Berkhamstead, Carringtons at 9–10
Belsize Park Gardens, Strachey family at 63, 106
Berkhamsted, Carringtons at 9, 10
Biddesden: accident at 298
  borrows gun from 299
  trompe l'œil painting 289, 293
Bingham, Henrietta:
  C's account of 234
  C's relationship with 208–9, 213, 214, 216, 217, 223, 224–5, 229
  Strachey's dislike of 208, 209
Birrell, Frankie 198
Birrell & Garnett, bookshop 198, 202, 220

Bloomsbury Group:
  and C's art xvii, xviii, 68, 222
  and C's sexuality 93
  discussion, intellectual 104, 105, 135
  francophile 68, 222
  Gertler on 49
  gossip and intrigue 92, 93, 126
  and Partridge 133
  and physical discomfort 104, 180
  reshufflings 247
  sexual relationships 93–4
  social class 126–7
  takes up C 61–3, 69–70, 104–5
Bloomsbury Portraits (Shone) xviii
Box, Mrs 118, 149, 150
Boxmoor Common, picnic at 227
Boyd, Phyllis, see Janzé
Brenan, Gerald 144
  LIFE:
  first meets C 151–2
  Strachey, Partridge and C visit (1920)
    157–9
  visits Tidmarsh (1921) 173–4
  falls in love with C 173–5, 178, 185,
    190, 200
  at Watendlath (1921) 178
  hears of Partridge's infidelity 184–5
  relationship with C 189, 190–91, 211,
    212–16, 218–20, 226–30, 234, 239
  forbidden from C 191, 195, 196
  Partridge and C visit (1923) 201–2,
    203–5
  in London 211, 212–16, 218, 222
  at Warren's End (1924) 213
  writes biography at St Theresa 226
  in Toulon (1926) 236
  resumes correspondence with C
    (1926) 236
  meets C in Paris (1926) 236–7
  breaks with C 240–41
  tries to resume friendship 251
  animosity towards C 257–8, 282
  writes autobiography 258
  engagement & marriage 282, 302
  C visits in Dorset 288
  and Joanna Carrington 302
  GENERAL REFERENCES:
  as actor 228
  and C's art 220–21
  on C's death 301
  C's letters to xvi
  C's portrait of 221
  and Partridge 151, 175, 190–91, 204,
    216
  and Strachey's death 292

Brett, Dorothy 51, 92, 93
  appearance 27, 28
  on C and Strachey xv–xvi, 23, 124
  at Garsington 87
  at Gower Street 94
  and Gertler 82
  in New Mexico 207–8
  relationship with C 23
Brooke-Pechell, Sir Roger 188
Brooke-Pechell, Valentine, see Dobrée
Brown, Frederick 20, 21, 25
Bussy, Dorothy 223
Bussy, Janie 223
  C's portrait of 221, 289
Bussy, Simon 68, 161–2, 223
Byng House, Gordon Square, C at 19,
  22, 35

Café Royal 41, 42
Cambridge:
  C visits with Strachey 111–12
  Gertler visits 49
  Strachey lectures at 180, 227
Cannan, Gilbert 53–5, 56
  and Gertler 76
  in love with C 59, 97
  portrays C 59, 97
Cannan, Mary 53, 140
Carrington, Catharine, see Alexander
Carrington, Charlotte Houghton:
  artistic talent 13, 24
  background 6–7
  conventionalism 9, 14, 157, 171, 235
  finds Tidmarsh for C 120
  illness 235
  marriage 6–7
  personality 6, 7, 9
  and public opinion 9
  relationship with C 3, 51, 58, 139,
    140, 235
  visits Sam in Spain 181
  widowhood 181
Carrington, Dora de Houghton:
  LIFE:
  childhood 3, 7–17
  education 11–12, 16, 73–4, 75
  at the Slade 19, 22–8, 30–43, 44, 50–
    51, 53, 60
  Rothenstein proposes 55–6
  sells first drawing 57
  at Hurstbourne Tarrant 60–61
  taken up by Bloomsbury 61–3, 69–70
  and Omega Workshops 68
  first meets Strachey 69–70, 75
  and the war 74, 80, 97–9

Carrington, Dora de Houghton—*cont*
LIFE—*cont*
visits Wales with Strachey 83, 84, 85, 88–91
searches for country cottage 94–5, 201–2
helps with wartime concert 98–9
at Tidmarsh Mill 122–3, 127, 129–32, 134, 135, 137–8, 197, 198
Spanish trip (1919) 143–5
in Cornwall with Partridge 149–50
Spanish trip with Strachey (1920) 157–9
at Gordon Square 164–8
marriage 168, 171
honeymoon 171–2
at Watendlath (1921) 175–80
hoaxes Clive Bell 185–6
visits Dobrées with Partridge and Brenan 187–8
punished by Ralph 191–2, 195, 196
Africa trip (1923) 198–9
France (1923) 199–200
Yegen (1923) 201–2, 203–5
at Ham Spray (1924) 211–12
negotiates with Frances 232–3
riding accident (1927) 238–9
difficulties with Partridge and Frances 246, 247, 248, 250, 271
needs physical relationship 254–5, 260, 262, 279, 281
France, with Johns (1929) xvi, xvii, 268–70
pregnancy 271–2, 273
grows closer to Strachey 275
'Reverse of the Medal' (1930) 276, 277–9
writes Strachey pastiche 288–9
and Strachey's last illness 291, 292–5
first attempts suicide 294–5, 296
longs for death 296–300
dies xxi–xxii, 238
ART:
ballet design 290
book-plates 255, 285
Brenan's portrait 229, 259
decorative work xvii, 40, 68–9, 142–3, 239, 250, 252, 255, 281
difficulties with 142, 253
drawings 19, 26, 31, 57
and emotional relationships 219, 222, 247, 304
exhibitions 66, 79, 149–50, 162, 165, 166, 222, 275

fears about 68, 69, 142, 161–2, 166–7, 196, 245, 253, 267, 270, 275, 289
flower paintings 221–2, 235, 289, 304
as gift for Strachey 142, 303
glass pictures 220–21, 255, 289, 293
influences on 87–8
Julia Strachey's portrait 259–60
landscapes 88, 101–2, 179–80, 207, 289
and marriage 163
oils 50, 131, 289
painting over canvases xviii, 222, 249
portraits 50, 114, 118–19, 161, 165, 216, 221, 229, 245–6, 289, 304
progression in 254, 304
serious painting xvii–xviii, 50, 68, 69, 101–2, 131, 187–8, 220, 235, 249, 289, 303
sexuality 179–80
shyness about 146
signboards 68, 166, 173, 177
Strachey's portrait 89, 103, 112
subjects 221, 253–4
tiles 255, 263, 280, 282
watercolours 101–2
woodcuts 68, 81, 113–14, 116
INTERESTS:
country life 57, 60, 134, 172–3, 239
cycling 12
film-making and cinema 267–8, 282, 290
horse-riding 135–6, 271–2, 298
music hall 268, 282
readings 26–7, 60, 100, 134, 255
theatre 290
travel 253
walking 12
PERSONALITY:
ambivalence xiv, 39, 40, 53, 110–11, 164, 228–9, 234, 251, 259
bisexuality 93, 179, 229, 238
competitiveness, lack of 175, 177
devotion xiv, 187, 256
femininity 252
independence 204, 205, 219, 254
infidelity xiv, 187, 212
lesbianism 184, 208–10, 214, 238, 251, 274
modernity xiv, 51, 73, 115
romance 214, 274
secrecy and untruth 14–15, 27, 67, 85, 88–9, 92, 110–11, 162, 177, 191, 256, 257, 273

sexuality xiv, 11, 39–40, 47, 52–3, 65–6, 73, 84–5, 93, 100–101, 115–16, 146, 148, 164, 274, 304
traditionalism xiv
voyeurism 278–9
waste, hatred of 139, 257
RELATIONSHIPS:

Gertler:
first meets 31
triangular relationship 31, 34–5, 47
marriage proposal 34–5
unwilling for sexual relationships 39–40, 45, 47
C meets Strachey 88–9, 100–101, 108–11
sexual relationship 100–101, 219
break with 108–11
tries to resume 119, 304
invites to Ham Spray 247

Partridge:
first meets 132–3, 138
Spanish trip (1919) 143–5
attracted to 146, 147, 153
sexual relationship 146
refuses marriage 160, 161, 167
at Gordon Square 164
marriage 167–8, 186, 189, 195
and P's infidelity 189, 198, 200, 204, 205, 206, 208, 216, 226, 230
at the end 295, 296, 297, 298

Brenan:
first meets 152
letters 152–3, 160, 174, 211, 215, 218, 236
soul-mates 174
relationship 174–5, 178, 214–16, 218–20, 236–7, 257
sexual relationship 189, 213, 214, 218–19
forbidden from 191, 195, 196
visits with Partridge (1923) 200, 203–5
neglects 212
conflict with 212, 216, 218
and Partridge 226–30
ends relationship 251, 257–8, 304

Penrose:
first meets 262
on board ship 262–3
film-making 267
pregnancy 272, 273
infatuation 173–4, 281

problems 276–9
ends relationship 283, 287, 304

Strachey:
love for 70, 73, 78–9, 90, 103, 107–8, 120, 124–7, 135–6, 149, 162–3, 164, 167–8, 183, 187, 206, 231, 236, 255, 260–2, 263, 298, 303, 304

GENERAL REFERENCES:
and ageing 251–2, 274, 276, 283
appearance 10, 23, 27, 58–9, 67, 70, 127, 152, 251–2
dependence on parents 84, 85, 88, 107–8, 134–5, 157
domestic duties 122–3, 130, 134, 150–51, 181, 183, 207, 209, 252–3, 265, 270, 279
drinking 236, 266, 269–70
dyslexia, possible xix
fear of the future 231, 249–50
female nature, loathing of xiv, 11, 65, 67, 135, 229, 271
financial matters 53, 112–13, 145, 177, 182, 196, 201, 255, 280
friendships 23–4, 29, 50–51, 58, 130, 134, 223
health 131–2, 143, 159–60, 180–81, 198, 234, 246, 248, 250
letters xvi–xvii, xviii–xix, 14–15, 133, 137, 146, 152, 234, 238
and love 304–5
and marriage 35, 65–6, 160, 162, 163, 165, 189, 194, 252
and menstruation 11, 65, 67, 187, 229
and motherhood 135, 163, 177
names, preoccupation with 15, 27, 57, 215, 263
pacificism 74, 98
poems 129, 156, 166, 281, 282, 296
portrayed in fiction xiv–xv, xvi, 59, 86–7, 142, 183
short stories, diary entries as 273–4, 276–9
solitude and loneliness 246, 248–50, 251, 256, 258, 266, 268, 274
virginity 79, 84–5, 90, 93, 100, 101, 141
as witch 258–9, 279
Carrington, Edward (Teddy):
at Cambridge 26–7
death 7, 80, 97, 106, 119–20
relationship with C 13
resemblance to Beakus 287
war service 56, 57, 80

Carrington, Joanna, Brenan's love for 302
Carrington, Lottie Louise (later Elmslie) 7, 140, 181–2, 235
  education 11–12
  shares house with C 35
Carrington, Louisa 3
Carrington, Noel 199
  on Charlotte Carrington 9, 235
  on children 271
  on C's relationship with father 8
  financial help from 112–13, 145
  on Fry 68
  in India 155
  marries 221
  and Partridge 132
  relationship with C 7, 8, 9, 16, 26
  returns to England 198
  on Samuel Carrington 6
  Spanish trip (1919) 143–5
  walking tour 115, 117–18
  war service 56, 57, 80, 98
Carrington, Sam (brother) 208
  war service 7, 80
Carrington, Samuel (father) 3–6, 7–8, 11, 13
  background 6–7
  death 138, 139
  ill-health 14, 56, 61
  in India 3–5
  marriage 6, 15–16
  personality 6, 8, 15–16
  relationship with C 7, 8–9, 11, 16, 139–40, 141
  religious belief 7
  similarity to Strachey 73
Carrington, Samuel Snr 3
'Cattle by a Pond' (1930) 289
Cézanne, Paul 26, 88, 142
Charleston Farmhouse, nr Lewes 95
  C visits 180
  life at 104
Charteris, Lady Violet 23–4
Chatto & Windus, publishers 127
Chelsea Palace Theatre, Concerts for the Front 98–9
Cheltenham: Carringtons at 138, 139, 235
Cholesbury: C at 54, 59
  Gertler at 53–4, 56, 99–100
Clair, René 290
clothes, recycling 139, 257
'Cockney Picnic, A' (1911) 26
Collie, Miss 12
contraceptives, use of 100, 101

Córdoba 158
Cornwall: Strachey and C in 118–19
Crome Yellow (Huxley) xiv
  C on 87
  C portrayed in 86, 87, 142, 183
  Garsington in 85
Cross, Paul 290
Crozier, Miss (potential servant) 147
Currie, John 42–3, 49
  murders Dolly and commits suicide 54, 97

'Dahlias' (1927) 254
'Dante's Inferno' (1911) 26, 254
Davidson, Angus 267
Davidson, Douglas 252
death, C's views on 216, 248–9, 285–6
Dobrée, Bonamy 172, 189, 194, 196
  Brenan visits 178
Dobrée, Valentine 171–2, 202
  Brenan visits 178–9
  C's affection for 184, 187
  and Partridge, 187–8, 190, 191, 192
  real name 198
  visits Brenan 184–5
Doggett, James 180
'Downs from Ham Spray in Winter, The' (1929) 289
dress, C's 22, 111, 127, 245, 274, 279, 286
Durbins 113
  Strachey at 88, 114

East India Railway Company 3–5
Edward VII, King 18
Edwardian London 18–19
Elizabethan and Essex (Strachey) 239, 252, 253
  success 255–6
Elmslie, Lottie, see Carrington
Elmslie, R. C. 65
Elvery, Beatrice, see Glenavy
Eminent Victorians (Strachey) 63, 81, 94, 114, 303
  success 132, 133

Falmouth: Strachey and C at (1926) 233–4
'Farm at Watendlath' (1921) 179–80
film-making, amateur 267–8
Flo, Ham Spray maid 270, 279
flowers, C's love for 221–2
Forster, E. M. 68, 74, 249, 270
  C's portrait of 221

France: and Bloomsbury 68, 222
  Johns and C visit (1929) xvi, xvii,
    268–70
  painting 222, 267
  Strachey, Sprott and C visit (1923)
    199–200
  see also Paris
Fraser-Simon, H. 98
Freud, Anna 186
Friday Club 42
Frith Street, C's studio at 113, 115
Fry, Roger
  and C 68–9
  C works for 114
  as critic 142, 195
  Gertler on 54
  at Hampton Court 111, 112, 114
  and Helen Anrep 213
  Omega Workshops 40, 68
  Post-Impressionism 18, 24–5
  translates Mallarmé 68
Fryern Court:
  Beakus and C at 266
  C paints at 267
  C visits 245–6, 253, 289

Garnett, David 'Bunny' 105, 198, 227
  bookshop 198, 202, 220
  on C xiv, 134
  C sends clothes to 139
  C's affair with 96, 304
  and C's death xxii
  C's portraits of 221
  edits C's letters 59
  first meets C 58–9
  on Garsington 74
  on Ham Spray film 267, 268
  paints at Garsington 62–3
  sends Henrietta to Tidmarsh 208
  sexuality 93
  on Strachey 90
  Strachey tells of love for C 83–4
  war work 79, 80, 95
  warns Frances of Partridge 202
  on Week-End Observer contest 288
Garnett, Ray 202, 227
Garsington Chronicle, The (1916) 85–6
Garsington Manor:
  and Bloomsbury group 74
  C at 74, 84–5, 86, 92–3, 102
  C excluded from 116
  in fiction 85
  Gertler at 82
  Gertler and C at 55, 62–3
  Strachey at 81, 116, 147

  wall of paintings 62–3
Gauguin, Paul 24, 25
Gertler, Golda 30
Gertler, Louis 30
  death 105
Gertler, Luke 302
Gertler, Marjorie, see Hodgkinson
Gertler, Mark:
  appearance 30
  art 37, 38, 49–50, 83, 108, 142, 302
  background 29, 45, 50, 56
  and Bloomsbury 49
  on Bloomsbury group 126
  and Cannan 53–5, 63, 76, 97
  death 302
  flirtations 47–8
  friendships 53, 55, 64
  health 30, 128–9, 180, 247, 302
  homophobia 93
  and John 41, 50
  marries Marjorie 47, 302
  and Marsh 49, 55
  and Morrells 55, 62–3
  self-doubt 37, 44
  social behaviour 61, 62
  and Strachey 63, 64, 75, 82, 88

  RELATIONSHIP WITH CARRINGTON 31:
  at C's death 302
  as C's friend 35–6, 39, 46, 48–9, 52,
    61, 66, 142
  as educator in art 32–4, 42, 47, 303
  ending of relationship 119, 128–9,
    142
  first proposes 35
  invited to Ham Spray 247
  jealousy of Nevinson 33–4, 36, 37–8,
    41, 43, 45–7
  poem on C 77–8
  sexual relationship with 39–40, 45,
    52–3, 65–6, 69, 76, 79, 84–5, 93,
    99–102, 103–4, 111, 146, 219
  spreads gossip about Partridge 185
  and Strachey 75–80, 103, 110, 113,
    119, 123–4, 128
  tries to part with 43, 82, 108–10
Gide, André 199
Glenavy, Beatrice, Lady 98, 99
Gordon Square:
  Partridge and C at 164–5
  Partridge and Frances at 233, 236
  Strachey at 166, 236, 239, 280
Gower Street: C shares house in 92, 94,
    112
Goya, Francisco 142, 145

Grafton Galleries, Post-Impressionist
   Exhibitions 24, 25
Graham, Harry 98
Granada 158
Grant, Duncan 61, 105, 165, 195
   art 87–8, 304
   at Asheham 69–70
   in France 68
   at Garsington 62
   lends C his studio 79
   paints at Garsington 62–3
   sexuality 93
   and Strachey's play 228
   war work 79, 80, 95
Gratton, Harry 99
Great Bedwyn 118
Greco, El 142, 145
Greville, Charles, Strachey edits 275
Grosvenor Gallery, C exhibits at 166
Guinness, Bryan 293
Guinness, Diana 293

Ham Spray:
   break-up, threatened 230, 231–3
   C alone in 236
   C dies at xxi–xxii, 301–2
   C's new studio at 255
   film-making at (1929) 267–8
   library 254, 255, 264–5
   life at 216–17, 223–4, 252, 253, 276
   new phase at 234, 235, 238
   redecoration 254, 264–5
   settling in at 211–12
   Strachey absent from 236, 246, 249,
      250, 254, 258, 263, 280
   Strachey dies at 292–5
   Strachey and Partridge buy 201–2,
      203, 204, 205–6, 210–11, 255, 299
   Strachey's plays at 225–6
   visitors to 220, 222–3, 240–41, 270,
      288
Ham village 118, 201
Hampton Court, C works at 68, 111,
   112
Havenhurst, Berkhamstead:
   Carringtons at 10
Henderson, Faith 94
Henry, Dolly 43
   murdered 54, 97
Hereford: Carringtons at 9
'Hermaphrodite Parties' 282–3
Hiles, Barbara (later Bagenal) 51, 61,
   159, 180
   appearance 27, 28
   at Asheham 69–70, 104–5

babies, birth 135, 177
   French trip (1923) 199–200
   illness 199–200
   motherhood 163
   relationship with C 22–3
   at Tidmarsh 122, 192
   in Wales 64–5, 83, 84, 85, 88–91
   war work 80
'Hill Town in Andalusia' (1924?) 207
'Hills in Snow at Hurstbourne Tarrant'
   (1916) 101–2
Hilton Hall 227
   film-making at 267
Hodgkinson, Marjorie (later Gertler)
   47, 247, 302
Hogarth House: Brenan and Partridge
   meet at 190
Hogarth Press:
   C's woodcuts for 68, 113–14
   Partridge at 163, 167, 173
   Partridge leaves 196
   Partridge unhappy at 175–6, 182–3,
      193
Holland: Sprott and C visit 266–7
Holroyd, Michael 172
honey labels, C's designs for 81
Hope-Johnston, John 200
Houghton, Charlotte, see Carrington,
   Charlotte Houghton
Humphries, Ruth (later Selby-Bigge)
   23, 40, 51
   pregnancy 65
Hurstbourne Tarrant (Hants.):
   C at 57, 60–1, 67, 92, 101, 113, 114
   C loots 122
Hutchinson, Mary 130, 183
   at Asheham 69–70
Huxley, Aldous:
   portrays C xiv, 183
   relationship with C 86–7, 141–2

India 4–5
Indian Mutiny (1857) 4
Inkpen Beacon 201
Inkpen village 201
Ireland: Strachey in (1930) 282
Italy: Partridge honeymoon (1921) 171,
   172
Ivy Lodge, Hereford: Carringtons at 9

Janzé, Henri de 184
Janzé, Phyllis de 184, 281
   C visits 195, 237
Joad, Marjorie 198, 228

John, Augustus 20, 22, 235
  C on 58
  C visits 245–6, 253
  C's letters to xvi
  French trip (1929) xvi, xvii, 268–70
  friendship with xvi
  and Gertler 41, 50
  paints T. E. Lawrence 267
  Strachey visits 107
  and women's dress 99
John, Caspar 286
John, Dorelia 235, 298
  aeroplane trip 286
  C decorates room for 264
  C visits 245–6
  C visits after Strachey's death 297–8
  C's relationship with 223
  French trip (1929) xvi, xvii, 268–70
  friendship with xvi, 245, 253
  at Ham Spray 223
  Strachey visits 107
  and Strachey's death 293
  visits Beakus's ship 267
John, Poppet xvi
John, Robin 200
John, Vivien xvi
  C's portrait of 246
Jones, Ernest 216

Keynes, Maynard 62, 63, 80, 90, 92, 94,
  128, 183, 195
  sexuality 93
Kirstein, Mina 208
Kitty, Ham Spray maid 270
Koteliansky, S. S. (Kot) 82

Lake District 161, 176
Lamb, Henry 222, 238, 270
  C paints panel for 274
  friendship with 245
  on Ham Spray 222–3
Lamb, Pansy 245
Lambeth Art School 13
Lambourne Downs 199, 235
Lane, Constance 48
Lawrence, D. H. 49
  and Bloomsbury xv
  C on 60
  first meets C 58–9
  and Gertler xv
  on *Mendel* 97
  in New Mexico 23, 207–8
  portrays C xiv–xv, 55, 59
Lawrence, Frieda, in New Mexico 23,
  207–8

Lawrence, T. E. 267
Legg, Donald 123
Legg, Mrs 123, 130, 146–7
  dishonesty 160–61, 223
Legros, Alphonse 20
Lehmann, Rosamond 245, 287
  at Ham Spray 298
Lewis, Wyndham, portrays C xiv
Lockeridge, Nr Marlborough, Strachey
  at 63
London Group exhibition (1920) 165,
  166
London heat 114
Lopokova, Lydia 195, 198, 290
'Love Locked Out' (Merrit) 58
Lucas, F. L. 180

MacCarthy, Desmond 25, 63, 228, 267
MacCarthy, Rachel 267–8
MacIver, Alan 161, 176, 177
Madrid 158, 159
Mallarmé, Stéphane 68
Manners, Lady Diana 23–4
Mansfield, Katherine 49, 102
  bisexuality 93
  C on 92–3, 94
  death 196
  and Gertler 61
  at Gower Street 94
  portrays C xvi
Mantegna painting, C restores 68
Marlborough fair, C visits 290
Marsh, Edward 49
  and Gertler 49, 55
Marshall, Frances, see Partridge
Marshall, Ray, see Garnett
Martin, Olive 238, 251
  comes to Ham Spray 224
  illness 265
  leaves 270, 272
Matisse, Henri 24, 25
Melville Nettleship Prize (1912) 31
Mendel (Cannan) 59, 76, 97
Merrit, Anna Lea 58
'Mill House at Tidmarsh, Berkshire,
  The' (1918) 131, 161–2
Mill House, Tidmarsh, see Tidmarsh
  Mill House
Monk's House, Rodmell, Woolfs at
  146
Moore, G. E. 48, 87
Morrell, Lady Ottoline 293
  on C xiv, 87
  and C's virginity 84–5
  dislike of C 92, 93, 116

Morrell, Lady Ottoline—*cont*
  and Gertler 55, 62–3
  in *Women in Love* xiv
Morrell, Philip 55, 74, 112
  and C's virginity 84–5
motor bike, C learns to ride 79, 80
'Mountain Ranges at Yegen, Andalusia'
    (1924) 180, 207, 222
Munich: C visits Alix in 241
Murry, John Middleton 49, 92, 94, 102,
    196

Nash, John 53, 61, 88, 102
  paints at Garsington 62–3
Nash, Paul 23
National Union of Women's Suffrage
    Societies 18–19
Nevinson, C. R. W. ('Chips'):
  art 37
  background 30
  and C 31–2, 33–43, 45–7
  and Gertler 29, 30, 31, 35, 36, 37, 40–
    41, 43, 45–7
  war service 64
New English Art Club 20, 24
  C exhibits at 57, 66, 79
New Mexico: Lawrences in 23, 207–8
nightmares, C's 135, 141, 206, 225, 246,
    247, 250, 251, 264
Nimes: Strachey and C in 254
'None of That' (Lawrence) xiv, xv
Normandy: C visits 195
Norton, Harry 116, 128, 130
Nys, Maria 102

Oliver, Noel 118, 119, 159, 160
Omega Workshops 40
  decorative art 67–8
'On a Picture of a Ship' 281
Oriental Club, London 232
Orpen, William 20

Pangbourne signboard, C paints 166
Pankhurst, Christabel 18
Pankhurst, Emmeline 18
Paris:
  C visits Brenan in (1926) 236–7
  Gertler and C plan visit (1912) 45
  Partridge and C visit (1925) 226
  Partridge honeymoon (1921) 171
  Strachey and C in (1920) 158, 159
  Strachey, Partridge and C in (1924)
    205
  Stracheys in (1926) 236

Partridge family:
  and C 182, 196
  wealth 196–7, 201
Partridge, Burgo 303
Partridge, Dorothy 143, 144, 145, 197
Partridge, Frances:
  on Beakus 262
  on C 27, 245
  on C's art 304
  on C's death xxi, xxii
  C's portrait of 216, 231
  and C's pregnancy 272
  C's relationship with 206, 208
  on C's suicide attempt 296
  C tries to find solution with 231–2,
    232–3
  as film actress 267
  on Fry 68–9
  on Garnett 96
  at Ham Spray 211, 216, 223, 246,
    247–8
  on Henrietta Bingham 209
  on Hermaphrodite Parties 282–3
  and Julia Strachey 223
  in Paris with Partridge and C 205
  Partridge in love with 202–3
  reads Brenan's diaries 258
  Strachey negotiates with 232
  and Strachey's death 292
  wears Brenan's scarf 257
  works in bookshop 198
  to Yegen with C (1923) 201–2, 203–5
Partridge, Ralph (Rex)
  LIFE:
  first meets C 132–3, 137–8
  Spanish trip (1919) 143–5
  in Cornwall (1919) 149–50
  Tidmarsh visits 138, 152, 154–7
  Spanish trip (1920) 157–9
  proposes to C 160, 162, 163–4, 167–8
  at Hogarth Press 163–4, 166, 167,
    175–6, 182, 193, 196
  marriage 168, 226, 227
  honeymoon 171–2
  infidelity 185, 188, 189, 190, 198, 200
  and Valentine Dobrée 187–8, 189,
    191, 192, 194, 196
  and C's affair with Brenan 190–3,
    194–5, 200, 203–5, 216, 217, 218,
    227
  to Spain with C (1923) 201–2, 203–5
  and Frances Marshall 202–3, 204,
    206, 216, 230, 231, 256
  as threat to happiness 206, 220, 230,
    256

film-making at Ham Spray 267
and C's pregnancy 271, 272
and Strachey's death 292, 295, 297
tries to prevent C's death 295, 296, 297, 298
and C's death xxi–xxii
marries Frances 303
GENERAL REFERENCES:
as actor 228
and Brenan 151, 175, 194–5, 218
and C's art xviii, 221
competitiveness 175, 177
finances 177, 182, 196–7, 201
military service 151
personality 155, 191
and Strachey 148, 154, 162, 231, 291
pen wiper, C as 148
Penrose, Alec 262, 267
titles for 282
Penrose, Bernard 'Beakus' 262
affair ends 283
amateur films 267–8
C's infatuation with 278, 279, 281
and C's pregnancy 272, 273
ill at Ham Spray 287
problems with 276–9, 281
relationship with 265, 286, 287
relationship, as drama 273–4
resemblance to Teddy 287
Penrose, Lionel 262
Penrose, Roland 262
Personal Record (Brenan) 180, 258, 267
Perugia 172
Phillips, Wogan 287
Picasso, Pablo 24, 226
Post-Impressionism 24–6, 31
Exhibition, First (1910) 18, 24–5, 37, 68
Exhibition, Second (1912) 37, 68
Poynter, Sir Edward 19–20
pregnancy, C's horror of 135
Principia Ethica (Moore) 48
Prix de Rome art competition 50, 52, 66
Proust, Marcel 68
Provence: Strachey and C in (1928) 253–4

Queen Victoria (Strachey) 127, 148, 180

Ramsey, Frank 267
Ramsey, Lettice 267
Ravenna 172
Reeves, George 115
Remembrance of Things Past (Proust) 68

Rendel, Ellie 239
Renoir, Pierre Auguste 266
'Reverse of the Medal, The' (1930) 276, 277–9
Reynolds, Michael 23
Rimbaud, Arthur 79, 80
Rimini 172
Ritchie, Philip: at Ham Spray 223
conversation 210
death 241
relationship with Strachey 210, 226
Rome: Strachey and Rylands in 275
Room of One's Own, A (Woolf) 267
Rothenstein, Albert 51, 57
changes name 58
lends studio 54
proposes to C 55–6
Rothenstein, John, and C's work 30
Rothenstein, Sir William 20
and Gertler 30
Rothsay Gardens, Bedford, Carringtons at 11
Royal Academy 20, 24
Royal Drawing Society of Great Britain and Ireland, prizes 16
Royal Free Hospital, London, C in 159–60
Russell, Bertrand 102
at Garsington 62
Rylands, George 'Dadie':
at Ham Spray 223, 226
in Rome (1930) 275
rooms, C decorates 252, 254, 264

Sackville-West, Eddie 282
Salisbury Picture Gallery, C shows at 275
Sanger, C. P. 210
Sans Pareil, C on board 262–3, 286
Sargant-Florence, Alix, see Strachey
Savernake: Strachey and C visit (1931) 286
Scala Theatre, London, Strachey's play at 228
Schwabe, Randolph 21
Scotland: C visits 133–4
Selby, Ruth, see Humphries
Selby-Bigge, John 51, 65
Senhouse, Roger 223
relationship with Strachey 241, 246, 256, 275, 276
Sepoy Rebellion (1857) 4
Seurat, Georges 266
Shalbourne, Brenan at 226

Shaw, George Bernard 185
Shaw, T. E. 267
Shearman, Monty 128
  in Holland with C (1929) 266–7
Stansfield, Miss 12
Steer, Philip Wilson 20–21, 22
Stephen, Adrian 105
Stephen, Karin 105
Stephen, Vanessa, see Bell
Stephen, Virginia, see Woolf
Stiles, Annie 147, 150, 161
  C's portrait of 166
  leaves Ham Spray 223–4
  London day out 197–8
Strachey, Alix 150, 192
  bisexuality 209
  C paints walls for 234
  C's love for xvii
  C's portrait of 114, 221
  friendship 120
  at Gordon Square 164
  gramophone, C decorates 239, 250
  illness 186–7, 189, 198–9
  at Marlborough Fair 290
  marriage 160
  personality 130–31
  plays joke on C 134–5
  at Tidmarsh 209
  in Vienna 186
  at Watendlath 175, 176–7
Strachey, Dorothy 161
Strachey, James 130, 150, 198, 239, 282
  African trip (1923) 198–9
  and Alix's illness 186
  in Cornwall 118, 119
  at Gordon Square 164
  on Henrietta 216
  and Lytton's death 292, 295
  marriage 160, 164
  in Vienna 164, 186
  at Watendlath 175, 176–7
Strachey, John 282
Strachey, Julia (later Tomlin) 282
  on C 251–2
  on C as witch 258–9
  C's friendship with 209, 223, 245
  C intrigues with 231–2
  C's letters to xvi
  C's love for xvii
  marriage 241
  C's portrait of 221, 259–60
  C's relationship with 237–8, 258, 260
Strachey, Lady:
  C's portrait of 165–6
  death 258

Strachey, (Giles) Lytton
  LIFE:
  proposes marriage to Virginia
    Stephen 64
  first meets C 69–70
  educates C 74, 75, 81–2, 162–3
  grows fond of C 78–9, 81
  in love with C 83–4, 90–91, 103–4,
    168, 231, 293
  visits Wales with C (1916) 83, 84, 85,
    88–91
  sexual relationship with C 90, 100
  country cottage, search for 91, 94,
    106, 115, 120–21
  fears C's love 107, 110, 120, 125, 126,
    167, 231
  takes C to Cambridge (1917) 111–12
  and war service 112
  stays in C's studio 113
  makes woodcut 116
  at Tidmarsh Mill 127, 129–31, 134
  literary success 132, 133, 147–8, 255–
    6
  relationship with C 137, 148, 164,
    192, 197, 225, 234, 239, 252–3,
    255, 286–7, 303
  Spanish trip (1920) 157–9
  buys Ham Spray 206, 231, 255, 299
  negotiates with Frances Marshall 232
  asks Partridge to exclude Frances 248
  and C's pregnancy (1929) 271–2
  grows closer to C 275
  death xxi, xxii, 285–6, 292–5
  and C's death xxii, 302
  GENERAL REFERENCES:
  appearance 63, 70, 138
  at Asheham 69–70
  country house visits 81–2, 133, 134
  country life 134, 197
  and C's art xvii, 221, 280, 289, 303,
    304
  C's conversations with 162–3
  C's letters to xvi, 116
  and domestic duties 265, 286
  at Garsington 62, 116, 147
  and Gertler 63, 64, 75, 78, 82–3, 128
  grave xxii
  health 63, 73, 89, 124–5, 134, 199,
    206–7, 226, 233, 252, 290–91
  and Henrietta Bingham 208, 209
  homosexuality 64, 70, 73, 93–4, 137,
    210, 241, 256, 303
  humour 225
  hypochondria 63–4
  intellectual circle 183

and Partridge 148–9, 154–6, 162, 231, 291
and Penrose 262, 272, 287
personality 63, 106, 225, 286
plays 225–6, 228
poems 156–7
and Senhouse 275, 276, 291
similarity to C's father 73
voice 63, 70, 138, 176
in *Women in Love* (Lawrence) xv
Strachey, Marjorie 150, 199
Strachey, Oliver 61, 86, 130, 131, 150
as shareholder 94, 122
Strachey, Pippa 150, 165
in France with Strachey 212, 236
as nurse 207, 292, 293, 295
Stratford-on-Avon: C visits 161
suffrage, women's 18–19
Sweden: Strachey and Senhouse visit 256
Sydney-Turner, Saxon 104–5, 150
film-making at Ham Spray 267–8
as share-holder 94

Tatooed Venus, at World's Fair 61–2
Tennant, Stephen 270
Tiber, Ham Spray cat 265, 275, 277, 288, 289
Tidmarsh Mill House 120–21, 172–3
boredom with 197, 199
C fears for 189–90, 192
C weekends at 164, 165
domestic problems 146–7
early days at 122–3, 127, 129–30, 131, 134, 135
Frances Partridge first visits 203
Partridge at 138, 145–6
shareholders 150
Strachey's fears for 192
visitors to 130, 138, 150–51, 180, 183, 195
tiles, C paints 68, 255, 263, 280, 282
Toledo 158
Tomlin, Garrow 286, 296
Tomlin, Stephen 'Tommy' 245, 282
C proposes ballet to 290
C's affair with 236, 304
film-making at Ham Spray 267–8
and Henrietta Bingham 209, 223
and Julia Strachey 238
and Lytton's death 292
marriage 241
supports C after Strachey's death 295, 296
at Tidmarsh 209

Tonks, Henry 20, 21, 22, 25
Tree, Helen Maud, Lady 274
Tree, Iris 274
at the Slade 23–4
Two Stories (Woolf) 113–14

University College London, Slade School of Fine Art 19–22

Van Gogh, Vincent 24, 266
Venice 172
Victoria, Queen 18
Vienna: Stracheys in 186

Wales, C and Strachey visit (1916) 83, 84, 85, 88–91
Waley, Arthur 270
Walton, Willy 270
Wantage 118
War and Peace (Tolstoy) 68
Warren's End: C visits Brenan at 213
Watendlath holiday (1921) 175, 176–80
Week-End Observer competition 288–9
Welcombe, nr Bude 118
Partridge and C visit 149
White Horse Hill, Brenan and C at 173, 241
Wilson, Angus 290
'Winter, The' (1928) 289
Wissett Lodge, Suffolk 80, 95
Strachey at 81–2, 83
Woman Who Rode Away and Other Stories, The (Lawrence) xv
Women in Love (Lawrence) xiv–xv, 55, 85
Women's Social and Political Union 18–19
Woolf, Leonard 62, 63, 167
on C 212
and C 193–4
C first meets 95–6
and C's woodcuts 113–14
last visit 299–300
and Partridge 175–6
personality 193
sexuality 93
Woolf, Virginia 167
on Bonamy Dobrée 172
C's affection for 175
and C's devotion to Strachey 125–7, 256
C's woodcuts for 113–14
on C 125, 146
on C's death xxii, 302
on C's sexuality 115–16

Woolf, Virginia—*contd*
  on C's suicide 296–7
  on Elizabeth and Essex (Strachey)
    255–6
  first meets C 95–6
  at Garsington 62
  last visit 299–300
  on *Mendel* 97
  and Partridge 175–6, 196
  on Partridge marriage 163, 167, 171
  personality 193
  relationship with C 193–4, 196
  sexuality 93
  and Shaw hoax 186
  on Strachey xxii, 146, 302
  Strachey proposes to 64
  and Strachey's death 293
  suicide 302

Woolsey, Gamel 282, 288
Wordsworth, Dorothy 161
Wordsworth, William 161
World's Fair, Islington (1915) C at
  61–2

Yegen 151
  C's landscapes of 206–7
  Partridge and C visit (1923) 201–2,
    203–5
  proposed visit (1923) 200
  Strachey and C visit with Partridge
    157–9
Yeomans Row, London, C's studio at
  79, 94

zeppelin, burning 99

...onfrey ...

...adcast on Channel 4

...vision Society Award) and

...(winner of the Whitbread Prize

...zed as Britain's leading theatre and

...y Harrison has written extensively for the

...eatre, the New York Metropolitan Opera, the

...annel 4, and for unique ancient spaces in Greece
and Austria. His *Theatre Works 1973–1985* is published
by Penguin and his theatre works *The Trackers of
Oxyrhynchus, Square Rounds, The Common Chorus, The
Mysteries* and *The Prince's Play* by Faber and Faber. His
film *Black Daisies for the Bride* won the Prix Italia in
1994; this and his volume of film/poems *The Shadow of
Hiroshima and other film/poems* is published by Faber and
Faber.

by the same author

poetry
THE LOINERS
PALLADAS: POEMS
FROM THE SCHOOL OF ELOQUENCE
CONTINUOUS
V.
SELECTED POEMS
A COLD COMING
PERMANENTLY BARD

plays
THE MYSTERIES
THE TRACKERS OF OXYRYNCHUS
THE COMMON CHORUS
SQUARE ROUNDS
THEATRE WORKS 1973–1985
LE ROI S'AMUSE / THE PRINCE'S PLAY

film/poems
BLACK DAISIES FOR THE BRIDE
THE SHADOW OF HIROSHIMA AND OTHER FILM / POEMS
(A Maybe Day in Kazakhstan, The Gaze of the Gorgon,
The Blasphemers' Banquet, Loving Memory)

TONY HARRISON

Plays Three

Poetry or Bust

The Kaisers of Carnuntum

The Labourers of Herakles

Introduced by
Michael Kustow

faber and faber
LONDON · BOSTON

First published in 1996
by Faber and Faber Limited
3 Queen Square London WC1N 3AU

Photoset by Parker Typesetting Service, Leicester
Printed in England by Clays Ltd, St Ives plc

A CIP record for this book
is available from the British Library
ISBN 0-571-17966-5

2 4 6 8 10 9 7 5 3 1

Contents

Introduction by Michael Kustow, vii

Poetry or Bust, 1

The Kaisers of Carnuntum, 61

The Labourers of Herakles, 115

INTRODUCTION
by Michael Kustow

POET BECOMES THEATRE-MAKER

At the last performance of *The Kaisers of Carnuntum* (just twenty-four hours after its world première), in a Roman arena outside Vienna, two performing bears broke loose backstage. Stagehands chased after them, one getting clawed. Barrie Rutter, playing Marcus Aurelius' thuggish son Commodus, was left alone on stage, flanked by three lions and a tiger, fortunately still in their cages. The actor Jaro Frank, who should have come on as Orpheus to deliver the play's *coup de grace* by impaling Commodus on a cello-spike, was busy chasing the bears, since he was also their trainer. Tony Harrison was about to step into the breach and deliver the death-blow himself when the animals were recovered and order, of a sort, was restored.

When you make theatre outside the walls of theatre, this is the kind of thing you contend with. In interviews with the Austrian press, Harrison had said, 'I want to reclaim this place of blood' – the Roman stadium on the outskirts of empire where humans and animals were slaughtered for entertainment. He didn't reckon how close he would get to re-enacting their bloody ceremonies.

This incident, skirting disaster, may stand as emblematic of the risks Tony Harrison ran in undertaking the radical shift in his theatre work evident in the three plays in this volume, performed between autumn 1992 and summer 1995. Through them, he moved on from being a poet at work in the existing theatre, providing texts for others, notably John Dexter at the National Theatre, to direct. During the same period, his work in film led him from being a poet collaborating with other directors to becoming a film/poet in his own right, director as well as screenwriter.

vii

In both film and theatre, Harrison becomes an *auteur*, testing the limits of stage and screen, deepening his themes and concerns as he pushes poetry into new territories.

His first step out of what Brecht called the 'apparatus' had been, with the support of the National Theatre and its studio, to develop and direct his own plays *The Trackers of Oxyrhyncus* (1988) and *Square Rounds* (1992), both in the National's Olivier Theatre. But the decisive shift came with the move outside the National, to a succession of non-theatre sites where he created theatre events as director, writer and not infrequently producer, working with a regular group of actors, designer, composer, even clog choreographer. The poet in the theatre became the poet as theatre-maker. These three plays are the first result.

During this period Harrison also made three film/poems for television: *Black Daisies for the Bride* (BBC, 1993, winner of Prix Italia best documentary and the Mental Health Media award for best drama); *A Maybe Day in Kazakhstan* (Channel 4, 1994); and *The Shadow of Hiroshima* (Channel 4, 1995). He co-directed the second and directed the third, as well as writing all three. His journey into film parallels his theatrical odyssey, and interplays with it. The heightened text and action he created on stage spurred the language and images on screen, as in his daring juxtaposition in *Black Daisies* of a music-hall song, memories of confetti and the faces and voices of Alzheimer's sufferers. The factuality of documentary film – human hurt and history happening before the lens – sharpened the focus of his plays, yoking classical heroes and myths to the actuality we know largely through television. In each medium, Harrison was essentially metaphorical, starting the action on one level and moving out to others, each play or film a springboard of volatile transformation.

And in a further interaction Harrison fine-tuned his most precious conception of the nature of theatre: its specificity, its uniqueness, its transience. This is exemplified by these three plays. One of them was performed just once, another only twice, the third for a handful of performances. All were conceived for specific places, audiences and histories, in Yorkshire, Austria and Greece.

Each of the places of these plays means something particular to him. Saltaire, the model mill-town, the place of wool-bales, sheds, clogs, the poignancy of the industrial revolution, and the sounding-board of native vowels, idioms and intonations, is Harrison's Yorkshire homeland, the site of origins. Carnuntum, which he discovered through the National Theatre tour of *Trackers*, is central Europe for this rooted yet cosmopolitan writer, a territory he knows well from having lived and taught in Communist Czechoslovakia. It also stands for Rome, Roman power and empire, the other face of antiquity for this scholar gypsy, Rome which in its stadia and on its stages acted out the killings that Greek tragedy only impersonated. The third site Delphi, indeed Greece as a whole, is Harrison's elected homeland, the source of his theatre's morality and aesthetic.

Concurrently with the making of the three plays in this volume, he applied these ideas to television, everything theatre is not: technology, mass-audience, pre-recorded. But Harrison conceived the action of his film *The Shadow of Hiroshima* as if it were happening on 6 August 1995, and insisted on it being broadcast that day, exactly fifty years after the atom bomb was dropped, because he wanted a commemorative act in a charged space – even in the jostled slot of a television schedule.

This concept of a charged space, a one-off incarnation, a positively single performance, goes deep into Harrison's theatre convictions. It's rooted in his vision of the place of the ancient Greek drama festival in the life of democratic Athens, when a trilogy of tragedies and a satyr play were performed in one all-day marathon performance. This was part civic ceremony, part religious tribute, part talent contest, and altogether a shared journey through drama into the myths and stories that fed personal and public life. Through dramatic action, Apollonian argument and Dionysiac song and dance, through the formality of masks and single-sex casting, and crucially through all the resources of language, audiences were drawn into the extremes of their common condition. Sometimes the plays were reminders, sometimes confrontations, sometimes ferociously ironic, sometimes raucously debunking, always hard-won affirmations in the teeth of what Aeschylus calls, in Harrison's version, 'Necessity: neck into the yoke-strap.'

Ancient Greek theatre, then, is the source of Harrison's once-and-only idea of time and place for these three plays. They are haunted by an idea from antiquity – faintly, in *Poetry or Bust*, the most genial of these plays, where busts of great writers from the past haunt the hero with dreams of everlasting fame, and three very down-to-earth muses visit the Airedale poet, John Nicholson:

Muse 3
There's not many left that still'll use
them metres that you used to get from t'Muse.

Muse 1
So here in Titus Salt's wool-combing shed,
we'll try to put some couplets in your head.

Muse 3
But no looking to the summits of Parnassus!
The Muses you've got now are local lasses . . .

Muse 2
Hail, Airedale Bard. Strive to be like these:
Homer, Aeschylus and Sophocles.

In the other two plays in this volume, the classical connection is much more central, as hugely aggressive

Herakles, superhero to the ancients, bestrides the stage, role-model for Marcus Aurelius' killer son in Carnuntum, or sprouts belligerently from his own statue in Delphi, a bridge between brutality then and now. It would be a mistake to connect these one-off pieces with contemporary performance art or 'site-specific' events; they may have some visceral qualities of the happening, the circus, the zoo and the demolition site, but they are formal classical works, rooted in history and text.

Poetry or Bust, chronologically the first of this trio, is a chamber-piece in comparison with the windswept arena dimensions of *The Kaisers of Carnuntum* or the hilltop building-site ceremony of *The Labourers of Herakles*. An indoors piece, devised for the former woolcombing shed of Salts Mill, Saltaire, half an hour from Leeds, it's also an inward work, dramatising personal themes Harrison has mined in his poetry: high art versus low, vernacular versus polite, north versus south, the scholar among the skinheads.

All these are explored through scenes and tableaux from the life of John Nicholson (1790–1843), 'the Airedale Bard', who aspired to join the gallery of busts of the mighty dead poets; sucked up to noble and metropolitan patrons; was politically wobbly, first writing fiery protests against child labour and then becoming a mouthpiece of the factory-owners; returned home and found his baby dead; and drowned while drunk in the river Aire, just down the hill from the mill where the play was performed.

It's a wry, affectionate portrait of a Yorkshire poet, an artistic precursor. The character of John Nicholson was winningly performed by Barrie Rutter, avuncular and driven, quixotic and somehow wounded. A group of young actors from Rutter's Northern Broadsides company played wool-sorters, poachers and muses, Nicholson's patrons, a portrait sculptor, his wife. Harrison, who also designed the show, painted the mill's concrete floor blue to represent the river Aire – and David Hockney, up for a performance, added ripples to it. Bales of wool were stacked up, clogs were donned to punctuate and syncopate the verse-rhythms – they all built the past of the place into the present, making theatre out of simple ingredients, like medieval mysteries whipped up out of everyday materials by ordinary people in a place marked by work, which had once helped to define a community.

The intimacy, tenderness and sadness of *Poetry or Bust*, its strong sense of a return to roots, may also owe something to the circumstances of its creation. It seems to me very much a pivotal play, the hinge between Harrison's texts for the National Theatre of Olivier, Peter Hall and Richard Eyre, and his current theatre-making. Though he may still revisit the National as playwright/adaptor (as in his 1996 adaptation of Victor Hugo's *Le Roi s'amuse*), his eye now seeks other spaces, other stages, a more poetic way of making theatre.

Chronologically, *Poetry or Bust* followed on Harrison's Olivier theatre production of *Square Rounds*, which was not a happy experience for him. This play, a dazzling, Meyerholdian dramatic disquisition about the creative and destructive powers of science, written in often pyrotechnic couplets, told the story of the inventors of the machine-gun and poison gas, and called for a cast almost entirely female and a spectacular illusionist and conjurer. These theatre ingredients were marshalled in the service of what John Arden, studding his early plays with ballad poetry, once called 'telling a sad tale gaily', an attitude which Harrison echoes when he praises the formality of the mask and of verse in Greek tragedy. The more horrible the story, the more highly wrought its telling.

In *Square Rounds*, this required distinctive performance skills – a relish and deftness in language, a choreographic elegance and a willingness to forgo questions of motivation and characterisation in favour of metamorphosis and transformation. Casting largely from the existing National Theatre company and quickly launching them into workshops, Harrison found it hard to find common artistic ground with some of his cast – a drawback in a piece whose central metaphor is a chorus of women from which principals emerge, a chorus only as good as its weakest link.

This unhappy working atmosphere must have been compounded also by Harrison's memories of the genesis of *Square Rounds*. He originally conceived it as the final play of his trilogy *The Common Chorus*, also commissioned by the National Theatre, and set on the perimeter of the Greenham Common air base – another example of Harrison yoking the theatre to a currently charged situation, like his Greek forebears. The first play in the trilogy was Aristophanes' *Lysistrata* (since published separately); the second, Euripides' *The Trojan Women*. *Square Rounds* was to have been the pay-off of the trilogy, a modern play with a classical structure in which a company of women camped round a nuclear air-base recount two lethal scientific inventions made by men on the threshold of the twentieth century.

The trilogy was never performed by the National Theatre, but at the end of 1992 Harrison was directing its amputated final play on the Olivier stage, with much anguish and not a little anger. *Square Rounds* opened to mixed and quite hostile reviews. I thought it was chillingly perfect, an astringent cabaret of carnage. But it could have had heart as well as virtuosity, tragedy as well as bitterness. These qualities were not released in this production of a searingly original play.

Following *Square Rounds*, when Harrison accepted a commission from the ebullient entrepreneur and owner of Salts Mills, Jonathan Silver, to write and direct a play set there (where his production of *Trackers* had already played), he went into it with a lot of emotion and unstaunched theatre appetite. That's why *Poetry or Bust* is such a passionate return to his vernacular and cultural roots. That's why it tells such a sour tale of a local poet seduced by the genteel metropolis. That's why I think it's such a pivotal piece of work, opening the door for Harrison from being poet-in-the-theatre to becoming poet-theatre-maker.

Bruised in London, the Yorkshire bard comes back home and, in a frenzy of work, writes and stages a play rooted in its location and locality, not in the London praised by his character, the upwardly-mobile Sir Francis Chantrey, a cynical society sculptor born in Sheffield, acclaimed in London:

> You should live in London. My chisel and your pen
> depend on the support of cultivated men.
> Poetry and sculpture, neither of our arts
> is much respected in provincial parts.
> Move to the metropolis! The river's Aire's
> a narrow market for poetic wares.
> Widen your horizons, lad. You ought to sell
> your creations to a London clientele.
> Go to the theatres. The Opera's a good spot
> to flog your poetry in. You'll sell the lot.

At this turning-point, Harrison even considered moving to Saltaire and running a company based there, a company that would build on the strengths of the ones he's worked with – Bill Bryden's Cottesloe group, for whom he wrote *The Mysteries*, the 'hairy-arsed football team' of actors for whom he conceived his masked and alliterative *Oresteia*, which Peter Hall directed, and the clog-dancers of *Trackers*, which he directed. A company like that would be a worthy successor to the troupes inspired by poetry and led by poets through history: the companies of Brecht, Lorca, Molière, Shakespeare, the Greeks, whom Harrison loves with a deeper understanding than John Nicholson's.

But at the outset of the nineties, when the Thatcherite market and the triumph of musicals and management as a philosophy had eaten into the theatre, he lacked angels – government funders who might back creative individuals, not just institutions, as they have done in France; or commercial backers, who would have found his theatre alien to the entertainment industry they knew. Even his most faithful patron, Jonathan Silver, would only fund single ventures, one at a time. So the dream of leading his own company, forming his actors, placing poetry and the poet at the heart of an ongoing theatre, planted in his place and language of origin, was shelved. For the time being, he plunged up to the elbows into the making of *Poetry or Bust*, writing and staging the whole thing in two weeks.

In *Kaisers of Carnuntum*, made for that perilous Roman stadium near Vienna, he brings to the stage the ultimate delinquent of the classical world, Commodus, son of the philosopher-king Marcus Aurelius, and a natural born killer. Marcus Aurelius mourned the transience of all things human in the *Meditations* that he wrote – in Greek – while commanding Carnuntum, the Roman frontier post against barbaric Germanic tribes. His son saw his first blood spilt in the very arena where the play happened. Later, he grew up to throw captive barbarians to the lions, butcher a hundred ostriches in a morning, and generally come on like Herakles, the warrior of Olympus.

Harrison is drawn to him, as he has been to a long line of outlaws and underdogs, from the skinhead who desecrated his parents' grave in *V* to the priapic satyrs attacking Apollo in *Trackers*. He's always interested in marginalised characters; finding that Commodus has been airbrushed from history, he writes this play to reinstate him in vivid, foul-mouthed flesh and blood, and to make us confront chasms of the human psyche we would rather deny.

The result is to revise the accepted portrait of Marcus

Aurelius, sanctified in the nineteenth century, notably by Matthew Arnold, as a contemplative, proto-Christian Caesar, a model for self-justifying empire-builders. In late twentieth-century Carnuntum, half an hour from Vienna, where the racist demagogue Jorg Haider wins 20 per cent of the votes of an amnesiac electorate, a play about historical forgetting and simplification has great resonance. And not only in Carnuntum.

With the help of Piero Bordin, producer of the Carnuntum festival which had come into being to present *Trackers*, Harrison assembled an enormous cast, including safari-park animals, the above-mentioned Czech lion tamer, hunting-horn bands, detachments of the local fire brigade and army, and choirs from Austria, Slovakia and Hungary, for Carnuntum lies between several national borders. At the heart of the production were some of Harrison's core team of regular collaborators: Barrie Rutter, his inspirational lead actor; Jocelyn Herbert, his long-term designer; Richard Blackford, composer for his last two films; and actors and technicians who had worked in earlier Harrison shows. More than a dozen people who are his nomadic troupe, his floating theatre company, forming, dissolving and reforming to make short-lived theatre interventions at sites around the world – '*kamikaze* performances', Harrison calls them.

Saturday, 3 June, 1995, the final performance at Carnuntum. Animals are everywhere: in magnified Roman mosaic images of men wrestling with wild beasts, or being savaged by them; and in the pad-pad of the live lion and tigers, caged beneath our feet as we sit in the cold night on terraced seating in the circular former military stadium. The animals pace back and forth as we wait for the play to start, they pant hard, they scratch at their bars – quite a change from the performance conditions Harrison had worked in at the Olivier auditorium.

The earth is covered with a big round canvas on which

is a world-map as the Romans saw the world. At its hub is
a model of the Roman Coliseum. Orpheus mounts it,
sounds his lyre. High on a tower above the arena Marcus
Aurelius sings, in unearthly falsetto, about the flow of the
nearby Danube and the flux of lives and empires:

> Every empire, Reich and Raj
> no matter how well-armed or large,
> is but a moment's brief mirage.
>
> All the emperors old and new,
> Caesar, Stalin, Ceausescu,
> transients all passing through.

With a swoop of searchlights and a stutter of gunfire,
Commodus thunders in, hauling a local road-sign with
tragic and comic masks indicating the amphitheatre we're
in. Barrie Rutter's imperial Roman bovver-boy is
horrendous to behold: shaven head, red Doc Martens,
purple boxer's robe and a pop-eyed grin like Mr Punch.
He has the lethal playfulness of Chaplin's Great Dictator.

First he softens up the locals with a gag or two about
their wine: 'You'll never find Marcus pissed in the arena /
on Petronell-Carnuntum *Grüner Veltliner*'. Then he grows
irate and hammers the road-sign designer to death with his
sign, for daring to portray this death-stadium as an art-
site:

> Oh why
> this modern squeamish need to Disneyfy
> this space that was made for men and beasts to die?
> This space wasn't built for tragic plays,
> for your Sarah Bernhardts or your Lord Oliviers,
> nor for your *Cosís* or your sopranos trilling,
> but built for just one purpose: killing, killing, killing!

This tireless creature, hauling lumps of meat from the tiny Coliseum and distributing them round the victory sites of his empire, where weeping women cradle them as lost sons and husbands; this beaming psychopath, stripping down to red lingerie and donning a Heraklean lionskin and club; whipping the audience into Nuremberg rally-style chants ('Thumbs down for kill, thumbs up for save'); this rough, dangerous, voluble, vernacular spellbinder becomes more than a modern match for Marlowe's Tamburlaine or King Herod of the mystery plays. The drive and impetus of Harrison's verse, ground out with force and delicacy by Barrie Rutter, becomes the seductive, garrulous, threatening voice in your head, the inexhaustible bully in the brain that rends and dismembers, forever spoiling for a fight.

Staging the story of Commodus in the actual space where as a child he must have seen buckets of blood gives *The Kaisers of Carnuntum* great resonance, amplified still more by the political implications of the site. The frontier near Carnuntum kept out the Czechs and Hungarians, 'barbarians' on the Cold War map, where our side was as pure as Marcus Aurelius, theirs as benighted as Commodus. With Communism gone, there's no grounds for demonising them and deifying ourselves. So the play's final confrontation of Marcus and Commodus, blood relatives bound in mutual contempt, mirrors the now unstable division between 'good' West and 'bad' East.

Commodus entices his father down from his tower, then taunts him to the point when he's ready to kill his son. As he raises the club of Herakles high in the air, we hear a woman character speak for the first time. It's Faustina, Marcus Aurelius' wife, condemned by subsequent history as a whore, who must have slept with Roman rough trade to spawn the un-Aurelian Commodus. 'To deify the one and demonise the other / in the end damns me, the blameless mother,' she cries. But, in a maddened gesture of desperation, Faustina is prepared publicly to accept the libel, so long as for once, for her alone, the father acknowledges Commodus as his son, accepts his Calibanic darkness as the ground of his Aurelian light. In the whipping wind, Sian Thomas, rising from her throne among us spectators, gives her cry the grief and urgency of Europe's crazed war-widows:

> Would it help the world pretending your pure semen
> did not create this blood-demented demon?
> If it would I'd swear the nympho whore Faustina
> fucked a fighting man from the arena.
> And if I swear my folly under oath
> it puts a boundary between you both,
> and raises up a future frontier post
> between the god-like and the gangster ghost.
> I'll let these stories go on being told
> to keep apart the iron age and the gold.
> If I agree to let these slanders thrive,
> will the future learn to hope, and thus survive?

Down in the arena, Marcus and his son approach each other, either side of the Danube's banks. 'Just one stride,' jeers the son, 'takes you from the savage to the civilised side.' When they do finally embrace, Commodus smears blood over his father's white suit, and is then killed, like a stuck-pig Samurai at the end of a Kurosawa film, by Orpheus and his cello-spike. Massed choirs exorcise his evil spirit in furious, percussive Latin, leaving his corpse slumped across the Coliseum.

Enthroned Aurelius enters, not pursued but pushed by a bear, followed by Harrison, who delivers an epilogue, and is then sent flying by Commodus resurgent, a horror-film revenant rising from his grave with a warning roar that reminds us, whether in sweet-sour Vienna, in nearby Bosnia, far-off Belfast or farther-off Oklahoma City, that the ghosts of Commodus are alive and furiously kicking.

The Kaisers of Carnuntum and the final play in this volume, *The Labourers of Herakles*, were sandwiched between two forays by Harrison into contemporary history through other media. In the run-up to Carnuntum, he researched, wrote and directed a Channel 4 film/poem for the fiftieth anniversary of the atom bomb dropped on Hiroshima. And immediately after the Herakles play made for Delphi, he set out for the heart of Europe in a helmet and flak-jacket, as part of his arrangement with the *Guardian* to write front-line poems from world crisis-points. ('What are you doing for a holiday?' I asked him at the end of the Delphi show, which once again had worn him out. 'Two weeks in Bosnia,' he muttered with a gritty grin.)

The cumulative experience of being in and reflecting on Hiroshima must have fed the ferocity of *The Kaisers of Carnuntum*, lending gravity and mass to its manically destructive protagonist. But now, instead of the windswept darkness of Carnuntum, Harrison brought his new play to brilliant, lucid light, high in the mountains of Apollo's shrine at Delphi.

Delphi, at the foot of Mount Parnassos, the site of Apollo's oracle, has an even deeper meaning for him than most places in Greece, for it's the site of the Castalian Spring. Pilgrims to the sacred shrine purified themselves in its waters. Believing in its powers to inspire the poetic imagination, Byron jumped in. As a young poet, Harrison slept by it under the stars, and he took a group of us to drink its waters, excitedly explaining that the women of nineteenth-century Delphi used the sacred spring to wash their clothes. When I lay down to drink, my sun-glasses fell off and broke. 'It's telling you to throw away your shades!' he cried, and led us up into the sanctuary, deciphering chiselled typography on the treasuries, memorials and monuments, picking out animals carved among the letters.

In the 1920s the Greek poet Angelos Sikelianos and his

American wife started a 'world university' at Delphi, and made the first modern stagings of Greek drama. Now there are annual festivals and conferences on Greek drama, and it was for the 1995 gathering that Harrison made *The Labourers of Herakles*. It was rather a special year at Delphi, a foretaste of an international festival called 'The Theatre Olympics', the brainchild of Greek director Theodoros Terzopoulos and Japanese director Tadaki Suzuki, who has mounted vivid versions of *The Bacchae, The Trojan Women* and many other Greek tragedies. It's a sort of club of world-class directors and playwrights, which in 1995 included Suzuki and Terzopoulos, Robert Wilson from America, Yuri Lyubimov from Russia, Heiner Müller from Germany, Nuria Espert from Spain, and Harrison – the group's only writer, now that Müller is dead.

They staged most of their productions in the stadium above the sanctuary, a massive space closed off by a distant wall of mountain rock, which Suzuki stunngingly lit up at the moment when Orestes murdered his mother. Lyubimov staged a high-spirited version of Aristophanes' *The Birds* as an aquatic cabaret in the garden pool of Sikelianos' mansion. Wilson's statuesque piece looked like early Martha Graham, solemn and monumental.

After several evenings slogging up to the stadium for shows which started late and went on for a long time, even the charm of seeing theatre under the stars began to wear off. There were too many expressionistic effects, too many sets and costumes that looked as if their designers had been studying the latest Venice Biennale, too much visual imagery, too little language.

Harrison's play was a counterblast in every respect. It was staged – on a shoestring, unlike the other well-funded troupes – in a building-site. Its set was a ring of cement mixers and a cement silo, with a Herakles logo. It was in no way an exercise of style, trying to flog some life into a well-worn classic; instead it built a modern theatre-piece out of all the existing fragments of Phrynikos, the earliest Greek tragedian. It was acutely aware of the proximity of Bosnia and of the discomfort of holding a cultural festival in Delphi while mass rapes were happening an hour's flight away, of the dissonance of celebrating classic European values while villages were being ethnically cleansed in the name of beliefs inseparable from those values.

And above all it was propelled by living language, the sinewy physicality of Harrison's verse and its local roots, a text which makes the actors perform with mouth and mind and whole body. Not an imposed physicality, like the scenic constructions and choreography of the many imagistic theatre productions at the Delphi festival, which often seemed merely spectacular. Instead, in the mud and cement of a half-finished building site, Harrison offered a physical immediacy that welled up from theatre poetry planted in vernacular and rising without losing its roots.

Aiming to be universal, many of the other productions seemed just grandiose; rooted in the specifics of language and location, Harrison's quite modest piece reached out to an international audience, and went in deep. Theatre born of and borne by language can communicate widely at a level below language. Harrison's plays may seem untranslatable, but the last thing they are is parochial.

Harrison's anticipation of being in Bosnia gave a transfusion of urgency to *The Labourers of Herakles*, pushing him to imagine an excruciating contemporary equivalent of the shirt of Nessus, the garment of flame that maddened and killed Herakles. 'The shirt of Nessus is the shirt of modern Europe's agony,' he writes in his stage direction. And his chorus of labourers hammer out agonised questions:

Who wove the caustic camouflage no cooling water quenches?
Muslims that are mouldering in mass-execution trenches.

Who wove the blistering blouson that Herakles can't loose?
The fingers of the raped girl who wove herself a noose.

Who wove this caustic camouflage consuming Herakles?
Sarajevo children his shells made amputees.

Who wove this caustic khaki that seals his maleness in?
The mother of the mortared mosque's dismembered muezzin
assisted by the convoys of those cleansed out of Knin.

Sung out by a bunch of building labourers trapped in the
cement foundations of the forthcoming new theatre of the
European Cultural Centre at Delphi, these lines have the
power and pulse of Duke Ellington or Count Basie, but
their exuberance encompasses a basinful of grief. On their
lift and roll a soloist can ride, like Big Joe Williams
shouting the blues above a big band, as Barrie Rutter's
Herakles did at Delphi, soaring out of the Nessus chorus
to voice an anguish that spans centuries:

I wear a fitted furnace. My scalded body squirms.
My ethnic cleanser's conscience crawls with caustic worms.
If you pull this garment from me, you'll pull away my skin.
This is Europe's conscience I'm cremated in.

   Cradled by the action, the music and the resonance of
their site which makes performance verge on ceremony,
language in these plays can take flight. These etched
couplets and triplets, these ferocious reiterations, are the
true music towards which all Tony Harrison's theatre
tends. It's a riff, a collier's rant, an antic hurdy-gurdy
music. You hear it in the Marsyas speech in *Trackers*,
where it plays the tunes of torturers and tortured. You
hear it in the tirades of child-slaughterer Herod in
Harrison's *The Mysteries*. Round and round it goes,
rhymes clicking into place like tap-dance heels and toes. At
the play's crisis it rises from deep down, with the force of a

Moby Dick. Its thrust and insistence feel masculine, its finesse and grief feminine. Always it stares into the heart of violence and crime, bearing witness to the very worst, yet testifying in its form to the very best in humanity.

Behind it lie echoes of poets and poet-playwrights through the ages: from the *stycomythia* of the Greek tragedians, a zig-zag of exchanged single verses turning up the temperature as the action nears its climax (Orestes and Electra in *The Oresteia*, irresistible in Harrison's National Theatre version as the lines were tossed and swung across waves of live drumming); from Anglo-Saxon poetry's alliteration, punching home perceptions, to the 'flyting' of the fifteenth-century Scottish bards Henryson, Dunbar and Douglas, poets whom Harrison calls 'northern internationalists', a phrase that might well apply to him; from Marlowe's magnificent stomps to early Shakespeare tableaux (the Father Who Has Killed His Son and Son Who Has Killed His Father scenes in *Henry VI*); from Molière's and Racine's *tirades*, wave after wave of rhyme mounting an assault on mind and heart, to Ibsen's memorable but perhaps mistaken farewell to verse drama in *Peer Gynt* and *Brand*; from the ghosts of ballad, song and stage icons that haunt Yeats's plays, to the macabre vaudeville of T. S. Eliot's *Sweeney Agonistes*, a sturdy Yankee theatre idiom he abandoned for something more genteel.

In our time, Harrison crowns this procession, reinventing a modern form rooted in ancient powers. Not the poet in the theatre, a stranger admitted into a universe of prose – that's how theatre critics used to talk of T. S. Eliot or Christopher Fry – but the poet/theatre-maker as an essential expression of theatre's deepest action in our lives.

March 1996

POETRY OR BUST

Poetry or Bust was devised for the former wool-combing shed of Salts Mill, Saltaire, two minutes away from the river Aire, where John Nicholson died. The play was commissioned by Jonathan Silver of Salts Mill and sponsored by Pace Micro Technology, whose premises occupy half of the former wool-combing shed where it was performed.

Poetry or Bust was first performed at Salts Mill on the 5 September 1993 with the following members of Northern Broadsides:

Ishia Bennison
Colin R. Campbell
Lawrence Evans
Maggie Jackson
Conrad Nelson
Edward Peel
Isobel Raine
Barrie Rutter
Andy Wear

Written, directed and designed by Tony Harrison
Music Conrad Nelson
Clogging Lawrence Evans
Stage Management Fraser Marlow

Lights up on Hall of Fame.
   *In a corner of the former wool-combing shed of Salts
Mill, Saltaire, is set the Hall of Fame. A red carpet with
nine draped marble busts. In front of them, unveiled, a
bust of Shakespeare on a plinth. There are two mirrors on
the wall and the iron columns are painted white and gold.*
   Enter **John Nicholson** (*1790–1843*).

John Nicholson

Here are the immortals, Fame's most sacred shrine.
The busts of the great bards. And one of them is
                                                        mine.
There's no need to give my name as you'll all know it;
you're all acquainted with the Airedale poet.
I'm sure you've all a favourite poem or two,
so I only need remind you of a few . . .

(*He quotes from* 'Airedale in Ancient Times':)

> 'AIREDALE IN ANCIENT TIMES.
>   By John Nicholson.

Lead me, O Muse, along Aire's winding course,
To sing of Gordale – its tremendous source,
But softer scenes on Malham Water view,
When its smooth breast reflects the azure blue.

O, Nature! Be my Muse – to touch the scene
Of Bingley's glories, which long since have been . . .'

As I'm your local bard, I see no need
to quote more from a poet that you all must read,

whose works must lie on every library shelf.
Your Airedale poet. John Nicholson, myself.
I need only do a couplet, make a start,
and you'll pick up a poem you know by heart.

(*He quotes:*)

'Where winding Aire, enamour'd of the place,
Moves on so slow, it seems to stop and gaze . . .'

I made the Muses visit these very river banks,
and made the Aire immortal. This was the Aire's
                                                              thanks.
Trying to drown me when, I confess, the worse for
                                                              wear,
I lost my footing and slipped into t'river Aire.

It was in the very river Aire that I'd invoked
where I, its great immortalizer, choked.
Fate like this can only seem perverse
to perish in the subject of your own immortal verse!
Midway between two banks why was I drowned
in the very river my poem made renowned?

Not two minutes' stroll from this shed here
to where there's now a footbridge and weir,
the very stretch Sir Titus chose as site
for what is now Salts Mill, I last saw the light.
A return for all my pains that seemed unjust
but for the compensations here of fame and bust.

Here are the immortals, Fame's most sacred shrine.
The busts of the great bards. And one of them is
                                                              mine.
Are you ready? Where's t'brass band, Lord Mayor,
to unveil the bust to t'bard who died in t'Aire?

Is it this? I hereby unveil
John Nicholson, that's me, poet of Airedale.

(He unveils all the busts in the Hall of Fame with increasing desperation until he realizes he must be in the front rank. Two busts remain still veiled.)

> Though I expected fame, how could I know
> Fame had a place reserved on the front row?
> Though modest fame had been my life's ambition
> I never hoped for such a proud position
> in the foremost rank of bards, so near
> to him who gave the world *King Lear*.
> Not first, that's always Shakespeare, but assigned
> a plinth and bust not all that far behind.
> The brother bards of Aire and Avon stand
> so close together, almost hand in hand.
> I expect you to applaud the sculptor's skills
> when I unveil my bust placed next to Will's.

(He unveils the bust. It turns out to be not his, but that of Sir Titus Salt.)

> It's Sir Titus! O, Sir Titus,
> Who put you here with all us famous writers?
> Now I know that my bust will be there,
> next to the famous founder of Saltaire.

(The bust of Sir Titus Salt appears to speak. Nicholson bends close.)

> What's that you're saying? I'm afraid it's true,
> when I slipped in the river, yes, I'd had a few.
> But this is no time for censure or for blame,
> when we're both together in the Hall of Fame.
> You always stood by me. Now that I've died,
> I bet that we're still standing side by side.
> Fame must have arranged that the wool-sorter
> would be immortalized beside his chief supporter.
> Thee and me, Sir Titus, eh? Marble next-door
> > neighbours.

7

I can hardly wait to see my sculptor's labours.

(*He unveils the last bust. It is that of a woman.*)

    There must be some mistake. I'm bound to be among
the Muses' chosen, the immortal throng.

(*Still no bust. He's now desperate. To the audience:*)

    The name's John Nicholson. Of course you know
                              it . . .
John Nicholson, the poet . . . the Airedale poet.

    When I tell you I'm John Nicholson who died on yon
                            Aire bank
just down the road from here and you look blank,
I have a sudden horror no one here could quote
even a couplet of the verse I wrote.

    Don't let me believe that no one reads
my verses, not in Bingley, Bradford, Leeds.

    I'd expect to haunt this mill and find my fame
everlasting, but not one person knows my name.
I'd have thought the Airedale poet, if anywhere,
would have been a legend in Saltaire.

    O Muses, pray assist your devotee,
to move those who've forgotten all my poetry.

(*Enter three* **Muses** *walking on the surface of the river
Aire. They bear on their heads, like girls practising
deportment, three tomes representing the world's great
poetry.*
    John Nicholson adopts 'Poet Addressing Muses' pose.)

    O Muses, come and lend me all your power.

Muse 1
Ay, we'll lend you a hand. You've got about an hour.

Muse 2

We used to be nine Muses, but now we're only three
and even that's too much for poetry.

Muse 3

There's not that much work in Yorkshire since tha
                                                    drowned,
there's not that many Airedale bards around.

Muse 1

I mean, you only need one part-time Muse
to squeeze royal birthday poems from Ted Hughes.

Muse 2

So we're glad to help. Just like old times,
helping a poet with couplets and with rhymes.

Muse 3

There's not many left that still'll use
them metres that you used to get from t'Muse.

Muse 1

So here in Titus Salt's wool-combing shed,
we'll try to put some couplets in your head.

Muse 2

But no looking to the summits of Parnassus!
The Muses you've got now are local lasses.

Muse 3

And we have to tell you that we let you drown
because we felt our bard had let us down.

Muse 1

We'll come out of retirement to inspire
what you will keep addressing as your 'lyre'.

Muse 2
Hail, Airedale bard. Strive to be like these,
Homer, Aeschylus and Sophocles.

(*Muse 2 presents John Nicholson with an enormous tome.*)

Muse 3
The greatest spirits, Rome's and ancient Greece's,
Milton, Shakespeare, all the masterpieces.

(*Muse 3 presents John Nicholson with an enormous tome.*)

Muse 1
And the fattest volume of the lot,
those bards who yearned for fame and time forgot.

(*Muse 1 presents John Nicholson with an enormous tome.*
Nicholson is precariously loaded with the three volumes.)

Muse 1
Look at the load they carry. It's no wonder
most would-be poets end up going under.

Muse 3
But remember the Airedale bard and us immortal
                                    daughters
started here in Bradford as wool-sorters.

(*The Muses are transformed to wool-sorters.*)

Muse 1
We'll be there when you arrive, and unless you run,
they'll be yelling . . .

(*Muse 2 slides open the mill door, revealing . . .*)

All Workers
tha's late again for work, John Nicholson.

(John Nicholson teeters across the stepping stones of the river and joins the other **Wool-sorters** *at the wool-laden sorting board.)*

Wool-sorter 1
Late again, our John?

Muse 1
    A neet wi t'Muse?

Wool-sorter 2
Nay more like another neet on t'booze . . .
He sups ale like other folk sup water.

Wool-sorter 3
I hope tha's a better bard than tha's a sorter.

John Nicholson
Ah wor reading all neet
by the candle leet.
The great spirits, Rome's and ancient Greece's.

Wool-sorter 4
This table's thick with 'ancient grease' from a million
                                        sorted fleeces.
If we don't meet our quota it'll be thy fault.

Wool-sorter 5
Ay! But he'll not be blamed. He's in wi' Titus Salt.

John Nicholson
'Tis cos I aspire
to the world of the lyre,
to the summits of Helicon's peak
and my bardic vigil . . .

Wool-sorter 1
                    . . . Just keep
your eyes on them shit balls in t'sheep.

(*The work goes on. John Nicholson falls asleep.*)

Wool-sorter 2
His eyes are half shut. He's asleep.

Wool-sorter 3
Ay, he spends half the neet with his nostrils stuck
into the pages of some stuffy book.

Wool-sorter 4
His mam said to him, 'No more candles for thee
to waste all neet on thy poetry.'

Wool-sorter 5
Dost tha know what he did? He scraped off this
                                        grease
that gets thick and hard when it oozes from t'fleece
and put a twist of wool in for a wick
and med hissen candles.

Wool-sorter 1
                    His mind's that quick
when he's reading his poets or making up rhymes,
and hungover or snoring at other times.

Wool-sorter 2
Like now, when he's dreaming of making his name
as summat else than a sorter of fleeces.

Wool-sorter 3
Ay, dreaming of immortal fame
and writing masterpieces.

Wool-sorter 2
These mill pillars here that flake with rust
to John are gilded columns round his bust.

Wool-sorter 1
This girder, this rusted iron support . . .

(*Wool-sorter 4 flicks his sweat-rag loose and it becomes
the cravat of* **The Patron.**)

The Patron
. . . is the gilded portico to the Muses' court.

Wool-sorter 1
He even scratches poems in t'congealed suint
with a skewer from t'sacks.

(*Muse 3 moves from the wool-sorting table across the
stepping stones of the river to an island of red carpet and a
column.*
*Wool-sorter 4 follows the Muse and on the centre of the
stepping stones is transformed from a Wool-sorter into*
The Patron.
John Nicholson follows the Muse and The Patron.)

John Nicholson
And dreams of gilt-edged pages, proper prints,
read by gents with good suits on their backs.

(*The Patron and Muse 3, now transformed into* **The Patron's
Wife,** *read together 'The Vale of Ilkley' by John Nicholson.*
*Wool-sorter 3 reads the title of the poem etched in the
hardened grease of the wool-sorting table. He is only semi-
literate and reads with difficulty.*)

Wool-sorter 3
'The . . . Vale . . . of . . . Ilkley.'

The Patron
'THE VALE OF ILKLEY.
By John Nicholson

Why does not some great bard, whose potent mind
No earthly passions in its sphere can bind,
Take the tun'd lyre, which wakes at genius' spells,
And sing in praise of Ilkley and its wells?'

John Nicholson
'Had I a Shakespeare's pen, a Byron's powers,'

The Patron
'Nor mountains, woods, nor valleys, trees, or flowers,
Nor all that poets have for ages sung,
Since Homer's harp or Sappho's lyre was strung,
Should tempt my Muse, on ocean or on shore,
Till I had sung the charms of . . .'

John Nicholson
                    'Ilkley Moor.'

The Patron's Wife
Oh, those charming verses. Whose are those?

The Patron
It's a rude wool-sorter's efforts to compose.

The Patron's Wide
Well, I'd say, for one untutored, he succeeds.

The Patron
The wonder is these days he even reads.
And you know I feel it might imbue a

14

certain *frisson* to know that it's a skewer
that our wool-sorter poet uses
as a quill to cultivate his charming Muses.
They tell me when he wrestles with his Muse
he etches his odes in a sort of waxy ooze
that sweats out of all the handled fleeces.
He actually writes in grease the fleece releases.
Isn't it amusing, to scratch in grease,
one's first clumsily composed poetic piece?

The Patron's Wife
It's disgusting. Why did you tell me that?
The very thought. *Verses* scratched in fat!
I fear, for me, your rude wool-sorter's Muse
has that awful, fleecy smell she'll never lose.

Don't give him any money, he'll spend it all on drink.

The Patron
I think this fellow's aspirations need support.

(*The Wool-sorters from the sorting table make the sound of money falling into John Nicholson's outstretched palm and the sound transforms the sorting table into the pub.*)

Wool-sorters
CHINK!

(*John Nicholson goes into the pub with his money.*
The Wool-sorters are singing the wordless tune to what will become the song 'O for an Everlasting Spring.')

Wool-sorter 1
Here's our John.

Wool-sorter 5
We need a drinking song.

Wool-sorter 4
Some words to fit our tune.

John Nicholson
            Won't take me long.
I'm the reigning prince of impromptu . . .
or I will be when I've had a pint or two
or three or four . . .

Wool-sorter 2
        Give our John a drink.

(*Muse 2 brings a drink to John Nicholson. She is to become* **Mary**, *Nicholson's first wife.*)

John Nicholson
Ay, give us a pot of ale. It helps me think.

(*John Nicholson and Muse 2/Mary exchange affectionate glances. Nicholson drinks his beer and stares up to the Muses.*)

Wool-sorter 3
Have you noticed how he looks up into t'skies
when he's making summat up?

John Nicholson
        I'll improvise.

(*He begins to improvise the song.*)

     'O FOR AN EVERLASTING SPRING.
        By John Nicholson.

O for an everlasting spring
Of home-brewed beer like this!
Then with my friends I'd laugh and sing,
And spend the hours in bliss;

Then come old Care, linked with Despair,
For I with thee made strong,
Would plunge them overhead in beer,
And make them lead the song.'

(*The Wool-sorters join in, all singing the song. It becomes
sadder and eventually they are all staring into their beer.*)

I was staring at this froth on that porter there,
thinking how it gets blown away by one slight puff of
air.

(*He improvises the second drinking song.*)

'The hard-working Yorkshire wool-sorter
Has here but little to stay:
For life's like the froth on that porter,
And quickly doth vanish away.'

(*The Wool-sorters sing the words that John Nicholson has
improvised.*)

Wool-sorter 1

Come on, our John, we depend on your good cheer
and drinking ditties when we quaff our beer.

(*To change the sad mood left by the second drinking song,
the Wool-sorters and John Nicholson sing again the first
drinking song.*)

'O for an everlasting spring
Of home-brewed beer like this!
Then with my friends I'd laugh and sing,
And spend the hours in bliss;

Then come old Care, linked with Despair,
For I with thee made strong,
Would plunge them overhead in beer,
And make them lead the song.'

*(The three Muses dance in the pub. Muse 2/Mary draws
John Nicholson into their dance. They dance together and
Muse 2/Mary leaves the dance and skips across the
stepping stones to the other side of the river.*

*Wool-sorters 3 stares into the thickened grease of the
sorting table and announces the next poem by John
Nicholson.)*

Wool-sorter 3
'LOVE.'

John Nicholson
'By John Nicholson.'

Muse 2/Mary
'LOVE.
By John Nicholson.'

John Nicholson
'Wild the night, my love, my Mary!
   But I promis'd thee to meet;
Winds and rain sound dreary, dreary –
   Yet thou listn'st for my feet!

Dark the woods which lie between us,
   High the rocks I have to pass,
Where the village swains have seen us,
   Each one happy with his lass.

Frail the plank across the river,
   Slipp'ry with a night of rain;
One false step – I'm gone for ever,
   Ne'er to meet my love again;'

Muse 2/Mary
'Frail the plank across the river,
   Slipp'ry with a night of rain;

18

One false step – I'm gone for ever,
   Ne'er to meet my love again;

Swollen the streams of ev'ry fountain;
   Trackless is the stormy moor;
Capp'd with mist the lofty mountain
   Which I have to wander o'er.

Though the winds be cold and dreary
   I have promis'd thee to meet;
If I reach my love, my deary,
   'Twill but make our bliss more sweet!

What the rocks or misty mountains?
   What the darkness of the woods?
What the roaring of the fountains,
   Though the rills be swoll'n to floods?

What the trackless moor or river,
   though some demon should appear?'

John Nicholson
'Can those stop me? O no, – never!
   Soon I clasp thee, Mary dear!'

(*Before John Nicholson can grasp Muse 2/Mary, she steps into the river and sings. Muses 1 and 3 join her in the song.*)

Muses

(*singing*)

'Then my plaid I will throw o'er me,
   Sing of Mary on the way;
Though great dangers lie before me,
   Yet I cannot, will not stay.'

(*Muses 1 and 3 veil Muse 2/Mary. She is dead. John Nicholson is alone with his grief on Nicholson's Rock.*)

John Nicholson

My Mary's dead, so is the child she carried.
Snatched away just after we were married.
My posterity, my future, in her womb,
gone with my dear Mary to the tomb.

Does all the sweetness of the world turn sour?
O Muses, come and lend me all your power.

(*The Muses turn their backs on John Nicholson.*)

Nothing made of flesh survives decay.
This rock will last. I'll carve in it a J,

(*John Nicholson begins to chisel the first letter of his name in the rock. The sound is made by the clogs of the Muses. It represents the theme of being immortalized in stone or marble.*)

and will come here when laden with my woe
and add the other letters . . . O . . .

(*The clogs make the chiselling sound.*)

and then the H and the N . . .

(*The clogs make the chiselling sound.*)

in rock that long outlasts the lives of men
In centuries to come, when I'm long gone,
men will come to Eldwick and read here JOHN.
And add to this the N. . .I. . .C. . .H. . .O. . .
L. . .S. . .O. . .N. . .

(*The clogs make the chiselling sound.*)

so posterity will know
that JOHN NICHOLSON spent here such lonely
hours
repeating his heartfelt prayer for Muses' power.
Should I add 'Poet' to my name or not,

in case in time to come the fact's forgot?

O Muses, come and lend me all your power . . .

(*Muse 2 makes three sharp stamps with her clogs to represent the gun of The Patron.*
    Wool-sorter 4/The Patron emerges to shoot gamebirds.
    *Wool-sorter 2/**Poacher** and Wool-sorter 3/**Poacher** continue the sportsman's salvoes by banging their clogs on the stones.*
    Wool-sorter 3 places one foot on the first stepping stone across the river to indicate the beginning of the Poachers' tentative trespass.
    The Patron shoots – game falls from the sky.
    The Patron announces the title of the next poem by John Nicholson.)

The Patron
'THE SPORTS OF THE FIELD.'

John Nicholson
'By John Nicholson.

When oaks are brown and birches bare,
    And not a bird is singing,
The sportsman drives away his care,
    The speckled woodcocks springing.

True joy he in the country knows,
    His faithful springers ranging
Among the hazel's yellow boughs,
    Or holly, never changing.

And when the long-bill'd woodcock springs,
    Mark! – the sportsman calling –
The blue smoke curls, – its useless wings
    through the trees are falling.

Full many a man at this would sigh,
    As sore against religion;
But at a feast just let him try
    Roast woodcock, grouse . . .

(*Wool-sorter 3/Poacher makes the sound of a gunshot
with his clog.*)

                                        or widgeon!'

(*The Patron drops the reward into the outstretched palm
of John Nicholson.*
    *The Wool-sorters from the pub make the sound of coins
falling into his palm.*)

Wool-sorters

                                        CHINK!

(*The Wool-sorters begin 'The Poachers' Song'.*)

    'So long as planets rise and set,
        Or tim'rous hares can run,
    The poacher true . . .'

(*John Nicholson cuts the song off in midflow.*)

John Nicholson
Sir, I've forsworn the fatal lure of drink.

The Patron
You know your fellow sorters trespass on my land,
bagging the hares and grouse the law has banned.
And I said to her Ladyship just the other day
our wool-sorter/poet's a poacher in his way.
They poach hares and grouse that don't belong.
You poach the gentry's diction for your song.
You're a poet/poacher. Your furtive view halloos
go poaching Parnassus for a posher Muse.
One might even say your rude wool-sorter's lyre

is made with strings of poacher's snaring wire.
They come for grouse and widgeon with their snares,
but fine poetic words are your trapped hares.
Jolly amusing parallel, don't you think?
Pursue the poacher's theme . . .

Poachers
CHINK!

Wool-sorter 3/Poacher
We'll give you the details

Wool-sorter 2/Poacher
If you provide the drink!

*(John Nicholson follows the Poachers into the pub, where
he acquires the details of their furtive craft.*
*The Wool-sorters, the Poachers and John Nicholson all
sing 'The Poachers' Song':)*

'So long as planets rise and set,
   Or tim'rous hares can run,
The poacher true will hang his net,
   And level sure his gun;
      The high park wall,
      Spring guns and all,
And keepers strong with beer,
      We value not,
      Nor shun the spot,
If hares are frisking near.'

(John Nicholson suddenly cuts off the song.)

John Nicholson
Don't sing those words in pubs. They don't belong
to beery boozers and the vulgar throng.
I want to see them bound in gilded pages,

23

read by connoisseurs through all the ages.

(*John Nicholson crosses the stepping stones to offer his poem 'The Poacher' to The Patron. He stands on the middle stone.*)

'THE POACHER.
By John Nicholson.

Inspired by drink, who can be silent long?
The poachers could not, but began this song:

'So long as planets rise and set,
    Or tim'rous hares can run,
The poacher true will hang his net,
    And level sure his gun;'

(*The Poachers sing:*)

'The high park wall,
    Spring guns and all,
And keepers strong with beer,'

(*John Nicholson stops them.*)

The Patron
'We value not,
    Nor shun the spot,
If hares are frisking near.'

(*John Nicholson turns on the Poachers with the following phrase from his poem:*)

John Nicholson
'Ye rustic plunderers,'

The Patron

(*continuing*)

'Who sport by night,

And fearlessly invade another's right,
. . .
If injur'd lords no punishment prepar'd
Drinking and poaching bring their own reward.'

(*The Poachers retreat.*
The Patron drops some coins into the outstretched palm
of John Nicholson.)

Poachers

CHINK!

(*The Wool-sorters sing 'The Poachers' Song'. John*
Nicholson cuts it off.)

John Nicholson
Sir, I've forsworn the fatal lure of drink.
I'm thinking of taking another wife, sir.

Wool-sorters

CHINK!

(*The Wool-sorters begin 'The Poachers' Song'. John*
Nicholson cuts if off.)

John Nicholson
Sir, I've forsworn the fatal lure of drink.
I have a wife and two bairns, sir.

Wool-sorters

CHINK! CHINK!

(*The Wool-sorters begin 'The Poachers' Song'. John*
Nicholson cuts it off.)

John Nicholson
Sir, I've forsworn the fatal lure of drink.
I have *five* children, sir.

Wool-sorters
CHINK! CHINK!

(*The Wool-sorters begin 'The Poachers' Song'. John Nicholson cuts it off.*)

John Nicholson
Sir, I've forsworn the fatal lure of drink.

(*This final phrase of John Nicholson earns him the sanctimonious approval of The Patron.*)

The Patron
'THE DRUNKARD'S RETRIBUTION.'

John Nicholson
'By John Nicholson.

Where is the ink so sable in its hue,
That can portray the picture dark and true;
The horrid state that language fails to tell,
The dark confusion and the earthly hell!
In such sad state how often I have thought –
O! that I could sink backwards into naught!
Reason o'erthrown and anguish in its place,
I thought myself below the reach of grace.
Despair o'erwhelmed my soul, and keen remorse;
To know I liv'd, became my bitterest curse;
My sorrowing friends appear'd my greatest foes,

(*The Wool-sorters commence the first bars of 'The Poachers' Song', which John Nicholson cuts off, continuing:*)

And chearfull songs but added to my woes.
. . .
The phantom trumpets, the imagin'd ban,
Methought I heard, which summon'd me to stand

High in the pillory – to meet disgrace;
My trembling heart shrunk back from every face.
Thus swiftly did imagination rove,
And o'er the prostrate throne of reason drove.
Afraid of poison from a mother kind,
I durst not drink, – suspicion fill'd my mind.
Each trembling leaf, if shaken by the blast,
Struck me with terror as I hurried past.
I deem'd myself the cause of all the guilt
That fills the earth – of all the blood e'er spilt,
And that kind heaven would design on earth to dwell,
Were I but hurried to the deepest hell . . .'

The Patron
While you embraced intemperance I'd no hope
you'd last in London. Now I think you'll cope.
You'll do well in London if you can resist
your fatal propensity for getting pissed.
If you really can resist the taproom's snare
you'll make your mark in London. But beware!
Go south! Sell volumes, find subscribers, find
more patrons of a cultivated kind.
Go to the capital. They're pretty rare,
your poetry readers round the river Aire.
Go to London.

Wool-sorters
CHINK! CHINK! CHINK!

John Nicholson
Martha, Martha, here.

(*Enter Muse* 1/**Martha**.)
                          Success! Success!
Twenty guineas. Not a penny less!
Treat the children.

Martha
It'll be a treat
for your children to get something to eat.

John Nicholson
From now on they'll be eating every day.
Fame and fortune are already on the way.

Martha
Twenty guineas with nine mouths to feed . . .

John Nicholson
Six guineas.

Martha
You said twenty.

John Nicholson
Well, you see, I'll need
fourteen for my journey.

Martha
Journey?

John Nicholson
Yes!
To the capital to build on my success.

(*The Wool-sorters help to effect the transition to London
by reprising 'The Poachers' Song'.*)

I'm off to London with my poetic gems
to immortalize the Aire down by the Thames.

(*John Nicholson gazes with wonder at the gilded columns
and the statues of the capital.
    The Wool-sorters walk along a roadway of fleeces*

which silences their clogs and they step on to the red carpet with all the busts. They are singing 'The Poachers' Song', which becomes quieter and quieter, representing the distance between Yorkshire and London:)

> 'What stop we at the rivers deep,
>   The frost or winter's snow;
> The lazy keepers soundly sleep,
>   When tempests wildly blow.
>   Of rain and hail,
>   Let Jove's great pail
> Be emptied from on high;
>   The darker night,
>   The more delight,
> And greater numbers die!'

(They become Workers in the sculpture yard of **Sir Francis Chantrey**. *Their clogs make the sound of chisels carving out the statues of those immortalized by fame.)*

London. John Nicholson enters the studio of Sir Francis Chantrey.

John Nicholson
Francis Chantrey?

Sir Francis Chantrey
            This is Sir Francis Chantrey, yes.
Whom do I have the honour to address?

John Nicholson
John Nicholson, the bard of t'river Aire.

Sir Francis Chantrey

(*dropping into native Yorkshire*)

Well, I'm 'The Sheffield Chiseller'. Put it there.

(*The sound of the Workers' chiselling made by their clogs.*)

Though I put poets and princes into stone,
my origins are Sheffield and as humble as your own.

John Nicholson
Are all these famous people that you're doing?

Sir Francis Chantrey
Everyone wants fame. The whole world's queuing.
All the most powerful, those nearest to the throne,
queuing for Chantrey to carve them out of stone.

(*The sound of chisels is heard again.*)

They know their mortal fate is just to moulder
unless Chantrey charms their likeness from a boulder.

(*The sound of chisels is heard again.*)

Sir Francis Chantrey

(*He indicates the stepping stones.*)

I've got a queue of stone blocks in the yard,
waiting to be royalty, politician . . . bard.

John Nicholson
One day when my poetic fame proceeds
beyond Bingley, beyond Bradford, beyond Leeds,
there'll be a statue, when I've made my mark,
proud and prominent in a Bingley park.
The bard who made a legend of the Aire

's bound to have a bust in Forster Square.
Every Yorkshire city will require
that statue of the bard with wreath and lyre,
or, dare I say it, within the Abbey's walls
or there with Dr Donne in his St Paul's?

To have one done, how much do people pay?

Sir Francis Chantrey
One hundred guineas, lad!

John Nicholson
              Nay, gerraway!

I'll never be able to afford
one hundred guineas stuck at t'sorting board.

Sir Francis Chantrey

(*He is walking on the stones.*)

This one's say, Lord Hume, that's Walter Scott.
I'll carve him a smiling mouth out of that spot.

(*He dances the chiselling rhythm on the stones.
The Workers in his yard respond by making the sound
of chisels with their clogs.*)

This one's a bishop. There's his eyes, his snout,
once I get my tools to carve 'em out.

The milk delivery boy of yesterday
rescues the high and mighty from decay.
Nobles of high rank and high degree
have no earthly future without me.

Once my magic chisel starts to chip,
that might be Lord Byron's nether lip.
And this great block some day
will get carved into that great blockhead, Castlereagh.

31

(*He dances the chiselling rhythm on the stones.*
    *The Workers in his yard respond by making the sound
of chisels with their clogs.*)

> Stand on that stone. Just think that you tread
> boldly and brashly on a noble's head.
> There's a king I'll carve with jewelled crown on,
> but now he's just for jumping up and down on.
> It gives me such pleasure: I can hop and skip
> on first the Lord's face, then her Ladyship.
> The stern judge with black gown and wig on
> is just someone I can do my Sheffield jig on.

(*He dances the chiselling rhythm on the stones.*
    *The Workers respond until the sound of the chiselling
reaches a crescendo.*)

> I can dance on all their faces. I can squash
> the stuck-up noses of the proud and posh.

John Nicholson
Oh, don't say things like that. That's Chartist talk!
They're hanging people like that up in York.
Your business'd go bust with them top dogs.

Sir Francis Chantrey
Ay, they'd decree that all the world wore clogs.
But I tell you, Nicholson, I bet
they'd soon be wanting their own stone statuette.
And Chantrey would be commissioned to create a
million marble busts of some dictator.
If your wool-sorters and wool-combers and their sort
overthrow the Crown, the Church, the Court,
they'd be the patrons that you'd have to please.
They'd be the masters gave you your new fees.

John Nicholson
Most of 'em can't read.

Sir Francis Chantrey
Well, you'll have to use
some girl from the mill to be your Muse.

(*He suddenly takes out sketchpad and pencil.*)

Stand still!

John Nicholson
What? Why?

Sir Francis Chantrey
Stand absolutely still!
If I were to sculpt you (I'm not promising I will),
that would be the stance that I'd propose:
'The Poet Addressing Muses' pose.
Your statue should stand like that beside the Aire,
eyes cast towards the Muses in poetic prayer.
That stone you stand on one day could be yours,
carved in your likeness, unveiled to loud applause.
So write some poems to please some local Lord.
Strive to be marble! Quit the sorting board.
You should live in London. My chisel and your pen
depend on the support of cultivated men.
Poetry and sculpture, neither of our arts
is much respected in provincial parts.
Move to the metropolis! The river Aire's
a narrow market for poetic wares.
Widen your horizons, lad. You ought to sell
your creations to a London clientele.
Go to the theatres. The Opera's a good spot
to flog your poetry in. You'll sell the lot.

Then I could get you a chap here to cast a
bust of you . . .

John Nicholson
of ME!!

Sir Francis Chantrey
            Not marble, mind, just plaster,
but something – summat – cheap you could afford,
to set 'em gawping back at the sorting board.

John Nicholson
Oh, thank you very much, Mr Chantrey, sir.
Won't my Martha be impressed when I show her.
A bust of the Airedale bard while still alive!
What a stir I'll cause up North when I arrive.
Wait till I get home and show our lass . . .

Sir Francis Chantrey
First get off to Drury Lane and earn the brass.

(*John Nicholson goes off.*
   *Sir Francis Chantrey hands over his sketchpad to one of
the Workers.*)

Worker 2
There's nothing on this drawing!

Sir Francis Chantrey
I know. I found that Yorkshireman so boring.
Knock up something for my fellow tyke.
I doubt it matters too much what it's like.
But make sure you get five guineas from the feller.

On second thoughts, go down into the cellar
and file down that cast we've got of Robert Burns
and flog it to that oaf when he returns.

34

*(The Workers in Chantrey's yard and the posed group of
the Muses become first the performers, then the elegant
audience at the Opera.)*

John Nicholson
After tonight the capital will know it,
the poetry of Yorkshire's greatest poet,
the greatest Airedale poet alive,
after a pint or two, or three or four or five . . .

*(He walks into the Opera foyer, drunk, and mixes among
the elegant gentry.)*

Those garments that you gorgeous ladies wear
were woven from alpaca made on t'river Aire.
Them fine dresses, that shirt and that coat
came from a Peruvian sort of camel-goat.
This sorter's finger and this sorter's thumb
first touched the llama woven round her bum.
That bodice round her bust, did you but know it,
was fingered first of all by t'Airedale poet.

In the hardened surface of fat residue
of llama fleeces shipped from far Peru,
I etched my poetic efforts, the sorter bard
who skewered his couplets into llama lard.

(He addresses the bust of Shakespeare:)

Even alpaca rots, but marble is for aye.
I'll be a bust like thee before I die.
Bingley's known nowt like it. I'll be t'first
lad out of Bingley to become a bust.
A bust from Bingley – Oh, to be
in marble form for all posterity!
Unless Chantrey chisels me a more enduring face,
I'm scared my name will sink without a trace.
Each new poem that I compose

transforms me line by line to one of those.

(*He leans closer to Shakespeare's bust to confide the following:*)

> I'm not at that late stage in my career
> to give the world my Hamlet or King Lear,
> but I wrote a play myself two years ago,
> I could recite it to you . . .

(*He makes as if to begin to recite his play and is apparently interrupted by something said by the bust of Shakespeare.*)

What's that? No!

(*He tries again.*)

> *The Siege of Bradford*, that's the title.
> Are you sure that you don't fancy a recital?
> All right, No!
> Honestly I'm not trying to compete.
> I am not fit to kneel down at your feet.
>
> I have to confess to you, Bill, when I drink,
> I see them llamas in a shocking shade of pink.
>
> There in the sorting table's hardened grease
> from the fatty matter oozing from the fleece
> used like a waxen tablet I incised
> with a skewer point my poems . . .

(*He starts selling his wares and shouts:*)

reasonably priced!

> I'm going to sell the lot. They all look rich.

(*He addresses the bust of the woman:*)

How many, Madam?

(*He listens to the bust's response.*)

None? You mean old bitch!

(*Enter a* **Constable**.)

Constable
Here, this foyer's not the place for ballad vendors.

John Nicholson
But I'm the Airedale bard!

Constable
God, defend us!

John Nicholson
I made the Aire immortal with my lyre!

Constable
You're also drunk and dressed in soiled attire.

John Nicholson
But I'm the Airedale bard!!!

Constable
You're permanently *barred*.

(*He indicates Shakespeare's bust.*)

I think it was your pal here who called the guard.

John Nicholson

(*being marched off*)

I'm going to be a bust from Chantrey's yard.

Constable
You're going to spend the night in Bow Street gaol
and sleep off the effects of all that ale.

(The Constable puts him in the cell and slams the door.
The door reopens and John Nicholson's head appears.)

John Nicholson
I'll be in marble when all of you are dust.
Tonight I may be busted, tomorrow I'm a bust.

(The prison door slams.
We hear John Nicholson singing drunkenly behind the
cell door.
Muse 1/Opera-goer removes her shawl and, becoming
Martha, folds the shawl into the shape of her dead baby.
The prison door opens. John Nicholson runs with the
bust back to Bradford and meets Muse 1/Martha carrying
her own dreadful bundle.)

Martha stays silent.

John Nicholson
Martha, Martha, the poems I've written
may start in Bradford but they'll conquer Britain.
I went into the Abbey and saw all the great,
the bards in marble with the heads of state.
I heard their spirits whisper, yea, oh, yea,
you'll be here with us, John Nicholson, one day.

(He notices that Martha is carrying something.)

What's that, our Martha, got a gift for me?

Martha
Yes, summat to inspire your poetry.

John Nicholson
I went to Francis Chantrey's famous sculpture yard

and found the genius who'll carve the Airedale bard;
a genius of the chisel (and a Sheffield lad!),
the greatest bust-creator Europe's ever had.
I hear his chisels tapping. It's a sound that draws
me onwards to posterity's applause.
I hear his chisel like a roll of drums
saying, O Fame, prepare! A new bard comes!

But to be going on with, Martha, see
look what I've brought from London.

Martha

What's that?

John Nicholson

Me!

I'll soon be famous, Martha, almost there;
they'll know me by the Thames as by the Aire.
You and the bairns are going to be that proud.

(*He looks more closely at the bundle in Martha's hands.*)

What's that, love?

Martha
Your baby in her shroud!

(*He drops the plaster bust of himself and hears it smash.
The breaking of the bust vies with Martha's news for his
full awareness and attention.*)

While you were pursuing your poetic fame,
I saw her spirit leave its feeble frame.
You've gained a plaster likeness, lost a wain,
who died while you were drunk at Drury Lane.
Her tiny corpse will rot a little faster
than that daft mug you've brought. She isn't plaster,
though she's as cold as marble, and as white.

She was warm flesh and blood till t'other night.
Call your Francis Chantrey, maybe – maybe
he can knock you up a marble baby.
I sometimes think that you'd prefer
a marble likeness to the living her.
You wouldn't need to work to earn a crust
to feed a never-hungry marble bust.
Nay, flesh with all its hungers can't compete
with marble busts. Busts don't have to eat.
Isn't it sad, my lass, tha didn't last to
plant a kiss on Daddy cast in plaster?
Well, John Nicholson, your fame has come too late
for little Martha. Martha couldn't wait.
Here's your daughter, Martha, dead and gone.

What can she ever be? A poem by Nicholson?

(*There is a long silence from John Nicholson.*)

John Nicholson

She will. The least a poet can do 's
commit her memory to the caring Muse.

(*He recites:*)

'ODE ON THE DEATH OF THE POET'S CHILD

A solemn scene was here!
Absorb'd in anguish wild,
Weeping upon the bier
Of his departed child,
The father stood – parental grief was there –
He kiss'd the corpse – a prey to sad despair.

O Death! O cruel Death!
In fearful garb array'd
How could'st thou snatch the breath
Of this sweet babe, here laid?
See, see thy victim! On her cold pale face,

A smile yet dwells, though clasp'd in thy embrace.

Clos'd are those sparkling eyes:
Fled is my baby's bloom;
Her cherub form now lies
Enshrouded for the tomb.

Martha is gone – has breath'd her last – her thread
Of life is spun – is snapp'd – the babe is dead.
Angels! take her soul above,
And, as you bear her through the sky,

Sing a seraph's song of love,
A song of heav'nly harmony.
Now let celestial music sound,
Strike, strike the lyre! Ye heav'nly choir!
Angelic music breathe around!'

Martha

Can't you do better for your child than that?
That's for the connoisseur in silk cravat.
That's for your Lords and Ladies, men of letters.
That's not for your bairn but for your betters.
You and them Muses! Just what are they like?
Do they give you this lyre you always strike?
How come I've never seen them Muses coming
and never heard this lyre you're always strumming?

'A smile yet dwells', 'A smile yet dwells', you write.
When did you see her smiling, the poor mite?
'A smile yet dwells'. How can you say she smiled?
You never even looked at your dead child.
Why not look at the child, or don't you choose
to break your rapturous gaze up to the Muse?
Did she dictate 'Closed are her sparkling eyes',
when yours were raised in rapture to the skies?
If you'd looked at your dead child and looked no higher,
you'd have spoken from the heart and ditched your lyre.

41

We've got six more children. Shall I let them die,
so you can raise your bardic eyes up to the sky,
and call on your childless Muses to assist
you write six elegies, then go get pissed?
How many children do we have to lose
before you find a way to t'proper Muse?
Can't you see one loyal, breathing woman
beats all the Muses that you always summon?

Never mind the man in the silk cravat.
I want a poem for me, John, us. You owe us that.

John Nicholson
Martha, the language that I use to speak to thee
flounders in the depths of poesy.
The words wool-sorters and their fellows use is
frowned on by the Goddess Fame and Muses.

Martha
Have you asked them lately? They might not agree.
And even if they don't, it's up to you. You're free.

(*Enter Muses.*)

Muses 1, 2 and 3
John Nicholson,

Muse 2
        to your profoundest shame,
you've chucked away your voice to follow fame.

Martha
You who wear the sorter's chequered brat
cater only for the crinoline,

Muse 3
        the cassock,

Muse 2

the cravat.

Martha
I see some Lord with silk scarf round his throat,
reading the poem for Martha that you wrote.

Muse 3
And allowing a feeling teardrop to be shed
over the touching verses he's just read.

Muse 2
Go to such gentlemen and touch your cap,
they'll give you a few coppers for that crap.

(*In the Hall of Fame/Opera, five* **Gentlemen** *open the
poetical works of John Nicholson and read out the title of
his poem.*)

Gentleman 1
'ODE ON THE DEATH OF THE POET'S CHILD.
By John Nicholson.'

Gentleman 2
'ODE ON THE DEATH OF THE POET'S CHILD.
By John Nicholson.'

Gentleman 3
'ODE ON THE DEATH OF THE POET'S CHILD.
By John Nicholson.'

Gentleman 4
'ODE ON THE DEATH OF THE POET'S CHILD.
By John Nicholson.'

Gentleman 5
'ODE ON THE DEATH OF THE POET'S CHILD.
By John Nicholson.'

(All the books are closed together.
John Nicholson walks over to Nicholson's Rock.
From the Hall of Fame, the Gentlemen change back to
Wool-sorters except for Gentleman 5/The Patron.
As they step off the carpet, we hear the clogs walking in
the rhythm of the Funeral March.)

Martha
When the angels call my lass to her last home,
she should go beneath the earth in this great tome.

(Muse 3 opens the great tome carried by Muse 2, and Muse
1/Martha places the dead baby into the vast volume.)

Muse 1/Martha
Take the poet's child and take her off in
Literature, your little lass's coffin.

(The procession gathers up the great tome and deposits it
in the skip.
The Muses, moving in the same rhythm as the Funeral
March, glide along the Aire away from the scene.)

The Patron
(quoting the poem)

'Now let celestial music sound,
Strike, strike the lyre! Ye heav'nly choir!
Angelic music breathe around!'

Wool-sorters and Muses
CHINK!

(John Nicholson is alone at Nicholson's Rock.)

John Nicholson

Little Martha's underneath a stone
carved with her name, as I have carved my own.
But she'll live until your day. Although she's dead,
she's become a poem that all of you have read.

O Muses –

Muse 1

For little Martha's sake and in her name,
serve the factory cause.

Muse 3

Forget your fame.

Muse 2

Use whatever you possess of poet's skills
to sing the plight of children in the mills.

(*The Muses draw John Nicholson towards the island of
plush where* **Richard Oastler**/*Wool-sorter 2 is.*
*Nicholson knocks on the door. The Muses' clogs make
the sound of knocking. Oastler answers the knock.*)

John Nicholson

The poet of the Aire and Ilkley Moor 's
here to help you, Mr Oastler, with your cause.

Richard Oastler

We can't pay you like other patrons can.

John Nicholson

I don't want money, sir, I'm a different man.
I want to serve the children. The Airedale lyre
's no longer twanged for drink or servile hire.
I want to help you change our mills' conditions.
I've set aside all other bard's ambitions.

Richard Oastler
I'm pleased to hear Fame's wrong in her report
of you as boozing bard who's bribed and bought.

John Nicholson
No longer, Mr Oastler, sir, no longer.
Adversity has made my purpose stronger.

Richard Oastler
Then use what's left of your poetic powers
to tell of children working sixteen hours
and often more, the whole time on their feet.

John Nicholson
My children work there too, we have to eat.

Richard Oastler
They fall asleep, get beaten if they nod.
Show these conditions, an offence to God,
are no better than the way we treat the Blacks.
A poet could put some fire in my attacks.
Show the world how Yorkshire's tiny slaves
go, as your own children might, to early graves.

John Nicholson
'THE FACTORY CHILD.
By John Nicholson.'

(*The Wool-sorters join John Nicholson and Richard Oastler in a 'political rally'.*)

Wool-sorters
'THE FACTORY CHILD.
By John Nicholson.'

Muse 1
'THE FACTORY CHILD'.

Muse 3
'By John Nicholson.'

John Nicholson
'Come join with me, give eloquence a tongue,
Unite with mercy to protect the young:

Talk of reform! then with the young begin,
Since negro slavery is proclaim'd a sin
By England's voice, pray let us look at home,
Nor send *our* youth by thousands to the tomb!'

Richard Oastler
'Worn out with cruel hardships, fierce disease
Feed on their vitals – death is a release.
The graves close on them – not a tear is shed,
And thousands thus are number'd with the dead.
Oh,'

John Nicholson
'England,'

Richard Oastler
'let this awful truth strike home,
Thy pride hath sent its millions to the tomb!
Send if thou wilt thy gifts beyond the sea,
But first resolve that'

John Nicholson
'BRITONS SHALL BE FREE!!!

Ye Bards of greater powers, take up the theme,
The Factory-Girl from Slavery redeem:

Strike your wild lyres, and let the inspired page
Plead for the Factory Child of tender age;
Plead till you see all injuries redrest;'

Richard Oastler
'Plead till you see the infant sufferers blest.'

John Nicholson
In true sobriety, I wrote this poem that reviled
all those who had enslaved the Yorkshire child.
My eyes stayed focused here. I didn't drink.
I finally forswore its fatal lure.

(*Another patron,* **Edward Baines/Wool-sorter 1**, *emerges from the island of red plush. He chinks coins in his open palm.*)

Edward Baines
                Chink! Chink!
Chink! Chink! Chink! Chink! Chink!
Twenty guineas (Chink!) if you rewrite
your version of the factory children's plight.
Is it that dreadful (Chink!), their true condition?
Couldn't you change your mind for a commission?
Chink! Chink! Chink! Twenty guineas for your
                                  pains.

John Nicholson
Perhaps I did exaggerate. Thank you, Mr Baines.

(*He takes the money.*)

> 'THE FACTORY CHILD'S MOTHER
> or, The Voice of True Humanity.
> A Poem by John Nicholson.
> Leeds 1832.'

Wool-sorters
'THE FACTORY CHILD'S MOTHER.
By John Nicholson.'

John Nicholson

(*declaiming the poem from the middle stepping stone*)

' 'Tis true that . . .'

Edward Baines
'agitation . . .'

John Nicholson

'. . . is come forth
Under the shape of mercy in the north;
But for that mercy never, never heed;
Can pomp and fulsome noise the hungry feed?
Do these subscribe to ease the sinking mind?
NO! these are air, and empty as the wind.
'Tis'

Edward Baines
'trade and wages'

John Nicholson
'make the cottage blest,
Then give us'

Wool-sorter 1
'commerce,'

John Nicholson

'throw to air the rest.
The man of feeling and the man of sense
Must calculate on shillings, pounds, and pence . . .
He dreads the parish, ever shuns its aid,

49

His children all must work, or how can debts be paid?

The father of the factory child can feel,
Wants not their aid, for few have hearts of steel;
They know their wants, their feelings do not sleep,
They know 'tis labour must their offspring keep.

The three great towns of Yorkshire now
In agitation meet,
To make the factory masters bow
In dust beneath their feet.

The helpless children laugh and sing
As often as they weep:
They know that trade's the safest wing,
And there they wish to keep.

Say not the masters all are knaves,
For that can ne'er be true:
They to anxieties are slaves,
And have enough to do.

Then why oppress the nation's stay,
Or tarnish their good name?
If you that talk were in their shoes
Would you not act the same?'

Edward Baines
'The spell is broke, the factory children know;
These see they wanted honour from their woe,
They now expect they to the mills are sent,
They must be houseless when there is no rent,
And greater joys have they each ended day
Than those who idle all their time away –
A glorious supper, and soft rest in bed,
Their labour not so hard as has been said;
Send them to any place, each factory child would fain
Return with joy to factories again.

Then why this fuss – why factory masters blame,
For fleeting honour, for an empty name?
Have eight around your table all to feed,
Then would you know what parents feel indeed . . .'

(*John Nicholson goes to Eldwick Rocks.*)

John Nicholson

O Muses, why have you left me so alone,
Staring at my name carved on this stone,
the sepulchre of one who's still alive?
How can I make my slipping fame survive?

O Muses!

(*He hears the Muses, or seems to hear them.*)

What's that?
                    Go back where you belong!
Where you first improvised a drinking song . . .

And yes? Go on!

(*The Muses turn away.*)

Before time (and drinking) spoils
those bardic features, get them done in oils . . .

I will. I will. And I know just the feller,
I drink with him in Bradford, William Geller.
Sssh! I think the Muses have some more to say.
No, I was mistaken, they've gone away.
Perhaps to inspire the painter who'll immortalize
the fire of inspiration in these eyes,
I'll have my portrait done, and then I'll show it,
to prove I've really made it as a poet,
at every inn I stop at on the way,
to show the doubters I'm a legend in my day.

(*He enters the pub. The Wool-sorters there, who have been singing, stop suddenly.*)

Come on, lads, let's sing my drinking song!

Wool-sorter 5
Piss off, Nicholson, you don't belong.

Wool-sorter 2
You couldn't compose a song now if you tried.

Wool-sorter 3
You've long crossed over to the other side.

Wool-sorter 4
We've got a poet who understands our needs.
Let me introduce the young James Ross from Leeds.

(**James Ross**/*Wool-sorter 3 climbs on to the pub table and declaims his poem attacking John Nicholson.*)

James Ross
'THE FACTORY CHILD'S FATHER'S REPLY
TO THE FACTORY CHILD'S MOTHER.
By James Ross.

One book he wrote and it he named
the Factory Infant's Mother.
Of which I hope he'll be ashamed
and never write another.'

(*The Wool-sorters repeat the words as a song.*
James Ross declaims his poem to the Wool-sorters.)

'Where, then, are the blessings this system creates?
In England? – or are they in some foreign states?
I kindly request Mother JOHN to look round,
And show to the world where such comforts are found.

Let her rise from her bed in a morning at five.

And witness poor children, like bees from a hive,
Dart in swarms through the streets at the bell's noisy
call,
Although hail, rain, or snow, in torrents may fall –
Sure her heart would then melt, t'were not harden'd
by gold,
To see such poor innocents pierc'd with the cold.

Declare ye that children shall never more be
Us'd worse than the Blacks whom you wish to set
free;
A sketch I could draw that would redden with shame
The cheek of each Briton, if worthy that name;

But when this rhyming money he had drunk,
And he to poverty again was sunk,
He straight resolv'd to get a few more gills,
By writing for the masters of the mills.

I need not spend much time, howe'er, to shew
Thy actions base, and cowardly, and low.
For all thy words and ways do make it plain
Thou only zealous art for SORDID GAIN.'

John Nicholson
James Ross! James Ross! No one knows your name.
You'll never have a bust in the Hall of Fame.
James Ross! James Ross! No one knows that feller.
He'll never get his portrait done by William Geller.

(*He begins to unroll his portrait.*)

Regard this marvel that I now unveil,
the bard who quaffed of Hippocrene.

Wool-sorters
And too much ale!

53

John Nicholson
This is 'The Poet Addressing Muses' pose.

Wool-sorter 1
More like 'Poet with Bit of Shit Beneath His Nose'.

Wool-sorter 2
Or 'Poet Wool-sorter Working with a Fleece
Who Can't Bear the Smell of Sheep Shit and Sheep
                                    Grease'.

Wool-sorter 1
. You once wrote us songs that still get sung,
until you learned to speak the sponsor's tongue.

Wool-sorter 4
One sponsor liked you drunk, one liked you dry.
You can't please both and only you would try.

Wool-sorter 2
You praised temperance as easily as beer
as long as it seemed to serve your poet's career.

Wool-sorter 3
As long as patrons dipped into their purses,
you'd write one thing and then reverse your verses.

Wool-sorter 5
You wrote *for* the Factory Acts you wrote against,
provided that your poems were recompensed.

Wool-sorter 3
You wrote that children were exploited, then for pay
you saw the same facts the exploiter's way.

(*Wool-sorter 2 takes the picture from John Nicholson.*)

Wool-sorter 2
The Poet Addressing Muses. You
make a truer picture torn in two!

(*Woolsorter 2 tears the portrait in half.*
The Wool-sorters stamp on the picture and dance across
the stepping stones. They crowd on to the carpeted island
of plush.
John Nicholson gathers up the three vast volumes of
Literature and carries them precariously to the centre
stepping stone. He sways and tries to keep his balance.)

Wool-sorter 4
That's the best pose yet: swaying in between
two banks of a river,

Wool-sorter 3/James Ross
where you've always been.

John Nicholson
My painting's torn in two, my bust's in pieces.
The Aire seems like a mass of heaving fleeces –
all those I ever fingered as a sorter.
Something's dragging me into the water.
I feel some awful power pull
my body into depths of greasy wool.

(*He falls into the river.*)

O Muses, those tomes you gave me weigh me down.
They're dragging me under and I'm going to drown.

Unless, unless, unless there's anybody here
who remembers my poetry, my head will disappear.

A poem. A few lines even. One!
One quotation from John Nicholson.

Only your memories can save

the Airedale poet from his watery grave.

(*The Wool-sorters hum the tune to the drinking song.*)

'Airedale in Ancient Times' by John Nicholson?

(*When no one responds, Wool-sorter 3/James Ross drops a volume from The Patron's library into the river.*)

'The Vale of Ilkley' by John Nicholson?

(*When no one responds, Wool-sorter 3/James Ross drops a volume from The Patron's library into the river.*)

'The Beauties of Bingley' by John Nicholson?

(*When no one responds, Wool-sorter 3/James Ross drops a volume from The Patron's library into the river.*)

'The Commerce of Bradford' by John Nicholson?

(*When no one responds, Wool-sorter 3/James Ross drops a volume from The Patron's library into the river.*)

'The Siege of Bradford' by John Nicholson?

(*When no one responds, Wool-sorter 3/James Ross drops a volume from The Patron's library into the river.*)
[*If anyone should happen to respond, John Nicholson will say:*

Thank you, Sir [Madam]. But at this late juncture your quote is like a lifebelt with a puncture.]

(*The Wool-sorters stop their humming.*)

Nothing! Nothing! Nothing! Not one quote
to help the Airedale bard to keep afloat.

Is there not a ripple left of my renown?
Are you going to sit there and let me drown?

O Muses, come and lend me all your power.

(*Enter the Muses as at the beginning, but this time singing the Mary song. John Nicholson kneels in the 'Poet Addressing Muses' pose.*)

O Muses, come and lend me all your power.

Muse 2
Sorry, John,

Muse 3
Time's up.

Muse 1
You've had your hour.

(*The Muses push John Nicholson down into the river.*)

Blackout.

Everlasting Spring (extract*)

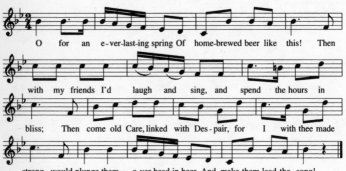

O for an e-ver-last-ing spring Of home-brewed beer like this! Then
with my friends I'd laugh and sing, and spend the hours in
bliss; Then come old Care, linked with Des-pair, for I with thee made
strong, would plunge them o-ver-head in beer, And make them lead the song!

*see p. 17

Then My Plaid (extract*)

rall.

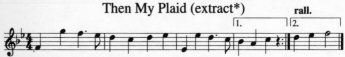

Then my plaid I will throw o'er me, Sing of Ma-ry on the way;
Though great dan-gers lie be - fore me, Yet I can-not, will not stay.

*see p. 19

The Factory Infant (extract*)

One book he wrote and it he named The Fac - to-ry In - fant's Mo-ther
Of which I hope he'll be a-shamed and ne - ver write a - no-ther.

*see p. 52

The Poacher's Song (extract*)

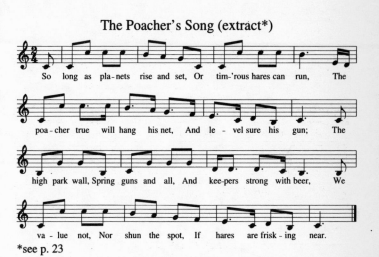

So long as pla-nets rise and set, Or tim-'rous hares can run, The
poa-cher true will hang his net, And le-vel sure his gun; The
high park wall, Spring guns and all, And kee-pers strong with beer, We
va-lue not, Nor shun the spot, If hares are frisk-ing near.

*see p. 23

The Disappearing Porter! (extract*)

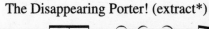

The hard-work-ing York-shire wool-sor-ter _ Has here but lit-tle to stay: _ For
life's like the froth on that por-ter, _ And quick-ly doth va-nish a-way.

*see p. 17

THE KAISERS OF
CARNUNTUM

The Kaisers of Carnuntum was first performed on 2 June 1995 in the Roman amphitheatre of Petronell/Carnuntum, Austria with the following company:

Orpheus Jaro Frank
Marcus Aurelius Conrad Nelson
Commodus Barrie Rutter
Julius Bollux Lawrence Evans
Faustina Sian Thomas

with students of the Vienna Music School and the Wiener Musikgymnasiums and the combined choirs of: Collegium Vocale Marchfeld (Conductor: Georg Kugi); Gesangverein Moosbrunn (Conductor: Roman Staller); Concordia Chorus Comaromium, the Hungarian Choir of Komarno, Slovakia (Conductor: Istvan Stubenidek). The choirs were coordinated and conducted by Georg Kugi. Bläsergruppen der Region Bruck am Leitha were under the direction of Herbert Nemeth.

Musicians Michael Garcia, Tim Wright
Cellists Alexander Kovalenko, Wolfgang Buxbaum, Toshi Yanakida, Michael Rachlin

Director Tony Harrison
Music Richard Blackford
Designer Jocelyn Herbert
Assistant to the Designer Polly Richards
Producer/Art Carnuntum Piero Bordin
Stage Management and Technical Direction Fraser
Marlow and Martin Walitza
Light Philip Harnoncourt
Sound Glenn Keiles
Scenery Building Oliver Aignier, Franz Himmelbauer,
Franco Kappl, Heinz Roderic Reisinger, Johannes
Stattman, Wolfgang Stückler
Choreography Lawrence Evans

Orpheus (Jaro Frank)

The Roman amphitheatre, Petronell/Carnuntum, Austria.
The amphitheatre has four tribunes of modern seating.
Behind each is a scaffolding 'border tower' of the kind
recently familiar to this part of the world. In the centre is a
map of the world as conquered by the Romans; in the very
centre of this, in Rome, is the Colosseum. Under each
tribune, covered with Roman gladiatorial mosaics, are
cages which contain lions and a tiger.

Lights down.
   For some moments in the darkness we hear the growling
of animals, the roaring of lions. It crescendos, gets a little
frightening . . .
   Spotlight on **Orpheus** *with lyre. He puts his finger to his*
lips and ssshhhs the crowd. Then he begins to play the lyre
and as he does so the roaring and growling grow a little
less.
   He plays to the crated and caged animals, and they
become quiet.
   He stands centre over the model of the Colosseum and
plays a kind of threnody for all slaughtered beasts.
   He puts his finger to his lips and ssshhhs the crowd,
then points with it to the Watchtower to reveal **Marcus**
Aurelius, *who is surveying what was once Carnuntum, the*
Roman frontier town. The emperor gazes at the Danube
and reflects, singing first a text from Meditations *in*
ancient Greek.

Marcus Aurelius

'παντα τα μεν του σωματος ποταμος, τα δε ψυχης
ονειρος και τυφως'.

(Book ii. 17)

'η γαρ ουσια οιον ποταμος εν διηεκει ρυσει'

(Book v. 23)

'ποταμος τις εκ των γινομενων και ρευμα βιαιον ο
αιων.'

(Book iv. 43)

(*A* **Chorus of Women**, *representing the flow of time and
the Danube, sing the same text translated into various
languages of Europe. Then Marcus Aurelius sings in
English:*)

Carnuntum, once here all around,
is now nowhere to be found
except in stones dug from the ground.

Carnuntum's ruin's no surprise.
These edifices I saw rise
were already ruins in my eyes.

The empires of the past all fell,
witness pathetic Petronell,
once my imperial citadel,

and recenter imperial powers
with barbed wire, checkpoints and watchtowers,
fell in ruins just like ours.

Every empire, Reich and Raj,
no matter how well armed or large,
is but a moment's brief mirage.

All the emperors old and new,
Caesar, Stalin, Ceausescu,
transients all passing through.

What are they now? Mere tales to tell
or immortalized as a hotel
like Carnuntum's Marc Aurel.

Time's vast Danube bears away
men and empires, and today
the same flux sounds in motorway.

(*Enhanced traffic flow from motorway as part of flow-music.*)

Listen, open borders, constant flux
of Viennese and Slovak trucks,
light after light, *lux* after *lux.*

Listen, open borders, no empires
to block the free flow of the tyres,
the hum of truth along the wires.

Welcome this ghost in clean white suit,
whose revered repute
is most removed from man as brute.

And time has made the white suit cleaner,
the philosophic soul serener,
with no bloodstains from the arena.

Pure philosophy has been my guide
when four of my five children died
and left but one son at my side,

that little boy who sat at my right,
watching men and wild beasts fight,
Here in this ruined Roman site.

And he'd whisper, 'Daddy, Daddy!'
flexing his then quite little body.
'Can I come with you to kill Quadi.

And kill Marcomanni like you do?'
I'd come to Carnuntum to subdue
those barbarians who now are you.

You Rome subdued, indeed despised
as barbarian hordes, I'm now surprised
to find, well, almost civilized.

Witness these melodic lutes
played by Orpheuses in suits
to move the stones and tame the brutes.

Rome had to be an Hercules
to turn barbarians like these
into cultivated Viennese.

(*The cellos play 'civilized' music.*
Marcus Aurelius is lost in reflective Stoic thought.
Suddenly there are sirens, machine-gun fire, sweeping
searchlights and the sound of a searching helicopter as if
someone unauthorized is crossing a border. A searchlight
picks up the figure of **Commodus**, *who is running carrying*
a roadsign with a picture depicting the amphitheatre and
two masks. It says on it AMPHITHEATRE II. *The sign has*
been rudely ripped from the roadside.

Breathless and angry, Commodus hollers in indignation:)

Commodus
Barred from <u>my</u> own empire, barred, barred
like a barbarian by the border guard.

(*He recovers breath and becomes more graciously inquisitive.*)

Is this Carnuntum? Thumbs up or thumbs down!
And is this the arena of that ruined Roman town?

(*He waits for an answer.*)

It is! It is! Is it really true
that this is Carnuntum Amphitheatre II?

I have something to tell you. But first
in Marcomannisch: *Ich habe Durst.*

Although I was here when I was very young,
I still have some smatterings of your barbarian
                tongue.

Ich habe Durst. Come now, which of you
can serve me up a strong barbarian brew?

(*A bottle of* Römerquelle Heilwasser *is thrown into the
arena.*

    *Commodus rushes towards the bottle eagerly and, being
so in need of a drink, is almost half-way through it before
he realizes it's only water. He looks at the label
contemptuously.*)

Though not averse to the people's fervent *Heil*
Heilwasser is not this emperor's style.
My father up his tower's the sort of feller
you should serve up this fizzy *Römerquelle.*
You'd never find Marcus pissed in the arena
on Petronell/Carnuntum *Grüner Veltliner.*

(*He holds up* Römerquelle *bottle.*)

All right, hands up anyone who thinks
that this *Wasser*'s what a Roman soldier drinks.
Don't imagine for a minute your average Roman
                squaddy
quaffed fizzy drinks to get fired up and go out and
                kill Quadi.
The last thing that you want with barbarian
                marauders
like the Marcomanni causing havoc on your borders,
and the Quadi also causing border troubles,
is a ghastly gassy drink with fucking bubbles.
When a Roman soldier went out to face the slaughter,
he didn't get fired up with 'healthy' fizzy water.
No, he wanted wine. And so do I.
Give me a bottle, someone. I'm so dry.
Who's going to be kind. Have we no wine?

(*A bottle of* Dreikaiserwein *is thrown from Tribune 3.*)

> A local white? That'll do me fine.
> And it says 'Kaiserwein', that's more like,
> a little local tribute to the Roman Reich.
> 'Kaiserwein'! I'm touched my status still can earn
> my own special vintage. *Danke schön!*

(*He drinks a little and approves. As he drinks, gargantuan glugs come from the speakers.*)

> Good that Carnuntum has found a special way
> of commemorating Commodus with his own *cuvée.*

> I expect you've put up statues, one or two,
> to commemorate my presence here in 172
> but for a start this special wine will do.

(*He drinks – gargantuan glugs – and feels better.*)

> You know, I must confess, I did have fears
> I might have been forgotten after all these years.
> How many is it now? Let me see . . .

(*counts*)

> One thousand, eight hundred and twenty-three!
> My father's always saying, once a man is rotten,
> it's not long before he's totally forgotten.

(*He waves the bottle at Marcus Aurelius, superior on his tower.*)

> I know it's only wine, but see how
> I'm still remembered on the barbarian Donau.

Marcus Aurelius
It does say *Drei*kaiserwein, not *Ein.*

Commodus
We'll put your head on the water, me on the wine!

(*He notices the head of Marcus Aurelius on the label.*)

Well, they've gone and put the father with the son.
His head on a bottle's not the most auspicious one.
Daddy's a killjoy, a conqueror of Germans,
less into piss-ups than preaching Stoic sermons.
He's too doom-laden an endorser, Dad's
not the most inspiring of Dionysian ads.
His head's a hindrance, won't help sales at all –
who'd stamp a condom with the face of Pope John
                                              Paul?
Of all the Kaisers you could have chosen he's the
                                              worst,
like having Gandhi to endorse a *Blut-* or
                                      Zungenwurst.

All this can be amended. I don't want to boast
but I'm the boozer who would suit a bottle most.
For now let's overlook it. *Prost!*
Welcome back Carnuntum's more glorious ghost.

(*He drinks, finishing the wine with a flourish.*)

Ave, Carnuntum, that has had the grace
to embellish this bottle with my imperial face.

(*He finishes off the dregs.*)

That's better! Now let's see
if the artist's likeness really looks like me.

(*He studies the label.*)

Here, just a minute. This one isn't me.
So who's the other Kaiser of the three?
Septimius Severus. Septimius. Septimius.
He was a bastard and probably abstemious!
Thank goodness you were wise to choose a
proper intemperate, unrepentant boozer
like me. COMMODUS PISSISSIMUS! What!

I thought this would be me here, and it's not.
DIO-fucking-CLETIAN, DI-
O Carnuntum, I think I'm going to cry,
you could be so cruel thus to pass me by.

(*He stares at the bottle.*)

Marcus Aurelius, 161–80 AD.
But who came in 180? Me! Me! Me!
It jumps from 180 to 193
to *Septimius*. They've left out ME.
Who was the emperor? I ask you, who
ruled from 180 to 192?

If I find that you don't know
there might be some troublesome *Ta en Karnounto*!

And to think I thought this former frontier post
was trying to be gracious to its greatest ghost.
I was touched that you'd planned as a little surprise a
special welcome drink for Carnuntum's favourite
                                                Kaiser.
And now I find I don't even rate a mention
on the *vino* of these Marcomanni *Untermenschen*.
The emperor's reception being somewhat rude
's put Commodus in a less accommodating mood.
You'd better show this emperor imperial respect –
and make sure you put his bonce on a bottle of good
                                                Sekt.
A gold medallion head with this imperial profile
those who know what's good for them will learn to
                                                Heil.
And make it not *Sehr Trocken* but absolutely BRUT.
Only the brutest of the brut will suit.
Then maybe I won't be brutish or go berserk
and bludgeon for his blunder this Herr Josef Köck.
I mean, I'm Hercules incarnate. I was made divine
and I don't get my kisser on Carnuntum's crappy wine!

(*then reflectively sinister*)

> I think that I might have to do a little work
> on the historical perspectives of Herr Josef Kock!

(*sulkily*)

> I've a good mind to leave and let my father speak
> to you for hours in ancient bloody Greek.
> His gloomy Stoic *contemptus mundi*
> makes every day he lives seem like a Sunday.
> I'll leave you to his mercies, then you'll know,
> after a few hours of *Ta en Karnounto*,
> which of your two Kaisers will give you the most fun,
> the philosopher father or the gladiator son.
>
> I'll see that proper punishments get meted
> if disrespect of that sort gets repeated,
> but I'll not let that serious slight
> spoil the fun I've planned for you tonight,
> and I assume you are assembled here because
> you're fully aware what this amphitheatre was,
> and that you followed this same sign as I did
> to find a sort of place where I presided,
> and so we should honour the designer whose design
> deserves your grateful thanks, and now gets mine.
> Out of my munificence I'd like to reward
> the gentleman who designed this helpful noticeboard,
> without whose help I would've never found my way
> among the miserable ruins Carnuntum is today.
> I have a generous Commodian urge to crown
> the man whose signpost led me through your town.
> Is the sign-designer here?

(**Sign-designer** *is, in the audience. He stands.*)

> Come this way, sir,
> I have a Commodian medal I should like to confer.
> Yes, sir, this way, let him past. Don't be afraid,

73

I want to bestow on you an imperial accolade.

(*Sign-designer makes his way into the arena and towards
Commodus, crossing a map of the world.
Commodus speaks to him, like a quiz-show host:*)

Tell everyone your name. *Wie heissen Sie?*
(as we said in Marcomannisch in 172 AD.)

Sign-designer
Ich heisse Franz.

Commodus
Franz, *Danke schon*
(that's all the Marcomannisch I could ever learn!).
You did your Roman emperor a very good turn.
You could say you're responsible for my return.
This sign that you (and *Römerquelle*) got erected
helped to get this emperor resurrected.
Marcomanni, Quadi, give Franz a big round,
without whose help I never would have found
my way back to Carnuntum and come here,
where as a boy I yearned to don my gladiator gear.

And this is Carnuntum, yes, it's really true,
that this is Carnuntum's Amphitheatre II.
And I found my way back because of you . . .
You brought me back, and as a little token
of my gratitude . . .

(*savagely*)

you get your brain-box broken!

(*Commodus kills the Sign-designer with one bloody blow
of the signpost. Cello music cuts off and the released,
agonized ghosts of beasts and men rise from the re-
blooded amphitheatre. The sounds of the ghosts of the*

74

Colosseum rise from the centre and mushroom out to all
four loudspeakers.)

Since I arrived I've been dying to bestow
on this poor bugger one death-dealing blow.
You get off, you Vindobona wets,
Fuck off to Vienna with your Haydn string quartets.

The idiot deserved to die. He led you all astray
and deceived you into thinking you were here to
watch a play.

(He indicates the comic and tragic masks on the roadsign.)

Look here! Look here! Tragedy and Comedy!
Well, you'll get nothing funny out of me.

It's good to smell fresh gore, and we've just begun.
This Sign-designer's only victim number one.
Why did I kill this fool? I'll tell you why.
Because this is a place for watching people die.
So far as I know, there has never been a
poetic play performed in this arena.
and yet this sign says it was. Oh why
this modern squeamish need to Disneyfy
this space that was made for men and beasts to die?
This space wasn't built for tragic plays,
for your Sarah Bernhardts and your Lord Oliviers.

(And I'll kill the first barbarian who mutters
that neither was it built to star your Barrie Rutters.)

Not for your *Cosis* or your sopranos trilling,
but built for just one purpose: killing, killing, killing!

I, by shedding this fresh blood, hereby
reconsecrate this place as one where creatures die.
As the great emperor/gladiator, I hereby restore
this Roman ruin to its real function: GORE!

And for Carnuntum's delectation I revive
for you, deprived of death in 1995,
the thrills we had when this place used to thrive.

(*He tears off the mosaic covering of the cages, revealing
lions and a tiger.*)

This is again a place of death and my soul salutes
the bravery of men (like me) who battled with fierce
brutes.
Make sure when you replace this idiot's sign
it has a roaring lion's head on, along with mine.
This miserable man (may he never rest in peace)
has got his Rome a bit mixed up with Greece.
It was Greeks who played around in masks like
these,
spouting their Aeschylus and Sophocles.

We got rid of the verbiage and hacked
our villains and our beasts in actual fact.
Where Greek tragic choruses bewailed their woes
became for Rome a place where real blood flows.
When the Greeks did death it was all pretend;
here beasts and bastards come to a real end.
And in all those theatres where the Greeks had been,
where Electra and Medea played the scene,
we put a bloodguard round, so front-row priests
didn't get splattered by the blood of beasts.
(You on the front row, by the way, better be alert
when I start clubbing lions, blood is bound to spurt.
You should have brought a brolly or a mac,
the blood will fly now Commodus is back.)

Greek bloodshed was all *ficta*, ours is *facta*;
we Romans really kill our tragic actor.

(*Musical flourish. Commodus indicates Orpheus.*)

The Greeks would have this fool torn apart offstage

and get some messenger to tell of the lions' roar and
rage.
Well, I'm a Roman and he's really going in
with these lions, who'll divest him of his skin.
He's stepped off that museum wall just up the road,
playing music to the animals and mosaically bravoed.
Calming beasts with music! Well, let's see
how this pretender fares against reality.

Art will have to acknowledge that it's truly beaten
when he plays his magic lyre but still gets eaten.
These musicians believe that they're immune
from animal attack if they play the Orpheus tune.
It's all a fairy-tale. No Orphean lute's
ever going to calm these ferocious brutes.
And I don't want any Orphean music taming
these wild animals; I want them enflaming.
I want a rowdy racket that can really reveille 'em,
not some Orphean form of animal Valium.

It would be another very Roman wheeze
to put a philosopher among beasts such as these.
I'd like to put my father in this cage
to see if his *Meditations* could calm the lion's rage.
I'd split my sides laughing, that would be a hoot,
watching philosophy face up to the brute.
I suppose he could always strike the beast a blow
with a rolled-up papyrus of *Ta en Karnounto*.
It would be wonderful to see them eat his words
and shit out that Stoic crap as steaming lion turds.

I've half a mind to leave and let this precious pair
be your chosen champions against the lion and bear –
but on second thoughts it wouldn't be quite fair.
I'm a Hercules and I couldn't guarantee
your safety with anyone but me.
When the chips are down and the fighting starts,

you won't get much protection from the gentler arts.
As far as music goes, I'm personally partial
to something much less smoochy and more martial.
So I've brought along my own more macho band
to reveille Roman ghosts . . .

(*He points to* **Trumpeters** *on the rim of the amphitheatre.*)

and there they stand.
My trumpeters' titanic tones will put you all in touch
with a past that's much more bloody and brilliantly
butch.
These trumpeters of mine that you see now surround
the amphitheatre are about to sound
a raucously reverberant reveille
to bring 50,000 ghosts to join my rally,
the ghosts of the Colosseum who'd sooner shout
bravo
to me the beast-dispatcher than to *Ta en Karnounto.*

Trumpeters, blow to the four quarters
and summon back my slaughterer supporters.
As you lot aren't too vocal, I'll have to summon back
my Commodus-coordinated Colosseum claque.

(*The Trumpeters blow and from the four speakers behind
the audience comes the roar of the 50,000-strong
Colosseum crowd.*
Lights come up on the Colosseum centrepiece.
*As the crowd goes on roaring, Commodus parades
round the world, the map of the Roman Empire, on the
amphitheatre floor. He does a sort of monstrous lap of
honour.*)

It's great to be back after all these years,
buoyed up by the mighty Colosseum cheers.
I think it's time for the emperor to demonstrate
the power that resides in the imperial Roman state.

(*He signals to the Trumpeters to prepare another set of fanfares. To Trumpeters in position 1, east:*)

Blow to the east beyond the Euxine Sea
and call the cohorts here to honour me.

(*The Trumpeters blow a fanfare to the east. After the call we hear marching feet, at first faint, then growing louder and nearer. Commodus, as if marching at their head, starts at the farthest point east and in time to their marching processes to the Colosseum centrepiece.*
  To Trumpeters in position 2, south:)

Blow to the south along the African shores
and bring Aethiopian legions to encourage the
                                      applause.

(*The Trumpeters blow a fanfare to the south. We hear the sound of marching feet, distant at first, then growing louder and nearer. Commodus marches as if at their head from the southernmost part of the Roman Empire map on the amphitheatre floor. When he reaches the Colosseum centrepiece, the marching feet emerge on the amphitheatre rim as soldiers in black riot gear.*
  To Trumpeters in position 3, west:)

Blow to the west and wake the EEC
to send its militias here to honour me.

(*The Trumpeters blow a fanfare to the west. The marching feet begin faint at first, then grow louder and nearer. Commodus marches as if at their head from the westernmost point of the Roman Empire map. When he reaches the Colosseum, the marching feet emerge as soldiers in riot gear.*
  To Trumpeters in position 4, north:)

Now summon the men I feel most sorry for,
those luckless legions who drew the shortest straw

and ended up in Britain, where barbarians abound,
and summon them to close the gap so that we
                surround
the amphitheatre, and let all their clubs be poised to
                clout
any yeller-belly who feels like walking out.

(*The Trumpeters blow to the north. Same routine.*
   *The assembled soldiers in their riot gear now surround
the whole arena, and they drum a rhythm with their clubs
on their shields.*
   *Commodus glories in his restored power. He summons
four* **Guards** *to him and indicates the body of the Sign-
designer.*)

First the boring part, drag this bugger's body off
and hack it into segments for these hungry beasts to
                scoff.
Drag this doomed Disneyfier off and bring him back
hacked into morsels for the lions' midday snack.
I know they'd've preferred him a bit warmer, but
I got so rattled that I had to crack his nut.

(*The body is dragged off to music and maybe a pre-reprise
of 'Unco Trahatur'.*
   *We hear the butcher's block and cleaver noises of a
body being chopped into pieces.*
   *A blood-dripping sack is brought back with an arm
sticking out. Commodus holds it aloft and takes it on a
tour of the arena.*)

I thought at first I'd let you watch his body being
                hacked
to wean you off Greek fiction and on to Roman fact,
but then I thought it better to do things inch by inch,
so that finally you'll thrill to what first made you
                flinch.
I'll re-educate you slowly and by gradual degrees

get you hooked on hacking and slough off Sophocles
to become the fervid, frenzied fans of snuffer
                                        Hercules.

(*The 'tour' ends with Commodus close to Orpheus.*)

And you are going to feed them, you with the lyre, I
                                        mean.
I'm appointing you the *Kommandant* i/c beasts'
                                        canteen.
Feed them these human gobbets. Let the lions crunch
the Sign-designer's remnants as a lightish lion lunch.

Orpheus
I daren't go in the cages. I'd be too afraid.

Commodus
Take your magic lyre with you. Give 'em a serenade,
then they'll grovel at your feet.

(*to audience:*)

                            Little does he know it,
but lions are partial to a nosh of poncy poet.

(*Commodus takes the lyre of Orpheus and on the
Colosseum adopts the stance of a lyre player about to
play, then reverts to using the lyre like a rock guitarist.
Orpheus is led by Guards to cages and Commodus plays
music intended to rouse the fury of lions.*)

I think you may be wondering why I've returned
                                        tonight.
Well apart from the matter of setting records right,
I owe a debt to Carnuntum I'm anxious to requite.
A debt to Carnuntum, I can hear you say.
Yes, to Carnuntum, and it's one that I'll repay.

It was here in this arena that my thirst

for blood and killing was awakened first.
I started here as an eleven-year-old spectator
and graduated to become Rome's greatest gladiator
at the Colosseum, where all the world's roads led,
when the Roman Empire painted the whole world
red.

Thank you, Carnuntum, my illustrious career
started with the beasts that I saw slaughtered here.
Thank you, Carnuntum, from the bottom of my
heart,

for getting my career off to a flying start.
This very spot in Carnuntum set me on the track
of gladiatorial glory, and I never once looked back.

(*He looks into the centre Colosseum and stirs about the
bits of bloody meat, representing the flesh of the many
varieties of beast from all over the Roman Empire
slaughtered by him.*)

These are my conquests. You could feed the Roman
army

if you processed all I've slaughtered into sliced salami.
The animals I've slaughtered in the Colosseum here
could keep the world's McDonald's in burgers for a
year.

The amount of meat in Rome's great arena's
enough to stuff the world on Vindobona-*Wieners*.

But every morsel of this mass of Colosseum meat
is meant to be a symbol of some barbarian defeat.
In caravans of crates from every far-flung corner
of our empire come the tons of fearsome fauna,
to demonstrate before the whole assembled nation
through dominated animals Rome's world
domination.

So when you see a creature, some fierce exotic,
caught

and crated and then, freighted, it's killed for more
than sport.

(*To illustrate his point, he picks up a bleeding piece of
meat, displays it triumphantly to the audience and walks
towards Britannia on the world map.*)

This bear I bashed and slashed came from over here,
Britannia, the most barbarian frontier.

(*He places the meat on the white circle with a bear
silhouette and returns to the Colosseum, where he selects
another, longer piece of meat.*)

This is the skinned tail steak of a crocodile
from Aegyptus, so when the Roman people *Heil*
Commodus, who clubs ten crocs, they know he rules
the Nile.

(*He deposits the meat on the white circle with a crocodile
silhouette, then returns to the central Colosseum and
extracts another lump.*)

These bashed-out Mauretanian dromedary brains
show Roman civilization's reach as much as roads or
drains.

(*He crosses from Africa to Spain.*)

And by this lump of bull I show I reign
Over the western world as far as Spain.

(*He dumps the bull meat on to Spain. He returns to the
Colosseum and takes out another piece of meat.*)

When I gut an aurochs, the cheering Roman folk
know it means Germania's beneath the Roman yoke.

(*He crosses from Germany to Syria.*)

My imperial domination of the East
's shown by these gobbets of their brother beast.

(*He drops the lion meat on the silhouette of the lion in
Syria, goes back to the Colosseum and picks up the
severed necks of two ostriches.*)

> A hundred ostriches in just one morning's session,
> slashed with a sickle in double-quick succession.

(*He waltzes with the ostrich necks and dumps them in
Libya, before returning to the Colosseum and selecting
two lumps of meat.*)

> These still-bleeding bits of bears and boars,
> shipped from Carnuntum from the Marcomannic
> > wars,
> were killed to show our people we had conquered
> > yours.

(*He drops the bloody gobbet on the white circle, then
stands in the centre of the Colosseum and triumphantly
surveys the Roman Empire.
We hear the singing voice of Marcus Aurelius.*)

Marcus Aurelius

'μη, τεκνον, προς αλλο πεφυκαμεν. εγω μεν ου μη
βλαβω συ δε βλαπτη, τεκνον.'

(Book xi. 18)

[trans: No, my child, we were born for something
different. It is not me who's harmed but you, my child.]

(*With the same text as their song, **Women** – representing
the conquered countries – pick up the pieces of meat from
each circle and wrap them in their national flags and begin
to process towards the Colosseum, which they circle,
cradling their butchered children. The subjugated Women
form a circle round the Colosseum facing the audience, to
whom they display their pitiful lumps of meat, as if they
were showing to the world a recently slaughtered child.
They turn and drop the meat in the Colosseum around the*

Commodus (Barrie Rutter) waltzes with the ostrich necks and
dumps them in Libya

feet of the triumphant Commodus, who is standing in its
centre. Commodus scares them away with a scream that
also removes the persistent voice of his father, Marcus
Aurelius.)

Commodus

I wish to be gracious, and in grateful recognition
of the part Carnuntum played in shaping my
ambition,
I hereby grant that you barbarians may
call Carnuntum Commodiana from today.

(fanfare)

And having dubbed you all Commodians, I'll bestow
upon you, gratefully, a gladiator show . . .
And just as a favour, to make me feel at home,
join your modern voices with those of ancient Rome,
and before we get down to business and begin
the bloody duels, I implore you, please, join in
and learn, before I let the monsters out on to the scene,
as a favour to your emperor, the Colosseum routine.

It goes like this. Thumbs up, spare! Thumbs down,
slay!
And I'd like a short rehearsal, if I may –
and my surrounding cohorts will show you the
way . . .
They'll show you with their batons the routine a
gladiator/emperor expects in the arena.

(He addresses the **Soldiers** *on the amphitheatre rim. On*
the command 'Spare!' they point batons vertically
upwards, and on the command 'Kill!' they turn their
batons downwards.)

First my cohorts! Spare! Kill! Spare! Kill!
That's the way we Romans show the people's will.

Now all of you together, *ein, zwei, drei*,
get those thumbs up high into the sky.
Thumbs up! Thumbs up! That means spare, set free.
So all together, once more. After me!

And if you turn your thumbs down that means kill
and if that's your heart's desire, kill I will.

So, once more, all together, hands in the air.
Thumbs up! Thumbs down! Spare! Kill! Spare!

For barbarians you're very bright! *Jawohl! Jawohl!*
You see how you Commodians have all in your
control.
What you say happens, a down-turned thumb
and some poor bugger's final moment's come.
Your collective wish is my command.
All you have to do is show it with your hand.
You see how democratic dealing death can be.
You decide, the people, not the emperor, me.

Good Commodians, now we're ready to begin.

(*To Guards and Trumpeters:*)

Trumpet in my club and lion skin!
And let Commodiana witness my transformation
into the god Hercules's incarnation.

(*Trumpeters play a solemn fanfare. Guards enter in stately
procession, bearing the club and lion-skin of Hercules.
Two Guards prepare to divest Commodus of his purple.
The procession is supervised by* **Julius Bollux**.)

When I don this skin all Commodiana sees
its greatest emperor, divine as Hercules.

(*To Guards on rim of amphitheatre:*)

Cohorts, take your batons and beat me a tattoo
as I am made divine in front of all of you.

(To Trumpeters:)

> And trumpets play a fanfare to give a solemn sign
> that Commodus is Hercules, hero and divine.

(The Guards/Soldiers beat a tattoo with their batons on their shields. The Trumpeters play a fanfare.

Julius Bollux helps to divest Commodus of his robe. He is revealed as wearing a woman's bra, suspender belt, and silk knickers and stockings. Commodus slowly becomes conscious of the laughter and sounds of ridicule, even wolf-whistles. His ceremonial composure becomes a cold fury.

Julius Bollux opens one of the many papyrus scrolls he burdens himself with as a portable library.)

Julius Bollux

Please, Commodians, composure. It may look

                      hideous

but it is authenticated in Aelius Lampridius!
In veste muliebri. Chapter 9.

Commodus

Go on, laugh. I dare you. Anyway, they're not mine,
I nicked them from Jorg Haider's washing line.
You Marcomanni and Quadi though, you're not too

                      hot

on your mythology, you barbarian lot!
If you ever read beyond the pages of *Die Presse*,
you'd know that Hercules was also a cross-dresser.
You'd know that Queen Omphale once made

                      Hercules

dress in lacy knickers just like these.

(He flexes his muscles and invites a woman in the audience to look at them.)

There you are, Madam. Have a look at these.
Aren't they the muscles of the he-man Hercules?
Hercules and me! So what if we're both benders,
who like ladies' lingerie, stockings and suspenders?
Rules are for weaklings. Oh yes, oh yes,
I cross all boundaries not just in dress.
And I admit I'm double-doored. Had piles of pokes
with birds as poker and as poked by blokes.
Commodus Fututor, known to shaft
both sexes, man and beast, both fore and aft.

So, you Pannonian piss-heads, just one laugh
at my lingerie, that laugh's your epitaph!
If any of you snigger at me as a perv,
that laugh'll get you lunched on by a *Löw*.
Let this club be a reminder that applause
is the appropriate reaction, not guffaws.
So cheer when you're told to, you backward
                                    barbarians,
you Austrians, Slovaks, Germans and Hungarians.

(*Julius Bollux opens a scroll. It reads* APPLAUS. *He holds it up to the audience to command them to applaud.*)

We're going to butcher beasts. We'll have a butcher
                                    beano
bloodier and realler than Quentin Tarantino.

(*Julius Bollux opens a second scroll and shows it to the audience. It reads* JUBELN (*cheer*).)

Here in Carnuntum's collapsed imperial ruins,
let's slaughter lions and butcher a few bruins.

(*Julius Bollux opens a third scroll and shows it to the audience. It reads* JUBELN LAUTER (*cheer louder*).)

This is Julius Bollux, my wizened hanger-on
and author of the *Onamasticon*.

Bollux's encyclopaedic compilation's
three times longer than Daddy's *Meditations*.
And would you believe that the dedicatee
of this momentous compilation is . . . me.
Come on, Bollux, show them how you reel
off an endless string of sycophantic *Spiel*.

Julius Bollux

Θεοειδης: godlike . . . deistic . . . theistic . . .
                                                    divine . . .
Δικαιος: just . . . virtuous . . . honourable . . .
                                                    fair . . .
Φιλανθρωπος: humane . . . charitable . . . loving . . .
                                                    kind . . .
Ημερος: merciful . . . forgiving . . . gentle . . .
                                                    benign . . .
Οξυς: intelligent . . . gifted . . . reasonable . . .
                                                    wise . . .
Ευβουλος: prudent . . . sagacious . . . knowledgeable
                                                    . . . astute . . .

(*As Julius Bollux reads from the scroll, it gets longer and
longer and Commodus walks around Bollux, swathing
him in his own papyrus until he looks like a mummy.*)

Commodus

That's enough, Bollux. No need to bore us
with the entire contents of your tedious thesaurus.

Name any author that you like and Bollux here can
                                            quote 'em.
And I take him to the Senate (where I have to call
                                            him Scrotum).
If I say, 'Bollux (or Scrotum), write me this or that in
good demogogic dictatorial Latin',
he'll spew me a speech out in only half a tick,
words pouring from his mouth like someone being sick.

Commodus (Barrie Rutter) commands Julius Bollux (Lawrence
Evans) to recite from his *Onomasticon*

He took Dad's dictation and he knows by heart
the whole of the *Meditations*, every boring part.
Sometimes when I'm bored and want a little show
I get Bollux to read *Ta en Karnounto*.

(*He raises his club.*)

And to caution little Bollux, as I caution all of you,
I simply shift my trusty club, just an inch or two.
All I have to do is move my club a fraction,
and obedient little Bollux leaps straight into action.

(*Julius Bollux begins to recite from Chapter 3 of the*
Meditations *in Greek, starting with the title.*)

Julius Bollux
'ΤΑ ΕΝ ΚΑΡΝΟΥΝΤΟ

Ουχι τουτο μονον δει λογιζεσθαι, οτι καθ' εκαστην
ημεραν απαναλισκετε ο βιος και μερος ελαττον αυτου
καταλειπεται, αλλα κακεινο λογιστεον, οτι, ει επι
πλεον βιοη τις, εκεινο γε αδηλον, ει εξαρκεσει εκεινο
γε αδηλον, ει εξαρκεσει ομοια αυθις η διανοια προς
την συνεσιν τωδν πραγματων και...και...και...'

(*Commodus gets bored with the performance and cuts it
short.*)

Commodus
I can fast-forward Bollux through the whole
of my father's philosophic scroll.

(*Julius Bollux pathetically tries to sort his shredded and
twisted papyri and remembers the dignity he once had as
the amanuensis of Marcus Aurelius.*)

Julius Bollux
His father's amanuensis and official memorizer,
the codex keeper to the contemplative Kaiser!

Commodus

Right, then, codex keeper – one, two, three and go!
Give me section 3 of *Ta en Karnounto*.

Julius Bollux

Ἱπποκρατης πολλας νοσους ιασαμενος αυτος νοσησας
απεθανεν και . . . και . . . και . . . και . . . και . . .

(*He takes a deep breath and continues.*)
και . . . Αλεξανδρος και Πομπηιος. και Γαιος
Καισαρ . . .'

(*Commodus stops him.*)

Commodus

You disappoint me, Bollux, I thought that you could
list
all the Kaisers whose arses creeps like you have kissed.
Perhaps your dancing's better. Dance me that exotic
Eastern dance I always find erotic . . .

Julius Bollux

Sire, I fear I'm rather past it.

Commodus

I think that just one blow
could even make a geriatric get up and go.

Julius Bollux

In that case, Sire, I can but try.

Commodus

Better, Bollux, dear. It's either dance or die.

Come on, Bollux, I command you as your ruler
to perform for my people and do the hula-hula.

Imagine that you're in the *Hawaiische Reitschule*!

93

(Julius Bollux begins to dance, He sees Marcus Aurelius descending from his watchtower. The emperor screams at Commodus:)

Marcus Aurelius

How dare you so disgracefully demean a
dignified imperial servant.

Commodus

Look who's joining us down in the arena!

Marcus Aurelius

I damn you, you've made me, the Stoic, shriek
and break the flow of my meditative Greek.

Commodus

I gloat that I can goad 'the god'. How glad
it makes me, maddening my meditative dad!
It's taken me some time. Everything I've done
was to make my father come and face his son!

Marcus Aurelius

I have been summoned here to Europe's aid
to find a new philosophy beyond free trade.

Commodus

If you were summoned, I was summoned too.

Marcus Aurelius

Who on earth would want to summon you!

Commodus

Not my father, true, too true!
But someone's summoned me, some welcoming well-
                                            wisher
leaves bouquets at my bust in the *Kunsthistorische*.

There are secret enclaves who worship my
                                   incarnation,
summoned as the saviour of a deeply troubled
                                         nation.
If not here then my ghost has come
to save Dalmatia and Illyricum.
Somewhere they'll welcome an Herculean Kaiser,
beast-batterer, cattle-clubber, civilizer.

Marcus Aurelius
Who would model his image on someone like you?

Commodus
Look in Josefplatz at Josef II.

Marcus Aurelius
Anyone in Vindobona sees him, yes, of course,
but the emperor's depicted on a horse,
with right arm raised (not too high), meant to be
modelled on the one in Rome of me.

Commodus
Maybe, but he's also depicted as Hercules,
the baby giving two snakes a fatal squeeze.

Marcus Aurelius
I didn't notice that.

Commodus
        You wouldn't, NO!

Marcus Aurelius
I'm up above, on top.

Commodus
            But I'm still there below.

95

All through history you're going to meet
the damned delinquent that you can't delete.

And where you have one image, I have at least a
score –
like me throttling monsters on *Michaelertor*.
Our Vindobona heirs identify
with me, the Herculeses on the *Reichkanzlei*.

Marcus Aurelius

One of the empires that succeeded ours
once, but no longer, one of the world's powers,
took Hercules as a symbol of its civilizing work
against their own barbarians, like the Turk.
And I think that you've been grossly impolite
to so debase the image before our hosts tonight.

(*Julius Bollux, edging back to curry favour with Marcus
Aurelius, produces another scroll from his scroll-bag.*)

Julius Bollux

Yes, and this philosopher, Herodorus, in a scroll
that would take more hours than my own to unroll,
so, if I may, I'll sum up: Herodorus sees
a *spiritual* symbol in the guise of Hercules.
And for Stoics like Your Highness the lionskin
which your son so sacrilegiously goes swaggering in
signifies the garb of reason . . .

Marcus Aurelius

                              stolen from a shrine
which Stoics like myself long held divine,
and the stolen club he carries is the soul
which keeps all base desires in control,
a strong soul to protect us and defend us
against vile lusts . . .

Commodus
                    So what are these suspenders?
Does your Herodorus tell you what they are?
Or the hidden meaning of Hercules's bra?
This club which signifies 'strong soul' to Stoic quacks
is the plain club that will give Bollux a few thwacks.
'Strong soul', my arsehole! You'll see what it means,
when I smash your skull to smithereens.

(*He pursues Julius Bollux, trailing scrolls, out of the arena.
He then patrols the audience, brandishing his club.*)

Anybody else who's in the slightest doubt
that this club is a club I'll more than gladly clout.

(*As he threatens the audience, Marcus Aurelius creeps up
behind him and snatches the club away. He swings it up as
Commodus sinks to his knees.*)

Marcus Aurelius
And let's see what you're like without
the club you so bravely brandish all about.

Isn't this the pose? The club poised up above,
ready to crash down . . .

Commodus
                    Not on the son you love!

Marcus Aurelius
I sometimes think you're not my son at all!

(*The voice of* **Faustina** *comes clear and commanding from
out of the imperial box:*)

Faustina
If you believe that, let your raised club fall!

There are followers of yours who just can't bear

97

The Empress Faustina (Sian Thomas)

to think that such a saint had such an heir.
And to preserve your role as Stoic saviour,
invented my lascivious behaviour.
It would keep the Stoic icon undefiled,
if adultery had doomed me with this child.

Alas, I can't collude with these deniers
of your son's descent. They're frightened liars.
To deify the one and demonize the other
in the end damns me, the blameless mother.
Though I bore you all your children and was chaste,
those who sanctify you had my fame debased.
History branded me the worst of wives and whores
because no one wanted to believe that he was yours.
But I, Faustina, am the only one
who knows that you're his father, you his son.
Those libels and those slanders are untrue.
I never slept with anyone but you.

You should thank fortune you can free
your reputation from paternity;
such freedoms are impossible to me.
Even if her son sheds millions' blood,
a mother can't deny her motherhood.
As babes they pressed the warm milk from our pap
before they pumped men's blood across the map.
Whatever boundaries they've gone beyond,
nothing ever breaks that early bond.
I'd be relieved if history released
me too from the burden of having borne this beast.

Sometimes when I imagine that I hold
my Commodus again a one-year-old,
I cradle carcasses whose eyes can't close,
to whom no gentle rocking brings repose.
I find my blood-flecked arms are full
of hacked-up bits of bear and bull,

meat bundled up in bloody rags
of boldly flown, but now abandoned flags,
and I have to add my bitter mother's cry
to this abattoir's black lullaby,
along with Klara and with Rosa,
each a *mater dolorosa*,
cradling Adolf's or Benito's tons
of other mothers' meat that once was sons,
and with Yekaterina, whose cradled darling
sucked milk, and then sucked blood as Joseph Stalin.

Would it help the world pretending your pure semen
did not create this blood-demented demon?
If it would, I'd swear the nympho whore Faustina
fucked a fighting man from the arena.
And if I swear my folly under oath,
it puts a boundary between you both,
and raises up a future frontier post
between the god-like and the gangster ghost.
I'll let these stories go on being told
to keep apart the iron age and gold.
If I agree to let these slanders thrive,
will the future learn to hope, and thus survive?

To free the dreamer fouled by his son's flaw,
I'll swear to the future, 'Yes, I was a whore!'

Now you are free to go your separate ways,
demon and deified, to future days.
Go in opposite directions, trace
the boundaries of our empire, then embrace,
and as one brief gesture for my eyes alone,
acknowledge to him and me he was your own.
Meet there in Carnuntum, where in 172
I sat in this very seat with both of you.
Here canopied with purple and with gold
and you, my child, not quite eleven years old.

Commodus

I remember! I remember, I sat there.
They dressed a man as Orpheus and a bear
ripped him to pieces though he played
with panicky desperation a lyre serenade.

Faustina

Yes, the first time that you'd seen a
man or beast destroyed was here in this arena.

Marcus Aurelius

I don't remember what the beasts were or who
                                     fought.

Faustina

No, you were, as always, lost in thought.
You were dictating with averted gaze what was to
                                     grow

into the chapter titled *Ta en Karnounto*.

Commodus

I was on his right. He spoke above my head,
so I had to listen to every word he said,
except when at those moments the crowd's roars
drowned out the Stoic apothegms and saws.
Since then, no matter how many beasts I've slain,
those boring banalities bombarded my brain.
No matter how loud the Colosseum cheers,
Ta en Karnounto still echoes in my ears.
I kill a hundred ostriches but can't get rid
of the *Meditations* I heard muttered as a kid.
Right there in this arena I heard Daddy drone
to his amanuensis from his golden throne.

Marcus Aurelius

(*singing*)
> 'παντα τα μεν του σωματος ποταμος, τα δε της ψθχης
> ονειρος και τυφος.'

(*His voice, singing about time being like a river, draws in
the voices of the Women singing under him and the cellos.*
   *Faustina directs the pair to part and meet in Carnuntum,
and the music of time and the river accompanies them on
their journey.*)

Faustina
Go in opposite directions, trace
the boundaries of our empire, and embrace
there in Carnuntum for my eyes alone.
Acknowledge to him and me he is your own.

Meet in Carnuntum and that done,
I'll tell the future world he's not your son.

(*She leaves with veiled face.*
   *As directed, Marcus Aurelius and Commodus, taking
different directions, walk the boundaries of the Roman
Empire on the mapped arena floor. Marcus Aurelius turns
to his right and proceeds along the coast of Spain, then
Britain, then back to where Carnuntum is marked on the
world map.*
   *Commodus turns left and proceeds along the coast of
Africa, through the Middle East, Greece and former
Yugoslavia, back towards where the Danube and
Carnuntum are marked on the world map.*
   *The music takes them all the way back to Carnuntum.
They stand facing each other across the Danube.*)

Marcus Aurelius
Listen to the Danube. Listen to the flow
that became time's symbol in *Ta en Karnounto*.

Why are you laughing?

Commodus
                Because Your Highness stands
with both feet planted in barbarian lands!

(*He points to Marcus Aurelius.*)

Barbarian!

(*He points to himself.*)

            And civilized!
                        Just one stride
takes you from the savage to the civilized side!
Come to Carnuntum! Step over the Donau,
and, for my mother's sake, embrace me now.

(*Marcus Aurelius steps over the Danube and embraces
Commodus. The embrace leaves blood on Marcus
Aurelius's white suit and he recoils in disgust.*)

Marcus Aurelius
Look what you've done to my best suit.
It's covered with blood. Oh, you brute! You brute!
I should have known embracing you would mean
my time-bleached suit of white would not stay clean.

When the time comes, and it will,
and you're not the one who's going to kill
but the one who's going to die,
you'll face death better with philosophy.
There'll come a moment when you'll know
the truth I contemplate in *Ta en Karnounto*.

Commodus
Go change your suit, and once again withdraw
back up your tower far removed from gore.
But I swear, when I start to club and batter

all these beasts, the blood is going to splatter
in all directions, and will even fly
to spray you where you are, however high.
I said I'd give these burghers here '*en Karnounto*'
a genuinely bloody gladiator show.
And so I will. It's time we saw released
the world's most dangerous and savage beast,
to be killed before your eyes in this place where
I saw my first man killed by a wild bear.
The man was dressed as Orpheus, whose guitar
didn't save his guts or get him far.

(*The lyre of Orpheus sounds. Enter Orpheus.*)

Orpheus
It got me far enough, and I survive
to haunt you still in 1995.

You promised the people here a savage beast
but the savagest beast of all has been released.
The beast that they'll see slaughtered is, I fear,
the beast in lionskin before me here.
And since you are a beast beyond the bounds
of music's soothing, civilizing sounds,
and since you seem untouched by music's charms,
you will have to be subdued by force of arms.

(*He strums his lyre, which plays the music we heard that
calmed the beasts at the beginning of the show, but then
the gentle music turns into the aggressive lyre sounds
which Commodus had created from the lyre. As he plays
the large crate opens to disgorge men in riot gear, this time
like massed gladiators surrounding a beast. They
overpower Commodus and muzzle and chain him like a
bear.*
*Orpheus leads him and the real Bear on a tour round
the arena.*)

Commodus (Barrie Rutter) muzzled like a bear, with Orpheus (Jaro Frank) and Bear

Commodus (Barrie Rutter) impaled on a white cello in the Colosseum

FINALE

*Orpheus secures the chain attached to the muzzle of
Commodus to the Colosseum then exits with the Bear.
Commodus, chained to the Colosseum, tries to reach the
club of Hercules, but the length of the chain prevents him;
it is just out of reach. Growling like an animal, cries come
from his throat and are heard reverberating through the
arena speakers.*

*Enter Orpheus, bearing a white cello with the pointed
end thrusting forward towards Commodus. He
approaches Commodus slowly and ceremoniously.*

*Commodus, like a doomed animal, runs from one side
to another, each time restricted by the length of the chain
securing him to the Colosseum. He stands, he approaches
the audience with the thumbs-up sign to encourage them
to make their will known to Orpheus, who will thus be
persuaded to spare him. He tries each section of the
audience in turn – no response. Orpheus makes the
thumbs-down sign, which the audience follow. Orpheus
rams the point of the cello through the guts of Commodus.
Exit Orpheus. Blood runs down the white cello.*

*With the death of Commodus and the beast safely
disposed of, the whole* **Chorus** *run into the arena and stop
before they reach the body in the centre. One woman
tentatively approaches the body and pokes it to see if it's
truly dead. The Chorus begins to sing 'Unco Trahatur'.*

Chorus

Parricidae gladiatoris memoria aboleatur,
Parricidae gladiatoris statuae detrahantur.
Impuri gladiatoris memoria aboleatur.
Gladiatorem in spoliario.
Carnifex, carnifex,
Unco trahatur.

Parricidae cadaver, unco trahatur

Gladiatoris cadaver, unco trahatur.
Gladiatoris in spoliario ponatur
Parricidae cadaver, unco trahatur.
Unco trahatur, unco trahatur.

Perroga, Perroga,
Omnes consemus unco trahendum.
Qui omnes occidit, unco trahatur.
Qui omnem aetatem occidit, unco trahatur
Qui utrumque sexum occidit, unco trahatur
Qui templa spoliavit, unco trahatur
Qui testamenta delevit, unco trahatur
Qui vivos spoliavit, unco trahatur
Parricidae cadaver, unco trahatur
Parricidae cadaver, unco trahatur
Parricidae cadaver, unco trahatur
Unco trahatur.
Unco trahatur.
Unco trahatur.
Unco trahatur.

(*The crowd parts to form a gauntlet of honour for the
approaching Marcus Aurelius, who enters in a golden
throne with wheels, accompanied by Orpheus and pushed
by a bear. As they reach the Colosseum, Marcus Aurelius
stops and takes up the lionskin from the arena floor and
drapes it over the grotesque corpse of Commodus and
then proceeds on his journey across the world in his
wheeled throne, still pushed by the bear.*)

Marcus Aurelius and Chorus
(*Singing*)

᾿εν και μονον φιλοσοφια!

(**Tony Harrison** *enters with the amphitheatre sign and
rams it in the heart of Commodus. He also carries the
script of* The Kaisers of Carnuntum.)

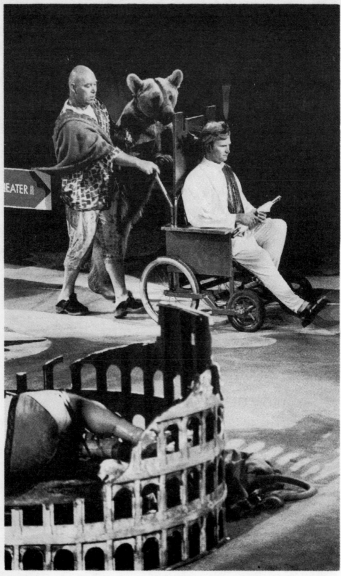

Enter Marcus Aurelius (Conrad Nelson) on a golden throne pushed
by a Bear with Orpheus (Jaro Frank)

Tony Harrison
At least it can be said this sign's now right.
A comedy and tragedy were enacted here tonight.

(After two beats of silence, with a bestial shriek the bloody body of Commodus rises from the Colosseum, swinging the signpost. Tony Harrison flees, scattering the pages of the play's script to the four winds.

Commodus removes his bear-muzzle, laughs and bows to the audience, indicating that the show is over.)

TONY HARRISON

Marcus Aurelius Looks at the Danube (extract*)

Marcus Aurelius: Pan - ta ta — men tou so-ma-tos — po-ta-mos —

ta deh tees psee-kees o - near - os

*see p. 65

M.A. keh tee-phos p —10″—

S All things of the body a river, all
things of the spirit dream and delirium*
p

A Was den Körper betrifft ist ein
schneller Fluss, was die Seele
angeht Träume und Dunst*
p

T All things of the body a river, all
things of the spirit dream and delirium*
p

B Was den Körper betrifft ist ein schneller Fluss,
was die Seele angeht Träume und Dunst*

* Repeat these phrases softly, freely, like the murmuring of a river

III

TONY HARRISON

Chorus of Subjugated Women (extract*)

*see p. 84

Chorus of Commodus' Condemnation (extract*)

Repeat as a canon: tenors lead, then basses, then sopranos and altos
together, two beats apart

*see p. 106

THE LABOURERS OF HERAKLES
or
Η ΑΥΤΟΨΙΑ ΤΟΥ ΦΡΥΝΙΧΟΥ

The Labourers of Herakles was first performed on an excavated site intended for the New Theatre of the European Cultural Centre of Delphi, Greece, on 23 August 1995, with the following company:

Labourer 1 Barrie Rutter
Labourer 2 Lawrence Evans
Labourer 3 Conrad Nelson
Labourer 4 Tim Wright
Labourer 5 Fraser Marlow

Director Tony Harrison
Designer Jocelyn Herbert
Music Richard Blackford
Choreography Lawrence Evans
Sound Glenn Keiles
Production Coordinator Trish Montemuro
Assistant to Designer Vicki Hallam
Stage Manager Fraser Marlow

The Labourers of Herakles was a co-production between the European Cultural Centre of Delphi and the Royal National Theatre Studio, London. The production was sponsored by the Herakles General Cement Company.

Grateful acknowledgements are due to Oliver M. McGoey and Balfour Beatty Amec for the generous loan of equipment and protective clothing.

A construction site in Delphi, where the foundations are being laid for a new theatre for the next millennium. It is to be based on the familiar shape of the ancient Greek theatre with a central circular orchestra.

There is a 'chorus' circle of nine cement mixers. Behind them is a 35-foot cement silo, with the logo of the cement company, Herakles: the head of Herakles wearing the traditional lionskin.

There are various wheelbarrows, planks, assortments of scaffolding, wooden and metal, and from the ground the protruding iron barley-sugar-shaped reinforcing rods for the concrete columns and foundations. Also a large pile of cement sacks, all with the Herakles logo, and three white Herakles cement sacks beneath cement mixers 4 and 6.

Enter five **Labourers.** *They begin to bang the drums of the cement mixers, or the bodies of the stacked wheelbarrows, to free them from the accretions of yesterday's set cement.*

The work becomes hypnotically more rhythmic with Labourers 4 and 5 banging the drums of the mixers, Labourer 2 the wheelbarrows, and Labourers 1 and 3 beginning to shovel the required portions of cement and gravel and sand into the cement mixers. Then, like a united chorus of mixers and men, the Labourers stand beside the turning mixers, beating a rhythm which reaches a crescendo, then suddenly stops.

Out of the silence a voice (Labourer 1) is heard singing from the cement silo the one surviving fragment of the Herakles tetralogy of Phrynichos.

Labourer 1
σωμα δ'αθαμβες γυιοδονητον
τειρει.

(*Labourer 1 moves from his cement mixer into the circle,
drawn by the voice of his ancient self. Then from the silo
comes the voice of Labourer 3.*)

Labourer 3
σωμα δ'αθαμβες γυιοδονητον
τειρει.

(*Labourer 3 moves from his cement mixer into the circle,
drawn by the voice of his ancient self. Then the voice of
Labourer 2 comes from the silo.*)

Labourer 2
σωμα δ'αθαμβες γυιοδονητον
τειρει.

(*Labourer 2 moves from his cement mixer into the circle,
drawn by the voice of his ancient self.
   There are also percussive sounds from the silo which
call Labourers 4 and 5. Each Labourer recognizes his own
voice in another form from the ancient past. Then they
hear a voice from the silo.*)

The Voice from the Silo
σωμα δ'αθαμβες γυιοδονητον
τειρει.

(*Labourer 1 assumes the stance of the 'wrestling* **Herakles**'
and adds the stage directions:)

Labourer 1
Ηρακλης Θανατον παλαιων νικα . . .

(*Labourer 1 assumes the stance of the Herakles who*

Statue of Herakles

wrestles with death, then with a thunderous rumble from the giant silo of Herakles, there is a loud crash as the worn timber planks at the centre of the cement mixers collapse to reveal an ancient statue of Herakles. It is as if the statue has come up through the silo from the underworld, where Herakles has been wrestling with death for the body of Alkestis.

A musical chord rivets the Labourers' attention to the revealed statue. They clear away the earth from it and stand it upright in the centre. Something makes them move away from it in awe.

Labourer 4 becomes possessed with the madness of Herakles and launches into a manic percussion solo, which utilizes everything on the construction site – wheelbarrows, cement mixers, scaffolding – as instruments. On Labourer 4's 'final round' of the cement mixers, the other Labourers start up the cement mixers, and Labourer 4 leaps on to the cabin roof of an earth-mover and drums the final rhythms with his feet on the metal cab. Finally he transfers his madness to Labourer 1, who has been assuming the pose of the classical statue.

During this 'madness' solo, Labourer 1 is frozen into the position of the statue of Herakles, with his shirt and shovel positioned like the lionskin and club of the statue.

Labourer 1 suddenly squares up to the statue and then demolishes it with violent blows from his shovel. He throws bits of the shattered statue into the turning cement mixers, thereby increasing their thunderous volume.

With the increase of sound from the manic cement mixers, Labourer 1 turns his murderous attentions to the sacks of Herakles cement, which he batters, throws, slashes and deguts in his frenzy, hauling out of the ripped open stomachs yards of red and white barrier tape, like guts. He seems to have slain all the cement sacks. He searches. Nothing. Then he notices two small sacks (representing children). He impales their little bodies on

the end of a pick. Red silk guts protrude from their gaping
wounds. Exhausted by the effort of killing, Labourer 1
adopts the pose of the statue of Herakles in the catatonic
aftermath of slaughter and devastation.

Enter Labourers 2, 3, 4 and 5, wearing protective dust-
masks.

Labourers 4 and 5 clear away the sacks of cement as if
they were putrefying bodies, throwing them into an open
trench as if for mass burial.

Labourers 2 and 3 clear the rubble of the dismembered
statue of Herakles and lay the fragments on the white
sacks of cement beneath cement mixers 4 and 6.
Labourers 3 and 4 are like those who search the rubble of
a gutted, devastated city looking for survivors or even
something familiar, and eventually they are like mothers
who search for their missing children. They pick up
various fragments of the statue, examine them and let
them fall. Then with a terrible cry they recognize the tiny
cement sacks that are the bodies of their children. They
take off their hard hats and dust-masks as a token of
respect for the dead. Labourers 4 and 5, who stand on the
rim, where the nine cement mixers are, also remove their
hard hats.

With a tragic shriek of recognition, Labourers 2 and 3
fall to their knees, and embrace and huddle to the cement
sacks (their dead children) in their grief. They each pull
from the gaping wounds of their babies a length of red
silk, which becomes their robe and a classical female
mask. They become the two **Women of Miletos***.*)

Women of Miletos
στρατος ποτ' εις γην τηνδ' επεστρωφα ποδι,
Ὑαντος δε γην ναιεν, αρχαιος λεως,
πεδια δε παντα και παρακτιον πλακα
ωκεια μαργοις φλοξ εδαινυτο γναθοις.

Labourer 3 (Conrad Nelson) and Labourer 2 (Lawrence Evans)
become the Women of Miletos (rehearsal photo)

(*At the end of the song Labourers 4 and 5 replace their
hard hats and start up the cement mixers. Labourers 2 and
3 as the Women of Miletos pick up the small cement sacks
that are their children and turn towards two revolving
cement mixers. They throw the sacks and the women's
masks into the revolving drums. Then they wash their
faces in the water drums, return to put on their hard hats
and boots, and resume their work as Labourers 2 and 3.*

*Labourers 4 and 5 tip their respective cement mixers,
which gush a stream of blood over the piled white sacks of
Herakles cement, and over the dismembered fragments of
the statue of Herakles.*

*Labourers 2, 3, 4 and 5 form a Greek frontier guard
against invading Persians, two behind the protection of
'sandbag' Herakles cement sacks and two standing at
attention, vigilant and on the look-out for Persian troops.*

Labourer 1 comes to life as the statue of Herakles.)

Herakles

When Greece squared up to Persia, the one and only
                                shrine
they sought protection from was Herakles's, mine.
Not all the Greeks, though, were steady devotees
of the one who masters monsters, Herakles.
Even Delphi's oracle advised the Greeks to flee –
not the advice that you'd ever get from me.
Appeasement of aggressors has been the fatal cause
not just of the Persian but your more recent wars.
Athens, though, resisted, and my huge figure rose
out of the swamps of Marathon to help defeat your
                                foes.

With club and lionskin the god/hero led them on
to pulverize the Persians here at Marathon.
Go to Marathon today and bend your ear
close to the ground and listen:

(The shrieks of **Persians** *from below the ground.)*

Persian fear!
Persian panic and their barbarian cries
seconds before darkness sealed their frightened eyes.
In the village that's now Varna every night
you can hear the fleeing Persians shrieking in their
fright,
wading, or trying to, through the marshy ooze,
Greek mud weighting down their oriental shoes.
The panic never fades, no matter if you pour
tons of cement above the shrieks of war.
You still hear the panic, the screaming wild and
shrill,
under modern Marathon the Persians panic still.

Even in Athens (but no friends of Herakles!)
reactionary voices said Greek cities should appease.
The appeasers were ready to let Ionia stay,
with no fellow Greek assistance, beneath barbarian
sway.
Medizing appeasers banned *The Fall of Miletos*
and fined, for his politics, the poet *Phrynichos*.
Though this poet wrote me four plays for myself
(which I trust, are on everybody's library shelf!),
showing my adventures for many years to come,
even, dare I say it, to the next millennium,
and, though I applaud he wrote Milesian scenes
to sting the cowardly appeasers, I'm not keen on the
means
he used to do it. He, Phrynichos, the first
to bring on wailing women, but what to me's the
worst –
it wasn't women sang the roles but dragged-up men.
Greek drama was never the same again!
And though he shamed appeasers with *Halosis*
Miletou,

for masking men as women, I'd've had the poet
                                    banned too.
While I don't share the scared appeasers' view,
or their reasons for banning *Halosis Miletou*,
I believe that men dragged-up as women undermined
the military effort, so I'd've had him fined.
The politics I approved of, what I found distressing
was all those men in drag, all that cross-dressing!

But if I'm being honest I'd have to confess,
despite my reservations about men in women's dress,
when the Persian envoys came once more to demand
the earth and water that were meant to stand
for our surrendered country, what did Athens do?
She remembered Phrynichos's *Halosis Miletou*,
and with Herakles's help, wise Themistokles
(Phrynichos's patron) beat Persian creeps like these.

(*The four* **Athenian Guards** *remove their Labourers' hard
hats, duck down and, putting their heads through a hole in
the orange plastic barrier netting, become robed Persians.
They each place a traffic cone on their heads as a Persian
pointed hat. Persian 4 knocks the bottom of a bucket out
to make a Persian drum, which gives the beat as the
Persians process round Greece as envoys collecting the
tokens of surrender, earth and water. The earth and water
are collected in the drum, which Persian 4 then uses as a
'shaker' to give the beat for their return to Persia, where
they present the symbolic earth and water to King Xerxes.
Persian 4 places the drum with the earth and water before
their king, before whom the dour Persians prostrate
themselves.*)

Herakles/Labourer 1

But Athens gave the Persians a flea in the ear.
We gave them Marathon, Salamis, Plataea.

ΗΡΑΚΛΗΣ

Labourer 3 (Conrad Nelson) as a robed Persian with a cone for his hat

(*On 'Plataea', Herakles throws a shovelful of sand at the prostrated Persians.*)

When they asked for earth and water, our response
was this –
we gave them Marathon, Plataea, Salamis.

(*On 'Salamis', Herakles throws a bucket of water over the prostrated Persians. The Persians scream, as if it were boiling oil that had been thrown over them. They become Labourers again.*)

Labourer 3
You stupid cunt!

Labourer 4
You barmy sod!

(*Herakles/Labourer 1 threatens them with the club of Herakles. He seems almost on the point of another outbreak of destructive madness.*)

Herakles/Labourer 1
Don't talk to me like that! I'm a fucking god!

(*The other Labourers back off from the danger.*)

Labourer 2
That was a stupid trick you played.

(*Herakles reverts to being Labourer 1 again.*)

Labourer 1
Let's get this fucking concrete laid!

(*Labourers 2, 3, 4 and 5 pick up their discarded traffic cones/Persian hats and, using them as megaphones, warn the audience that the concrete, that will form the orchestra of the theatre for the next millennium, is about to be laid.*)

Labourers 2, 3, 4 and 5
Attention! Attention! We're now about to lay
the concrete orchestra where choruses will play.

(*The concrete orchestra is laid.*
The Labourers contemplate the results of their labours,
the first layer of the orchestra for the theatre of the next
millennium.)

Labourer 1
Well, there it is! The orchestra's first layer.
The world's great actors will perform on there.

Labourer 2
They'll be inspired there.

Labourer 1
                And so they oughta!
We mixed that concrete with Kastalia spring water!

Labourer 4
Well, there it is.

Labourer 2
            Well, at least a start,
though I've got no fucking interest in stuff like art.

Labourer 5
Well, there it is.

Labourer 3
            Another layer or two
and the orchestra's all ready for *Halosis Miletou*.

Labourer 2
Will you go and see a play?

Labourer 3
No, I've never been
once to the theatre.

Labourer 5
And it's not my sort of scene.

Labourer 3
No, there's nothing in the theatre for me.
I'd sooner watch the fucking football on TV.

Labourer 1
Before it gets monopolized by the cultural élite,
let's mark these foundations with the imprint of our
feet.
Then when the first Agamemnon walks towards the
axe,
little will he know it, but he'll be walking in our
tracks.

Labourer 2
Yes, when this theatre gets its official première
the feet of us labourers will be in the bottom layer.

Labourer 3
When the first chorus treads this orchestra before us,
we can say, 'Ah, yes, but we were there before the
chorus.'

(*The Labourers step on to the concrete and relish the fact
of initiating the space. They reprise the fragment of the*
Alcestis *of Phrynichos, but this time as if it were nothing
but a rowdy drinking song.*
*They take off their hard hats and bow to the audience.
They then attempt to leave, but find their feet are stuck
fast in the cement.*)

131

Labourer 1
I hate to say it, but I think we're fucking stuck.

Labourer 2
Fuck!

Labourer 3
Fuck!

Labourer 4
Fuck!

Labourer 5
Fuck!

All
FUCK!

Labourer 1
Let's shout for help.

Labourer 2
No one's going to come
to rescue us till next millennium.

Labourer 3
βοηθεια!

All
BOHθEIA!

Labourer 5
Not a sound!

Labourer 4
There's nobody here for miles around.

Labourer 4

What about all that lot over there?

Labourer 2

All they're allowed to do is sit and stare.
However deep the sorrow, or severe the pain,
they think we're only here to entertain.

Labourer 1

Did they stop Herakles when they saw him don
the shirt of Nessus with the fiery poison on?

Labourer 2

And did they save Agamemnon? Did they? No!
They let him walk right into the murderous axe-
                                                    blow.

Labourer 3

You never get spectators to stand up and shout
to Agamemnon, 'Don't go inside! Watch out!'

Labourer 1

No audience in Delphi, Athens, Epidaurus
has ever been more useful than the helpless chorus
at saving Agamemnon from the fatal chop
or yelled at Clytemnestra, 'Stop! Stop! Stop!'
or stopped wide-eyed Cassandra from being hacked.
They're audience. They're not allowed to act.

Labourer 2

We need a *deus ex machina* or a *dea*
or just the fucking *machina* to lift us out of here.
But are they going to help us, seeing us so stuck
in our concrete *kothurnoi*?

All
                    Are they fuck!

Labourer 3
Not one of them 's ever going to intervene.
They've been programmed not to stop the scene.

Labourer 4
Even to save us from starvation?

Labourer 5
                                    Ay!
They're just going to sit there and watch us starve
                                                and die.

Labourer 3
What're we going to do to pass the time until . . .
until . . . that's *if* somebody comes?

Labourer 2
                          They will . . . They will!

Labourer 1
Don't be too sure of that. God knows what we'll do.

The Voice from the Silo
Do ολα τα δραματα τον *ΦΡΥΝΙΧΟΥ!*

Labourer 1
(*counting one in modern Greek*)
ενα!

The Voice from the Silo
ΑΛΚΗΣΤΙΣ!

(*The Labourers clap a rhythm.*)

Labourer 1
Ηρακλης Θανατον παλαιων νικα.

All
σωμα δ'αθαμβες γυιοδονητον
τειρει.

Labourer 1
(*counting two in modern Greek*)
   δυο!

(*The Labourers clap a rhythm.*)

All
  Orcum . . .!

(*The Labourers have a vision of* **Death/Thanatos** *coming towards them.*)

   . . . *gladium ferentem . . . quo crinem Alcesti abscidat . . .*

Labourer 1
(*counting three in modern Greek*)
   τρια!

The Voice from the Silo
ΑΝΤΑΙΟΣ Η ΛΙΒΥΕΣ.

(*The Labourers wait for inspiration. It seems to be coming, then doesn't.*)

Labourer 1
(*counting four in modern Greek*)
   τεσσαρα!

The Voice from the Silo
ΔΑΝΑΙΔΕΣ.

(*The Labourers sing silently, then with voice:*)

All
... εγκαρπα ...

Labourer 1
(*counting five in modern Greek*)
πεντε!

The Voice from the Silo
ΠΛΕΥΡΩΝΙΑΙ.

(*Labourers 2 and 3 sing and the rest of the Chorus point to the cities blazing along the seashore.*)

Labourers 2 and 3
στρατοσ ποτ᾽ εις γην τηνδ᾽ επεστρωφα ποδι,
Υαντος ος γην ναιεν, αρχαιος λεως,
πεδια δε παντα και παρακτιον πλακα
ωκεια μαργοις φλοξ εδαινυτο γναθοις.

Labourer 1
(*counting six in modern Greek*)
εξι!

Labourer 3
(*speaking*)
κρνερον γαρ ουκ
αλυξεν μορον, ωκεια φλοξ κατεδαισατο
δαλου περθομενου ματρος υπ᾽ αινας κακομαχανου.

Labourer 1
(*counting seven in modern Greek*)
επτα!

And now the most tantalizing play by far
in the entire ancient Greek dramatic repertoire.

The Voice from the Silo
ΤΑΝΤΑΛΟΣ!

(*The Labourers anticipate their play. Nothing happens.
Labourer 1 asks the audience to help.*)

Labourer 1
Ολοι μαζι!

All
(*plus audience hopefully*)
ΤΑΝΤΑΛΟΣ!

Labourer 2
. . . εφεδρανα . . .

(*The Labourers register amazement at this speech.*)

Labourer 1
(*counting eight in modern Greek*)
οκτω!

The Voice from the Silo
ΦΟΙΝΙΣΣΑΙ!

(*The Labourers adopt the 'Persian position', with hands
raised.*)

Labourer 2
(*setting the scene*)
Ευνουχος στορνυς θρονους της της αρξης παρεδροις.

Labourer 3
ταδ' εστι Περσων των παλαι βεβηκοτων.

The Labourers stuck in the cement perform a fragment of the
Phoenissae of Phrynichos

(*He emits a shrill Persian scream.*)

Labourer 2
αλλελλει την Ξερξου ητταν.

Labourer 1
(*counting nine in modern Greek*)
εννια!

Labourer 3
Σιδωνιον αστυ λιπουσα
και δροσεραν Αραδον.

Labourer 1
(*counting ten in modern Greek*)
   δεκα!

Labourer 2
κα⍳ Σιδωνος προλιποντα ναον.

Labourer 1
(*counting eleven in modern Greek*)
   ενδεκα!

Labourers 2 and 3
(*singing*)
   ψαλμοισιν αντισπαστ' αειδοντες μελη.

Labourer 1
(*counting twelve in modern Greek*)
   δωδεκα!

Labourer 5
σφηκωσαι.

(*The Labourers clap their hands to show the end of each fragmentary play.*)

Labourer 1
(*counting thirteen in modern Greek*)
   δεκατρια!

Labourer 2
λαμπει δ'επι πορφυρεαις παρησι φως ερωτος.

(*The Labourers all clap.*)

Labourer 1
(*counting fourteen in modern Greek*)
    δεκατεσσαρα!

Labourer 3
τα γε μην χεινια δουσας, λογος ωσπερ λεγεται.
ολεσαι καποτεμειν οξει χαλκω κεφαλαν.

(*The Labourers all give a bloodcurdling scream, then
clap.*)

Labourer 1
(*counting fifteen in modern Greek*)
    δεκαπεντε!

(*The Labourers listen, then burst out laughing. They
suddenly put their hands over their mouths.*)

Labourer 1
I'm sorry if we're laughing, but it's just because
fragment fifteen's from the *comic* Phrynichos.

(*counting sixteen in modern Greek*)
    δεκαεξι!

Labourer 4
ταυρος αργιμητης.

(*The Labourers all clap.*)

Labourers 2 and 3
(*singing*)
    εσθλων απαγγελτηρα μαλλον η κακων.

(*The Labourers all clap.*)

Labourer 3
αξιος θεας.

(*The Labourers all clap.*)

Labourer 5
αμαρτολη.

(*The Labourers all clap.*)

Labourer 1
(*counting seventeen in modern Greek*)
δεκαεπτα!

Labourer 2
επτηξ 'αλεκτωρ δουλον ως κλινας γενη.

(*The Labourers all clap.*)

Labourer 1
(*counting twenty in modern Greek*)
εικοσι!

Labourer 3
ω φιλτατ'ανδρων, μη μ'ατιμασας γενη.

(*The Labourers all clap.*)

Labourer 1
(*counting twenty-one in modern Greek*)
εικοσι ενα!

Labourer 2
εγω δε, μισει γαρ μ', εξ ομματων.

(*The Labourers all clap.*)

Labourer 4
εξωστρα.

Labourer 1
(*counting twenty-two in modern Greek*)
εικοσι δυο!

Labourer 5
ιδριδες.

(*The Labourers all clap.*)

Labourer 1
(*counting twenty-three in modern Greek*)
εικοσι τρια!

Labourer 2
σεμελη.

(*The Labourers all clap.*)

Labourer 1
(*counting twenty-four in modern Greek*)
εικοσι τεσσαρα!

All
(*whispering*)
ψελια . . .

(*The Labourers make to clap but freeze in mid-movement.*)

The Voice from the Silo
ΑΛΩΣΙΣ ΜΙΛΗΤΟΥ.

(*The Labourers chant the title of the lost play of Phrynichos, then fall silent and desolate.*)

Labourer 1
Phrynichos won't free us. We're still stuck.

Labourer 2
Fuck!

Labourer 3
Fuck!

Labourer 4
Fuck!

Labourer 5
Fuck!

All
FUCK!

(*Enter* **Tony Harrison** *to speak as* **The Spirit of Phrynichos**.)

The Spirit of Phrynichos
And you'll be staying stuck until you do
more than the title of *Halosis Miletou*.
Although I speak in English and not in ancient

                       Greek,
it's the poet Phrynichos on whose behalf I speak.
To honour Phrynichos, who gave theatre a start
in redeeming destruction through the power of art,
and, witnessing male warfare, gave the task
of mourning and redemption to the female mask,
to honour such a poet, all modern actors need
to celebrate his genius, and get their spirits freed
from Europe's impasse, where art cannot redeem
the cry from Krajina or the Srbrenica scream,
all modern poet and actors need to do,
to perform the sadly missing *Halosis Miletou*,
is to incline their heads north-west a few degrees,
to see the moral madness of the modern Herakles.

The Spirit of Phrynichos (Tony Harrison) 'Once more the mourning women trudge the roads / of murderous Europe. Look at them, and sing your odes!'

(*The Labourers turn their heads north-west towards
former Yugoslavia, then turn back towards the audience.*)

The Spirit of Phrynichos
The spirit of Phrynichos cries out, 'Cast aside
mythology and fables and look at genocide!
Cast aside mythology and turn your fearful gaze
to blazing Miletos, yesterday's, today's.'

(*The Labourers turn again towards former Yugoslavia,
then turn back towards the audience.*)

Once more the mourning women trudge the roads
of murderous Europe. Look at them, and sing your
                                                    odes!

(*Exit the Spirit of Phrynichos/Tony Harrison.*)

Labourer 3
Who the fuck was that?

Labourer 2
Who was who?

Labourer 1
Perhaps it was the poet of *Halosis Miletou*!
Delphi's full of ghosts. It must have been
one of the ancient spirits that you've seen.

Labourer 3
He spoke to us?

Labourer 1
Go on, what did he say?

Labourer 3
He said we might get free, if we did a play.

Labourer 1
US? I don't believe it.

Labourer 4
Get away!

Labourer 2
I don't believe it. Didn't hear a thing.

Labourer 3
He said, 'Learn to mourn like women. Look at war,
and sing!'

Labourer 1
I'm a labourer of Herakles, and a labourer lays
fucking concrete. He doesn't act in plays.

Labourer 2
The ancient Delphi theatre had a sculptured frieze
depicting the labours of the hero Herakles.
The frieze for this, us labourers, poor sods,
cemented as a sacrifice to drama's bloody gods.

Labourer 1
I'm fucking freezing, never mind frieze!
Pass me my shirt, if you can reach it, please.

(*The Labourer nearest the army-surplus camouflage shirt
of Labourer 1 reaches out of the concrete circle, picks the
shirt up and passes it to Labourer 1. Labourer 1 puts on
the shirt. Pause. Then Labourer 1 lets out a bloodcurdling
scream. The shirt of Nessus is the shirt of modern
Europe's agony. Labourers 2 and 3 sing a duet about the
shirt of fire. They have the voices of women.*)

Labourers 2 and 3

Who wove the caustic camouflage no cooling water
quenches?

Muslims that are mouldering in mass-execution
trenches.

Who wove the blistering blouson that Herakles can't
loose?

The fingers of the raped girl who wove herself a
noose.

Who wove this caustic camouflage consuming
Herakles?

Sarajevo children his shells made amputees.

Who wove this caustic khaki that seals his maleness
in?

The mother of the mortared mosque's dismembered
muezzin,
assisted by the convoys of those cleansed out of Knin.

When the former Yugoslavs started slaughtering each
other,
who was left to mourn them but the daughter, sister,
mother?
When all the men are massacred in Miletos, or
elsewhere,
who is left but women to keen in their despair?
This was the truth that Phrynichos first knew
when female masks first mourned *Halosis Miletou.*

(*Labourer 1/Herakles utters another terrible scream, then,
weakened by his agony, falls silent. He pauses a while
before speaking:*)

Labourer 1/Herakles

I wear a fitted furnace. My scalded body squirms.
My ethnic cleanser's conscience crawls with caustic
                                                worms.
If you pull this garment from me, you'll pull away
                                            my skin.
This is Europe's conscience I'm cremated in.

From Ibn El Ass, who lit the fire that caused the loss
of millions of papyri, including Phrynichos,
in Alexandria's library, because nobody needs
so many different volumes, if he only reads
the one book that gives everything that any man
could want for in life's guidance, the Koran,
to one today who mortars mosques and uses
                                        bulldozed blocks
to erect a hurried edifice that's strictly Orthodox,
cementing over cemeteries with centuries of dead,
and over sacred ancestors puts parking lots instead,
we've all been sent a garment of agony like this.
This is the shirt of *Miletou Halosis*,
a material that's tailored from woven lengths of hell.

My soul chokes with rancid smoke. I smell! I smell!

My body's flayed red-raw by revengeful racist rage,
bellowing with bloodlust all through our blighted
                                                age.

And officials with the suits and ties of Nessus on
walk the corridors of power in Washington and
                                                Bonn,
In London and in Paris, in New York at the UN,
the shirt of fire's the fashion for flame-tormented
                                                men.

Monsters uniformed in famished flames that feast
on their flesh walk from the West and East,

and like the eagles sent out by Zeus, they come
to meet here in Delphi for the next millennium,
and, their bodies torched red-raw by torturing
remorse,
quench their scalded skin in the one and only source
that could ever cool it, the Kastalia spring,
where the scarred soul of Europe may learn again to
sing,
and inhuman monsters may turn once more to men
and mourn the gutted cities that will not rise again.

(*Enter Tony Harrison with the club of Herakles, which
Labourer 1/Herakles lights with a match and transforms
into a torch.*)

Labourer 1

The Greek shrines gutted by the Persians, after
Plataea,
had their holy fires rekindled with the Delphic flame,
from here.

The fire that burned Miletos and the flame
that makes me writhe with anguish are the very same
element that we hold up here tonight
as a beacon for the future with its ambiguous light.
This fire for the future that still comes flickering
through
drew its first furious flame from . . .

All

Halosis Miletou.

Labourer 3

(*singing*)

> *Halosis Miletou*,
> a title with no play,

and those who can't bear art so true
would ban it still today.

Halosis Miletou,
a banned play to embrace
the horrors that begin anew
when race abuses race.

Halosis Miletou,
a play once banned, now lost,
but its message still shines through
in times of Holocaust.

Halosis Miletou,
a title with no play
but the text's in front of you
in Bosnia today.

Labourer 1

(*holding up the torch*)
Now the power to free us is entirely yours.
Fine us and ban us. Or give us your applause.

Halosis Miletou

Ha - lo - sis mi - le - tou, a tit - le with no play, and those who can't bear art so true would ban it still to-day. Ha - lo - sis mi - le - tou, a banned play __ to em-brace the hor-rors that be - gin a-new when

CHARLIE MOON AND
THE BIG BONANZA BUST-UP

BY THE SAME AUTHOR

Here Comes Charlie Moon

CHARLIE
MOON
AND
THE BIG
BONANZA
BUST-UP

written and illustrated by

Shirley Hughes

RED FOX

A Red Fox Book
Published by Random Century Children's Books
20 Vauxhall Bridge Road, London SW1V 2SA

A division of the Random Century Group

London Melbourne Sydney Auckland
Johannesburg and agencies throughout the world

First published by The Bodley Head 1982
Red Fox edition 1992

13 5 7 9 10 8 6 4 2

Printed and bound in Great Britain by
Cox & Wyman Ltd, Reading, Berkshire

ISBN 0 09 992670 9

Characters in this Story

Charlie Moon, a boy hero

Ariadne, his cousin

Dodger Best, his friend

Linda, a lovely children's librarian

Norman, Charlie's uncle,
temporarily employed as a waiter

Owen Bowen, Linda's uncle, an artist

Mr Dix, Owen Bowen's landlord, an art dealer

Duggie Bubbles, a famous TV magician

Charlie's Mum, a hairdresser

Trevor and Ray, two mysterious men

A Lady Illustrator

For all children's librarians
with admiration and gratitude

Contents

1 Bonanza Blues, 11

2 A Ghost is Heard, 18

3 Smells and More Smells, 26

4 Fire Down Below! 34

5 The Magician Appears, 39

6 Stuck in the Mud, 44

7 Our Mums Wouldn't Like It, 49

8 Fishy, 56

9 Very Fishy, 61

10 Haunted, 67

11 Dark Doings, 74

12 Bonanza Day, 81

13 Horsing Around, 87

14 Mixed Infant, 91

15 Smile, Please, 97

16 Black Magic, 102

17 A Game of Grandmother's
    Footsteps, 112

18 Escape! 119

19 A Little Celebration, 122

1 Bonanza Blues

It was pitch dark inside. Charlie couldn't see anything except a bit of back belonging to his friend, Dodger Best. They were trying hard to walk out of step. It wasn't easy. Charlie hung on to the belt of Dodger's jeans and stumbled along as best he could but he kept falling over Dodger's feet. Dodger's muffled voice came back to him through the stuffy blackness telling him what to do.

"Come on, Charl. It's like the opposite of marching, see. I lead with the left foot and you go off on the right. Ready?"

"O.K., but go a bit quicker, will you?"

They started off again, one two, one two. Charlie kept remembering a poem he knew:

"Will you walk a little faster?" said a whiting to a snail. "There's a porpoise close behind us, and he's treading on my tail."

There wasn't a porpoise behind them, but an even stranger creature: Charlie's cousin Ariadne, wearing her home-made robot suit. He could hear her breathing heavily as she clanked along.

"Faster, Dodger," he urged.

"I can't."

"Go *on*."

Dodger suddenly quickened his pace alarmingly. Now he was going too fast for Charlie to keep up. They lurched forward, quite out of control. Then, without

warning, Dodger stopped dead. Charlie's left foot tangled with his right one. They swayed about, trying to keep
their balance. Ariadne, stepping up briskly behind, cannoned straight into them. There was a great tinny crash,
a ripping of cloth, a thudding of wild kicks. Under a rain
of heavy objects they all hit the floor.

Charlie was the one underneath. He couldn't even
struggle. He just lay there trying not to be squashed to
death by Dodger and promising himself never to be the
back legs of anything ever again. Especially not a horse.
More especially not if Dodger was the front legs. He
wasn't a reliable person to go about with at the best of
times, what with holding his breath between one lamp-
post and another on the way to school or suddenly
deciding to sidle about like a crab. You never knew
when he was going to have a stop-and-go phase. Being
inside the same skin with him was a mistake from the
beginning, thought Charlie bitterly. Next time, at the
very least, it was front legs or nothing.

(12)

At last Linda, the children's librarian, wrestling with zips and fastenings, managed to rescue them and get them on to their feet. There were books all over the place. They'd been accidentally knocked off a nearby display stand. Luckily all this had happened in the small room across the passage from the main library, the one where Linda sometimes read stories aloud to them. The door was firmly shut, so the people who were choosing their books didn't rush across to demand who was making all the noise. Even so, Linda looked anxiously towards the door.

"Come on, you three, we'd better get this lot tidied up right away," she said. "Charlie, Dodger, you start piling up all those books—very carefully, mind—and I'll rearrange them as they were. Ariadne, you'd better get the costumes back into their boxes. I hope nothing's been damaged. The horse suit is only borrowed and I've promised to return it in good condition."

Linda had borrowed the costumes for the Book Bonanza which was going to be at the end of this half-term week. She had hired the big hall which was next door to the library, and there were going to be lots of stands with all kinds of books on them—ghost books and fairy-tale books and books about snakes and racing cars and magic and Egyptian mummies and monsters from outer space. There were going to be badges and stickers and some real writers and artists too. Linda was organizing it all. She had a lot of good ideas, like having some people in fancy dress walking up and down outside the hall with notices telling everyone about the Book Bonanza and getting them to come inside. This was where Charlie, Dodger and Ariadne came in. Today was supposed to be a sort of rehearsal.

"Thank goodness my notice is O.K.," said Ariadne, leaning it tenderly up against a wall. "It took me hours to do. Typical of you to go falling over it, Charlie Moon." She always thought that things which happened to Charlie quite accidentally were "typical". It was her favourite word. The other was "pathetic". Worse still, she'd just discovered another one: "nauseating". "You're absolutely *nauseating*," she would tell Charlie, whenever she could steer the conversation round to it. He wasn't quite sure yet what it meant, but he knew it wasn't a compliment.

They got the books back on to the shelves. Linda looked worried. Her hair was all on end. It was short and curly all over like a red setter that's been out in the rain, only it smelt much nicer.

(14)

"There's only a few days to go and so much to do," she said.

"Is Duggie Bubbles really coming?" asked Charlie and Dodger for about the twentieth time.

Everyone knew about Duggie Bubbles because they'd all seen him doing magic tricks on television. He was going to be the star attraction of the Bonanza. Charlie was planning to be a television conjuror too, so he was anxious to pick up some hints. You were supposed to have a top hat, which Charlie hadn't, but he was working on that. He'd also spent his Christmas book-token on a book by Duggie Bubbles himself called *Magic for Boys and Girls*. But the chapter about cutting a hole in a large white handkerchief hadn't been a success because he'd kept getting the hole the wrong size. Mum had been very cross when she'd found out what had happened to all her good linen handkerchiefs.

"Yes, he's really coming," said Linda, "and so is that lady illustrator. They're going to use the platform. Everything's got to be absolutely ready by then. Oh, dear!"

They all liked Linda. She could read aloud ever so well. Listening to her was as good as a play. Dodger sometimes hung about at the back pretending he was doing something else, but really his ears were flapping. They all wanted to help with the Bonanza. But now it was nearly time for the library to close, so it was too late to do any more today.

They were just finishing tidying up when there was a
great roaring noise outside. A powerful engine splut-
tered a couple of times and then shut off.

A fierce figure appeared in the doorway, covered from
head to foot in shiny black plastic, with a helmet under
its arm and its face covered like a bandit's with a white
silk scarf. But inside it was only Norman, Charlie's
young uncle. He quite often dropped in to collect
Charlie from the library. This was because he hoped to
linger about, chatting to Linda.

Charlie, Dodger and Ariadne ran out at once to
admire Norman's big motorbike. Dodger stroked its
shiny tank lovingly. Bending his knees and gripping
imaginary handle-bars, he pretended to zoom off, leaning over sideways as he cornered at 80 m.p.h.

"I hope he's brought the spare crash helmet so I can
have a ride," said Charlie.

This afternoon they were all in luck. Linda had invited
everyone to have tea with *her* uncle, Mr Owen Bowen.
Unlike Charlie's Uncle Norman, who was young,
Linda's uncle was very old. He was often at home and
liked to be visited.

Norman was in a good mood.

"O.K., Charlie, get this helmet on. I'll give you a lift round there," he said. With Charlie snug and secure on the pillion, he kicked the starter and revved the engine very loudly two or three times.

"See you there, folks," shouted Charlie above the din, with a careless wave.

The admiring group on the pavement watched as they roared away up the quiet road and disappeared round the bend. Even Ariadne was impressed.

2 A Ghost is Heard

Linda's Uncle Owen Bowen lived quite nearby on the
top floor of a big old house. He was lucky with his view
because his room overlooked the most beautiful river in
the world: the steely, oily, muddy, tidal, glittering River
Thames. The other houses along this River Walk were
mostly very grand. Some elegantly furnished rooms
could be glimpsed through the freshly painted windows.
But the house where Uncle Owen Bowen lived stuck out
like a rotting tooth in a row of gleaming white ones. Bits
of the front seemed to be falling off into the basement
area. The windows of the downstairs rooms, which were
all empty, had bedraggled lace curtains drawn tightly
across them.

Charlie and Norman arrived first, of course, and had
to wait on the pavement until Linda, Ariadne and
Dodger came strolling along the River Walk to join
them. The row of doorbells next to Uncle Owen
Bowen's front door bore the fading names of lodgers
who had all gone away. It was no good ringing any of
them because they were all disconnected, like Uncle
Owen himself. He never seemed to hear anything that
went on down in the street. They had to shout up to the

windows for a long time before his face appeared over the balcony. Then he dropped the front door key down to them.

The most difficult thing about getting through the hall was the smell. Or smells. Was it tom cats, dead rats, mouldy kippers or simply very old socks? Or all four? It was hard to tell. Every time they came there the smells seemed to be different. Today there was an ancient heater at the bottom of the stairs which smoked and stank gently, adding to the already over-laden air. As usual, all the children held their noses on the way upstairs.

"I'b nod breadigg add all," Charlie told Dodger, scarlet in the face as they reached the first landing.

"Neidder ab I," answered Dodger between clenched teeth.

"Dawseatigg!" muttered Ariadne.

(19)

Uncle Owen Bowen was hovering outside his room at the top of the house, waiting to welcome them. What a relief it was to be there. Inside, with the door shut, there was no smell at all except for a pleasant whiff of oil paint and turpentine. It was a lovely room. From the balcony outside you could see right up to the great iron bridge with its fairy-tale towers, and the moored barges, and the river slipping past. Near the window Uncle Owen Bowen had his easel and his paints and brushes, neatly arranged upright in big jars. Charlie had never seen so many interesting objects collected in one room. There was the stuffed pike in a glass case, the brass letter-scales, the fourteen old clocks (none of them going), the banjo, the tailor's dummy and the model ship. There were also stacks and stacks of pictures, framed and unframed, not only hung all over the walls but leaning up against them too. Uncle Owen had painted quite a few of these himself. Hanging over the massive sideboard was a birdcage, inside which lived, not a parrot or a budgie, but Uncle Owen's best false teeth and his gold-rimmed glasses. His sight was bad, so he kept them there for safety in case he lost them.

"I've got in some rock cakes for your tea," said Uncle Owen Bowen. "The home help bought them for me."

They ate standing up or wandering about the room because all the tables were too full already to put plates on them. This suited everyone very well, especially Dodger. There was nothing he hated more than a set meal. Uncle Owen Bowen had given them up years ago.

"I like this picture," said Ariadne, pausing in front of the easel. "Are you working on it now, Mr Bowen?"

"Yes, yes. River with pleasure boat. Greens and

blues. Light's a bit unreliable today, though."

"It's lovely. I like the way the clouds are flying up out of the top of the canvas."

"It's coming along, coming along. Must get the paints away before Mr Dix comes. Said he might drop in later, and he'll be ever so cross if he sees them."

"Why *should* he be cross?" asked Ariadne, indignant.

"Mess—paint on the carpet—smells. He complains about the smells. Oh dear, yes."

"But oil paints smell lovely," said Linda.

"Doesn't like them." Uncle Owen Bowen's pale eyes started nervously. His chin disappeared into his neck rather like a goose, which gave him a permanently startled look anyway. The very mention of Mr Dix made him nervous. Mr Dix was the owner of the house. He had bought it with Uncle Owen Bowen in it. There had been some other lodgers too, but they hadn't liked the way Mr Dix had kept popping in to check up on their habits. So one by one they had all packed up and moved out until only Uncle Owen was left. He had lived there all his life and didn't know where to go.

"Mr Dix says that Beauty's making the hall smell," said Uncle Owen. Beauty was his old cat. "But I have to let her go up and down so she can get out through her cat door."

"That old stove down there's smoking badly," said Norman. "Looks a bit dodgy to me."

"No, no. Mr Dix gave that to me himself. Good of him. Second-hand of course but he said it had cost him a lot. Beauty feels the cold terribly, you know."

Charlie knew Mr Dix. He didn't seem like a specially good person. He lived on a barge which was moored nearby, and he was always shouting at Charlie and Dodger whenever they played near that part of the river. Mr Dix had bought Uncle Owen Bowen's house so he could move in himself and do the old place up as a posh hotel. But he couldn't get people to pay a lot of money to stay there if Uncle Owen was messing about on the top floor, painting pictures. Mr Dix kept suggesting to Uncle Owen that he should go into a Home, but he wouldn't. He had an old friend who was in one he said, where the head nurse was a regular sergeant-major. Nobody there was allowed to use a small box of water-colours, let alone oil paints. Charlie wondered why so many things that seemed worth doing counted as making a mess, like practising conjuring, or Norman taking his motorbike to pieces in the front room.

Ariadne asked Uncle Owen if they could see some more of his paintings. She was keen on art. Uncle Owen let them turn some of the canvases that were stacked against the wall face forwards so they could look at them. They were nearly all of the river: on misty days and grey days, or in sparkling sunshine, with boats going up and down, and the water all jumping points of light. They admired them all, one by one.

"Did you do this one too, Mr Bowen?" asked Norman with interest. He was looking at a small chalk drawing hanging on the wall opposite the window. It was of a young lady with dark red hair.

"No, no. That's very old. It's of my grandmother, Lily Bowen. Linda's great grandmother. The Stunner, she was called. She was an artist's model. Drawn and painted by all the famous artists of her time. Stunner was their nick-name for a good-looking young lady in those days, and she was the most stunning stunner of them all."

Linda happened to be standing next to the drawing. Turned towards the light she looked just like the lady in the picture, except that her hair was short and curly and Lily Bowen's was long.

"Lovely," said Norman. Charlie hadn't known until now that Norman was keen on art. He'd never mentioned it.

"I don't think I ever had a great grandmother," said Dodger. "I've got a gran, but we've moved such a lot that I don't see her very often."

"Lily used to live by the river," Uncle Owen told them. "She was a mudlark's daughter."

"What's a mudlark?" they all wanted to know.

"Poor people who used to go down to the river at low tide and search for things in the mud that they might be able to sell. Rubbish and things that people had thrown away. Coins sometimes, if they were lucky. A famous artist saw Lily when she was helping her mother with the mudlarking and cleaned her up so he could paint her."

"Did she marry him?" asked Ariadne promptly.

"No, no. He married someone else. A richer lady. And Lily married George Bowen who kept a pub. But she wasn't happy. Not happy at all, I'm afraid."

"Poor lady," said Ariadne.

"After she died," said Uncle Owen quietly, "her ghost was supposed to haunt the river at low tide, down where she used to do her mudlarking. The place where the famous artist first found her."

They all fell silent, looking at the little drawing. Outside the spring dusk was starting to fall and the colours of the opposite bank of the river, so bright an hour ago, were ebbing away to grey like the tide. Overhead there was a faint scuffling noise, like footsteps walking in tissue paper. They began on one side of the ceiling and worked their way slowly over to the other, paused, then started again, then stopped.

"Who's that up in the attic, Uncle Owen?" asked Linda.

3 Smells and More Smells

There was nobody else in the house at all, as far as Uncle Owen knew. But he had heard that noise at dusk before.

"The place is full of smells and now it's got strange noises as well. I can't make it out," he said. They listened again. Now the noise had stopped the silence seemed ghostly too. Charlie had a nasty chilly feeling in the back of his neck.

"Perhaps it's Beauty catching mice," suggested Ariadne nervously.

But Charlie knew it couldn't be Beauty because he'd seen her sitting on the railings down below in River Walk. He couldn't help thinking about that sad, dead Lily and wondering if, rather than haunting the river mud, she'd taken to following Uncle Owen Bowen about instead. Just then there was a louder, creaking step on the landing and a knock on the door that made them all jump.

"Afternoon, all," said Mr Dix, stepping in without being asked. He was not a welcome sight. But it was a relief, at least, that he wasn't a ghost.

Mr Dix wore heavy dark glasses. When you looked into his eyes all you saw were two tiny reflections of yourself. He also wore a peaked cap which he never removed, indoors or out. It made him look rather like a sea-captain, an idea which he encouraged because he liked standing about on the deck of the safely-moored barge where he lived, pretending he was at sea and bossing an imaginary crew. Very little of his face was visible except for his jutting jaw.

"Good afternoon, Mr Dix," said Uncle Owen, hovering about in front of his easel and paints in the hope that they wouldn't be noticed. But it was too late. Mr Dix was already bearing down on them.

"Sorry to see you've got those paints all over the place again," he said to Uncle Owen, ignoring the others. "I could smell them half way up the stairs, you know. I'm a reasonable man, I hope. Don't like to interfere with tenants. Never did. But this is my property and we can't have oil paint smelling the place out and getting all over the carpet, can we?"

"Not on the carpet," murmured Uncle Bowen, shuffling his feet. "Most careful, I do assure you. A cup of tea, Mr Dix?"

"Haven't time, I'm afraid. Madly busy. Just dropped in to remind you about that drawing."

"Drawing?"

"You know. The little chalk drawing of the girl over there."

"Yes, yes. My grandmother. We were just looking at it when . . . I was telling these young people here . . . I mean . . . Mr Dix is an art dealer, you know," Uncle Owen explained to his guests.

Mr Dix nodded briefly.

"I've managed to get a few pounds for your river paintings from time to time, haven't I, Mr Bowen? I just wondered if you'd decided to sell that little drawing. It's a bad time, of course, but I might be able to find a buyer for it."

"Er, no, I don't think so, Mr Dix, thank you very much. I'm rather fond of it, you see."

"Oh, Uncle, you *can't* sell The Stunner!" cried Linda. "I couldn't bear you to part with it!"

"Pity. I might be able to get quite a good price, you never know," said Mr Dix. "And, considering your rent arrears, Mr Bowen . . ."

"I think it may be quite valuable," said Uncle Owen Bowen, "by such a famous artist . . ."

"Pity it's not signed," said Mr Dix, "that brings the value down a lot, of course. But I tell you what. Let me

have it valued for you. I know an expert—a customer of mine—who'll do that for me as a favour. No charge. And there's no need for you to sell if you don't like the price."

"Well . . ." Uncle Owen took the drawing down from the wall and held it in his hands, peering at it.

"I can have it back to you the day after tomorrow," said Mr Dix persuasively. And somehow, before they knew it, he had the drawing under his arm.

"Oh, Uncle!" said Linda.

It was too late again.

"I'll just make another pot of tea," said Uncle Owen apologetically, as he shuffled off into the little kitchen next door.

"You needn't worry, dear," Mr Dix told Linda. "This drawing's quite safe with me, you know, safe as houses. In fact, it's probably a lot safer than with your uncle here, bless him. A dear old soul, we all know, but he's slipping a bit. Memory isn't what it was. Wandering." He tapped the side of his temple. "I've noticed it quite a bit recently. He shouldn't be here on his own, you know."

"I don't think his memory's that bad," said Linda. "He's certainly quite able to make up his mind about selling that drawing. And he doesn't have to if he doesn't want to."

(29)

Mr Dix ignored this remark.

"Shouldn't be on his own," he repeated. "I don't like it. As his landlord I feel responsible. Never know what kind of damage he's likely to do now he's getting so forgetful. And he can't look after the place properly, you know. The house smells terrible. I shall be in trouble with the Health authorities if I don't do something about it."

"He's got the home help once a week."

"Well, it's not enough. I wish you'd get him to reconsider a Home. Otherwise I may have to take action. See if you can't persuade him to be sensible, dear—face up to his age." He pressed Linda's arm in a familiar way but she withdrew it quickly.

"Well, I mustn't stop. Can't wait for your uncle to make the tea, I'm afraid," said Mr Dix coldly. "And get him to watch those messy oil paints, won't you?" Without saying goodbye he was off, clattering down the stairs with The Stunner under his arm. They all looked at the small empty patch on the wallpaper where she had hung.

"Perhaps she'll start haunting Mr Dix for a change," said Ariadne.

Dodger was getting restless. All this talk of paintings and people in olden times had begun to bore him. He was inventing a complicated game of hopscotch, using the faded bunches of flowers on Uncle Owen's carpet.

"Come on, Charlie," he said. "My Mum wants me back by half past six. Let's go and play out for a bit."

All three children said goodbye and thank-you to Uncle Owen Bowen before, holding their noses like divers, they rushed downstairs and into the street. It was good to be outside again and take in great gasps of river air. It wasn't dark yet, though some windows along the River Walk were already lighted and encouraging sounds of supper on the way and snatches of radio music floated out into the dusk. Between the street and the river embankment itself there were some bits of garden with low walls and railings. Some had rowing boats drawn up in them, some had flowers and white-painted

seats. The garden opposite where Uncle Owen Bowen
lived was full of weeds and tangled bushes. It had an old
rotting shed which Charlie and Dodger used as their
Club Headquarters when Mr Dix wasn't looking.

Charlie and Dodger started a game called "Fire Down Below". You had to move about without touching the ground, pulling yourself along the railings, balancing on walls, leaping from one gatepost to another. If your foot touched the pavement you were on fire. If it touched three times you were all burnt up. Ariadne climbed on to the shed roof. She was the umpire.

"You're burning!" she shouted to Charlie as he stumbled for a second, just brushing the ground with his toe. "You've lost one life! You're on fire!"

Charlie clung to the railings. It was a very realistic game. He could even smell the smoke. So could Ariadne. From where she was sitting she could see right over the river on one side and all the houses on River Walk on the other. Surely it wasn't pretend smoke she could smell?

It was real, all right. And it was pouring out of Uncle Owen Bowen's front door.

4 Fire Down Below!

"Fire!" shouted Ariadne.

Charlie and Dodger thought this was part of the game.

"Not fair! I never touched the ground," called Dodger.

"A real fire, you pathetic idiot! I can see the smoke." Ariadne was already scrambling down from the shed. Then Charlie realized what was happening.

"Come on, Dodger, quick!" he said.

Together they all ran back to Uncle Owen Bowen's front door. Black oily smoke was billowing out into the street.

"It's from that old stove, I think," cried Ariadne. "Oh, Charlie, whatever shall we do?"

"Better not try to go in there ourselves," said Charlie. "Must tell the others. They can't have smelled it yet up all those stairs. If only one of these doorbells worked." He was pressing them all frantically, one by one, but it was no good. He stepped back into the street. "Hey, Norman!" he yelled at the top of his voice. "Lindaaaaah!" Putting his fingers into his mouth, he managed one of his piercing whistles.

Greatly to their relief, the faces of Norman and Linda

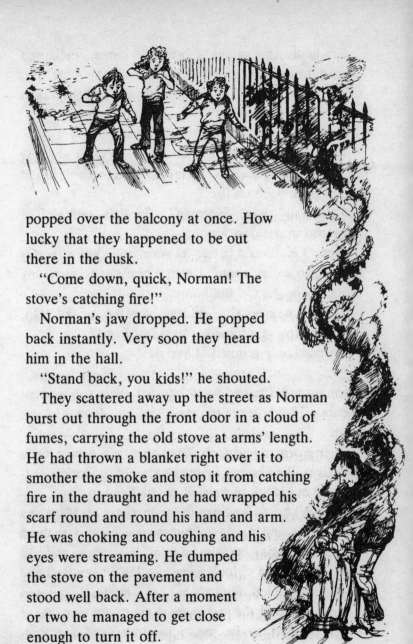

popped over the balcony at once. How
lucky that they happened to be out
there in the dusk.

"Come down, quick, Norman! The
stove's catching fire!"

Norman's jaw dropped. He popped
back instantly. Very soon they heard
him in the hall.

"Stand back, you kids!" he shouted.

They scattered away up the street as Norman
burst out through the front door in a cloud of
fumes, carrying the old stove at arms' length.
He had thrown a blanket right over it to
smother the smoke and stop it from catching
fire in the draught and he had wrapped his
scarf round and round his hand and arm.
He was choking and coughing and his
eyes were streaming. He dumped
the stove on the pavement and
stood well back. After a moment
or two he managed to get close
enough to turn it off.

(35)

Gradually the smoke subsided. Norman collapsed against the railings, mopping his face with his scarf. The situation was saved. The whole operation had only taken a few minutes.

"Is the fire out?" asked Ariadne, scared.

"Yes. It didn't burst into flames, but it was just going to. Lucky you kids called me in time, or the whole house would have been on fire."

"You all right, Norman?" Linda's white face appeared in the doorway.

"I'm O.K. You'd better let your uncle know there's nothing to worry about. But tell him not to have any more old heaters in the house."

"Thank heaven the children saw the smoke. Oh, Norman, you've probably saved our lives!"

Norman only grinned at her.

Norman and Charlie were late for their supper that evening. They'd seen Linda and Ariadne off on the same bus.

Then Norman had gone ahead on his motorbike while Charlie walked home, saying goodnight to Dodger outside the big block of flats where he lived.

Charlie's home was over the shop where his Mum had her hairdressing business. Norman was living with them for the time being because he'd just left college and had come to London to look for a job. He'd been studying something called Philosophy but, although he and Charlie scanned the newspapers every evening, there never seemed to be any jobs advertised for Philosophers. So Norman was being a waiter, part-time, instead.

Charlie's Mum was a bit cross about them being late but she'd kept their supper hot: mince, tomatoes and mashed potatoes. Norman and Charlie were tired out. It had been a long day. They ate on the sofa in front of the television. The programme that was just coming on was a magic show. First the screen was full of silver bubbles and then, who should be smiling at them from it but Duggie Bubbles himself.

"Hey, there he is!" said Charlie, speaking with his mouth full and leaning forward excitedly. "He's coming to our Book Bonanza. We're going to see him real, doing his tricks."

Duggie Bubbles had shoulder-length blond hair and a black velvet suit and he smiled all the time. He seemed to be all teeth and smiles. Smilingly, he amazed everyone with lightning card tricks, pulled yards and yards of silk scarves, coloured streamers and live birds out of a top hat and turned a vase of paper flowers into a white rabbit by whisking a cloth over them and tapping them with his little wand.

"It all seems so easy," said Charlie enviously. "It never works like that when I try to do it."

"Looks as though he's going to do a Houdini act now," said Norman.

Still smiling, Duggie Bubbles removed his jacket and allowed himself to be firmly tied up with ropes and shut into a big wooden box, which was secured with more ropes and even chains and padlocks. Everything went dark, with only a spotlight shining down on the box. There was a tense moment of silence. Then a roll of drums, a loud fanfare of music and the lights blazed again as Duggie Bubbles stepped out from behind some curtains, absolutely free! His hair was a little ruffled and he was sweating lightly, but his smile was as broad as ever.

"How does he do it, Norman?" asked Charlie.

"Perhaps there's a hole in the bottom of the box," suggested Norman. But it had already been proved to the viewers that this was not so.

"I'm going to ask him how he does it when I see him," said Charlie.

"Magicians never tell," said Norman.

5 The Magician Appears

The next morning Charlie put on his favourite cap with the big peak and his Superman T-shirt, packed his roller-skates and a couple of cheese sandwiches into his canvas shoulder-bag, and set out for the big hall next to the library. He'd promised to help get the Book Bonanza ready. This probably meant running about and fetching things.

Linda was in command when he got there, and Ariadne was already busy moving piles of books about. Dodger had turned up too, although he hadn't been asked. This was because he often got rather wild and over-excited at Bonanzas. Strictly speaking, he was also on the library black-list for returning some books late and in a nibbled condition. Dodger had insisted that his dog, Prince, had done it. But everybody knew that no pets whatever were allowed in the block of flats where Dodger lived. Dodger's dog was an imaginary one, who followed him about. The real-life Book Nibbler was actually Debbie, Dodger's little sister. But in spite of all this Linda still had rather a soft spot for Dodger, which was why she was letting him be the front legs of the horse. So she sighed and said all right, if he really *was* going to help she supposed he might as well stay.

There were books everywhere, beautiful new shiny ones with brightly coloured covers, being unpacked from boxes all ready for sampling. Ariadne kept getting side-tracked by one she simply had to read and settled down on the floor with it, where people kept tripping over her.

Display stands were arranged all round the hall, and there was a platform at one end with curtains, just like a proper stage. In fact, it *had* once been a stage because long ago the hall had been a theatre. It had a gallery and boxes on either side of the stage where the audience used to sit. Linda had had the good idea of making some book displays in these boxes. One of them was a Haunted House, for mystery stories. The students from the Art College had made some lovely ghosts and bats and other spooky things out of paper, and rows of hairy spiders on strings. Charlie and Dodger were set to work with a pair of steps, hanging up the spiders. They looked great, dangling all around.

"Pass us up some more drawing-pins, Dodger," said Charlie, perched up astride the balcony rail.

Dodger rushed down the steps, tore about looking for the drawing-pin box, and tripped over Ariadne, who happened to be lying under the steps, deep in a ghost story. The steps wobbled and crashed over, leaving Charlie stranded high above their heads.

"Ouch! Watch what you're doing!" yelled Ariadne.

"Hey! Get me down!" shouted Charlie.

"Oh, dear, oh, *dear*!" said Linda.

At this moment, who should appear as though by magic, but Duggie Bubbles himself! The real thing, in person, teeth and all. He looked much the same as he did on television, except that he was wearing a sparkling white suit instead of a black one. He was still smiling.

"Gosh!" gasped Charlie. He swung himself over the side of the rail, hung on to a carved pillar and slid down it to join the others.

"Miss Linda Bowen? I believe you're the organizer?" said Duggie Bubbles, pumping Linda's hand.

"Oh, yes. How do you do? We weren't expecting . . . I mean, this is a lovely surprise." Linda was all pink and flustered.

"I was just passing on my way to the studios so I dropped in to see where you want me to do my act, signing and so forth, and check up on one or two points," Duggie Bubbles went on. "Is this the stage? Small, isn't it? You'll be expecting a big crowd, naturally. I'll be bringing my own equipment and I'll need proper facilities for it, storage and so on. There'll be full

(41)

press coverage, won't there?"

"Oh yes, I've told the local paper . . ."

"I'd rather imagined that the National Dailies would be in on it. And you'll be laying on television coverage, of course?"

"Well, I . . ."

"I usually like—Good heavens! What are those spiders doing up there?"

"The children were putting them up."

"Oh, I see. Great, kids, great!" For the first time he beamed his smile towards Charlie and Dodger. Ariadne, who was skulking in the background, wasn't included.

"Coming along to have your books signed, are you? Bring your friends—all the fans! Only you'd better have those spiders down when I'm doing my act," he said, turning to Linda again, "rather distracting, you know. Want to get everyone's full attention on me, don't we? Now, if you could just show me the stand where I'm going to sign the books. You've got them all prominently displayed?"

Talking all the while, he allowed himself to be led over to where Linda was arranging a display of all his books.

"It's not quite ready yet, I'm afraid," she apologized.

"Well, that's obvious, dear, isn't it? I see you've got *Magic for Boys and Girls* here, but what about my other book, *Out of My Hat*? The one with the big picture of me on the front?"

"It's ordered. We've got a very good local bookseller here and he'll have it by Saturday, I'm sure."

"It's a particularly good one of me. The fans all like

(42)

that one. You'll see that it's laid on, won't you, there's a good girl." He paused for the first time and glanced round the hall. "Bit chaotic here, isn't it?"

"We've only just started to get it ready this morning. Everyone's working really hard."

"Kids under foot don't help, do they?"

"Children are supposed to be who it's *for*," murmured Linda.

"Will you sign my magic book, please, Mr Bubbles?" asked Charlie, inserting himself into the conversation at this point.

"Afraid I've got to rush now, Sunny Jim," answered Duggie Bubbles, glancing at his watch. "Bring it to the Bonanza and I'll sign it then."

"Are you going to get shut into a box and then get out again, like you did on television?" Dodger asked him.

But Duggie Bubbles was already on his way, disappearing down the hall.

"You'll get all this properly organized by Saturday won't you?" he called back to Linda. "I like my personal appearances to go off properly. And it gives you librarians a chance to do something else except sit about and read books, doesn't it?"

"Goodbye, Mr Bubbles," said Linda politely.

"Nauseating," said Ariadne. "Typical. I might have known it."

"He's ever so good on television," said Charlie. "And he's going to sign my book at the Bonanza, he said so."

6 Stuck in the Mud

"Two very rough-looking men called on me this morning," Uncle Owen Bowen was telling Linda. "Kept asking for Mr Dix. I told them to go over to the barge. Wouldn't let them in, you know. Mr Dix wouldn't like it. Oh dear, no."

"Never mind, Uncle. I don't expect they'll come back," said Linda reassuringly. She was only half listening. Worries about the big Book Bonanza were occupying most of her mind.

They were all eating a sandwich lunch in the little bit of overgrown garden between Uncle Owen's house and the river. It was a welcome break after all the hard work they had done that morning. Uncle Owen had set up his easel by the river wall and was painting the view up towards the bridge. It was low tide. The sun was out, lighting up mirror-like patches of water in the black mud. Mr Dix's barge was moored up high and dry, directly in front of them. It was a smart craft with neat curtains in the port-hole windows and potted geraniums on the deck, more like a bungalow than a boat. Uncle Owen kept glancing anxiously in that direction.

"He's found out about my stove catching fire, you

know," he told them. "Made a terrible fuss about it. Said it was all my fault."

"But I thought he gave it to you in the first place?"

"Says I'm getting forgetful. Smells seem to be getting worse too. And the noises. Sometimes I think I'm starting to imagine things."

"Don't worry, Uncle," said Linda, standing up. "I'm afraid I really must go. There's such a lot to do. Why don't you children stay here? I'll pop back for you at teatime."

Charlie and Dodger thought this was a good idea. They were getting rather tired of helping and wanted to roller-skate on the River Walk. The only trouble was that Dodger hadn't got any skates. He had to take turns with Charlie's. They set off, arguing loudly. Uncle Owen returned to his painting. Ariadne stretched out on the grass nearby with a book. Suddenly the early afternoon peace was broken as Mr Dix banged open his cabin door and strode up on to the deck of his barge. He stood there looking at them with his legs planted well apart, like a captain on a bridge. He was clearly in a bad temper.

"May I ask what you're doing on my private property, Mr Bowen?" he called out. "This garden isn't a public park, you know."

Uncle Owen started guiltily.

"Just doing a little oil painting, Mr Dix. River scene, you know. Such a good light today."

"You have no right to use this garden, Mr Bowen. I've told you before. No lodgers have a right to use the garden. It's in the agreement."

"Sorry, sorry. Always used to paint in this garden. Ever since I've lived here. Very fond of the view, you see."

"People will think I'm running some sort of an art school here," said Mr Dix crossly. "Some sort of hippy colony, with that child lying about all over the grass as though it was her own back yard. And is that the remains of a picnic I can see? Really, Mr Bowen, I must ask you to go, and take her along with you. Right away, if you don't mind."

Uncle Owen did mind. He looked as though he wanted to cry. Mr Dix had really upset him. It was humiliating. With trembling hands he began to pack up his box of paints. Ariadne closed her book. Her lips moved silently to sound her favourite word: "Nauseating!" She stepped forward to help Uncle Owen. His big wooden palette, with its lovely sticky mess of colours still wet, and a fistful of long brushes were lying balanced on the edge of the river wall. While Uncle Owen was fumbling with his easel a spiteful gust of wind whipped up from the river. It blew the canvas face down on to the ground. The easel toppled over and knocked the palette,

and the brushes with it, over the edge. They lay there, stuck down in the river mud between the embankment wall and the barge.

"My palette! My best brushes!"

This was the last straw for Uncle Owen. He sat down on the wall and covered his face with his hands.

"Now look what's happened!" cried Ariadne angrily. "Please, have you got a ladder or something on your barge?" she asked Mr Dix. "The wall's too steep and slippery for me to climb down, and we've got to get them back before the tide comes in!"

But Mr Dix was stonily unsympathetic.

"I'm afraid I can't help you. They'll just have to stay where they are," was all he said.

"But there must be a way of getting down there!" said Ariadne desperately. "I'll run and fetch Charlie and Dodger."

"No. No good," said Uncle Owen wearily. "We'll have to do as Mr Dix says. Leave them where they are. There's no way of reaching them."

"But you won't be able to paint without them!"

Uncle Owen didn't reply. Slowly he began to pick up his canvas and easel from the muddy ground.

At this moment Charlie was swooping like a gull on wheels up at the far end of River Walk, with Dodger running close behind. They were too far away to see what was happening to poor Uncle Owen. But they were not the only roller-skaters out that afternoon. A pair of slithering figures appeared round the corner, at the other end of the walk: two men, one tall and thin with a sly face hunched into his collar, the other tubby and unshaven. They both seemed to be having a lot of difficulty in standing upright. Reeling, clutching one another for support, hanging on to railings and lamp-posts to stop themselves from falling, they edged their way determinedly along.

"Let *go* of me, Trevor. You'll have us both over."

"Terrible idea, this was, Ray."

"Shut up and try to act naturally. We'll get noticed."

At last they reached the railings outside Uncle Owen's front door and hung there, sweating and panting.

"What do we do now then, Trevor?"

The tall man adjusted his beret, clicking his teeth with irritation.

"We skate up and down, Ray, as I told you. Keep our eyes on the barge. Look as though we're enjoying ourselves."

"This isn't doing my weak ankles any good."

"Never mind your weak ankles. Keep skating."

7 Our Mums Wouldn't Like It

Linda had never seen Uncle Owen Bowen so sad as
when she returned at teatime. There seemed to be
nothing anyone could do to cheer him up. Charlie and
Dodger were keen to try and slither down the wall when
Mr Dix wasn't about, but Uncle Owen wouldn't hear of
it. He said he didn't want them to do anything dangerous. And anyway, how would they ever get up again?
There were no steps anywhere near that part of the river.
But he had used that palette for years, and brushes were
expensive things. Too expensive for an old man to replace easily. He couldn't hide his distress. All the while,
from the balcony outside his room at the top of the
house, they could see the river tide rising.

It was getting dark. Time for the children to be going
home. Kind-hearted Linda, though she was tired, said
that she would stay a while and see to Uncle Owen's
supper. Ariadne, Charlie and Dodger said goodnight,
but they lingered uncertainly outside Uncle Owen's
front door. The River Walk was empty. The mysterious
roller-skaters were now nowhere to be seen.

"What are we going to do?" said Dodger. "That
palette thing and the brushes are going to be washed

away when the tide gets to them. And painting pictures is what Mr Bowen really likes doing, isn't it? Just like we like roller-skating. I suppose he's a bit too old for that," he added.

But even Charlie was at a loss for an idea this time.

"I can't stay any longer," Ariadne told them. "*Typical* of my family to be having guests this evening. They'll go on and on at me if I'm not back in time. And I'm late already."

"You'd better go," said Charlie. "Dodger'n me'll think of something." But he didn't sound very confident.

"Pathetic!" muttered Ariadne. And this time she didn't mean Charlie.

Dodger and Charlie hung about in the street after Ariadne had hurried away to catch her bus. They were plunged in gloom.

"Let's have one more look before we go. See how far the tide's come up," Dodger suggested.

"Better make sure Mr Dix doesn't catch us," said Charlie.

Together they slipped quietly through a gap in the railings into the overgrown garden, and crept through the rank undergrowth of brambles and stinging nettles to a vantage point they knew of behind the old shed. From here they could get a good view of Mr Dix's barge without being spotted. The deck of the barge was empty. But light shone from the port-holes of the cabin. Mr Dix was still at home.

Charlie crept silently along in the shadow of the low river wall until he reached the point, just near the gang-

plank of the barge, where Uncle Owen's palette and brushes had fallen.

He peered over the edge. The light was failing, but he could still see them, lying there in the mud. The river was rising fast. Some other barges further up the river were already gently afloat. Charlie looked about him desperately for inspiration. And just at the end of the gangplank, on the deck of the barge, there it lay: a coiled-up length of rope.

Charlie took his roller-skates out of his canvas shoulder-bag and put them down in the grass. He crept back to Dodger.

"I've got an idea. You'll have to keep watch."

They crept back to the gang-plank. Step by step Charlie edged his way silently along it. The lighted portholes of the cabin were just below, uncomfortably close. He picked up the rope. But with it he managed to dislodge a pot of geraniums, which rolled over on its side and along the deck. Charlie froze. They both fixed their eyes on the cabin door. But there was only the lapping of the water. After a pause, Charlie came softly back, carrying the rope.

Making it secure was a problem. There didn't seem to be anything to tie it to. If only he'd attended more carefully to all those things they'd told him about knots at Scouts. But Dodger surprised him by having a good idea too. He took one end of the rope right across the garden to the railings and wound it round and round one

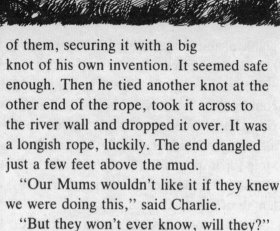

of them, securing it with a big knot of his own invention. It seemed safe enough. Then he tied another knot at the other end of the rope, took it across to the river wall and dropped it over. It was a longish rope, luckily. The end dangled just a few feet above the mud.

"Our Mums wouldn't like it if they knew we were doing this," said Charlie.

"But they won't ever know, will they?" answered Dodger.

Charlie slung the empty shoulder-bag over his head, gripped the rope with both hands and scrambled over the edge. He swung down, then braced his feet against the embankment wall like a rock-climber. He closed his eyes for a moment, hoping that the railing and Dodger's knot were as strong as he thought they were. Then he started to lower himself down, bumping and slithering now and again, trying to make as little noise as possible. He could see Dodger's white face peering down over the wall, anxious but reassuring. At last he reached the bottom of the rope and dropped the last few feet, landing ankle-deep in black slime.

Uncle Owen's palette and brushes lay just near his feet. He picked them up and, messy as they were, quickly stuffed them into his shoulder-bag. Now came the really difficult bit. Summoning all his strength, he leapt for the end of the rope. His arms seemed to be being pulled out of their sockets as he spun round, trying to re-establish his foothold on the wall. Then came the climb up, hand over hand.

"Come on, Charlie. You're doing fine!" Dodger whispered to him hoarsely.

The way back seemed endless. His arms were aching terribly. Three quarters of the way he stopped climbing and dangled in space, too tired to go on. He was exactly level with one of the port-holes of Mr Dix's barge. Luckily the light which shone out of it just missed him as he hung there against the wall. But he could see inside quite easily. Mr Dix was at a table, bending over something. He was drawing a picture! Charlie couldn't see his face, or what kind of picture it was. But, propped beside his drawing-board, was something that Charlie recognized at once. It was a small chalk drawing, not in a frame, but unmistakable: The Stunner!

Charlie was shaking all over when, with a final enormous effort, he managed to reach the top of the rope. Dodger's hands gripped his arms and helped him to heave himself over the wall. They both flopped on the ground, Charlie still clutching his shoulder-bag, too tired to move.

"You got them then, Charlie?" whispered Dodger presently.

"Yes, palette and all the brushes, I think," panted Charlie, tipping them out on to the grass.

"Great! Bit messy, aren't they?"

"Mr Bowen won't mind. Hey, Dodger, I saw inside that cabin place. I saw Mr Dix, but he didn't see me. He was drawing . . ."

"Perhaps he's another of these artists," said Dodger, not much interested in this piece of information. "Lucky he didn't look out and see you! Let's go and give these things back to Mr Bowen. He'll be ever so pleased."

"It's getting dark. There isn't time tonight," said Charlie, jumping up and grabbing his roller-skates. "My Mum'll be really mad if I'm not home soon. We'd better hide these things behind the shed. We can get them tomorrow morning and give him a surprise then."

"What about the rope?"

They'd forgotten about the rope. There followed a

terrible struggle to untie it from the railings. Charlie's weight had pulled it tight. At last they managed to wrestle it undone. They didn't want to risk creeping along Mr Dix's gang-plank again, so they left it neatly coiled by the river wall. Then they plunged into the undergrowth to a spot behind the shed, a safe hiding-place for Uncle Owen's precious things.

By now it was getting really late. The slick black water reflected the lights from the barges and the young May moon. Charlie and Dodger squeezed back through the railings and scampered away up the street to their waiting suppers. The overgrown garden was full of quiet shadows: two shadows in particular, one long and thin, another squat—Trevor and Ray, no longer pretending to roller-skate, but still watching and waiting. They too had seen what Charlie had seen through the lighted port-hole window.

8 Fishy

When Charlie woke up the next morning his Mum was already busy in the shop, vigorously rubbing up ladies' heads into snowy wigs of white lather. The smell of shampoo came wafting up the stairs. Charlie wondered if she was still cross with him for getting home after dark the night before. She worried about this sort of thing, and worrying always put her in a bad temper. Still, it had been worth it. The first thing Charlie did was to ring up Ariadne and tell her how he and Dodger had got Uncle Owen Bowen's palette and brushes back for him. He made a lot of the dramatic bits, how he had swung like Tarzan over a dizzy drop, which would have meant certain death if he had slipped. Ariadne was furious that she'd missed it.

"And to think I had to spend the whole evening being polite to grown-ups and answering all those questions about how I'm getting on with my 'cello lessons and whether I like my school," she said bitterly. "I couldn't even watch television! It's too nauseatingly pathetic!"

"Meet you at Mr Bowen's house this morning," said Charlie. "We can give him back his things then—give him a nice surprise."

When he rang off he remembered he hadn't mentioned what he had seen through the lighted cabin window. But the thought of it kept buzzing at the back of his mind. It was still bothering him when Norman, who had been working late the night before, emerged for his breakfast. So Charlie told him all about it.

"That Dix character's a bit fishy if you ask me," said Norman, carefully spreading plenty of butter and marmalade on a thick piece of toast. "Linda gets worried about the way he goes on at her uncle all the time. Pretends he's going off his head, which he isn't. Although it would suit old Dix if he did. He can't wait to pack the old man off into a Home so he can move in himself and posh the place up. You can see that a mile off."

"He'd taken that drawing out of its frame, the one of The Stunner, you know, that looks just like Linda."

Norman did know.

"But I didn't know Mr Dix was an artist too. He's never mentioned *that* before. Could you see what he was drawing?" he asked.

"No, he was bending right over it. The Stunner was propped up next to him."

"Fishy," said Norman again, chewing thoughtfully.

"We're going to give Mr Bowen back his things this morning," Charlie told him.

"Think I'll look in there myself. I've got the morning off," said Norman. "Will Linda be there, do you think?" he added casually.

"I don't know. She's busy with the Bonanza. It's

tomorrow, you see!"

When Norman had finished breakfast they went round to River Walk on the motorbike. Ariadne and Dodger met them on Uncle Owen Bowen's doorstep. Together they managed to persuade the old man downstairs and over to the garden.

"It's a surprise," Charlie explained. "We've got your palette and brushes back! Dodger and me rescued them last night before the tide came in."

"Wait there while we get them for you!" said Dodger excitedly.

Uncle Owen Bowen was quite bewildered. He could hardly believe the good news. He stood obediently by the old shed while Charlie and Dodger ferreted about in the nettles.

"We left it just here, I think," whispered Dodger, searching frantically.

"I thought you'd marked the place," said Charlie.

"No, I didn't. It was too dark."

They were getting very scratched and stung. The palette and brushes didn't seem to be where they had left them.

"Come on, Charlie. We're waiting for the surprise," called Ariadne.

"*All right!*" shouted Charlie. He was beginning to get agitated. "It must be somewhere here, Dodger," he hissed.

"Want any help?" said Norman.

Uncle Owen waited eagerly while they all searched. They worked their way right along the back of the shed. With a horrible sinking feeling Charlie began to think that the palette and brushes had disappeared.

"Are you sure you left them here?" Norman asked.

"Course I am." Charlie was in agony. The adventure of the night before and Uncle Owen's surprise seemed to be going all wrong. Already the old man's face was starting to crumple into disappointment, as though this was some kind of cruel practical joke. Norman was kicking the brambles aside. He looked at the muddy ground.

"That's funny," he said. "There's a lot of footprints which look too big to be yours or Dodger's. Somebody else must have been here."

(59)

At that moment a whoop of delight came from Dodger.

"Hey, look! They're here!" He was holding up the palette and brushes. "They were in quite a different place to where we left them, all scattered about. I just saw the edge of the palette poking out from the grass underneath this bush, as though someone had thrown them down here."

Uncle Owen was as pleased to see his precious things as though they had given him a hundred pounds. At once he was wreathed in smiles. Filthy as they were he kept fingering them as though he couldn't believe his eyes.

"So *grateful*. So *kind* of you to take the trouble. So *brave*," he kept saying, beaming at Charlie and Dodger. "This must be my lucky day. I thought these were lost for ever, and now I can start another painting. And, do you know, I've got my grandmother's portrait back too! Mr Dix brought her back to me earlier this morning. You must all come up and see her."

Still thanking them enthusiastically, Uncle Owen led them all proudly back to the house and upstairs to his room. There, hanging in her frame in the usual place on his wall, was The Stunner.

9 Very Fishy

"I was *so* pleased to see her again. I missed her almost as much as I did my old palette and my brushes. Now I've got them all back. I just can't believe it!"

"Couldn't Mr Dix sell her then?" asked Norman.

"No, no. Showed it to his friend the expert and, what do you think? He found out that it's a fake! Completely worthless! Not worth more than a few pounds. And all these years I've been thinking it was the real thing. Pre-Raphaelite, you know."

Charlie didn't know. He felt very confused altogether. But Uncle Owen went on happily,

"Of course, my sight isn't what it was. And somehow, you know, I don't really mind a bit. It's a likeness of Lily Bowen, the only one I have, and that's all I care about. I'm glad she isn't valuable. If she had been, I might have been tempted to sell her, you know. And I'd much rather have her here on my wall."

"Well, if you look at it that way, Mr Bowen, I suppose it is a bit of luck," said Norman doubtfully.

Ariadne was silent. But while the others were chatting she stood for a long time in front of The Stunner, peering at her intently.

"I'm glad you've got her back," she said at last.

"The strangest thing of all," Uncle Owen told her, lowering his voice, "is that I've been hearing those noises overhead again. Muffled footsteps. Bangs and thumps. In the evening when there's nobody here, only Beauty and me. It's as though Lily's been trying to tell me something. That she didn't want to be sold at all. That she wanted to come back here with me. Now perhaps she'll stop," he added.

"I hope so," said Ariadne.

Norman said he thought he would go round to the hall and see if he could help Linda with the Book Bonanza, and the children said they'd all come along too. Leaving Uncle Owen happily washing his brushes and rubbing linseed oil lovingly into his palette, they went downstairs. The smells were getting worse. Although the old stove was gone it had left blackened marks on the walls and ceiling, from which bits of old paper hung down in sad festoons. What was left of the carpet was full of holes. A door leading off the hall, down to dark basement regions, lurched drunkenly off its hinges.

"This place is a slum," said Norman, indignantly. "I think Mr Dix is letting it go like this so Mr Bowen will have to move. I keep telling Linda to try and get him to complain to the authorities, but he won't. He's afraid of Mr Dix."

"I wouldn't live here for a million pounds," said Dodger. "My Mum's always going on about the state of the lift in our flats. But she'd have a fit if she saw this. I wonder what's down there?" He peered fearfully down the basement stairs.

"Dare you to go down and see," said Charlie.

"Not likely."

"Go on. I dare you."

"Why don't you go, if you're so brave?" retorted Dodger. At this moment two green eyes appeared in the gloom. They both jumped back hastily. But it was only Beauty, Uncle Owen's old cat. She ran through Charlie's legs, crouched down and regarded them balefully for a moment, and then disappeared upstairs.

Norman went on ahead to the hall on his motorbike, leaving the children to follow on foot.

"You know, there's something very funny going on in that house," said Ariadne as they walked along.

"Mr Dix is acting fishy. Norman said so," said Charlie. And he told her what he had already told Norman, about all he had seen through the port-hole of the lighted cabin the night before.

"He was drawing a *picture*?" said Ariadne. "I thought he was meant to be an art dealer, not an artist."

"Perhaps it's his hobby," said Dodger. "There's going to be a Hobbies competition at the Bonanza tomorrow. A quiz, too, with prizes. I'm going in for everything. The only trouble is," he added, "that I haven't actually got a hobby. But roller-skating's going to be, when I get my new skates. My Dad's going to get me some really good ones. The expensive kind with precision bearings. Much better than your old ones, Charlie."

Dodger's Mum and Dad both had good jobs and earned a lot of money, so Dodger nearly always got the things he wanted. Their flat was stuffed with colour tellys, video cassettes and stereo systems. Even Dodger's little baby sister had her own transistor. But they didn't have time to talk to him much and they never told stories, as Charlie's Mum did sometimes when she was in a good mood. Charlie liked the true ones best, about all the awful things she did when she was a girl.

Ariadne wasn't listening to Dodger. She was thinking hard. She walked more and more slowly, until in the end she stopped altogether.

"I'm going back to Mr Bowen's house," she told them.

"What for?" asked Charlie, surprised.

"Won't be long. See you later," was all Ariadne said, and, before they could stop her, she was hurrying back the way she had come.

They had closed Uncle
Owen's front door firmly
behind them, as usual,
when they left.
But when Ariadne arrived back at the house she was
surprised to find it slightly open. She walked quietly
inside. The hall was empty. Some instinct stopped her
from calling out. Instead, she tiptoed over to the foot of
the stairs. On the half-landing above her she saw a
kneeling figure, his shadow cast up strongly on to the
peeling wall. It wasn't Uncle Bowen. It was Mr Dix.

There didn't seem anything else for Ariadne to do but
to stand there, watching, unable to go forward or back.
Mr Dix was far too intent on what he was doing to notice
her. He appeared to be burying something under a
floorboard. After a while he stood up and carefully
replaced the board, stamping it into place with his feet.
Ariadne felt as if she was frozen, like the lady in the
Bible who was turned into a pillar of salt, quite unable to
move. Mr Dix was about to turn round. Then their eyes
would meet. Then . . . But when Mr Dix had finished,
he turned the other way without once glancing in her
direction. His footsteps went echoing up the three flights
of stairs to Uncle Owen Bowen's room at the top of the
house. Ariadne could hear their voices, and she could
tell by Mr Dix's tone that he was complaining again.

She crept up on to the half-landing. It was easy to see which was the loose floorboard. She scrabbled at it hurriedly, breaking her fingernails on its rough edges. Now she felt like somebody in a detective story, galvanized into swift action. What had Mr Dix been hiding? Something he didn't want anyone to know he possessed. Jewellery, wads of pound notes, a priceless painting? The floorboard came up. She peered down into the hole, then reeled back on her heels.

What Mr Dix had hidden there was a mouldy kipper!

10 Haunted

Ariadne ran straight round to the hall to tell the others all about her discovery.

"Fishy," remarked Norman.

"It certainly was fishy. It smelt absolutely *nauseating*," Ariadne told him.

"Why should Mr Dix want to put a mouldy kipper under the floorboards of his own house?" Charlie asked. "It smells bad enough in there as it is."

"That's it!" shouted Norman suddenly. "Perhaps he's trying to make the smells *worse*, on purpose, so he'll have a better excuse for getting Mr Bowen out."

"That would be typical," said Ariadne. "I'll bet you're right."

"There was that old stove," Norman went on more thoughtfully, "the one that caught fire. Perhaps Mr Dix put it there specially so it would smoke and give him another excuse to complain. And to think it nearly set the place on fire!"

They all looked at each other, struck silent by such villainy.

"There's something even more fishy I've been wanting to tell you about," said Ariadne at last. "I've been thinking. You know Mr Dix borrowed The Stunner, and now he's given it back to Mr Bowen saying it's a fake, that it isn't worth anything. Not by a famous artist at all, or so his expert friend said. But I had a really good look at it when we were there this morning, and there's something funny about it. It looks different."

"How do you mean, different?" Charlie asked.

"Well, it's really hard to say. But I've looked and looked at The Stunner before—the day when Mr Bowen was telling us all about Lily being a mudlark, you know—and this morning I thought the drawing didn't look the same as it did before. One or two pencil strokes round the edges are different and it's sort of flatter, somehow. You have to look awfully hard to see. Mr Bowen would have noticed himself, of course, but he's a bit absent-minded at the moment."

"He's always forgetting where he's put his glasses," said Dodger.

"I wasn't quite sure. But when you told me, Charlie, about seeing Mr Dix through the port-hole last night, and how odd it was that he had The Stunner propped up beside him when he was drawing, I suddenly thought I wanted to go back and have another look. But I couldn't, because that's when I saw Mr Dix on the stairs."

Charlie and Dodger listened to all this open-mouthed. It was just a bit too difficult to get the hang of all at once.

"Do you mean," said Norman slowly, "that Mr Dix might have been *copying* The Stunner? That he might have given Mr Bowen a fake and kept the real one?"

"Well, he's clever enough to do it," said Ariadne.

"He knows Mr Bowen's sight is bad. Perhaps he thought he'd never notice the difference."

"This is serious," said Norman. "If you're right it's a matter for the police. We must tell Linda about all this. But she's so busy with the Book Bonanza at the moment, I don't want to worry her till it's over. And we can't mention anything to Mr Bowen yet because he gets so anxious and upset, especially about anything to do with Mr Dix. We've got to make sure. We can't go accusing anybody of anything until we've got absolute proof. Now remember, you lot, not a word to anyone for the moment until I can think what to do."

They all promised.

"Fancy all this fuss about a little chalk drawing," Dodger said to Charlie later, as they were humping books about. "My Mum puts all my drawings in the bin."

"You've got to get famous or dead before they're valuable," Charlie told him.

"Well, even if I was both, it won't do me any good if the binman's got them," said Dodger bitterly. "My baby sister usually nibbles them round the edges, too. I don't suppose even that famous artist our teacher was telling us about— you know, the very thin chap, Lean Ardo what's-his-name . . ."

"Da Vinci, I think. The one who tried to invent wings."

"Yes, him. Well, I don't suppose even *he* could have got to be such a famous artist with my Mum and sister around."

"Perhaps he didn't have a Mum, or a sister. Perhaps he could just stay at home all day and paint pictures and invent things."

"Must have been great. Even if he did get thin with nobody to cook his dinners."

That evening, after supper, Norman couldn't settle down to anything. He paced restlessly up and down the sitting-room, frowning deeply and nibbling potato crisps. They helped him to think.

"I'm going for a walk down to the river. Maybe have a chat with Mr Bowen," he said at last.

"Can I come?" asked Charlie promptly.

"It's too late for you to be going out," said Mum, looking sternly round her newspaper. "You've got a big day tomorrow at the Book Bonanza. I'm not having you up till all hours, getting tired out, even if it is half-term."

"But I'm not getting tired out. I'm not in the least bit tired," Charlie protested. "*Please*, Mum. I'll be with Norman."

"We won't be long," Norman said.

Mum wavered for a second and Charlie, taking up the advantage with a skill born of long experience, was already putting on his anorak.

"You've got to be in bed by nine," Mum called out after him as he and Norman ran downstairs.

It was dark now. Down on the River
Walk the old-fashioned street-lamps were
already lit. There were very few people
about, only a few strollers on their way
to the pub on the corner. Uncle Owen Bowen's
house was shrouded in darkness. Norman and
Charlie stood in the street, looking up at
his window, but the light was out.

"Must have gone to bed already," said
Norman. "We'd better not disturb him. I
wanted to get another look at The Stunner
but it'll have to wait till tomorrow, I
suppose."

They retreated to the other side of the
street and leant against the garden railings
in the shadow of a straggling elder bush,
smelling the night river smells and wondering what to do next. Just then a familiar
figure turned the corner and walked briskly
up the street towards them—peaked cap,
dark glasses, jutting jaw. Mr Dix himself!

Norman and Charlie instinctively
drew back into the shadow. Mr Dix
hadn't seen them. He stopped under
a street-lamp, glancing up at
the house. After a moment he
felt in his pocket, produced
a key, and let himself in.

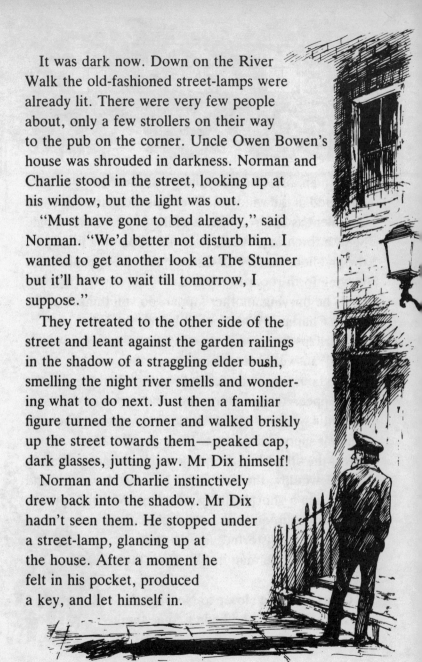

Norman and Charlie waited and watched. No lights appeared in the windows. The house remained as black and silent as before. After a while they could see a pale light, a torch or a candle perhaps, appearing fitfully on the first floor landing. It disappeared, then reappeared, moving from room to room.

"Is he burying another kipper, do you think?" whispered Charlie. "Why doesn't he put the lights on?"

"Perhaps he doesn't want Mr Bowen to know he's there," answered Norman.

The house went quite dark again. Then, eerily, the light appeared once more, this time in one of the three tiny attic windows above Uncle Owen's room, the attic that was supposed always to be empty. It started to move across the breadth of the house and back again, showing in one window then another. Up and down, up and down, like a ghost walking. Suddenly Mr Dix's profile was thrown up quite sharply against the pane, slightly distorted, like an evil caricature of the man inside. Then the light went out.

Charlie moved closer to Norman. He was very glad that he hadn't come there alone.

"It's scary. Do you think Mr Bowen's awake?"

"No wonder he feels haunted," muttered Norman. "But it's not the ghost of Lily Bowen who's doing the haunting. It's Mr Dix."

"I'd put my head under the blankets if I was in there," said Charlie. But Norman was furiously angry.

"He ought to be had up, frightening an old man like that. It's downright cruel."

"Perhaps he's coming down again," said Charlie. "He'd better not catch us here watching the house."

"Things are fitting together like a jigsaw puzzle," said Norman. "Come on, Charlie, we'd better be going home. I've got to think."

But another piece of the jigsaw, unknown to Norman, was close at hand. They were not the only watchers on the River Walk that night. Two pairs of eyes followed them as they hurried away under the lamplight. Trevor and Ray, crouched in the rank grass of the overgrown garden, stirred stiffly in their hiding place as they watched them out of sight.

11 Dark Doings

"I thought they'd never go," said Ray. "Thought we were stuck here in this blooming grass like a couple of broody swans. Ooo, my leg's gone to sleep."

"Get up, quick. We've got to get going. Wasted enough time as it is," snapped Trevor.

"It's too late, man. Dix is over at the house. He might be back any minute."

"It's our last chance, isn't it? You want to be in on this deal, don't you?"

"Yes, Trevor."

"Well, come *on*, then."

They started to move like two bobbing shadows along the river wall towards the gang-plank of the barge.

"I can't feel my leg at all," whispered Ray, bent double.

"You and your leg. It's always something with you. We wasted all yesterday messing about on those roller-skates with you complaining about your bruises. Then you had to go and sit on that old palette when we were hiding behind the shed and get colours all over the seat of your trousers."

"Wish I hadn't thrown that thing into the bushes now. Might have been worth a bob or two. Brushes too."

"A few bob!" spat Trevor scornfully.

They reached the gang-plank and paused there, eyeing the cabin door. The port-holes were dark. The tide was coming in, and the barge was already lifting on the lapping water. There was no other sound or movement.

"You're sure he's still got the drawing in there?"

"Yeah, sure. We saw him doing the copy, didn't we? And we've been watching him ever since. He hasn't left the barge except to go over to the house. But he's one of the quickest workers in the business. He'll be getting rid of it like a hot potato, tomorrow probably. He's been putting out feelers already, trying to see what kind of price he can get for it from a crooked dealer."

Ray giggled. "You ought to know all about *that*," he said.

"Quick, before he gets here. That cabin door's probably locked but I can get it open in no time. You stay on deck and keep watch."

Trevor hopped silently on to the gang-plank and padded along it like a lean cat. Ray followed, making the boards bend and creak. Together, they were outlined sharply against the sky. Trevor landed lightly on the deck. Ray paused, balancing uneasily.

"You two want something?" said a clear voice suddenly from the bank behind him.

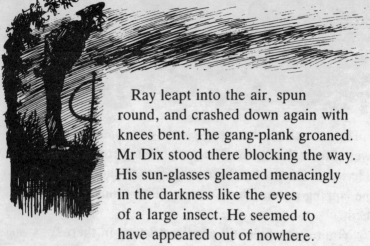

Ray leapt into the air, spun
round, and crashed down again with
knees bent. The gang-plank groaned.
Mr Dix stood there blocking the way.
His sun-glasses gleamed menacingly
in the darkness like the eyes
of a large insect. He seemed to
have appeared out of nowhere.

"Gas Board!" cried Ray. "We're from the Gas
Board—"

"At this time of night?" Mr Dix took a step forward.

"Just checking. Looking for a leak. Trevor—we've
done it wrong again, Trevor—Trevaaaaah . . ."

Trevor reacted more directly. At the sound of Mr
Dix's voice he leapt back on to the gang-plank and
sprinted along it, cannoning into Ray and throwing him
completely off-balance. Locked together, they waltzed
wildly. Then Trevor jerked himself free. Reaching the
bank, he met Mr Dix head on. For a few dangerous
moments they grappled silently.

Ray struggled to keep his footing on the gang-plank, arms out, beating the air like wings. Then he toppled slowly sideways and disappeared from view. A huge splash followed as he hit four feet of water between the barge and the river wall.

Meanwhile Trevor had managed to heave Mr Dix into an elder bush where he collapsed heavily backwards into the headily-scented flowers. Seizing his chance, Trevor tore across the garden and, taking the railings like a hurdler, was away up the deserted street.

"Get him! Stop him, can't you?" roared Mr Dix, but nobody heard. He fought his way out of the bush and began to give chase, shedding white blossoms behind him. Unable to jump the railings, he used some regrettably ugly language as he fumbled with the gate.

By this time Ray had surfaced in the river and was staggering about, spewing dirty water and shouting to Trevor to get him out. But Trevor was already well out of earshot.

Charlie and Norman were on their way home up one of the narrow streets which led away from the river. They heard the cries echoing distantly from River Walk, then swift footsteps running up the street behind them. Norman glanced round, surprised. Then he gripped Charlie's arm.

"Seems to be somebody chasing us. Quick, Charlie. Better be on the safe side. Can you make it to the corner, double quick, do you think?"

Charlie obediently broke into a jog-trot. They could hear Trevor gasping and heaving for breath as he loped up behind them. Norman and Charlie quickened their pace to a run. Trevor was gaining on them. They were nearly at the corner, where the brighter street lights shone, when he drew level with them. Ahead they could see a bus just pulling away from the kerb. Trevor shoved his way violently between them, sending Charlie reeling against the wall, and ran on into the main road. For a moment or two he sprinted level with the moving bus. As it accelerated he put on a desperate spurt and took a flying leap on to the platform. He nearly missed his footing but the conductor caught his arm and hauled him aboard. They saw his white face looking back at them before he disappeared up the stairs.

"*He* was in a bit of a hurry," said Norman. "You all right, Charlie?"

Winded, Charlie was leaning against the wall.

"He didn't half give me a shove," he said, rubbing his elbow. "Worse than the dinner queue at school."

"Must have been his last bus. I'm glad he wasn't chasing us, anyway," said Norman. He took Charlie's arm. "We've got to get you home. Your Mum said nine o'clock, and there'll be terrible trouble if we're late."

But before Charlie could collect himself another flying figure came up the street behind them. It was Ray, oozing water, his clothes flapping desperately about him. He lolloped towards them like a creature risen out of the primeval mud.

"Trevor, wait for me," he was shouting, "Trevaaaah . . ."

Charlie was flung against the wall a second time as he plunged past. Reaching the corner, Ray paused for a moment, moaning, then ran off in the direction of the vanishing bus. Norman helped Charlie to his feet for a second time.

"Nutter night," he said. "They're everywhere. It'll be Things from Outer Space next. Come on, Charl."

They were just turning into the main road when some-body, walking briskly in the other direction, bumped straight into them. For the third time that evening Charlie was nearly knocked off his feet.

"Sorry," said the man briefly, hardly bothering to stop. He didn't recognize Charlie, but Charlie recognized him.

"Hey, Norman, do you know who that was?" he said, staring after him in surprise.

Norman was in no mood for guessing.

"The Incredible Hulk, of course," he said, dragging Charlie forward by the arm. Charlie allowed himself to be dragged, but he was still looking back over his shoulder.

"Didn't you see?" he said excitedly. "It was Duggie Bubbles! I know it was. I saw him quite close up at the hall yesterday. I wonder what he's doing down here?"

"Another disappearing act, probably," answered Norman, striding purposefully homewards.

12 Bonanza Day

Charlie woke up the next morning still thinking about Duggie Bubbles. He had been dreaming that he was sitting on the lid of a box, trying to keep it shut, while Duggie Bubbles, who was inside, kept trying to jump out like a jack-in-the-box. Later in the dream Charlie found himself trying to do magic tricks before a huge audience, but everything he did kept going wrong. Now, fully awake, he remembered it was Bonanza day, and it was late already.

He hurried out of bed and searched about for his favourite book. It was extra large and brightly coloured: *Magic for Boys and Girls*. He was beginning to think that seeing Duggie Bubbles on the way home last night had all been part of his dream. But he was determined to get his book signed at the Bonanza. Mum had told him that signed books were sometimes valuable. He had written his own name already, in bold writing on the fly-leaf: "This Book Belongs to Chas. L. G. Moon." That signature was going to be famous too, he was quite sure.

The first thing he saw when he reached the hall was Ariadne, already encased in her robot suit, walking up and down on the steps in front of the main entrance. She

had a blue light on her head which flashed on and off when she pressed a button inside. The Bonanza hadn't opened yet but already quite a few people had collected and were watching her with curiosity.

"Where's Dodger?" Charlie shouted into one of her small coffee-strainer ears.

"Round the back," came Ariadne's voice, rather muffled, from inside. "He's getting into his half of the horse. Linda's there too. You'd better hurry."

Charlie couldn't resist giving a few raps on her plastic casing. Ariadne flashed her light at him fiercely. Secretly he was rather jealous. Being inside a robot seemed much more fun than the back legs of a horse. He had tried to talk Dodger into letting him be the front part, but it hadn't worked. When Charlie found him in the dressing-room place behind the hall he had already got the head on. The front legs were crumpled round his ankles like concertinas.

"Hee-haw, hee-haw!" he went when he saw Charlie, clattering the huge set of grinning teeth.

"You're a horse, not a donkey," Linda told him. She looked tired and bothered, but pretty, too, in her nice pink dress. "Now be careful with that costume, you

(82)

boys. The Library Service are having Cuts, so we can't afford to replace it if it gets damaged. Here, Charlie, let me hook you up."

Charlie put down his Magic book in a safe place until later, when Duggie Bubbles was due to arrive. There was a great deal of frantic activity going on all around them. Busy helpers were running in and out, and Linda was answering their questions and giving last-minute instructions as she helped Charlie into his back legs. Once inside, he had to hold on to Dodger's waist firmly. He could see very little, although there were some air-holes so he could breathe.

"For heaven's sake don't go walking backwards," Linda warned Dodger sternly, "and give plenty of warning when you're going to stop."

She fixed large notices on either side of them: "Book Bonanza Today!"

They were off, cantering down the passage, with Dodger whinneying realistically and Charlie behind swishing his tail. The Bonanza had officially begun.

Down on the river, the morning was still and calm. A few seagulls rode the water behind the barge, hoping for breakfast. Mr Dix opened the cabin door a few inches and peered round. Then, having made quite sure that he was not being observed, he locked the door carefully behind him and walked on to the deck. He carried a large book casually under one arm, as though he was planning a morning stroll to the library. He hadn't called the police to report the intruders the night before. He had very special reasons of his own for not doing so. Having chased after Trevor a little way, he had given up and returned to the barge in the hope of cornering Ray. But he was too late. Ray had found a rope-ladder hanging down into the water from another barge a little further up-river. Somehow he had managed to heave himself up it, dodge round the gardens, and make off.

Mr Dix crossed the gang-plank and let himself out through the garden gate. He glanced up and down the street a couple of times, then set off at a leisurely pace. As soon as his footsteps had died away round the corner, two faces slid into view at pavement level, looking after him through the railings of a basement area. Trevor was as foxily alert as ever under his clamped-down beret, but Ray was bleary-eyed and sulky.

They climbed up stealthily to street level and hesitated there for a moment. It was very risky to have come back,

but Trevor had decided to take a last desperate chance. Ray had been against it. He had wanted to stay in bed and nurse his aches after the strenuous events of the night before. Being a burglar didn't suit him. He much preferred a more peaceful way of making a living. He and Trevor ran a dubious Antique shop together, where they sold things which might or might not have been stolen by somebody else. They never tried too hard to find out where they'd come from. Trevor knew just where he could sell a valuable drawing if he could get hold of one. But today it was far too dangerous to try to break into the barge again in broad daylight. So Trevor started off up the street after Mr Dix.

"It'll be all up if he sees us this time," said Ray, hobbling after him. "He'll recognize me for sure and you, too, probably. He'll have us arrested."

"Call the police? You must be joking. He doesn't want to have anything to do with the law, any more than we do." Trevor paused on the corner and peeped round. "Nasty questions. Trouble. The last thing he wants."

"What'll we do if we catch up with him?"

"We're *tailing* him. Just keep out of sight and do as I say."

"I think I've done my back in, Trevor. Felt it go as I hit the water last night."

"So it's your back now, is it?" said Trevor unsympathetically. "What I've ever done to deserve such a useless, gutless, witless partner I don't know. I'd have that drawing by now if I was working on my own."

"I wish you were," said Ray.

A huffy silence followed between them. Lurking in and out of doorways, they followed Mr Dix's progress. Once or twice he glanced back over his shoulder but Trevor managed to keep out of sight, bundling Ray with him. When they reached the busy High Street it became easier not to be spotted, although once or twice they nearly lost sight of him amongst the shoppers. Through a street market and down another side-street, they arrived at the main square. Suddenly Mr Dix seemed to disappear. Anxiously Trevor quickened his pace. Forgetting all caution, he craned his neck above the crowd. Ray caught his arm.

"There he is, Trevor," he said, pointing. "On the steps of the hall over there, where all those flags are. Book Bonanza it says. He's going in there!"

"Come on, then," said Trevor.

13 Horsing Around

Mr Dix was paying his entrance money for the Bonanza when Ariadne clanked past. She was so astonished when she saw him that she nearly dropped her banner. For a moment they came face to face, regarding one another. But Mr Dix was not the kind of person to be amused by an outlandish figure in fancy dress. He pushed on past her into the crowded hall.

Ariadne watched him carefully through her tin visor. He began wandering round the exhibition, stopping now and again to idly flip through a book on one of the stands. Children swarmed everywhere, chatting excitedly, devouring books, collecting badges, filling in quizzes and popping balloons. Ariadne started to make her way round the backs of the stands, pretending she was circling the hall with her banner. She was watching his every move. He strolled round casually in the throng, but he kept glancing about, his dark glasses ranging the hall for something. Or somebody. Once or twice he raised his eyes suddenly from a book and nearly caught Ariadne peering at him from behind the display, but she hurried on, flashing her light innocently.

She noticed that he carried a book under his arm. She

(87)

couldn't get near enough to read the title. But when a newly-arrived class of primary school children momentarily surrounded Mr Dix and swept him along in their midst, she managed to jostle near enough to read: *Magic for Boys and Girls* by Duggie Bubbles.

"That's odd," said Ariadne to herself, "very odd. Not at all typical. Oh dear, I wish Norman was here."

Charlie, meanwhile, was already feeling hot and tired inside the back legs of the horse. They had been capering up and down the steps of the hall for some time, displaying their notices and trying to attract the crowds. Dodger, quite carried away with his part, was whinneying gaily, browsing in people's shopping baskets for carrots and gnashing his teeth at them. He caused quite a stir. One little girl even timidly offered him a lump of sugar, which Dodger accepted with a great show, tossing his mane and licking his chops. All this was rather boring for Charlie, who felt that his supporting role of back legs offered no such artistic scope. All he had to do was to hold on to Dodger's belt and go wherever he was led, occasionally kicking out his legs. He was just thinking of suggesting that they have a breather and go to see if there was any free orange drink going in the back room, when they were violently cannoned into by Trevor and Ray, who were running up the steps in a great hurry.

Dodger was caught off-balance and
fell back on to Charlie. They sat down
heavily, Dodger in Charlie's lap. The
two men tripped over both of them.
Together they all rolled down several
steps on to the pavement.

"Hey, mind my ears!" shouted Dodger,
forgetting for the moment that he was
supposed to be a horse. Charlie was
furious. He couldn't see anything. What was more, this
was the fourth time he'd been knocked over in the last
twenty-four hours. Blindly he fought his way out from
the tangle of limbs. At this moment one of the seams on
the horse costume gave way under the strain and
Charlie's head popped through, about where the saddle
ought to have been. Trevor and Ray stumbled to their
feet and ran on up the steps without a backward look.
The same two men!

"Those two again!" muttered Charlie, scowling.
"They seem to be making a hobby of pushing me over.
How many more times are they going to try it?"

"Get your head down," Dodger hissed at him.
"You're spoiling everything."

Charlie popped back inside and followed obediently
after Dodger as he trotted back up the steps and into the
hall in the direction of the back room. They had both had
enough of being a horse for the moment. It was certainly
time for a breather.

(89)

"What are those two doing here, anyway?" wondered Charlie aloud as they were sucking up their orange drink. They were both still wearing their horse's legs while a lady helper was kindly doing some running repairs to the torn seam. Dodger had thankfully removed the head, which sat on the table, grinning amongst the general confusion.

"Perhaps they're following you about," Dodger suggested. "Perhaps they've got up a special club to go about pushing you over. Some boys did that to me once in the school playground. It was awful. But me and my gang fought them off in the end."

"But they didn't even know it was me," said Charlie. "And they don't look like the sort of people who'd be interested in Book Bonanzas. When we get into our costume again let's go and find out what they're doing."

14 Mixed Infant

A puppet show was in full swing. Trevor and Ray were stalking the main hall, keeping well to the side among the ornate pillars. They had already spotted Mr Dix who was still loitering rather aimlessly among the stands.

"What's he want to come in here for?" whispered Ray hoarsely. "It's all kids' books in here." Pausing, he pulled one down from a nearby display. "Fairy-tales! I like those. Giants, witches, princesses and that. I always wanted to be a writer of children's stories you know, Trevor. Just look at these lovely pictures!"

He began to turn the pages with interest until Trevor grabbed the book and thrust it back on the shelf.

"Keep watching Dix," he said irritably. "Don't take your eyes off him."

They began to work their way round behind the stands, still trying to keep Mr Dix in view without being seen. Every so often they passed and repassed Ariadne who was still circling in the opposite direction.

"A robot!" cried Ray, turning to look at her with delight. He seemed to have quite forgotten about his bad back. "Look, Trevor, flashing blue light and all. Clever, isn't it?"

"Reminds me too much of a police car," muttered Trevor, pushing him roughly on.

Charlie and Dodger, back again in their horse costume, were hovering behind them in the shadows.

"What are they doing?" whispered Charlie. It was maddening not to be able to see, and to have to rely on Dodger to tell him everything that was going on. Dodger poked his horse's head round a pillar.

"Just walking round. Seem to be looking for somebody."

"Let's follow them."

They set off at a stately pace, daintily picking up their feet. Ariadne, manoeuvring on the other side of the hall, seemed to be making some kind of signals at them, waving her robot arm frantically. But Dodger couldn't understand what she was pointing at.

The puppet show drew to a close, amid noisy applause. Linda's voice came over the loud-speaker, announcing the next event. The Lady Illustrator had arrived and was going to draw some pictures for the younger children in the smaller room off the main hall. There was a general move in that direction. The spaces round the stands suddenly emptied out. Trevor and Ray were dangerously exposed to view, and, what was worse, Mr Dix seemed to be heading straight for them.

"Quick, Ray, he'll see us. Get out of the way," said Trevor.

They shuffled into a crowd of parents and small children who were filing into the smaller room, where an easel had been arranged with a large piece of blank paper pinned to it. The Lady Illustrator was there already, felt pen in hand.

"Now make yourselves comfortable, everybody," called Linda, who was there to introduce her.

Trevor and Ray lowered themselves uneasily on to cushions on the floor among a drove of toddlers. The grown-ups, perched at the back of the room on chairs and tables, shot them an odd look or two, but the Lady Illustrator started off at once with some bright chat. She was large and artistic-looking, dressed in a colourful tent-like garment and hung about with beads. The effect was of an Indian squaw who was accidentally wearing her own wigwam. She asked the children what they would like her to draw. Some of them were too shy to suggest anything, but after some encouragement the braver ones began to call out some ideas.

"Draw a monster!"

"Draw Red Riding Hood!"

"Draw a wolf!"

The Lady Illustrator worked away obligingly, filling page after page with large felt-pen sketches. Sometimes she paused to answer questions about books and drawing. The children were getting braver and more inventive.

"Draw Rumpelstiltskin!"

"Draw my auntie's budgie!"

"Draw the centre-forward of our team, scoring a lovely goal!"

The Lady Illustrator's hair had begun to escape rather wildly from her bun. The floor was covered with pictures. Ray leant forward with interest. He would have liked to ask her to draw something for him but he knew it would make Trevor cross. A small stir was created at the back of the room as a horse's head appeared inquisitively round the door, but Linda hurried over to it.

"You can't come in here, you two," she whispered. "Go back outside *at once*!"

"What are they doing in there, anyway?" Charlie wanted to know.

"Just Art, that's all," said Dodger.

Now Linda and the Lady Illustrator unrolled a huge piece of paper on the floor. Felt pens were liberally distributed amongst the audience. The Lady Illustrator started to sketch the long shape of a dragon, stretching from head to tail almost the length of the room. Every-

body gathered round and began to join in, filling in the
details for themselves. There was a great deal of interested chatter.

"I'm drawing a man with a spear chasing the dragon
from behind."

"My man's shooting arrows."

"This is lots and lots of smoke coming out of his
mouth . . ."

"And burning flames . . ."

"I'm doing his big pointed teeth."

"Lend us the red a minute, will you?"

"Hang on, I want it for all the dripping blood."

The Lady Illustrator hovered encouragingly, helping
the younger ones with a shape here and there. Trevor
began to eye the door, shifting restlessly on his cushion.
Ray couldn't resist the temptation to pick up a green felt
pen and, hoping that Trevor wasn't looking, he carefully
began to fill in some neat scales on the dragon's tail.

"We've got to get out of here," muttered Trevor.
"For Pete's sake, Ray, stop messing about. We've
probably lost Dix by now, and you're acting like a
mixed infant."

Ray reluctantly gave up his pen to the little girl next to
him, and he and Trevor edged their way towards the
door.

(95)

Charlie and Dodger were patrolling about outside. Dodger caught sight of them as they slipped out of the door into the main hall. The crowds were denser than ever. Children of all ages, Mums, Dads, Grandpas and Aunties milled happily round the stands, browsing and choosing. Before Trevor and Ray could sight the figure of Mr Dix, there was a commotion over by the main entrance. People were gathering, craning over one another's shoulders. A voice on the loud-speaker announced:

"Your attention, please, everyone. Duggie Bubbles has just arrived! He'll be signing your books at the big stand in the centre of the main hall. Don't miss the Magic Show, which will follow shortly."

Charlie tugged at Dodger's belt.

"Come on, Dodger. Never mind about those two now. We've got to get out of this suit quickly. I want to get my book signed."

15 Smile, Please

The drawing session was over. Willing helpers were clearing up. The Lady Illustrator was being revived with cups of tea. Linda hurried over to welcome Duggie Bubbles and to check for the hundredth time that everything was ready for him on the stand. He was already surrounded by a crowd of children, waving books and bits of paper, and he was signing busily, chatting to reporters from the local paper and flashing porcelain smiles about him, all at the same time.

"Now don't push, children. Just make a little space and wait your turn," said Linda. Organizing a Book Bonanza was even harder work than she had imagined.

Charlie, freed from his role as back legs, shot up to join the queue, clutching his copy of *Magic for Boys and Girls*. Dodger, determined not to be left out of anything, followed close behind. The press of people round Duggie Bubbles was growing all the time and, in spite of Linda's words, there was a certain amount of excited jostling. Charlie found himself being pushed against someone, and nearly fell over for a fifth time with sheer astonishment when he saw who it was: Mr Dix! He turned his dark glasses towards Charlie for a moment, but if he recognized him he had certainly decided to ignore the fact.

"What's *he* doing here?" whispered Dodger from behind. "There seem to be some awfully funny people at this Bonanza."

"*I* don't know. Perhaps he's studying to be a magician, like I am," Charlie whispered back. But he was too busy trying to keep his place in the queue to bother about Mr Dix. He badly wanted to get to Duggie Bubbles and ask him how he did that trick of being tied up in a box and getting out again. He wanted to try it sometime, but he had privately decided not to ask Dodger to be his assistant. Something was bound to go wrong if he did. Mr Dix had somehow managed to push ahead of them. Now he was already thrusting his copy of *Magic for Boys and Girls* into Duggie Bubbles' hands. Charlie, not to be outdone, ducked under his outstretched arm.

"Hold it a minute, Duggie," said a news photographer. "Let's have one of you holding up your books and some of the kids . . . you, with the cap, and you . . . would you mind stepping to one side a moment, sir?"

He pushed Charlie and Dodger into a group with Duggie Bubbles in the centre, holding up two copies of *Magic for Boys and Girls*, one in either hand.

"Let's have a big smile, now!" said the photographer.

The camera flashed. Mr Dix skulked in the background, his jaw set angrily.

"Hey, Charlie, we're going to be in the newspaper!" said Dodger, all agog.

"About that trick, the one where you get shut in the box," Charlie began. "Please can you tell me . . ."

But Duggie Bubbles didn't seem to be listening. He was still smiling and signing, but his face was half turned towards Mr Dix. They exchanged a few quick words over Charlie's head. Then the crowd pressed forward impatiently and Charlie's chance was lost.

"There were lots of things that I wanted to ask him about, and now I'll never find out," Charlie grumbled to Dodger when he found himself pushed out to the edge of the crowd again, with his book under his arm.

"Typical!" commented a voice from behind them. It was Ariadne of course. She was still wearing her robot suit, but she had propped her banner up against a pillar and was watching events from the side of the hall. "There are some fishy things going on at this Bonanza, Charlie, if you ask me. I've been following Mr Dix around for ages but I still can't make out what he's doing here. He certainly doesn't seem much interested in the books."

"And we've been trying to track two *very* fishy characters who keep pushing me over," said Charlie. "Only we've lost them now," he added.

"Pathetic!" said Ariadne. "Oh, dear. I can't think what we ought to do now. It's awfully bad for my brain being inside this robot suit. If only Norman was here."

"He is," said Dodger. "Look, over there."

"Thank *goodness*," said Ariadne with relief. They all hurried over to where Norman was examining a pop-up book with great interest.

"Got off early from work," he told them. "Thought I'd come along and see what's happening. Where's Linda?"

All three children started to talk at once, each telling him something different. But their voices were drowned by another announcement on the loud-speaker:

"The Duggie Bubbles Magic Show will begin in five minutes on the stage at the end of the main hall. Take your places, please."

"Come on, let's try and get near the stage," said Charlie, dragging Norman's arm. "We'll tell you everything later. I want to watch all the tricks from really close up so I can see how he does it."

There was a rush for seats. There weren't enough for everyone. Charlie nimbly threaded his way through the crowd and just managed to bag a place in the second row. Dodger immediately plumped himself down in the row behind him, but Norman and Ariadne were somehow left behind.

"Where are they?" said Charlie, craning his neck. "I hope they don't get left in the standing-room-only."

There was a buzz of excitement all about them. Some helpers were setting up the stage for Duggie Bubbles' act. There was a small table with a fringed cloth, some screens and a trolley with all sorts of strange objects on it. On either side of the stage there were displays with huge posters of Duggie Bubbles' larger-than-life-size smiling face and many copies of *Magic for Boys and Girls*.

"Let's see where he's written his name in your book," said Dodger, leaning over the back of Charlie's seat. Charlie opened his copy at the front page.

"I've been fiddled!" he cried furiously. "This isn't my book! Look, it's got Duggie's signature in it all right, but it hasn't got mine. I wrote it in specially, 'This Book Belongs to Chas. L. G. Moon'. I've got the wrong book!"

"Well, it looks much better than your old one, anyway," said Dodger. "Yours had all that marmalade and tomato ketchup spilt on it. Hey, when's this show going to begin?" He stood up in his seat, trying to catch a glimpse of Duggie Bubbles in the wings.

"But I don't *want* this one," muttered Charlie indignantly, flicking through the pages. "I *liked* my old one. What's this, then?"

He had come across a loose leaf of paper, concealed between two of the pages. It was just smaller than the size of the book, quite thin, and overlaid with a sheet of tissue paper. Charlie folded it back. A face looked up at him that he knew well, a very pretty face, framed with long curly hair: The Stunner.

16 Black Magic

Ariadne had been separated from Norman in the rush
for seats. She was trying to make her way among those
people who were standing at the side of the hall, to get
nearer to the stage, when a burst of applause greeted the
appearance of Duggie Bubbles himself. He launched at
once into a flow of jokes and patter, at the same time
doing some astonishing things with playing-cards, shuffling them with the greatest skill, picking aces out of his
ears, his hair, and what seemed like empty air. He
followed with a rapid succession of tricks with coloured
balls (which appeared from some equally extraordinary
places), and tossed a silk cloth over a transistor, which
was blaring out military marches at full blast, and threw
the whole thing into the air, making the set disappear

abruptly and the music with it. Before
the audience had finished applauding,
he was pouring out all kinds of coloured
liquid into glasses and making those
disappear too. And never once did he
stop smiling and cracking jokes.

Then came the familiar empty top
hat from which he began to pull

yards and yards of multi-coloured
silk handkerchiefs, paper
flowers, strings of sausages, miles
of streamers, and, finally, two snow-
white live doves. One of them strutted,
cooing, across the stage. The other
fluttered up to the rail of one of
the old theatre boxes and perched there,
calmly preening its feathers.

The audience were all intent on
Duggie Bubbles as he started yet another
trick. He was keeping them all laughing.
But Ariadne was looking up. Behind
the curtains of the box she had
caught sight of something. A man's
figure was standing there, half hidden
in the shadows. When he moved slightly,
the glasses gleamed. Mr Dix, like a
Demon King waiting in the wings, was
staring down at the stage.

Ariadne tried to attract Norman's attention. She could see him over the tops of people's heads, standing next to Linda, but she couldn't get near them. Every time she tried to wave, her suit made a noise like a binful of old tin cans.

"I've just got to get out of this thing," said Ariadne to herself. She edged her way over to the exit and set off down the corridor to the small untidy helpers' room behind the stage.

Ariadne was not the only person who had seen Mr Dix up there. Trevor and Ray, in a dark corner beside the display of posters, were still hot on his trail.

"There he is!" whispered Trevor.

"Where?" said Ray, gazing about him.

"Shhhh, shhhh!" said all the people round about.

Trevor was already pushing his way through them towards a side exit.

"I can't think why we're *bothering*," said Ray, lowering his voice to a piercing whisper as he struggled behind. "He's probably flogged that drawing by now."

"*Would* you mind being quiet?" said a lady threateningly.

Up on the stage Duggie Bubbles was saying, "Now, I'm going to ask a member of the audience to step up here. Don't be shy, now—any boy or girl—what about you, young man? Would you come up and give me a hand?"

"He means you," said Dodger, giving Charlie a shove from behind.

"What?" said Charlie, startled.

"That's right," said Duggie. "The young man in the red cap. We've met before this afternoon, haven't we? Bring your book with you."

Bewildered, and clutching the copy of *Magic for Boys and Girls* with The Stunner still between the pages, Charlie found himself being helped up the steps and on to the stage. Beaming, Duggie Bubbles was pumping him by the hand.

"Now, what's your name? Charlie? This is Charlie, everyone! Give him a big hand now!"

Charlie smiled foolishly as everybody clapped, but the clapping soon turned to laughter as, when Duggie released his hand, he found himself holding an egg. It seemed to have appeared out of nowhere. He was even more surprised when Duggie pulled another one out of his left ear. And before he could wonder how it got there Duggie said,

"Would you mind lending me your handkerchief? I've got a shocking cold," and he began to pull one coloured silk handkerchief after another out of Charlie's back pocket.

Charlie stood there with the book under his arm, blinking with amazement. Things were happening too quickly. The events of the last few minutes seemed unreal, as though he had truly been bewitched. Only Dodger's face, open-mouthed, in the audience below, seemed to make sense.

Mr Dix had shrunk back into the shadows of the box. Quietly he opened the door at the back and slipped out. He paused at the top of the flight of stairs which led down to the corridor below, listening. There seemed to be nobody about. Everyone was watching the show. Gales of laughter came from the hall as Duggie Bubbles pulled more and more extraordinary things out of Charlie's pockets. Suddenly Mr Dix heard footsteps running along the corridor and up the stairs towards him. As they drew nearer he heard a voice saying,

"I think I ought to go home, Trevor. Sitting on that floor hasn't done my back any good, you know—"

Trevor and Ray came round the turn in the stairs and they all met face to face. Mr Dix recognized them both instantly. He towered above them, dark with rage.

"You! Following me about, are you? Spying on me, eh? Tried to break into my barge last night, didn't you? Well, I'm going to settle you two, once and for all!"

But Trevor and Ray had already turned in their tracks like lightning and were scrambling back down the stairs the way they had come. With Mr Dix after them, they swerved into the corridor and tore off towards the helpers' room at the other end. Ariadne was just coming out. They cannoned into each other head on.

"Quick, Ray!" gasped Trevor, pushing her roughly out of the way. He wrenched open a small door on his right and both men tumbled down the dark flight of steps which led into the space under the stage. Ariadne flattened herself against the wall as Mr Dix rushed past in hot pursuit. He disappeared after them like an angry ferret down a rabbit-hole.

Ariadne tip-toed to the door and peered after them into the darkness below. The sounds of a struggle had broken out. She could hear them scuffling and blundering about.

"Typical!" she commented under her breath.

Meanwhile, on the stage above, Duggie Bubbles had taken the book from under Charlie's arm and was hold-

(108)

ing it up to the audience.

"Here it is, folks: *Magic for Boys and Girls*! All the secrets of wizardry and illusion! Let me show you . . ."

Before Charlie could stop him, he began to turn the pages. As he did so clouds of confetti flew out and drifted like snow across the stage.

"There's plenty of good card tricks in here," said Duggie, as, from another opening, he drew out four aces, "but you have to be very careful about taking this magic book up to bed with you at night, you know, Charlie, very, very careful indeed."

Out of the book came a folded piece of paper. Duggie shook it open. It was not, as Charlie had expected, The Stunner, but a huge concertina of black tissue paper on which was painted a grinning skeleton with gangling arms and legs.

The thumps and bumps that were going on under the stage were drowned in applause as Duggie handed the book back to Charlie, and he made his way back to his seat.

"How on earth did he do it?" said Dodger, awe-struck. "I was watching him all the time and I never saw him put all those things in between the pages."

But Charlie didn't answer. He was searching through the book, page by page. Suddenly he leapt to his feet with a wild shout, as though he'd been scalded. The Stunner had disappeared!

"Sit *down*! We can't see!" chorused the children in the row behind.

But Charlie wouldn't sit down. This was all just too much. He felt as though he was going to burst. Scarlet in the face, he stormed back up the steps and on to the stage, stopping Duggie Bubbles dead in mid-patter.

"The drawing! Where's that drawing?" shouted Charlie. He was so furious he felt like a giant. The very boards seemed to be trembling under his feet. The audience, thinking that this was all part of the show, clapped him good-humouredly.

The commotion under the stage was getting louder. The boards were trembling all right, as Trevor and Ray crashed about in the dark beneath, grappling grimly with

Mr Dix. Just then Ray struck out with a wild swinging blow, missed, and fell flat on his face, bringing Mr Dix down with him. Trevor staggered against them, clutching at a wooden lever for support. It gave way. There was a strange clanking noise and a groaning of old boards. A trap-door in the stage above swung open, and Duggie Bubbles disappeared abruptly from view. Charlie found himself alone on the stage, staring down at a heap of wildly waving arms and legs in the pit which had opened at his feet.

17 A Game of Grandmother's Footsteps

The audience loved it. They clapped loudly. It seemed like the perfect ending to a Magic Show for the Magician himself to disappear. This was even better than television.

"Something's gone terribly wrong!" gasped Linda, clutching Norman's arm. Together they hurried out of a side exit and ran to the door which led down under the stage. There they met Ariadne, still peering down the steps with some interest.

"A big fight," she told them briefly, "Mr Dix and two other men. And I think there's someone else in there now, but I can't think how he got there. It's too dark to see who's winning."

The sounds of struggle and terrible oaths which came from below were getting louder and louder. At last one figure broke free and lumbered up the steps. It was Ray. He was wild-eyed, his sleeve was ripped, and he was covered in cobwebs and grime. Closely on his heels followed Trevor, in a similar sorry state. One after another they pushed past the little group at the top of the steps and ran off at full speed in the direction of the main exit. A third figure staggered out after them. Without his

(112)

cap or his dark glasses, Mr Dix was almost unrecognizable. He was very nearly bald and his eyes seemed nakedly small and deep-set, like those of an angry gorilla. His teeth were bared in a snarl of rage. He didn't look in the least like his usual self, but, for a split second, Ariadne thought he seemed oddly familiar. He gave them all a furious, lowering look before pursuing Trevor and Ray down the corridor at amazing speed.

"Are you all right, Mr Bubbles?" called Linda anxiously from the top of the steps.

"What do *you* think?" answered a hollow voice from the gloom below.

In the hall above the audience were still applauding, half hoping for an encore. When none was forthcoming they began to drift happily away. It had all been a huge success. They had never expected, when they paid their entrance money, that the Book Bonanza was going to be quite such a lively event as this.

Charlie stood hesitating on the stage, all his anger suddenly deflated. Too many weird things had happened all at once. He felt so bewildered he was ready to cry. He had even begun to wonder if he really had found The Stunner's picture inside that book, or if he'd imagined the whole thing. Dodger scrambled up on the stage to join him.

(113)

"That last bit was great, wasn't it?" he said, peering down the trap-door. "I never expected him to do that."

Down below Linda and Norman were helping Duggie Bubbles up the steps and leading him away to the helpers' room at the back of the stage. Luckily he was more or less unhurt. Landing on top of Ray had cushioned his fall. Linda apologized over and over again, and flustered helpers rushed for cups of tea and brandy.

Dodger wandered curiously about the stage. He peered into Duggie Bubbles' top hat and cautiously touched one or two other props, half afraid that some magic might suddenly rise up out of them and take him unawares. But Charlie hadn't the heart to investigate. He had decided in the last half hour that he didn't want to be a conjuror any more. Making magic was altogether too difficult, and, even if you could make it, still harder to control. And being on stage with a real magician hadn't been any fun at all. It had just made him feel foolish. He wandered off across the stage, miserably kicking up some bits of confetti which were still lying there.

"Hey, look, Charlie!" called Dodger. "Here's that skeleton thing that he pulled out of the book!" And he jerked the paper concertina open with a flourish. Some-

thing fell out of it and drifted across the stage, coming to rest at Charlie's feet. He picked it up. Then he let out a yell of triumph.

"It's The Stunner!" he shouted. "I was right! He *did* take it after all!"

"Not that drawing again," said Dodger. "I just can't understand why everyone goes on about that silly old drawing."

All the same, he followed Charlie as he rushed off to the helpers' room to find Norman, waving The Stunner. Linda, Norman and Ariadne were hovering attentively about Duggie Bubbles, who was slumped in an armchair. He wasn't smiling any more. His eyes popped and his jaw hung slackly, making him look more like a discarded ventriloquist's dummy than a magician.

"Here's The Stunner . . ." began Charlie breathlessly. "Got her back . . . found her in my Magic book . . . only it turned out not to be my Magic book after all . . . couldn't tell you, Norman, because then I had to go up on the stage and be magicked at myself . . . and when I got off it again, it wasn't there, you see, and so . . ."

Nobody was listening to this explanation, even if they could have followed half of what Charlie was trying to tell them. They were all staring at The Stunner. Ariadne was the first to recover from her surprise. She took the drawing out of Charlie's hand and looked at it carefully.

"I think it's The Stunner, all right, the real one," she said. "I *am* glad to see her again."

"We've just found it, up on the stage," Charlie explained. "Inside that skeleton thing."

(115)

Now they all turned to Duggie Bubbles. His expression was blank. He was the only one among them who had showed no surprise at Charlie's dramatic entrance.

"I never wanted it," he said. "Didn't want anything to do with it. Never saw the wretched thing until today."

"It's Linda's uncle's drawing," said Norman quietly, "and apart from being valuable, it's very precious to him for family reasons. At the moment he still hasn't realized that he's been robbed of it, because there's a clever fake hanging on his wall in its place, put there by Mr Dix. We couldn't tell you, Linda, until after the Bonanza was over. We didn't want to worry you, and anyway, we weren't sure. But now perhaps you'd like to explain, Mr Bubbles, what it's doing here."

Duggie Bubbles' face had lost all its doll-like pink colour. He looked suddenly grey, and years older.

"It'll be the end of my career if this goes any further. I'll be finished if the papers get hold of it . . ." His voice trailed away miserably. They waited. "You see," he said, "Duggie Bubbles is my stage name. My real name's Douglas Dix. Howard—that's Mr Dix—is my older brother."

"I *thought* there was something familiar about him when I saw him without his dark glasses!" said Ariadne.

"I don't see him very often. We've never got on well. He's a lot older than me, and I don't like some of the ways he has of making money," Duggie told them. "Anyway, being seen about with him wouldn't have been very good for my image. But he rang me up out of the blue the other day and said he wanted me to keep something for him. For safety, he said. A small drawing. Said there were some people he didn't trust watching the barge, and he had to get rid of it as soon as possible."

"Why didn't he ring the police?"

"Oh, he'd never do that. He doesn't like to involve the police for, er, personal reasons. I didn't like it at all. But he puts a lot of pressure on. Says he knows things about me that would ruin my career. So I said I'd go down to the barge and collect it from him. Last night, that was. But when I got near to the river there seemed to be a spot of trouble going on. Some sort of fight. So I beat it as fast as I could. You can't afford trouble in show business, you know."

"We were there too," put in Charlie, "I saw you. Do you remember, Norman? And those two men, the ones that kept pushing me over. They were here today, at the Bonanza."

"They must have been the same two who were watching the barge. They must have been after The Stunner too," said Norman.

"Probably," Duggie agreed. "My brother telephoned me again early this morning. Sounded pretty anxious.

(117)

Said he was being watched all the time, but that he was going to get to the Book Bonanza somehow—he knew I was making a personal appearance there—and smuggle the drawing to me in a copy of my book. He wanted me to hang on to it for him until the coast was clear."

"So *that's* what Mr Dix was doing at the Bonanza," said Ariadne. "I followed him all afternoon, but I never guessed he had The Stunner inside that book."

"And we were following those two men, who were following Mr Dix . . ." said Charlie.

"Until he turned round and caught them at it. Just like a game of Grandmother's Footsteps!" finished Ariadne.

"I thought I'd let Howard slip me the drawing," Duggie continued, "but I didn't want to have anything to do with stolen goods. I was going to make him give it back, or return it myself if I could find out who it belonged to. I would even have gone to the police, even if he is my brother. But when I got hold of the book, the drawing wasn't inside. It was the wrong copy. They must have got muddled up when the news photographer was taking the picture. We realized that as soon as we looked inside and saw this kid's name."

"Chas. L. G. Moon," Charlie prompted him.

"Howard was furious. I've never seen him in such a rage. He threatened to ruin my act. So I had you up on stage and got it back."

"But how did you do it?" Dodger wanted to know. "I was watching you every second."

But Duggie Bubbles wasn't telling him that.

"I'm a magician, aren't I?" was all he said.

18 Escape!

Trevor and Ray had reached the River Walk, pouring sweat and sobbing for breath, but still running. Twice they had nearly managed to throw Mr Dix off the scent, skidding round corners, dodging down side-roads, running the wrong way up one-way streets, scattering shoppers at every turn. But he had clung on relentlessly. Though he was the older man by far, rage seemed to fire his pace.

"Oooh, my back! My legs! My weak ankles!" cried Ray piteously as he puffed behind Trevor, but Trevor didn't seem to hear. He was making for a small wooden landing-stage which stuck out from the river embankment between two moored barges. A ladder led down to the water, where a small boat, which belonged to one of them, was tied up. Mr Dix was gaining on them rapidly. They scrambled over a low wall, and across somebody's garden, recklessly treading down the plants. They had reached the landing-stage when Mr Dix caught up with them. Trevor was already half-way down the ladder. Ray was hopping about on the platform above. His shoe had come off. A split second before Mr Dix made a grab at him, he picked it up and hurled it. It caught Mr Dix a

stinging blow on the side of his head. He staggered about, cursing.

"Wait for me, Trevor!" Ray's voice was a high-pitched scream.

He slithered down the ladder and gave a great leap into the boat. It rocked dangerously as he landed in it, nearly capsized, but not quite. It turned round twice, quite out of control, drifting away from the landing-stage. They had no oars. Trevor, hunched in the bows, was paddling with his hands for all he was worth. Ray lay flat on his back in the bottom of the boat, moaning.

"Paddle, Ray, you daft idiot, for pity's sake, paddle!" shouted Trevor.

The boat drifted out a little way and seemed to waver uncertainly. Ray dragged himself up over the side and flapped a hand hopelessly in the water. His weight listed the boat over to one side. It spun round once more. Then, quite suddenly, a swift current caught it and they were carried out into the main course of the river, away on the out-going tide.

Mr Dix was forced to stand there and watch them go. He couldn't contain his fury. Lifting his arms to heaven, he let out a wild cry. He shook his fists in the air. He literally capered with rage. But his foot caught against Ray's discarded shoe. He staggered for a moment, then tipped headlong over the edge of the landing-stage into the river below. Great ripples marked his fall. When at last his dripping head emerged from the filthy water, he was just in time to hear Ray's voice, carrying faintly back over the tide,

"This isn't doing my rheumatism any good, you know, Trevor . . ."

19   A Little Celebration

A few days later, a little celebration was about to take place at Uncle Owen Bowen's. His room had been slightly tidied up and the table was laid with all sorts of delicious food: egg sandwiches, sausage rolls, plenty of chocolate biscuits and a big fruit cake with nuts and cherries on top. There was fizzy lemonade and even a bottle of wine for Uncle Owen himself. Linda had taken him for a stroll by the river. This was supposed to be so the children could get everything ready, but it was really so that Norman could have time to return The Stunner to her original frame and rehang her on the wall without Uncle Owen ever knowing the difference.

"But *why* can't we tell him?" Charlie wanted to know. "It was so exciting about Duggie Bubbles disappearing through the stage and me finding her and everything."

"People as old as Mr Bowen aren't as fond of excitement as you are," Norman told him. "They like a more peaceful kind of life. It's all thanks to you we got her back for him, Charlie. And we'd never have found out what was going on here if it hadn't been for you, Ariadne, and Dodger too. But Linda thinks it's better if he never knows about The Stunner being taken from him. It would only upset him. But we'll have to see that he doesn't let her out of his hands again."

"But what about Mr Dix?" asked Charlie.

"Vanished. Scarpered. Completely disappeared. Or so Linda's just been telling me," said Norman, working away busily. "Nobody's seen him since the day of the Bonanza. I think that magician brother of his, Duggie Bubbles, has told him to get out of London quickly, before there's trouble. Or he might have decided for himself that things were getting too hot for him. He must know by now that he's lost all hope of getting The Stunner for himself, and, what's more, we could have the law on him for forgery if he shows his face here again."

"What are you going to do with that copy?" Ariadne wanted to know.

"Put it in a package and post it through the letter-box of his barge, I suppose," answered Norman. "It's all locked up and empty there, Linda says. Only a few empty milk bottles left on the gang-plank." He carefully straightened the real Stunner in her frame on the wall and stood back to admire his handywork. "Lovely, isn't she?" he said, but he was looking over at the door, where Linda had just appeared, rosy-cheeked and looking rather stunning herself, with Uncle Owen following close behind. He beamed with pleasure at the sight of the loaded table.

"A party! How *kind* of you all. I love parties. Used to go to a lot of them at one time. What a wonderful cake! When can we start?"

(123)

As all the chairs were occupied by stacks of paintings, they began at once, without bothering to sit down.

"A very curious thing about Mr Dix," said Uncle Owen, munching away happily. "Nobody can understand why he left so suddenly. Overnight, without a word, not even to me! A neighbour of mine said she saw him running down the River Walk, dripping wet and shouting, but that must be just wild gossip, of course. Extraordinary fellow. But, do you know, the people from the Welfare Service have been round to see me, and they say I can stay here as long as I like! And, I must admit, it's lovely here without Mr Dix. I can paint down by the river whenever I want to now. Quite like old times. Beauty thinks so too, don't you?" He bent down to offer a piece of roll to the old cat who was purring about his legs.

"Linda and I'll decorate the hall for you when we've got some time off, if you like," Norman offered.

"You're too kind, too kind. Do you know, the whole house has changed since Mr Dix went away? Even the smells seem to have disappeared. And I never hear those footsteps overhead at night any more. I really think Lily must be quite at rest at last."

They all looked at The Stunner. A pale rippling light was thrown up from the river on to the wall where she hung. Even Dodger stopped short, with a chocolate biscuit half-way to his mouth, and gazed at her, as though he'd just caught sight of her for the first time.

"I *think* I see why you were making all that fuss," he said at last, through a mouthful of crumbs, "about her being pinch—" but here Charlie nudged him warningly in the ribs with his elbow, "—about her hanging there," he corrected himself quickly. "She does look rather a pretty kind of lady."

"Not half bad," agreed Norman.

"Beautiful," said Ariadne. "I'm so glad she's yours, Mr Bowen."

"She's only mine in a way," said Uncle Owen, filling his glass. "Art belongs to everyone, really, you know. Especially to you young people—to you, Ariadne, my dear, and Charlie and Dodger here. It gets handed on from us older people to you young ones because it *belongs* to you. It's not something chilly or stuck-up or always in a glass case. It changes all the time. And it's not only painting, it's singing and dancing and books and libraries and telling stories and acting plays and getting a good tune out of a musical instrument. It's yours by right, and it's worth sticking up for and never letting anyone take away from you. Because it's the best present you'll ever have."

"Here's to Art, then," said Norman, raising his glass.

"And here's to *you*, Mr Bowen," said Charlie Moon.